T0261201

Office 2004 *for* Macintosh

THE MISSING MANUAL

*The book that
should have been
in the box*

Office 2004 for Macintosh

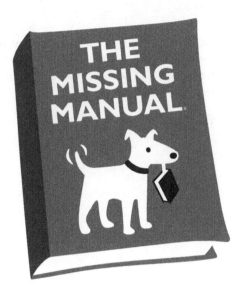

Mark H. Walker and Franklin Tessler

POGUE PRESS™
O'REILLY®

Beijing • Cambridge • Farnham • Köln • Sebastopol • Tokyo

Office 2004: The Missing Manual

by Mark H. Walker and Franklin Tessler

Copyright © 2005 O'Reilly Media, Inc. All rights reserved.
Printed in the United States of America.

Published by O'Reilly Media, 1005 Gravenstein Highway North, Sebastopol, CA 95472.

O'Reilly Media books may be purchased for educational, business, or sales promotional use. Online editions are also available for most titles (safari.oreilly.com). For more information, contact O'Reilly's corporate/institutional sales department: 800-998-9938 or corporate@oreilly.com.

February 2005:   First Edition.

Missing Manual, the Missing Manual logo, and "The book that should have been in the box" are registered trademarks of O'Reilly Media, Inc.

Many of the designations used by manufacturers and sellers to distinguish their products are claimed as trademarks. Where those designations appear in this book, and O'Reilly Media was aware of a trademark claim, the designations have been capitalized.

While every precaution has been taken in the preparation of this book, the publisher assumes no responsibility for errors or omissions, or for damages resulting from the use of the information contained herein.

ISBN: 978-0-596-00820-8
[LSI]

[2012-06-29]

Table of Contents

Introduction 1
Keeping Up with the Macs 1
What's New in Office 2004 4
The Very Basics 6
About This Book 7

Part One: Word

Chapter 1: Basic Word Processing 13
Creating and Opening Documents 13
Word Processing Basics 19
A Window into Word 21
The Views 32
Every Conceivable Variation on Saving 35
Printing 38

Chapter 2: Editing in Word 55
The Many Ways to Select Text 55
Moving Text Around 58
Navigating Your Documents 66
Finding and Replacing 71
Spelling and Grammar 79
Five Ways to Type Less 90

Chapter 3: Formatting in Word 105
The Formatting Palette 105
Character Formatting 106
Lists 112
Paragraph Formatting 116
Document Formatting 130
Section Formatting 132

Chapter 4: Styles, Page Layout, and Tables 137
Styles 137
Page Layout 144
Automatic Hyphenation 149
Text Boxes 151
Pictures and Drawings 158
Charts, Spreadsheets, and Equations 160
Tables 160

Chapter 5: Comments, Change Tracking, and Versions 175

Comments 175
Change Tracking 178
Comparing Documents 185
Versioning 186

Chapter 6: Notebooks, Outlining, and Master Documents 189

Notebook Layout View 189
The Outliner 200
The Document Map 207
Master Documents 209

Chapter 7: Advanced Word Processing 217

Headers and Footers 217
Footnotes and Endnotes 221
Line Numbers 225
Templates 226
AutoSummarize 234
Fields 237
Bookmarks 242
Captions 244
Cross-References 248
Creating a Table of Contents 251
Indexing 256
Data Merges 263
Macros 279

Chapter 8: Word Meets Web 285

Word as Web Browser 286
Creating a Web Page in Word 287
Graphics, Sounds, and Movies 295
Hyperlinks 300
Web Forms 307
Saving Web Pages 308

Part Two: Entourage

Chapter 9: Entourage Email and Newsgroups 315

The Big Picture 315
Setting Up Entourage 318
Sending and Receiving Mail 325
Newsgroups 370

Chapter 10: Calendar, Tasks, and the Project Center..................383
The Calendar..383
Recording Events..386
What to Do with an Appointment...392
Saving Calendars as Web Pages...399
Tasks..401
Office Notifications...406
Project Center..410
Accessing Projects from Other Office Programs.................................422

Chapter 11: Address Book and Notes.............................425
Address Book..425
The Note Pad...440

Chapter 12: Advanced Entourage....................................443
Palm Synchronization...443
About Conduits...444
Multiple Identities..450
Finding Messages...452
Links...456
Categories...458
Checking Your Spelling...459
The Script Menu...460

Part Three: Excel

Chapter 13: Basic Excel 465
Spreadsheet Basics...465
Formula Fundamentals..484
Excel, the List Maker..496

Chapter 14: Formatting and Charts................................509
Formatting Worksheets..509
Charts...528
Printing Worksheets..543

Chapter 15: Advanced Spreadsheeting...........................551
Workbooks and Worksheets...551
Advanced Formula Magic..562
Working with Databases..567
Opening the Excel Toolbox..572
Macros: Making Excel Work for You...592

Part Four: PowerPoint

Chapter 16: Basic PowerPoint 599
Triple View 599
Step 1: Specify a Design 599
Step 2: Writing the Outline 605
Step 3: Building the Show 608
How to Build a Slide 613

Chapter 17: Advanced PowerPoint 627
Making a Slideshow 627
Multimedia Effects 640
Printing Your Presentation 650

Part Five: Microsoft Office as a Whole

Chapter 18: The Project Gallery and Toolbox 657
The Project Gallery 657
Toolbox 663
Reference Tools 665
Projects Palette 667
Compatibility Checker 668

Chapter 19: Customizing Office 669
Customizing Your Toolbars 669
Redesigning Your Menus 674
Reassigning Key Combinations 677

Chapter 20: The Graphics Programs of Office 679
Inserting a Graphic 679
The Clip Gallery 680
AutoShapes and WordArt 682
Lines and Shapes: The Drawing Toolbar 684
Formatting Pictures and Drawings 687
The Picture Toolbar 693
Object Linking and Embedding (OLE) 694

Chapter 21: AppleScripting Office 699
What is AppleScript? 700
Installing and Running Office Scripts 702
Starter Scripts 706
Learning More 715

The Missing Credits

About the Authors

Mark H. Walker is a veteran computer book author, Microsoft Office aficionado, Virginia Tech football fanatic, and all around technosapien. He has authored over 40 computer related books including *How to Use the Internet, The Visio Bible,* and *Visio 2003 Inside Out.* His articles have appeared in *Family Software, Alaskan Airlines, Smart Solutions,* and *Playboy,* and he is a regular columnist for *PC Gamer* and *The Armchair General.* He lives in the beautiful hills of south-central Virginia with his lovely wife, three daughters, four dogs, two cats, and a horse. Email: *mark@markhwalker.com.*

A native of Montreal, **Dr. Franklin Tessler** (PowerPoint chapters) has been a writer for Macworld magazine since 1986. Over the years, he has written numerous feature articles and reviews, and has lectured extensively about how to create and deliver electronic presentations. Dr. Tessler is currently a Professor of Radiology at the University of Alabama in Birmingham, where he resides with his wife and two children. Email: *mmbook@ftessler.com.*

Paul Berkowitz (author of the AppleScript chapter and technical editor for Entourage chapters) has tech-edited other O'Reilly books, including *AppleScript: The Definitive Guide* by Matt Neuburg and *AppleScript: The Missing Manual* by Adam Goldstein, and has also done technical proofreading for Apple and Microsoft. He is well-known as the author of over 100 AppleScripts for Entourage. In his "other life," Paul is a classical pianist and Professor of Piano at the University of California in Santa Barbara, where he now lives happily ever after. Email: *berkowit28@mac.com.*

About the Creative Team

Nan Barber (editor, copy editor) co-authored *Office X for the Macintosh: The Missing Manual* and *Office 2001 for the Macintosh: The Missing Manual.* As the principal copy editor for this series, she has edited the titles on iPhoto, Mac OS X, AppleWorks 6, iPod & iTunes, and Windows XP. Email: *nanbarber@mac.com.*

Rose Cassano (cover illustration) has worked as an independent designer and illustrator for twenty years. Assignments have ranged from the nonprofit sector to corporate clientele. She lives in beautiful Southern Oregon, grateful for the miracles of modern technology that make working there a reality. Email: *cassano@cdsnet.net.* Web: *www.rosecassano.com.*

Phil Simpson (design and layout) works out of his office in Stamford, Connecticut, where he has had his graphic design business since 1982. He is experienced in many facets of graphic design, including corporate identity, publication design, and corporate and medical communications. Email: *pmsimpson@earthlink.net*.

Acknowledgments

I've been doing this stuff for quite awhile, but have never had as much fun, or worked with such talented people as those that I've found at O'Reilly. I'd like to thank Sarah Milstein and Nan Barber for giving me this opportunity, and especially Nan for all her help, encouragement, and expertise. Thanks also to my agents, Neil and Lynn, to Shannon Mapp at Edelman PR, and to the rest of the team that brought this book to fruition: Phil Simpson for layout; John Cacciatore and Stephanie English for their proofreading smarts; technical reviewers John McGimpsey and Paul Berkowitz; indexer Julie Hawks; and Caroline Savello, InDesign expert extraordinaire.

Finally, none of this would be possible without gobs of support from my wife, kids, friends, and God. Thanks all.

—Mark H. Walker

Special thanks to Nan Barber for asking me to do this work to begin with: her confidence was inspiring. I'm also enormously grateful to my wonderful wife and children for putting up with all my late hours at the Mac.

—Franklin Tessler

The Missing Manual Series

The Missing Manuals are conceived as superbly written guides to computer products that don't come with printed manuals (which is just about all of them). Each book features a handcrafted index, cross-references to specific page numbers (not just "see Chapter 9"), and an ironclad promise never to use an apostrophe in the possessive word *its*. Current and upcoming titles include:

AppleScript: The Missing Manual by Adam Goldstein

Windows XP Hints, by Preston Gralla

Mac OS X: The Missing Manual, Panther Edition by David Pogue

iLife '04: The Missing Manual by David Pogue

iPhoto 4: The Missing Manual by David Pogue & Derrick Story

iMovie 4 & iDVD: The Missing Manual by David Pogue

iPod & iTunes: The Missing Manual, 2nd Edition by J.D. Biersdorfer

GarageBand: The Missing Manual by David Pogue

Mac OS X Hints, Panther Edition by Rob Griffiths

FileMaker Pro 7: The Missing Manual by Geoff Coffey

Dreamweaver MX 2004: The Missing Manual by David Sawyer McFarland

Windows XP Home Edition: The Missing Manual, 2nd edition by David Pogue

Windows XP Pro: The Missing Manual, 2nd Edition by David Pogue, Craig Zacker, & L.J. Zacker

Introduction

Microsoft Office has penetrated the business world with a universality rivaled only by the personal computer itself. In most Mac- or Windows-based corporations, anyone *not* using Word, Excel, and PowerPoint at work is considered a weirdo. For that matter, a few people use them at home, too.

Office has been on the Mac in one form or another since 1989, but it gained greater acceptance with the release of Office 2001, which was the debut of Entourage—the all-in-one email-cum-personal-information-manager-program. But before the year 2001 was even torn off the calendar, Office X exploded onto the scene with some of the first—and best—productivity programs available for the Mac's new operating system, Mac OS X. With each new version, Microsoft has not only given Office greater speed and more new features, but has strived to make them all work better together. The result is the topic of this book—Office 2004.

Keeping Up with the Macs

Building on Office X, which incorporated new Mac OS X features like Quartz graphics, Office 2004 includes more innate Mac OS X features than ever. For instance, there's now Unicode support and thus the ability to use the Mac's Character Palette (see Figure I-1). The Thumbnails pane in Word is a dead ringer for the Thumbnails pane in Mac OS X's Preview program (not to mention Adobe Acrobat). Finally, Microsoft has outfitted Office 2004 with full AppleScriptability.

Furthermore, much of what's new in Office 2004 is unique and innovative. From the new Notebook layout and audio notes features in Word, to the all-encompassing Project Center in Entourage, there's less reason than ever to click out of Office to get things done on your Mac.

What's New in Office 2004

The shimmering, Aqua-enhanced splash that Office X made on the scene was a hard act to follow, but Microsoft gave Office 2004 significant improvements over its predecessor, Office X. Some, like Notebook Layout view and the Project Center, are eye-catching, but others are less readily apparent. Here's a list of the most interesting new features.

Word

- **Notebook Layout view.** More than just a new view that looks like lined paper, Notebook Layout view is a quick way to take, outline, and organize notes. The view features a formatting palette that's slimmed down to the essential functions, and the ability to take audio notes right in your document with a single click of your mouse. Just the ticket for those long social studies lectures or business meetings.

- **Improved Change Tracking.** Change Tracking is now much more stable, and boasts a revamped toolbar that makes its features more accessible. You can now display changes in balloons that float in the document margins, which makes them easier to spot. On the downside, inserted and deleted text can be harder to deal with. (If you don't like the change, worry not. You can always tell Word to track changes more like the old-fashioned way.)

Note: If you're just now switching from Windows to Mac, give thanks. Word's Change Tracking feature now looks and works more like its Windows counterpart.

- **Remodeled Formatting Palette.** Subtle changes makes text syles easier to apply and modify. The new Add Objects panel means fewer trips to the menu bar to insert things like AutoText and Drawing objects.

- **Smart Buttons.** A Smart Button pops onto your window just after Word makes an AutoCorrection. With a quick click of the mouse, you can choose to accept or reject the suggestion. Smart Buttons also let you determine the formatting of pasted text.

- **Send as HTML mail.** With one swift command, you can plunk your fully formatted Word text into the body of an email, ready for sending.

Excel

- **Page Layout View.** The cool Page Layout view that you've used in Word is now available in a tasty new Excel 2004 flavor. You can review, change, and redesign your workbooks onscreen, confident that they'll print just as they're displayed.

- **Cool Charts.** Now you can add charts to your Excel spreadsheet with just a single click in the Formatting Palette. You'll find everything from area charts to line graphs waiting for your instant gratification.

- **Smart Buttons.** Just as in Word, these small pop-up tools let you perform quick formatting-on-the-fly without a side trip to the menu bar.

PowerPoint

- **Presenter Tools.** These new tools help keep presenters organized by displaying, in a private window, the slide currently being shown and what's in the queue. There's also an onscreen clock and a place for notes that only the presenter can see.

- **Better Transitions.** Microsoft has worked hard to make PowerPoint prettier, and it shows. PowerPoint includes smoother transitions and more than 200 animations. That's enough to dress up even the Gettysburg Address.

- **New Design Templates.** Can't get started? Just don't have any ideas for your presentation's format? PowerPoint now has over 100 templates for your presenting pleasure.

Entourage

- **The Project Center.** The big kahuna for people who use Entourage to organize their lives. The Project Center provides the ability to organize and track any kind of pursuit, project, or endeavor in one convenient location. Better still, the Project Center works across the entire Office suite, so it can keep track of your files, remind you when meetings and milestones occur, share documents with fellow employees, and more. (Sorry, Entourage still can't write the final report for you.)

- **New View.** Entourage now offers a three-pane view, with the preview pane on the right side of the window. Microsoft claims that people read short lines more easily, so their three-pane view is the way to go.

- **Archiving.** If you're buried in email overload, Entourage has made it easier to store away old email, contact, and project data in exported archive packages, keeping your hard drive clean and your data safe.

- **Improved Calendar Printing.** With improved calendar printing, you gain more control over more layouts.

- **Microsoft Exchange Server.** You can now connect to an Exchange Server, just like all those Windows Outlook people you work with. (Unfortunately, this book doesn't tackle the behemoth that is Exchange Server; see page 380.)

Office as a Whole

- **Unicode Support.** Now that Office has jumped on the Unicode bandwagon, you can type in virtually any language using the Mac's keyboard layouts without any additional software. It also helps make Office work with Exchange Server (see above), and the Mac OS X Character Palette (Figure 1-1).

- **Toolbox.** The Toolbox provides a window into Office's new Project Center, a gateway into a set of improved reference tools, a method to check the compatibility of your documents, and quick access to your Scrapbook (another new feature in Office 2004). You can drag snippets of text, pictures, and lots more into the Scrapbook, and then access them from your other Office programs.

- **Compatibility Reports.** Although Office 2004 can open and work with documents from Office 98, 2001, and X for Mac; Office 97, 2000, and XP for Windows; and AppleWorks 6, certain program features can hamper the process. New compatibility features help you find—and fix—such problems.

- **New Project Gallery options.** As described on page 657, the Project Gallery offers a wider variety of templates and wizards, in addition to new options that let you access the Project Center, customize the Project Gallery to suit your tastes, and avail yourself of new Office training tools.

- **AutoUpdate.** Don't be left behind when Microsoft comes out with a stability-enhancing or bug-fixing update. This new mini-program lets you know as soon as one's available. (See the box on page 8.)

The Very Basics

You'll find very little jargon or nerd terminology in this book. You will, however, encounter a few terms and concepts that you'll see frequently in your Macintosh life. They include:

- **Clicking.** This book offers three kinds of instructions that require you to use the mouse or trackpad attached to your Mac. To *click* means to point the arrow cursor at something onscreen and then—without moving the cursor at all—to press and release the clicker button on the mouse (or laptop trackpad). To *double-click,* of course, means to click twice in rapid succession, again without moving the cursor at all. And to *drag* means to move the cursor while keeping the button continuously pressed.

  When you're told to ⌘-*click* something, you click while pressing the ⌘ key (next to the Space bar). Such related procedures as *Shift-clicking, Option-clicking,* and *Control-clicking* work the same way—just click while pressing the corresponding key in the lower corner of your keyboard.

- **Menus.** The menus are the words in the lightly striped bar at the top of your screen. The menu titles are slightly different in each of the Office programs. You can either click one of these words to open a pull-down menu of commands (and then click again on a command), or click and *hold* the button as you drag down the menu to the desired command (and release the button to activate the command). Either method works fine.

- **Keyboard shortcuts.** Every time you take your hand off the keyboard to move the mouse, you lose time and potentially disrupt your creative flow. That's why many experienced Mac fans use keystroke combinations instead of menu commands wherever possible. ⌘-B, for example, is a universal keyboard shortcut for boldface type throughout Office 2004 (as well as in most other Mac programs). ⌘-P opens the Print dialog box, ⌘-S saves whatever document you're currently working in, and ⌘-M minimizes the current window to the Dock.

When you see a shortcut like ⌘-W (which closes the current window), it's telling you to hold down the ⌘ key, and, while it's down, type the letter W, and then release both keys.

- **Pop-up buttons.** The tiny arrows beside many of Office 2004's buttons are easy to overlook—but don't. Each one reveals a pop-up menu of useful commands. For instance, the arrow button next to the Undo button on the Standard toolbar lets you choose any number of actions to undo. Meanwhile, the arrow next to the New button in Entourage lets you specify what *kind* of item you want to create anew—an appointment for the calendar, an address book entry, and so on.

- **Choice is good.** Microsoft wouldn't be Microsoft if it didn't offer you several ways to trigger a particular command. Sure enough, everything you could ever wish to do in Office 2004 is accessible by a menu command *or* by clicking a toolbar button *or* by pressing a key combination. Some people prefer the speed of keyboard shortcuts; others like the satisfaction of a visual command array available in menus or toolbars.

One thing's for sure, however: You're not expected to memorize all of these features. In fact, Microsoft's own studies indicate that most people don't even *know* about 80 percent of its programs' features, let alone use them all. And that's OK. Great novels, Pulitzer Prize–winning articles, and successful business ventures have all been launched by people who never got past Open and Save.

On the other hand, as you skim this book, be aware that the way you've been doing things in Word or Excel since 1998 may no longer be the fastest or easiest. Every new keystroke or toolbar you add to your repertoire may afford you more free time to teach ancient Greek to 3-year-olds or start your own hang-gliding club.

As for the programmers in Redmond, let them obsess about how many different ways they can think of to do the same thing. You're under no obligation to try them all.

About This Book

Office 2004 comes in a shiny, attractive package adorned with a distinctive stylized "O" logo. What you won't find inside, however, is a printed manual. To learn this vast set of software programs, you're expected to rely on sample documents in the Project Gallery, a PDF guide, and built-in help screens.

Tip: You can learn how to use Office's Help system in this book's Appendix B, which you can download from the "Missing CD" page at *www.missingmanual.com*.

Although Office Help is detailed and concise, you need to know what you're looking for before you can find it. You can't mark your place (you lose your trail in the Help program every time you close an Office program), you can't underline or make marginal notes, and, even with a laptop, reading in bed or by firelight just isn't the same.

The purpose of this book, then, is to serve as the manual that should have accompanied Office 2004. Although you may still turn to online help for the answer to a quick question, this book provides step-by-step instructions for all major (and most minor) Office features, including those that have always lurked in Office but you've never quite understood. This printed guide provides an overview of the ways this comprehensive software package can make you act like a one-person, all-purpose office.

About the Outline

- This book is divided into five parts, each containing several chapters.

- Parts 1 through 4, **Word, Entourage, Excel,** and **PowerPoint,** cover in detail each of the primary Office programs. Each part begins with an introductory chapter that covers the basics. Additional chapters delve into the more advanced and less-frequently used features.

- Part 5, **Office as a Whole,** shows how the programs work together for even more productivity and creativity. For example, it covers the Project Gallery and Toolbox, the graphics features that work in all Office programs, how to customize Office's menus and keystrokes, and more.

Tip: Three appendixes await you on the "Missing CD-ROM" page at *www.missingmanuals.com* in electronic form: Appendix A explains the Office online help system; Appendix B offers guidance in installing, updating, and troubleshooting the software; and Appendix C, "Office 2004: Menu by Menu" describes the function of each menu command in each of the four major programs, with cross-references to the book in your hands (where these features are discussed more completely).

UP TO SPEED

Office Up to Date

Writing complex software is never easy—and few companies write more complex software than Microsoft. It's also no wonder that few companies issue more "Service Packs" and updates than Microsoft—with the possible exception of Apple. You'll do yourself a big favor by making sure that you have the most updated versions of both Office 2004 and Mac OS X).

To get the latest Office update, go to *www.microsoft.com/mac* and look under "Quick Downloads" at the right of the page. When you reach the download page, follow the instructions onscreen.

Of course, you can avoid all that hassle if you wish. When you install Office 2004, it automatically installs Microsoft's AutoUpdate for Mac. After that, your Mac will periodically check Microsoft's Web site and prompt you to download the latest updates to your Office suite. You can determine how often you want to check for updates by double-clicking the Microsoft AutoUpdate icon in your Applications folder—daily, weekly, or monthly. Or turn on the Manually radio button. That way, AutoUpdate will run only when you launch it and click Check for Updates.

With the help of AutoUpdate, you'll always have every update and fix that Microsoft makes to Office 2004, including the first and most important update, Service Pack 1. Among other things, you'll find that Word crashes a lot less often.

There's no downside to installing Service Pack 1 (although it did interfere with Word's ability to insert hyperlinks into documents, an effect which is hopefully only temporary; see page 300). In fact, this book assumes that you've already done so.

About→These→Arrows

Throughout this book, and throughout the Missing Manual series, you'll find sentences like this one: "Open the System folder→Libraries→Fonts folder." That's shorthand for a much longer instruction that directs you to open three nested folders in sequence. That instruction might read: "On your hard drive, you'll find a folder called System. Open that. Inside the System folder window is a folder called Libraries. Open that. Inside *that* folder is yet another one called Fonts. Double-click to open it, too."

Similarly, this kind of arrow shorthand helps to simplify the business of choosing commands in menus, as shown in Figure I-2.

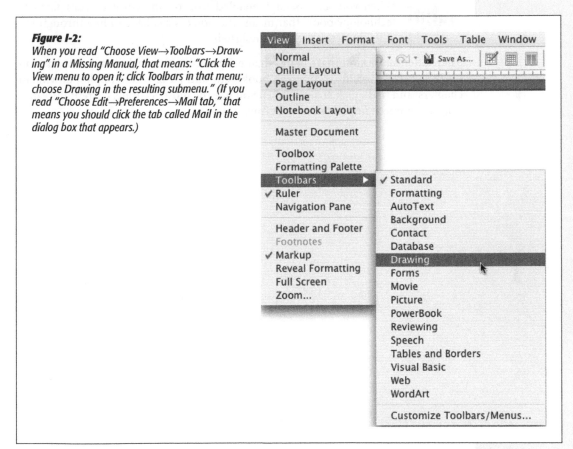

Figure I-2:
When you read "Choose View→Toolbars→Drawing" in a Missing Manual, that means: "Click the View menu to open it; click Toolbars in that menu; choose Drawing in the resulting submenu." (If you read "Choose Edit→Preferences→Mail tab," that means you should click the tab called Mail in the dialog box that appears.)

About MissingManuals.com

At the *missingmanuals.com* Web site, you'll find news, articles, and updates to the books in this series.

But if you click the name of this book and then the Errata link, you'll find a unique resource: a list of corrections and updates that have been made in successive printings of this book. You can mark important corrections right into your own copy of the book, if you like.

In fact, the same Errata page offers an invitation for you to submit such corrections and updates yourself. In an effort to keep the book as up to date and accurate as possible, each time we print more copies of this book, we'll make any confirmed corrections you've suggested. Thanks in advance for reporting any glitches you find!

In the meantime, we'd love to hear your own suggestions for new books in the Missing Manual line. There's a place for that on the Web site, too, as well as a place to sign up for free email notification of new titles in the series.

Safari-Enabled

 When you see a Safari®-enabled icon on the cover of your favorite technology book, that means the book is available online through the O'Reilly Network Safari Bookshelf.

Safari offers a solution that's better than e-Books. It's a virtual library that lets you easily search thousands of top tech books, cut and paste code samples, download chapters, and find quick answers when you nee the most accurate, current information. Try it free at *http://safari.oreilly.com.*

Part One: Word

Chapter 1: Basic Word Processing

Chapter 2: Editing in Word

Chapter 3: Formatting in Word

Chapter 4: Styles, Page Layout, and Tables

Chapter 5: Comments, Change Tracking, and Versions

Chapter 6: Notebooks, Outlining, and Master Documents

Chapter 7: Advanced Word Processing

Chapter 8: Word Meets Web

Basic Word Processing

S kip these next few chapters. You don't need them. After all, everyone knows how to use Word to type a letter to Mom, tap out a report on the Komodo dragon, or clack out a recipe. But listen closely, my Padawan: much more than a typewriter, Word is. Granted, Word is a great tool for projecting your prose onto paper. But you can also use it to chart the Sweet Sixteen as they struggle through March Madness, snap off a To Do list that's as attractive as it is helpful, or put together a company newsletter that gets you noticed. Word offers the basic features of a desktop publisher, Web page designer, graphics utility, Dictaphone, and about a million other programs rolled into one convenient—if somewhat large—package.

The next few chapters teach you how to unwrap that package and put it to good use. From typing your first word to formatting complex layouts and creating templates for mass-producing your own favorite documents, these chapters will teach you everything that you've ever wanted to know about Word...and perhaps more. So, on second thought, you better not skip them.

Creating and Opening Documents

There are at least four ways to create a new document from scratch. They are as follows:

- Choose File→Project Gallery and click the Word Document icon, as described on the next page.

- Choose File→New Blank Document.

- Press ⌘-N.

• Click the New Blank Document button (the very first icon) on the Standard toolbar that appears just beneath your menu bar.

However you do it, the result is a lemony fresh, empty document.

Tip: In fact, this new document is not really empty at all. Behind the scenes, it's already loaded up with such settings as a default font, margin settings, keystroke assignments, macros, style sheets, and so on. It inherits these starter settings from a special document called the Normal template.

You can read much more about Templates on page 226. For now, though, it's enough to know that you can modify the Normal template so that each new document you open automatically contains your own favorite settings.

The Project Gallery

The first thing you see when you initially launch Word is the Project Gallery (see Figure 1-1), where you indicate what kind of document you wish to create.

The Project Gallery is your entry point to the many types of documents Office 2004 (not just Word) is equipped to handle. Your choices include Web pages, business cards, spreadsheets, and even email messages. (For more detail, see Chapter 18.)

When the Project Gallery opens, the Word Document icon is highlighted as shown in Figure 1-1. If you click Open (or press Return or Enter) now, a new blank Word document opens, just as if you'd chosen File→New Blank Document (or pressed ⌘-N).

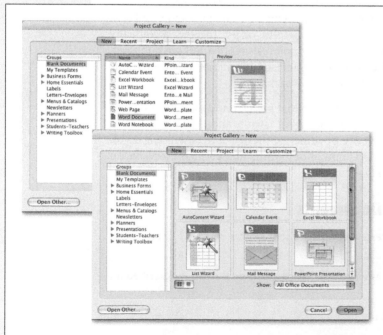

Figure 1-1:
The Project Gallery opens automatically when you first launch Word. When you wish to open another new document, just open the Project Gallery again by choosing File→Project Gallery or pressing Shift-⌘-P.

Left: The List view (use the lower-left pop-up menu) offers a better overview than the Catalog view and saves you some scrolling.

Right: The Catalog view, where you can really see what you get.

Opening any kind of document in the Project Gallery works the same way: Click the list items in the Category list on the left until you see the desired template or document type on the right. Then double-click the document icon to open it.

Opening Documents with the Open Command

If you're entering the world of Word for the purposes of editing an existing document, just double-click the document in the Finder (or click it in the Dock, if that's where you stashed it). If you're already in Word, though, simply choose the fastest of the following options:

• Click the Open button in the Project Gallery

• Choose File→Open

• Press ⌘-O

• Click the second (arrow-from-folder) icon on the Standard toolbar

No matter which method you use, Mac OS X's standard Open File box appears (Figure 1-2). It has a column view, just like the OS X Finder, and a pop-up menu to make it easier to access the document you seek. (See *Mac OS X: The Missing Manual* for a complete list of Save and Open dialog box features.) Once you've located the document you want in this dialog box, double-click to open it.

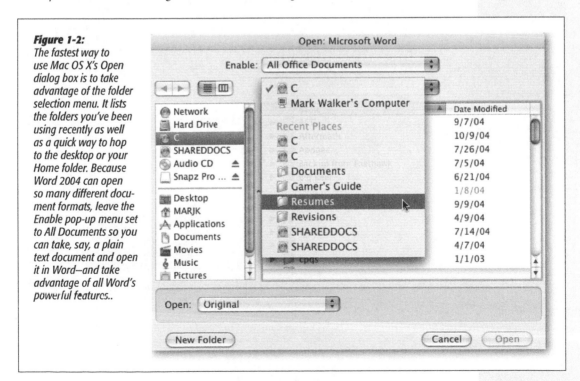

Figure 1-2:
The fastest way to use Mac OS X's Open dialog box is to take advantage of the folder selection menu. It lists the folders you've been using recently as well as a quick way to hop to the desktop or your Home folder. Because Word 2004 can open so many different document formats, leave the Enable pop-up menu set to All Documents so you can take, say, a plain text document and open it in Word—and take advantage of all Word's powerful features..

Tip: When you choose File→Open, Word shows you the contents of the folder you last opened. But if you keep all your Word files in one folder, you might rather see *that* list of files when you use the Open command.

To make it so, choose Word→Preferences. Click the File Locations button (in the list at left), then Documents, then Modify; navigate to and highlight the folder you use most often, and then click Choose. From now on, choosing File→Open automatically uses your favorite starting folder.

In addition, Microsoft has added the following special features of its own to the Open dialog box:

- **Enable.** Use this pop-up menu (at the top of the Open dialog box) to choose which kinds of documents you want to see. The setting "All Readable Documents" lets the Open dialog box display any possible document on your Mac that you can open in Word—not just Microsoft Office documents, but text files, JPEG graphics, HTML Web page documents, and so on. If you know that the document you're seeking is of a certain type, you might save time by telling Word to show *only* those choices (other kinds of documents are "grayed out.") No need to waste time browsing through, say, HTML files when you're looking for an Excel document.

GEM IN THE ROUGH

In Search of Files

The Open dialog box offers a streamlined means of traveling directly to the document you want to open—assuming you remember where you stored it. Until Word 2004, the Open dialog box offered a powerful but somewhat clunky Find File feature that searched your Mac for Word files containing certain properties or even keywords. Microsoft has consigned Find File to the feature graveyard, but you can achieve the same end using Mac OS X's built-in Find function.

Click the Finder icon on the Dock and then choose File→ Find or press ⌘-F. Doing so opens the Find dialog box. To find a file, type the portion of the file name you remember into the text entry box to the right of the search parameter boxes. If you think you know which folder the document might be in, click the Add button at the top of the dialog box and choose a folder location.

Word searches and displays a list of all files that have those characters in their titles. The Commands pop-up button lets you open, or even delete (Send to Trash) a file, right from within this dialog box. You can, however, get much more specific in your search, and doing so often gives you more closely focused results. Conversely, searching in too tight a band sometimes yields no results at all. Nevertheless, altering the parameters in the Find dialog box can often lead to the results that you want.

Use the first pop up menu (top left in the "Search for items whose" panel) to set your initial parameter. What you choose here determines what choices you'll get in the next pop-up menu. For example, choose Size and the pop-up menu gives you a choice between "is less than" or "is greater than." If you're searching for certain letters in the Name or Content of the file, type them in the text field that appears at far right. If you remember you worked on a document recently (or a long time ago), a Date Created or Date Modified search might be the quickest way to locate it. If you change your mind about using a certain criterion, select it and click the minus button to delete it.

Click Search (or just press Return) when you're done, and a list of matching documents pops up in a new window. For the full story on all Mac OS X features, check out *Mac OS X: The Missing Manual* by David Pogue.

Tip: Don't miss the "Recover text from any file" option listed in this pop-up menu; it's a spectacular tool. It lets you extract recognizable text from *any file* and place it into a new window. It was intended to rescue usable prose from a corrupted Word document, of course, but it means what it says: *any file.*

- **Folder Selection Menu.** The pop-up menu underneath the Enable pop-up menu allows you to quickly select a folder. You may then browse its contents in the center panel. This list includes the folders that you've recently visited—handy stuff for accessing commonly used folders.

- **Open.** This pop-up menu lets you choose one of the three different ways Word can open the same document. **Original** opens the document itself; **Copy** opens a copy, leaving the original untouched; and **Read-Only** opens the document but doesn't let you make changes to it.

  Most of the time, you'll open the original and get to work. But opening a *copy* is a convenient way of leaving an electronic paper trail of your work. No matter how many changes you make or how badly you mess up a document, you still have an unsullied copy saved on your Mac. To save changes you've made to a Read-Only document, you must first save it under a different title.

- **View Buttons.** The two List View and Column View buttons at the top left of the Open File dialogue box switch the view from the list to the vertical dividers, as shown in Figure 1-3. Clicking the list icon displays the folders and documents in

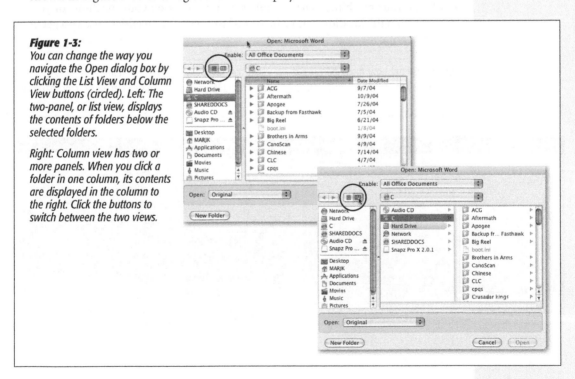

Figure 1-3:
You can change the way you navigate the Open dialog box by clicking the List View and Column View buttons (circled). Left: The two-panel, or list view, displays the contents of folders below the selected folders.

Right: Column view has two or more panels. When you click a folder in one column, its contents are displayed in the column to the right. Click the buttons to switch between the two views.

the selected location. Click the flippy triangle to view a folder's contents, which will be displayed below and indented from the folder (just like the list view in Finder windows). Clicking on the three-pane column icon displays the files in multiple panels. In this view, clicking on a folder in the center panel displays its contents in the right panel. Column view is better for diving through swarms of nested folders, while list view lets you see more documents onscreen, total.

• **New Folder.** Creates a—you guessed it—new folder in the selected location. For example, you know you want to save your document into a folder called Resumes04 in your Job Search folder...but you don't have a folder called Resumes04. No problem: Navigate to the Job Search folder and click the New Folder button. Type the new folder's name in the little message box that appears, and click Create to birth the folder.

Returning to Favorite Documents

Like most people, you probably work with the same documents and templates over and over again. Word knows that and offers two shortcuts to retrieving files that you've used recently or that you intend to use frequently.

The Recent Files list

First, there's the list of recently opened Word documents at the bottom of the File menu. Just choose a file name to open the corresponding document, wherever it may be on your machine. (That is, unless it's no longer *on* your machine, or you've moved it from the location from which you last opened it, in which case you get only a cheerful error message.)

Tip: You control how many documents are listed here by choosing Word→Preferences→General. Set the "Recently used file list" number to 0 if you don't want Word to track your files at all, or 9 for maximum tracking.

FREQUENTLY ASKED QUESTION

Purging the Recent List

I'm not so sure I want my boss seeing which files I've been working on recently. Is there any way to delete the document names listed in the File menu?

You bet. Open any Word document. Choose Word→Preferences→General tab. Turn off "Recently used file list" and press Return. The list of names at the bottom of the File menu disappears, and Word stops remembering them.

To cover your tracks even more completely, choose Word→Preferences→General tab again. Now turn on "Recently used file list" again. Word again starts listing files that you open—but that last embarrassing batch remains gone.

Of course, you can avoid the whole issue by writing your Milla Jovovich love letters at home, but what fun its that?

The Work menu

Word's Work menu is one of the program's best, but most overlooked, features. It's simply a list of the documents you use most often. This is where you can store your book outlines, templates for your invoices, or the different drafts of your thesis. Figure 1-4 illustrates how to install new documents to the list.

Note: The Work Menu lists the Word documents you ask it to. Although useful, it's not even in the same organizational ballpark as Office 2004's Project Center, which compiles a folder of all Office files related to a specific project. For more information on the Project Center, see Chapter 10.

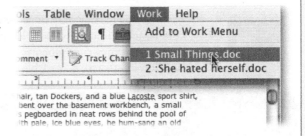

Figure 1-4:
To add to the Work menu, open the document (save it, if you haven't done so). Choose Work→Add to Work Menu. Now click the Work menu again; the name of your document appears, ready for opening just by choosing its name.

You can remove a document from the Work menu just as you'd remove any Word command: by pressing Option-⌘-hyphen. The cursor turns into a thick, black – sign. Use it to choose the name of the document you wish to banish from the Work menu. After your selection, it goes away for good (the menu listing, not your actual document).

Word Processing Basics

Once a document is onscreen, your administrative efforts are complete, and the creative phase can begin. While odds are good that you've word processed before, Chapter 2 still covers the nuts and bolts of editing in detail.

As a reminder, here are the very, very basics of word processing:

- **Don't hit Return at the end of a line.** Word automatically wraps the text to the next line when you reach the edge of the window.

- **Don't type hyphens to break end-of-line words, either.** To divide words at the end of lines, use Word's hyphenation feature, as described on page 149.

- **Press Return at the end of a** paragraph. To create a blank line between paragraphs, don't press Return twice; that can cause awkward problems, such as an extra space at the top of a page. Instead, change the paragraph's *style* to leave more space after each paragraph, as described on page 119. Using this more advanced and graceful method also lets you edit, add, and subtract paragraphs at will. As you do so, the spacing between the paragraphs remains consistent.

- **For similar reasons, don't press Tab to indent the first line of a paragraph.** If, instead, you set a *first line indent* using the Formatting Palette, as described on page 121, Word automatically creates the indents each time you start a paragraph. Indents created this way remain consistent as you edit the document. In addition, the amount of indentation you choose is not dependent upon the positions of your tab stops.

- **Don't press Return at the end of a page.** Word automatically wraps the text to the next page. If you want your next thought to start at the top of a new page, choose Insert→Break→Section Break (Next Page) instead. Now, no matter how much you edit before or after the section break, your new section always starts at the top of a new page.

- **Press the Space bar only once—not twice—after punctuation such as periods, colons, and semicolons.** Double-spacing after punctuation is a holdover from the days of the typewriter, when you had to manually add extra space after punctuation for an attractive, readable result. On a Mac, Word automatically places the

---

Document Protection

Word makes it easy to open documents; almost too easy, if you're trying to keep certain documents private or unmodified. Never fear: Word offers three levels of document-protection features designed to keep spies and busybodies out of your files.

- **Suggest Read-Only.** When someone tries to open a document protected in this manner, a dialog box politely suggests that he use the read-only option. That person can make changes, but can only save the file under a new name. The original, read-only file remains intact. To save a file this way, choose File→Save As; click Options, and then click the Security category. On the Security panel, turn on "Read-only recommended," and press Return. Click Save or press Return to complete the process.

- **Password to Modify.** This trick makes Word ask for a password at the moment the document is opened, using a dialog box like the one shown here. Readers to whom you give the password can edit the document and save the changes just as you can; for everyone else, the document opens as read-only, as described above. To protect a

document this way, choose File→Save As; click Options. In the Security dialog box, type in a password in the Password to Modify box. Click OK or press Return. Word asks the forgetful among us to retype the password. Do it.

- **Password to Open.** This highest level of document protection requires readers to enter a password before they can even open the document. In the Save As dialog box, click Options, and then click the Security category. On the Security panel, type a password in the "Password to open" box and press Return (or the mouse-happy can click OK). Re-enter the password when Word asks for it, click OK, and your document is protected.

If you use one of the password methods, write the password down and keep it somewhere safe. If you lose the password, don't bother calling Microsoft. They can't help you open the protected document, and even Recover Text From Any File doesn't work on *these* files. (You could probably find a few thousand Internet hackers that could handle it for you, but that's a different book. Anyway, writing down your password is easier.)

---

correct amount of space after each period or other punctuation mark. Adding an extra space is superfluous, clutters your file with extra characters, and cramps your thumbs.

- **Save early, save often.** Choose File→Save (or press ⌘-S) after every paragraph or sentence.

A Window into Word

The tools you use most often—those for navigating your document and for basic formatting—are clustered around the main text window, which is shown in Figure 1-5.

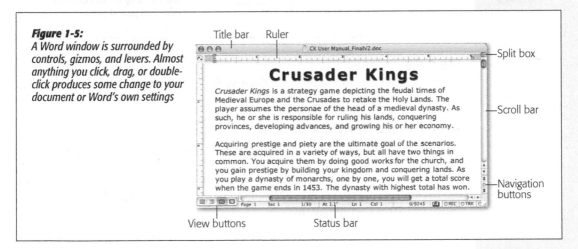

Figure 1-5:
A Word window is surrounded by controls, gizmos, and levers. Almost anything you click, drag, or double-click produces some change to your document or Word's own settings

Title bar   Ruler

CK User Manual_FinalV2.doc

Crusader Kings

Crusader Kings is a strategy game depicting the feudal times of Medieval Europe and the Crusades to retake the Holy Lands. The player assumes the personae of the head of a medieval dynasty. As such, he or she is responsible for ruling his lands, conquering provinces, developing advances, and growing his or her economy.

Acquiring prestige and piety are the ultimate goal of the scenarios. These are acquired in a variety of ways, but all have two things in common. You acquire them by doing good works for the church, and you gain prestige by building your kingdom and conquering lands. As you play a dynasty of monarchs, one by one, you will get a total score when the game ends in 1453. The dynasty with highest total has won.

—Split box
—Scroll bar
—Navigation buttons

Page 1   Sec 1   1/30   At 1.1"   Ln 1   Col 1   0/9245   REC   TRK

View buttons   Status bar

Title Bar

Word 2004's title bar does all the usual Mac things—sends the window to the Dock when double-clicked, moves it when dragged, and so on—but it has a few unheralded powers, too. It also performs like a Mac OS X *folder* window in two key respects:

- To find out which folder your document is nested in, ⌘-click the document's title. As shown in Figure 1-6, a pop-up menu appears, identifying your document *icon's* location on the hard drive. Click any folder or drive on the list to open it into a new Finder window.

- See the tiny Word icon next to the document's name in the title bar? That's your *document proxy icon,* which works just like the *folder* proxy icon in every Finder window title bar. As shown at right in Figure 1-6, you can drag that icon just as you would any icon in the Finder. You might do so to move the current document to a different folder, to copy it to a different disk, or even to drag it directly to the Trash. In true Mac OS X fashion, you see a translucent ghost of the icon as you move it. (You have to hold the cursor down on this icon for about one second, making it turn dark, before you can drag it in this way. If you drag it too quickly, Word thinks you're simply trying to move the window on the screen.)

Tip: The document proxy icon appears faded out (disabled) whenever you've edited your document without
saving the changes. (And you can't drag it to move, copy, or trash your document when you haven't saved
changes.) Only when you choose File→Save (⌘-S) does the icon spring to life, ready for dragging.

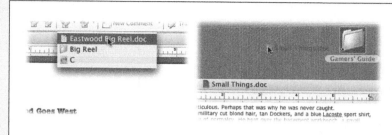

Figure 1-6:
Left: When you ⌘-click the document name, you can choose and open, in a Finder window, any folder or disk in the list.

Right: After holding for a second, you can drag the tiny icon anywhere on your desktop.

The Ruler

The ruler across the top of the page displays the current settings for margins, tabs, and indents. See page 116 for details on how to use and change these settings.

Scroll Bar and Navigator Buttons

Figure 1-5 shows the *Navigator buttons*—double arrows flanking a little round button at the lower-right of the Word window. When you first open a document, these Navigator buttons act as Page Up/Page Down buttons. But once you've used the Find and Replace command (see page 72), or in some other way changed the *browse object*, the double arrows act differently.

For instance, after you've used Find and Replace, clicking the Navigator buttons takes you from each occurrence of the word you're trying to find to the next. For more detail on the Browse Object feature and Navigator buttons, see page 69.

Split Box

Figure 1-5 also shows the small blue *Split box* at the upper-right of the window. When you point to it, the cursor changes to a double-pointing arrow. Dragging that arrow divides the window into two panes, each with its own, independent, vertical scroll bar. (Choosing Window→Split, or pressing Option-⌘-S, accomplishes the same thing.)

This is a great arrangement when you're working at the end of a long document and need to refer to material earlier in the document. You can use the upper window to scroll through the entire document, while meanwhile back at the lower window, you can continue typing without losing your place.

Tip: It's often faster to simply *double-click* the Split box. Doing so gives you two evenly split panes of the window; to adjust their relative proportions, just drag the *resize bar* (the gray dividing line between the panes) up or down.

Double-click this dividing line a second time to restore the window to its single-pane status. (The *bottom* half of the window disappears, even if it contained the insertion point–a potentially alarming behavior.)

Drag the light gray bar between the two panes up or down to adjust their relative sizes. Like the scroll bars, the Page Up, Page Down, and arrow keys work as usual *within* each pane, meaning you can't use them to travel from one pane to the next. To switch *between* panes, you can use the mouse, or just press F6, which acts as a toggle key to the other pane and back again.

To restore a split window back to a single one, drag the resize bar all the way to the top of the window, double-click the resize bar, or press Option-⌘-S again.

Window Menu

You can't split a window into more than two panes—nor create *vertical* panes—using the Split box as described above. However, you can get these effects using the Window menu (see Figure 1-7).

Figure 1-7:
If your screen is cluttered with documents and duplicate windows, the Window→Arrange All command turns each window into a screen-wide strip and stacks them from top to bottom. It's not a very convenient arrangement, but at least you can see what you've got. You can now resize and arrange them as you wish.

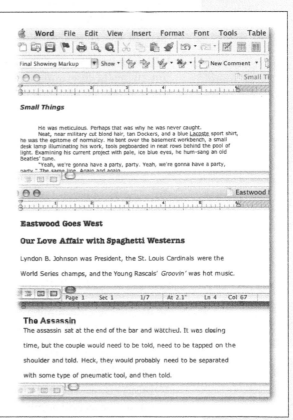

Choosing Window→New Window creates a clone of your document window, which you can scroll, position, or zoom independently; each can be in a different Word *view*, too (one in Outline view, one in Normal, and so on). The new windows are different peepholes into the same document; remember, you haven't created a new document. Therefore, any change you make in one window appears in both windows simultaneously. When you use File→Save, you save *all* the windows.

There's almost no limit to the number of windows you can create in this way. You can place two windows side by side and work on the first and last pages of your document at the same time, or you can create five windows, each scrolled to a different region of your manuscript. The title bar identifies the windows as "Introduction:1," "Introduction:2," and so on.

To reconstitute your document, just close the extra windows.

Status Bar

The light gray bar running across the bottom of the window (see Figure 1-5) is called the *status bar*. Divided into segments by etched vertical lines, the status bar presents a variety of statistics about your current location within the document.

- **Page 1, Sec 1.** At the far left is the number of the page that contains the insertion point (not necessarily the page you're looking at), followed by the section number. If you haven't divided your document into *sections* (see page 132), which is likely, then the section readout always says Sec 1.

- **1/30.** The third set of numbers looks like a fraction; it shows the page number containing the insertion point (again) followed by the total pages. For instance, if you're at the end of a three-page letter, this readout says 3/3.

Tip: Double-click anywhere in the first two segments of the status bar to open the Go To tab of the Find and Replace dialog box, described on page 68. The idea, of course, is to provide you with a quick way to jump to a different page of your document without scrolling.

- **At 1.1".** The status bar's second segment provides information about your insertion point's location on the current page. The first number is the distance, in inches, from the top of the page to the insertion point. It tells you where you're "at" along the length of your page, which could conceivably be useful if, for example, you need to determine column inches for a newspaper.

- **Ln 1.** The second number identifies the current *line* of your document, counting down from the top of the *printed page* (not the window) to the insertion point. It's useful when the number of lines is important, such as when placing a personal ad, if you're a lawyer, or just curious (you know who you are).

- **Col 1.** This peculiar statistic reveals the number of characters you've typed from the left margin.

- **0/9245.** The next divided segment of the status bar shows two numbers divided by a slash; the second number shows the total number of words in your document (journalists, kneel!), and the first indicates which word contains your insertion point, as counted from the first word of the document.

If these numbers are blank, it's probably because your word count feature is turned off. To turn it on, choose Word→Preferences; in the Preferences dialog box, click the View button. Turn on Live Word Count (under "Window") and click OK. Now, when you start typing, the word count number is revised after every few words that you type; hence the name "Live Word Count."

Tip: Double-click the word-count segment to summon the Word Count dialog box, which provides the number of pages, paragraphs, lines, and other countable items, as well as the word count. (It's the same box that appears when you choose Tools→Word Count.)

By the way, if you first highlight some text in your document, the number before the slash tells you how many words are in the selected passage.

- **The little book.** This icon is the spelling and grammar–checking status indicator. As you type, a little pencil moves across the pages, indicating that Word is checking for spelling and grammar errors. Most of the time, when you're at rest, a red X appears on the book icon, meaning that Word has found an error somewhere in your document. (That is, an error according to Word's sense of grammar.) When you've just completed a grammar check and made no new errors, the icon shows a checkmark instead of an X.

  To review Word's spelling and grammar flags starting from the beginning of the document, double-click the book icon. At each error, a pop-up menu offers alternative spelling and punctuation choices and commands that lead you to relevant spelling and grammar dialog boxes (see page 79).

Note: If you don't see the little book icon, it may be because you've turned off "as you type" spelling and grammar checking (Word→Preferences→Spelling & Grammar panel).

- **REC.** This button shows the status of the macro recorder (see page 279). It's almost always off (hollow). Clicking it on opens the Record New Macro dialog box, in readiness to create a new macro. See Chapter 7 for a full explanation of macros and how to record them. When the button is on (green), you're recording a macro.

- **TRK** corresponds to the Track Changes command (see page 179). When TRK is turned on, your own edits show up in a different color, so that your collaborators can see exactly which changes you've made.

Tip: Clicking the TRK indicator turns on revision tracking (or, if it's on, turns it off). That's a *huge* timesaver if you're used to turning on tracking in the usual way (Tools→Track Changes→Highlight Changes; turn on "Track changes while editing"; click OK).

- Clicking the **EXT** button turns your cursor into a high-powered text-selection tool. Normally, when the EXT is off (hollow), clicking in your text just places the insertion point there. You have to drag the mouse to select anything. But when you click EXT, the button turns green and you enter Extend Selection mode. Your insertion point, wherever it is at that moment, marks the beginning of a new selection. Clicking the mouse, pressing the arrow keys, or even pressing the Page Up and Page Down keys highlights text and keeps it highlighted until you turn EXT off again.

Extend Selection mode is useful for selecting large amounts of text with a minimum of mouse work. (The Cut, Copy, and Paste commands work as normal in extend-selection mode.)

Tip: You can duplicate the mouseless-selection convenience of Extend mode without having to remember to click EXT again when you're done. Just hold down the Shift key to select text using the arrow keys and Page Up/Down keys.

- **OVR** stands for *overtype* mode, another slightly peculiar editing mode. In overtype mode, when you click within existing text, what you type *replaces* what was typed there before. This arrangement is the opposite of the normal mode, where what you type is inserted *between* existing letters. Click OVR to turn overtype mode on (green) and off (hollow).

  By the way, there's nothing worse than entering overtype mode by *accident*. Suddenly your typing eats away at whatever perfectly good prose was already there. Keep your cursor well clear of this status-bar doohickey or at least keep your eyes on the keyboard.

- **The stack of papers.** If you've created multiple *versions* of the current document (a feature described on page 186), you'll see an icon that looks like an overlapping stack of documents. Double-clicking it calls up the Versions dialog box, in which you create and manage your various versions of a file.

Tip: You may need to enlarge the document window to see all of the status-bar icons. Just drag the resize box at the lower-right corner of the window.

- **Tiny floppy disk.** This fleeting icon appears only when Word is automatically saving your document during idle moments, thanks to its background-saving feature (page 35).

- **Printer icon.** A printer-shaped icon indicates your background printing status, which appears only when you're printing. You can watch the progress of your printout by examining the Dock icon of Print Center, Mac OS X's printing software.

Tip: If you don't find any of these status indicators particularly helpful—and you'd rather dedicate the screen space to your writing—just hide them. Choose Word→Preferences, click the View tab, and turn off the "Status bar" checkbox near the bottom of the dialog box. Then click OK.

Standard Toolbar

Word 2004 can slip in and out of many guises—a picture or movie editor, a database manager, or a Web browser, to name just a few. Each primary function comes complete with its own *toolbar* filled with icons relevant to that task.

If all these icons were available all the time, your screen would be filled with toolbars. As a result, you'd have to do all your typing in a leftover space the size of a Triscuit. Fortunately, Word 2004 is very considerate of your screen real estate. You can open, close, resize, reshape, or relocate toolbars at will, like so:

- To open a toolbar, choose View→Toolbars and choose a toolbar from the submenu. Alternatively, carefully Control-click one of the etched dividing lines on any open toolbar and choose from the resulting list. Believe it or not, you can also see the toolbar list by Control-clicking any blank space on the Formatting Palette (page 105).

  Word comes with 25 toolbars, including the Standard toolbar; you can also design new toolbars of your own (see Chapter 19). There's no limit to the number you can have open at once. To close a toolbar, click the tiny close button in the upper-left corner, just like any other Mac window, or choose its name a second time from the View→Toolbars command.

- Each toolbar has a place where it likes to appear. The Drawing toolbar, for example, opens vertically at the far left of the screen the first time you use it. However, you can move toolbars anywhere you like. To move a toolbar around onscreen, drag the textured bar at the top (or left side), just as though it's a shrunken version of a standard Mac title bar. As you drag a toolbar near one of the screen edges, or near another toolbar, it jumps neatly into place.

- To resize a toolbar, drag the tiny, striped, lower-right corner. You can change most toolbars from a long, narrow bar (either horizontal or vertical), into a squarish palette.

- If you forget the name of a *button*, just point to it without clicking and wait one second; a yellow screen tip appears.

The Standard toolbar is the only one that opens by default when you create a new Word document; it has icons for printing, saving, and other tasks that you perform frequently. Each button on it instantly does something that would normally take two or more mouse clicks: opening a new blank document, opening an existing file, saving the document, and so on.

From left to right, the buttons on the Standard toolbar are:

- **New Blank Document, Open, Save.** These buttons correspond to the equivalent commands in the File menu.

- **Flag for Follow Up.** This button opens the Flag for Follow Up dialog box (also available at Tools→Flag for Follow Up), where you set a date and time. Word automatically creates a reminder on your Entourage calendar. When the appointed moment arrives, a reminder dialog box opens to remind you that it's time to quit procrastinating and finish up your work; see page 406 for a full description of this feature.

- **Print.** This button isn't the same thing as the File→Print command; it's a much more streamlined function. It prints the current document—all pages, one copy. For more control over what Word prints (number of copies, which pages), use the File→Print command (⌘-P), which opens the Print dialog box (see page 39).

- **Print Preview.** This button is another avenue into the printing process. It opens up the document in a window that offers a full view of the page, and a toolbar with various print commands. See page 42 for more on using the Print Preview feature. (*Keyboard shortcut:* ⌘-F2 or Option-⌘-I.)

- **Web Page Preview.** This button—a globe signifying the World Wide Web with a magnifying glass for *preview*—shows you what your document would look like if translated into a Web page. Like its menu equivalent (File→Web Page Preview), the button launches your Web browser and displays the document in a new browser window. (For those people unaccustomed to using their word processors for churning out Web pages, there's much more on this topic in Chapter 8.)

- **Cut, Copy, Paste.** These buttons correspond to the Big Three of the Edit menu. Cutting, copying, and pasting are described on page 58.

- **Format Painter.** Just as you can pour color onto a selected area in a painting program, you can also "pour" a set of formatting choices onto any number of words or an entire paragraph. See page 121 for details.

- **Undo.** Clicking this curved arrow undoes your last bit of typing, pasting, and so on. The tiny triangle next to it, however, is where the power of Undo is truly unleashed.

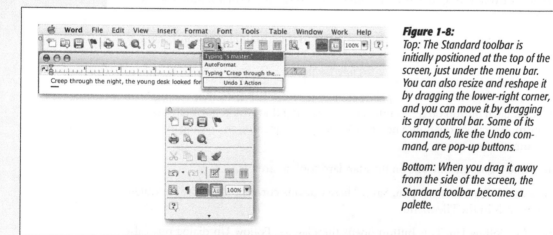

Figure 1-8:
Top: The Standard toolbar is initially positioned at the top of the screen, just under the menu bar. You can also resize and reshape it by dragging the lower-right corner, and you can move it by dragging its gray control bar. Some of its commands, like the Undo command, are pop-up buttons.

Bottom: When you drag it away from the side of the screen, the Standard toolbar becomes a palette.

Clicking on the Undo triangle pulls down a list that displays, in reverse order, the last several steps you took in Word—from major style changes to single deletions. You can retrace your steps pages and pages into the past. As you drag down this pop-up menu, the button at the bottom of the list (see Figure 1-8) tells you how many things you're about to undo. Letting go of the mouse button triggers Undo. If you change your mind, be sure to move the cursor off the Undo list until the button says Cancel before letting go. (*Keyboard shortcut:* ⌘-Z or F1, either of which only undoes one action at a time.)

- **Redo.** This button and triangle let you *redo* whatever you've just undone. If you just undid your last 10 moves, for example, you can drag the Redo list as far as "Redo 10 Actions." As with the Undo list, you can scroll up and down in this list to redo as much or as little as you like. (*Keyboard shortcut:* ⌘-Y or Option-Return, either of which only redoes one action at a time.)

- **Tables and Borders.** Clicking this button turns the cursor into a pencil, ready to draw a *table* anywhere in your document, and opens a palette of all the tools necessary to work with a table. See page 160 for full detail on using tables.

- **Insert Table.** Another quick way to create a table is to click this button, whose pop-up menu is a small expanse of white squares. Drag over the squares to select the table size you want: 2 x 2 (two rows by two columns), 3 x 3, and so on.

Tip: Don't feel cramped by the 4 x 5 shape of the pop-up menu itself. If you drag beyond the boundaries of the proposed 4 x 5 grid, the pop-up menu itself expands until it's enormous.

POWER USERS' CLINIC

Secrets of the Re-branching "Undo" Tree

Having a multiple-level Undo is great; there's no debating that a program with one is much better than a program without one.

But the multi-Undo can also be frustrating in one occasional circumstance. Imagine something like this: You decide that you really wanted paragraph 13 the way you originally wrote it. Trouble is, you've since rewritten it and made hundreds of other changes to the manuscript. How can you recapture the glory of paragraph 13 the way it was two hours ago?

Unfortunately, you can't use a thousand Undos to recreate it. Remember, you've done a lot of great work in the meantime, in other paragraphs that you want to keep. If you were to Undo all the way back to paragraph 13, just for the purpose of restoring it, you'll also lose all the other paragraphs you've written or edited in the meantime.

The sneaky solution is this: Undo all the way back to the point where paragraph 13 was originally by pressing ⌘-Z over and over again—all the while coolly watching all your editing work disappear. When you finally see paragraph 13 return to its original version, highlight the paragraph and copy it (⌘-C).

Now redo all the changes, using ⌘-Y repeatedly until Word beeps, indicating that you've restored the document to its latest condition.

Finally, highlight paragraph 13 (which is back to its unsatisfactory version) and paste over it (⌘-V), replacing it with the good, earlier version. Fortunately, all those Redos don't affect what you copied to the clipboard.

When you release the mouse button, a table of the size you selected appears in your document at the insertion point. See page 160 for more on the Table tool.

- **Columns.** This button's pop-up menu lets you create columns; drag down and across to choose the number of columns you want. (You can drag beyond the borders of the pop-up menu if four columns across aren't enough, you crazed designer, you.) When you release the mouse button, you find yourself in Page Layout view, with your entire document divided equally into the number of columns you chose. For details on using columns, see page 146.

- **Navigation Pane.** New to Word 2004, this viewing tool gives Word the click-a-thumbnail-to-jump-to-a-page convenience of programs like Adobe Acrobat and Apple's Preview program. Clicking the magnifying glass over a page icon displays the Navigation Pane to the left side of your document. The pane is a big help when working with long documents. It lets you go to a page by quickly scrolling to it in the left pane, and then clicking it to view in the main pane. Select the view you want from the pop-up menu at the top of the pane. Thumbnail (small page pictures) or the old standby Document Map (outline of the document) are the choices.

- **Show/Hide ¶.** Clicking this button exposes paragraph markers (¶) and other nonprinting characters. This display is useful when, for example, you're copying a paragraph and want to make sure you're copying *all* the formatting. (Word stores formatting for each paragraph in the invisible ¶ mark that follows it.) Click it again to render the characters invisible once again. (*Keyboard shortcut:* ⌘-8.)

- **Toolbox.** New to Office 2004, the red toolbox icon opens a multipurpose palette of tools. Here you can access your Scrapbook text, images, and objects (page 679). It's also where you conduct compatibility reports (page 668) that troubleshoot documents from earlier versions of Word or on computers that have been lured to the dark...er, PC, side. The Toolbox also provides a gateway into the world of the Office 2004 Project Center, which is covered in more detail in Chapter 10, and

---

DON'T PANIC

Who's Got The Buttons?

Those of you that are used to Office X are wondering where your beloved Drawing and Dictionary buttons have gone. Well, although they are MIA from the Standard toolbar, they are still alive and well in Word 2004. You may open the Drawing Palette by choosing View→Toolbars→Drawing. See Chapter 20 for the skinny on using the Drawing feature.

Choosing Tools→Dictionary is now the quickest way to open the Dictionary tools. You can also click the bookshelf icon in the Toolbox palette (page 663) if it's open. Click one of the words in the scrolling list in the top pane to read a brief definition at the bottom. Office's Dictionary is an abridgement of the Encarta World English Dictionary (*www.encarta.msn.com*). The definitions may not be comprehensive enough for card-carrying word nerds, but they're ideal for those times when you want to look up a word but just don't want to leave your chair. (See page 665 for more detail on using Office's reference tools.)

a window into Word 2004 reference tools, which presents itself in greater detail in Chapter 18.

- **Formatting Palette.** This button displays or hides the Formatting Palette (see page 105). It's the same as choosing View→Formatting Palette, but quicker.

- **Zoom.** There are two ways to zoom (enlarge or shrink your document's representation on the screen) from the toolbar. First, you can enter a number in the box and press Return. (100% is roughly life-size; 125% is a more comfortable size on high-resolution monitors.)

Second, you can select a magnification from the pop-up menu. Page Width magnifies or reduces your view so that it fills the document window, no matter how wide or narrow you've made it. Even if you make the window bigger or smaller, Word automatically adjusts the text so that it always neatly fills the window, with nothing chopped off and no extra space.

In Page Layout view, you get a Whole Page command in this pop-up menu, too. It does the same thing as Page Width, but in both dimensions; in other words, Word scales the picture of your document so that the entire page fits within the window. Similarly, the Two Pages command forces two side-by-side pages to fit inside your window—a terrific option if you're the proud owner of one of Apple's gigantic flat-panel screens. (Make your window as wide as possible before choosing this option; otherwise, the font may become too small to read.) These and more zoom options are also available by choosing View→Zoom.

Note: Zooming never changes the actual printed size of your document. It only makes the type larger or smaller onscreen, as though you're moving closer to the page or farther from it.

- **Office Assistant.** This classic Help symbol—the question mark in the speech balloon—turns Max, the Office Assistant, on and off. (See Appendix B on the "Missing CD" page at *www.missingmanuals.com* if Max turns *you* off.) Whether you use Max or the Help system index, this button is the way to fire it up.

Note: Not all of the buttons on the toolbar have keyboard shortcuts. In fact, two of them don't even have menu equivalents: Format Painter and Show/Hide ¶. (Of course, you can always *add* these commands to your menus, as described in Chapter 19.)

Clicking the tiny triangle at the right end of the Standard toolbar reveals some extra buttons, plus commands that allow you to customize the toolbar (see Chapter 19). The extra buttons, accessible only by clicking the triangle, inexplicably remain hidden no matter how you resize the Standard toolbar. That's unfortunate, because some of them are just as useful as the buttons that are continually visible.

- **Spelling and Grammar.** Like choosing Tools→Spelling and Grammar, this button initiates a spelling and grammar check starting from wherever you are in the document. See page 79 for more detail.

- **Hyperlink.** This button (the globe with a chain link on it) opens the Insert Hyperlink dialog box, also accessible by choosing Insert→Hyperlink. This feature lets you create underlined links either to Web sites, other files on your Mac, or even other places in the same document (see Chapter 8).

- **Web Toolbar.** Clicking this little icon summons the Web toolbar—like choosing View→Toolbars→Web, but faster. The Web toolbar (see page 286) comes in handy if you've added any hyperlinks to your document.

- **Scrapbook.** In a way, the Scrapbook replaces the Office Clipboard. You may drag and drop just about anything in the Scrapbook, from pictures to documents. Then use the Scrapbook to organize it. See page 663 for more detail. Choose Tools→ Scrapbook to open it.

- **Insert Excel Spreadsheet.** This button lets you create an Excel worksheet right in your Word document. (Since you're merely embedding the spreadsheet there, you must open Excel in order to edit it.) When you choose this command, Excel launches and opens a worksheet where you can enter your spreadsheet data. (This technique is a handy way to send income tax information in a letter to an accountant, for example.)

When you're done inputting numbers, close the worksheet; the resulting spreadsheet appears in your Word document. To edit the spreadsheet later, double-click the table to launch Excel. (To insert other kinds of Excel items into Word, choose Insert→Object.)

- **Close.** Like the File→Close command, this button closes the current document and gives you a chance to save it. (It's probably not worth asking who at Microsoft thought that it might be simpler to use this difficult-to-reach button to close a window, instead of simply clicking the close button at the upper-left corner of every Word window or pressing ⌘-W.)

- The next two buttons, **Envelopes** and **Labels,** open their respective dialog boxes, which can also be found on the Tools menu. As described on page 273, these features make creating, aligning, and printing envelopes and labels more painless than ever before.

- The final extra button, the universal magnifying glass icon for **Find,** is yet another way to open the Find and Replace dialog box, as described on page 72. (*Keyboard shortcut:* ⌘-F.)

Formatting Palette

For details on this final, very important Word interface component, see page 105.

The Views

Word can display your document in any of five different views, including the just-introduced Notebook Layout view. Each offers different features for editing, reading, and scrolling through your work. Some people spend their entire lives—or at least their Mac lives—in only one of these views, while power users may switch regularly back and forth between them.

In any case, using the views feature doesn't change your actual document in any way; regardless of what view you're using, the document *prints* exactly the same way (the two exceptions: Outline and Notebook view). Views are mostly for your benefit while still preparing the document onscreen.

Here are the five Word views, as they appear in the View menu.

Tip: You can also switch views by clicking one of the four icons at the very lower-left corner of your document window. (Except Online Layout view, which you can only get to via the View menu.)

Normal View

Normal view presents the Standard toolbar, the Ruler, and all the window accessories described in the previous section (see Figure 1-5). In Normal view, your entire document scrolls by in a never-ending window, with only a faint dotted line to indicate where one page ends and the next begins. Normal view is where you can focus on *writing* your document. Many page-layout elements, including headers and footers, drawing objects, and multiple columns, don't appear at all in Normal view. As a result, Normal view offers the fewest distractions and the fastest scrolling.

Online Layout View

This view shows what your document will look like if you convert it to a Web page, as described in Chapter 8. (And if you'd never in a million years dream of using Microsoft Word as a Web-design program, then this is only the first of many discussions you can safely skip in this book.)

For example, in Online Layout view, you don't see any page breaks, even if a particular page requires 47 consecutive feet of scrolling; as far as Word is concerned, that's what the Web is like. The Ruler goes away, too, because Web pages don't actually offer true indents or tabs. (Your existing tabs and margins still work, but you can't make changes to them in Online Layout view.) Any backgrounds, drawings, and images you've added to your document are visible, and look as they would when your document is viewed in a Web browser.

Note: The little row of view buttons disappears when you're in Online Layout view. It's not your fault. You can switch out of this view only by using the View menu.

Page Layout View

This view offers a second ruler along the *left* side of the page—a vertical ruler. (The parts of the ruler that are your page margins are blocked out with diagonal gray stripes.) In Page Layout view, you can see—and manipulate—everything. You can adjust margins by dragging them as described in Figure 1-9. You can edit headers and footers by double-clicking where the cursor changes (see page 218). You can create drawing objects by clicking View→Toolbars→Drawing (see Chapter 20 for more detail on drawings), and move them around by dragging. To see more of your page at once while in Page Layout view, simply change the Zoom box setting in the Standard toolbar.

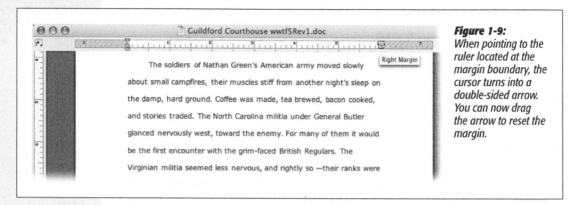

Figure 1-9:
When pointing to the ruler located at the margin boundary, the cursor turns into a double-sided arrow. You can now drag the arrow to reset the margin.

Outline View

In Outline view, Word automatically formats your paragraphs into outline form, saving you from remembering whether your next point should be labeled I., a., i., or whatever. Outline view lets you move your topics and supporting facts up and down, in and out of the hierarchy, using the mouse or keyboard—and remembers everything on the fly. Chapter 6 contains a full tutorial on using Word's outliner.

Notebook Layout View

New to Word in 2004 is Notebook Layout view. You may want to use this layout for your personal or scholastic note-taking needs, or an information organization tool. This view allows you to draw images directly on the Notebook using the Scribble tool, and reorganize notes or even entire sections with a simple drag and drop. Choosing this view converts your document to a notebook complete with lined pages, and places the Notebook Layout tools on the toolbar. See Chapter 6 for more details on the Notebook Layout view.

Note: Notebook Layout view offers many of the features of a full-fledged note-taking program, such as Circus Ponies' Notebook or Microsoft's OneNote. You can use it to take notes and rapidly rearrange them, organize graphics and photos, sketch out ideas, and even dictate notes to yourself using the new Audio Notes feature. Unless you require specialized features like custom covers or notebook sharing, you can organize your life without investing 50 bucks in a separate notebook program.

Master Document View

Master Document view is Outline view writ large. Where Outline view treats each *paragraph* as a movable, draggable entity, Master Document view allows you to manipulate entire *documents* within a giant, overarching master file. If you write a novel as a master document, for example, each *chapter* could be considered a subdocument.

Each chapter would have its own custom-tailored headers and footers, but the book would have a consistent look because all chapters would use the same master template. (Not to mention how much easier it is to change the character's name throughout the entire novel when all the chapters are contained in a single file.)

See Chapter 6 for the full story on working with master documents.

Every Conceivable Variation on Saving

The first thing to do with a completed file—or even a file just underway—is, of course, to save it onto the hard drive, preserving it in case of an unforeseen system crash or accidental surge-suppressor power-switch toe-press. However, if you're still not in the habit of pressing ⌘-S every few sentences, paragraphs, or minutes, Word's AutoRecovery feature may save your hide.

Tip: If you have more than one Word document open at a time, hold down the Shift key as you choose File→Save. The Save command becomes Save All, which saves the changes to all open documents one by one. When you hold down Shift, you'll also notice that Close becomes Close All.

AutoRecovery

At preset intervals, Word saves the current document into a separate AutoRecover file. If your Mac freezes, crashes, or blacks out in a power failure, the AutoRecover file opens automatically (once *you've* recovered, that is). If you're satisfied that the "Recovered" file is the most recent and the one you want to keep, save it under a new name and continue working. (The file under the old name is the file as it was when you last conducted a real Save.)

WORKAROUND WORKSHOP

Who is that computer and why is it staring at me?

Meet Max, the Microsoft Office for Mac mascot. This little animated, QuickTime-generated character acts as doorman to the Word Help system. Plus, when you're not using him for his day job, he entertains you with various antics as you type. (Attempts to entertain you, anyway.)

You either love him or you hate him. If Max gets on your nerves, you can dismiss him like any other window by clicking his close box. (Ever the friendly one, Max makes sure to wave goodbye before he leaves.)

Clicking inside Max's window does the same thing as choosing Help→Microsoft Word Help: It gives Max a speech balloon that helpfully asks, "What would you like to do?" Whatever you type appears in the balloon and, when you click

Search, triggers a search of the Word Help system. (See Appendix B on the "Missing CD" page at *www.missingmanuals. com* for more on the Word help program.)

Clicking the Search button on the standard toolbar, however, calls up Max and his type-your-question balloon again, even if you've shut him down with the close box.

If you'd rather never see him, even when you click the Search button, here's the permanent solution: Choose Help→Use the Office Assistant to remove the checkmark and turn Max off until you turn him on again. Now when you choose Help→Search Word Help, Word takes you directly to the Microsoft Office Help window, with a Max-free search function.

Although AutoRecovery functions in the background as you work, it produces a momentary and detectable slowdown. In other words, you want Word to save often, but not *too* often. To set the AutoRecover interval, choose Word→Preferences and click the Save button. Under "Save options," turn on the "Save AutoRecover" box and enter a preferred number of minutes in the adjoining box.

Save As Options

The first time you save a document, or anytime you choose File→Save As, you open the Save dialog box (see Figure 1-10).

The first thing to do is choose a disk or folder for storing your newly created document (see Figure 1-10). Next, click in the Save As box (or press Tab so that it's highlighted) and then name your document. (You certainly can do better than *Document1*.) Use the Format pop-up menu below to save your document into a different word processing file format, if you like (Figure 1-10).

Tip: If you frequently save documents in a different format, you can change the default setting so that you don't have to choose the preferred format every time the Save As box appears. Click the Options button in the Save As dialog box, which is a shortcut to the Word→Preferences→Save panel (that is, click the Save button on the left side of the dialog box). There you'll find a pop-up menu called "Save Word files as," which lets you specify the format you prefer.

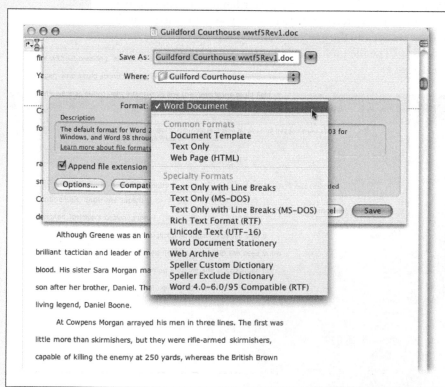

Figure 1-10:
Word can convert your document into many formats. If you save it as a "Word document" (the proposed choice), then any recent version of Microsoft Word–specifically Word 98, 2001, or X (on the Mac), or Word 97/2000/XP (Windows)–can open it without any conversion or translation. To share with earlier versions of Word, choose their names from the pop-up menu.

Finally, you'll generally want to leave the "Append file extension" checkbox turned on. It tacks a three-letter extension (*.doc* for standard Word files, *.dot* for templates, and so on) onto your file names—an essential feature that (a) lets Windows PCs identify the file, and (b) makes Mac OS X itself much happier. You can hide these suffixes, if you like, either globally in Mac OS X (choose Finder→Preferences) or on a file-by-file basis (highlight the file, choose File→Show Info, and choose Name & Extension from the pop-up menu). The appropriate extension-hiding controls appear before you.

Tip: It's also a good idea to run a compatibility report if you're sending the document to people using a different version of Word. Do so by clicking the Compatibility Report button at the bottom of the Save As dialog box. Word runs a compatibility test and serves notice if it finds any issues. (You can do the same thing from the Compatibility tab of the Toolbox. For details, see Chapter 18.)

Fast Saves

In the olden days of Word, two conflicting urges generally raged inside you when working on long documents: the instinct to use the Save command often, and the instinct *not* to, since every save took longer and longer as the document grew.

Microsoft's solution was the *fast save* feature. In a fast save, Word doesn't bother saving the entire document. Instead, it saves just the changes you've made since your last save, by tacking that information onto the *end* of the document file. That's why a fast-saved document takes up more disk space than one saved the regular way—and why a fast save is quicker than a standard one.

Tip: Not only does the fast-save feature create larger files, it also poses a hypothetical security risk. Because material you've deleted is still contained, technically speaking, in a fast-saved document, a savvy villain could use a program like CanOpener (or even Word's own "open any file" option) to see every word you'd ever typed into the file.

You can solve both problems at once by using the File→Save As command as the last step before you're ready to submit a document. Doing so creates a new, non-fast-saved document that's both compact (in terms of disk space) and purged of all obsolete text.

You can turn this feature on and off like this:

1. Choose Word→Preferences→Save panel.

2. Turn the "Allow fast saves" box on or off. Click OK.

Fast saving doesn't work for documents shared over a network. Furthermore, you should always perform a full save when saving a document for the last time, as described in the tip above.

Backing Up

No discussion of saving would be complete without a word about backing up your work. Saving preserves your document in its current condition; backing up creates an additional, *extra* copy of the same file. For an extra measure of security, you can place this extra copy on a Zip disk, an external hard drive, or even your electronic iDisk (see *Mac OS X: The Missing Manual*) in case something goes wrong with the copy on your Mac's hard drive.

Word can create backup copies automatically. Here's the process:

1. **Choose File→Save As and click Options.**

   You can also access this tab of Save options by choosing Word→Preferences→ Save panel.

2. **Turn on the "Always create backup copy" box and click OK. Click Save.**

   Word saves both the current document and an identical backup copy in the same folder; the duplicate has "Backup of" in front of its file name.

From now on, Word will automatically update the backup whenever you save the original document, providing a useful "last saved" version.

Note: When you turn on "Always create backup copy," the "Allow fast saves" box is automatically turned off (see above). Backups can only be created during full saves, not fast saves.

Printing

Even in our era of email, you can't use a Mac for very long without printing something. As with so much else in Word, printing can be as simple or as complicated as you care to make it.

The Print Button

Printing doesn't get any simpler. Click the printer icon on the Standard toolbar to print one copy of your document. No dialog box, no page ranges, no options.

GEM IN THE ROUGH

Slick Saving Tricks

In general, renaming or moving the Finder icon of a document that's open and active is a no-no. But in Word, you can be rather cavalier. With a Word document open on the screen, try switching back to the Finder and renaming its icon. When you return to the Word document and next use the Save command, the Word document instantly takes on the new name you gave it in the Finder!

Now try switching to the Finder and moving the icon into a different folder. When you return to Word, Microsoft's magic is on display yet again—if you ⌘-click the title of your Word window, you'll see that the program somehow knows about the icon's new location without missing a beat.

Another gem in the rough: When you close a document without first saving changes, Word displays the usual "Do you want to save the changes?" dialog box. Your choices—Don't Save, Cancel, and Save—can all be triggered from the keyboard. Just press D, C, or S, respectively.

File→Print

This method is still simple, but more specific. Choose File→Print (or press ⌘-P) to open the Print dialog box, where you can tell Word how many copies of which pages of your document to print (and which printer you want to use, if you have several).

The Print dialog box is comprised of a series of *panels* that you expose by choosing from the pop-up menu in the middle of the box. This remodeling was much more than cosmetic, however, as you can now do things from the Print window (such as add a border or create an Adobe Acrobat [PDF] document), which used to require opening a separate dialog box—or a separate program!

The features in the Print box vary depending upon which printer you chose above, but here are a few of the classics.

Copies and Pages

This panel is the preselected pop-up menu choice when the Print dialog box opens. Often, these are the only settings you need.

- **Copies.** Enter the number of copies you need. Hit Return to print, or Tab to move on to more settings.

- **Collated.** Turning on this box prints out each copy of your document in page order. For instance, if you print multiple copies of a three-page letter with collating turned off, you'll get two copies of page one, two page twos, and so on. With collating turned *on*, you'll get page one, page two, page three, followed by another complete set of pages one, two, and three, and so on.

- **Pages.** The All button is initially selected, but you can also hit Tab and enter page numbers for a page range. For more control over which pages to print, read on.

Tip: If you don't see "Print odd/even pages only" or other common printing options, choose Microsoft Word from the pop-up menu, as described in Figure 1-11.

- **Range.** Clicking this button activates a text box where you can be more specific about which pages you want Word to print. Actually, you can be very specific. To print an individual page, type its number in this box (*12*, for example). Separate additional single pages by commas. (Typing *12, 20*, for example, prints one copy each of page 12 and page 20.) You can add ranges to your print batch as well, by using hyphens, like this: *12, 20, 25-30, 100-102*. This selection would print page 12, page 20, pages 25 through 30, and 100 through 102.

Layout

This menu choice offers a shortcut to a feature formerly available only in the Page Setup dialog box: the ability to print more than one Word page on each sheet of paper—a great paper-saving tool for printing rough drafts.

The Layout panel also contains a surprise: the Border menu. You can choose one of four simple page border options (single hairline, double hairline, and so on). The beauty and power of this menu is that you can apply the border to only one print job, or only one *page,* without actually changing your document in the Borders and Shading dialog box. (When you choose a border type from the menu, the preview box at the left presents an idea of what the border will look like.)

Output options

This sheet contains the key to one of Mac OS X's best features: its ability to turn your Word document into a PDF (Acrobat) file.

Because all Macs and PCs can view Adobe Acrobat documents, you can attach a PDF file to an email and know that your recipient, no matter what kind of computer he has, will be able to open and read it, with all your fonts and layout intact. That makes PDF an ideal format for resumés, flyers or brochures, booklets, and other documents that need to look good for their intended audiences.

To "print" your Word document as an Acrobat file, simple click the Save as PDF button at the bottom of the Window or turn on Save as File and choose PDF from the Format pop-up menu.

Print settings

The options in this panel depend on the kind of printer you've selected. Here's where you can choose from a list of paper types (plain, glossy, and so on), and whether you want to use black and white or color. Choosing the print option that matches the type of paper you're using effectively changes settings in the printer (amount of ink released, printing speed, and so on) to achieve the best results on that paper. If you're using photo paper to print out digital photographs, for example, it's especially important to specify that here.

It's also where you can adjust print *quality,* high for good looks, low to save ink when printing out rough drafts or file copies.

Advanced settings

This panel, too, appears only for certain printers. It may provide finer control over quality, such as letting you specify the exact dpi (number of dots per inch) that the printer uses. For a professional-looking invitation or newsletter, for example, use at least 300 dpi.

Microsoft Word

This panel lets you restrict your printout to odd or even pages, as described in Figure 1-11. It also offers the **Print what** pop-up menu, which is usually set to Document. However, this menu lets you print out some fascinating behind-the-scenes Word information sheets. They include:

- **Document Properties** provides a page of statistics for the pathologically curious. In addition to the usual number of pages, the title, and the author, you can see how many editing changes you made, and how many minutes you've spent on the document.

- If you have tracked changes or comments visible in Word's reviewing feature (see page 176), choose **List of Markup** to print out lists of the comments, additions and deletions that appear in the document. (They print on separate pages, not the way you see them onscreen.)

- If you do a lot of work with **Styles** (if you're charged with keeping them consistent in all your company documents, for example, or if you're just a total control freak), this choice lets you print a list of all styles the current document uses, complete with a full description of each. (Much more on Styles in Chapter 3.)

- Similarly, if you've created a lot of **AutoText entries** in your copy of Word 2004 and you're getting confused, this option prints out a list of them. You can get the same information by choosing Tools→AutoCorrect→AutoText tab and scrolling through the list.

  If you're one of those power users who uses more than one *global template* (see page 228, this command is the way to create a separate AutoText cheat sheet for each template. It's also a quick way to print a list of all your address-book contacts, since they're considered AutoText entries; that way, you can review the list and decide which ones you want to add or delete.

- **Key Assignments** produces a handy cheat sheet to remind you of the keyboard-shortcut keystrokes you've created, as described at the end of Chapter 19.

This panel also contains the **Word Options** button, which opens the Print tab of the Preferences dialog box. Click the button, which, misleadingly, does not immediately print, but rather opens the Preferences window.

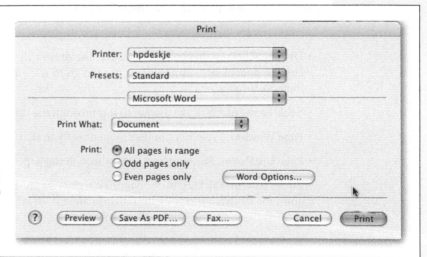

Figure 1-11:
The ability to choose odd or even pages is hidden behind the easily over-looked Microsoft Word pop-up menu choice. To print double-sided pages, print the odd pages first, then turn them over, rein-sert them into the printer, and then print the even sides. (Experiment with just a couple of pages first until you figure out how to get them right side up on both sides.)

Summary

This command calls up a box showing all current print settings: number of copies, page range, layout options, and so on. It's a quick way to review all your choices with one stroke of the pop-up menu. You can't print this information, and probably won't need to. Use the Custom option (described below) to save your favorite settings.

Saving custom settings

You've gone through every choice on the pop-up menu and gotten everything just the way you want it. For instance, you know you'll always print two copies, always want them collated, and almost always want to print with black ink (saving the more expensive color ink for photographs). To save this combination of settings for repeated use, choose "Save As" from the pop-up menu *after* you've set all the other panels to your liking. Fill in a name for your presets, and you're good to go.

From then on, all you have to do is press ⌘-P and choose the name from the Presets menu in the Print dialog box. Then press Return to print, or you can go on to adjust any of the settings if you need to deviate from your usual custom set (print three copies instead of your usual two, for example).

Preview

The Preview button is your gateway to the magnificent built-in Mac OS X print preview function. Click the button to get a picture of what your page will look like when printed. Mac OS X actually creates a PDF file of your document on the fly, and pops it open in your Mac's Preview program. Accordingly, you get to use all of Preview's bells and whistles—things Word's built-in Print Preview never dreamed of. You can flip forward and backward through your recently viewed pages, type in a page number to jump to it, page through your document a page at a time, zoom in and out, and even choose a page to view from a drawer containing each page in the document. And, oh yeah, you can also print the document if you so desire (click the Print button).

The Preview toolbar includes the following buttons:

- **Drawer.** Clicking this button slides out the drawer that displays the pages of the current document. Simply click a page to go to it—a convenient way to preview long documents.

- **Back/Forward.** Click the arrows to flip through the document pages.

- **Page Window.** Type in a number to go directly to that page.

- **Page Up/Down.** Pages up and down through the pages displayed in the drawer.

- **Zoom In/Out.** Clicking the + magnifying glass zooms in on the document. That's good for studying images within the document, or when you left your glasses in the bedroom. Clicking the – glass zooms out.

- **Tool Mode.** The Tool Mode offers three modes. The left button (a cross) activates the hand, which allows you to move and scroll through the document. Click the center A button to activate the text tool that allows you to select text within the document. The dotted square on the right enables you to select a section of a page (to zoom in on, for example).

Note: Yes, you can also turn your Word files into PDF documents using the Print dialog box as described on page 40–but this way, you're allowed to review it before committing.

Save as PDF, FAX, and Cancel

The last items in the Print dialog box are the Save as PDF, FAX, and Cancel buttons, each of which gives you a different way to exit the dialog box and share your document (or not).

- **Save as PDF** saves your file as a PDF, which is useful when sending documents to folks with incompatible software, or when you want to ensure that it arrives looking like as it did when it left your computer. Just click the button, choose a save location, type a name for your document, and click Save.

- **FAX** does just that—faxes your document. Clicking this button pops open another window in which you may fill out pertinent fax details, including the recipient, subject, and finally send your document (if your Mac's dial-up modem is connected).

- **Cancel**. Click here if you have reconsidered the whole printing thing (pressing Esc also dismisses the Print dialog box).

File→Page Setup

Some of the settings that appear when you choose Page Setup are a function of your printer's software, not of Word. As in the Print dialog box, choose your printer from the pop-up menu at top to see exactly what's available. Generally, however, you'll find options like these:

- **Paper Size.** Make sure the page size here matches what you've got in your printer. You can choose envelopes as well as paper, but if you use Word's envelope feature (see page 273), this setting is taken care of automatically.

- **Orientation.** You can change the direction that Word prints the "page" on the paper ("portrait" vs. "landscape" mode).

- **Scaling.** Most of the time, you print at 100%, but in some cases this might not be your best option. For instance, if your document is just two lines too long to fit on one page, try printing at 90%. (You'll know if you've adjusted the document correctly by checking the File→Print Preview before committing the document to paper.)

You can set custom page sizes by clicking Custom Paper Size as shown in Figure 1-12. Turn on "Use custom page size" and enter the dimensions of your paper. Remember that width is the measurement of the edge that you feed into the printer.

After setting up your page, click OK (or press Return) to save your page settings. Click Reset to return all settings to their original configuration.

For more advanced settings, choose Microsoft Word from the Settings menu. If you need to adjust the document's margins before printing, clicking the Margins button is a quick way to open the Format→Document→Margins tab, as described on page 130). Finally, if you find yourself frequently changing from the default settings to your own configuration (2 Up, 99% reduction, and so on), click the Default button to make that your *new* default page setup. Word asks if you want to change the default settings for all new documents based on the Normal template (in other words, all new, blank Word documents that you open).

Note: Clicking Default in the Page Setup dialog box changes the defaults only for the settings *in the Page Setup dialog box.* If you took a side trip to the Margins dialog box, those settings won't be affected. To change the default margins, click Default in the Format→Document→Margins tab itself.

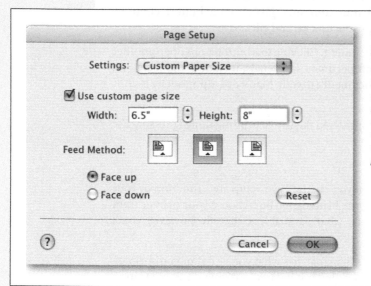

Figure 1-12:
Don't worry about the Feed Method unless you're printing on very nonstandard-sized paper. After you've entered the page measurements for width and height, you need to instruct Word how the paper is going into the printer (all the way to the left of the tray, for example), and which side of the page (Face up or Face down) your printer prints on.

Finally, as in the case of margins (page 130), the Page Setup dialog box gives you a chance to apply these settings to the entire document, or just "This point forward" (as the "Apply Page Setup settings to" pop-up menu puts it). This feature may come in handy if you have letters and envelopes together in the same document, for example.

Print Preview

Word's Print Preview feature was created in the old days, before Apple added a system-wide Preview function to Mac OS X itself. Now you have a choice of either.

Like the Mac OS X version, the built-in Word view lets you see an onscreen representation of how your document will look on paper—a terrific way to avoid wasting paper on printouts that get chopped at the margin or contain straggling one-line hangovers on the last page. To see for yourself, choose File→Print Preview or click the

Print Preview button on the Standard toolbar. (*Keyboard shortcut:* ⌘-F2.) A special preview window opens, displaying a full view of one page of your document.

Because most windows are smaller than 8.5" x 11", the image is probably reduced. You can see the percentage of reduction in the Print Preview toolbar, as shown in Figure 1-13. (Unlike most toolbars, you can't choose this one from the View menu; you must open the Print Preview window to see it.)

Figure 1-13:
When you're ready to print, click the printer icon on this toolbar to access the Print dialog box. You can dismiss the Print Preview window by clicking the close box, pressing Esc, or clicking back in any other document window.

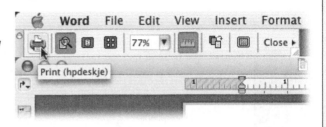

For a closer look at a certain word or a particular portion of your document, click the magnifying glass icon (Figure 1-13), and then click the page. The cursor changes into a magnifying glass and, with each click, toggles between the original view and the enlarged one. You can also change the view size by typing a percentage in the Zoom box (also shown in Figure 1-13). Remember, 100% is not necessarily life-size; it's the size that allows you to see one full printed sheet at a time.

If your document is going to be bound with facing pages, you can see how the two-page spread will look by clicking (and holding the cursor down on) the Multiple Pages pop-up button. Drag to highlight two or more panes, and then click; Word simultaneously displays that number of pages.

The most powerful button on the Print Preview toolbar is the Shrink to Fit button. When the last page of a document contains just a few lines, you may want to avoid wasting that whole extra piece of paper. Or suppose you've been given a five-page limit, and you're just a couple of paragraphs too long. If you have neither the time nor the inclination to edit down your document, you can click the Shrink to Fit button. Word adjusts the type sizes, across the entire document, just enough to eliminate that last fraction of a page.

Note: If you don't like the effect of Shrink to Fit, you can choose Edit→Undo Shrink to Fit, press F1, or press ⌘-Z. But once you save and close the file, you can't restore the original font sizes with the Undo command. You must do so manually.

Pointing to the other buttons on the Print Preview toolbar, without clicking, prompts their identifying screen tip labels. These other buttons include:

- **View Ruler.** Click to make both horizontal and vertical rulers appear. As shown in Figure 1-14, you can use these rulers to adjust the margins of your document quickly and easily.

- **Full screen.** Because of the reduced view, Microsoft offers you this one-click way to maximize the available screen space. Clicking here collapses your tool palettes, enlarges the window to the edges of your monitor, and hides Word's usual assortment of status bars around the window edges.

- **Close button.** Click to return to whatever view you were using before opening the print preview.

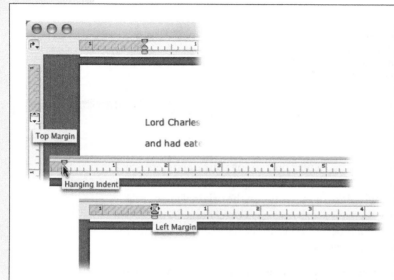

Figure 1-14:
Top: It's easy to adjust the top margin; just drag the intersection of the white and gray–striped regions on the rulers (you can see the special cursor shape at left).

Middle: Finding the spot to drag is extremely important, especially when adjusting the left margin; this screen tip indicates you're about to drag on the wrong spot. The indentation markers on the ruler don't do anything to the overall page margins.

Bottom: When you've found the correct location, your cursor changes shape, as shown here, and a screen tip appears.

Print Preferences

Believe it or not, Word 2004 offers yet another swath of printing settings—none of which even appear in the usual Print and Page Setup dialog boxes.

Specifically, the controls that govern the printing of fields, hyperlinks, drawings, and other advanced features are tucked away in the Word→Preferences dialog box, as shown in Figure 1-15.

- When **Update fields** is turned on, Word checks all the *fields* in your document (page 237) and verifies they contain the most recent information. The date is updated, for example, and captions are renumbered.

- Turning on **Update links** tells Word to check all hyperlinks (page 300) in the document and fix any whose destination document *on your hard drive* has moved. (Word can't update *Web* links this way, alas. Instead, you have to update Web links manually, as explained on page 309.)

- **Reverse print order** tells Word to print starting with the last page first. If your printer puts out sheets right side up, with each new sheet on top of the previous one, this option saves you from shuffling the pages into their proper order.

- Turning on **Document properties** prints the information from the General, Summary, and Statistics tabs of the File→Properties dialog box onto a separate sheet at the end of the document.

- When **Field codes** is turned on, Word prints the field codes (see page 238) instead of the *results* of those codes. For instance, a Date field would print as { DATE \@ "M/d/yy" * MERGEFORMAT } instead of 10/31/05.

- Turning on **Drawing objects** prints all images, including drawings, paintings, Clip Art, and WordArt. Turning it off suppresses images and prints text only.

- When **Hidden text** is turned on, any hidden text (page 112) in your document prints, along with all the other text.

- **Print data only for forms** suppresses the main text of the form document and prints only information that has been entered into form fields, as described on page 242.

- The precision that the Mac can use to place characters onscreen is limited to the screen's resolution of 1/72 of an inch. But with **Fractional widths** turned on, the printer possesses much greater precision and flexibility to place each character in its typographically correct position on the page. For the best-looking printouts, turn on Fractional widths just before printing.

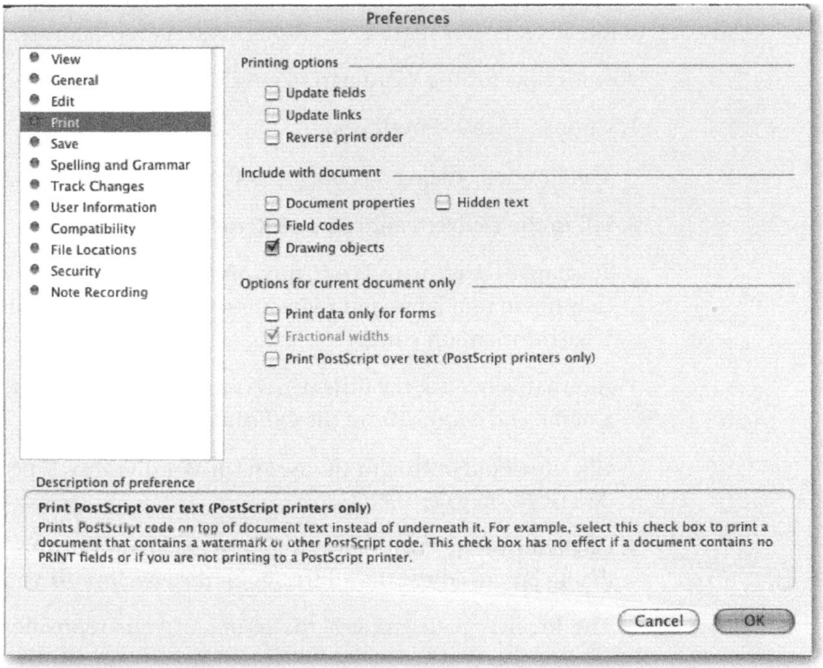

Figure 1-15:
The three checkboxes under "Options for current document only" need to be turned on each time you use them. You can also access this dialog box by clicking the Word Options button in the Microsoft Word panel of the Print dialog box.

Note, however, that when Fractional widths is turned on, Word's approximation of the printed appearance can result in overlapping, awkward-looking spacing on the screen. (Interestingly, when you switch to Page Layout view, Word *automatically* turns on Fractional widths, because Page Layout view is intended to show you how the page will look when printed.)

If you're not connected to a PostScript printer and have not used any PRINT fields in your document, the **Print PostScript over text** box is grayed out. If you have—you desktop publishing professional, you—turning on this box prints watermarks and other PostScript-generated figures *on top of* the text.

Printing Envelopes and Labels

There's a big temptation to just hand-letter your envelope, but Word makes it so easy that there's no need to settle for anything less than a professional-looking, printed envelope. Moreover, the Labels command is equipped for printing business cards, Rolodex cards, and other odd-shaped items. These are tools worth learning.

Tip: You can also print a whole mass of labels or envelopes at once, based on addresses in your Office Address Book; see page 439.

Printing envelopes

Before starting, inspect your printer and the envelope you're going to use. Practice fitting the envelope into the feed slot. Check the printer's manual to see if you need to flip any levers or mash any buttons to accommodate envelopes.

Now it's time for the Word part of envelope printing, as follows:

1. **Choose Tools→Envelopes.**

   The Envelope dialog box opens, as shown in Figure 1-16.

2. **Fill in the Delivery address and Return address boxes.**

   To change the return address, turn off the "Use my address" box. (Word automatically fills in your name and address as you entered them in the Word→Preferences→ User Information panel.)

   Alternatively, click the little person icon located next to the address box to select a name and address from the Office Address Book.

   Click the Font button to choose any of Word's fonts, type styles, and font sizes, as described on page 106.

3. **Click one of the Position buttons; use the arrow buttons in the Address Position dialog box to adjust the addresses on the envelope, if you wish.**

   The Preview pane displays the results of your repositioning actions. Click OK when done.

4. Click Page Setup or Custom in the Printing Options pane.

If your printer has an envelope slot, and you're using a standard envelope size (as opposed to an oddly shaped greeting card envelope, for example), you're in luck. Click Page Setup and choose the envelope size in the Print dialog box (#10 is a standard business envelope). Click OK to return to the Envelope dialog box.

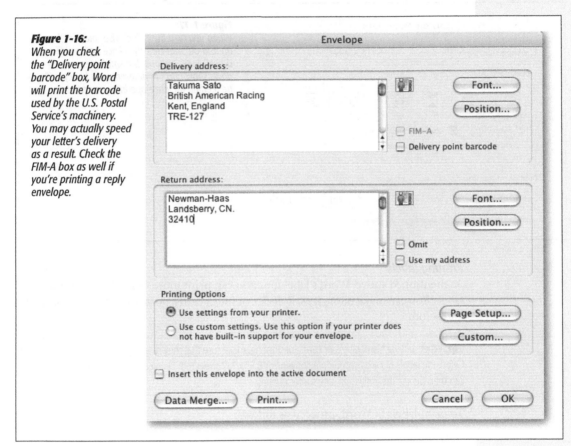

Figure 1-16:
When you check the "Delivery point barcode" box, Word will print the barcode used by the U.S. Postal Service's machinery. You may actually speed your letter's delivery as a result. Check the FIM-A box as well if you're printing a reply envelope.

Click Custom if your printer doesn't have an envelope feed or doesn't accommodate your size envelope. In the Custom Page Options dialog box (Figure 1-17), choose the "Envelope size" menu, and then click the preview window that most closely resembles how you plan to insert that envelope into your printer's feed. Click OK when done.

You're almost ready to print. When you do, Word will create a new document to hold the envelope text. To store the envelope in the same document that you've been working in, check "Insert this envelope into the active document."

5. **If you'd like to use the envelope you've just set up in a *data merge* (see page 263), click Data Merge to open the Data Merge Manager and use the envelope with a list of addresses.**

Otherwise, click Print or OK to print the envelope with the current address.

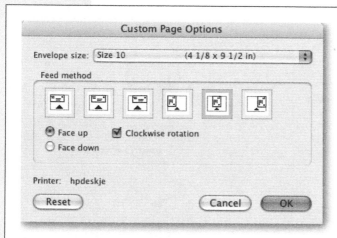

Figure 1-17:
When you turn the "Clockwise rotation" box on and off, and click the "Face up" and "Face down" radio buttons, the small preview windows show you the differences in how you'll be feeding the envelope into your printer.

Printing labels

As mentioned above, Word's label function can print more than plain white address labels. You can make name tags, Rolodex or index cards, postcards, floppy disk labels, and so on.

Tip: When buying blank labels or cards for printing, make sure that they're going to work with your printer. Often, the labels or cards come on a convenient 8.5" x 11" sheet that fits nicely into your printer's feed. You can then detach the individual labels after printing.

To print labels in Word, proceed as follows:

1. **Choose Tools→Labels.**

   The Labels dialog box opens, as shown in Figure 1-18.

2. **Type an address—or other label information—into the Address window.**

   See Figure 1-18 for full detail.

3. **Click Options in the Label pane to tell Word what kind of label or card you're using, as shown in Figure 1-19.**

   The choices may seem overwhelming, but Word can help. Once you've chosen a manufacturer and item number, click Details to see a preview (with measurements) of the label itself.

If you have an odd-sized or unidentified label, click New Label. Word opens a dialog box in which you can enter your custom dimensions. (You'll need a ruler to measure the label itself in this case; however, Word has enough built-in labels that you'll rarely need to get this creative.) Click OK.

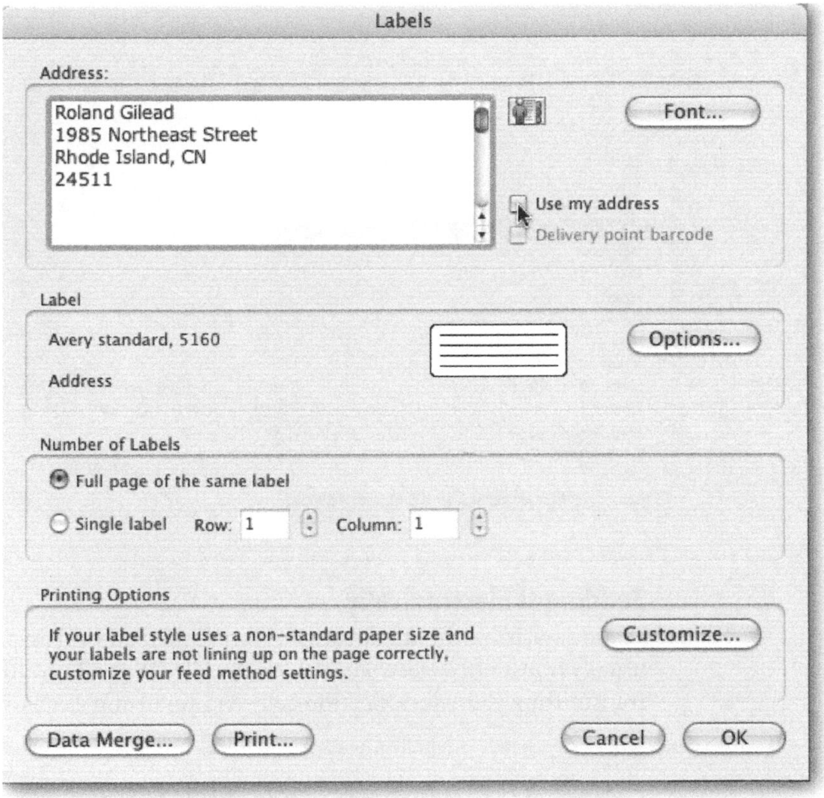

Figure 1-18:
When typing in the Address window, click Font to use any of Word's fonts or text formatting. Check the "Use my address" box to have Word insert your name and address from the Word→Preferences→User information tab (which is also reflected in the Entourage Address Book entry you created for yourself). Click the contact icon to choose a name and address from the Entourage address book.

If your odd-sized labels come on odd-sized sheets (something other than 8.5" x 11"), click Customize in the Printing Options pane. Here you set the page size and feeding method, as described earlier and illustrated in Figure 1-20.

4. **If you're printing only one label, click the "Single label" radio button and choose a row and column to tell Word where to print the label.**

This way, if you have a sheet with some blank labels left over, you can have Word print on one of those remaining labels. No waste!

If you're printing more than one label, on the other hand, click Data Merge and use the Data Merge Manager (see page 263) to give Word a list of addresses to use.

5. Click Print or OK when done.

To avoid wasting labels, print on a blank piece of paper first. Hold the printed sheet over a label sheet (preferably against a window or light) to see if the labels are going to line up. If they don't align correctly, choose Tools→Labels, click Options, and click Details to adjust the print area and spacing of each label.

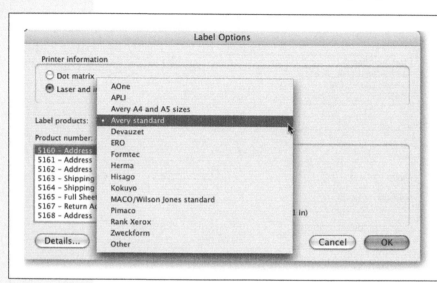

Figure 1-19:
Choose the name of the manufacturer from the "Label products" menu before choosing from the "Product number" list. Look on the label package for this information.

Sending It Electronically

These days, it's rare that a document is sent into the world on paper or disk. Instead, it's usually transmitted electronically. Word's File→Send To command offers two ways of transmitting your work electronically: via email and as a PowerPoint presentation.

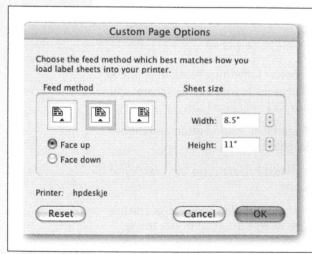

Figure 1-20:
Practice on a blank sheet of paper to determine whether your printer feeds face up or face down, and which corner the labels start to print from. Then use the buttons in this dialog box to match Word with what your printer is doing. If you're using one of the standard label types, you probably won't have to bother with these settings.

- **File→Send To→Mail Recipient (as Attachment).** This long-winded command launches Entourage and opens a new email message. The document you were just working on in Word is automatically attached to the message, and your address book is open—ready and waiting for you to choose a recipient from your list of contacts. (See Chapter 11 for more on Entourage's Address Book.) Congratulations—you've just saved several tedious steps.

- **File→Send To→Mail Recipient (as HTML).** This alternative offers a prettier, though riskier, way of emailing a Word document. It converts the Word text into HTML and plunks it directly into the body of an email message. Why riskier? Because your recipient won't be able to see it if her email program's HTML options are turned off or nonexistent.

- **File→Send To→Microsoft PowerPoint.** You can import a Word outline into PowerPoint for conversion into a slideshow, but why go to all the trouble? When your Word document is ready to become part of your big show, choose this command. PowerPoint opens with your Word document now displayed as a PowerPoint presentation. See Chapter 16 for full details on working with your document in PowerPoint.

Tip: If you don't see this PowerPoint option, try opening and closing PowerPoint once. Then quit and relaunch Word. That should make the menu command appear.

Editing in Word

Despite all the whiz-bang, 21st-century innovations in Word 2004, some things haven't changed, including...well, typing and clicking. The basics of adding, deleting, and moving text around work essentially the same way as they did in Word 1.0, which fit on a single floppy disk and had to be started up with a hand crank.

Most of the editing and formatting techniques in Word and the other Office programs require a two-step procedure: select, then do. That is, first select the thing (word, paragraph, sentence) that you intend to act upon, then use keystrokes or menu commands to tell the Mac *what* to do to it.

The Many Ways to Select Text

Dragging with the mouse is the way most people first learned to select text. In this time-honored method, you click at the start of where you want to select text, and while holding down the mouse button, drag until the text in question is highlighted.

Note: Don't forget Word's multi-selection feature, which has been around since Word X. You can select bits of text far apart from each other simultaneously and then cut, copy, and paste them all at once. You can grab a single sentence from the first paragraph of a document and a couple sentences from the second—and scrap everything else (see page 58).

Assuming you mastered dragging a long time ago, here are some more streamlined ways to select text. (Some of these moves are second nature to power users.)

- **Shift-arrow.** If you undershoot or overshoot the mark when dragging manually, don't start over—just remember the Shift–arrow key trick. After you release the mouse button, don't click again or do anything else. Hold down the Shift key and then press the arrow keys to expand or shrink the size of the selection—one character or line at a time. Add the Option key to expand or shrink the selection one *word* at a time.

- **Dragging with the mouse and Option key.** When dragging with the mouse, you'll notice that Word highlights text in one-word chunks, under the assumption that you'll very rarely want to edit only the first syllable of a word. Even if you begin dragging in the center of a word, the program instantly highlights all the way from the beginning to the end of that word, including the space after it. Usually, this behavior is what you want, and lets you drag somewhat sloppily.

Tip: If you dislike the way Word automatically selects in one-word increments, you can turn it off by choosing Word→Preferences and clicking the Edit tab. The checkbox called "When selecting, automatically select entire word" is the on/off switch for this feature.

Every now and then, however, you *do* want to edit only the first syllable of a word—perhaps to correct a typo. In those situations, Word's tendency to highlight the entire word can induce madness. On those occasions, press the Option key as you drag. Word responds by respecting the precise movements of your mouse.

Tip: Option-dragging *vertically* is a sneaky trick that lets you highlight only a tall, skinny block—a useful way to shave off the garbage characters at the beginnings of the lines of text you've pasted in from an email message, for example.

- **Clicking with the mouse.** Using the mouse and *not* dragging can save you time. Double-click a word to select that one word as a whole. Triple-click to select an entire paragraph.

  With one paragraph selected in this way, hold down Shift and click the mouse elsewhere, even pages away, to select more text in one-paragraph increments.

- **Using the Shift key and the mouse.** By using the Shift key, you can enjoy all the convenience of using the mouse without the wrist-wearying effort of holding down the mouse button. Just click at where you want to start selecting, hold down the Shift key, then click the mouse a second time where you want the selection to end (even if you had to scroll the document between clicks). Word highlights everything between the two clicks. If you overshoot the mark, you can back up in one-unit (letter, word, paragraph, whatever) increments by holding down Shift and clicking back into the selection. (Unfortunately, you can't change the *beginning* of the selection using this method.)

- **Using Shift with other keys.** If you do a lot of word processing, you may find it faster to keep your hands at the keyboard as much as possible, without stopping to grasp the mouse. In fact, it's possible to select text without using the mouse at all. Just use the arrow keys to get to where you want to begin selecting. Hold down the Shift key and use the arrow keys to adjust the size of the selection—line by line for the up and down arrow keys, and one character at a time for the right and left arrow keys.

If you hold down Option and Shift, the right and left arrow keys select in one-*word* increments, and the up and down arrow keys select in one-*paragraph* increments. (Your original selection is preserved, however, even if it was only part of a paragraph.)

You can use the Shift key with the Home, End, and Page Up/ Page Down keys as well. **Shift-Home** or **Shift-End** selects from the insertion point to the beginning or end of the line.

Shift-Page Up/Page Down selects one "screenful" (about half a page, depending on your monitor size) up or one down from the insertion point.

- **Using ⌘ with the mouse.** Here's a great command to memorize: ⌘-click anywhere within a sentence to select exactly that sentence, neatly and quickly, period and all. ⌘-click again to select a different sentence.

- **Using the selection strip.** To the left of your text, just inside the left window edge, is an extremely thin margin—an empty white space about an eighth of an inch wide. It's an invisible but extremely useful tool called the selection strip. (In Page Layout view, the selection strip is beefier—about as wide as the visible margin.)

When your cursor ventures into this area, the arrow pointer points to the *right* instead of left as usual. Now you can click once to highlight a single line of text, twice to select a paragraph, or three times to select the whole document.

Tip: ⌘-clicking in the selection strip also highlights the entire document—unless a bunch of text is already selected. If that's the case, ⌘-clicking selects an additional *line* instead. As for the peculiar highlighting that appears when you Option-⌘-click in the selection strip: Well, you tell *us* what Word's doing.

You can also drag vertically through the selection strip to highlight a vertical chunk of text—one of this strip's most frequent uses. (As always, you can click there once, then Shift-click elsewhere in your document to highlight all lines of text between the two clicks.)

- **Using Extend mode.** Turning on the EXT button in the Status bar (see page 24) or pressing F8 activates Extend mode, the most powerful (if disorienting) way to select text. Position the insertion point where you want to begin selecting, activate Extend mode, then use the arrow and Page Up or Down keys to select text automatically. You know you're in Extend mode when the EXT button in the Status bar is on. To cancel Extend mode, click the button (or press ⌘-period to turn it off).

Exactly as when you're *not* in Extend mode, pressing the Option key with the arrows forces Word to select in one-word (right and left arrow) or one-paragraph (up and down arrow) increments.

Note: Early versions of Word let you use the numeric keypad as cursor keys. By pressing Shift-Clear, you brought out the pad's second personality as a navigation keyboard, where the keys surrounding the 5 key acted as cursor keys, the 0 key acted as Insert, and so on. But Microsoft evidently fielded one too many desperate tech-support calls from customers who'd entered this mode accidentally, and couldn't figure out why they could no longer type numbers with the numeric keypad. Ever since Word 2001, the number keypad has done just one thing—type numbers.

Multi-Selection

To use Word 2004's multiple-selection feature, highlight a piece of text using any of the methods described above that involve the mouse. Then press ⌘ as you use the mouse to select more text. Bingo: You've highlighted two separate chunks of text.

For instance, drag to select part of a sentence. Then scroll down a couple of pages and, while pressing ⌘, triple-click to select another entire paragraph. Finally, you can ⌘-double-click a single word to add it to the batch selection.

Note: Selecting text using the Shift key and keyboard, then pressing ⌘ and using the mouse to select additional areas creates (or adds to) a multi-selection. Multi-selections must be in the same document (you can't select text simultaneously in different windows).

When you're done selecting bits of text here and there, you can operate on them en masse. For example:

- You can make them all bold or italic with one fell swoop.

- When you cut, copy, or paste (as described in the next section), the command acts upon all your multi-selections at once.

- You can drag any *one* of the highlighted portions to a new area, confident that the other chunks will come along for the ride. All of the selected areas will wind up consolidated in their new location.

Tip: This feature has special ramifications for the Find command described on page 72. The Find dialog box contains a "Highlight all items found" checkbox. It makes the *software* perform your work for you, simultaneously highlighting every occurrence of a certain word or phrase within the entire file.

Moving Text Around

Three commands—Cut, Copy, and Paste—appear in every word processing program known to humankind, Word included. But Office 2004 has more powerful ways of manipulating text once you've selected it.

Copy (or Cut) and Paste

To copy text, highlight it as described above. Then choose Edit→Copy (or click the corresponding Standard toolbar button), click the mouse or use the arrow keys to transport the insertion point to your new location, and choose Edit→Paste. A copy of the original text appears in the new locale. To move text instead of copying it, use Edit→*Cut* and Edit→Paste; the selected text moves from one place to another, leaving no trace behind.

Alternatively, after selecting the text, you can also Control-click the selection (or click the right mouse button if you have one), and choose Copy or Cut from the contextual menu. Similarly, when you arrive at the place where you want to paste, you can Control-click, then select Paste.

If this procedure sounds like a lot of work, you're right—especially if you're trying to choose these menu commands using a laptop trackpad. Cut/Copy and Paste is the sequence you'll probably use extremely often. By learning the keystroke equivalents, the time you save avoiding the mouse really adds up. For example:

Function	Command	Keystrokes
Copy	Edit→Copy	⌘-C or F3
Cut	Edit→Cut	⌘-X or F2
Paste	Edit→Paste	⌘-V or F4

The Paste Options smart button

No matter which Cut/Copy and Paste method you use, you'll notice a small, square button hovering over the surface of your document just by where you pasted. This is Word 2004's Paste Options smart button, shown in Figure 2-1.

Figure 2-1:
Appearing immediately after you paste, the Paste Options smart button lets you choose exactly how you want imported text to look with a simple click of the mouse. Instant gratification!

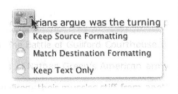

Clicking this button provides three options: Keep Source Formatting, Match Destination Formatting, and Keep Text Only. If you choose Keep Source Formatting, the text looks just like it did when you lifted it from its previous residence. Go this route if you liked the way the original text looked, and wish to import that styling into your current document. For instance, if you spent a lot of time getting the formatting of your newsletter heading just right, and now want to use it again in next month's issue, use Keep Source Formatting to preserve your hard work.

Conversely, if you choose Match Destination Formatting, your text takes on the formatting of its new surroundings. This selection is a popular choice because it lets you import text from disparate locations without that imported-from-disparate-locations look.

The final option, Keep Text Only, does just that—keeps the text only, eliminating any additional formatting, such as bold, italics, and so on. You may need to click Keep Text Only *after* you choose to retain source destination formatting. Although those options format text as described above, they do not remove bold, italics, underlining, and so on. For example, if you imported text that was 14 point Verdana bold and pasted it into the middle of your 10 point Times font, selecting Match Destination Formatting would convert the text to 10 point Times, but you would then need to select Text Only to clear the bold.

Note: Smart buttons are a new feature in Office 2004 that let you tell Word how to handle pasting and AutoCorrect options (page 91) on the fly. (If you're a PC veteran, this is nothing new to you.)

Paste Special

The Edit→Paste Special command dictates—as described below—how your text looks and acts once it reaches its final destination. The options include pasting the information as either a linked object or embedded object, and various types of text formatting. Your first choice is to decide whether to paste your text directly into the document or paste it as a link. To choose, click the appropriate radio button in the Paste Special dialogue box. Here's what the choices mean:

- **Paste.** Creates an embedded object. When you click an object you've pasted this way, the *source* (original) program opens in a separate window, where you can edit the object without actually leaving Word. When you make changes in that window, you're also making those changes in the source file (if there is one). Think of it as the opposite of a linked object, described below.

- **Paste Link.** Creates a linked object that refers back to the source file. In other words, an inserted Excel object is merely a *link* to the original Excel file, and you can't click to edit it in Word. Instead, Word opens the source (original) file where you can make changes to the file itself. See Object Linking and Embedding in Chapter 18 for more detail.

- **Display as Icon.** If you choose Paste Link, you may also want to check the Display as Icon box. Doing so displays your pasted object as an icon representing the program from which it was drawn. Essentially, your Word document is the "launching pad" for the linked document. Double-click to open it.

After choosing Paste or Paste Link, you must choose from the following options in the right panel of the Paste Special dialog box.

- **Microsoft Word Document Object.** This command nests one self-sufficient Word document inside another, which Microsoft calls an *embedded object*. See page 694 for more detail.

- **Word Hyperlink.** Inserts a hyperlink as discussed in the next section.

- **Formatted Text (RTF).** RTF stands for Rich Text Format, a file format that Microsoft devised to simplify the transfer of formatted text documents between incompatible programs. An RTF file is a lot like a text file, except that most common formatting specifications—bold, italic, font selections, line breaks, style sheets, and so on—survive the conversion to RTF and back again. Every modern word processor, for Mac or Windows, can open and export RTF documents. You'll rarely need it for transferring text between programs, thanks to the Styled Text feature offered by most Mac programs (see below).

Note: Once upon a time Rich Text Format (RTF) was a big deal. The computing world was full of different word processing programs, and different operating systems to run them on. RTF was the common file that most programs could read. But now (at least since Word 98), most programs can open and read files from other word processing programs, like AppleWorks. You'll rarely use RTF, if at all.

- **Unformatted Text.** Paste this way when you want to paste the text without any formatting (font, bold or italic, Word styles, and so on). Text pasted as unformatted picks up the current font, style, and formatting at the insertion point wherever you paste it. (Unformatted text does carry its own paragraph breaks.)

- **Picture.** When pasting text *as a picture,* from that moment on, Word treats it just like a picture (and switches you into Page Layout view). Text pasted in this way plays with your head a little bit, since you don't get an insertion point for editing when you click inside the text. Instead, the Picture toolbar appears and the Formatting Palette's image tools (like Image, Size, Rotation, and Ordering) come into view (see page 693). Accordingly, you can use any of the Picture toolbar tools (color adjustment, brightness, contrast, and so on) to change the look of the text. (The Watermark toolbar icon is especially handy in this instance. It's harder to guess, on the other hand, what the Fix Red Eye button does to pasted text.)

  What you can never do again is *edit* the text—check spelling, delete words, and so on. But once you have text just the way you want it, Paste Special→As Picture is a great way to create a poster, letterhead, watermark, or any document that you *don't* want anyone to edit later.

Note: The Office Clipboard, which debuted in Office 2001, is with us no longer. It has been replaced by Office 2004's Scrapbook, which works about the same, but better. Get the whole Scrapbook story on page 663.

The Mac OS X Clipboard, by the way, is still alive and well. Unfortunately, it only remembers the last item pasted to it. To view the Mac OS X Clipboard, in the Finder, select Show Clipboard from the Edit menu.

- **Styled Text.** This option preserves all font and paragraph styles in the pasted text. This Macintosh-only feature explains why you can copy some text from, say, a Web page or email: When you paste it into Word, the font sizes, boldface, and other formatting arrives intact.

  Most modern Mac programs, including word processors and page-layout programs, automatically copy styled text to the Clipboard whenever you copy.

- **HTML Format.** Use this option when you're creating a Web page (see Chapter 8) and pasting in text from another type of document. Word adds HTML formatting commands to the text you're moving.

Paste as Hyperlink

This command is at the heart of a truly wild Word feature, one that lets a Word document become a living table of contents—a launcher—for the chapters in your book project, pages on the World Wide Web, people in your email address book, or even applications on your hard drive.

Note: If you've installed Service Pack 1 (see page 8), you may find the Paste as Hyperlink command not working very well. Presumably, Microsoft is working on it. Check *www.microsoft.com/mac* for more details.

Text that's pasted as a hyperlink remembers where it came from, wherever that may be. Here are the kinds of hyperlinks possible in Word:

- **Within the same document.** Select some text, choose Edit→Copy, then use Edit→ Paste as Hyperlink. Text that you've pasted as a hyperlink becomes a blue, underlined link to its point of origin.

  For example, using Paste as Hyperlink, you can paste text from the last chapter of your book into the introduction. From then on, you can click the link to jump directly to the last chapter. You can also use this command to construct a "live" table of contents, as shown in Figure 2-2.

  When you position the cursor over a hyperlink without clicking, a yellow screen tip balloon identifies the name and location of the file it's connected to.

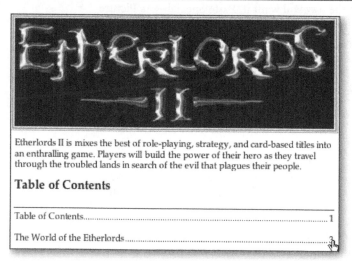

Etherlords II is mixes the best of role-playing, strategy, and card-based titles into an enthralling game. Players will build the power of their hero as they travel through the troubled lands in search of the evil that plagues their people.

Table of Contents

Table of Contents...1

The World of the Etherlords...3

Figure 2-2:
To create this linked table of contents, the headings from each section of the training manual were copied (Edit→ Copy) and pasted as hyperlinks (Edit→ Paste as Hyperlink). When you move the cursor over one of these links, it turns into a pointing hand. When you click it, you jump to that heading in the document.

- **Between two different Word documents.** You can use the same technique to create a link between two different Word documents, even if they're on different disks. When you click the hyperlink, Word opens the document.

Note: If you click a link to a file on a removable disk (such as a Zip or floppy) that isn't currently in the drive or a LAN station (a drive or folder on a computer on your home or office network) that you're not currently connected to, an error message appears.

Editing a link can be tricky, since you can't exactly click it to plant the insertion point or drag it to highlight some text. If you try, you'll simply trigger the link itself. The secret is to Control-click (or right-click) the link and choose Hyperlink→Edit Hyperlink from the contextual menu. A dialog box appears that lets you easily edit the link's text.

Drag-and-Drop

Drag-and-drop is the easiest way to move text from one place to another, especially if both the starting and ending locations are onscreen simultaneously. Because it lets you grab chunks of text and drag them directly around the paragraph or sentence before you, drag-and-drop is an extremely direct and satisfying way to rearrange your prose. As a bonus, drag-and-drop doesn't involve the Clipboard; whatever you've most recently copied or cut to the Clipboard remains there, ready for pasting, no matter how many times you drag-and-drop in the meantime.

After highlighting some text, position the cursor anywhere within the highlighted area. Press the mouse button and drag carefully. A dotted outline of the original text block moves as you drag, along with a non-blinking insertion point at your arrow-cursor tip. Move the mouse until the insertion point is where you want the relocated text to *start*. When you release the mouse button, the text jumps immediately into its new location. (If it didn't wind up exactly where you intended, choose Edit→Undo move, or press ⌘-Z or F1, to return everything to the way it was.)

FREQUENTLY ASKED QUESTION

Linking Word to the Web

When I copy a link from a Web site to paste into a Word document, the Paste as Hyperlink command is grayed out. I want to create a tutorial in Word that new employees can read on their computers. I want to link it to Web sites that the employees can refer to for more information. How can I do this if the command is grayed out?

Don't make things harder for yourself! You can create a link to the Web in any Word document simply by dragging the link from Internet Explorer into your document. (If you want the actual URL—beginning with *http://www*—to appear in your Word document, drag the actual address out of the

browser's address bar. If you want the plain-English name of the Web page to appear instead, drag the tiny @ icon in the address bar instead.)

When you click the resulting link in Word, your browser opens and takes you to the Web page specified by the link. (If you're not already online, the Mac may or may not dial up the Internet in the process, depending on your settings in the PPP tab of the Network panel of System Preferences.)

Note: This trick also works in recent versions of Safari and OmniWeb for Mac OS X. Just drag the little icon from the address bar.

Note: Within a Word document, drag-and-drop acts like a *Cut* and Paste operation—your text *moves* from one place to another. When you drag while pressing the Option key, however, or whenever you drag-and-drop between Office programs (see below), drag-and-drop acts like *Copy* and Paste—the original text remains where it was. (Drag-and-drop also acts like Copy and Paste when you drag between different open Word documents.)

Drag-and-drop between programs

In addition to working within Word, drag-and-drop also lets you drag text or graphic elements *between* Office programs. Position the two windows side by side, select your text or graphic, and then drag the highlighted block toward the destination window.

Note: Ever want to drag text to a window that's buried beneath several others? With Panther's Exposé feature you can, as shown in Figure 2-3.

Watch what happens before you let go of the mouse button:

- If you're dragging to an Excel spreadsheet, a dotted outline appears around the destination cell.

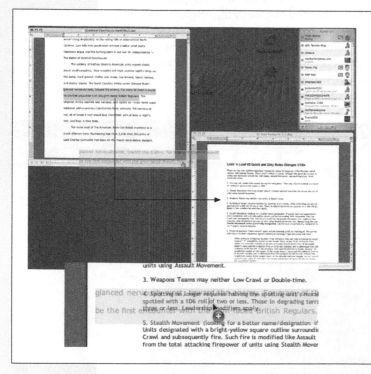

Figure 2-3:
Take advantage of Mac OS X 10.3's Exposé to drag selected text to a buried window.

Top: First select the text, then click and start to drag. As you do, press the F9 key. Exposé displays all the active windows in miniature form. Move the cursor to the destination window, and wait a couple of seconds...the window under your cursor starts to blink and moves to the front.

Bottom: Wait until you get the green + sign before depositing your text.

- If you're dragging to an Entourage email message, a gray line appears around the message, subject, or address text boxes. You can drop text into any of these locations.

- If you're dragging into a PowerPoint presentation, you can drop your text into a slide, notes area, or list. A colored outline indicates where the dragged material will appear when you let go of the mouse.

When your desired destination is appropriately highlighted, let go of the mouse button; your text appears in its new home.

Tip: Don't feel limited to dragging and dropping within Microsoft programs. Almost every modern Macintosh program can accept drag-and-drops. For example, you can drag from Word into AppleWorks (for Mac OS X or Classic), an America Online email, SimpleText, TextEdit, and Stickies. Conversely, Office 2004 programs can also accept drag-and-drops from other drag-and-drop–savvy applications. (When you drag into America Online for Mac OS X, the text appears as an uneditable picture instead of text. Still, your recipient will be able to read it.)

Dragging and dropping to the desktop

When you drag and drop a chunk of selected text outside the boundaries of your document and onto the desktop, Word creates a *clipping file* (see Figure 2-4). Clipping files are pieces of text-in-waiting that you can later drag and drop.

Figure 2-4:
As a bonus, when you drag and drop to the desktop, Word copies the text to the clipping file; it doesn't cut it, so you can store a clipping for safekeeping before you edit the original.

GEM IN THE ROUGH

Cut Out to Be Smart

Have you noticed that when you cut and paste in Word, your pasted text is always perfectly spaced? In other words, when you paste a word with a space after it in front of a period, the extra space magically disappears and the period comes right smack after the word, where it belongs. And when you paste one word after another, a space appears between the two words, even if you forgot to put one there yourself. (Don't try that in TextEdit.)

That's Word's Smart Cut and Paste feature. You turn it on and off by the checkbox on the Word→Preferences→Edit panel—but turning it off is probably a bad idea. The golden rule of computing: Whenever your software offers to take over boring, microscopic, annoying work for you, let it.

Later, when you drag a clipping file back into a document, Word pastes a copy of the clipping text; the clipping file remains on the desktop, where you can use it again and again. In effect, you can use your desktop like a giant pasteboard to store boilerplate paragraphs that you use frequently. In fact, dragging the clippings to the Dock keeps them handy, but still out of the way.

Note: In Mac OS X, the Finder names every clipping "Picture Clipping," even if it contains text. Be sure to rename your clippings quickly and carefully so that you can remember what's in them. (You can rename a clipping file as you would any Finder icon: For example, click its name once, then twitch the mouse to make the "renaming rectangle" appear.)

You can also create clipping files from Word pictures or drawing objects. Just select the object and drag it to the desktop. (Mac OS X names it a *picture clipping,* as shown in Figure 2-4.)

Navigating Your Documents

Word 2004 offers a multitude of ways to navigate your document, some of which aren't as immediately obvious as the scroll bar.

Tip: Using the scroll bar has its own reward: As you drag the "elevator" scroll-box handle up and down, a pop-out screen tip balloon identifies the major headings in your document as you scroll by. By scanning this readout, you'll know exactly where you'll be when you stop scrolling.

What the Keys Do

It's by far one of the most frequently asked questions among new (and even some veteran) Mac fans: What on earth are all of those extra keys for on the standard Mac keyboard?

In many cases, the answer is "nothing." In most Mac programs (games excepted), such keys as the F-keys on the top row and the Num Lock key don't do anything at all. In Office, however, there's scarcely a single key that doesn't have a function. For example:

- **Esc.** Short for "Escape," this key provides a quick way of dismissing a dialog box without having to click the Close or Cancel button. It also closes a menu that you've pulled down, once you've decided not to use it. Esc acts the same as the ⌘-period key combination that Mac fans know and love.

- **Home.** This key moves the insertion point to the beginning of the line it's currently in. (You were expecting it to take your insertion point to the top of the document, weren't you? It's a trick; to do that, press ⌘-Home.)

- **End.** The End key, if you have one, takes you to the end of the current line. The ⌘-End combination takes you to the very end of the document.

- **Ins.** The Ins key (short for Insert), if you have one, is a very quick shortcut to the Paste command—even quicker than ⌘-V, and more intuitive than F4.

- **Delete.** The Delete key acts as a backspace key. It backs over and erases the last character you typed. In Word 2004, in fact, ⌘-Delete comes set to delete the entire *word* before the cursor, which is often far more useful than deleting just one character—especially when you're in the middle of a writing frenzy.

- **Forward Delete.** This key deletes the character to the *right* of the insertion point— not a function to which most Mac fans are accustomed, but an extremely useful one once you know it. For example, when trying to correct a typo, you sometimes place the insertion point on the wrong side of the letter you want, especially when you're working with italics. In such cases, one tap on this key does just the trick. (Many Mac keyboards lack this key; if you have a numeric keypad, you can use the Clear key instead, as described next, or—if you're using a laptop—you can use fn-Delete.)

- **Clear.** This key acts as a forward delete key, too. On desktop keyboards, it shares a space with the Num Lock key.

POWER USERS' CLINIC

The F-keys

On some Macs, they're tiny; on others, they're full-sized. On some Macs, you have 12 of them; on others, 15. They're the function keys (or F-keys) stretched along the topmost row of your keyboard.

Once you're familiar with the many benefits of the F-keys, you may become addicted. The following is how the function keys come defined in a new copy of Word 2004—but remember that it's easy enough to change their functions (see Chapter 19).

F1 means Undo (the same as ⌘-Z). (There's no predefined F-key for Redo, although ⌘-Y or Edit→Redo are on hand if you change your mind again.)

F2, F3, and F4 correspond to the Cut, Copy, and Paste commands described earlier in this chapter (⌘-X, ⌘-C, and ⌘-V).

You're entitled to wonder, by the way, why you might use the F-keys for simple functions like copying and pasting when you're already in the habit of using the ⌘-key combinations.

The answer is on your keyboard: Many Mac laptops have only one ⌘ key—on the left side. If you have one of these, you'll probably find the single F-key to be more convenient than a two-key combination.

F5 (Go To Same, also ⌘-G) calls up the Go To tab of the Find and Replace dialog box (see page 68).

F6 (Other Pane) moves the insertion point to the other pane of a split window. You can use Shift-F6 to return to the original pane, but why? Hitting F6 a second time performs the same function.

F7 (Proofing, also Option-⌘-L or Tools→Spelling and Grammar) takes you to the first instance of a misspelling or instance of questionable grammar (as defined by Microsoft), and calls up the Spelling and Grammar dialog box.

F8 (Extend Selection) puts you in Extended selection mode, as described on page 25.

F9 now belongs to Mac OS X 10.3's Exposé feature (see Figure 2-3). It's still part of some keyboard shortcuts for Word's fields feature (see page 237).

F10 does nothing in Word. (Along with F9 and F11, it's part of Exposé.)

F11, like F9, works in Exposé when alone, or for working with fields, in combination with other keys (page 237).

F12 (Save As) opens the Save As dialog box. (Note there is no F-key shortcut for the Save function.)

- **Help.** Pushing the Help button opens the Word Help window or Max the Mac Plus's "What's your question?" window (depending on whether or not you have Max activated, as described on page 31). If the dog ate your Help key, ⌘-/ does the same thing.

- **Page Up and Page Down.** These keys move you up and down in the document, one screen at a time. (If you actually do want to jump from the top of one page to the top of the next, use the Navigator buttons instead, as described on page 69.)

Tip: Remember that you can combine some of these keystrokes—Home, End, Page Up, Page Down—with the Shift key to *select* text instead of simply scrolling.

Keystrokes: The Missing Manual

Microsoft apparently employs seething crowds of programmers who do nothing but dream up keyboard shortcuts for every conceivable Word function. With the Shift, Option, and ⌘ keys in various combinations, for example, the top-row function keys described in this chapter have second, third, fourth, and fifth functions—far more keyboard shortcuts than any human being could possibly remember (or fit in a 700-page book).

To print out a list of all Word shortcut keys for future reference, choose Tools→ Macro→Macros. Choose "Word commands" from the "Macros in" pop-up menu, click ListCommands in the macro list, then click Run. In the dialog box that appears, click "Current menu and keyboard settings," then click OK. When the dialog box goes away and the shortcut key list appears, press ⌘-P or click the Print button in the Standard toolbar.

The list is several pages long and contains commands you may never use. But when you find yourself using the same menu commands over and over, it's worth taking a look to see if a keyboard shortcut exists.

The Go To Command

The scroll bar and arrow keys can get you pretty close to where you want to go in a long document, but now you can get there with much greater precision by telling Word. Double-clicking the Status bar (see page 24), pressing ⌘-G (or F5), or choosing Edit→Go To opens the Go To tab of the Find and Replace dialog box, as shown in Figure 2-5.

The Go To tab looks simple, but there's quite a lot you can do with it:

- **Enter a page number.** If you know what page you want to access, just enter the number in the "Enter page number" box and hit Return (or click Go To if you're a mouser).

- **Jump a certain number of pages forward or back, as described in Figure 2-5.**

- **Step through your document page by page.** Just keep pressing Return (or Enter) without doing anything else in between—after entering 1, for example, in the

"Enter page number" box. (Microsoft calls this "browsing.") Of course, a less dialog box–intensive method of jumping from one page to the next is to use the Navigator buttons described below.

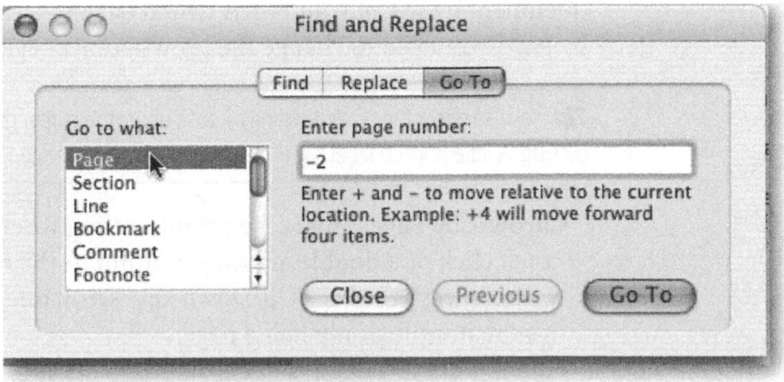

Figure 2-5:
Typing -2 in the "Enter page number" box will scroll the document back exactly two pages. It also moves the insertion point back. Choose your unit of measure (pages in this example) in the "Go to what" box.

• Choose a specific item type to go to in the "Go to what" box at the left. It can be as much as a section (see page 132) or as little as a line. You can check all your comments (see page 175) or footnotes at once by hitting Return repeatedly after selecting your unit of choice. (Jumping from one Heading, Graphic, Table, Comment, or Footnote to the next can be particularly useful in complex documents.) Or if you have placed Bookmarks in the document (Insert→Bookmark), you can jump to a previously placed bookmark (page 242).

The Navigator Buttons

All these nifty browsing features are also available by mouse, at the lower-right corner of every Word window, as shown in Figure 2-6. In the same illustration, you'll see the double-headed arrows called Navigator buttons. By choosing an item in the "Go to what" box (see Figure 2-6), you can click the Navigator buttons to move forward and backward from one to the next.

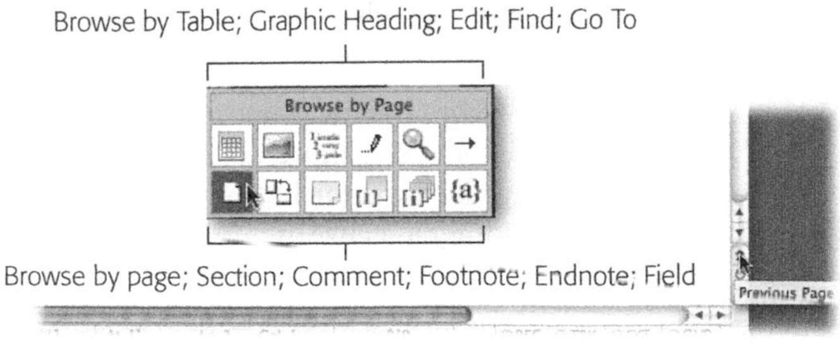

Figure 2-6:
The icons on the Select Browse Object palette (left) match the item types in the "Go to what" box. Once you've selected an item, you can click the Navigator buttons (right) to step directly to the next or previous one of the chosen item—Browse by Page in this example. This palette also contains shortcuts to the Find and Go To dialog boxes.

Browse by Table; Graphic Heading; Edit; Find; Go To

Browse by page; Section; Comment; Footnote; Endnote; Field

As shown at the left in Figure 2-6, click the tiny round Select Browse Object button to choose *how* you want the Navigator buttons to take you through your document. Just click one of the icons (described below) in the pane that pops up.

Changing the browse object affects all open documents. If you've been browsing a big document by *sections*, and then switch back to a shorter one that you want to review by *page*, you need to change the browse object again.

Tip: You can check the current setting by positioning the cursor over one of the double-arrow buttons without clicking. A little pop-up label says "next page," "previous page, " or whatever.

- **Browse by Page.** This is the default setting when you open a new document. With each click of a double arrow, you jump to the top of the next (or previous) page. (By contrast, the Page Up/Down keys scroll one *screen* at a time, even if that means you're jumping only half a page.)

- **Browse by Section.** When this setting is selected, the Navigator buttons take you from the top of one *section* to the next. Needless to say, it's most helpful if you've actually used section breaks in a document (see page 132).

- **Browse by Comment.** Word's Reviewing features (see Chapter 5) let you attach comments to a document, so that you can provide typed feedback to the author. Either way, this setting lets you skip from one such comment to the next, bypassing the remainder of the text. (It's a very good idea to use Browse by Comment before you send a document out into the world.)

- **Browse by Footnote, Browse by Endnote.** Similar to Browse by Comment, these settings take you directly from one note to the next. See page 221 for more on footnotes and endnotes.

- **Browse by Field.** When you've used the Data Merge feature (page 263) or otherwise placed *fields* in your document (page 237), you can use the Navigator buttons to skip from one field to the next. This browse feature is really quite useful, since fields can look exactly like ordinary text and be easily missed. When browsing with this feature, Word helpfully highlights fields as it finds them.

- **Browse by Table.** This feature makes the Navigator buttons jump directly from one *table* to the next.

- **Browse by Graphic.** Choosing this browse object does nothing unless your document contains pictures, drawings, paintings, or scanned photographs. If it does, then the Navigator buttons move you from one graphic to another, skipping everything in between.

- **Browse by Heading.** This command is actually a two-in-one browse object. If you're working in Outline view (see page 34), the Navigator buttons move the insertion point item by item, hitting each entry in your outline.

  This browsing method also works if your document's *styles* (see page 137) include any Heading styles. Use these preformatted font styles to set off chapter titles, captions, or subtopics. When you browse by heading, your insertion point skips from one heading to the next, bypassing all the mere mortal body text in between.

- **Browse by Edit.** Unlike the other browse objects, this one possesses a limited short-term memory. Word only remembers the last three places you clicked in your document. Check out the sidebar on the previous page for details.

Tip: Even though you've selected a browse object, you're not stuck with using the mouse to click the Navigator buttons. The keyboard shortcut ⌘-Page Up or Page Down takes you from one item to the next.

Finding and Replacing

When editing a document, sometimes you know exactly what you want to revise, but just don't know where it is. For instance, you want to go back and read the paragraph you wrote about *mansions*, but you don't remember what page it's on. Or suppose you've found out that you misspelled Sarah's name all the way through an article. Now you have to replace *every* occurrence of Sara with Sarah—but how do you make sure that you've got them all?

That's where Find and Replace comes in.

GEM IN THE ROUGH

Back to Where You Once Belonged

The Go Back command is unique to Microsoft Word, and it's fantastically useful. No matter where you are in a document, this command scrolls directly back to the last place you clicked (usually the last place you edited text)—even if it was in another open document.

You'll find this command useful in a number of circumstances: after splitting and unsplitting the window, and then finding yourself deposited in the wrong part of a document; when you've just opened up a document that you were editing yesterday and want to return to the spot where you stopped; when reconsidering an edit after scrolling to a new location; and so on.

Better yet, Word doesn't just remember the last place you clicked; it remembers the last *three* places. Each time you use the Go Back command, your insertion point jumps among these four places—the last three edits and your current position—even if that means bringing different document windows forward.

You can trigger the Go Back command by pressing Option-⌘-Z, or Shift-F5, or using the Navigator buttons described above. If you fall in love with this feature, as you might, consider changing the keystroke to something easier to remember. (See Chapter 19 for instructions on changing a keystroke.)

Find

If you just want to find a certain word (or even part of a word), choose Edit→Find (or press ⌘-F). The Find and Replace dialog box opens, as shown in Figure 2-7. Type the word you're looking for, and then click Find Next (or press Return or ⌘-F).

Tip: If you turn on "Highlight all items found in Main Document," the Find Next button changes to say Find All. Now Word will select all occurrences of the search term simultaneously. At that point, you can bold them all, italicize them all, cut them all, or perform other kinds of neat global maneuvers.

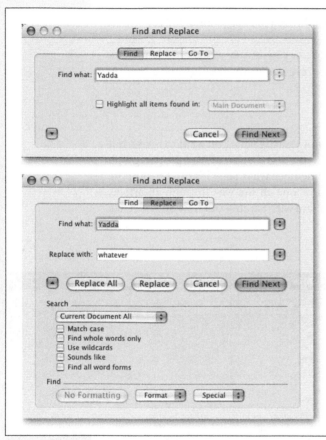

Figure 2-7:
Top: The Find dialog box.

Bottom: The expanded Replace box. The Format and Special menus at the bottom of this dialog box let you search for a font, typestyle, paragraph break, and so on. If you'd like to find all your italics and change them to boldface, or find all the dashes and delete them, this is the way to do it.

Now Word searches for your search term, starting from the position of the insertion point. If it finds what you're seeking, it scrolls to and highlights each occurrence of that word or phrase in your document. (If it doesn't find any occurrences, an error message tells you so.)

If Word finds an occurrence, but it's not the one you had in mind, you can keep clicking Find or hitting Return to find successive occurrences. When Word reaches the end of your document, it starts searching again from the beginning. When it finally wraps around so far that it finishes searching the whole file, another dialog box lets you know.

The Find box remains onscreen throughout the process, but don't let that stop you; you can pause and edit your document at any time. Just click in your document window, sending the Find box to the background. To resume your search, click the Find dialog box to bring it forward, then click Find Next.

Tip: The keystroke Shift-F4 (or Shift-⌘-Y) means "find the next occurrence of whatever I just searched for." The advantage is that it works even after you've closed the Find box altogether—and even if you performed your search hours ago (provided you haven't closed the document).

Replace

Although you can do edits and replacements in conjunction with the Find command as explained above, Word has a more streamlined process for making the same replacement over and over. Choosing Edit→Replace (Shift-⌘-H) opens the Replace tab of the Find and Replace dialog box.

Note: Before the dawn of Mac OS X, Word's Replace keystroke was just ⌘-H. Of course, Apple has now claimed ⌘-H as its universal Hide command, so Microsoft was forced to change the Replace keystroke to Shift-⌘-H.

It takes the Word veteran some time to unlearn ⌘-H for Replace. However, a few dozen shocks of seeing all your open Word windows disappear (and having to bring them back by clicking the W icon in the Dock) should train you to use the new protocol.

Once again, start by typing the word or phrase you want to replace in the "Find what" box. This time, however, you press Option-Tab to jump into the "Replace with" box; now type the new, improved replacement text.

When you click Find Next or press Return, Word searches the document and stops at the first match. Now there's a decision to make. After examining the highlighted phrase in context, click one of these buttons:

- **Replace.** This button means, "Replace this search term with my replacement text, then find the next occurrence of the search term."

Caution: If you simply press Find Next or Return, Word doesn't make the replacement. You must click the Replace button (or press ⌘-R) each time.

- **Replace All.** If you don't need this occurrence-by-occurrence interview, and you're sure you want to replace every occurrence of the search term in the entire document, click Replace All (or press ⌘-A).

  Be very careful, however: In most cases, it's safer to check each case to make sure the replacement is appropriate. For instance, if you're replacing "rite" with "right," Word will change even "criteria" to "crightria," giving quite an unexpected surprise to your editor, professor, or boss. Use Replace All only when there's little chance for that kind of confusion. Even so, you should proofread carefully afterward... even if that's not your favorite way to spend a Friday afternoon.

- **Find Next.** Suppose that, as you're searching for every occurrence of "Sara" to replace it with "Sarah," Word finds and highlights the first four letters of the word Saratoga. Clearly, you don't want Word to change this occurrence. In that case, just click Find Next (or press Return) to leave this occurrence alone and jump to the next one.

Advanced Find

Clicking the Expand button (the blue button with the down arrow on it) at the bottom of the Find or Replace tab makes the dialog box sprout an additional, secret panel. (Pressing ⌘-M does the same thing.) It offers the following precision controls for narrowing your search even further:

- The **Search** pop-up menu tells Word where to search. **Current Document All** starts the Find function from the very beginning of the document. **Current Document Down** and **Document Up** search forward and backward from the insertion point, and **All Open Documents** searches from the beginning of each document in the order that you opened them, moving automatically from one to the next.

- Turn on **Match case** when you want to find or change words only when they're capitalized a certain way; for instance, when you want to find the name Mike but skip over words like "mike."

- **Find whole words only** (⌘-Y) is a very powerful safety option. It tells Word to only look for the search term if it's separated from surrounding text by a space or punctuation mark—if it's a whole word unto itself, in other words. If you're

---

FREQUENTLY ASKED QUESTION

Converting Quotes from Curly to Straight, or Vice Versa

I need to convert all of Word's automatic, typographically correct "curly quotes" into Internet-friendly "straight quotes" before posting my work on a Web page or sending it by email. How do I do that?

As you've noted, Word converts your quotes automatically as you type, curling open and close quotes (and single quotes) as appropriate. To turn this feature off, choose Tools→AutoCorrect, click the AutoFormat As You Type tab, and turn off "Straight quotes with curly quotes."

You can also leave this feature turned on, while making the occasional curly quote straight—such as when you want a " mark to designate inches. The solution is simple: Just after

typing the quote mark, press ⌘-Z or F1. Word straightens it instantly.

But to perform global surgery on an entire document, turning all curly quotes into straight ones, for example, choose Tools→AutoCorrect, click the AutoFormat As You Type tab, and turn off "Straight quotes with smart quotes." Click OK.

Now choose Edit→Replace. In both the "Find what" and "Replace with" boxes, type ' or ", and then click Find Next or Replace All. Word straightens all single or double quotes, as appropriate. (To curlify all straight quotes, repeat the procedure with the "Straight quotes with smart quotes" checkbox turned on.)

---

searching for the word "men," for instance, turning on this box prevents Find from stopping on (or, worse, replacing) "menu" and "document."

- Checking **Use wildcards** (⌘-U) lets you use special characters to *stand in* for actual letters, in cases where you're unsure of the right letter or want to look for more than one spelling at a time. For example, *?* stands in for any one letter or character. Entering *f?r* in the "Find what" box finds occurrences of "far," "for," "ferry," and so on. You can use * to represent any string of one or more letters (or other characters). Thus, entering *c*r* would find words like "car," "carrier," and "rancor."

When you'd settle for finding any one of several *specified* characters, put them in brackets. For instance, use *f[au]nny* to find all occurrences of both "fanny" and "funny" in your document.

Finally, an exclamation point indicates that you want to find any character *except* the one in the brackets. For example, *[!f]unk* finds "hunk," and "spunk," but not "funk."

Tip: There are several more wildcard characters in Word, which you can use—independently or in combination—to send Word on incredibly complex, convoluted searches. For a list of all wildcards, enter *wildcards* in the Office Assistant's or Word Help window's Search box, choose "Advanced search methods" and click the flippy triangle next to "Wildcard characters you can use when searching."

- **Sounds like** (⌘-S). Turn on this box and enter a phonetic spelling for the word or words you're hunting for. Entering "thare" finds every occurrence of "there," and "their," but not "they're." Go figure. This option really comes in handy when you can't remember the spelling of a name; enter "lee" to find Ms. Li, for example.

- **Find all word forms.** This rather intelligent option finds all those irregularly spelled English nouns and verbs. For instance, if you're trying to find all the places where your article mentions running, type *run* and turn on this box. Word finds "ran," "runs," and "running"—but not "runner."

Finding by Format

Word is sometimes described as the Feature List That Ate Cleveland. Dozens or hundreds of features lie untapped by the vast majority of its owners.

But here's a buried feature that's well worth noticing: It's the Format pop-up button at the bottom of the Find dialog box, which lets you search for text according to its *formatting* (alone, or in combination with words typed in the "Find what" box). By opening this Format menu (or pressing ⌘-O), you'll see that Word lets you search for:

- **Font.** Finds occurrences of, say, Times or Palatino, as well as font *characteristics* like bold, italic, blue, 12-point, double-underline, shadow, and so on—in any combination.

- **Paragraph.** Locates paragraphs according to their indentation, line spacing, leading, outline level, page breaks, and so on.

- **Tabs.** Searches for tab stops by position and type.

- **Language.** Searches for text you've designated as being in a certain language (by highlighting the text and then choosing Tools→Language).

- **Frame.** Locates any *frame*, according to any of its attributes. (These days, most people use Word's text boxes instead of frames; see page 151.)

- **Style.** Lets you search for, or replace, any of your document's styles (see page 137).

- **Highlight.** Finds text you or a colleague has highlighted using the Highlighter tool on the Reviewing toolbar (page 176).

Tip: Once you've popped open the menu with ⌘-O, you can "walk" down its commands with the arrow keys. Press Enter when you've snagged the one you want.

This powerful feature is instrumental in dozens of situations. Sometimes it's useful when you just want to *find* something, like this:

- Type *the* in the "Find what" box. Choose Format→Style and choose one of the heading styles you've used in your document. (See page 137 for more on styles.) Word finds the word "the" only when it occurs in a heading.

- Click inside the empty "Find what" box; choose Format→Font. In the resulting dialog box, click Italic, and then click OK. Word will now find every italicized word in the document, one by one.

The uses of this feature become even more amazing when you use the Replace function at the same time:

- Suppose that, in keeping with your newspaper's style guide, you decide to put Microsoft's company name in bold type, everywhere it occurs. Type *Microsoft Corporation* in the "Find what" box. Click in the "Replace with" box, choose Format→Font, choose Bold in the Font Style box, and click OK. Now, when you click Replace All, Word changes all occurrences of the phrase "Microsoft Corporation" to boldface.

Tip: You don't have to type *Microsoft Corporation* again into the "Replace with" box; if this box is empty, since you specified a format, Word assumes that you don't intend to change the text itself.

- You want to create a quick table of contents document. You decide that the easiest way is to remove all the words in your document that *aren't bold*, leaving behind only what appears in bold type (your headings, that is).

  Leave both the Find and Replace boxes empty. Click in the "Find what" box, choose Format→Font, click NotBold, and click OK. By leaving the "Replace with" box empty, you're telling Word to *delete* every occurrence of the specified "Find what" item (in this case, text that's not bold). When you click Replace All, Word vaporizes all the body text of your document, leaving behind only the boldface type.

- Click in the "Find what" box and choose Format→Tabs. Word displays a dialog box similar to the one where you set tabs (see page 122). Type .5 in the "Tab stop position" box and click OK. Use the radio buttons in the "Find Tabs" dialog box to tell Word what kind of tab you're searching for. Word will not find tabs if the alignment doesn't match. Click in the "Replace with" box, choose Format→Tabs, and type *1* in the "Tab stop position box."

  Finally, click OK. Word finds all the paragraphs with half-inch tabs and changes them to one-inch tabs.

- Someone has turned in an article to you that contains headings. But rather than using the Heading 1 *style* (see page 137), the author used simple boldface formatting for the headings. As a result, you can't use Word's Outline view to see just the headings.

  The solution is simple: Click in the empty "Find what" box. Choose Format→ Font, choose Bold in the "Font style" box, and click OK. Now click in the empty "Replace with" box; choose Format→Style, select the Heading 1 style, and click OK. Now, when you click Replace All, Word changes all bolded paragraphs to the Heading 1 style.

Your formatting selections are displayed just below the "Find what" box. Click No Formatting to erase them (in readiness for a different search, for example).

Note: If you've set up an elaborate string of formatting characteristics (Palatino, Heading 1 style, 12 point), there's no way to delete only one of them; you must click No Formatting to delete all of them and build the list again.

Finding Invisible Characters

The Special menu at the bottom of the Find and Replace dialog box lets you incorporate non-alphanumeric "characters" into your search. It also lets you search for document features that have nothing to do with words, such as column breaks, paragraph breaks, and hyphens.

When you choose one of these items from the Special menu, Word places its character code in the "Find what" box. You can use more than one of these choices and use them with wildcards, as described above.

Tip: Once again, you can manipulate this list with the keyboard. Press ⌘-E to open the Special pop-up menu, and then use the arrow keys to highlight the commands on it.

The Special menu really demonstrates its power in Find and Replace operations. Some examples:

- Suppose your document is filled with typographically correct dashes, which may turn into gibberish if posted on a Web page or emailed. To convert them into double hyphens, click in the "Find what" box and choose Special→Em Dash (for a long dash, like this —) or En Dash (for a shorter dash, like this –). Click in the

"Replace with" box and type two hyphens (--). When you click Replace All, Word replaces dashes with hyphens.

Tip: To replace both kinds of dashes in one pass, choose one after the other in the Special menu. Now place brackets around them in the "Find what" box.

- To take out column breaks and let the text reflow, click in the "Find what" box and choose Special→Column Break. Click in the "Replace with" box and choose Special→Paragraph Mark to ensure that the paragraphs in the newly joined columns don't run into each other.

- A Word document may look fine if there's just one press of the Return key after each paragraph, as the style in question may have built-in "blank lines" between paragraphs. But if you try to paste the document's text into an email message, you'll lose the blank lines between paragraphs.

   The solution is to replace every paragraph mark with *two* paragraph marks before copying the document into your email program. Click in the "Find what" box and choose Special→Paragraph Mark; then click in the "Replace with" box and choose Special→Paragraph Mark *twice*. Word replaces every paragraph mark (which Word represents with the code $^\wedge p$) with two consecutive paragraph breaks ($^\wedge p^\wedge p$).

- To reduce typing, insert abbreviation codes into a Word document, then replace them with much longer passages of boilerplate text. Before searching, copy the replacement text to the clipboard, type the abbreviation code into the "Find what" box, click in the "Replace with" box, and choose Special→Clipboard Contents. Finally, click Replace All.

Tip: You'll see the Special→Clipboard Contents command only when you've clicked in the "Replace with" box. In other words, you can't search for something you've copied to the clipboard. That's unfortunate, since almost everyone, sooner or later, comes across a Word document filled with some strange symbol—little white squares, Symbol-font squiggles, or some other mysterious character. It would be nice if you could copy one instance to the clipboard, so that you could replace all instances with, say, nothing.

In such situations, you can usually get away with *pasting* the copied mystery symbol directly into the "Find what" box.

To undo selections you've made from the Special menu in the Find and Replace dialog box, select and delete the characters that Word placed in the "Find what" or "Replace with" boxes.

Spelling and Grammar

Whatever your document—term paper, resumé, or letter to the milkman—typos can hinder its effectiveness and sully your credibility. When you let mistakes remain in your document, your reader may doubt that you put any time or care into it at all. Word helps you achieve the perfect result by pointing out possible errors, leaving the final call up to you.

Tip: A spelling-related feature (new since Word 2001) may have been benefiting you without you even noticing. When you incur a typo that even a Sominex-drugged reader would notice, such as *wodnerful* or *thier,* Word makes the correction automatically, instantly, and quietly. (Press ⌘-Z or F1 immediately afterward if you actually intended the misspelled version.) Technically, Word is using its spelling dictionaries as fodder for its AutoCorrect feature, as described on page 91.

As a bonus, the spell checker in Word 2004 is smart enough to recognize run-together words (such as *intothe* and *giveme*) and propose the split-apart versions as corrected spellings.

There are two basic modes to Word's spelling and grammar features:

Check Spelling as You Type

Word's factory setting is to check spelling and grammar continuously, immediately flagging any error it detects as soon as you finish typing it. Each spelling error gets a red, squiggly underline; each grammatical error gets a green one. These squiggly underlines (which also appear in the other Office programs) are among the most noticeable hallmarks of Office documents, as shown in Figure 2-8.

Figure 2-8:
Top: When Word is set to check spelling and grammar as you type, errors are underlined as you go. Control-clicking each error opens a contextual menu that contains suggested spellings and commonly used Spelling and Grammar commands.

Bottom: Choosing "About this sentence" prompts the Office Assistant to explain the grammatical issue (bottom). Press Option-F7 to move on to the next error.

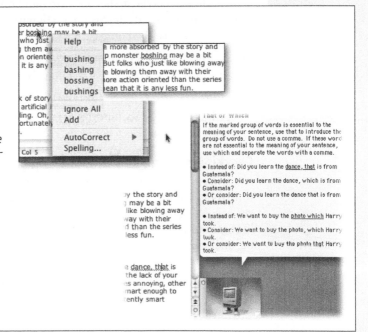

If you can spot the problem right away—an obvious spelling error, for example—simply edit it. The squiggly underline disappears as soon as your insertion point leaves the vicinity. It's often more fun, however, to Control-click (or right-click) each error (see Figure 2-8), which opens a contextual menu to help you handle the correction process. Here are the commands you'll find in this contextual menu:

- **Help** opens the Word Help system, as described in Appendix B (see the "Missing CD page at *www.missingmanuals.com.*)

- The next segment of the contextual menu contains spelling suggestions from Word's dictionary. It says "(no spelling suggestions)" if Word has none.

  If one of these suggestions is the word you were trying to spell, click it. Word instantly replaces the error in your document, thus evaporating the squiggly line.

- Choosing Ignore All from the contextual menu tells Word to butt out—that this word is spelled exactly the way you want it. Once you've chosen this command, the underlines disappear from *all* occurrences of that term in *this* document. (If you use the same spelling in a new document, however, Word will flag it as an error again. To teach Word the word forever, add it to the custom dictionary, as described next.)

- As you've probably figured out by now, Word underlines a word not necessarily because it's spelled incorrectly, but because it's not on Word's list of correctly spelled words. Occasionally, you have to "teach" Word a new word. The Add command does exactly that.

  Word maintains word lists called custom dictionaries. When Word checks a word's spelling as you type it, the Add command on the contextual menu instantly adds that word to the current custom dictionary. You can also edit a custom dictionary directly, as described on page 86.

- The **AutoCorrect** pop-up menu provides access to matching choices from Word's AutoCorrect list (see page 91). Often, but not always, these choices are the same as the alternate spellings from the custom dictionary.

- **Spelling** opens the Spelling dialog box and performs a spelling and grammar check on whatever you selected and clicked.

Checking Spelling and Grammar All at Once

If it annoys you when Word flags incorrect or unusual spellings as you type, there's something you can do about it. Turn that feature off, as described in Figure 2-9, and check spelling on demand—once at the very end, for instance. If that's the way you like it, choose Tools→Spelling and Grammar (or press F7, or Option-⌘-L) to open the Spelling and Grammar dialog box (Figure 2-9).

Word scans your document, starting at the insertion point, and displays errors one by one in the "Not in dictionary" box, as shown in Figure 2-9. As a courtesy, Word shows you the "error" in context, placing the whole sentence in the text box with the specific spelling error shown in red. Your options are as follows:

- Click **Ignore** (⌘-I) to skip over the error without doing anything. If you don't want Word to flag this particular error again (in this document), click **Ignore All** (⌘-G).

Figure 2-9:
If you want Word to check spelling only and keep its grammatical comments to itself, uncheck the "Check grammar" box (⌘-K) in the lower-left corner.

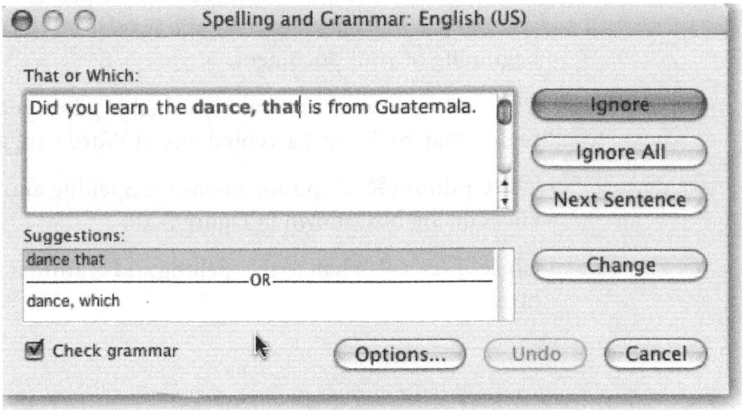

- As described under "Check spelling as you type," clicking **Add** (⌘-A) adds the highlighted word to the custom dictionary. From here on out, in every document, Word will understand this spelling to be a correct one.

- In the lower Suggestions list box, Word shows you some similarly spelled words from your main and custom dictionaries. Using the mouse or the up/down arrow keys, highlight one of them and click **Change** to accept that spelling just this once, or **Change All** (⌘-L) to swap all occurrences of the highlighted word—in this document only—with the selected suggestion.

- If you agree that something is misspelled, but you don't see the correct spelling in the Suggestions list, you can make the correction directly in the top text area, using any of Word's editing tools. (This is a handy trick when Word discovers a typo like ";lkjijjjjjjj"—a sure sign that you'd fallen asleep on the keys. Just drag across the mess—right there in the dialog box—and press the Delete key to fix the error.)

  Then click Change or Change All, as described above, to apply your change to the document itself. You can also click **Undo Edit** (⌘-U) if you change your mind. (The Ignore button changes into Undo Edit as soon as you start typing in the window.)

- Whether you make a choice from the Suggestions window or make a change in the editing window, clicking the **AutoCorrect** (⌘-R) button tells Word to make the change from now on, using the AutoCorrect feature (see page 91). When you do so, Word enters your typo/correction pair to its AutoCorrect list, which you can view by choosing Tools→AutoCorrect and scrolling through the list. (See page 91 for more information on working with the AutoCorrect dialog box.)

- The **Undo** (⌘-U) button is a lifesaver for the indecisive. After you've made a correction, after you've clicked Change, even after you've created a new AutoCorrect pair, you can click Undo and take back your last change. Better still, the Undo command works even after you click Change, and Word has moved on to the next error. In that case, Word backtracks to the previous change and undoes it. In fact, you can keep on clicking Undo and reverse all the changes you've made since the beginning of your document.

The Undo button is particularly valuable when you're spell checking rapidly and realize that you've just accepted one of Word's suggestions a bit too hastily.

- The **Options** (⌘-O) button opens the Spelling and Grammar panel of the Preferences dialog box, shown in Figure 2-10.

- **Close** (Esc) calls a halt to the spelling and grammar check and dismisses the dialog box.

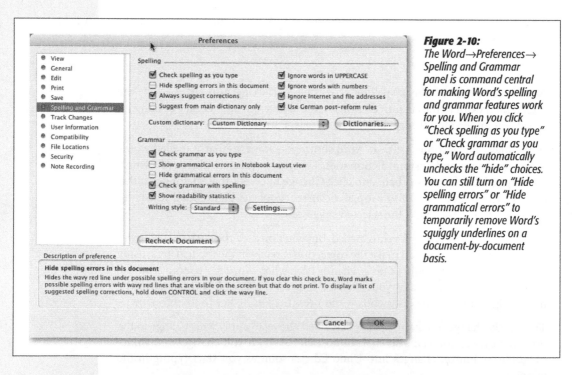

Figure 2-10:
The Word→Preferences→ Spelling and Grammar panel is command central for making Word's spelling and grammar features work for you. When you click "Check spelling as you type" or "Check grammar as you type," Word automatically unchecks the "hide" choices. You can still turn on "Hide spelling errors" or "Hide grammatical errors" to temporarily remove Word's squiggly underlines on a document-by-document basis.

When you're running a spelling and grammar check, the Office Assistant balloon often opens to explain the grammatical principle at work. Turn the Office Assistant off (see page 35) if you have no use for this reading material.

Over the years, Word's grammar checker has grown smarter and less likely to underline perfectly correct sentences or make incorrect suggestions. Sometimes, however, you still need to rely on your own knowledge of grammar (and a healthy dose of common sense) in order to decide when to accept Word's suggested grammar changes—and when to click Ignore.

Spelling and Grammar Options

To tell Word how much (or little) help you need with your spelling and grammar, choose Word→Preferences; in the Preferences dialog box, click the Spelling and Grammar button. You'll find these options:

- **Check spelling as you type** turns on and off the red, wavy underlines that mark spelling errors in all Word documents.

- **Hide spelling errors in this document** turns off "Check spelling as you type" in the current document only.

- **Always suggest corrections** prompts Word to show you alternative spellings during spelling checks that use the Spelling dialog box. Without this option, Word will flag errors without proposing suggestions.

Note: Control-clicking a squiggly-underlined word produces spelling suggestions regardless of the "Always suggest corrections" setting.

- **Suggest from main dictionary only** instructs Word to use only the list of words that came installed with it, ignoring your custom dictionaries. (See page 86 for more detail on custom dictionaries.)

- Turn on **Ignore words in UPPERCASE** if you frequently use acronyms or stock symbols (such as WFMI or ADM). Otherwise, Word interprets them as misspelled words.

- Turn on **Ignore words with numbers** if you'd like Word to leave words like 3Com and R2D2 alone.

- **Ignore Internet and file addresses** governs whether or not Word interprets URLs (*www.missingmanuals.com*) and file paths (Macintosh HD:Documents:Tests) as spelling errors. Because it's unlikely that most Web addresses are in Word's dictionaries, you'll usually want this option turned on.

- **Use German post-reform rules.** Turning on this box tells Word to use the new German spelling rules that were instituted in the 1990s—in Germany. (So if it works only on German-language Macs, why you still can turn it on with English-language Macs? As a conversation starter, perhaps.)

- **Custom dictionary.** See page 86 for a full explanation of this feature.

- **Check grammar as you type** turns on and off the green, wavy underlines that mark what Word considers grammatical errors in all Word documents.

- **Show grammatical errors in Notebook Layout view.** In Word 2004's new Notebook Layout view (page 189), many of your notebook ramblings are incomplete thoughts, little more than notes to yourself, stuff that you either don't need (or don't want) Word to check for grammatical correctness. If you don't want Word to check grammar in Notebook Layout view leave this box turned off. (Word still checks grammar in all the *other* views, just like normal.)

- **Hide grammatical errors in this document** turns off "Check grammar as you type" in the current document only.

- Turn off **Check grammar with spelling** to proceed through spelling checks without stopping for grammar issues.

- **Show readability statistics** may please educators and testers, but is probably of little value to anyone else. If you turn on this checkbox, Word applies a readability formula to the document. ("Check grammar with spelling" must be on as well.) The readability formula calculates an approximate grade level based on the number of syllables, words, and sentences in the document. These statistics are displayed in a box at the end of the spelling and grammar check.

Word uses one of two formulas to interpret the results. The *Flesch Reading Ease* score uses a scale of 0 to 100, with 100 being the easiest. A score of 60 or 70 indicates text that most adults could comfortably read and understand. The Flesch-Kincaid Grade Level Score, on the other hand, calculates grade level according to U.S. averages. A score of 8, for example, means that the document is on the eighth-grade reading level. If you're writing the minutes for your recent MENSA meeting, this reading level may seem a little low; for a general audience, though, it's a good level to shoot for.

GEM IN THE ROUGH

Checking Foreign Language Text

The spell checkers in ordinary word processors choke on foreign terms. But not Word—it actually comes with different spelling dictionaries for dozens of languages. The program can actually check the English parts of your document against the English dictionary, the French portions against the French dictionary, and so on—all in a single pass.

This amazing intelligence works only if you've taken two preliminary steps. First, you must install the foreign-language dictionaries you intend to use (they're not part of the standard installation), using the technique described in Appendix A on the "Missing CD" page at *www.missingmanuals.com*.

Second, you must tell Word which language each passage is in. To flag a certain word, passage, or document as Danish, for example, first highlight it. Then choose Tools→ Language; in the resulting dialog box, select the language and click OK.

You've just applied what Microsoft calls language formatting—that is, you've flagged the highlighted text just as though you'd made it blue or bold. From now on, your spell checks will switch, on the fly, to the corresponding spelling dictionary for each patch of foreign language text in your document.

Either way, remember that this is a software program analyzing words written by a human being for specific audiences. By no means, for example, should you base somebody's entrance to a school on these scores—they're only crude approximations of approximations.

Writing Styles

As it's probably occurred to you by now, grammar can be very subjective. Contractions, for example, aren't incorrect; they're just appropriate in some situations and not in others. In an academic or medical paper, long sentences and the passive voice are the norm (but still less than ideal); in a magazine article, they're taboo. On the other hand, other kinds of errors, such as writing the contraction "it's" when you mean the possessive "its," are things you *always* want to avoid. And when writing poetry or a play in dialect, the usual rules of grammar simply don't apply.

In other words, there are different writing styles for different kinds of documents. Word 2004 not only recognizes that fact, it lets you choose which one you want to use in a given situation. Better still, it lets *you* decide which grammatical issues you want flagged.

To select a writing style from Word's preconfigured list, choose Word→Preferences→ Spelling and Grammar. In the resulting dialog box, choose a writing style from the pop-up menu near the bottom of the box under Grammar.

To customize writing styles to your own needs, thus becoming your own grammar czar or czarina, click Settings. The Grammar Settings dialog box opens, as shown in Figure 2-11. (If the Grammar settings are dimmed in the dialog box, it's because the Grammar module isn't installed. See Appendix A for installation instructions.)

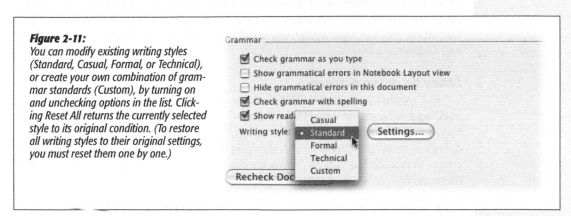

Figure 2-11:
You can modify existing writing styles (Standard, Casual, Formal, or Technical), or create your own combination of grammar standards (Custom), by turning on and unchecking options in the list. Clicking Reset All returns the currently selected style to its original condition. (To restore all writing styles to their original settings, you must reset them one by one.)

The choices you make from the pop-up menus under Require apply to all writing styles. Each menu gives you a chance to customize points of style that are more a matter of individual choice than grammar. By default, Word doesn't check for any of the three Require items listed here: whether you put a comma after the second-to-last item in a list (as in: *planes, trains, and automobiles*), whether punctuation goes inside or outside of quotation marks, or the number of spaces between sentences.

If you learned how to write in England, you probably put periods and commas *after* the quotation marks at the end of a quote. In the United States, punctuation is expected to go *before* the quotes. Choose "inside" or "outside" from the second pop-up menu to have Word check if you're doing it consistently, one way or the other.

If you're sending your text to an editor or layout person for desktop publishing, you'll probably be asked to put just one space between sentences; you probably learned how to type with *two* spaces after every period. You can choose 1 or 2 from the bottom menu to instruct Word to check the spacing for you.

You can create your own unique style by choosing Custom from the pop-up menu at the top of the box and turning on any combination of options. When you click OK, the custom style applies to your document; you can't name the style or create more than one custom style at a time.

Custom Dictionaries and Preferred Spellings

As noted earlier, Word maintains a list of thousands of words that it "knows" how to spell. When it checks your spelling, Word simply compares the words in your document to the words in the list.

To teach Word the words that you use frequently, you have two options: You can add them to a *custom dictionary,* or, if you have large batches of words that you only use for specific situations, you can create multiple custom dictionaries. Then choose which dictionary you wish to apply to the document you're currently working on.

You can't add words directly to Word's *main* (built-in) dictionary, which is permanently "hard-wired"—specially encoded for speed. In fact, you aren't even allowed to see the main dictionary. However, when you add words to a custom dictionary, Word uses them seamlessly along with the main dictionary (as long as you haven't turned on the "Use main dictionary only" box in the Word→Preferences→Spelling and Grammar panel).

Editing the custom dictionary

To add words to a custom dictionary, choose Word→Preferences, then click the Spelling and Grammar panel (Figure 2-10). Now click the Dictionaries button. In the Custom Dictionaries dialog box that opens (Figure 2-12), one custom dictionary, by default, is listed and checkmarked, meaning that it's currently in use. Any words that you've ever added to Word's dictionary during a spell check appear in this custom dictionary.

To review the list of words, click Edit. (If a message appears to warn you that Word will now stop checking your spelling, click Continue.) Suddenly, all your added words appear listed in a new Word document, which you're now free to edit. You can add, delete, and edit words using any of Word's editing tools; just remember to use the Return key to ensure each word is on a separate line.

Creating a new custom dictionary

In some cases, you may want to create a new custom dictionary for specific projects. For instance, suppose that you're writing something in a foreign language or a paper filled with technical terms. If you add these foreign or technical terms to the same custom dictionary that you use for everyday correspondence, they'll show up in spell checks and sometimes even create false errors.

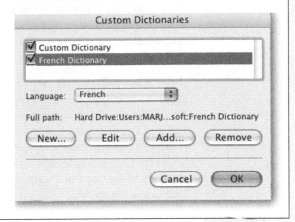

Figure 2-12:
The checked boxes show the custom dictionaries currently in effect. Uncheck one if you would like Word to stop using it in spell checks. For example, if you turn off French Dictionary, Word will interpret French words as spelling errors.

To create a new custom dictionary, click New in the Custom Dictionaries dialog box (Figure 2-12). Type a name for the new dictionary, and then click Save. Word saves the new custom dictionary in your Home folder's Library→Preferences→Microsoft folder.

Now you can add words to the custom dictionary in one of two ways:

- To add new words occasionally, in the course of your everyday writing career, click the name of the new dictionary in the Custom Dictionaries dialog box. (Turn off any other dictionaries that may be listed in the box. Otherwise, Word will add newly learned terms to the default custom dictionary, for example, instead of your own foreign/technical one.) Then just go to work in your document. Whenever you check spelling, choose Add to place the unfamiliar term in your new custom dictionary.

- You can also add words all at once, by selecting the custom dictionary in the Custom Dictionaries dialog box and clicking Edit as described above. If there's a list of vocabulary words or technical terms in front of you, simply type or paste them into the text document that is the custom dictionary. Just make sure that each word is on a separate line before you click Save.

You can also copy and paste words from one custom dictionary into another. Thus, you can always copy the contents of the original custom dictionary into your specialized dictionary, so that you'll have constant access to all your preferred spellings.

Tip: When editing custom dictionaries, you can access them easily by going directly to the Library→Preferences→Microsoft folder in your Home folder. You'll see icons marked with "ABC," which you can open in a program like TextEdit and edit away.

You can also rename these files. For example, if you've created new custom dictionaries, you may want to rename the default custom dictionary "original," "default," or "old."

Adding and removing custom dictionaries

After creating a new custom dictionary, you may decide to exclude it from certain documents. To do so, turn off its box in the Custom Dictionaries dialog box as described in Figure 2-12.

If you select a dictionary and click Remove, it disappears from this list and no longer appears in the pop-up menu in the Preferences→Spelling and Grammar panel. This is the way to go if you never again want this custom dictionary as an option and don't want anyone else to see it in Preferences. However, a removed custom dictionary doesn't go away forever. It remains in the Library→Preferences→Microsoft folder (in your Home folder), or wherever you stored it on your Mac's hard drive. To return it to the Custom Dictionaries dialog box, click Add and choose it in the Add Dictionary dialog box.

Foreign language dictionaries

If your new dictionary is in a foreign language, there's an extra step. After creating the new custom dictionary, as described above, select the new foreign dictionary in the Custom Dictionaries dialog box. Then choose the appropriate language from the Language pop-up menu. Now Word will know to apply the correct spelling rules for that language.

Choosing custom dictionaries before spell checking

From now on, before you check spelling, you can specify which custom dictionaries you want Word to consider as it pores over your document. To do so, choose Word→Preferences→Spelling and Grammar panel, and then choose a custom dictionary from the pop-up menu.

Exclude dictionaries

As noted earlier, you can't edit the built-in Word dictionary. The previous discussions guide you through *adding* words to Word's spelling wisdom—but how do you *delete* a word from the built-in dictionary? After all, as noted above, the main dictionary is a hermetically sealed, specially encoded, untouchable entity that you can't edit using any tool known to man.

The answer: by creating an *exclude dictionary.* This is a special kind of dictionary document format that stores the words that you want Word to flag as spelling errors. Whereas a custom dictionary "teaches" Word which words are spelled correctly, the exclude dictionary teaches Word what spellings are *wrong*, even though Word's main dictionary lists the spelling as correct.

For instance, say you prefer "focussed" to "focused." The second spelling, "focused," is the one that comes installed in Word. You should put the word "focused" into the exclude dictionary, so that Word will question that spelling during spell checks, giving you a chance to change it to "focussed."

To create an exclude dictionary, open a blank document. Type or paste in any standard spellings that you want Word to treat as errors. For instance, if you work for the Trefoil Theatre, you'll want to put "Theater" in the exclude dictionary. (The exclude dictionary is case-sensitive; if you want Word to flag both "focused" and "Focused," for instance, you must type both versions into the dictionary.)

When your list of excluded spellings is complete, choose File→Save As. In the Save box, navigate to the Home Folder→Library→Preferences→Microsoft folder. Before saving, also do the following:

- Type a name for the exclude dictionary. "Exclude dictionary" is fine.

- Most importantly, you must choose a special format for this dictionary. In the Format pop-up menu, choose Speller Exclude Dictionary.

Click Save. You have to quit and relaunch Word for the exclude dictionary to take effect.

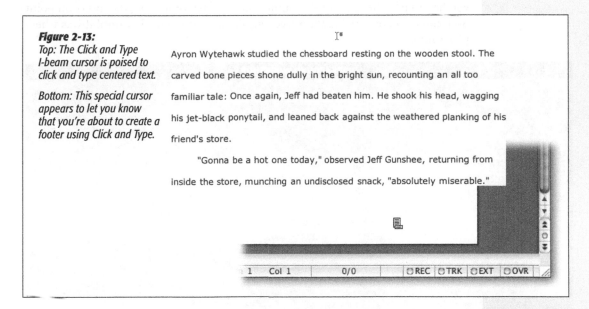

Figure 2-13:
Top: The Click and Type I-beam cursor is poised to click and type centered text.

Bottom: This special cursor appears to let you know that you're about to create a footer using Click and Type.

Ayron Wytehawk studied the chessboard resting on the wooden stool. The carved bone pieces shone dully in the bright sun, recounting an all too familiar tale: Once again, Jeff had beaten him. He shook his head, wagging his jet-black ponytail, and leaned back against the weathered planking of his friend's store.

"Gonna be a hot one today," observed Jeff Gunshee, returning from inside the store, munching an undisclosed snack, "absolutely miserable."

1   Col 1   0/0   ◯REC ◯TRK ◯EXT ◯OVR

Five Ways to Type Less

At first glance, the Word window looks much like any computer screen. You type, and letters appear, just as in that classic Mac word processor, TextEdit. But there's actually much more to it than that. While you're typing, Word is constantly thinking, reacting, doing things to save you precious keystrokes.

As noted earlier, for example, Word corrects obvious spelling errors as you go along. But it also lets you create your own typing shortcuts, and even tries to anticipate your next formatting move, sometimes to the frustration of people who don't understand what the program's doing. The more you know what Word is thinking (it means well, it really does), the more you can let Word do the work, saving those precious brain cells for more important stuff—like writing or remembering to get the kids to soccer practice.

Click and Type

In olden days, our screens gave us a continually blinking insertion point, located in the upper-left corner of the screen. That's where you typed, no questions asked or answers given. If you wanted to type in the middle of the page—for example, to create a title page of a report—you couldn't just click there and start typing. Instead, you had to take the ludicrously counterintuitive step of moving the insertion point over and down by tapping the Space bar, Tab key, or Return key until it was where you wanted it.

WORKAROUND WORKSHOP

Telling AutoCorrect to Shut Up

Sometimes Word is more diligent in correcting errors than you'd like. What if you're trying to type a letter to a Mr. Porvide, and Word changes it to Provide? Or maybe you work for a company called Intelligance, and you're tired of changing the "e" to an "a" every time Word helpfully "corrects" it.

You don't want to turn AutoCorrect off, because you want Word to catch all your other typos. You could press ⌘-Z after Word makes each change, but that gets wearisome about the 35th time. Fortunately, there's a solution.

Click the Exceptions button on the AutoCorrect tab (see Figure 2-15). Then click the Other Corrections tab. Type your preferred spelling into the "Don't correct" text box and click Add. If you have many preferred spellings that you'll need to reeducate Word about, turn on the "Automatically add words to list" checkbox. Now, each time Word makes an incorrect correction, click the Undo button on the Standard toolbar, choose Edit→Undo, or press ⌘-Z. Intelligance turns back into Intelligance, for example, and Word automatically adds your exceptional spelling to its AutoCorrect Exceptions list.

But you're not done yet, since the substitution pairs in the AutoCorrect dialog box (Figure 2-15) override the list in the Exceptions box. In other words, even though you've listed a preferred spelling as an exception, Word will still make the correction, and change Porvide to Provide, for example. The final step, then, is to delete the original AutoCorrect substitution pair. Choose Tools→AutoCorrect→AutoCorrect tab, scroll down until you find the offending correction pair, click to select it, and then click Delete. You may now Porvide to your heart's content.

But in Word 2004, Click and Type assists location-challenged typists the world over by letting them reach their desired insertion point just by double-clicking. Here's how it works:

1. **Switch to Online view or Page Layout view.**

   These are the only views where Click and Type is available; choose from the View menu to change views.

2. **Move the cursor around on the blank page, letting it hover for a second at the point where you'd like to place some text.**

   In some cases, you'll see the cursor change to indicate that Word is about to provide some free formatting help. If your cursor is near the left or right margin, Word assumes that you want your text to be left- or right-aligned; you'll see tiny left- or right-justified lines appear next to the hovering insertion point (see Figure 2-13). When you hover in the middle of the page, the insertion-point icon changes to centered text. If your cursor is near the top or bottom of the page, the cursor changes shape again to illustrate that you're about to edit the document's *header* or *footer* (see page 217).

   If Word guesses wrong about the alignment, you can always adjust the text alignment later using the Alignment and Spacing tools in the Formatting Palette (see page 117).

3. **Double-click.**

   The insertion point turns into a standard blinking bar, and you're ready to begin typing. (If the insertion point doesn't end up quite where you wanted it, just double-click again.)

Note: Behind the scenes, Word actually fills the page with Tabs and Returns, exactly as you did manually in the old days; that's how it gets your insertion point to the spot where you double-clicked. Knowing that (or *seeing* that, by clicking the ¶ button on the Standard toolbar) makes troubleshooting or adjusting Click-and-Typed text much easier.

To turn Click and Type on and off, choose Word→Preferences→Edit panel. Turn on or uncheck the "Enable click and type" box.

AutoCorrect

Word seems psychic at times. You type *teh*, and Word changes it to "the" before you even have a chance to hit Delete. You start to type the name of the month, and all of a sudden today's date pops up on the screen— and you didn't even know what day it was.

You're witnessing Word's AutoCorrect and AutoType features at work—two of the least understood and most useful tools in Word's arsenal. They can be frustrating if you don't understand them, and the writer's best friend if you do.

Think of AutoCorrect as Word's *substitution* feature. All it does is replace something you're typing (the typo) with a replacement that Word has memorized and stored (the correct spelling). The correction takes place as soon as you type a space after the incorrect word; no further action is required from you. And it happens so fast that you may not notice you've just been autocorrected unless you're watching for the blue bolt that slides under the word as Word analyzes it. If the correction isn't what you were expecting, click under the word to reveal the AutoCorrect smart button, as shown in Figure 2-14.

Crucial Tip: If you retain one tip from this book's advice about Microsoft Word, remember this: *You can undo any automatic change Word makes,* under any circumstance, by pressing ⌘-Z or F1 just after Word makes it. That goes for automatic capitalization help, spelling help, formatting help, curly quote help, and so on. (It's also even faster than using the smart button shown below.)

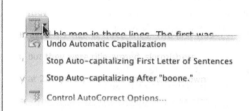

Figure 2-14:
Hover your mouse over text Word autocorrects to display the AutoCorrect smart button. As Yoda would say, "Helpful it is." The provided options are contextual, but include undoing the action that Word has done, a heartfelt offer to stop doing it in the future, and a link to the AutoCorrect dialog box.

Word maintains a file of common misspellings and their corrections. That's why Word makes certain corrections and not others: Not all possible error/correction combinations that you need come installed on the list. To see this list, choose Tools→ AutoCorrect and click the AutoCorrect tab (Figure 2-15). (Here you'll also find the most important checkbox in the world of AutoCorrect: the master on/off switch, called "Replace text as you type.")

The first three checkboxes cover capitalization errors; they save you from the errant ways of your pinky fingers on the Shift keys. When the first two boxes are turned on (see Figure 2-15), Word makes sure that you get a capital letter at the beginning of every sentence, whether you hold the Shift key down too long ("Correct TWo INitial CApitals") or not long enough ("Capitalize first letter of sentences").

Tip: Efficiency-addicted Word fans eventually stop capitalizing the first letters of sentences altogether. Word does it automatically, so why twist your pinkies unnecessarily?

If you turn on "Capitalize first letter of sentences," bear in mind that Word assumes every period is the end of a sentence. So why doesn't it auto-cap the first word after you type *U.N.* or *Jan.?* Because it's smart enough not to auto-cap after all-cap ab- breviations (U.N.), and because it maintains a list of lowercase abbreviations that *shouldn't* be followed by capitals. (To see the list, choose Tools→AutoCorrect, then click Exceptions; you can add your own abbreviations to this list, too.)

If you turn on "Automatically use suggestions from the spelling checker," AutoCorrect will go above and beyond the list of substitution pairs in this dialog box. It will use Word's main dictionary as a guide to proper spelling and automatically change words that almost, but not quite, match ones in the dictionary. (When Word can't decide on a match, it simply squiggly-underlines the misspelled word in the document.)

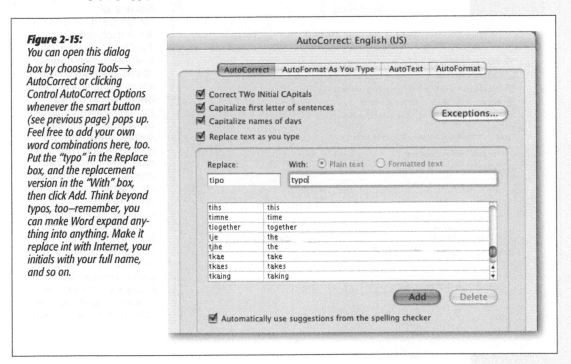

Figure 2-15:
You can open this dialog box by choosing Tools→ AutoCorrect or clicking Control AutoCorrect Options whenever the smart button (see previous page) pops up. Feel free to add your own word combinations here, too. Put the "typo" in the Replace box, and the replacement version in the "With" box, then click Add. Think beyond typos, too—remember, you can make Word expand anything into anything. Make it replace int with Internet, your initials with your full name, and so on.

AutoText: Abbreviation Expanders

AutoText is another Word feature that automatically changes what you've typed, once again delighting the expert and driving novices batty. In short, it's an abbreviation expander.

Figure 2-16 shows AutoText in action.

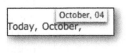

Figure 2-16:
You're typing along. Suddenly you see a floating yellow screen tip just above the insertion point. That's Word's AutoText feature in action. It's proposing a replacement for what you just typed today's date, in this case. If you want to accept the suggestion, press Return or Enter; if not, just keep typing and pretend the screen tip never happened.

AutoText works by maintaining a preinstalled list of commonly typed terms and their replacements. You can also add your favorite terms to the list—the name of your company, your phone number, email address, and so on (see Figure 2-17). You can also add longer items—entire paragraphs, full addresses, lists, and even graphics, as described on page 96.

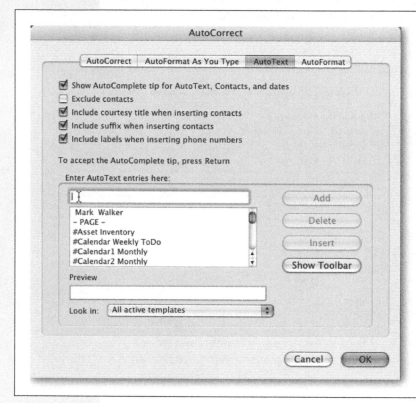

Figure 2-17:
This tab (Insert→AutoText→ AutoText tab, or Tools→ AutoCorrect→AutoText tab) is where you choose words, phrases, and fields to insert into your document without typing. You can also add your own items to the list by typing them into the "Enter AutoText entries here" box and clicking Insert. Select and click Delete to banish from your list any items you never use. You can also insert Auto-Text items into your document from this tab. Press the down arrow or Page Down key to scroll down until your desired entry appears in the Preview box (you can also use the scroll bar). Hit Return to drop the entry into your document; it lands wherever your insertion point has been blinking.

Setting up an AutoText entry

Word comes set up with dozens of ready-to-use AutoText entries; in fact, it's more powerful in Office 2004 than in previous versions. It completes not only the names of days of the week and months of the year, but also today's date and names from your Entourage address book (see Chapter 11).

But the real joy of becoming an AutoText addict is creating your own abbreviations. You can use AutoText to save form letters or contracts that go on for pages and pages, and then dump them into your documents just by typing a few keys. If you're a lawyer, realtor, or medical professional who's not using AutoText to save time on boilerplate copy, you're missing out on a great timesaver.

To create a new entry, select a block of text (from a word or two to many paragraphs) and choose Insert→AutoText→New. (If the AutoText toolbar is visible—to make it so, choose View→Toolbars→AutoText—you can just click its New button.) Name your selection carefully, since the name you choose is the abbreviation that will trigger the expansion. Choose something easy to remember, but not something that you might type unintentionally. Click OK.

Tip: If you've carefully formatted the copy that you want to use as AutoText—with different type styles and colors, for example—you can preserve that formatting no matter what the style of the document you eventually use it in. Click the Show/Hide button (a ¶ symbol) on the Standard toolbar or Formatting Palette. Now when you select the text, select the gray ¶ symbol at the very end along with it; the selection's formatting will come along into AutoText.

Triggering AutoText entries

You can drop any item in the list into your document in one of two ways.

- **AutoComplete.** It doesn't get any less labor-intensive than this. When you type the first four letters of any word on the AutoText menu, AutoComplete, if turned on, shows you the full, expanded version in a pop-up screen tip (see Figure 2-16), hovering above the area where you're typing.

  To accept it, just hit Return; Word finishes the typing for you. If you don't want the choice that AutoComplete is offering, just keep typing (or hit Esc). If you inadvertently accept a completion that you didn't want, just press ⌘-Z to undo it. You can also choose Edit→Undo AutoComplete.

  There's little downside to leaving AutoComplete turned on. After all, you can ignore all of its screen tip suggestions, if you dislike the feature. But to turn off even these suggestions, you'll find the on/off switch by choosing Tools→AutoCorrect→

POWER USERS' CLINIC

AutoText Toolbar

If you use AutoText frequently, or when you're first using Word 2004 and adding lots of new entries, consider keeping the AutoText toolbar visible at all times. Choose View→Toolbars→ AutoText, or click Show Toolbar on the AutoText tab of the AutoCorrect dialog box (see Figure 2-17).

The first button on the toolbar, which looks like an A (representing text) and a mechanical cog-wheel (representing automation), calls up the AutoText tab, saving you several clicks.

All your AutoText entries are found under the All Entries

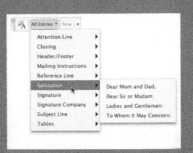

menu, making them more easily accessible than the Insert→ AutoText submenu.

The New button is usually grayed out. It's active only when you select a word, phrase, paragraph, or graphic. Clicking New brings up a dialog box where you can confirm, and name, your selection as a brand-new AutoText entry, never to be typed in full again. (The first four letters of the name entered here will trigger AutoComplete, so make sure to use the first four letters of what you want to type, or something equally easy to remember.)

AutoText tab. It's the "Show AutoComplete tip for AutoText, Address Book Contacts and dates" box (see Figure 2-17).

- **Choosing from AutoText menu.** Choose Insert→AutoText. The current AutoText items are listed in the submenus that have arrows. Drag through the submenus until you find the entry you want to avoid typing, and click it to drop it into your document. Your choice appears wherever you left your insertion point, and it inherits whatever text style and formatting is in place at that point.

AutoText graphics

Despite its name, AutoText can automate more than just text. It can easily store frequently used graphics, as well. Create a drawing in Word (see Chapter 20), or paste a graphic from another program into a Word document—a logo that you've created in a drawing or painting program, your scanned signature, or a favorite photograph, perhaps. Click the graphic to select it, then choose Insert→AutoText→New (or click the New button on the AutoText tab or toolbar).

You can't insert an AutoComplete graphic by typing. So, to drop it into a document, you must choose its name from the Insert→AutoText submenu (or the AutoText toolbar).

AutoText fields

Some of the preinstalled AutoText entries are *fields*: placeholders that, when you print, Word fills in with the date, type, page number, and so on. Word lists them in the Header/Footer section of the AutoText submenu, because that's where you're most likely to use them.

For example, you can place a page number at the top of each page by putting a—*PAGE*—AutoText field in the header. To remind yourself (and everyone else) who wrote

---

POWER USERS' CLINIC

AutoText for Polyglots

If you have the English version of Office 2004, and you never type in any language other than English, this sidebar is not for you.

But suppose you're typing a letter to your lover in Paris, only to realize—*sacre bleu!*—that the entries listed in the AutoText tab of the AutoCorrect dialog box are in English, and will do you no good at all.

Not to worry. Instead of using the AutoText tab, use the submenus on the Insert→AutoText menu, or the All Entries menu on the AutoText toolbar. Those menus reflect the language currently in effect at the insertion point, while the

list in the AutoCorrect box always reflects the language of the version of Word that you've purchased.

How does Word know which language you're typing in? You told it so by highlighting the foreign language text, choosing Tools→Language, and then selecting a language in the dialog box that appears next. So, before typing your letter to Jean-Marie, choose Tools→Language, select French in the list that appears and click OK. *Et voila!*—your choices on the AutoText submenus and AutoText tab are in French. (If you've already begun typing in French, be sure to select that text first. Otherwise, Word will think it's very poorly spelled English.)

---

a particular document and when, place the "Author, Page #, Date" AutoText in the footer. (Word uses the name you entered when first setting up Office. To override that name, enter a different name in the Word→Preferences→User Information panel.)

Project Gallery Templates

A *template* is like Word stationery: It's a special kind of document with formatting and preferences options set the way you like them. A *wizard,* on the other hand, is Microsoft's term for a series of interview-style dialog boxes that request information from you and process your responses.

The templates in Office 2004's Project Gallery combine the two features, with the ultimate aim of, once again, saving you much of the grunt work of typing and formatting. Here's how you might use one of these template/wizard combos to create a business brochure:

1. **Choose File→Project Gallery.**

   The Project Gallery opens, as described on page 14. Except for Blank Documents and My Templates, all the Groups in the list box at the left contain lists of built-in templates (see Figure 2-18).

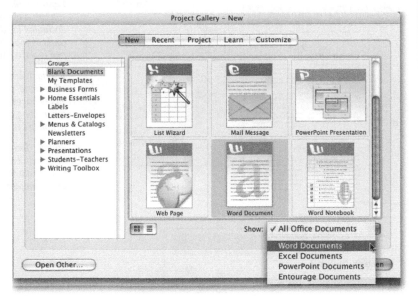

Figure 2-18:
Click the "flippy triangles" next to the groups to see a larger selection of templates. To see only the ones that work in Word, select "Word documents" from the Show pop-up menu at the bottom of the Project Gallery.

2. **Double-click Business Forms, then click Brochures.**

   Word displays a list of prefab brochure designs. (If you're not seeing the thumbnail images, make sure the View pop-up menu says Catalog.)

3. **Double-click the brochure design you want.**

The template's wizard windows open. Some of the wizard fields may be already filled in, using information from the Word→Preferences→User Information tab or from the last template you used.

The Content tab collects information, such as your name and address, that will be inserted into corresponding fields in the template.

4. **Fill in the blanks; specify the tables or other elements you want in your finished brochure.**

As you make changes to the wizard, you can see them reflected in the new document window behind the wizard window. However, you can't click in or scroll the new document while the wizard remains open.

5. **Click the Layout tab to add a preformatted order form, price list, or one of the other professional brochure elements.**

Word 2004 anticipates some of the more complex features you're likely to include in a brochure. You can choose a table (such as an event schedule or price list) or form (such as an order form or sign-up form), as shown in Figure 2-19.

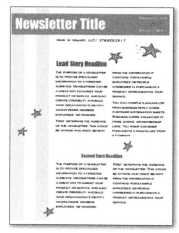

Figure 2-19:
Top left: A template is a canned Office document filled with "dummy" text. You could, if you wish, simply drag through it and replace it with new text of your own.

Top right: The Newsletter Wizard, on the other hand, presents a dialog box full of empty boxes (fields) to fill in, partially automating the process of replacing the template's text.

Bottom: The template has turned into a meaningful document, with your own text substituted for what was previously in the template.

If you have the option of changing the color scheme, the wizard offers you a Theme & Color tab. (You do, in the case of the brochure.) If you like, click the tab and specify a different color scheme or graphic design theme.

6. **Click Save & Exit.**

    The wizard closes. (If you click Cancel, the wizard closes, and everything that was in the template disappears, leaving a blank document.)

Finally, you arrive in your new document—a heavily formatted Word file, almost ready to print, but filled with dummy text and placeholder images. Although this dummy text isn't going to be around very long, it's worth a quick read. It contains advice and tips for your own writing (such as "This is a good place to briefly, but effectively, summarize your products or services").

If you've prepared your letter, newsletter or other text in another document, open that document and select the text. Choose Edit→Copy or press ⌘-C. Return to the template, select the prefab dummy text that you want to delete, and choose Edit→ Paste or press ⌘-V. You may have to adjust the size of the text boxes by clicking on them and dragging their handles.

AutoFormat

Has this happened to you?

- You type a numbered list, and suddenly the next number in sequence appears on its own.

- You type a Web address, and suddenly Word turns it into a blue, underlined, working hyperlink (that you can't edit, since clicking inside it opens your Web browser).

- You type an email smiley—which looks like :)—and Word, on its own, decides to replace your punctuation symbol with an actual graphic smiley face, like ☺.

- You start typing a letter, and Office Assistant Max offers to help. How did *he* know you're writing a letter—and how do you convince him that you're perfectly capable of formatting a letter on your own?

Tip: Remember: Just because Word steps in and formats something for you doesn't mean you're stuck with it. You don't even have to backspace over it; just press ⌘-Z or F1 (or choose the "change back" from the smart button menu). Whatever it is that Word just did—making a smiley face, turning a URL into blue underlined text, numbering a list—is restored to the way you originally typed it.

All of these behaviors—considered helpful by Microsoft and unspeakably rude by many Word users—are triggered by a technology called AutoFormat. This tool doesn't have to be annoying. In fact, once you learn the workings behind AutoFormat, you can control and use it to your own advantage.

There are two ways to use AutoFormat: You can have Word autoformat words and
paragraphs as you type them, or you can autoformat manually, in one pass, after the
typing is complete.

Autoformatting as you type

To turn AutoFormat on and off, choose the Tools→AutoCorrect→AutoFormat As
You Type tab. There they are: the master on/off switches for all of Word's meddlesome
behavior (see Figure 2-20).

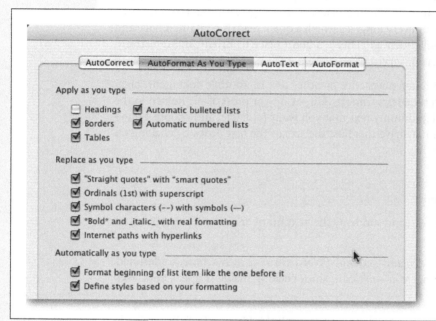

Figure 2-20:
*There are two separate
tabs in the AutoCorrect
dialog box for the two
different ways of using
AutoFormat. This one,
called AutoFormat As
You Type, and the one
on the far right, simply
called AutoFormat. Here
you can turn on and off
the formatting-on-the-
fly changes that Word
offers to make. (As with
the AutoCorrect feature
described on page 92,
this box may open when
you click "Control Auto-
Correct Options" on the
smart button menu.)*

To turn AutoFormat off completely, uncheck *all* the boxes and click OK.

You should also turn AutoFormat off if your document is destined for plain text, or
if you're going to paste and format it in a different program anyway. Also, be aware
that curly quotes and bullets can turn into funny characters when pasted into an
email. (They look fine in Entourage email, but your recipient's email program may
not translate them properly. And borders don't work at all.) Later, you can turn the
same plain text into a nicely formatted Word document by conducting a single Auto
Format pass, as described below.

There's a checkbox for each feature that Word can autoformat. Here's what each
AutoFormat option does:

- **Headings.** If you type a short phrase and press Return, Word interprets it as a
  heading and applies a big, bold style (Heading 1) to it.

- **Borders.** Word draws a bold horizontal line across the page when you type three hyphens in a row (or three underlines) and press Return—a handy way to break up sections in a document, if that's indeed what you want.

  AutoFormat also creates a double line if you type three equal signs (===); a dotted line for asterisks (***); a wavy line for tildes (~~~); and a triple, picture frame-like line for number signs (###). (Press Return after the symbols.) Later, you can reformat the line or turn it into a full border by clicking in the paragraph and using the Borders and Shading tools on the Formatting Palette (page 125).

  The first time it makes the change, Word asks your permission. Click Yes. After that, Word will do it without asking.

- **Tables.** This feature lets you create Word tables (see page 160) by using typed characters instead of the Draw Table tool. Type a plus sign (+) to start the table, a row of hyphens (---) to set the width for the first cell, another + sign to end the cell, more hyphens, and so on. The line must begin and end with + signs. To create the next line, click below this first row and start typing + signs and hyphens again. You can also switch to using Word's table tools to reformat or expand the table at any time.

Note: Because Word's table feature is so easy to use, it's hard to imagine why anyone would create a table using + signs and hyphens. The answer is that tables sent by email, as well as those posted on Web pages and newsgroups, *already* use this format. By pasting them into Word and performing an AutoFormat pass, you turn existing Internet tables into proper Word tables. Few people build a *fresh* table using this method.

- **Automatic bulleted lists.** When you type a common "bullet" character, such as *, -, >, or =>, and follow it with a space or a tab, then some text, and then press Return, Word changes the character to its proper bullet symbol (• or ❑, for example). It also switches to the ListBullet style in your document's template (page 226). When you type a return at the end of a line, Word continues with the next bullet. Press Return twice to end the list.

  You can also start a bulleted list by inserting a bullet of your choice. Choose Insert→ Symbol (page 224) followed by *two* or more spaces and your first list item, then press Return. You can even use pictures as bullets; just choose Insert→Picture→ Clip Art, and then click Web Bullets and Buttons in the Category pane. Now select a bullet by clicking it. (Keep them small; a graphic used as a bullet must be no more than one-and-a-half times the line height of your text.)

- **Automatic numbered lists.** When you type a number followed by a period (or a hyphen, close parenthesis, or close angle bracket [>]) and a space or tab, Word understands that you're starting a numbered list. After you press Return, Word automatically types the next number in the series and applies a ListNumber style (page 137) from your document's template. Pressing the Return key twice in a row instructs Word to end the list.

- **"Straight quotes" with "smart quotes."** When you type a quotation mark (Shift-apostrophe), Word replaces the double-apostrophe straight quotes with more attractive, typographically correct curly quotes.

  Most of the time, this is a useful option. If you're going to email the document, however, turn this feature off. (See page 74 for details.)

- **Ordinals (1st) with superscript.** If you type "1st," Word instantly changes it to 1st.

- **Symbol characters (--) with symbols (—).** When you turn on this box, Word changes a single hyphen to an en dash, like this – , and two hyphens to an em dash, like this — . It's a handy feature, especially because the keystrokes for those dashes are so hard to remember (Option-hyphen and Shift-Option-hyphen, respectively).

Tip: Grammatically speaking, an en dash is used to indicate a range or gap in a sequence ("The poetry reading went from 6:30 p.m.–11:00 p.m., and featured a reading from pages 23–142 of *Letters My Father Never Wrote Me*"). The em dash is the real dash, which indicates a pause for impact ("I can't stand readings—especially poetry").

- ***Bold* and _italic_ with real formatting.** When Word encounters words bounded by asterisks and underscores, it changes them to boldface and italics, respectively.

  You may already be familiar with the use of asterisks and underscores for emphasis on the Internet. For the same reason, you can use this feature during a final Auto-Format pass (see below) to reformat text you've copied from an email or chat room. (Few people use this feature *while typing*, since it's easier to press ⌘-B for bold or ⌘-I for italics. Most people use it only when massaging text from the Internet.)

- **Internet paths with hyperlinks.** When this box is checked, Word changes URLs that you type (*www.msn.com*, for instance) into working hyperlinks. Hyperlinks are usually formatted in blue and underscored, unless you change these settings in the Format→Style dialog box (see page 307).

- **Format the beginning of a list item like the one before it.** This option combines automation with the freedom of doing your own formatting.

  For example, suppose you want to start each item in your list with a Roman numeral, followed by a space, followed by the first word in bold, followed by a period and the rest of the sentence in plain text. To begin, type the first item that way and press Return. Word asks if your intention is to start a numbered list. Click Yes and continue. Word starts a new list item every time you hit Return. Press Return twice to end the list.

  The key is to start the first item with a number or bullet to let Word know that you're starting a list. If you want the first word or words to appear in, for example, bold (like the first sentences in this bulleted list), you must follow it with a period, colon, hyphen, dash, or other punctuation mark.

- **Define styles based on your formatting.** Here's the most powerful option on the AutoFormat tab. It tells Word to update the document's styles (see page 137), based on the formatting done directly in the document. For example, if you change your first heading to 14-point Helvetica Bold, Word applies that font to *all* occurrences of that style; you've just redefined the style, in fact. This option *overrides* any formatting you've done in the Styles dialog box, so use it with caution.

Tip: Consider memorizing AutoFormat "cues" for other AutoFormat options, too (in addition to using asterisks for bold and underlines for italic). For instance, if you frequently make bulleted lists, try to get in the habit of typing an asterisk for a bullet, knowing that Word will automatically change it to •.

To see the list of Word's autoformatting cues, type *formatting automatically* into the Search box of Word's Help window or the Assistant's Help balloon. Click Search. In the resulting list of links, click "Results of formatting a document automatically." The resulting Help window contains a table correlating what you type with Word's automatic replacements. Peruse this table and memorize the characters to type for your favorite kinds of borders, bullets, and so on. You can now format complex documents without ever reaching for the mouse.

Autoformatting in one pass

Even if you don't like Word making changes as you type, you can still benefit from AutoFormat—by running your finished document through what you might call its AutoFormat-O-Matic. For instance, you can take text that uses the Internet style for *bold* and _italic_ and have Word change them into proper **boldface** and *italics*. AutoFormat can also clean up a document by changing URLs into live hyperlinks or adding attractive bullets to lists, all at once.

First, choose Tools→AutoCorrect→AutoFormat As You Type and turn off all the boxes; now Word won't make any of these corrections *during* your typing.

When you're ready to autoformat, click the AutoFormat tab; the checkboxes here correspond, for the most part, to those described above. You're offered only a couple of new ones here. They are as follows:

- **Other Paragraphs.** Ordinarily, Word's AutoFormat feature applies a Heading style to whatever it recognizes as a heading, and a List style to anything it recognizes as a list. But if you turn on this option, Word also applies other styles when autoformatting. For example, Word can format plain text to your default Body Text font and paragraph style.

    Word does this by comparing the text in the document to the styles in your Normal template (see page 232) and automatically applying the closest matching style. If this box is turned on and the document appears to be a letter, Word also applies letter features such as Inside Address.

- **Preserve Styles.** Turn on this box if you've already done some formatting of your own in the document *before* starting the AutoFormat pass. Word won't change the style of any text you've manually formatted.

When you click OK, you won't notice any changes in your document; all you've done is specify what will happen when Word *does* conduct its editorial pass through your document. To trigger that event, choose Format→AutoFormat. Choose a document type from the pop-up menu—General document, Letter, or Email—which tells Word what kind of document it's going to be autoformatting. For instance, if the document is a letter, Word knows to apply letter styles such as Inside Address and Closing. If you choose Email, Word eliminates formatting options that usually don't work in email, such as first-line indents. (Clicking Options returns you to the AutoFormat tab described above.)

If you choose "AutoFormat and review each change," Word opens a dialog box that shows each change Word is about to make; you can choose to accept or reject it. If you choose "AutoFormat now," Word goes through the document and prepares all autoformatting changes without pausing. You can also click Style Gallery to apply one of Word's document templates (see page 226), with all its colors and fonts, to the finished document.

Formatting in Word

Formatting is a way to inject your style into the documents you create. Whether it's a newsletter for your college football fan club, or a white paper for your Fortune 500 business, formatting lets you transform that boring 12-point Times into something bold (pun intended) and exciting.

Word offers independent formatting controls for each of four entities: *characters* (individual letters and words), *paragraphs* (anything you've typed that's followed by a press of the Return key), *sections* (similar to chapters, as described on page 132), and the entire *document*. Attributes like bold and italic are *character* formatting; line spacing and centering are *paragraph* attributes; page numbering is done on a *section-by-section* basis; and margin settings are considered *document* settings. Understanding these distinctions will help you know where to look to achieve a certain desired effect.

The Formatting Palette

The Formatting Palette, which is the envy of Windows users the world over, puts Word's most common formatting commands within easy reach (Figure 3-1). It opens when you first open a Word document. If it's been hidden, you can bring it back by choosing View→Formatting Palette or clicking the Formatting Palette button on the Standard toolbar. Both methods alternately hide and show the palette.

The options on the Formatting Palette change depending on what you're doing. When you click a photo or drawing, for example, the palette changes to show the tools you need to work with graphics. Most of the time, however, the Formatting Palette displays the commands you most frequently need to work with fonts, paragraph formatting, and other elements of text.

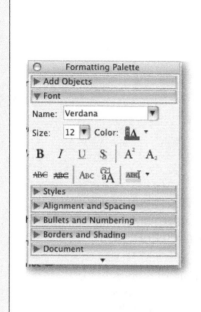

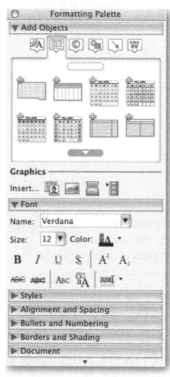

Figure 3-1:
In Word 2004, almost every conceivable formatting control resides in a single convenient window, a jam-packed command center called the Formatting Palette. Left: The Font panel offers the quickest way to restyle your text.

Right: The Add Objects panel, new in Word 2004, lets you insert Drawing objects, Tables and other special items without a trip to the Insert menu.

Clicking the close button makes the Formatting Palette genie back into its toolbar button in true Mac OS X fashion.

Character Formatting

The Font panel of the Formatting Palette—the one that's open the first time you use the Formatting Palette—deals mostly with what your letters, numbers, and other characters look like.

Choosing Fonts

Installing Office 2004 adds 76 fonts to your Library→Fonts folder—an unannounced gift from Microsoft.

To change the font of the text you've already typed, select the text first, using any of the methods described on page 55. If, instead, you choose a new font in the middle of a sentence or even the middle of a word, the new font will take effect with the next letter you type.

Now, open the Font menu to reveal your Mac's typeface names in their own typefaces. This what-you-see-is-what-you-get (WYSIWYG) fonts feature has a few ramifications, such as:

- If you have a very long list of fonts, you don't have to scroll all the way down to, say, Zapf Chancery. Once the menu (or Formatting Palette pop-up list) is open, you can *type* the first letter or two of the target font. The menu shifts instantly to that alphabetical position in the font list.

- You can open the font list faster if you *don't* use the WYSIWYG fonts feature. Pressing Shift when opening the Font menu or Fonts list in the Formatting Palette

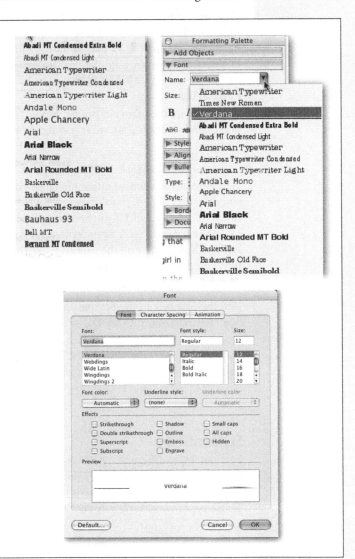

Figure 3-2:
Top left: When you pick from the Font menu, you get to see what each font looks like.

Top right: If you use the Formatting Palette to choose a font, the fonts you've used most recently are conveniently grouped together at the top.

Bottom: The Font dialog box (Format→ Font or ⌘-D). Not only are there more font style options here than in the Formatting Palette, you also receive a preview at the bottom of the box. If you like what you see, click OK.

allows you to see all the fonts listed in plain type. But honestly, the difference is negligible.

This is also the solution for the person trying to figure out the name of a font that shows up as symbols. (You can turn off the WYSIWYG feature for good by choosing Word→Preferences→General panel and turning off "WYSIWYG font and style menus," then clicking OK.)

- Once you've turned off WYSIWYG font menus, you can still summon the WYSI-WYG font when you *do* want it by pressing Shift when opening one of the Font menus.

Even the Formatting Palette doesn't offer every possible font manipulation tool; for that, you'll need the Font dialog box, as shown in Figure 3-2. To open it, choose Format→Font or press ⌘-D. In the following pages, you'll read about both the Formatting Palette and the more complete controls available in the Font dialog box.

Font Sizes

Font sizes are measured in points. A point is 1/72 of an inch in letter height, but you don't need to know that; what you *should* know is that most text is printed at 10- or 12-point sizes.

Some fonts (New York) look too large at 12 point. Other fonts (Times and Times New Roman) are almost uncomfortably small at 10 point. Print a test page to be sure, since the font size may look different on paper than on the screen, depending on your monitor's resolution. (If you have a high-resolution monitor, your tendency will be to make the font too large in order to achieve a comfortable size to read on the screen. Rather than increasing the font size, use the Zoom box (page 31) to verify that your font will print out in a proper size.)

To select a font size, choose one from the list in the Formatting Palette, type a size into the Size box in the Formatting Palette, or choose a point size in the Font dialog box (Format→Font or ⌘-D).

Tip: You can always bump selected text to a slightly higher or lower point size by pressing Shift-⌘->(that is, period) or Shift-⌘-< (comma) for larger and smaller type, respectively. Each time you press the combination, the text grows or shrinks by the intervals listed in the Formatting Palette's Size box (from 12 to 14 to 16, for example).

Styles of Type

You can apply different type styles to your regular, unembellished font for emphasis or effect. Most font styles are available in the Formatting Palette with a single click; a few extra ones reside in the "Font style" box in the Font dialog box (see Figure 3-2). Those type styles, as they appear in the Font dialog box, are as follows:

- **Regular** denotes plain, unadulterated text. Not bolded, not underlined.

Tip: You can return to plain text at any time without even opening the Font dialog box. Just highlight the text you've been playing with in your document and choose Edit→Clear→Formats or Clear Formatting from the Style menu in the Formatting Palette (*Keyboard shortcut:* Shift-⌘-N).

The Clear Formatting command, however, takes you all the way back to the Normal *style* (see page 137), which generally means your 12-point body type. To strip font effects from selected text without changing its underlying style definition (such as 24-point Futura for a headline), press Control-Space bar instead.

- **Italic** is commonly used for foreign words and phrases, as well as the titles of books, movies, and magazines. *Shortcuts*: Click the capital I in the Formatting Palette, or press ⌘-I.

- **Bold** is the most common way of making a single word or phrase stand out from the surrounding landscape. Use bold for emphasis. *Shortcuts*: Click the capital B in the Formatting Palette, or press ⌘-B.

- **Bold Italic** is a beautiful effect for headings and headlines. Use either method described above to choose both bold and italic, one right after the other. You'll know you've got it when both the B and the I are highlighted in the Formatting Palette. In the Font dialog box, just choose Bold Italic.

- **Underline.** Clicking the underlined U in the Formatting Palette, or pressing ⌘-U (Shift-⌘-D for a double underline), draws a line under the text, as well as the spaces between words. In the Font dialog box, use the "Underline style" pop-up menu to choose from a number of fancy underscores, and to specify whether you want Word to underline the words only, not the spaces.

You can also choose a color for the underline itself in the Font dialog box; see the next section for more detail.

UP TO SPEED

What's Normal?

When opening a new blank document, notice the name in the Name box located in the Formatting Palette: Normal. Word's idea of normal is black, 12-point Times.

But who's to say what's normal? You may prefer a soothing blue color. Or you may want to use boldface all the time, since you find it easier to read. You may want to make Sand your signature font—forget boring old Times! Fortunately, it's easy enough to specify your preferred typeface whenever you start a new document.

Choose Format→Font to open the Font dialog box. Now you can choose a font, color, size, or any of the other effects described in this section. When you've selected the font you want, click Default at lower left (shown in Figure 3-2). Word asks if you're sure that you want all new documents to use this font, as shown here. Click Yes. (Technically, you've just redefined the Normal style; see page 137 for more on the canned sets of formatting characteristics known as styles.)

Typing in Color

Color is a great way to liven up your documents—an increasingly valuable option in a world where many documents are read onscreen and color printer prices drop each year.

Click the tiny "Font color" color swatch or pop-up menu in the Formatting Palette or the Format→Font dialog box to survey your selection of 40 colors, as shown in Figure 3-3. To choose a color, just click it.

Tip: When using Word to prepare a document for the Web, remember that colors look different on different computers. For example, someone viewing your page on a Windows machine or an older monitor may see your true colors very differently.

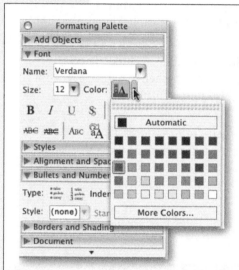

Figure 3-3:
From the Formatting Palette's font color button, Word offers quick access to 40 commonplace colors. To choose from a broader rainbow, click the More Colors button. Doing so opens the Apple Color Picker dialog box, which offers several different ways to specify any color under the sun, as described on page 689.

Special Text Effects

Bold and italic offer enough variety for most documents, but many more buttons await in the Formatting Palette, and still more choices in the Font dialog box. Some of them, such as Outline and Shadow, are clearly just for show (they usually look amateurish in printed documents); others, such as Subscript and All Caps, are invaluable tools.

Here are the options, in order, as they appear in the Font dialog box:

- **Strikethrough** and **Double strikethrough** indicate that something's crossed out, but you don't want to delete it outright. (Word's change-tracking feature adds strikethrough style to deleted text automatically; see page 181.) *Shortcuts:* Click the A̶B̶C̶ or A̶B̶C̶ buttons on the Formatting Palette.

- **Superscript** and **Subscript** shift characters slightly higher or lower (respectively) than the other text on its line and slightly decreases their size—perfect for chemical formulas and exponents. (You don't need these effects for footnotes, as Word handles footnote formatting automatically, as described on page 221.)

You can make letters or symbols super- or subscripted, too, not just numbers—very handy if you like taking things to the Nth degree. *Shortcuts:* Click the A^2 or A$_2$ in the Formatting Palette, or press ⌘-= for Subscript or Shift-⌘-= for Superscript.

- **Shadow** and **Outline** reverse the color of the type, making the letter white and the outline black (or whatever text color you're using). Shadow creates a heavier outline that makes the words appear slightly raised. Both were popular when the Mac first appeared, but seem dated now. *Shortcut:* For Shadow, click the shadowed capital S on the Formatting Palette; there's no shortcut for Outline.

- **Emboss** and **Engrave** make letters appear slightly raised or carved out, as if with a chisel. They work best on a colored background, such as on a Web page. On a white background, the words gain a subtle drop shadow. (These infrequently used effects are available only in the Font dialog box, not on the Formatting Palette.)

Small Caps, All Caps

Word offers several variations on the when-to-capitalize scheme you probably learned in English class. For example, you can apply either of these formats to text you've highlighted (or are about to type):

- **Small Caps** creates a formal look for headings and letterheads; all the letters are capped, but "lowercase" letters are shown in smaller capitals, SOMETHING LIKE THIS. *Shortcut:* Click the ABC button on the Formatting Palette.

- **All Caps** simply converts highlighted text to all capital letters. You can choose "All caps" in the Font dialog box, or click the a→A button in the Formatting Palette.

Even though the visual result is the same, there's a big difference between using the All Caps style and simply typing some words with the Caps Lock key down. Text you've formatted as All Caps is still, in Word's brain, actually mixed upper- and lowercase letters. It thinks you've applied the all-cap format just as a visual, the way

POWER USERS' CLINIC

Drop Caps

Have you ever wished you could duplicate those extra-large capitals that start the chapters of so many books (like this one)? Unfortunately, just enlarging the point size of the first letter doesn't work. True drop caps, as they're called, are not only large, but they drop below the other letters on the line; hence the name.

But Word 2004 can do it. After typing the first paragraph of your chapter, choose Format→Drop Cap. Choose one of the drop-cap styles, then adjust the Options settings

(font, number of lines to drop down, and distance from text) until you've got the look you like. When you click OK, Word sends you into Page Layout view—if you weren't there already—where the drop cap appears as an independent graphic box that you can enlarge or drag as you would any graphic (see Chapter 20).

If you return to Normal view, you won't see the drop cap in its correct position; that's perfectly normal, so to speak.

you'd apply bold or blue or underlining. That is, by turning off the All Caps style, the text reverts to the capitalization you originally used when typing it—something you can't say about text you typed with the Caps Lock key.

You can therefore search for text in the All Caps style using the Find and Replace command, or define it as part of a *style* (see page 137).

Tip: To change the capitalization of words you've already typed—or to fix an email message that arrived IN ALL CAPITAL LETTERS—highlight the text and then choose Format→Change Case. By choosing from the list in the Change Case dialog box, you can make Word instantly "retype" the text as all lowercase (all small letters), all uppercase (all caps), Sentence case (where the first letter of every sentence is capitalized as usual), or Title Case (where the first letter of every word is capped).

(Unfortunately, these options aren't terrifically smart; Sentence case still leaves names and the word *I* lowercase, and Title Case doesn't leave small words like *of* and *the* lowercase.)

The most interesting choice here is tOGGLE cASE, which reverses the existing capitalization, whatever it may be.

Hidden Text

Word's Hidden Text feature can remove your personal notes and reminders from plain sight in a document. You can make the hidden text reappear only when you want to; you can also choose whether or not you want it to show up when printed.

To turn certain text invisible, first select it. Choose Format→Font→Font tab. (There's no button for hidden text on the Formatting Palette.) Turn on the Hidden box and click OK; the text disappears until you choose to show it. (To turn hidden text back into normal text, show the hidden text as described next, select it, choose Format→ Font→Fonts tab, and turn off the Hidden box.)

When you want Word to display the text you've designated as hidden, use either of these techniques:

- Choose Word→Preferences→View tab. Turn on "Hidden text" and click OK.

- Click the Show/Hide button (¶) on the Standard toolbar (or the Document section of the Formatting Palette).

Either way, hidden text appears with a dotted underline to distinguish it from the rest of the text.

Tip: Whether or not hidden text *prints* is up to you. To print hidden text along with the rest of the document, choose Word→Preferences, click the Print button, turn on the Include with Document→Hidden text box, and click OK.

Lists

If you're in the business world, or even the business of organizing your thoughts, you can't go far without using numbered or bulleted lists.

Bulleted lists are an attractive way of presenting nuggets of information. Here's a great example:

- Each paragraph is indented from the left margin (like this one) and is preceded by a *bullet* (the round dot shown at left).

- You can always create a numbered list by typing a number at the beginning of each line, but it won't be nicely indented.

- You may know how to create a bullet (·) at the beginning of every line by using the keyboard shortcut Option-8. But again, that won't produce the clean left margin on your bulleted paragraphs.

- Furthermore, creating lists manually can get messy. For example, inserting an item between two existing ones in a numbered list requires some serious renumbering. And if you want your list indented, you'll have to fiddle with the indent controls quite a bit.

Word has partially automated the process. A quick way to start a numbered or bulleted list is from the Formatting Palette. Open the Bullets and Numbering panel by clicking anywhere on the Bullets and Numbering title bar, and then click one of the list icons (next to where it says Type, as shown in Figure 3-4). Word promptly indents the paragraph containing the insertion point and adds a bullet (or the number 1). Even the indenting is perfect: The second and following lines of a list item start under the first letter, not all the way back to the left margin. To start a new list item, just hit Return. When you're finished building the list, press Return once more and then click the same icon in the Formatting Palette a second time.

Figure 3-4:
Click the Bullets and Numbering title bar to expand the panel. The panel provides a bucketful of listing options. For example, you may choose a type of list (numbered or not), its indent, and even the number to begin your numbered lists with. Or if you aren't in a bulleted state of mind, choose "none" to remove a bullet.

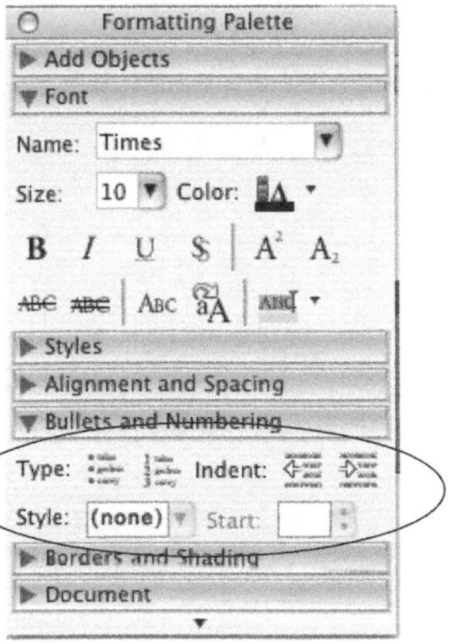

If you create a *numbered* list this way, Word does the numbering automatically as you go. Better yet, if you insert a new list item between two others, Word knows enough to renumber the entire list.

The pop-up menus and icons in the Bullets and Numbering panel control different aspects of how your list will look (the *entire* list, no matter which individual list line contains your insertion point).

- **Style** specifies the kind of numbering (Arabic numerals, roman numerals, and so on), or the size and shape of the bullet.

- **Start** tells Word what number to start the list with.

- The **Indent** icons increase or decrease your bullet's indent.

- The **Type** icons tell Word whether you want to start an unnumbered bulleted list (the Bullets icon) or a numbered list (Numbering icon). For more detail on bullets see below.

Extra Features in the Bullets and Numbering Dialog Box

The Formatting Palette is ideal for quickly designing a list, but the Bullets and Numbering dialog box offers even more options. Open it by choosing Format→Bullets and Numbering (see Figure 3-5).

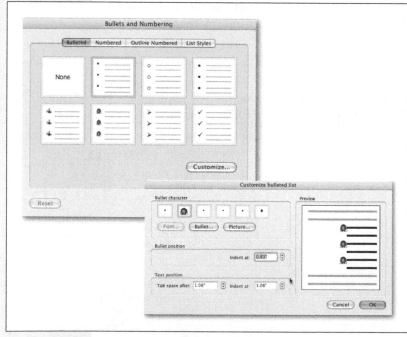

Figure 3-5:
Top left: After you've customized a bulleted or numbered list (see below), clicking Reset returns a list icon to its original configuration.

Bottom right: Clicking the Font button opens the Font dialog box (see page 107). You can then choose bold, italics, or even a different font altogether for your new bulleted list style. The Preview window shows you a representation of how your numbered list will look relative to the surrounding text.

Customizing a bulleted list

Bulleted lists as delivered by the Formatting Palette are fine, but there may come a day when simple black, round bullets just don't cut it for the radical new-age business plan you're writing up. In such cases, click the Bulleted tab in the Bullets and Numbering dialog box. If one of the styles appeals to you, choose it by clicking; then click Customize to open the dialog box shown at bottom in Figure 3-5. Watch what happens in the Preview box as you make changes:

- **Bullet character.** Choose an alternate bullet symbol, or click the Bullet button to open the Symbol dialog box (see page 224), where you can choose any character in any font to become your new bullet.

- **Bullet position.** The indentation point of the bullet is measured from the left margin.

- **Text position.** The text indentation is also measured from the left margin. It's usually indented farther than the bullet; note how, in Figure 3-5, the text position indent is a larger number than the bullet position one.

Click OK to return to the Bullets and Numbering dialog box. The bulleted list style now appears as one of the eight list icons (see Figure 3-5), easily accessible if you want to use the same style of bulleting later in the document. Click OK again to apply the new bulleted style to the current paragraph.

Customizing a numbered list

Like the Bulleted tab, the Numbered tab in the Bullets and Numbering dialog box presents a selection of eight preconfigured list styles (one of which is None). Click the one that suits your purposes, or at least comes the closest. Click Customize to open a dialog box much like the one at the bottom of Figure 3-5—but this one, of course, applies to numbers:

GEM IN THE ROUGH

Picture Bullets

There are a host of bullets preinstalled in Word, both in the Bullets and Numbering dialog box and in the Symbol dialog box, as described on page 224. For added creativity, insert a picture bullet, as in the example shown here.

To do so, choose Format→Bullets and Numbering→Bulleted tab. Click Picture. Now you can choose any graphics file on your Mac; Word starts you off with a folder full of its own preinstalled picture bullets. Choose one of those to add the selected picture as a bullet to the current paragraph. Otherwise, navigate to your own picture file (something

you've scanned, drawn, or downloaded from a Web site, perhaps), select the file in the list box, and click Insert.

More often than not, the typical picture will be unreasonably large for a bullet. Click to select it and drag the resize handles (at its corners) to make it smaller. In fact, you can actually edit the picture right within Word; see Chapter 20 for full detail on Word's picture tools.

It may sound like a lot of work, but you only have to do it once. When you press Return to make another list item, Word automatically continues using the edited picture bullet.

- **Number format.** You can't edit the number or numeral shown here, as it's determined by your choices in the "Number style" and "Start at" tools. You can, however, type additional text into this window, such as the words *Figure, Item,* or *Commandment*—whichever word you want to appear before the number in each list item.

- **Number style.** This pop-up menu lets you choose Arabic or roman numerals, letters (*A, B, C,* and so on), or even words (*First, Second,* and so on).

- **Start at.** Usually, you'll start at 1, but you can also start at 0 or any other number by entering it in the box or choosing it with the arrows.

- **Number position.** Choosing Left, Right, or Centered from the pop-up menu aligns the number relative to the space between "Aligned at" and "Indent at."

- **Aligned at.** This is the distance from the left margin to the numbered item. For instance, if you choose Left from the number position menu and .5" for "Aligned at," the number itself will be placed half an inch from the left margin.

- **Text position.** This is the distance from the left margin to the text part of the numbered item. The larger you make this measurement, the farther from the number the text begins.

Click OK to return to the Bullets and Numbering dialog box; the custom numbered list style now appears as one of the eight list icons (see Figure 3-5). Click OK again to apply the new numbered style to the current paragraph.

Tip: If there's more than one numbered list in your document—if you're writing, say, a book about Office 2004 that contains many numbered tutorials—you'll need a way to make the numbering start over at 1 for the second list. (Otherwise, Word will cheerfully keep your number sequence going all the way through a document.)

To tell Word to start over, click the first item in the *second* list and choose Format→Bullets and Numbering. Click the radio button for "Restart numbering," or press ⌘-R. ("Continue previous list" gives the list item the next number in the series, no matter how many pages have elapsed since the first part of the list.) Click OK.

Paragraph Formatting

The lower half of the Formatting Palette pertains mostly to settings that affect entire *paragraphs.* Just as the Formatting Palette's top section offers the most useful controls of the Format→Font dialog box, its second section offers a subset of the Format→Paragraph dialog box (Figure 3-6).

And just as character formatting applies *either* to highlighted text *or* to text you're about to type, paragraph formatting applies to only a selected paragraph (the one containing the blinking insertion point), several selected paragraphs, or the paragraph you're about to type (from the insertion point's location).

Alignment and Spacing

When you click the Alignment and Spacing title bar, the Formatting Palette almost doubles in size (Figure 3-6, right). All the commands here pertain to how your text lies on the page.

Horizontal

These icons illustrate how your paragraph will be aligned with the left and right page margins: left aligned, centered, right aligned, or fully justified. (*Justified* refers to straight margins on both sides. Word automatically adjusts the spacing between letters and words to make the right margin come out even, exactly like a newspaper. Justification works best if you turn on hyphenation, too, as described on page 150.)

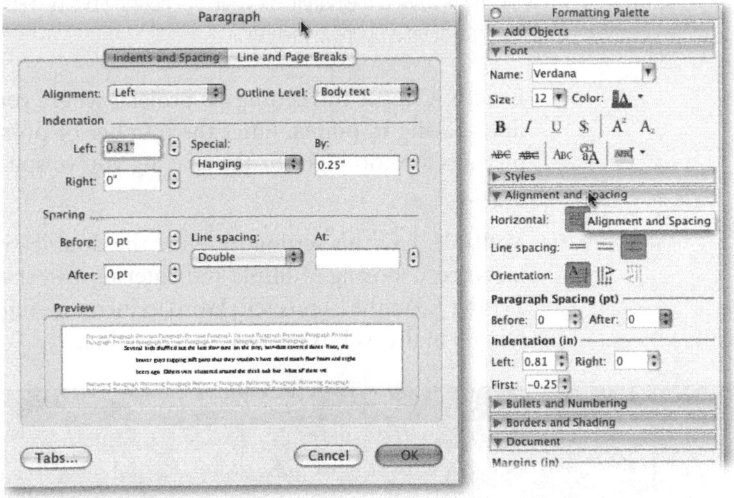

Figure 3-6:
Left: The Paragraph dialog box offers dozens of controls that apply to the selected paragraphs.

Right: The expanded Formatting Palette reveals the most useful controls. For example, the controls at the bottom of this panel are a quick way to change indents.

You may find yourself changing alignment frequently when writing something like a newsletter, in which it's common to go from a centered headline to a left-aligned article to a justified column of classified ads. Fortunately, alignment is fully equipped with keyboard shortcuts: ⌘-R right-aligns the current paragraph, ⌘-L is for left alignment, ⌘-E centers the current line or paragraph, and ⌘-J justifies the current paragraph.

Line spacing

Word's factory setting is for single-spaced lines, like the ones in this book. If you like more space between lines, or if you're required to use double-spacing for schoolwork or legal work, use these icons to change the spacing. The three line-spacing controls on the Formatting Palette correspond to single-spaced, one-and-a-half-spaced, and double-spaced text.

Choosing Format→Paragraph→Indents and Spacing tab (Option-⌘-M) generates even more spacing options. As shown in Figure 3-6, you can choose a setting from the pop-up menu under "Line spacing" and, to get even more specific, type an exact number in the At box.

- **At least.** Choose this setting to add graphics or vary font sizes within a paragraph. In the box, type a minimum number of points (12 is a good size for single spacing). Word now will automatically adjust the spacing to accommodate any larger items in a line.

Tip: Here's a trick you can use in this or any Office 2004 measurement text box: You don't have to be content with *points* as the units. After typing the number you want, type *cm, mm, in,* or *pi* for centimeters, millimeters, inches, or picas, respectively. The software makes the conversion automatically. (You can also change the proposed measurement value by choosing Word→Preferences→General panel and using the "Measurement units" pop-up menu.)

- **Exactly.** Choose this setting for projects where you've been asked to use a specific line spacing in points. Enter the number of points in the box. (If any letters or pictures are too high for the spacing you've specified, they'll simply be decapitated.)

- **Multiple.** Use this setting to refine the double-single-triple spacing system. For instance, choosing Multiple and entering *1* in the At box denotes single spacing. Typing *1.3* in the At box tells Word to increase single-spacing by 30 percent. Specifying *3* in the At box creates triple spacing.

POWER USERS' CLINIC

Windows, Orphans, and Paragraph Relationships

Ordinarily, when your text reaches the bottom of the page, Word chops a paragraph in half, if necessary, so that it continues on the top of the next page. The result isn't always especially good-looking, however; it may leave what publishers call a widow (the last line of a paragraph at the top of a new page) or an orphan (the first line of a paragraph all by itself at the bottom of a page). You can avoid these problems by highlighting a paragraph (or paragraphs), choosing Format→Paragraph→Line and Page Breaks tab, and turning on "Widow/Orphan control." This control instructs Word to allow no less than two lines at the top of any page before a paragraph break.

Similarly, to keep any paragraph or group of lines unbroken, just select any number of paragraphs or lines, choose Format→Paragraph→Line and Page Breaks tab, and turn on the "Keep lines together" box.

Another easily avoided typographical problem: a heading at the bottom of a page whose body text is split onto the next page. The solution: Select the heading, choose Format→Paragraph→Line and Page Breaks tab, and turn on "Keep with next." (It means, "Keep with next paragraph.")

Sure, these tools are useful when applied to individual paragraphs, but they're especially ideal for defining styles (see page 137). For example, you may as well turn on "Keep with next" for all of your heading styles, since it's never pretty when a heading appears on one page and its body text appears on the next.

Finally, you can change line spacing using the keyboard: ⌘-1 tells Word to single-space the current paragraph, ⌘-5 is for one-and-a-half space (1.5, that is), and ⌘-2 results in double-spacing.

Orientation

The Orientation icons on the Formatting Palette aren't actually paragraph-specific, like the other controls in their section. In fact, they work very differently depending on what you're editing:

- In a table cell, they rotate the text in the selected cell (see page 168).

- If you've divided your document into sections (page 132), you can use one of these icons to rotate *entire pages* within a document—to get a couple of horizontally oriented (landscape) pages in a document whose pages are otherwise oriented vertically (portrait). Here's the trick: Before using the Orientation controls, insert a "Section Break (Next Page)" break before and after the pages you want rotated (page 132).

- If your document has neither tables nor section breaks, these icons rotate your *entire window* by 90 or 180 degrees. They don't affect how the document is *printed;* for that purpose, use the Orientation icons in the File→Page Setup dialog box. Instead, this feature rotates the image of your document onscreen to make it easier for you to edit the *text* that you've rotated 90 degrees, such as the vertical label of a table cell.

In other words, if you were hoping that these icons would let you rotate, say, a particular heading, thus mixing text direction on a single page, forget it; Word can't do it. Your best bet is to fill your page with a borderless table (page 166) that confines the rotated text to a cell of its own.

Paragraph Spacing

If you're in the habit of pressing Return twice to create space between paragraphs, it's time to consider the automatic alternative. The Paragraph Spacing tools on the Formatting Palette let you change the amount of space that appears, automatically, before and after the current or selected paragraph. (The same controls show up in the

---

POWER USERS' CLINIC

Formatting Revealed

In looking at a Word document, there are very few outward cues to tell you what's going on in terms of formatting—since you can't see the behind-the-scenes formatting parameters. However, when troubleshooting a formatting snafu, you might want to see exactly what Word is thinking.

You can. Choose View→Reveal Formatting. The cursor turns into a small word-balloon. If you click the balloon on any word or in any paragraph, it opens into a larger balloon listing all of its font and paragraph formatting specifics: font, type style, indents, spacing before and after, and so on. You can click as many places as you like. As soon as you start to type again, or if you click anywhere outside the margins, Reveal Formatting turns off and the balloon goes away.

Format→Paragraph→Indents and Spacing tab, as shown in Figure 3-6.) When you click the arrows beside the Before and After boxes, the spacing increases and decreases in 6-point increments. For finer control, you can enter any numbers you wish into the boxes. (4 to 8 points is a good place to start.)

Change the spacing in the Formatting Palette or Paragraph dialog box at the outset of your document, or press ⌘-A to select all existing paragraphs first. The advantage of doing it this way is that the extra space is added automatically, with no danger of accidentally deleting any of the extra line breaks. Furthermore, if you change your mind about the extra space, you can press ⌘-A and readjust the paragraph spacing, without having to delete any extra line breaks.

Indentation

To the horror of academics and typesetters everywhere, most people indent the first line of each paragraph by hitting the Tab key. Trouble is, Word's default tab stops are set at half-inch intervals—much too wide for professional use.

It's a far better idea (from the purist's standpoint, anyway) to use Word's dedicated indenting feature, which lets you specify individual *paragraph* margins (and first-line indents) that are independent of the document margins (see page 130).

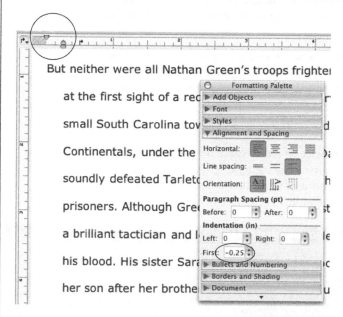

Figure 3-7:
Top: A paragraph with a hanging indent of a quarter-inch, and a right indent of a half-inch, as shown on the ruler.

Bottom: The Indentation settings on the Formatting Palette for the paragraph shown. To create a hanging indent, you must type a negative number in the First box.

Tip: If you do indeed press Tab to begin a paragraph, Word tries to guide you toward the proper way. It automatically moves the first-line indent marker (see Figure 3-7) to the first tab stop on your ruler. Now you've got a quick way to correctly indent your paragraphs. Adjust the marker (making the indent *smaller*, for best results) and then type away. All subsequent paragraphs will have the same first-line indent.

If you'd prefer that Word abandon this behavior, choose Word→Preferences→Edit panel and turn off "Tabs and backspace set left indent." Now the Tab key and indents are totally disconnected.

There are two ways to adjust indents for highlighted paragraphs: by dragging the indent markers on the ruler (Figure 3-7), or by setting numerical values (in the Formatting Palette or Format→Paragraph→Indents and Spacing tab). When you want to give a paragraph its own distinctive style, use one of these indents:

- **First line indent.** Drag the top-left marker (the first-line indent handle) to where you'd like the first line of each paragraph to begin. One-quarter inch is a typical amount. To set an exact measurement, adjust the First indent setting in the Formatting Palette (or choose "First line" from the Special pop-up menu in the Paragraph dialog box).

- **Hanging indent.** As illustrated in Figure 3-7, you create a *hanging indent* by dragging the lower, house-shaped marker. (The square left-indent marker moves along with it.) To set an exact measurement, type a negative number into the First box on the Formatting Palette (such as *-.25"*); or, in the Paragraph dialog box, click the Indents and Spacing tab and select Hanging from the Special pop-up menu.

- **Left and right indents.** Left and right indents are the internal left and right margins for a paragraph. Most people aren't aware of them, because they usually match the right and left margins of the *document*. But there are times when you want a paragraph to be narrower—either indented from the left margin or on both

---

GEM IN THE ROUGH

Format Painter

It could happen to anyone. You finally have a paragraph exactly the way you want it. In fact, you want to use these settings for all the paragraphs you've previously typed.

Instead of going back to change them one by one, now is the time to use the Format Painter. Select the text you worked so hard to perfect. (If paragraph formatting is involved, just click somewhere in the paragraph; if it's just the font characteristics you want to copy, then select a few letters or a word.)

Once you've selected the text, click the Format Painter—the paintbrush icon in the Standard toolbar. Now you can perform the following:

Drag across the text that you want the new formatting applied to. As you let go of the mouse button, Word applies the formatting.

To copy the new formatting to a large amount of text or to nonadjacent paragraphs, double-click the Format Painter; it's now locked on. (A tiny + symbol on the toolbar icon alerts you that it's locked.) From now on, every paragraph you click or blurb you select will get the new formatting—that is, until you click the paintbrush again or press ⌘-period.

Press Esc or ⌘-period to cancel the Format Painter; press ⌘-Z or F1 (repeatedly, if necessary) to back out of what you've just done.

---

sides—such as when creating a *block quote*, for example (a longish quotation that you want separated from the rest of the text).

To adjust the paragraph margins for highlighted text, drag the left and right indent markers (identified in Figure 3-7) on the ruler, or change the Left and Right settings on the Formatting Palette. (The Indents and Spacing tab of the Paragraph dialog box offers the same options.) The distances you specify here are measurements from the document's right and left margins, not from the edges of the paper.

Tip: You can also drag the first-line indent or left-indent marker *left,* into the margin, to make a line or paragraph extend into the margin. This is called a *negative indent,* which gives the effect of a hanging indent without changing the left margin. However, if you have a narrow left margin and use negative indents, you may get an error message when you print the document. That's because the negative indent is too close to the left edge of the page.

Tabs

To tell the truth, the era of the Tab key is fading.

In the typewriter days, it was useful in two situations: when indenting a paragraph and when setting up a table. But in the Microsoft Age, newer, far more flexible tools have replaced the Tab function in both of those circumstances. The indentation controls described above are much better for paragraph indents, and the Table tool (page 160) is a far superior method of setting up tabular data.

Still, millions of people are more comfortable with the tab-stop concept than Word's newfangled tools. This section shows how those tools work (and assumes that you remember how tab stops work on typewriters).

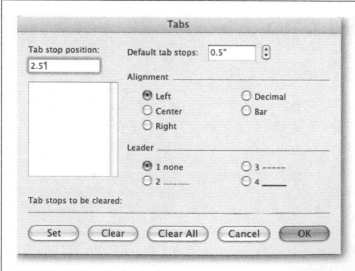

Figure 3-8:
You can change the spacing of the default tabs in the "Default tab stops" box (or by clicking the arrows next to it). You can also add a tab leader—that is, a dashed line, dotted line, or under-line that automatically fills in the gap between the end of your previous typing and the tab stop.

Default tabs

Every Word document has a ruler (choose View→Ruler if you don't see it), which starts out with an *invisible* tab stop every half inch across the page. These are the *default* tab stops. You can prove that they exist by pressing Tab over and over again, watching as the insertion point moves from one to the next, exactly as on a typewriter.

But the default tab stops aren't permanent; they start to disappear when:

- You choose Format→Tabs to open the Tabs dialog box (Figure 3-8) and change their default placement (in the "Default tab stops" box). You can do this by clicking the arrow buttons beside the box or by entering a new setting.

- You set new tab stops, as described next. When doing so, all of Word's default tab stops to the *left* of your hand-placed tabs disappear. For instance, when you set a new tab at .75" from the margin, the default tab stop at .5" goes away; when you press Tab, the insertion point goes straight to .75" (All remaining default tab stops to the *right* of the new tab remain in place until you add more new tab stops.)

Setting tabs

The quickest way to set new tab stops is by using the ruler; just click anywhere in its tick marks to place a new tab stop. After tabs are set, you can reposition them by simply dragging them along the ruler. To delete one, drag it directly down *off* the ruler until it disappears into thin air.

To place tabs more precisely, choose Format→Tabs (or double-click any tab stop on your ruler) to open the dialog box shown in Figure 3-8. Any hand-placed tab stops are found in the list at the left, according to their distances from the left margin.

To create a new tab, type its location in the "Tab stop position" box, choose an alignment (described next), and click Set (or press ⌘-S). To delete a tab, click it in the list and then click Clear (or press ⌘-E). To change a tab's position, clear the existing tab and type the new position in the "Tab stop position" box. To delete *all* tabs in the list, click Clear All (⌘-A). Press Return or click OK when you're ready to close the Tabs box.

Tab types

When clicking a tab stop in the dialog box list, you'll be shown its *type*. As illustrated in Figure 3-9, pressing the Tab key doesn't necessarily align your insertion point with the *left* side of your tab stop. The following types of tab alignments help you arrange text on the page:

- **Left (⌘-L).** This is the kind of tab stop you're probably used to. When you press Tab and then start typing, your text flows rightward from its origin beneath your tab stop.

- **Centered (⌘-N).** The text is aligned with the tab stop at its centerline, creating a balanced effect that's ideal for things like invitations and brochures.

- **Right (⌘-R).** When you press Tab and then start typing, your text flows *left*ward from its origin beneath your tab stop. Several of these rows together create a neat right margin.

- **Bar (⌘-B).** This kind of tab stop isn't a tab stop at all. Instead, it's a method of producing a *vertical line* down your page, directly beneath the tab stop. You don't even have to press Tab to get this vertical line; any paragraph that contains this tab type on the ruler continues the line down through the page. (Insert your own joke here about picking up the bar tab.)

- **Decimal (⌘-D).** This behaves exactly like a right tab stop—until you type a period (a decimal point, in other words), at which point your text flows to the right. In other words, this very useful tab type lets you neatly align a series of numbers (such as prices), so that the decimal points are aligned from row to row.

You don't have to use the Tabs dialog box to change tab-stop types, by the way. If you repeatedly click the *tab well* at the upper-left corner of the ruler (see Figure 3-9), Word displays the icon of each tab type until you stop. If you click the spot on the ruler where you want the tab, you'll plant that tab type. For example, to set a left tab at 1/4", click the tab button until the left-tab arrow appears, then click at 1/4" on the ruler.

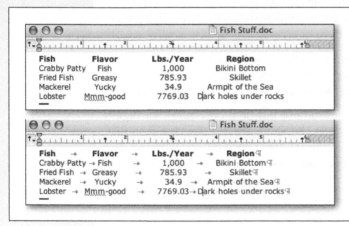

Figure 3-9:
Top: Using different tab types, you can make your text align neatly from one line to the next.

Bottom: By turning on the Show ¶ option (on the Standard toolbar, for example), you see the tiny gray arrows that indicate where you pressed the Tab key to jump from one of these tab stops to the next.

Applying tabs to paragraphs and styles

When you set, clear, and move tabs, the changes apply to the paragraph that contains your insertion point. Often, however, you'll want to use the tab settings for many paragraphs—or an entire document. Here are the ways you can accomplish that:

- **Set the tabs before you start typing.** This is a common trick if, for example, you need to insert a little columnar table in the middle of a report. Every time you press Return to begin a new line, the same tab stops will be available.

- **Select all paragraphs.** If you've already done some (or a lot of) typing, select the paragraphs by dragging over them, or press ⌘-A to select the entire document. Set tabs as described above.

• **Make tab stops part of a style.** If you make your preferred tab stops part of a *style* (see page 137), you can apply them to any paragraph just by clicking that paragraph and choosing from the Style menu on the Formatting Palette. If you're *really* attached to certain tab stops, you can even make them part of your Normal style.

Borders and Shading

Black text on a white page is clear and easy to read, but it can get monotonous. When a little zest is required, try using borders, background shading, and fill patterns to emphasize various parts of your document. For instance, light gray background shading can highlight a useful list in the middle of your article. A plain border can set off a sidebar from the body of your text. And a fancy border can be part of an invitation.

Text and paragraph borders

To put a border around some text, first select the text in question; to put a border around an entire paragraph, just click anywhere in the paragraph. Click anywhere in the Borders and Shading title bar on the Formatting Palette to expand its panel, as shown in Figure 3-10. The controls are:

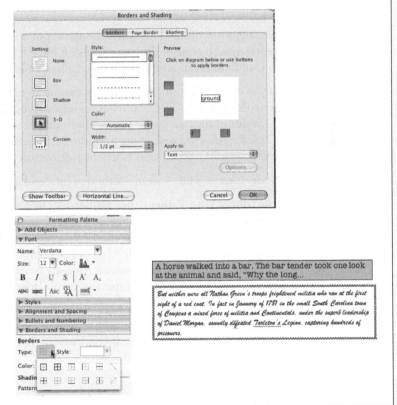

Figure 3-10:
Top: As you work, watch what happens in the Preview box at the right of the dialog box. The only way to see how the final result really looks, however, is to return to your document.

Bottom left: The Formatting Palette, expanded to show the border controls and the Type pop-up menu—the first step in applying a border.

Bottom right: Borders and shading vary from the ridiculous to the sublime. Here are two examples of borders used to different effect. Above, 15% gray shading, 1 point from text, .5 point border. Below, 3/4 point double wavy-line border, 12 points from text, no shading.

- **Type.** Clicking the square icon next to Type opens a palette of placement choices for your border: a square, a line above or below, and so on. Click the one you want. The light dotted line, No Border, automatically disables the remaining controls described here.

- **Style.** This pop-up menu shows a selection of solid, dashed, and multiple-line styles to apply to the border you've just specified.

- **Color.** Clicking the color square displays Word's standard palette of 40 colors. You can choose one, or click More Colors to use Office's color-picking tools, as described on page 689.

- **Weight.** This control denotes the thickness of the line in points (to 1/72 of an inch). The pop-up menu shows a variety of thicknesses ranging from 1/4 point to 6 points.

Extra features in the Borders and Shading dialog box

For more customization options than those available on the Formatting Palette, highlight the paragraphs you want to change and choose Format→Borders and Shading. The dialog box shown in Figure 3-10 opens. When you click the Borders tab (Figure 3-10), you see these options:

- **Setting.** Most of the time, you'll choose to put a *box* around your paragraphs, as represented by one of the lower icons on the left (Figure 3-10). The shadow and 3-D options create a very professional, modern look.

  If you choose Custom, Word doesn't assume anything—not even that you want a four-sided box. As the Custom button implies, you can use a different line style on each side of the box—solid top and bottom and dotted on the sides, for instance. Click the sides you wish to use from the buttons in the Preview panel, then design each one in the Style panel. Click the side button again to make changes.

- **Style.** Choose a line style, a width in points, and a color.

- **Horizontal Line.** Rather than a border, this tool adds a horizontal line *under* the paragraph in question. The line is actually a picture embedded into your document; that's why the lines you choose from are stored in a clip art folder. You also have the option of turning on "Link to File" to make the line a *linked object* instead of an embedded one. These lines are mostly intended for use on Web pages. (See page 694 for more detail on linked and embedded objects.)

- **Options.** Clicking Options opens a dialog box where you can choose how far away from the text you want to set your border. The default settings are 4 points on each side, 1 point top and bottom. If you have room, consider increasing the amount of space between the text and border for a clean, elegant look.

Note: If your text is in a *text box* (see page 151), don't add a border around it—you'll just end up with two borders. Text boxes come with *built-in* borders, which you can format using the line tools on the Drawing toolbar and the Colors and Lines tab of the Format→Text Box tab.

That said, you *can* put borders on parts of the text *inside* text boxes. (If you also want to hide the border surrounding the text box, click the border, then choose No Line from the Line Color palette on the Drawing toolbar.)

Once your border is complete, click OK. You can now use the tools in the Borders and Shading section of the Formatting Palette (or the Tables and Borders toolbar) to make further refinements.

Page borders

When it's time to create a title page, certificate, or phony diploma, nothing says "professionally published" more than a handsome border around the edges of your page. To add one, choose Format→Borders and Shading→Page Border tab. (The Formatting Palette has no controls for adding a page border, but if you decide to add one at the last minute, you can add a quick and dirty border from the Print dialog box, as described on page 40.)

Most of the tools for designing a page border are the same as those for a paragraph border (described previously). But there are subtle differences: Page borders trace the page margins, regardless of the size or amount of text on the page, and the page border changes size automatically as you change the margins (page 130).

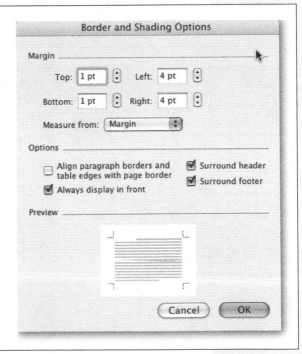

Figure 3-11:
The Margin settings control the distance of the text from the margin (or the paper edge, depending on what you choose from the "Measure from" menu). The border, however, still hugs the margins. In other words, when you increase the Margin settings in this dialog box, the text area will decrease as it moves farther in from the page margins. (Yes, some of the text may flow onto the next page as a result.)

The Page Border tab contains a few extra features specific to page borders:

- **Art.** The Art pop-up menu offers dozens upon dozens of small clip-art border motifs in repeating patterns (little marquees, banners, and—for those Halloween party invitations—black cats).

- **Apply to.** This menu on the Page Border tab lets you put a border on the first page of your document or section only. (Can you say "title page"?)

- **Options.** The Options button opens a dialog box with settings that control how the border frames the page, including the Margin settings described in Figure 3-11.

"Align paragraph borders and table edges with page border" does more than align them; it actually *connects* them if they're adjacent. Thus, the side borders of a paragraph will extend out to and meld with the side borders of the page.

Turn on "Always display in front" unless you plan to place text boxes or images *over* the page border. (If you do so, you may want to give the border a lighter shading or lighter color.)

The "Surround header" and "Surround footer" options determine whether the page border encompasses the header and footer (see page 217) along with the rest of the page.

Shading

When you decide to fill in a gray or colored background behind a paragraph or text box, the key words to remember are *light* and *subtle*. Patterns and shading can make text difficult to read, and the interference is often worse on the printed page than on the screen.

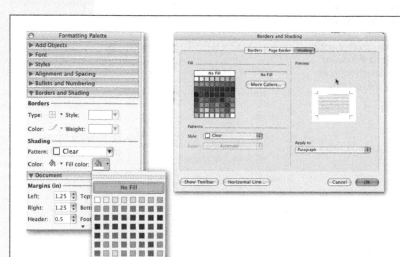

Figure 3-12:
Left: The Formatting Palette reveals that even if you don't think you're using a pattern, you are. Text with no background or a plain, unshaded fill color has a clear pattern. The Fill color is a background that underlies both text and any pattern you apply.

Right: The Borders and Shading dialog box offers more options.

To put a fill or pattern behind text, you must first select the text (or click anywhere in a paragraph). Click anywhere in the Borders and Shading title bar on the Formatting Palette to expand the panel, as shown in Figure 3-12.

- **Pattern.** The Pattern pop-up menu offers a long list of choices, from Clear (no pattern), to a series of percentages of *halftone* shading (like newspaper photographs), to line patterns such as diagonal stripes. Most of the time, you're probably best off leaving this pop-up menu alone; use the "Fill color" control instead for a professional, even tint.

Tip: Choosing "Solid (100%)" from the Pattern pop-up menu will result in solid black behind your text. Ordinarily, your text would therefore disappear completely, but Word thoughtfully makes the text white, producing an effect called *reversed type,* like this.

- **Pattern color.** If you decide to choose a pattern, the "Pattern color" pop-up menu becomes active. The color you choose here becomes the "black" color of the pattern you chose from the Pattern pop-up menu.

- **Fill.** This is the color that appears behind text or under any pattern you've chosen. You can choose from 40 colors and 24 grayscale shades.

Note: There's a difference between choosing No Fill and White fill color. No Fill is transparent, meaning when you layer a picture beneath text with no fill, you can see the picture. On the other hand, when you layer something beneath text with White fill, the fill blocks out whatever's below.

You can combine these options in fascinating and grisly ways. For example, any pattern you choose overlies the fill color of your paragraph, even if that's No Fill, in which case all you see beneath the pattern is the color of the paper. When you choose one of the percentage shadings from the Pattern pop-up menu, you're choosing a percentage of black or color to overlie the fill color.

Extra features in the Borders and Shading dialog box

A few extra features are available only in the Format→Borders and Shading dialog box. For example:

- You can control how far the fill extends beyond the text. For example, after choosing a fill color, choose Format→Borders and Shading→Borders tab. You'll notice that the None border setting is chosen. However, you can now click the Options button and adjust the "From text" settings, as described on page 125. The settings will apply to the boundary of the fill, as if it were an invisible border.

- Also in the Borders and Shading dialog box, the Horizontal Line button opens a "Choose a Picture" dialog box showing the decorative horizontal lines in Word's clip art gallery. Select one and click Insert to place the line across the text at the insertion point. (You can't make borders with these lines, just horizontals.)

Document Formatting

When you start with a blank document, Word provides a one-inch margin at the top and bottom of the page, and a stately one-and-a-quarter inch margin at each side.

Most people never change these settings. In fact, in its own, almost accidental way, Microsoft has dictated the standard margin formatting for the world's business correspondence. But if you learn how to work with margins—as well as paragraphs and indentation—you can give your document a distinctive look, not to mention fit much more text on a page.

Margins

You can adjust the margins of a Word document in either of two ways: by entering exact measurements (in the Formatting Palette or the Document dialog box), or by dragging the margins directly onto the ruler.

To use the numeric option, choose Format→Document→Margins tab, or click the Document title bar on the Formatting Palette. There you'll find individual boxes that let you specify, in inches, the size of the left, right, top, and bottom margins.

To set your margins by dragging, which produces immediate visible feedback, you must be in Page Layout view (View→Page Layout).

- **Left, Right, Top, Bottom.** To set margins by dragging, point to the line where the ruler changes from white to striped, without clicking. (The striped area is *outside* the limits of the margin.) When the cursor changes to a box with double arrows, drag the margin line to any point on the ruler you wish (see Figure 3-13). Now you can change the margins on both the horizontal and vertical rulers.

Tip: You may find it extremely hard to adjust the left margin, since the trio of *indent* markers (Figure 3-7) lies directly on top of the blue/white boundary. Let the cursor hover until the Left Margin screen tip appears and the cursor shape changes as shown in Figure 3-13. You may even find it worthwhile to move the first-line indent handle out of the way while you adjust the margin.

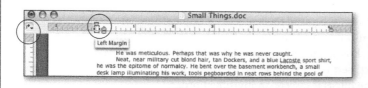

Figure 3-13:
The house-shaped controls in the top ruler set indents (page 120). Drag the blue/white boundaries (circled) in either ruler to adjust the margins.

- **Header and Footer.** Headers and footers (see page 217) appear *within* the normal margins. For instance, if you've set the bottom margin for 1", you can have the page number (footer) appear a half-inch from the edge of the paper—half an inch below the bottom of the text. To do so, set the Footer margin for 0.5", as shown in Figure 3-13.

Tip: When you've got your margins just the way you want them, you can make that setting the default for all new documents you open. Just choose Format→Document and click Default at the lower left of the Document dialog box.

Gutters and Mirrors

Word's *gutter* and *mirror* margin features make margins work when your document is destined to be bound like a book.

In an open book, the *gutter* is the term for the inner margins where the pages attach to the spine. Usually, the gutters have to be wider than the outer margins to allow room for the binding and the spine. (You may want to talk to your publisher—the fine people at Kinko's, for example—to learn about margin requirements.) Word can add this extra space automatically. For instance, if you set a gutter space of 0.25", Word will *add* a quarter-inch to the gutter margin on each page.

Another useful tool for book margins is the *mirror margin* feature, which is designed to let you set up margins that are uneven on each *page*, but reflected on each two-page *spread* (see Figure 3-14).

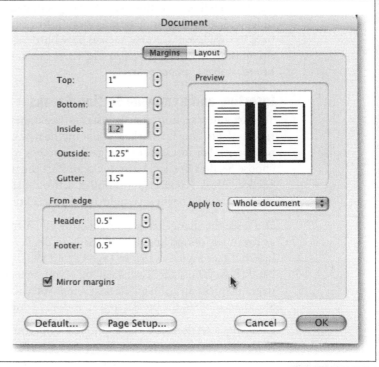

Figure 3-14:
A quick way to open this dialog box is to double-click on the ruler located along the top-left side of the page. The gutter is an extra area for binding; the mirror margins feature is handy when you want the outer and inner margins to be uneven.

Section Formatting

The Formatting Palette doesn't say anything about *section* formatting. In fact, most people have never even heard of it.

Still, section formatting is important in a few special circumstances, such as these:

- Sections allow you to divide a document into chapters, each with its own headers or footers.

- Sections let you change from, say, a one-column format for your opening paragraph to a three-column format for the body of the article. They also let you insert a landscape-orientation page or two into a paper that's primarily in portrait orientation.

- Sections give you flexibility in printing. You can print your title page on colored paper from a different paper tray on your printer, for example.

- You can set different margins for each section of your document. This might come in handy if your training manual contains multiple choice quizzes for which you could really use narrower page margins.

The bottom line: A section is a set of pages in your document that can have its own independent settings for page numbering, lines, footnotes, and endnotes. It can also have its own layout features, such as page borders, margins, columns, alignment, text orientation, and even page size. Finally, it can have its own printer settings, such as orientation and paper source.

Inserting and Removing Section Breaks

To start a new section, choose Insert→Break, then choose one of the Section Break *types*—depending upon where you want the new section to begin (relative to the current page). For instance, to change the number of columns in the middle of a page, choose Section Break (Continuous); to start the next chapter on a new page, choose Section Break (Next Page). If you're self-publishing a novel, remember that new chapters usually begin on a right-hand page; choose Section Break (Odd Page).

You'll see the change reflected right away. In Normal view, a section break shows up as two finely dotted lines labeled "Section Break (Next Page)" or whatever kind you inserted (see Figure 3-15). In Page Layout view, you see only the *effect* of the page break; if you chose the "Next Page" type, your text abruptly stops in the middle of one page and picks up again on the next. But if you click the Show/Hide (¶) button on the Standard toolbar, the breaks appear as double dotted lines, just as in Normal view.

Choosing a section type may sound like a big commitment, but don't fret—you can always go back and change it. To do so, click anywhere in the section that you want to *change*—that is, just after the section break itself—and then choose Format→ Document→Layout tab. Choose a new section type from the "Section start" menu. (This menu offers an additional section-break option: New column, which is useful solely if you're designing your document with multiple columns, as described on page 146. To make an existing column start at the top of the page, click it and choose "New column.")

To remove a section break (in either Normal or Page Layout view) click on the double dotted line and press Del (forward delete) on extended keyboards, or fn-Delete for PowerBooks. Or you can select the section break by clicking before it and dragging through it, and then pressing Delete.

Caution: Deleting a section break, or the last paragraph marker in a section (click ¶ to see it), also deletes its formatting. The section *before* the break will take on the formatting of the section *after* it. The sudden appearance of 24 pages of a two-column layout, for example, can be disconcerting if you're not prepared for it, to say the least.

Figure 3-15:
Top: Create a section break by choosing from the Insert menu (there's no dialog box for it).

Bottom: An example of a "Next page" section break, shown here separating the table of contents from the text. You see the handy guides automatically in Normal view; in Page Layout view, turn on the Show/Hide ¶ button in the Standard toolbar to make them appear.

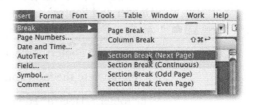

Formatting Within Sections

To change formatting or other settings within a section, such as page numbering or headers and footers, just click in the section and use the commands in Word's dialog boxes and toolbars. Settings like margins, alignment, columns, and page orientation, plus any feature involving numbering, such as page and line numbering, headers and footers, and so on, operate independently of the other sections in the document.

Page numbering across sections

When you use a header or footer and page numbers in your document, you can either number each section independently or number the document continuously from beginning to end. For example, suppose you've written a term paper with an introduction in its own section, which you want to number with Roman numerals. (You want regular Arabic numerals for the body of the paper.) Here's how you'd set things up:

1. **Click at the end of the introduction and choose Insert→Break→Section Break (Next Page).**

   The double dotted lines appear, assuming you're in Normal view (click the Show/Hide if you don't see them).

2. **Click anywhere in the introduction (*above* the section break) and choose View→ Header and Footer.**

   The header and footer areas of your page appear, as described on page 217. The Headers and Footers toolbar opens, too.

3. **Scroll down to the footer on one of the pages in the introduction. Click in it.**

   The footer is labeled "Footer – Section 1."

4. **On the Headers and Footers toolbar, click Insert Page Number (the # icon), then click the Format Page Number icon (shown in Figure 3-16).**

   The Page Number Format dialog box opens, also illustrated in Figure 3-16.

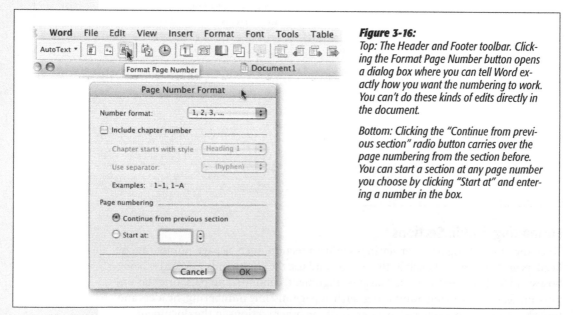

Figure 3-16:
Top: The Header and Footer toolbar. Clicking the Format Page Number button opens a dialog box where you can tell Word exactly how you want the numbering to work. You can't do these kinds of edits directly in the document.

Bottom: Clicking the "Continue from previous section" radio button carries over the page numbering from the section before. You can start a section at any page number you choose by clicking "Start at" and entering a number in the box.

5. From the "Number format" pop-up menu, choose "i, ii, iii…"; click the "Start at" radio button. Click OK.

The number *i* appears in the box, which is right where you want the numbering for the introduction to begin.

6. On the Headers and Footers toolbar, click the Show Next button (you've just done the same thing as clicking in one of the footers in the second section), then click the "Same as Previous" icon, so that it's no longer highlighted.

This button is about halfway across the toolbar; use the screen tip balloons to find it (point to each icon without clicking).

7. Again on the toolbar, click Insert Page Number, then click Format Page Number.

Again, the Page Number Format dialog box appears.

8. This time, choose the Arabic numerals (1, 2, 3, …) from the "Number format" pop-up menu. Click the "Start at" radio button; make sure *1* appears in the box. Click OK.

Now, no matter how you add material to, or remove material from, the introduction and the body of your paper, the introduction will be numbered starting on page i. The numbering of the main body, meanwhile, will start over with 1. Should you change your mind and decide to number your paper consecutively from the intro to the end, you won't have to remove the section break. Just click one of the footers *after* the section break, click Format Page Number, and select the "Continue from previous section" radio button.

Styles, Page Layout, and Tables

After you've polished the *content* of your document, it's time to work on the packaging, and Word 2004 includes the wrapping paper, ribbon, and bows that can take you beyond simple word processing deep into the realm of page design and layout.

For example, an endless block of text running across the page is fine, but columns of text are more professional looking, easier to read—and much less boring. Or perhaps you'd like to add some well-placed borders, but you've never been sure how to work with them.

This chapter builds on Chapter 3's formatting lessons and teaches finishing touches that give your document polish and flair.

Styles

Creating Word documents usually requires a small assortment of formatting styles, which you'll use repeatedly. In a short piece, reformatting your chapter titles (for example) is no big deal; just highlight each and then use the Formatting Palette to make it look the way you like.

But what about long documents? What if your document contains 49 chapter headings, plus 294 (or even 295? Gasp!) sidebar boxes, captions, long quotations, and other heavily formatted elements? In such documents—this book, for example—manually reformatting each heading, subhead, sidebar, and caption would drive you crazy. Word's *styles* feature can alleviate the pain.

A style is a prepackaged collection of formatting attributes that you can apply and reapply with a click of the mouse. You can create as many styles as you need: chapter headings, sidebar styles, whatever. The result is a collection of custom-tailored styles for each of the repeating elements of your document. Figure 4-1 should clarify all of this.

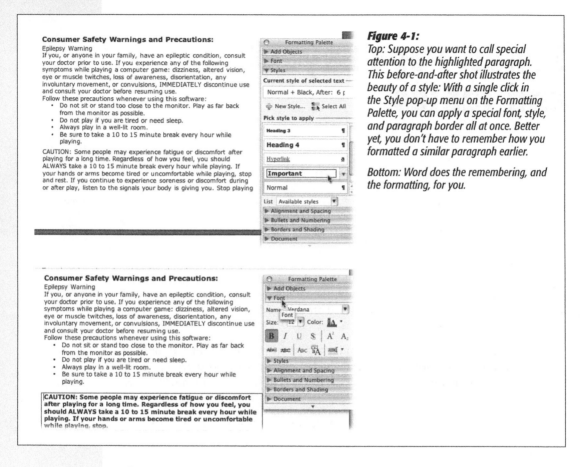

Figure 4-1:
Top: Suppose you want to call special attention to the highlighted paragraph. This before-and-after shot illustrates the beauty of a style: With a single click in the Style pop-up menu on the Formatting Palette, you can apply a special font, style, and paragraph border all at once. Better yet, you don't have to remember how you formatted a similar paragraph earlier.

Bottom: Word does the remembering, and the formatting, for you.

After creating your styles, just apply them as needed; they stay consistent throughout the document. During the editing process, if you notice an accidentally styled, say, headline using the *Subhead* style, you can fix the problem by simply reapplying the correct style.

You'll appreciate styles even more when it comes time to change the formatting of a particular style. If you change a style's description, Word offers to change *every occurrence* of that style in your document.

Styles aren't one of Microsoft's ease-of-understanding masterpieces, but they are getting better. Grasping how they work, where they're stored, and when they change explains many of Word's idiosyncrasies, and pays off handsomely in the long run.

Where Styles Are Stored

Every document has a collection of ready-to-use, built-in styles, whether you're aware of it or not. (To be more precise, every document is based on a *template* that stores a canned set of styles, as described on page 227.) Word opens each new blank document with the *Normal* paragraph style selected.

The styles available in your document reside in several places: in the Style panel of the Formatting Palette, the Formatting toolbar, the Ruler toolbar, and the Format→ Style dialog box (see Figure 4-2).

Tip: There are many more styles in the Style dialog box than in the Formatting Palette or the toolbar menus, which contain only a selection of the most useful styles. To see a more comprehensive list of styles without opening the Style dialog box, just Shift-click the Formatting toolbar's Style menu arrow, or choose All Styles from the Formatting Palette's pop-up menu.

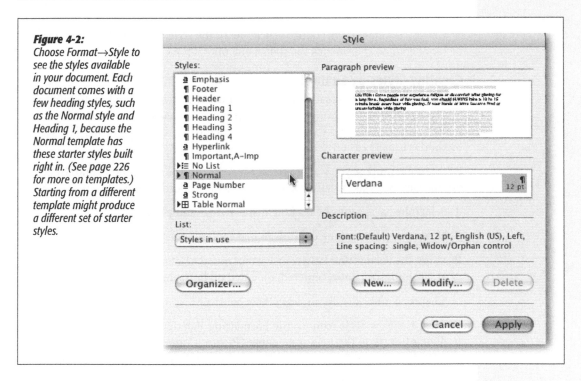

Figure 4-2:
Choose Format→Style to see the styles available in your document. Each document comes with a few heading styles, such as the Normal style and Heading 1, because the Normal template has these starter styles built right in. (See page 226 for more on templates.) Starting from a different template might produce a different set of starter styles.

Applying Styles

To apply a pre-existing style to text you've already typed, highlight the text. For example, drag through some text, or click once inside a paragraph to select it. (You can also choose a style for a new paragraph *before* you begin typing it.)

Note: If you click twice to select a word, the style will only apply to that word. Clicking once within a paragraph, however, will apply the subsequently chosen style to the entire paragraph. No fuss, very little muss.

Now choose a style from one of Word's style boxes, using one of the following methods (listed in ascending order of speed):

- Press Shift-⌘-S to highlight the Style menu in the Formatting toolbar and then use the up and down arrow keys to step through the styles in the list until the one you're seeking is highlighted. Press Return to apply the style. You can also use the mouse to scroll through this list.

Tip: You can save time by typing the name of the style and then pressing Return. For this very reason, some people use very short style names when they format a style. For instance, if you name a style GX, you only have to press Shift-⌘-S, type *gx*, and Return to apply the style—never having touched the mouse. Better yet, give the style *two* names, separated by a comma—one in English for your own reference in using the Style menus, the other its "keystroke name." For example, your Sidebar style might be called *Sidebar, sb*.

- Use the scroll bar next to the Style list in the Formatting Palette, then click the style name to apply it.

- Choose Format→Style; double-click one of the style names in the Styles list box (see Figure 4-2)—or click the style name once, then click Apply.

Creating Styles by Example

There are two ways to create styles: You can use the Styles dialog box to build one, or you can "create by example"—that is, you can format the text in the document the way you want it, and then tell Word to memorize that formatting. The second method is usually easier.

For example, suppose you want to create a style for illustration captions. Start by typing out the caption, making sure you end with Return in order to create a paragraph.

1. **Select the paragraph (by clicking inside it, for example).**

   Now use the formatting controls to make it look exactly like you want it.

2. **Using the Formatting Palette or Format menu, choose the Century Gothic font, at 10-point size, italic, centered, indented on both sides.**

   Chapter 3 offers details on using these controls.

3. **Click the New Style icon on the Formatting Palette to bring up the New Style dialog box, type the new style name (*Picture Caption,* for example), and click OK. (If the Formatting toolbar is open, you can simply type the new name in the Style box and then press Return.)**

   To apply this style more quickly in the future, consider assigning it two names separated by a comma—the second one can be an abbreviation (see the Tip above).

That's it...your style is now ready for use.

Creating Styles in the Dialog Box

For more style control, use the Style dialog box. To use it, choose Format→Style and then click New (or press ⌘-N) or click the New Style icon in the Style pane of the Formatting Palette. The New Style dialog box opens, as shown in Figure 4-3.

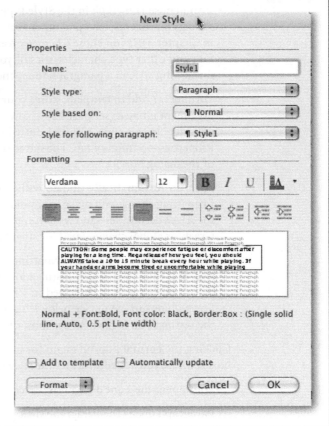

Figure 4-3:
As you develop your new style, the preview window in the middle of the New Style dialog gives you live feedback, so you can see exactly what you're creating. Below, the written definition of the style changes to indicate, in somewhat technical terms, the specifics of your formatting choices.

Use the various controls here to define this new style:

- **Name.** Give your style a name that reflects its usage: Headline, Sidebar, and so on.

- Style **based on.** Choose Normal or whatever existing style is closest to what you envision for the new style. Basing your new style on an existing one has two payoffs. First, it saves you time, since some of the formatting is already in place; second, when you modify the underlying style (such as Normal), all styles *based* upon it change as well, keeping your document design coordinated. For example, if you base a heading on the Normal style, and then change the Normal font to Palatino, the heading style's font changes to Palatino, as well.

- **Style for following paragraph** is a big timesaver. Let's say the new style you're creating is a heading, and after each heading, you always return to typing in Normal style. Instead of manually changing the font back to Normal after each use of the Heading style, just choose Normal here. Now, whenever you press Return after using the heading style, the font automatically returns to Normal.

- If you chose *Paragraph* in the **Style type** menu, the style will include the current settings for indents, tabs, and other aspects of paragraph formatting (as described in Chapter 3). If you chose *Character* formatting, then Word memorizes only the font and other type characteristics of your new style. You can apply a character-formatting style in a paragraph independently of the paragraph style.

- Turning on **Add to template** stores your new style in the *template* on which your document is based (see page 226). Now, all new documents based on this template will include this style. (To find out which template you're using, choose File→ Properties→Summary tab. The name of the template is shown near the bottom of the dialog box.)

- Turn on **Automatically update** with caution. When this box is turned on, any formatting change you make to any *one* occurrence of text in this style will change the style's definition—and with it, *every* occurrence of the style in your document. Great for global changes; bad for singular changes.

- New for Word 2004 is the **Formatting** panel that allows you to set the font type, size, and color; paragraph justification; line spacing; and indent. These options, all of which are fully described in Chapter 3, have always been available in the Format pop-up menu (see below), but this new panel gives you quicker access to the settings you're likely to use most often.

Clicking the **Format** pop-up menu (or pressing ⌘-O) gains you access to the dialog boxes, where you actually format the style you're building:

- **Font** opens the Font dialog box, described on page 107.

- **Paragraph** opens the Paragraph dialog box, described on page 116.

- **Tabs** opens the Tabs dialog box, described on page 122.

- **Border** opens the Borders tab of the Borders and Shading dialog box (page 125).

- **Language** provides foreign language choices for your style, for the benefit of the spell checker and other proofing tools.

- Placing a **Frame** around a paragraph gives it some of the qualities of text boxes. (Frames are an early Word feature that most people have abandoned in favor of text boxes; see page 151.)

- **Numbering** opens the Bullets and Numbering dialog box, which is described on page 114. The menu option's name, "Numbering," is only half accurate, since it's used for bulleted lists as well as numbered ones.

- **Shortcut Key** opens the Customize Keyboard dialog box (see page 677), where you can assign a keyboard shortcut to this style. For example, you can assign Control-⌘-Z to your favorite heading style and apply it with a quick tap of the left hand. If you frequently change styles as you type along, or if you have trouble using a mouse, this feature is a godsend.

When you click OK after making changes in any of these formatting dialog boxes, you return to the New Style dialog box, where the description information tells you which characteristics you've assigned to this style.

When you click OK again to return to your document, the newly created style's name appears along with all the others in the Formatting Palette. It's now ready to apply.

Changing, Deleting, or Copying Styles

There are several ways to change an existing style, but here are two of the quickest:

- Select text in your document and then, in the Formatting Palette as shown in Figure 4-4, click the little triangle next to the style's name; choose Modify Style in the pop-up menu that appears. When the Modify Style dialog box opens, make your changes, and then click OK to update the style.

Figure 4-4:
To modify selected text, click on the triangle to the right of the style's name and select Modify Style from the subsequent pop-up menu. This is a new feature in Office 2004, so it may catch old-timers by surprise. (Life is like that.) On the bright side, you get this nifty dialog box where you can accomplish almost everything you can in the Format→Style dialog box, only more quickly.

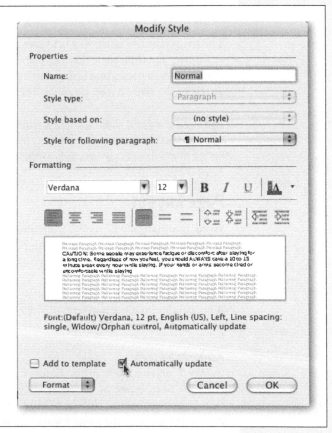

• Choose Format→Style; click the style's name in the Styles box; click Modify (or press ⌘-M); and use the Format menu to make changes to the font, paragraph, and so on, just as if creating a new style (as described above).

Deleting styles

To delete unwanted styles, choose Format→Style, then click the style in the Styles list box and click Delete.

Note: Word won't let you delete certain built-in styles (such as Normal, Heading 1, 2, and 3, and so on). If you click one of these styles, the Delete button is grayed out.

To delete multiple styles, choose Tools→Templates and Add-ins and click Organizer (or press ⌘-O). (If you're in the Style dialog box, just click the Organizer button.) The Organizer opens, as shown on page 230. In the list box for the current document, ⌘-click the styles you want to delete, then click Delete. (If the styles you wish to delete are consecutive, click the first one, then Shift-click the last style name; click Delete.)

Transferring styles

Once you've cultivated a crop of magnificent styles, you may want to spread their sunshine to other documents. You can do so in the Organizer dialog box, described in the previous paragraph and on page 230, but that's a lot of trouble.

The sneaky, much faster way is to *copy* paragraphs formatted in the styles you want to transfer and then paste them into another document. Word automatically adds the pasted styles to the second document's list of styles. (If the document already contains a style of the same name, it ignores the newly pasted one.)

Tip: If you're confused about which styles you've applied where, try this: Choose Word→Preferences→View panel. Set the "Style area width" to about one inch, then click OK. Now Word opens a new strip at the left side of your document window that identifies the style of every paragraph!

Page Layout

Word automatically flows text from line to line and page to page. Nice, huh? However, an important part of document design is placing text right where you want it, breaking it up, and generally controlling the flow.

Inserting Breaks

A *break* is an invisible barrier that stops your text in its tracks, and then starts it again on a new line, column, or page.

Paragraph break

In Word, pressing Return (or Enter) creates a paragraph break. Although you may not have been aware of the term, they're created every time you end a paragraph. Unless you've chosen a different "following paragraph" style (see page 142), the new paragraph assumes the same formatting as the previous.

Line break

Pressing Shift-Return inserts a *line break*. It's similar to a paragraph break except that the text on the new line remains part of the original paragraph, and retains its style and paragraph formatting. No matter how you edit the surrounding text, the line break will remain where you inserted it—until you remove it, of course.

Page break

Choose Insert→Break→Page Break (or press Shift-*Enter*) to force a *hard* page break. No matter how much text you add above the break, the text *after* the break will always appear at the top of a new page.

Use a page break when, for example, your report has a separate title page. Inserting a hard page break at the end of the title page text forces the body of your paper to begin on page 2. You may also want to start a new page for each topic in a document, if you're writing a manual on chores for the kids, for example. In this case, you could start a new page for the cleaning instructions for each room in the house.

Tip: In Page Layout view, page breaks are generally invisible. The text just ends in the middle of a page and won't go any further, which can be disconcerting if you've forgotten about the page break you added.

To view the dotted lines that represent a page break, choose View→Normal, or click the Show/Hide ¶ button on the Standard toolbar.

Column break

To jump text to the top of a new *column* (in multicolumn layouts like those described in the next section), choose Insert→Break→Column Break. Word ends the current column and, when you start typing again, hops you over to the top of the next column at the top of the page.

If you choose this option when you're not using multiple columns (see page 146), it behaves like a hard page break. (On the other hand, if you later switch to a two- or three-column format, the column break behaves like a normal column break. If you plan to make two different versions of your document—one with columns and one without—you may therefore want to use column breaks instead of page breaks.) *Keyboard shortcut:* Shift-⌘-Return.

Section break

A *section* is like a chapter—a part of a document that can have formatting independent of the other parts. For example, each section can possess unique margins, page numbering, pagination, headers and footers, even printing paper size. See page 132 for more detail on sections.

To begin a new section, insert a section break by choosing Insert→Break→Section Break and then the specific type of break that you want (see page 132).

Caution: When deleting a break as shown in Figure 4-5, bear in mind that the usually invisible ¶ marker at the end of a paragraph "contains" the formatting for the paragraph that comes before it. If you join two paragraphs or sections together by backspacing until there's no break between them, they blend into one and take on the formatting of the *second* section or paragraph.

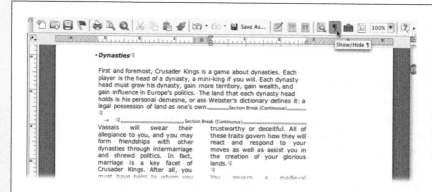

Figure 4-5:
Click the ¶ (Show/Hide) on the Standard toolbar to see which breaks are where in your document. This is the surefire way to eliminate breaks you want removed. Now that you can see them, you can delete or backspace over them.

Working with Columns

If you're putting together, say, a newsletter, some classified ads, or the rule book for the computer game you've just designed, you can give your publication a professional look by pouring it into multiple parallel *columns* (see Figure 4-6). Newspapers and magazines, for example, use columns in their layouts because the shorter lines are easier to read, and...well, they've always done it that way.

Tip: You can see multiple columns only in Page Layout view (View→Page Layout). Only one column per page appears in Normal view, much to the confusion of anyone creating columns for the first time.

Adding columns using the Standard toolbar

The quickest way to create columns is via the Columns button on the Standard toolbar, as shown in Figure 4-6. If you want your entire document in columns, make sure nothing is selected; if you want columns for only part of the document, select that text.

Then click the Columns pop-up button on the Standard toolbar. Now drag downward and across to highlight the number of columns you'd like to use, as shown in Figure 4-6. If you need more than four columns, drag beyond their borders to expand the choices to five or six.

When you release the mouse, Word divides your text into columns of equal width. (If you highlighted only part of the document, Word automatically creates invisible *section breaks* above and below the selected portion; see page 145.)

Adding columns using the Columns dialog box

Although the Columns pop-up button on the toolbar is quick and easy, Word, as usual, offers far more control if you're willing to visit a dialog box. To use this option, select text or click in your document and proceed as follows:

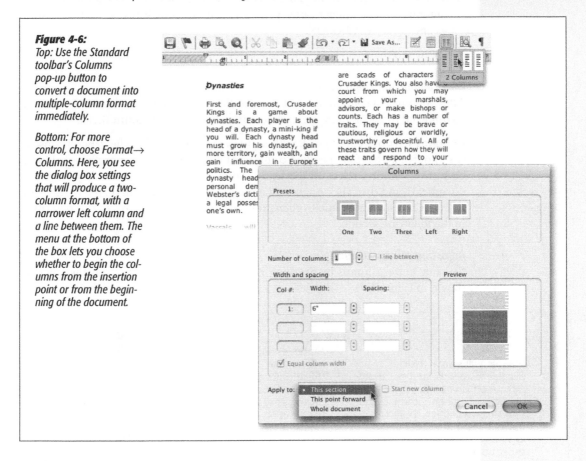

Figure 4-6:
Top: Use the Standard toolbar's Columns pop-up button to convert a document into multiple-column format immediately.

Bottom: For more control, choose Format→Columns. Here, you see the dialog box settings that will produce a two-column format, with a narrower left column and a line between them. The menu at the bottom of the box lets you choose whether to begin the columns from the insertion point or from the beginning of the document.

1. **Choose Format→Columns.**

   When the Columns dialog box opens (see Figure 4-7), the number of columns is preset to One, meaning that your text takes up the entire width of the page.

2. **Choose one of the icons at the top of the dialog box, or enter a number in the "Number of columns" box.**

   The buttons labeled Two and Three create two or three columns of equal width. Left and Right mean, "Give me the number of columns I've specified in the 'Number of columns' box, but for some visual spice, make the first column half as wide, or twice as wide, respectively, as the other columns."

3. **Click the arrow buttons next to the Width box for each column or the spacing boxes.**

Width boxes are available for the number of columns you've requested. The Preview box displays the results. To create columns of equal width at any point, check the "Equal column width" box.

4. **If you so desire, turn on "Line between" to draw a thin vertical line between columns (it only appears after you have written enough text to spill into your second column). Click OK.**

You return to the document, where the fancy columns are now in place.

How columns look and flow

After you finish a column, the text flows to the top of the next column. To end one column and move on to the next, choose Insert→Break→Column Break.

Columns start out left-aligned, with an uneven right margin. The general consensus, though, is that fully justified columns offer the tidiest, most professional look. To justify columns, select all the text in your columns (⌘-A if that's your entire document), and then click Alignment and Spacing→Justification on the Formatting Palette. (Turn on automatic hyphenation, too, for better word spacing, as described in the following section.)

Adjusting column widths

You can resize columns by dragging the column margin markers on the ruler, as shown in Figure 4-7.

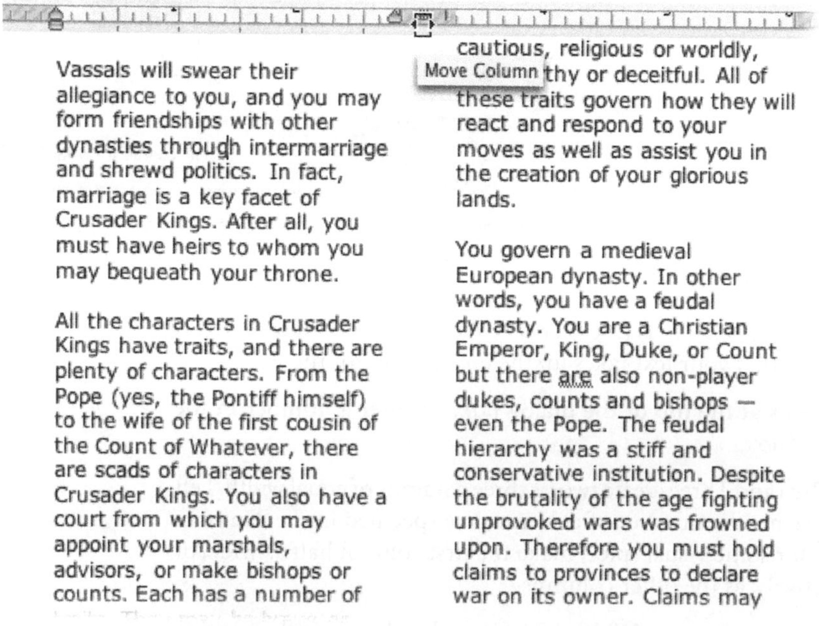

Vassals will swear their allegiance to you, and you may form friendships with other dynasties through intermarriage and shrewd politics. In fact, marriage is a key facet of Crusader Kings. After all, you must have heirs to whom you may bequeath your throne.

All the characters in Crusader Kings have traits, and there are plenty of characters. From the Pope (yes, the Pontiff himself) to the wife of the first cousin of the Count of Whatever, there are scads of characters in Crusader Kings. You also have a court from which you may appoint your marshals, advisors, or make bishops or counts. Each has a number of

cautious, religious or worldly, Move Column thy or deceitful. All of these traits govern how they will react and respond to your moves as well as assist you in the creation of your glorious lands.

You govern a medieval European dynasty. In other words, you have a feudal dynasty. You are a Christian Emperor, King, Duke, or Count but there are also non-player dukes, counts and bishops — even the Pope. The feudal hierarchy was a stiff and conservative institution. Despite the brutality of the age fighting unprovoked wars was frowned upon. Therefore you must hold claims to provinces to declare war on its owner. Claims may

Figure 4-7:
The quickest way to adjust column widths is by eye. First choose View→Page Layout. Then place the cursor over the ruler near the column boundary that you'd like to adjust (at the top of the page). When the cursor turns into a double-arrow box, drag to move the column margin.

Using the Format→Columns dialog box to resize columns gives you better control over the measurements, and provides access to the "Equal column width" feature (see Figure 4-7). If you turn on this box, the columns remain the same width no matter what; if you resize one of them using the arrow buttons, the others automatically grow or shrink to match.

If you don't turn on "Equal column width," you can resize each column individually; the other columns grow or shrink to fill the page width. You can also adjust the spacing with the arrow buttons (or by entering numbers in the boxes), and glance at the Preview pane to see the effects of your changes. The total width of the columns and spacing always equals the full text width on the page: the width between the left and right indents.

Tip: If you're experiencing trouble getting your column lengths to come out even at the bottom of the page, check the Paragraph Spacing (under Alignment and Spacing in the Formatting Palette). Leaving just a small amount of space before and after each paragraph makes it easier for Word to balance the columns.

Automatic Hyphenation

When you're using columns, the hyphenation feature (which automatically breaks longer words at the right margin) creates a straighter, almost even right margin (see Figure 4-8). It also provides more regular spacing within each line in *justified* text (text that's stretched to be flush with both margins).

Word normally doesn't insert hyphens until you type them—or until you turn on the automatic hyphenation feature. To do so, choose Tools→Hyphenation, then turn on "Automatically hyphenate document." When you click OK, Word scrutinizes the document and hyphenates words where necessary, using its built-in dictionary as a guide to "legal" syllable breaks. Word will continue hyphenating automatically as you edit and add on to your document.

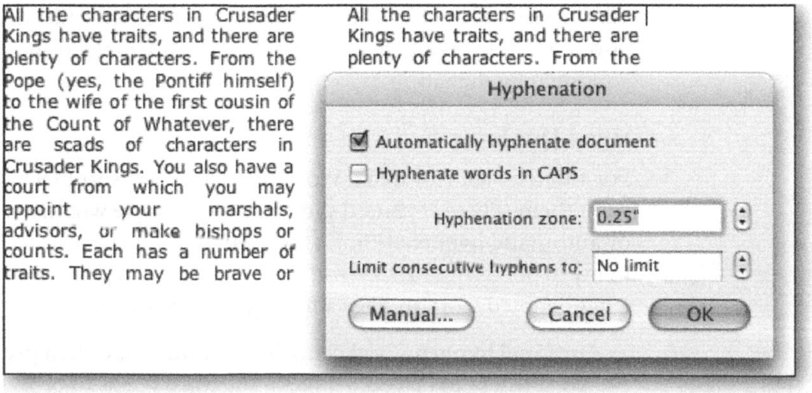

Figure 4-8:
Top left: By default, hyphenation is turned off, so that if a word is too long, Word moves it down to a new line. The result can be ugly gaps between words.

Bottom: Turning on "Automatically hyphenate document" can produce much better-looking spacing (top right).

Hyphenation Settings

Before clicking OK, be sure to review the following hyphenation settings:

- Turning *off* "Hyphenate words in CAPS," leaves your acronyms whole; that's probably what you want it to do.

- The "Hyphenation zone" is the amount of space allowed at the end of a line before Word inserts a hyphen. The larger you set this number, the fewer hyphens you'll end up with in your document. The smaller the number, the more even the right margin will be—and the more hyphens you'll have.

- Set "Limit consecutive hyphens" to 2 or 3. If you set it to more than that, all the hyphens at the end of consecutive lines will look like a little ladder climbing up the page (a big no-no in professional publishing).

Undoing hyphenation is easy: Just choose Tools→Hyphenation and turn off the "Automatically hyphenate document" box. Word returns your document to its pristine, pre-hyphenated condition.

Manual Hyphenation

The automatic hyphenation feature is an all-or-nothing deal, in that it applies to the entire document, or not at all. If you'd like more say in Word's hyphenation propagation (say that three times fast with a mouthful of Skittles), use manual hyphenation. Doing so lets you say Yea or Nay to each word that Word wants to break up.

Here's how: Choose Tools→Hyphenation and click Manual. Word goes through your document, stopping at each word it wants to hyphenate, just as in a spell check. In the Manual Hyphenation dialog box that appears, you can click No (don't hyphenate), Yes (hyphenate at the blinking hyphen), or use the arrow keys to move to the point where you want Word to put the hyphen; *now* click Yes. Clicking Cancel both dismisses the dialog box and ends manual hyphenation.

If you expect to conduct major editing after hyphenating manually, then consider another hyphenation pass. Unlike automatic hyphenation, manual hyphenation doesn't add or remove hyphens automatically as your text reflows during editing. (You can also rehyphenate only *parts* of the document by selecting the text before performing a manual hyphenation.)

Hard Hyphens

For the true control freak, Word offers two ways to place hyphens right where you want them. These keyboard shortcuts are effective whether or not you use the manual or automatic hyphenation features. For example, if you feel your document has too many hyphens in a row, even after your manual hyphenation pass, you can still change a hyphenated word to have a nonbreaking hyphen.

- **Optional hyphen.** By clicking inside a word and then pressing ⌘-hyphen, you tell Word where to place a hyphen *if* the word needs to be hyphenated. As you edit the document, if the word moves away from the end of a line, the optional hyphen disappears, returning only if the word needs to be divided again.

- **Nonbreaking hyphen.** Click inside a word and then press Shift-⌘-hyphen. You've just told Word that you *do not* want to break this word up—ever.

To delete optional hyphens and the oxymoronic nonbreaking hyphens, click the Show/Hide (¶) button on the Standard toolbar. The invisible hyphens become visible (they look like an L-shaped bar and an approximately-equal sign, respectively) and are ready for you to delete.

Note: If Hyphenation is grayed out on the Tools menu, you may be in Outline or Master Document view, where hyphenation is unavailable.

Text Boxes

Putting text in a box of its own, sitting there independently on the page, represents a quantum leap in text-flow management (see Figure 4-9). You can now format and color a text box independently from everything else on the page, as well as use drawing tools on it. In other words, text boxes let you think outside the box.

Note: A text box is fundamentally different from a paragraph with a *border* around it, although text boxes can (and often do) have borders. For one thing, you can't drag to resize a bordered paragraph, or flow text around it, as you can with a text box. On the other hand, if all you want is a border and none of the other fancy features, then creating a border around a plain old paragraph is the easiest way to do it.

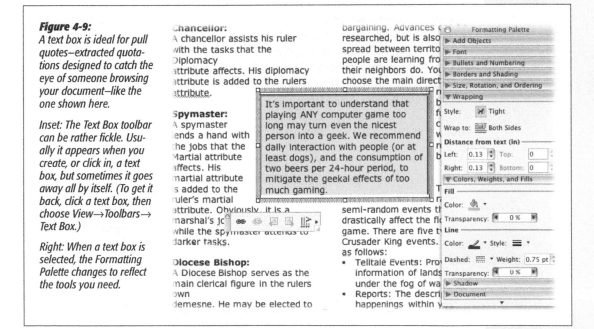

Figure 4-9:
A text box is ideal for pull quotes—extracted quotations designed to catch the eye of someone browsing your document—like the one shown here.

Inset: The Text Box toolbar can be rather fickle. Usually it appears when you create, or click in, a text box, but sometimes it goes away all by itself. (To get it back, click a text box, then choose View→Toolbars→Text Box.)

Right: When a text box is selected, the Formatting Palette changes to reflect the tools you need.

Text boxes also emulate the way desktop publishing programs such as Quark XPress and PageMaker handle text. If you've never used professional desktop publishing software, consider this your initial training.

Note: Text boxes completely disappear in Normal view. To work with text boxes, make sure you're using Page Layout view (View→Page Layout)—or be prepared for some surprises when you first see the printout.

Creating Text Boxes

To start a text box in your document, choose Insert→Text Box. (Another avenue: If the Drawing toolbar is open (page 684), click the Text Box button, which looks like a capital A with an I-bar next to it.)

Move the mouse to where you'd like the box to appear, and drag diagonally; Word shows you the rectangular outline of the box you're creating. The box is complete when you let go of the mouse, though you can always resize or move it later. To place text inside your new text box, click inside it and type or paste.

Tip: To enclose existing text in a text box, first select the text, then choose Insert→Text Box or click the Text Box button. Your text appears in a small text box, which you can then resize.

The Text Box Toolbar

The diminutive Text Box toolbar appears when you first create a text box, as shown in Figure 4-9. Its buttons let you:

- **Link and unlink text boxes.** *Linking* text boxes sets up an automatic text flow from one to another, exactly as in PageMaker, Quark XPress, or any newspaper on earth that makes you "Continue on page 13A." As you add text to the first text box, overflow text falls into the second one, even if it's many pages away. Most people never suspect that Word is even capable of this page-layout feature, perhaps because it's buried in this shy toolbar.

Tip: The Text Box toolbar only appears as an option in the View→Toolbars menu if your cursor currently resides in a Text Box.

To link two text boxes, click the first box, and then click the Create Text Box Link button (see Figure 4-9). The cursor turns into a pitcher, as if to pour text into the next box. Now click the second box. Excess text flows automatically from the first box into the second. (Press Esc or ⌘-period to back out of the process.)

Tip: There's nothing preventing you from repeating this process, linking three, four, or many text boxes together into a continuously linked chain. You may drive your readers crazy, but you can do it.

To break a link between two boxes, click anywhere in the first of the two boxes and click the Break Forward Link button. The text from the second box now flows back into the first one, leaving the second box (and any subsequent boxes) empty.

- **Navigate from one text box to another.** The next two buttons on the Text Box toolbar (see Figure 4-9) come in handy if there are many text boxes distributed far and wide in your document. They step you forward and back through the text boxes, skipping over everything in between.

- **Change text direction.** Clicking this button rotates the text within the box (and all others linked to it), as shown in Figure 4-10.

Tip: You can also find many of the above commands by Control-clicking the border of a text box.

Figure 4-10:
Clicking "Change text direction" on the Text Box toolbar or Formatting Palette (or choosing Format→Text Direction) allows you to create eye-catching mastheads like this one. You can make text read top to bottom, bottom to top, or back to normal. (You can't turn text upside down.) Use this trick for creative layout effects for newsletter mastheads or letterheads.

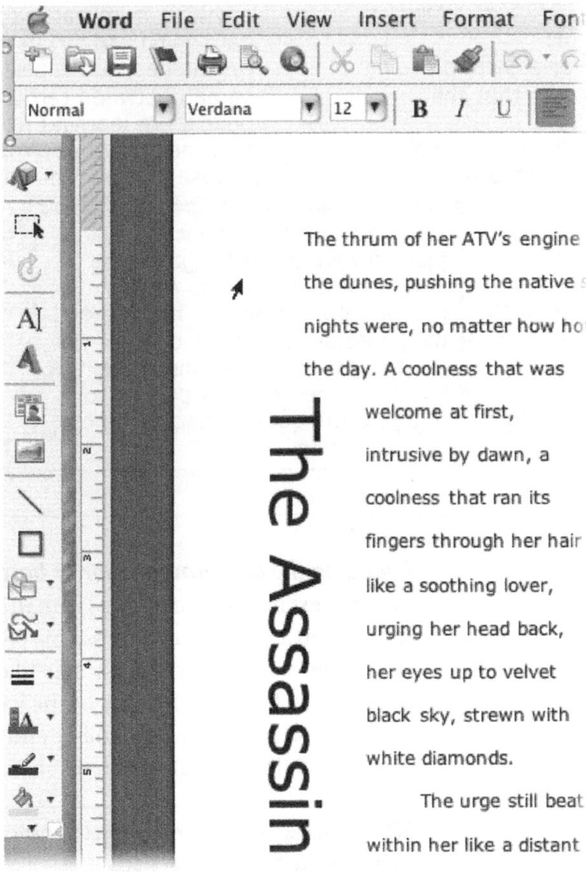

Formatting Within Text Boxes

To format text within text boxes, just select the text first. The tools on the Standard toolbar and the Formatting Palette pertain to the text within a box, so long as the insertion point is in that box.

Tip: Choosing Edit→Select All or pressing ⌘-A, while the insertion point is in a text box, effectively selects all the text in that box *and* any boxes that are linked to it.

To adjust the margins within a text box, choose Format→Text Box. (This choice only appears when the insertion point is within a text box.) Now click the Text Box tab, as shown in Figure 4-11. The settings you establish in these boxes control the distance between the borders of the text box and the text itself.

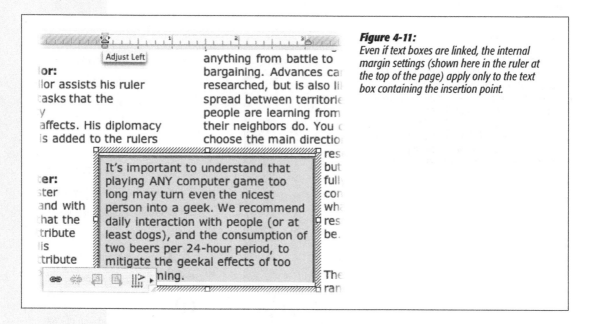

Figure 4-11:
Even if text boxes are linked, the internal margin settings (shown here in the ruler at the top of the page) apply only to the text box containing the insertion point.

Changing the background color or border style

When a text box is selected, the Formatting Palette changes to offer specialized controls for formatting its line thickness, line color, and background ("Fill") color or pattern. In fact, because a Word text box is like a cross between a text block and a *drawing object* (see Chapter 20), many of the icons on the Drawing toolbar affect text boxes. For example, the Drawing toolbar and Formatting Palette offer 3-D and shadow effects, which look dynamite on text boxes.

Tip: To use the drawing tools on a text box, make sure to select the box itself, not the text inside it. To do so, position the cursor on the box's outline until the cursor turns into a hand, and then click. (When you click *inside* the box, the tools on the Formatting Palette turn back to text tools.)

Sizing text boxes

If you can't see all the text in a box, you can either link it to another text box or just make the original box bigger. Here's how: Select the box by clicking it, and then drag any of the tiny white resize handles at its borders. Or, for numerical precision, use the boxes on the Formatting Palette's Size section; the relevant portions of the Formatting Palette are shown in Figure 4-9.

Working with Linked Text Boxes

Microsoft calls a group of linked text boxes a *story.* There's no limit to the number of text boxes you can link together—just keep creating new ones and linking them (page 152) until there's room for all your text.

Copying linked text boxes

You can copy or cut an entire story (or part of one) to paste into another document. To do so, select the text *box* (not the text) of the first box in the story and Shift-click any additional text boxes you want to copy. Once they're selected, you can copy or cut and paste the chain of boxes using any of the copy/paste methods described in Chapter 2. Use this method if, for example, you want to copy a series of text boxes and then change the text inside of them. This saves you the work of creating and sizing new text boxes.

Note: Word can't link text boxes across documents in order to keep the text flowing "live" from one to the next.

To cut or copy the *text only* from a story, click in any box in the chain and choose Edit→Select All (or press ⌘-A). Now when you use the cut or copy and paste commands, you'll be pasting just the text, not the boxes.

Deleting one text box in a chain

If you delete one box in a story, the text remains intact, flowing from beginning to end through the remaining text boxes in the chain. Select the box that you want to delete by holding the cursor over the box's boundary until it changes into a hand icon; click the box edge. Then choose Edit→Clear (or press Delete). If necessary, enlarge the remaining linked text boxes to show all of the story.

Grouping text boxes

You can *group* text boxes and then operate on them as a unit—the only problem is selecting them. As noted above, the trick is to click their *borders;* Shift-click to select the additional boxes that you want to group. Once they're selected, choose Group from the Draw pop-up button on the Drawing toolbar or Formatting Palette, or right-click and choose Group from the shortcut menu. (If you change your mind, the Ungroup and Regroup commands are on this same menu.)

When you drag a grouped text box, they all move together. When you drag the sizing handles, they all grow or shrink by the same amount. Likewise, when you use the color and fill commands, they act upon all boxes in the group.

Text Wrapping and Layering

Whether you're creating a Web site or printed document, one of the most enjoyable parts is putting in a few images—photos, clip art, or drawings. But too often, the text and graphics don't harmoniously share the space. Many people find topics like *text wrapping* too intimidating to bother learning.

Don't be one of them. Word 2004's layout features are more intuitive than ever, especially for you, the wise and discriminating Mac user.

Wrapping text around things

The "things" around which you can wrap text are clip art from Word's own collection (see page 680); drawings you've made in Word or any drawing program; AutoShapes from the Drawing toolbar; or text boxes. (See Chapter 20 for a review of the various graphic objects you can place into a Word document.)

The best way to configure the text around your text box or picture is with the Format dialog box. To get started, select the graphic or text box you want to wrap your text around. Ignore the text for now—just worry about getting the picture where you want it on the page. Then proceed as follows:

1. **Click to select the graphic or text box, then choose Format→whatever.**

   In other words, choose Format→Picture, Format→Object, Format→AutoShape, or Format→Text Box. The wording of the bottommost choice on the Format menu depends on the item you've selected. In any event, the appropriate Format dialog box now appears (Figure 4-12, left).

2. **Click the Layout tab. Choose one of the text-wrap styles by clicking its icon.**

   These wrapping controls correspond to those on the Formatting Palette, also shown in Figure 4-12. For example, choose Tight if you'd like the text to hug the outlines

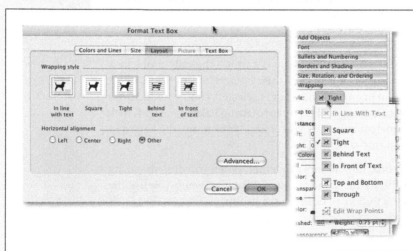

Figure 4-12:
The wrapping controls in the Format dialog box lets you bend text to your will. Your text can leave a hole for the graphic (Square), hug its irregular sides (Tight), sit superimposed (Behind Text), hide beneath by the graphic (In Front of Text), or treat it as just another typed character (In Line With Text).

of an irregularly shaped object. Choose Behind Text to create a watermark, or choose Square for a neat, businesslike look.

3. **To keep the object right where you placed it on the page, click Other under "Horizontal Alignment."**

The other buttons move the object to align with the left margin, center line, and right margin, respectively.

4. **Click Advanced.**

A new dialog box appears (see Figure 4-13).

5. **Make the changes you want, as shown in Figure 4-13; click OK twice.**

Figure 4-13:
Left: A Word clip art inserted into a document; left alignment, tight wrapping, one side only, 0.25" from text.

Right: The Advanced Layout tab contains additional options. For example, you can wrap text on one side only, instead of both sides (if the text wrapping is down one side of a column, perhaps). "Largest only" wraps text only on one side—the side that has the most room, even if that changes in the middle of the object. This is a good choice for irregularly shaped objects. Distance from text lets you choose how close you want the text against the object it wraps—in hundredths of an inch.

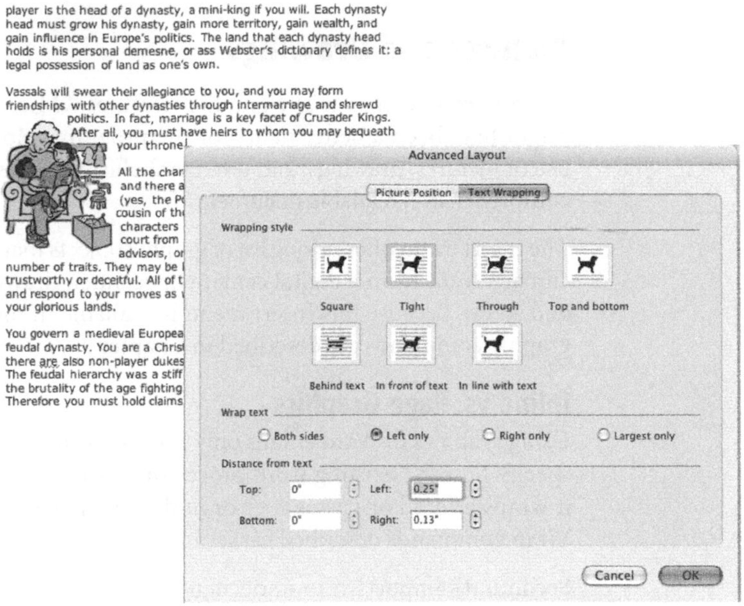

Layering text with graphics

Most of the time, you'll want to wrap text *around* objects. But sometimes, for effect, you'll put text right *over* an object, or vice versa. To pull this off, use the "Behind text" or "In front of text" options shown in Figure 4-13.

If superimposing a graphic has made the text difficult to read, there are a couple of fixes. Either lighten the object beneath the text, or, if the text has a fill, change it to a clear or semitransparent fill.

- To lighten an object, select it. If it's a picture, click the Image title bar on the Formatting Palette, then click the Mode icon, and then select Watermark. Clicking color Adjustment on the Formatting Palette and choosing the Saturation radio button is another way to lighten a picture. Then use the Setting slider to lighten the image as much as you need.

- If the object is a drawing or AutoShape, you can use the Transparency slider on the Formatting Palette to make it easier to see through. (The slider has no effect on lines. For less-intrusive, thinner lines, use the Weight box on the Formatting Palette, or choose a lighter color in the Line Color box.) You can access the same controls by choosing Format from the Draw pop-up button on the Drawing toolbar.

Tip: You can even layer text with text—a great trick when using your company's name as a watermark on your letterhead, for example. To do so, make a text box containing the logo, apply a light color or light shade of gray to it in the Formatting Palette, and choose "Behind text" from the Style pop-up button in Formatting Palette's Wrapping section. Drag the logo into place.

Pictures and Drawings

Word comes with so many graphics features, "Microsoft Word and Picture 2004" might have been a better name for the program. More and more often, the skilled use of pictures, drawings, and other embellishments is necessary in the creation of a comprehensive, readable document.

The Insert menu offers a long list of graphic objects that you can pop onto a Word page: clip art, scans from a digital camera or scanner, drawing objects called AutoShapes, and so on. Because this Insert menu is available in most of the Office programs, its graphic commands are described in Chapter 20.

Inline vs. Page Graphics

Using graphics in Word entails only a few special pieces of knowledge. First, you can specify how the existing word processor text interacts with each graphic—whether it wraps around or passes over or under the image. (That's the purpose of the Text Wrap commands described earlier in this chapter.)

Second, it's important to understand that you can paste a graphic in either of two ways:

- As an **inline** graphic, one that sits right in the text. If you delete or insert text in preceding sentences, the graphic moves backward or forward as though it's just another typed character.

- As a **page** graphic, one that's married to a particular spot on the *page*. If you add or delete text, nothing happens to the graphic; it remains where you inserted or pasted it.

Note: Page graphics don't appear in Normal view, Outline view, or Master Document view. To see them, you must switch into Page Layout view, Online Layout view, or the print preview.

The distinction between inline and page graphics has been a source of confusion since Word 1. And Microsoft continues to fiddle with the design of the controls that let you specify which is which.

In Word 2004, the scheme is simple, as long as you understand the technical difference between the two kinds of graphics that Word handles.

- **Drawing objects** always begin life as *page graphics,* floating on the page with no relationship to your text. (Drawing objects are graphics that *you make yourself,* right in Word, using the tools on the Drawing toolbar. They include AutoShapes, text boxes, arrows, rectangles, freehand lines, and so on.)

- **Pictures** always begin life as *inline graphics,* embedded right in a line of text. (Pictures are images you import from other sources; they include Word's own Clip Art gallery, scans and other digital photos, Photoshop files, and the like.)

Tip: See Chapter 20 for more detail on the distinction Word makes between drawing objects and pictures.

Converting Inline Graphics into Page Graphics

Just because drawings start out floating on the page and pictures start out hooked into your text doesn't mean they have to stay that way. It's easy enough to convert an inline graphic into a page graphic or vice versa. Here's how:

1. **Double-click the graphic.**

   In order to double-click a *drawing,* you obviously need to *see* the drawing, which means you need to be in Page Layout or Online Layout View. You can double-click *pictures,* and thus access all formatting tools, in any view except Outline or Master Document.

   In any case, the appropriate Format dialog box appears.

2. **Click the Layout tab.**

   The dialog box shown in Figure 4-12 appears.

3. **To convert a page graphic to an inline graphic, click "In line with text"; to convert an inline graphic to a page graphic, click any of the remaining Text Wrap icons. Click OK.**

   Word automatically switches views, if necessary, so that it can display the graphic in its new environment. Thus, your former inline graphic is now floating on the page in Page Layout view, or your former page graphic is now just another typed character in Normal view.

Tip: You can also select the picture, and then click the Wrapping title bar in the Formatting Palette. Click the Style menu button, and then select "In line with text."

Charts and Spreadsheets

Word's Insert→Object command lets you embed a variety of data—charts, equations, graphics, and other Office documents—from other Office programs right into a Word document.

You'll find a complete description of this feature, which technically is called Object Linking and Embedding technology (abbreviated OLE and pronounced "oh-LAY"—pass the tacos, please), in Chapter 20.

Tables

How do you use Word to create a résumé, agenda, program booklet, list, multiple choice test, Web page, or other document where numbers, words, and phrases must be aligned across the page? In the bad old days, people did it by pressing the Tab key to line up columns. As Figure 4-14 illustrates, this method is a recipe for disaster. (Unfortunately, thousands of people *still* use this method—or, worse, they still try to line up columns by continuously pressing the Space bar.)

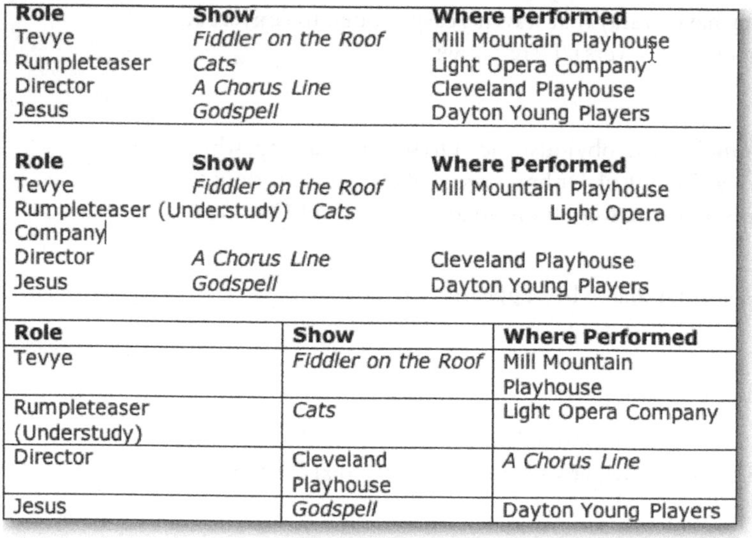

Role	Show	Where Performed
Tevye	*Fiddler on the Roof*	Mill Mountain Playhouse
Rumpleteaser	*Cats*	Light Opera Company
Director	*A Chorus Line*	Cleveland Playhouse
Jesus	*Godspell*	Dayton Young Players

Role	Show	Where Performed
Tevye	*Fiddler on the Roof*	Mill Mountain Playhouse
Rumpleteaser (Understudy)	*Cats*	Light Opera Company
Director	*A Chorus Line*	Cleveland Playhouse
Jesus	*Godspell*	Dayton Young Players

Role	Show	Where Performed
Tevye	*Fiddler on the Roof*	Mill Mountain Playhouse
Rumpleteaser (Understudy)	*Cats*	Light Opera Company
Director	Cleveland Playhouse	*A Chorus Line*
Jesus	*Godspell*	Dayton Young Players

Figure 4-14:
Top: If you use tabs to set up a table, things may look good at first—as long as every line fits within its space and you never plan to insert any additional text.

Middle: Here's what's wrong with the tab approach: When you insert the word Understudy into one of the columns, it pushes too far to the right, causing an ugly ripple effect.

Bottom: If you use a table, you never have this kind of problem. Just type as much text as you like into a "cell," and that row of the table will simply expand to contain it.

Using Word's *table* feature is light-years easier and more flexible. As illustrated in Figure 4-14, each row of a table expands infinitely to contain whatever you put into it, while everything else on its row remains aligned. Tables also offer a few simple spreadsheet features.

Creating Tables

There are two ways to insert a table: You can let Word build the table to your specifications, or you can draw it more or less freehand.

Inserting a table

The quickest way to insert a table is to use the Insert Table pop-up button on the Standard toolbar (see Figure 4-15).

If the toolbar isn't visible, choose Table→Insert→Table. The Insert Table dialog box opens, also shown in Figure 4-15.

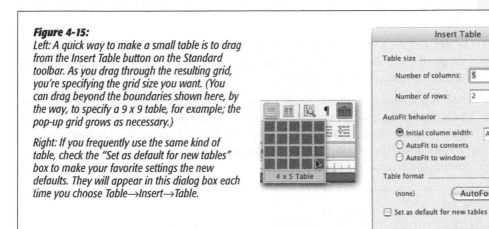

Figure 4-15:
Left: A quick way to make a small table is to drag from the Insert Table button on the Standard toolbar. As you drag through the resulting grid, you're specifying the grid size you want. (You can drag beyond the boundaries shown here, by the way, to specify a 9 x 9 table, for example; the pop-up grid grows as necessary.)

Right: If you frequently use the same kind of table, check the "Set as default for new tables" box to make your favorite settings the new defaults. They will appear in this dialog box each time you choose Table→Insert→Table.

After choosing the number of rows and columns you want (you can always add more later), click an AutoFit radio button to instruct Word how to size the columns across your table. If you know how wide in inches you'd like each column to be, click "Initial column width" and set a measurement in the size box. "AutoFit to contents"

Figure 4-16:
The light gray markings shown here appear when you click the Show/Hide ¶ button on the Standard toolbar or Formatting Palette. To select an entire column.

Fish¤	Flavor¤	Lbs./Year¤	Region¤	⌐
Crabby Patty¤	Fish¤	1,000¤	Bikini·Bottom¤	⌐
Fried Fish¤	Greasy¤	785.93¤	Skillet¤	⌐
Mackerel¤	Yucky¤	34.9¤	Armpit·of·the·Sea¤	⌐
Lobster¤	Mmm-good¤	7769.03¤	Dark·holes·under·rocks¤	⌐
¶				

creates skinny columns that expand as you type into them, and "AutoFit to window" (the easiest way to go if you're not sure) spaces the selected number of columns evenly across the page. You may also select the table (or a part of it), right click it, and choose "Distribute Columns Evenly" from the shortcut menu. The table appears in your document at the insertion point when you click OK. Figure 4-16 depicts a small 5 x 4 table.

Drawing a table

Word's Draw Table tool gives you free rein to form the table of your dreams—the trick is learning to control it.

To summon this toolbar, click the Tables and Borders button on the Standard toolbar, choose View→Toolbar→Tables and Borders, or choose Table→Draw Table. The Tables and Borders toolbar opens and the cursor turns into a pencil. (Press Esc whenever you want the normal cursor back.)

When you drag the pencil horizontally or vertically, it draws lines; when you drag diagonally, it draws boxes. Using these techniques, you can design even the most eccentric, asymmetrical table on earth.

The tidiest way to begin drawing a table is to drag diagonally to create the outer boundary (Figure 4-17, top), then drag horizontal and vertical lines to create the rows and columns. Drawing your own table is the best option when you want a variety of widths in your rows and columns, as shown in Figure 4-17, rather than evenly spaced ones.

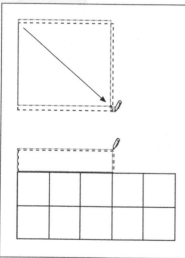

Figure 4-17:
Top: Drag diagonally to create the outer border of your table.

Bottom: The Draw Table tool lets you create rows and columns of any size and shape just by drawing them, but to be honest you can get similar effects, with much less drama, by using the Insert→Table command, as described on page 161.

To remove a cell or line you've just drawn, hold down the Shift key (or click the eraser tool on the Tables and Borders toolbar) and drag it across a line. The line promptly disappears. Be aware, however, if you erase the line between two cells, they merge.

When you're finished with your table's framework, you can dismiss the Tables and Borders toolbar. On the other hand, if you leave it open, you'll have buttons for sorting and formatting your table, or drawing more tables, ready at hand. The insertion point is now blinking in your new table, all set to begin typing.

If you really make a mess of things, press ⌘-Z to undo what you've done, one step at a time. Alternatively, vaporize the entire table by clicking inside it and choosing Table→Delete→Table.

Typing into tables

To type into a table cell, click in that cell. You can use the up or down arrow keys to change rows; press Tab and Shift-Tab to jump forward or backward through the cells. (There's not much call for tabs within cells—after all, you've *already* aligned the text the way you like it. But if you need a tab character, press Option-Tab.)

Note: Pressing Return or Enter *doesn't* take you to the next cell; it puts a line break in the *current* cell instead. Get in the habit of pressing Tab to move on to the next cell.

You can also navigate like this:

To move to:	Press these keys:
First cell in the row	Control-Home
Last cell in the row	Control-End
Top cell in the column	Control-Page Up
Bottom cell in the column	Control-Page Down
Highlight whole table	Option-Clear
Next cell	Tab
Previous cell	Shift-Tab

As you type, text wraps within the cell, forcing the row to grow taller as necessary. To widen the cell as you type, choose Table→AutoFit→AutoFit to Contents. (Even then, the cell will widen only until the table reaches the edge of the page—then the text will start to wrap down.)

Of course, this automatic wrapping is the principal charm of tables. But if you find yourself wishing Word would *not* wrap text in this way, select the cells in which you want wrapping turned off, and then choose Table→Table Properties→Cell tab. Click Options and uncheck the Wrap Text box. You can still enter as much text in a cell as you like, but the cell won't expand downward to show it—it'll just disappear beyond the cell boundary.

Selecting cells

To cut, copy, or drag material from cells in a table, you must first select it, as with any other Word text. Because it's a table, however, you have the following options:

- Drag the mouse—down, across, or diagonally over the cells you'd like to select.

- Click at the top of a column—the cursor changes into a downward-pointing arrow—to select an entire column. Likewise, click at the left of a row—the cursor changes into a right-slanting arrow—to select an entire row.

- Click the thin, invisible *selection bar* at the left edge of a cell to highlight that cell. (Double-click the selection bar to highlight a whole row.)

- Click one cell, row, or column, and then Shift-click another to extend the selection by additional cells, rows, or columns.

- Option-click anywhere in a column to select the entire column.

- Triple-click the cursor at the beginning of any row to select the entire table. In Page Layout or Online Layout view, you can also click the table move handle (at the upper left) to select the entire table.

- Use the Shift key in conjunction with any of the navigation keystrokes described above.

Sizing rows and columns

You can make a row taller or shorter, or a column wider or narrower, much the way you adjust Word's text boxes or margins. Point to any line or boundary of a table without clicking, then drag when the cursor turns into a double-sided arrow.

You can also rely on Word's own automatic table features to help you design the table. They include:

- **Balanced columns.** If a symmetrical, balanced look is what you crave, Word can automatically arrange the rows or columns across your table so that there's equal space between them. First select the rows and columns that you want to balance, then choose Table→AutoFit→Distribute Rows Evenly or Distribute Columns Evenly. (Corresponding buttons on the Tables and Borders toolbar and Formatting Palette can do all this with a single click; you can even right-click and choose this option from the shortcut menu.)

- **Automatic sizing.** Often, you want the columns to stretch and shrink depending on what you type into them. Or, you just don't know in advance what size you want or need the columns to be. In such cases, choose Table→AutoFit→AutoFit to Contents. As you work, the columns will stretch to just the width necessary to accommodate the contents. For maximum room, Table→AutoFit→AutoFit to Window stretches your columns—no matter how many of them there are—to fill the page from margin to margin.

  At any time, you can resize the table using the mouse; doing so overrides and cancels the previous AutoFit setting. When you have the column widths right where you want them, choose AutoFit→Fixed Column Width. The same menu choices are available on the Tables and Borders toolbar (click the little arrow next to the Insert Table button) as well as the bottom of the Formatting Palette. Or simply right-click and choose this option from the shortcut menu.

- **Numeric precision.** To set row and column sizes using exact measurements, select the rows or columns in question and then choose Table→Table Properties. The resulting dialog box (see Figure 4-18) contains size boxes where you can enter exact measurements.

  For columns, you can also specify a percentage of the table width instead of a measurement in inches. For rows, you have the option of setting an exact measurement, or an "At least" measurement. When "At least" is chosen, the cells in that row will stretch downward to wrap text as you type—even if you've turned off "Wrap Text" on the Cell tab.

- **The whole table.** To resize the table as a whole, drag the lower-right corner. The rows and columns remain evenly spaced, or in whatever proportions you have chosen.

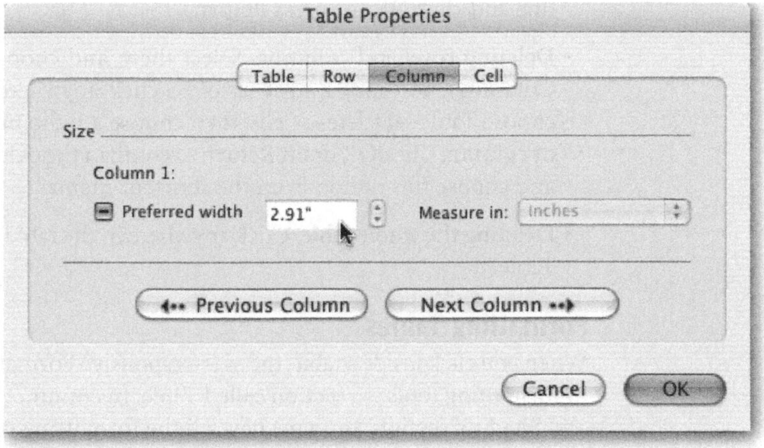

Figure 4-18:
When using the Table Properties dialog box, you can select a group of rows and columns and size them all at once, or you can use the Previous and Next buttons to work on each row or column one at a time.

Adding rows and columns

If you run out of room and need more rows at the *bottom* of your table, it's easy to add more: Click the lower-right cell and press Tab. A new row appears, identical to the one above, ready for your typing.

To add a new row or column *anywhere* in your table, click in the table and then use the Table→Insert submenu. Choose one of the options from the menu that appears: "Insert Columns to the Left," for example. (These commands are also available in the Insert Table pop-up button on the Tables and Borders toolbar and the Formatting Palette.)

Adding multiple rows or columns at either end of your table, or anywhere within it, is a two-step process. First, highlight the *same number* of rows or columns as the ones you want to insert; to add two rows, select two existing rows.

Next, choose Table→Insert, and one of the submenu options (Insert→Rows Below, for example). Word instantly creates the requested number of new, empty rows or columns.

Inserting individual cells works much the same way. Insert one cell at a time by choosing Table→Insert→Cells, or by using the Insert Table menu on the Tables and Borders toolbar. To insert multiple cells, select the equivalent number of *existing* cells at the desired location in your table before choosing from the menu.

Of course, you may find it more fun simply to click the Draw Table tool on the Tables and Borders toolbar and *draw* the extra columns and rows onto your table.

Deleting table parts

It's easy to dismantle a table in various ways:

- **Deleting cells.** Select one or more cells and choose Table→Delete→Cells. Word asks if you want to move the remaining cells up or leftward to fill the void; choose one and click OK (or press Return).

- **Deleting rows and columns.** Select them and choose Table→Delete→Rows (or Columns). You may find it faster to click anywhere in the row or column and choose Table→Delete→Cells, then choose a radio button to delete the *entire* row or column. Click OK or hit Return to confirm the deletion. You can also right-click and choose this option from the shortcut menu.

- **Deleting the whole table.** Click anywhere in the table and choose Table→Delete→ Table.

Formatting Tables

When you click inside a table, the ever-responsive Formatting Palette sprouts a new set of formatting tools—a section called Table. In conjunction with the existing Borders and Shading section, you now have all the formatting controls you need.

To use them, begin by highlighting the cells, rows, or columns that you want to work on. Now you're all set to format any of these table elements:

- **Table border or gridlines.** The Borders tools let you choose a line style (solid, dashed, and so on), color, and weight (thickness in points). Clicking the Type button triggers a menu where you can choose which sides of the table you want borders to appear on. For instance, you may want only vertical lines inside the table and no outside border. Or you may want a heavier top border on the top row of cells only. (The same border formatting tools appear on the top row of the Tables and Borders toolbar.)

FREQUENTLY ASKED QUESTION

The Thin Gray Lines

I like the concept of a table, but I don't want thick black lines in my résumé (or Web page). How do I get rid of them?

You're right: Unless you intervene, these lines will actually print out. One of the quickest ways to delete the borders and gridlines is to click inside the table and then choose Format→Borders and Shading. The resulting dialog box, click None, then click OK.

Even then, however, you may still see thin gray lines. These don't print; they're just on the screen to help you understand the "tableness" of your table. You can hide even these lines, if you like, by choosing Table→Gridlines so that the checkmark disappears.

At this point, you might want to consider clicking the Show/Hide (¶) icon on the Standard toolbar. The end-of-row and end-of-cell marks become visible, defining the bounds of your table.

Tip: You can also eliminate certain table lines entirely. Just click the eraser tool on the top row of the Tables and Borders toolbar, and drag along each line you want to disappear from the table. Doing so *merges* the table cells (page 170).

- **Background shading in cells.** Shading in a table is similar to a *fill* (see page 129), except that you don't use the Fill palette; you use the Shading palette in the Formatting Palette (or Tables and Borders toolbar). You can choose from 40 colors and 24 shades of gray, or choose More Colors to use Word's color pickers (see page 689).

Autoformatting tables

With creative combinations of borders, lines, and shading, you can make a table look right for anything from Citibank annual reports to *Sesame Street*. When you're in a hurry, though, choose a Table AutoFormat for instant good looks.

Click anywhere in your table and choose Table→Table AutoFormat. There's a long list of potential formats in the list box of the Table AutoFormat dialog box. Simply click on each for a preview. If you want to use *some* of the features in the format but not others (font, color, and so on), then just turn on the boxes for the ones you wish to use.

Tip: Turning on AutoFit is a good idea, since it ensures that the new format will exactly fit the existing information in your table, instead of vice versa.

Many of the formats have a different typeface or shading applied to the top (heading) row, first column, last column, and so on. The checkboxes in the "Apply special formats to" section control whether you accept those features with the rest of the format. For example, if you're not using the last row of your table for totals, don't turn on the "Last row" box.

Table headings

For the purposes of Autoformatting, Word considers the first row of a table to be a heading. But what if your table is longer than a page? Wouldn't it be nice if Word could *repeat* the column titles at the top of each page? Well, it can, thanks to the Heading Rows Repeat feature.

Select the top row of your table (and any additional rows you want to repeat). Then choose Table→Heading Rows Repeat; that's all there is to it. When your table flows onto a new page (page breaks you insert yourself don't count), the heading will appear at the top of each new page of your table.

Cell margins and spacing

To enhance the look of your text in a table, adjust the gap between the characters and the borderlines. You can also put a little space around the outside of each cell—an especially attractive effect on Web pages (see Chapter 8).

Just select one or more cells and choose Table→Table Properties→Cell tab. Click Options, and set measurements in the size boxes for the distance between the text and the top, bottom, left, and right edges of the cell. The "Same as the whole table" box changes the margins of the selected cell to match the default cell margins for the table. To set the default margins for all cells in the table at once, choose Table→ Table Properties→Table tab; click Options and enter measurements in the "Default cell margins" boxes.

To add more spacing around the *outside* of cells, click anywhere in the table and choose Table→Table Properties→Table tab. Click the Options button and turn on "Allow spacing between cells"; enter a setting in the size box. When you click OK, that amount of white space will surround each cell, simulating the effect of thicker cell walls. Usually .1" or less looks good. More space than that creates a waffle-like effect, as illustrated in Figure 4-19.

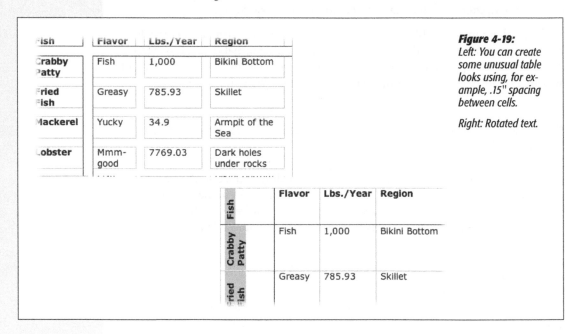

Figure 4-19:
Left: You can create some unusual table looks using, for example, .15" spacing between cells.

Right: Rotated text.

Text formatting within cells

Like text anywhere else in Word, you can change the direction and alignment of selected text in a table using the Format→Text Direction command—a terrific effect for row or column labels (Figure 4-19, right). In the resulting dialog box, choose the text orientation—horizontal, vertical, or bottom-to-top—and click OK.

You can also make the text in selected cells hug the left or right side of its cell, center it in the middle, or make it stick to the "floor" or "ceiling" of a cell. After selecting the cells, click the arrow button next to the alignment button on the Tables and Borders toolbar and choose the alignment pattern you're seeking. Align Top Left, for example, aligns text to the top and left margins of the cell, so that the text starts in the upper-left corner.

Table layout on the page

When you created your table, you probably dragged it where you wanted it, or built it starting from the insertion point. To position it exactly where it looks best on the page and apply advanced features like text wrapping, use the tools in the Table→Table Properties→Table tab, shown in Figure 4-20.

- **Size.** Use this box to set a width for the entire table. (It says "Preferred width" because it may change if you use the AutoFit feature, as described on page 161.)

- **Alignment.** Choose left, centered, or right alignment. "Indent from left" tells Word where to start aligning, measured from the edge of the page. (If your table already spans the page, margin to margin, you won't see any difference.)

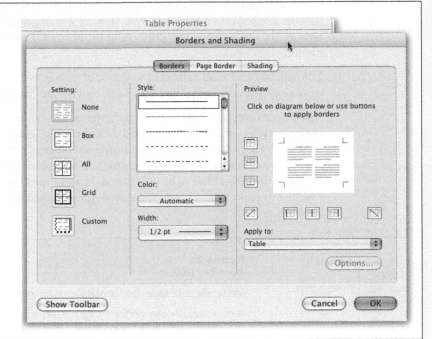

Figure 4-20:
The Table Properties Clicking the Borders and Shading button in the Table Properties dialog box opens a box where you can choose lines and fills for the table, as well as page borders.

- **Text Wrapping.** For large tables, you'll usually choose None. If you choose Around, the Positioning button becomes activated; clicking it opens a dialog box where you can use advanced layout features like those described on page 157.

Nested tables

A *nested table* is a table-within-a-table, or, more specifically, a table within a *cell* of another table. This feature is especially valuable when you're using Word as a Web-design tool. For example, you can create a table with four large cells to divide your Web page into quarters, and put a smaller table in each one.

To create a nested table, click in the cell where you want the table to start, then click the Insert Table button on the Tables and Borders toolbar. Choose the number of rows and columns for your nested table. Now you can click in one of the nested cells and start typing. (Because the nested table must remain within one cell, either resize the cell to hold the nested table, or choose Table→AutoFit→AutoFit to Contents to allow the holding cell to expand.)

Merging and splitting cells

Merging and splitting are nothing more than ways of subtracting or adding columns en masse. Merging cells (or rows or columns) turns two into one, and joins their contents together. Splitting cells (or rows or columns) divides them, forcing their contents into the cell above or to the left of the split.

Start by highlighting the cells, rows, or columns you want to merge. Then choose Table→Merge Cells, or click the Merge Cells button on the Tables and Borders toolbar; the selected cells instantly merge. Another way to proceed: Use the eraser tool to remove the line dividing two cells, columns, or rows. This lets you see directly how merging cells works.

The quickest and most satisfying way to split cells is to draw new lines right smack across existing cells, using the Draw Table tool on the Tables and Borders toolbar.

If you need computer-aided precision, however, you can split cells, rows, or columns perfectly evenly by selecting them and then choosing Table→Split Cells (or click the Split Cells button on the Tables and Borders toolbar). In the Split Cells dialog box, choose the number of rows and columns you want *each* cell to be divided into. For example, the cells at the right in Figure 4-21 were split into two columns and one row; the one row that was selected stayed one row, and the two columns became a total of four.

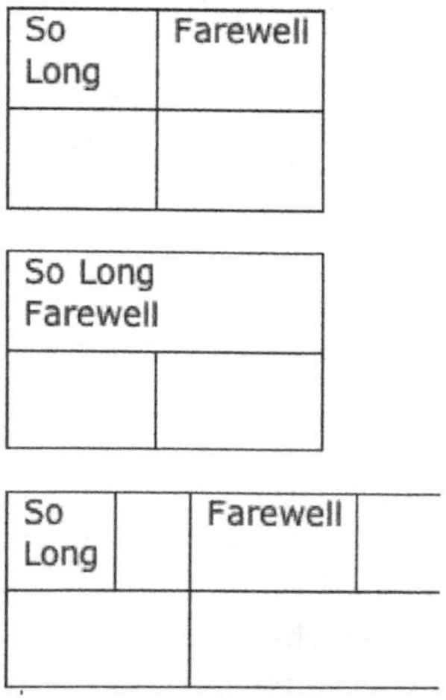

Figure 4-21:
Top: A 2 x 2 table.

Middle: The same table after merging the top two cells.

Bottom: The table after splitting the top two cells in two. If the "Merge cells before split" box had been turned on in the Split Cells dialog box, Farewell would immediately follow So Long in the upper-right cell.

Tip: You can also split a table, creating a blank line between its top and bottom portions—a great trick when you need to insert some regular text into the middle of it. Just click where you want the split and then choose Table→Split Table.

Converting text to a table

Sometimes you want to create a table from information that's already in Word, such as a table that a novice Word person (perhaps even a younger you) created by trying to line up text with the Tab key. At other times, you've got a table and want to extract its information *without* maintaining its tableness (before importing into a page-layout program, for example, because page-layout programs don't understand Word tables). Word is happy to be your obedient servant.

The key to turning highlighted text into a table is the Table→Convert→Convert Text to Table command. Presumably, the text is a list, a number of words separated by tabs, or some other vaguely table-like blob of text. In the Convert Text to Table dialog box, start with the "Separate text at" settings. Choose the most logical place to divide your selected text into cells. If that's not a paragraph, comma, or tab, then click Other and press the key that represents your choice—Space bar, Return, period, and so on.

Word automatically suggests the number of columns you'll need to hold all the text, though you can also specify the number of rows and columns you want, too. You also have the chance to use the AutoFit and AutoFormat features now—or you can always save them for later. Click OK to begin the conversion process.

If the table doesn't look quite as you had hoped, examine it and learn how Word interpreted your choices in the Convert Text to Table dialog box. Then press ⌘-Z to undo the conversion and try again with different selections. Or just reformat your table using the tools described in this section.

Converting a table into text

Converting a table to text is easier still. Click the table and choose Table→Convert→ Convert Table to Text.

Your only decision is how to divide the contents of one cell from the next—you don't want them all to run together, of course. You have a choice of paragraph marks (each cell's contents will become a new Word paragraph), tabs, commas, or any other character you enter in the Other box by pressing its key. If you choose tabs, the result is what you've heard described as *tab delimited text*—that is, one tab separating each word or phrase that formerly occupied a cell on a single row, with a Return character at the end of each line.

Formulas in tables

Word isn't Excel, but Microsoft is at least aware that you may want to perform simple math from time to time. Fortunately, a table can carry out many of the most common spreadsheet tasks with the help of functions and operators. You can add up a column of numbers, for example, or have Word average them and display the results.

To add a column of figures, click in the bottom cell of the column (making sure that it's blank, of course) and click the AutoSum (Σ) button in the Tables and Borders toolbar or Formatting Palette (see Figure 4-22, top). Your answer appears immediately against a gray background (which doesn't print). This gray box indicates that you're dealing with an uneditable *field* (see page 253).

Note: This kind of field doesn't update automatically. If your table numbers change, you must repeat the click on the AutoSum button (or click the field and then press F9).

For more complex formulas, click the cell where you want to place the results of your calculations and choose Table→Formula. Word's guess at what formula you're looking for already appears in the Formula window. If that's not right, press Delete, type an equal sign to begin your formula, and build it with the following (see Figure 4-22):

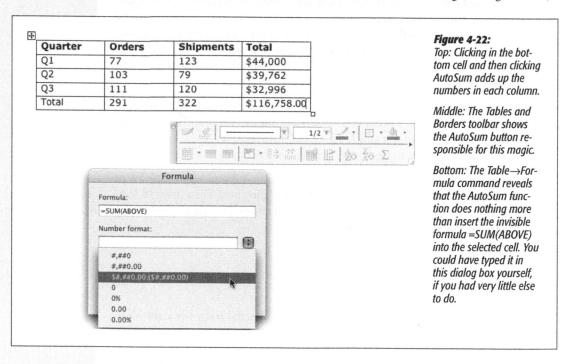

Figure 4-22:
Top: Clicking in the bottom cell and then clicking AutoSum adds up the numbers in each column.

Middle: The Tables and Borders toolbar shows the AutoSum button responsible for this magic.

Bottom: The Table→Formula command reveals that the AutoSum function does nothing more than insert the invisible formula =SUM(ABOVE) into the selected cell. You could have typed it in this dialog box yourself, if you had very little else to do.

- **Cell references.** Cells in Word tables are named the same way as in Excel spreadsheets, except that you can't see the row letters and column numbers. The columns are named A, B, C, and so on, from left to right; the rows are numbered 1, 2, 3, and so on, from top to bottom. The upper-leftmost cell is A1.

  To refer to the entire column above the formula cell, use the expression *(ABOVE)*; to refer to the entire row, use *(LEFT)*. For a *range* of cells (a block of them), use a colon to separate the top-left and lower-right cells of the range, such as A1:B2 to name a four-cell range.

- **Operators.** *Operators* are symbols like + for addition, – for subtraction, * for multiplication, / for division, and > for greater than. To view a complete list, type *Mathematical and relational operators* into the search box of Word's Help system. Using operators in combination, you can set up a table cell to add sales tax (* 1.05) to a subtotal column, for example.

- **Functions.** Choose formulas from the "Paste function" list in the Table→Formula dialog box. These are the same as the Excel formulas described in Chapter 13.

- Click the arrow next to the **Number format** box to tell Word what you want the results to look like—AutoFormatted with a dollar sign, with commas, and so on.

Click OK to place the formula in the current cell. See Chapter 13 for much more on using formulas in Office 2004.

Sorting tables

If your table contains names, dates, or other listed items, you may want to arrange them in numerical or alphabetical order. To do so, click the table and choose Table→ Sort.

In the "Sort by" box, Word helpfully suggests that you start with "Column 1," the first column on the left. All the columns in the current table are listed in a menu; click the arrows to choose one. For instance, to sort chronologically, choose the column that contains your dates. You can sort by Text (alphabetically), Number, or Date; just choose the one that matches your data.

You can choose second and third sort columns as well. For example, after the first column sorts by date, you may want to sort names alphabetically *within* each date. Use the "Then by" boxes to set up these second and third internal sorts.

Click OK to begin the sort. (Note that you can't sort columns—only rows.)

Comments, Change Tracking, and Versions

M ost of the time, you create documents in Word 2004 to send or show to other people. (The exception: Keeping a diary in Word. You know who you are.)

In the real world of which Rob Thomas sings, more and more people find it valuable to be able to mark up and revise such distributed documents. Thanks to the features described in this chapter, you, the original author, can peruse others' edits, and incorporate or delete them. Whether you're working with one partner or an entire team, Word's collaboration features make it easy to track the revisions and versions of the electronically transmitted documents that you create.

Comments

Often when reviewing someone else's document, you'll want to add comments without making them a part of the text itself. You'll have a query for the author, an idea, a suggestion, or a joke—the kind of thing that you'd write in the margin or on a sticky note if you were working on paper. Fortunately, the days of typing boldfaced or bracketed comments directly into the text are long over.

Adding Comments

To add a single comment in Word, select the applicable text and then choose Insert→ Comment (or press Option-⌘-A). Doing so triggers one of two things, depending on your selection in Word→Preferences→Track Changes. If you've turned on "Use balloons to display changes," your comment appears in a balloon at the side of the page. Otherwise, the Reviewing pane opens at the bottom of the document window, as shown in Figure 5-1, with an insertion point at the beginning of a new comment line marked with your name and the current date. Colored brackets (you can set the color at Word→Preferences→Track Changes) bookend the originally selected text. Type your comment, then press F6 to return to the main (upper) pane of the document window (or just click there).

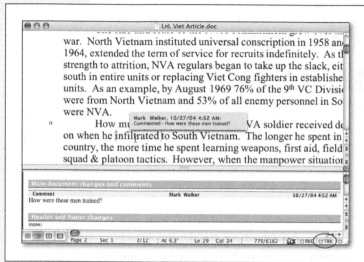

Figure 5-1:
Top: A document showing the brackets that designate comments, as well as the split-window Reviewing pane. When you point to a highlighted phrase, the comment appears at your cursor in a screen tip.

Circled at bottom: the TRK indicator on the window's status bar. Clicking it represents a quick way to turn change tracking on and off. Clear, as shown here, means off; it turns green when you click to turn it on.

If you plan to make more than a few comments, however, you may find it more convenient to open the *Reviewing toolbar,* which lets you add a comment with a single click. After selecting the text you'd like to praise, criticize, or deconstruct, proceed as follows:

1. **Choose View→Toolbars→Reviewing.**

   The Reviewing toolbar opens.

2. **Click the New Comment button on the Reviewing toolbar (see Figure 5-2).**

   Word splits your window, showing the Reviewing pane at the bottom (unless you turned on comment bubbles as described on the previous page).

3. **Type your comment; click back in the upper pane of the document window to return to it.**

   You can also press F6 to toggle between the two panes.

4. **When you're finished adding comments, close the Reviewing pane by clicking its icon on the Reviewing toolbar.**

   If you're typing your comments into a balloon, just click outside the balloon or press Esc to return to the document's main body.

Word 2004 greatly enhances the reviewing toolbar (Figure 5-2), adding some all-new, improved ways to access Word's reviewing features, which include both Comments and Change Tracking, described later in this chapter. The pop-up menu on the left of the toolbar provides the following viewing options:

- **Final Showing Markup.** If you've chosen to use balloons (as shown in Figure 5-2), and you're in Page Layout view, the text deleted by your reviewer/editor appears in balloons, and inserted text and formatting changes show up in the text itself. If not, the text and changes appear as indicated in Word→Preferences→Track Changes. Use this to quickly analyze what the editor has done to your precious prose.

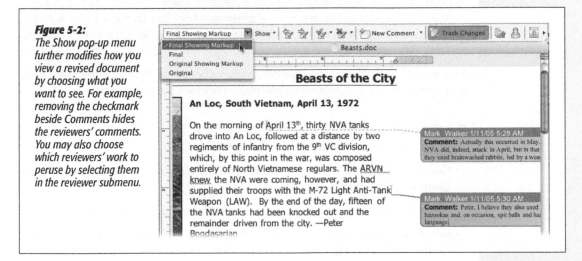

Figure 5-2:
The Show pop-up menu further modifies how you view a revised document by choosing what you want to see. For example, removing the checkmark beside Comments hides the reviewers' comments. You may also choose which reviewers' work to peruse by selecting them in the reviewer submenu.

- **Final.** This reveals how your document would look if you accepted all of your editor's changes and comments. Use this when it's just too darn painful to review them.

- **Original Showing Markup.** This is like Final Showing Markup turned inside out and viewed with a mirror. If you've chosen to use balloons, and you're in Page Layout view, *deleted* text is shown in the document, and inserted text and formatting changes are pumped into the balloons. If not, the text and changes appear as indicated in Word→Preferences→Track Changes. This option is best for reviewing both the new and original text at the same time.

- **Original.** This displays your virginal document, before your editor or reviewer improved or destroyed it (depending on your point of view). Use this to see how the document would look if you rejected all changes.

Reviewing Comments

When you open a document with comments, the Reviewing pane doesn't automatically open. Instead, what you see depends on your document view. In the Normal, Outline, and Notebook views, you'll see brackets surrounding sections of text that have comments. Hovering your cursor over the brackets reveals the comment. In Page Layout view, you'll see the brackets connected to comment balloons in the document's margin, indicating the comments.

If you like, you can open (or close) the Reviewing pane, where all the document's comments are listed sequentially. To do that, click the Reviewing pane button on the Reviewing toolbar, shown in Figure 5-2, or, if time is not at a premium, click the Show pop-up menu on the Reviewing toolbar and choose Reviewing pane.

Note: Some folks don't like the Reviewing pane eating half their viewing space. If you're one of them, you may prefer to add comments in attractive text bubbles, which are new in this iteration of Office, instead of the Reviewing pane. To make it so, select Word→Preferences and click Track Changes at the left. At the bottom of the Track Changes panel, turn on "Use balloons to display changes." You can then see the balloons, but only in Page Layout view.

If you've used Word for Windows, you may find these balloons look familiar. If you're a confirmed Mac-head, you may prefer the pop-up comment boxes from previous Word versions. You're not alone.

Deleting comments

To delete a comment do one of the following:

- Control-click (or right-click) within the comment's bracketing and choose Delete Comment from the shortcut menu.

- Click the Reviewing toolbar's Reject Change/Delete Comment button.

- Select the comment or the comment's title bar in the Reviewing Pane, and then Control-click and select Delete from the shortcut menu.

- Click the "X" button in the comment's balloon.

Navigating Comments

The main document pane and the Reviewing pane have independent vertical scroll bars. You can move around in each one using any of Word's usual navigation tools (see page 69). You can also use the Previous Comment and Next Comment buttons on the Reviewing toolbar (Figure 5-2), or the Navigation Buttons described on page 69, to hop from one comment in the document to the next. (The main document window scrolls automatically to keep up.)

If the Reviewing pane isn't visible, choose View→Toolbars→Reviewing, or Control-click (or right-click) the group divider on any toolbar and select Reviewing. Now you can edit comments—yours or anyone else's—or click Delete Comment (on the Reviewing toolbar) to do away with a comment completely.

Change Tracking

When it's time to mark up a document for revision, many people who otherwise use their Mac for everything still turn to paper, pencil, and highlighter. After all, marking up a printout lets you see both the original and your handwritten edits at a glance. And when you collaborate with others on a paper or project, you can use different colored ink to differentiate the various editors.

The problem with the paper method is that you eventually have to retype the document, incorporating all the handwritten comments, into Word.

To avoid all that hassle, you can simply edit onscreen in Word. Word has tools that highlight text in a multitude of colors and see at a glance who made what changes. Even better than paper, Word can automate the process of comparing and merging edited documents. On the downside, it's tough to make origami from your monitor.

Getting Ready for Change Tracking

In order for Word's change-tracking tools to work properly, you must tell Word how you want your name to appear (when it's used to "sign" comments and changes) and how to display the changes.

Identify yourself

Especially if you're working with others, Word needs to know who you are so that your name can be attached to your version and your changes. To ensure that Word knows your inner authorness, choose Word→Preferences→User Information panel. If your name isn't already there, fill in the panel. Word will use the name or initials in the author box to identify and label any changes and comments you add to the document. Click OK when you're finished.

Note: The User Information tab and your own address book "card" in Entourage are linked; that is, when you change User Information, you also change your Entourage "this is me" card, and vice versa. (You tell Entourage which set of contact information is yours by opening the card with your info and choosing Contact→This Is Me.)

Turning on change tracking

Suppose you receive a document from a colleague who's asked you to help clean up the prose. If you just dive right in, editing away, she'll have no way of spotting the changes you made. When you intend to review a document, whether it's your own draft or a Word document given to you by someone else, you must ask Word to track your changes *before* making them. Here are three ways, presented in order of speed:

• By far the easiest way to activate change tracking is to click the Track Change button on the Reviewing toolbar. If the Reviewing toolbar isn't visible you need either (a) another cup of coffee or (b) to turn it on by selecting View→Toolbars→ Reviewing.

• Turn on the tiny TRK button on the status bar at the bottom edge of your document window (Figure 5-1). (The button turns green when you click it.)

If you prefer the long way, however, you can go the dialog box route and gain some additional options, as described next.

1. **Choose Tools→Track Changes→Highlight Changes.**

   The Highlight Changes dialog box opens, as shown in Figure 5-3.

2. **Turn on "Track changes while editing."**

   You also have the option to turn "Highlight changes on screen" on or off. If it's *off*, you won't see any special markings as you edit the document; the usual coloring and other annotation formatting won't appear. You'll feel as though you're editing a Word file *without* change tracking turned on. (The only difference: Every now and then, Word will abruptly refuse to let you backspace any farther than you have. That's because your insertion point has collided with a deleted word—which you can't see because it's currently invisible.)

   Behind the scenes, though, Word will indeed record every change you make. At any time, you or a collaborator can choose Tools→Track Changes→Highlight Changes and turn "Highlight changes on screen" *on* again to make them show up.

   Now proceed as described in "Making Changes," below.

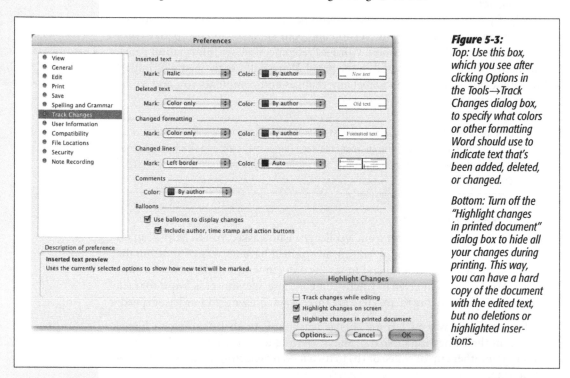

Figure 5-3:
Top: Use this box, which you see after clicking Options in the Tools→Track Changes dialog box, to specify what colors or other formatting Word should use to indicate text that's been added, deleted, or changed.

Bottom: Turn off the "Highlight changes in printed document" dialog box to hide all your changes during printing. This way, you can have a hard copy of the document with the edited text, but no deletions or highlighted insertions.

Making Changes

After turning on change tracking, edit the Word document as usual. Use any of the tools described in Chapter 2, including inserting text, formatting it, and deleting large blocks of text or even entire pages. Word keeps track of it all, as shown in Figure 5-5.

Changing tracking options

The Track Changes dialog box in Figure 5-3 and the sample document in Figure 5-4 show Word's factory settings for onscreen changes, which are as follows:

- Word places a thin vertical line in the margin where *any* kind of change has been made.

- Text you've inserted is italicized and color-coded by author. Text typed by the first person to review the document appears in red, the second author in blue, the third in pink, and so on, for up to eight authors. Then Word starts over again with red.

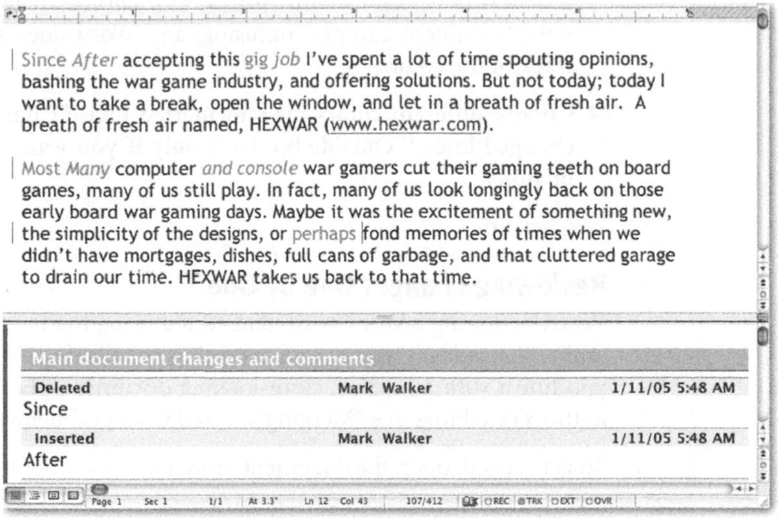

Figure 5-4:
If your work comes back heavily marked up by your editors, don't feel too depressed. Keep in mind two things: (a) The changes are probably for the better, and (b) editors are just that way, it's nothing personal. You can see the annotations both in the text itself and in the Reviewing Pane. (You can open this pane by clicking the pane-like button at the far right of the Reviewing toolbar.)

Since *After* accepting this gig *job* I've spent a lot of time spouting opinions, bashing the war game industry, and offering solutions. But not today; today I want to take a break, open the window, and let in a breath of fresh air. A breath of fresh air named, HEXWAR (www.hexwar.com).

Most *Many* computer *and console* war gamers cut their gaming teeth on board games, many of us still play. In fact, many of us look longingly back on those early board war gaming days. Maybe it was the excitement of something new, the simplicity of the designs, or perhaps fond memories of times when we didn't have mortgages, dishes, full cans of garbage, and that cluttered garage to drain our time. HEXWAR takes us back to that time.

Main document changes and comments		
Deleted Since	Mark Walker	1/11/05 5:48 AM
Inserted After	Mark Walker	1/11/05 5:48 AM

Page 1   Sec 1   1/1   At 3.3"   Ln 12   Col 43   107/412   REC TRK EXT OVR

- Deleted text is color-coded by author.

- Formatting changes (to boldface or italic, for instance) don't leave any visual trace (bolding and italicizing aside) except for the thin margin line (unless you're using Page Layout view, where text balloons also describe the change). You can change this setting, however, as described next.

Note: Word 2004 incorporates some semi-jarring changes for those of you that have grown comfortable with Word X's way of doing things. For example, the standard settings no longer indicate deleted text with the telltale strikethrough. Now, if your reviewer deletes text, in Normal view it appears in a different color, while in Page Layout view, it pops up in a balloon in the margin. Yet fear not, if these changes disturb you, you can reset them to Word X style—or any way you like—in the Word→Preferences→Track Changes panel.

Here is how to work with these options:

1. Choose Tools→Track Changes→Highlight Changes. Click Options.

The Track Changes dialog box opens (see Figure 5-3).

2. **For each kind of change, use the pop-up menu to indicate a highlighting style.**

   For instance, you could choose "strikethrough" for "Deleted text" so that it looks like it's been crossed out. Choose underlining for "Inserted text" so you won't confuse it with normal italicized text. The pop-up menus offer different marks for each context.

3. **If you don't want to use Word's "By author" color system, as described above, choose different colors for "Inserted text" and "Deleted text."**

   Unless everyone in your work group can agree on a different color scheme, it's probably best to stick with Word's color choices. Having different editors in the same document can get confusing, and Word does an efficient job of keeping track of the colors.

4. **Choose different colors for reformatted text ("Changed formatting") and the changed lines ("Outside border") only if you want to make these items more obvious.**

5. **Click OK.**

Reviewing Changes One by One

When reviewing a Word document edited using the tracking feature, it's easy to examine the changes one by one, accepting or rejecting each proposed revision, until you finish with a normal, clean-looking document. (For documents with multiple authors or editors, see "Merging Tracked Changes" below before proceeding.)

To get started, open the document or merged document.

Reviewing changes: light edits

If there's only light editing, the easiest way to approve or reject each change is simply to Control-click the changed text; from the contextual menu, choose Accept Change or Reject Change. When you accept a change, Word removes the color and marking and turns the change into normal text. When you *reject* a change, Word removes the marked or colored text and restores the original.

Reviewing changes: heavier edits

If there are many changes, you may as well pull out the heavy artillery—the Reviewing toolbar. Choose View→Toolbars→Reviewing to display the Reviewing toolbar. The Word 2004 version of the toolbar has everything you need. From here you may choose how to view your reviewer's edits, page through the edits and comments, and attach the document to an instant message or email.

1. **Click at the beginning of the document; click the Next icon on the Reviewing toolbar.**

   Word scrolls to the first change and highlights it.

2. **Click the Accept Change icon (with the checkmark) or the Reject Change icon (with the x) on the Reviewing toolbar.**

   Again, when you accept a change, Word turns the change into normal text. When you reject one, Word restores the original.

   If you change your mind after accepting or rejecting a change, press ⌘-Z to undo it.

3. **Click the Next Change icon and continue the process.**

   If change tracking is turned on, any new editing you do will be highlighted on the screen with your author color. To eliminate this during your last pass, click the Track Changes button on the Reviewing toolbar to turn it off, or turn off the TRK indicator in the Status bar at the bottom of the document. If the Status bar isn't visible, click Word→Preferences→View, and make sure Status Bar (under Window) is turned on.

   After you've reached the end of the document, but missed reviewing some changes along the way, Word asks if you want to return to the beginning.

4. **Click OK.**

Accepting or Rejecting All Changes

If you trust your editors completely, you can accept or reject *all* changes in a document, all at once. You don't even have to look at them first (although you should, unless you're sure your editors are *much* smarter than you are). Word also makes it possible to view the document as a whole, with or without all changes. Choose Tools→Track Changes→Accept or Reject Changes to open the dialog box. You can also accept or reject all changes from the Reviewing toolbar. Just click the arrow next

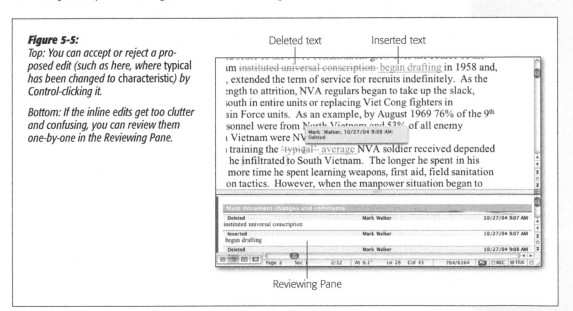

Figure 5-5:
Top: You can accept or reject a proposed edit (such as here, where typical *has been changed to* characteristic*) by Control-clicking it.*

Bottom: If the inline edits get too clutter and confusing, you can review them one-by-one in the Reviewing Pane.

Deleted text   Inserted text

Reviewing Pane

to the Accept Change icon, and choose "Accept All Changes in Document" from the pop-up menu.

1. **Choose a way to view the document.**

   The dialog box now onscreen is small for a reason: It's designed to be moved aside, so that you can survey the document before making the radical move of accepting or rejecting all of the edits that have been made to it.

   To help you with this pursuit, you're offered three radio buttons. They let you see the document with all changes highlighted (as shown in Figure 5-5), as if all changes were accepted ("Changes without highlighting"), or in its original state before any changes were made. These humble-looking radio buttons are one of the most powerful aspects of the change-tracking feature.

2. **To go ahead and make all proposed changes, click Accept All. To return the document to its original condition, click Reject All.**

   Word asks if you're sure before proceeding. Remember, even after accepting all or rejecting all, you can change your mind by clicking Undo.

3. **Click Close.**

Merging Tracked Changes

One of the most common scenarios for using change tracking is to email or otherwise transfer the same original document out to several reviewers, each of whom peppers it with edits and comments. If they all came back on paper, it would be quite a challenge to sort through and incorporate all the good ideas.

In Word, it's easy to merge the edited documents together, one by one. To do so, open the original file—or any one of the edited documents—and proceed as follows. Choose Tools→Merge Documents.

1. **Word opens the Choose a File dialog box, where you'll choose the first file to merge into the currently open document.**

   When you find the file, double-click it.

2. **Word begins the merging process.**

   When it's over, the original document contains both its own tracked changes *and* those merged in from the second document, but will only display one set of formatting changes on the same text (although both are listed in change balloons in the Page Layout view). Word will, however, ask you which to display. The changes from different authors appear in different colors.

3. **If you have more files to incorporate, repeat steps 1 and 2.**

When all the documents are merged, place your insertion point at the beginning of the document and review the changes as described on the preceding pages.

Comparing Documents

The merging process described earlier in this chapter works well if *all* documents have been edited using Word's change-tracking feature. But often enough, you wind up with two drafts of a document, one of which has been edited (by you or somebody else). Word's Compare Documents feature can help you see where edits have been made—a feature that has saved the bacon of more than one lawyer in back-and-forth contract negotiations.

To use it, round up both the edited version and your original or master copy and proceed as follows:

1. **Open the changed copy of the document. Choose Tools→Track Changes→Compare Documents.**

   Word opens the Choose a File dialog box. Here's where you select the *original* document—the one you want to compare the edited version to. The original could be the one that's never been edited, or one that's been edited with change tracking, or even one that's been merged. Just make sure that you've reviewed it and accepted or rejected all tracked changes before you begin the comparing process.

2. **When you locate the original version of the document, double-click it.**

   Word compares the two documents and creates a *new* document based on the *second* document, with tracked changed inserted as if the *first* document were created by editing the second.

If there were already tracked changes in either of the documents, Word ignores them and gives priority to the actual, unmarked text. If either of the documents has untracked changes, Word asks before proceeding with the comparing process. Usually, you'll want to click OK and go ahead. The unmarked changes may be edits you made to the document while you were writing it, before you started the reviewing process.

COMPLIANT USERS' CLINIC

Quicker Document Dispatch

Word 2004 lets—nay, encourages—you to email or Instant Message (IM) your documents right from the Reviewing toolbar. Granted, you could already do things like that—like attaching a document to an email in Entourage or sending a file via your MSM chat window—but the remodeled 2004 Reviewing toolbar makes these moves much easier. To email a document, click the paper-with-envelope-with-arrow icon in the Reviewing toolbar. Doing so pops open an Entourage email with the document already attached (that's *so* cool). Type your message, select a recipient, and click Send.

To send the document via IM, you (and your recipient) must have an MSM Messenger account (available at *www.microsoft.com*). Click the IM icon (a blue Weeble-like person), select the file recipient, and your document is now prepped for sending. Once your intended target accepts the file, it zips across the Internet. No fuss, and much less muss than in Word X. It's all part of the evil empire's desire to keep you in the Office/MSM loop for all your work and play. (Well, maybe not *all* your play.)

Versioning

The File→Versions command performs a kind of temporary Save, by creating a snapshot of your document at a moment in time—without actually creating a new document. All versions of a document are stored in the same file on your hard drive with the same file name; even though it may contain eleven different drafts, you still see only a single icon in the Finder.

Saving versions, in other words, creates listings in the Versions dialog box, not separate document files. Thus, you can save as many versions as you like without losing them or creating a mass of documents on your hard drive.

Caution: All this convenience comes at a price. Documents containing lots of versions are prone to corruption.

Saving a Version

Suppose you open your first draft of a document. You're about to do some heavy editing, but you're not sure you're going to like your own new direction. By saving the current draft as a version, you'll always be able to return to the document the way it used to be.

To save a version of the document you're working in, proceed as follows:

1. **Choose File→Versions.**

   The Versions dialog box opens, as shown in Figure 5-6.

2. **Click Save Now.**

   The Save Version dialog box opens. Type some comments that will help you remember what the version is all about (such as *Halloween V: Romantic comedy approach*), then click OK.

UP TO SPEED

Preparing to Send a Reviewed Document

If someone else will be merging the reviewed documents, there are a few things you can do to make his job easier when you send your edited copy:

Make changes visible. Choose Tools→Track Changes→ Highlight Changes, or click Highlight Changes in the Reviewing toolbar, before you send your document off. That way, the recipient can see immediately that it's been edited.

Change the name. Add your initials to the file's name in the Finder, for example, so that it won't be confused with the original during the merging process.

Send the most recent version. As you edit the document, you can freeze it in time by using Word's versioning feature (described later in this chapter). When you're ready to return your final edits, choose File→Versions and open the version that you want to submit. Choose File→Save As and save it as a separate document under a new file name before you send it off. Using this method, you still have a record of all versions you created, but your recipient only gets the one you intended to send out. (What's more, using the Save As command produces a much smaller file.)

You have just saved a version.

You can now forget all about the Versioning feature. To save, choose File→Save (⌘-S) as usual. When you open a document that has versions, Word always shows you the latest draft.

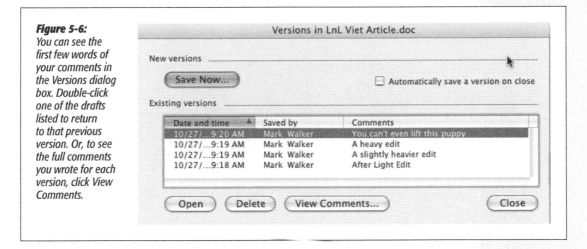

Figure 5-6:
You can see the first few words of your comments in the Versions dialog box. Double-click one of the drafts listed to return to that previous version. Or, to see the full comments you wrote for each version, click View Comments.

Opening a Version

To return to a version, open the document and choose File→Versions. Double-click the name of a version in the list. To help you keep track of what's going on, Word opens the selected draft in a separate window. Both the latest document and your selected earlier version are now visible, with their windows tiled one above the other. (The date and time stamp in the window identifies the earlier version.)

Spinning Off a Version

The beauty of saving lots of versions is that you can open any one of them and save it as a separate document at any time. To do so, open a version as described above. Click the version's window and choose File→Save or Save As (or press F12). A standard Save sheet opens in the version's window, where you can choose a name and location for the new document.

GEM IN THE ROUGH

Automatically Saving a Version

You don't have to remember to save a version every time you cultivate a new draft of your document; Word can do so automatically.

Just choose File→Versions, and then turn on "Automatically save a version on close" in the Versions dialog box (Figure 5-6). Click OK. From now on, Word saves a new version every time you close the file—a logical time to do so, preserving each session's editing efforts as a separate draft. (You don't have the opportunity to name each automatic draft, so Word calls each one "Automatic version." It does, however, date-stamp each one in the Versions dialog box.)

Deleting a Version

If you have too many confusing versions in the Versions dialog box, you can delete some of them. To delete a version, select it and click Delete. Word asks if you're sure (you can't undo this deletion). Continue selecting and deleting as many versions as you wish.

Click OK to exit the Versions dialog box.

Notebooks, Outlining, and Master Documents

Have you ever sat down at your Mac and pounded out a polished white paper, 25 page essay, or bestselling novel in one smooth pass, your words flowing logically from start to finish? Probably not. Human thoughts often fragment, and despite their disjointed nature, these shards of logic frequently represent the foundation for annual reports, term papers, and books. Microsoft understands, and has provided tools for better capturing and organizing those thoughts. Enter Word's Outliner and its spin-offs the Document Map, Master Documents, and the shiny new Notebook Layout view.

Outlining is simply a way of organizing your ideas, and Notebook view is a great tool for capturing those ideas, rearranging them, and even voice-recording your thoughts. As your document grows and reaches completion, the Document Map—which resides in Words 2004's new Navigation Pane—lets you fly through your document, and Master Document lets you and your co-workers create the mother of all documents.

Note: New to Word 2004, Notebook layout is a curious hybrid to be sure. On one hand, it appears that Microsoft wanted to make a utility that works as the human brain does—a way to capture your stray thoughts on "paper." Unfortunately, it lacks the ease of use and advanced features of a full-fledged note-taking and organizational tool, like Circus Ponies' NoteBook or the depth of word processing ease available in other Word views. But hey, it's a step in the right direction.

Notebook Layout View

Notebook Layout view is perhaps the most radically new feature in Word 2004. From its cool spiral edge to its ability to take "dictation," Notebook Layout view is Microsoft's

---

attempt to let your computer work as you do. To that end, they designed something where you can take notes quickly and rearrange them as you wish.

Opening Your Notebook

Choose File→Project Gallery, click the Word Notebook icon, and begin typing. Each new block of text starts out as Note Level 1, as you can see by a quick glance at the Formatting Palette. By hitting Tab, you can indent text under a heading to indicate that it applies to, and should be grouped with, that header, as shown in Figure 6-1. This is great stuff when taking notes in class, at a meeting, or just jotting concepts

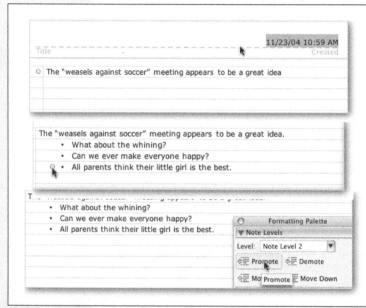

Figure 6-1:
As you type into a freshly created Notebook document, text flows onto the page automatically set to Note Level 1. After you finish the sentence or thought, press Return, and then Tab, to indent the next section of text, shown at center. You can also set the level of text with the Note Levels on the Formatting Palette, shown at bottom right.

UP TO SPEED

Where Did My Text Go?

Notebook Layout is a possessive view, and doesn't take kindly to other intruding views. It likes it best when you begin in Notebook Layout and stay there. When you change from other views to Notebook Layout, several things occur. Right off the bat, as shown here, Word asks if, in essence, you're really sure you want to do this. It opens a box asking if you wish to start a new, Notebook Layout view document, or convert the existing one. It then adds, almost in a whisper, "Some formatting may be lost in the conversion."

You don't say.

Pictures and text boxes will frequently get shoved about by the conversion. Even more important, much, if not all, of the template formatting in your non-Notebook Layout view document will be lost. In other words, all those carefully crafted headers, bullet lists, and captions will morph into plain, everyday text. So, before you convert, make sure it's something that you really want to do. Otherwise, it's best just to start from scratch in Notebook Layout view. That way you know what you are getting.

from your head. Additionally, you can click the little button to the left of each block of text and move it wherever you want on the page.

If you already have a non-Notebook Word document in front of you, select View→ Notebook Layout to open Notebook Layout view. Alternately, you can click the Notebook Layout view Icon (it's on the far left) at the bottom left of your page. Or, for the keyboard- and shortcut-crazed among you, Option-⌘-B also takes you to the Notebook Layout view. However you invoke the view, the first thing you see on your Notebook Layout view journey is the pop-up message shown in Figure 6-2.

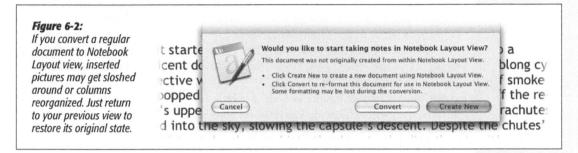

Figure 6-2:
If you convert a regular document to Notebook Layout view, inserted pictures may get sloshed around or columns reorganized. Just return to your previous view to restore its original state.

However you get there, once you arrive in Notebook Layout view, you see a clean new sheet (assuming you're starting with a new document) of lined notebook paper. Kinda makes you want to take a pen to your computer screen, doesn't it? But please, despite the temptation, don't scrawl "Jimmy likes Mary" or "Mr. Robinson is a nerd," on your computer screen. Replacing computer screens gets real expensive, real quick.

Like much of Word 2004, the Notebook Layout view is intuitive. As you type, words dance (or spew—mood depending) onto the page. You'll notice, however, that each paragraph, block of text, or picture is marked with a clear/gray bubble in the left margin. The bubble is similar to the little rectangle you see in Word's Outline view (page 201), but much easier to use. Furthermore, you can take that bubble and drag (it turns blue) your text wherever you like on the page. In fact, there's much more

---

POWER USERS' CLINIC

Pen to Screen

Although you can't take a Sharpie marker to your computer screen (well, actually you can, but it's not recommended), there is a way to write into Notebook Layout view. The view supports Mac OS X's handwriting recognition program, Ink. Thus, if you have a Wacom tablet, you can pick up a stylus and "write" in Notebook view. Ink changes what you write into typed letters. To do so, connect your Wacom tablet to your computer and install the software. Turn on handwriting recognition in the Ink System Preferences panel, and you're ready to write.

You can also draw on your notebook, by clicking on the Scribble icon on the toolbar. Choose the pen thickness and color from the pop-up menu, and commence writing. Unfortunately, Word doesn't convert characters drawn this way into letters. They appear as AutoShapes (see the box on page 680 for the full story).

---

you can do with your text than reposition it, and most of those capabilities reside on a new toolbar aptly named the Notebook Layout Standard toolbar, as shown in Figure 6-3.

The Notebook Layout Toolbar

The Notebook Layout view significantly changes the Standard toolbar into something that's tailored to the view at hand. Everything you need waits for your click on the toolbar or folds neatly into the ever-useful Formatting Palette.

Note: In addition to the transformation of the Standard toolbar, you'll notice that most of Word's other toolbars become completely unavailable when you're in Notebook Layout view. Check the View→Toolbars menu—they're just not there. Apparently, Microsoft wants to get all possible distractions out of your way when you're taking notes. On the other hand, if you're used to using Word's more advanced features like Change Tracking or even Style formatting, you may find Notebook Layout view more of a hindrance than a help.

- **Scribble.** A pen icon represents the Scribble tool. Click here to turn your mouse into a pen with which you can draw on your document. The mouse changes to a four-point crosshair that lets you pinpoint exactly where you're sketching. Press and hold the left mouse button to draw.

  It's convenient for drawing quick graphical marks, such as arrows, or circling important sections of your document, but it's a tad too cumbersome to write

---

POWER USERS' CLINIC

What's that Pen Doing?

The pen actually draws a shape that you can subsequently select and drag to new locations or even resize. On one hand that's great, giving you gobs of flexibility. On the other hand, it's not so great. Since the shape is, in essence, a hand-drawn picture, Word treats it as one. For example, if you circle a word, you'll find that the word disappears because the shape is now in front of it. To place it behind, you must chose Format→AutoShape, click on the Layout tab, and then move the shape "Behind Text." A bit counter-intuitive, no? Of course, if you have

the AutoShape's Fill properties set to "no fill," you won't have these problems. You'll be able to spot the word through your circle.

The shape you've drawn becomes like any Word AutoShape. In essence, it's a drawing object, and you can format it like one. To format the shape, choose Format→AutoShape. The Format dialog box (see page 156) opens, where you can choose how text will flow around the shape, whether it will reside in front of or behind the text, and all the other familiar formatting features.

---

more than a word or two. The pop-up menu beside the Scribble icon presents thickness options for your pen's point, and you can also choose an ink color on the palette that pops beside each pen thickness. The Scribble pop-up menu offers the following options:

Fine Point. Draws a thin line. You can also click on the arrow to the right and choose a color.

Very Fine Point. You guessed it—draws an even thinner line. Again, click on the arrow to the right for your color perusing enjoyment.

Medium Point. The point of choice for those who like fat pens.

- **Eraser.** The Eraser removes AutoShapes drawn with the Scribble tool. It's very simple. Click the Eraser, and then click the object to remove it. Faster than a Red Sox World Series sweep, and twice as easy.

- **Select Objects.** Click the Select Objects icon, and your cursor changes to a hand when it passes over an object, such as an inserted picture. You can then click and drag the object. To be honest, this tool is only marginally (if at all) faster than selecting the object with the mouse pointer and then moving it.

- **Audio Note Toolbar.** Clicking the microphone displays the Audio Notes toolbar. Using this toolbar, you can make your computer take dictation. For more details, see page 197.

- **Quick Search.** As described in Figure 6-3, the Quick Search is a very useful tool that cuts the clicks from thought to located word.

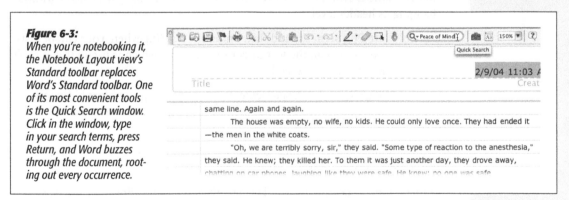

Figure 6-3:
When you're notebooking it, the Notebook Layout view's Standard toolbar replaces Word's Standard toolbar. One of its most convenient tools is the Quick Search window. Click in the window, type in your search terms, press Return, and Word buzzes through the document, rooting out every occurrence.

Organizing Your Notes

Notebook Layout view comes into its own when you are either taking notes on your laptop during a meeting or trying to get your arms around that huge project your boss dropped in your lap. It's not a view you'll often use when composing your entry into the romance novel field. But that's okay; Notebook does what it does pretty darn well, by automatically and clearly applying outline levels to every thought you type.

The cool thing about all this leveling business is the flexibility it provides when you're viewing and organizing your Notebook document. If a heading, any heading, in the document has *subheadings* beneath it, Word tags the heading with a big blue flippy triangle, as shown in Figure 6-4. You can click this triangle to expose or hide the subheadings.

Note: Levels are kind of like golf. The lower the number, the better (more important) the level. Level 1 is the highest level, level 2 is next, and so on.

Setting Text Levels with the Keyboard and Mouse

You can set text levels with various combinations of the Tab key, as described below. You can, of course, highlight text and drag it with the mouse, just like any other text, but you may find it quicker to learn a few shortcuts and never take your hands off the keys as the ideas come gushing out.

- **Tab.** Pressing Tab *demotes* the text one level of importance and tucks it neatly beneath the text above it.

- **Shift-Tab.** Pressing Shift-Tab *promotes* the text one level, moving it back out toward the margin, where items of greater importance reside.

- **Control-Tab.** Indents the first line of text one tab without changing the level.

- **Control-Shift-Up arrow.** Moves the selected paragraph up. Note that this keystroke physically moves the paragraph; it doesn't change its header level.

- **Control-Shift-Down arrow.** Moves the selected paragraph down, again without changing its header level.

- **Control-Shift-Plus sign.** Expands text under the heading where your cursor rests. This maneuver shows all the text under the heading, which is useful if you can't quite remember what you typed.

- **Control-Shift-Minus sign.** Collapses text under a heading, therefore hiding all text but the heading itself. Useful if you want to condense your notes into a smaller space.

- **Control-Shift-A.** Expands *all* text under *all* headings. Great if you want to see *everything* you've written.

- **Control-Shift-<Heading Level>.** Displays the selected heading level. For example, Control-Shift-1 displays all the Level 1 headers.

Setting Text Levels with the Formatting Palette

The easiest way to elevate or reduce the importance of text is with the Note Levels section of the Formatting Palette. To open Note Levels, click the flippy triangle on the Note Levels tab.

To promote (raise the level of) text, click anywhere in the text line, and then click the Promote icon. To demote the text, click in the text line and click the Demote icon. If you need to demote or promote text several levels, it's easier to use the level pop-up menu on the Note Level section. Just click the arrow to the right of the level window and then click on the level you desire. You can also press Tab (to demote) or Shift-Tab (to promote), as described earlier. Keep pressing until you reach the desired level. (Additionally, you can press Tab or Shift-Tab *before* typing a heading.)

The Move Up and Move Down icons don't change a level's level, so to speak, but rather alter the position of the text on the page, one line at a time. If you want to move the text up, select it and click Move Up. You can do the same thing by clicking on the clear/gray bubble to the left of the text and dragging it to the new position.

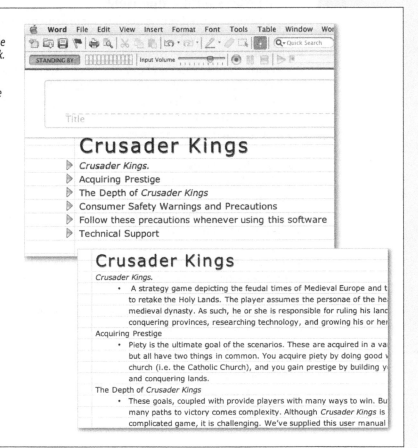

Figure 6-4:
You can expand or collapse the subheadings in your Notebook. At top left, headings are collapsed, displaying only the top-level text. After clicking the flippy triangle, the subheadings pop out, as shown in the bottom-right shot. Note that it's possible to have several levels of embedded headings. Wherever there are subheadings, you'll see the renowned flippy triangle.

Sorting Headings

As you've probably gathered by now, there are myriad ways to sort your headings and organize and reorganize your notes. You can drag notes (and objects), promote and demote headers, and move them up and down. It's cool, it's easy, and it's fast.

What's even faster is Notebook's ability to sort your data via the sorting function that's added to the Formatting palette whenever you work in Notebook Layout view. Select the section you wish to sort (the sorting commands sort a selection, not the entire document), open the Sorting panel by clicking the flippy triangle next to sorting, and click either Ascending or Descending.

- Ascending places the lowest header at the top of the page, and the highest at the bottom. It also sorts alphabetically within the header. For example, it would place a heading beginning with "Aplomb," before a heading beginning with "Zealot."

- Descending places the highest header (Note Level 1) at the top of the page, and the lowest at the bottom.

Placing Notes Beside Your Notes

Okay, you've organized your notes into some form of logic. Everything to do with the company party is listed under the Level 1 heading of Company Party, and all things pertaining to the boss's favorite client is tucked under the client's name. But what if you have some questions about items in both categories, need to remind yourself to order the party's food, and prepare a report for that number one client, and just keep in mind what is what, and set priorities for both? There are two ways of quickly transforming your notes into a to-do list: the Note Flags feature in Notebook Layout view, or by marshalling the forces of Entourage.

Flagging Action Items

The Note Flags panel of the Formatting Palette contains a pop-up menu that contains checkboxes and other items for just about every flagging purpose. Place a flag in the margin next to anything in your notebook by first clicking the text (anywhere in the text line), and then selecting the flag from the list.

Note: You can't apply a flag to a graphic. If you select a graphic, the Formatting Palette no longer includes the Note Flags section. You may, however, click on a line near the graphic and place your flag there.

The checkboxes are great for placing beside items on your Notebook list. Once placed, you can click the box to place a check in it. So, after you've finished that step in the project, you can check it off. Instant gratification!

Important Enough to Track in Entourage?

Pretty icons beside your notes are all well and good, but what if you want to take your reminder out of Word and into the real world? If you use Entourage to organize your life, you could launch that program and start a new task. Fortunately, there's no need to subject yourself to that kind of strain. Just click Create Entourage Task in the Note Flags section of the Formatting Palette. Doing so opens a dialogue box in which you can set the date and time when you wish to be reminded of the selected text.

This cross-program feature is a great timesaver and an ideal way to follow up on the notes that you took at yesterday's meeting. Simply click in the line of text you wish to remember, let's say "Prep sales report for Olsen by Tuesday," click Create Entourage Task, and set an appropriate reminder, for, say Tuesday morning.

Typing Less with Audio Notes

Hey, that's what everyone wants to do. Spend a little less time clacking on the key-board and a little more time living a private version of the Corona commercials. Well, Notebook Layout view can't get you away from the office, but it can get your hands off the keyboard with the Audio Notes toolbar and its capabilities. For example, you're sitting in that three-hour, Monday night sociology class. Just call up Word, open a new document in Notebook Layout view, turn on Audio Notes, and let it run. Then, as you type notes, Word automatically inserts icons that link to an audio snippet of whatever it was recording when you were typing.

The beauty of this arrangement is that you don't have to worry about typing every word the professor drones. Just type main points that you can click and listen to on the recording to refresh your memory later. You can also link audio notes to previously written text—something that's convenient if you wanted to connect a complex description to a point that you briefly touched on in your written notes. Here's how to enter your audio notes and listen to them later.

Entering an Audio Note

To enter an audio note, click in the text where you wish to insert the audio note, click on the microphone to display the Audio Notes toolbar and click the Record button, and start speaking (or you may need to *stop* talking so that your microphone can hear the important stuff). Or, just click the microphone and type away. Word automatically creates new audio notes every few lines. Click Stop (the blue square on the Audio Notes toolbar) when you wish to stop recording. When you pass the cursor over the text, the blue speaker pops into the left margin.

Listening to an Audio Note

To listen to a note, click the blue speaker icon in the left margin of the page. Your recording fills the air, and if you wish it to fill a little more or less, you can adjust the volume on the Audio Notes toolbar. In fact, there are a bunch of things that you can do on that toolbar, conveniently described below. To display the toolbar, click the Audio Notes toolbar icon. The toolbar, as shown in Figure 6-5, swims onto your screen.

Figure 6-5:
The Audio Notes toolbar (shown here divided in half to fit on the page) provides the controls needed to insert sound into your document. Keep an eye on the Size measure as you record: larger files take longer to save and email.

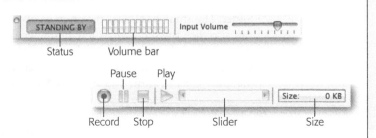

Tip: Perhaps you'd like to share your verbal brilliance with someone who doesn't have access to your computer. Don't worry, Word 2004 has you covered. You can export your audio notes to another medium. Choose Tools→Audio Notes→Export Audio. Word exports *all* the audio in the notebook document as an MP4 file to a location of your choosing. After you've done that, you can burn the MP4 to a CD and take it wherever you like. It's a dream come true for those folks who truly do like to hear themselves talk.

The Audio Notes Toolbar includes several functions:

- **Recording Status.** Located on the far left of the toolbar, the status bar shows whether you are in Standing By (not recording) or Recording mode.

- **Volume.** The Volume bar measures how loudly the computer hears you (or whatever it's hearing). For example, if you clap, the bar spikes (swings to the right). If you get really quiet, centering yourself in that peaceful place that only you know, the bar settles to the left…at least until your kids storm into the room, screaming that their big brother threw the cat into the tree.

- **Input Volume.** The input volume slider sets the input volume. Move it to the left if you're loud (or a close talker), move it to the right if you have one of those small, breathy voices like your cousin Sue.

- **Recording Button.** As you might expect, the recording button starts the recording process. Click it and talk normally (unless you're Cousin Sue, in which case you'll need to speak up). Watch the size display on the right of the toolbar as you talk. Try not to make your notes too big; less than 50 KB is a good rule of thumb.

- **Pause Button.** Pauses the recording. Use it if you either wish to return later to add to your audio note or if the cat has your tongue. The point is that pausing the recording lets you add more material to the same recording when you resume. If you click the Stop button, you'll need to start a new recording.

- **Stop.** Stops the current recording.

- **Play.** The Play button plays the selected recording. A small speaker that appears as you pass your mouse over it designates an audio note. Select an audio note and click Play to hear it. Double-clicking the speaker also starts playback.

- **Slider.** This small bar tracks the progress of the currently playing audio note. You can also slide the slider anywhere in the window to begin the audio note at that point. That trick can be quite useful if you left a contact phone number at the very end of a 30-second message. No need to listen to all that stuff at the beginning—just place the slider near the end and click Play.

Tip: Although the blue speaker pops up whenever you pass your mouse over an audio note, it's much easier to draw attention to the note with a line of text such as, "Monday meeting," or whatever. In fact, you can also flag it as discussed previously. For example, put a yellow checkbox beside all your audio notes so you can spot them without mousing around for the speaker icon.

Manipulating Notebook Sections

By now you're a pro at putting words onto notebook pages. It's also important to understand how to manipulate the pages themselves, specifically how to make changes to entire sections by adding improvements such as headers, footers, or removing the characteristic lined paper look. Notebook Layout view pages, referred to as sections, are an important organizational tool.

Note: Notebook pages really aren't–pages, that is. The Notebook Layout's sections are continuous sheets of paper, kind of like a Web page. In fact, you can't insert a page break (page 145) into a notebook. If you convert the notebook to a different Word view, such as Normal or Page Layout, you'll see that, behind the scenes, Word delineates each tabbed section with a section break (page 145).

Labeling Sections

A title resides at the top of each section. Initially—because Wood 2004 can't read your mind—it's blank (the title, not your mind), but you can fill it in by clicking in the title block (as shown in Figure 6-6), and typing whatever you wish. This label doesn't, however, change the title on the tab located on the right of the notebook page. To change these tab titles, Control-click (or right-click) the tab, and then choose Rename Section. Type your new tab title and press Return.

Note: You can turn off the section tab titles, if you wish. You may want to do so if you have a lot of them, or if you're very familiar with the sections. In general, it's best to leave them on. To turn them off, click the Show Section Tab Titles in the status bar. When the tab titles are on, the button glows green, and, well, you can see the tab titles. When off, the button appears clear and the tab titles are replaced by consecutive numbers.

Reordering the sections of your notebook is simple. Click on a section tab and drag it to its new location.

Figure 6-6:
It's a good idea to rename your sections to something useful. Dates are a good idea, as are categories.

To Line or Not to Line

Notebook Layout view's factory settings include lined paper. It's a curious, if understandable, decision by Microsoft. Curious, because on a computer, you don't need lines to keep your writing even; understandable, because it's a notebook view, and the lines make your computer screen look like a notebook.

Note: In fact, the lines do have an effect on the text placed on them. Text is positioned exactly between the lines, so if you increase the space between the lines (using the Rule Lines panel of the Formatting Palette), you'll increase the space between each line of text.

You can change the appearance of the lines in the Rule Lines section of the Formatting Palette. Click the flippy triangle next to Rule Line to display the section. You can choose from three styles: Standard, Outline, and None.

- **Standard.** This factory setting gives each page lines that look like notebook paper, with text spaced between the lines. It's great most of the time you're in Notebook view, because it reminds you you're supposed to be, well, taking notes.

- **Outline.** The lines are replaced with thick bands. Really, it's a personal preference thing.

- **None.** Removes all the lines. If the lines bug you, choose this setting and get a clean sheet of paper on which to type.

- **Distance.** Sets the spacing between the lines, in points (page 109). Obviously, the larger the number, the greater the spacing.

Numbering Pages

Oddly enough, you can choose to number your notebook pages in a footer, even though you'll only see this page number when you either print your notebook or switch to another view, such as Page Layout view. Numbering is a good idea if you intend to print your document, so you'll know you've got all the pages in the correct order.

To include page numbers, click the flippy triangle next to Footer in the Formatting Palette. The footer options are either None (no footer), or Page Numbers. Choosing Page Numbers plops them at the bottom of your pages. You can also choose to have Word begin renumbering the pages with each new tabbed section.

The Outliner

Your teachers were right: The more time you spend on the outline, the less work you'll have to do when it comes time to writing your actual paper, story, article, or book. Word's automated Outline view frees you from the drudgery of keeping track of all the letters and numbers in an outline, while encouraging you to categorize and prioritize your ideas.

Note: Before Notebook Layout view, the Outliner used to be the only way to organize your thoughts with levels. And it is still a darn good way to do so. Although you can't use audio notes in the Outliner, it does give you access to more of Word's other features. For example, you can't insert hyperlinks in Notebook Layout view, but you can in the Outline. Neither can you apply Styles to the Notebook (that's one of the reasons it sloshes around your intricately formatted documents), but you can in the Outliner.

Building an Outline

To outline your document from the beginning, open a blank document and choose View→Outline, or click the second tiny icon at the lower-left corner of your document window. (You can also apply Outline view to an existing document, which is described later in this section.)

Whenever you switch to Outline view, the Outline toolbar appears (see Figure 6-7). When you first start typing, your words are formatted as Heading 1—the highest level in the outline hierarchy. (Outline headings correspond to Word's built-in heading styles.)

Now you're ready to build your outline. Press Return after each heading. Along the way, you can create the subheadings using either the mouse or the keyboard, as described next.

Figure 6-7:
Top: A full-fledged outline in progress. The most important buttons on the toolbar are identified here.

Bottom: By clicking the big 1 on the toolbar, you hide all but the primary Level 1 headings, which offers an easy overview of your document. You can drag topics around using the + signs as handles.

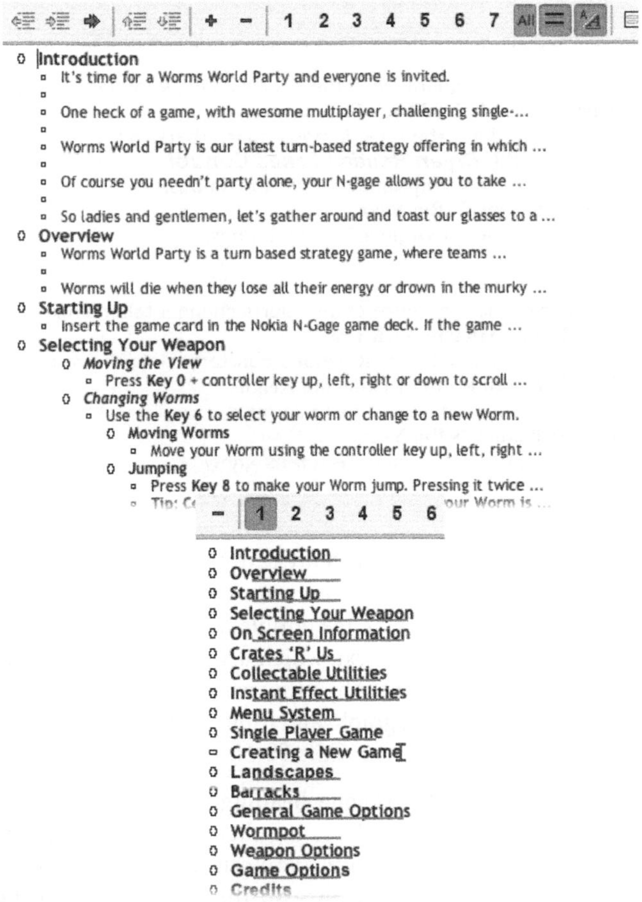

- **Promoting and demoting.** Moving topics out toward the margin (toward Heading 1, making them more important) or inward (less important) promotes or demotes them, identical to the same functions in the Notebook Layout view (page 189).

To promote or demote a heading, click within it and then press Tab (to demote) or Shift-Tab (to promote). Keep pressing until you reach the desired level. (You can also press Tab or Shift-Tab before typing a heading.)

Or, if you're a mouse-driven kind of person, click the Promote and Demote buttons at the left of the Outline toolbar (see Figure 6-7). Keyboard Shortcuts: Shift-Control-left arrow to promote; Shift-Control-right arrow to demote. You can also drag with the mouse, as shown in Figure 6-8.

> **Tip:** You can promote or demote an entire batch of headings at once. Drag through an outline to select certain headings, or neatly select a heading and all of its subheadings by clicking the + symbol. (To eliminate subtopics from the selection, first click the + sign, then Shift-click where you want the selection to *end.*)

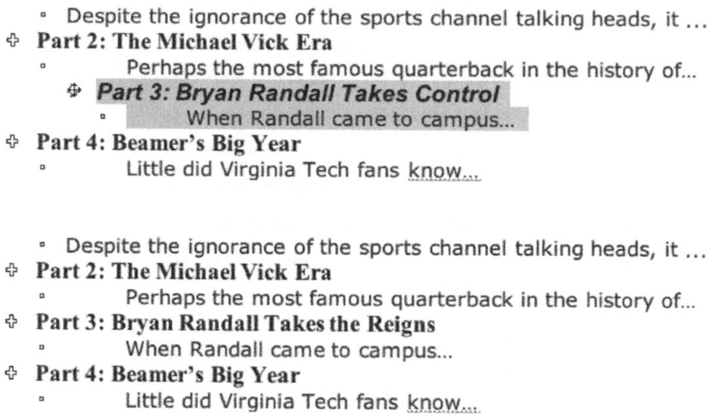

- Despite the ignorance of the sports channel talking heads, it ...
- **Part 2: The Michael Vick Era**
    - Perhaps the most famous quarterback in the history of...
    - *Part 3: Bryan Randall Takes Control*
        - When Randall came to campus...
- **Part 4: Beamer's Big Year**
    - Little did Virginia Tech fans know...

- Despite the ignorance of the sports channel talking heads, it ...
- **Part 2: The Michael Vick Era**
    - Perhaps the most famous quarterback in the history of...
- **Part 3: Bryan Randall Takes the Reigns**
    - When Randall came to campus...
- **Part 4: Beamer's Big Year**
    - Little did Virginia Tech fans know...

Figure 6-8:
Top: You can promote a heading just by dragging it. As you drag the icon next to a paragraph, the cursor turns into a four-sided arrow. Now drag the margin line out to the desired level.

Bottom: When you release the mouse, you've just promoted the heading—to Level 1, in this case. A paragraph of body text turns into a heading using the same technique.

- **Inserting body text.** You wouldn't impress many people if you wrote nothing but headlines. Fortunately, you can flesh out your headings with regular body text by clicking the double-arrow icon on the Outline toolbar. (It stands for Demote to Body Text, which actually demotes the text to the Normal style.) Use this style, denoted by a tiny white square in Figure 6-8, for the actual, longer-than-one-line paragraphs and thoughts that constitute the main body of your writing. *Keyboard shortcut:* Shift-⌘-N.

- **Rearranging headings.** To move topics up and down on the page without promoting or demoting them, just drag them by the + and − handles (see Figure 6-8). Alternatively, you can select the topic or topics and click the Move Up and Move Down arrows on the Outline toolbar. *Keyboard shortcuts:* Control-Shift-up or -down arrow.

- **Breaking up headings.** You'll probably come across instances, especially when outlining an existing piece of writing (see below), in which you need to separate one sentence from the previous one in order to make it a new topic. Just click before the first letter of the sentence and then press Return to put it on a new line.

Collapsing and expanding an outline

The whole point of creating an outline is to organize the topics you're presenting, to ensure that all the major points are there and to arrange them in a logical order. Therefore, it's helpful to see just your main points at a glance, unencumbered by the minor details. Here are ways you can control how much you see:

- **To show only Level 1 headings:** To get a quick "big picture" view of your outline, click the large numeral 1 on the Outline toolbar, or press Shift-Control-1; now Word shows *only* your Level 1 headings, the real main points of your document. Everything else is temporarily hidden.

  Similarly, clicking 2 (or pressing Shift-Control-2) shows heading Levels 1 *and* 2, so you can check how your subtopics are looking, and so on. (Figure 6-7 illustrates this trick in action.)

- **To collapse only one section of an outline:** Double-click the puffy + sign next to it. All subtopics of that heading disappear, leaving just a gray bar behind as evidence that something's been hidden. To expand it again, double-click the + again. (Double-clicking a minus sign doesn't do anything, since there's nothing to collapse.) This trick is helpful when you're closely examining a small portion of a long outline and just want to move some minor details temporarily out of your way.

- **To view first lines only:** Click the Show First Line Only button on the Outline toolbar, or press Shift-Control-L, to make Word hide everything but the first line of every paragraph—whether it's a heading or body text.

- **To hide all body text:** You can collapse all the material that you've relegated to body text so that only headings are visible by clicking the All button on the Outline toolbar (or pressing Shift-Control-A).

- **To expand everything:** In an outline where you've collapsed at least one heading somewhere, the All button takes on a different role. Clicking it now expands any headings or body text that have been collapsed. Click All or press Shift-Control-A to get everything out in the open and return to work. (If you click All again at this point, it hides all body text and returns to its role as body-text toggle.)

Tip: If the heavy boldface type and dark fonts make your outline hard to read, click the Show Formatting button on the toolbar. It displays all headings in plain, unformatted type.

Outlining an Existing Document

Say you've been typing away on your latest essay or annual report, and you're stuck. You've run out of ideas, and the ones you did have no longer look so clear now that you see them onscreen. It's still not too late to apply the organizational power of an outline. Just choose View→Outline; Word displays your document in outline format, using your own line breaks, indents, and headings as a guide. Now you can use the navigational tools described to reprioritize and clarify your thoughts.

Numbering an Outline

If what you remember about outlining came from high school English class, you may be wondering about the I's and a's and funny little iii's that you were taught to use as outline numbers. Not only can Word number your headings and subheadings

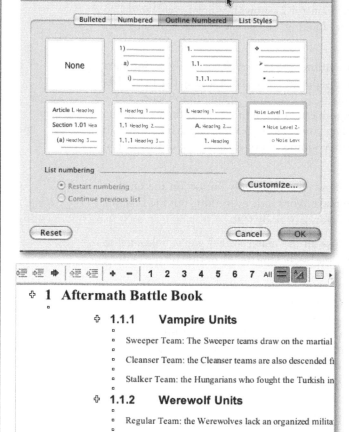

Figure 6-9:
Top: When this dialog box appears, choose one of the seven outline styles; the ones on the bottom row add numbering and apply heading styles to the text on each level. There's also an option for automatically adding the "Article" and "Section" labels used in legal documents (Article 1, Article 2...), and another for using Outline format for chapter headings. If one of the illustrated numbering styles fits your needs, click it and then click OK. If not, see "Customizing an Outline" in the next section. Click OK when you're set.

Bottom: The resulting outline is numbered automatically, according to the style you've selected.

automatically, but it can also automatically renumber the outline as you move topics around.

To add numbering to an outline, choose Format→Bullets and Numbering→Outline Numbered tab. Then proceed as shown in Figure 6-9.

Now continue working as usual with your outline. Even if you drag topics around or insert new ones, Word automatically updates the numbering.

Renumbering a numbered outline

You can't edit a numbered outline in your document; when you click the numbers or letters, nothing happens.

But what if you're starting a new section with a completely different outline in it, and want the numbers to start all over again? Click in the heading whose number you wish to change. Then choose Format→Bullets and Numbering→Outline Numbering tab, and click Customize. To change the number of the current heading, you must first change the number in the "Start at" box, as shown in Figure 6-10. Any numbered headings following this one will be numbered in a continuing order.

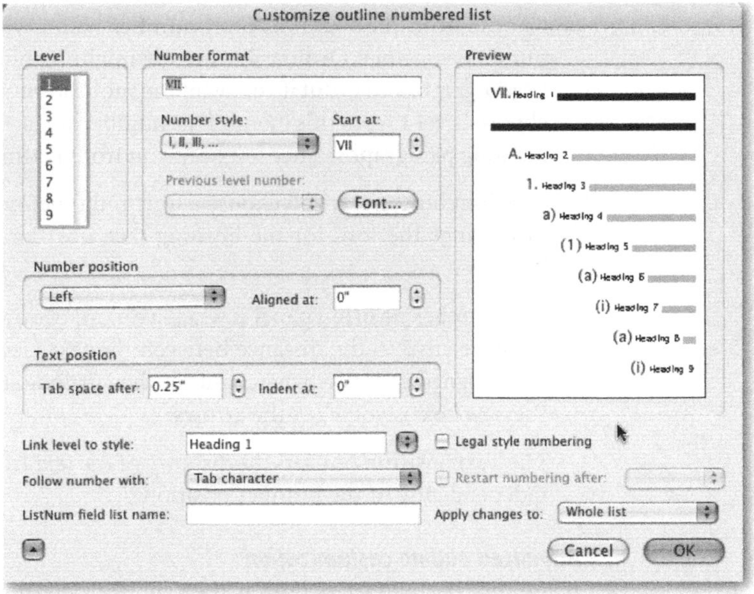

Figure 6-10:
The "Apply changes to" menu lets you make only part of a document into an outline. If it's grayed out, try selecting some text before opening the Bullets and Numbering dialog box and the Customize tab. (Click the blue expand arrow at lower left to view these choices.)

Customizing an Outline

The seven built-in numbering formats cover most purposes, especially if you're creating the outline for your own benefit. But if you've been asked to turn in a document in outline format, if you're using Word to create a legal document, or if you're one of those people who just can't leave well enough alone, you may need to tinker with the outline's AutoFormatting to get just the right result.

Using the Custom Outline dialog box

To set up an unusual numbering style for your outline, choose Format→Bullets and Numbering→Outline Numbered tab, and click Customize.

When the Custom Outline dialog box first opens, as shown in Figure 6-11, the settings you see pertain to the numbering style you've chosen in the Bullets and Numbering dialog box, and to the current heading level at the insertion point.

In the Level box at the left, choose the outline level you want to tailor. For instance, you can live with Word's built-in typeface for chapter titles, but want your secondary headings to look different. In that case, leave Level 1 alone and click the 2 in the Level box. The Preview box presents an example of the current numbering; it changes as you make changes in the Custom Outline dialog box.

- The **Number Format** panel shows the numbering style—letter, Roman numeral, and so on—for the current level.

- Word generally begins counting headings with the number 1. But if you want to print out an outline that's supposed to be a continuation of another document, you may want its numbering to start with, say, 17. That's the number you type into the **Start at** box.

- Choose from the **Previous level number** menu when you want to display level numbers together. Ordinarily, the title might be numbered 1, and the three subheadings a, b, and c. But if you want the subheads numbered 1a, 1b, and 1c instead, choose Level 1 from this menu. This numbering tactic is useful when your outline has long paragraphs, since it'll keep you from getting lost in the levels.

- The **Font** button lets you choose a font and typeface for the outline *number* only. (To change the font for the heading *text*, use "Link level to style" as described below.)

- The **Number position** panel is where you can choose left, centered, or right alignment, relative to the distance between the text (see below) and the left margin. The **Aligned at** box is where you set the left indent. Watch what happens in the Preview box as you click the arrows.

- The **Text position** box sets the distance of the text from the left margin. It operates independently of the number position.

Advanced outline customization

If you click the blue arrow button, the dialog box expands, sprouting a handy fold-out panel that offers even more intimidating-looking options.

- In the **Link level to style** menu, you can choose to apply any of the styles in the current document template (see page 226) to the level that you're formatting.

- The **Follow number with** menu lets you insert a tab, a space, or nothing at all between the number and the text. (You do it here because you can't directly format outline numbers in your document, not even in Outline view.)

- The **ListNum field list name** box lets you insert a *second* number into an outline numbered item.

- Check the **Legal style numbering** box to apply legal style (no letters, no capital Roman numerals) to any numbering style. This box grays out the "Number style" menu and gives Legal style numbering complete control.

- When you choose a new level in the Level box, the **Restart numbering after** box is turned on by default. That's because each subtopic is numbered from the beginning, under the main topic that contains it (1a, 1b; 2a, 2b)—unless you take a unique approach to counting, you wouldn't want your headings to go 1a, 1b, 2c, 2d, for example. Thus, under subheading (a), sub-subhead numbers start again with i, ii, iii, and so on, as shown in Figure 6-10.

Click OK to close the Customize box and apply your selections from the Bullets and Numbering dialog box. If you plan to always use the outline in Outline view, you're done; otherwise, consider switching into Normal or Page Layout view for further refinement. You'll discover that the nice, even indenting of your various headings in Outline view may not exist in Normal or Page Layout view. As a result, you may have to adjust the indentation of your various heading styles to make the indenting levels correspond in the other views.

The Document Map

The Document Map doesn't actually look like a map. It looks like a portable table of contents that's open as you read, similar to the left-side table of contents list you might find in an Adobe Acrobat (PDF) document. This unusual view can save you hours of laborsome scrolling (see Figure 6-11).

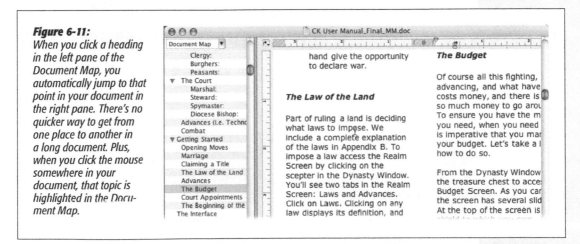

Figure 6-11:
When you click a heading in the left pane of the Document Map, you automatically jump to that point in your document in the right pane. There's no quicker way to get from one place to another in a long document. Plus, when you click the mouse somewhere in your document, that topic is highlighted in the Document Map.

What's in the Document Map

In essence, the Document Map is a navigating pane revealing just the headings in a document. A heading, in this case, can be any text in one of Word's built-in heading styles, a style you've *based on* one of the built-in heading styles, or text to which you've applied an *outline level*.

Viewing and Navigating the Document Map

To see the Document Map, you must open the Navigation Pane. You can do that by either choosing View→Navigation Pane or clicking the Navigation Pane icon on the Standard toolbar. A narrow panel with its own vertical scroll bar opens on the left side of your document window. From the little menu at the top of the pane, choose Document Map. (Your other choice—the Navigation Pane—is described on page 30 and in the box below.)

The Document Map doesn't have a horizontal scroll bar at the bottom; if you can't read the full text across the Document Map pane, drag the narrow gray bar—the resize bar—to widen its pane. However, you can read the full text of any topic without re-sizing: point the cursor at any line, and a screen tip appears, revealing the full text.

The flippy triangles in the Document Map work just like those in any Finder window: Click one to reveal or conceal all its subtopics. If you're a fan of contextual menus, you can also Control-click—or right click—a heading in the Document Map, choose Expand, Collapse, or any of the level headers that you'd like to see.

Because the items shown in the Document Map have levels, like headings and outline topics, you can collapse or expand the entire "outline" so that, for example, only the Level 1 and Level 2 headings show up, exactly as you can in Outline view. To do so, Control-click in the Document Map pane and choose a heading level from the con-textual menu (as mentioned above). If you choose Show Heading 4, for instance, the Document Map displays only Levels 1 through 4, hiding everything else.

To dismiss the Document Map, choose View→Navigation Pane again, double-click the resize bar, or click the Navigation Pane icon in the Standard toolbar.

GEM IN THE ROUGH

Navigation Pane's Thumbnails

For those of you who are truly visual creatures, Microsoft has included a special treat in Word 2004—the Navigation Pane's Thumbnail view as shown here. To use it, click the pop-up menu at the top of the Navigation Pane and choose Thumbnail view. The Thumbnail view displays a miniature picture of every page in your document. To go to the page, just click on it. If a page isn't visible, use the scrolling bar to move to it.

The Thumbnail view is more than just another pretty face. It's a great way to hunt for pages in a long document. For example, let's say that you can't remember the exact page where you inserted the picture of Sra Pezzini in your dissertation on the effect of modern pop-culture on comic book art. Just select the Thumbnail view, and scroll through the dissertation until you find Witchblade's alter ego's picture.

Customizing the Document Map

By default, the Document Map shows up as black Lucida Grande text with blue highlights.

To jazz up the Document Map font (or just make it less ugly), choose Format→ Style and choose Document Map in the Styles list box. Click Modify to bring up the Modify Style box.

Now choose Font from the Format menu. Whatever font, color, size, case, or text effect you specify now will apply to all text in the Document Map.

Tip: At this point, you can even change the highlight color, which appears when you click a heading in the Map. Click OK; then, from the Format pop-up menu, choose Borders. Click the Shading tab in the resulting dialog box. Choose a new fill color as described on page 689.

Click OK, OK, and Close when you're satisfied. (Clicking Apply changes the current paragraph in your main document to the Document Map style; that's probably not what you want to do.) If you have a change of heart at this point, press ⌘-Z to restore the Document Map to its original, bland condition.

Master Documents

In the beginning, there was Word 5.1. It had fonts, sizes, styles, tables, and graphics.

But the people weren't satisfied. They wanted to bind together many different chapter documents into a single, unified book. They wanted to knit together files written by multiple authors who had edited their respective sections simultaneously on the network. They wanted to print, spell check, or find-and-replace across dozens of different Word files at once, or generate tables of contents, indexes, and cross-references for all component Word files at once.

On the sixth day, Microsoft created the Master Document. (Really, it looks like they created it on the fifth day. They saved the sixth for Notebook Layout view and Halo 2.) Master documents are the logical extension of the Notebook Layout view train of thought. Notebook is perhaps the simplest form of outlining, while the Outliner is more capable, more complex. On the other hand, Master documents are the Mother Lode of document organization.

Without a doubt, a Master Document looks much like an outline. However, each heading in the Master Document can refer to a section or an entirely different *Word file*. As in the Document Map, you click these headings in Master Document view to travel directly from one part of the overall document to another.

In essence, a Master Document is a binder containing the individual Word files that comprise it (which Microsoft calls *subdocuments*). Each subdocument can be formatted independently, moved or removed, split up, or combined with another subdocument—all while remaining safely under the umbrella of the Master Document. The Master Document concept is slightly alien, difficult to understand, and sometimes a bit flaky; but if you're putting a book together, Master documents may be the only way to go.

Caution: Danger Will Robinson. Master documents are sometimes a cause of document corruption. When you're using this feature, back up your work even more frequently than usual.

Creating a New Master Document

To start building a Master Document, open a new document and choose View→ Master Document. The Master Document toolbar appears, and your document is set up for outlining (see Figure 6-12).

Setting up your über-document is exactly like creating an outline (see page 201), in that you use all the same techniques. Each heading, however, will eventually become the name of a separate file on your hard drive. Because a Master Document will wind up as a herd of individual files, you'd be wise to save it on your hard drive in a folder of its own; the subdocuments will wind up there, too.

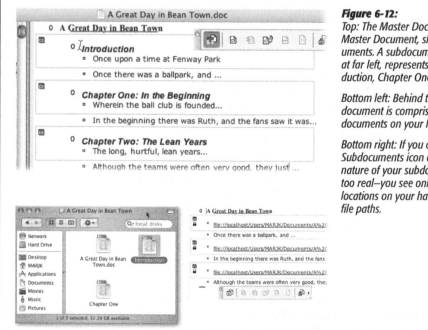

Figure 6-12:
Top: The Master Document toolbar and a Master Document, showing three subdocuments. A subdocument icon, like the ones at far left, represents each document. (Introduction, Chapter One, and so on.)

Bottom left: Behind the scenes, each master document is comprised of individual Word documents on your hard drive.

Bottom right: If you click the Collapse Subdocuments icon on the toolbar, the nature of your subdocuments becomes all too real—you see only hyperlinks to their locations on your hard drive, spelled out as file paths.

Spinning off a document

To spin off a particular heading as a subdocument, click it and then click the Create Subdocument button on the Master Document toolbar (see Figure 6-12). (You can also highlight several headings at once before clicking the Create Subdoc-

---

ument button. Just make sure the first heading is at the level you'll want represented as subdocuments.)

A light gray box that defines the boundaries of the document appears onscreen; you can type or paste into it. Behind the scenes, you've just created a new, linked file icon in your Master Document's folder (Figure 6-12, bottom left). You or your network comrades can edit these individual files independently; whenever you open up the Master Document, you'll see the changes reflected.

Note: Subdocument files are stored in the same folder as the Master Document and behave like perfectly normal Word files. But don't drag their icons to another folder; rename them by clicking the icon's name, and so on. If you do, the Master Document won't be able to find them. Instead, move and rename subdocuments using the techniques described later in this section.

The safest way to copy a Master Document and all its subdocuments to another location is to select them all and move them all at once. Better still, just move the folder that contains them.

Incorporating a document

You can turn an existing Word document on your hard drive into a new subdocument, too. Just click the Insert Subdocument icon on the Master Document toolbar to open its dialog box. When you navigate to and select a file and click Open, the contents of the document appear in your Master Document as a subdocument, just like all the others.

Viewing Master Documents

Master Documents look and act vastly different in each of Word's views. If you can remember to switch into the correct view, you've won more than half of the Master Document battle.

- **In Normal view**, subdocuments become *sections* (see page 132), with a section break separating each. Use Normal view to type and edit your document. Be careful not to remove the section breaks. Removing them will inadvertently combine the Word documents that make up your Master.

  If, in Normal view, your document looks like a series of hyperlinks, with no other text, you have two choices: Click on a hyperlink to open that subdocument in a new window, or choose View→Master Document and click the Expand Subdocuments button. Now when you return to Normal view, the text in your Master Document will flow continuously, with a section break between subdocuments.

- **Online and Page Layout views** function just as they normally do. Your document appears to be a seamless whole, with no visible breaks between subdocuments.

- **Outline view** turns the Master Document into one big outline; here too, if you see hyperlinks instead of text, expand the subdocuments as described above. This view is useful for organizing your document at any stage of the process because it's so easy to drag-and-drop. In Outline view, subdocuments are represented by continuous section breaks.

- If you convert your Master Document to **Notebook Layout** view (page 190), you get a beautiful notebook with each subdocument in a tabbed section of its own.

Note: If you sense a pattern here, you're right. A subdocument in Master Document view and a tab in Notebook Layout view are both represented, in Normal view, by continuous section breaks (page 145).

Working with Master Documents

In Master Document view, not only can you see all your subdocuments, you can also open them, arrange and organize them, and control access to them.

Opening and expanding subdocuments

When you click the Collapse Subdocuments button (first on the Master Document toolbar), something odd happens: Each subdocument is listed as a blue, underlined hyperlink, with only its heading visible (Figure 6-12, bottom right). The rest is collapsed, exactly as in an outline. The text of the hyperlinks can look unfamiliar to you, since they are the *folder path* and *file name* of the subdocument. Clicking a link opens the subdocument in its own window.

You also see a padlock icon next to each heading. It's a bug; that document is not, in fact, locked in any way. If you double-click it (to open the file into its own window) or expand it, you'll find that it's easily editable.

Tip: You *can* lock a subdocument so that it's protected from errant mouse clicks in Master Document view; just click in the heading and click the padlock icon on the toolbar. Even so, double-clicking that heading opens it into its own window, which is easily editable. In other words, the Lock function doesn't offer what you'd call government-level security.

But when you open a subdocument into its own window, the padlock in the Master Document indicates that you (or anyone else) cannot edit the same document in Master Document view. The lock feature is really effective only when sharing a Master Document over a network, where it prevents two people from editing the same document at the same time.

Once you've collapsed your subdocuments, you can drag their little document icons up or down to rearrange them (or press Delete to remove them).

When you then click the Expand Subdocuments button on the Master Document toolbar (the very first icon again), the subdocuments open within the Master Document window. A light gray box outlines the contents of the subdocument in outline form.

Moving and renaming subdocuments

Don't rename or move a subdocument in the Finder; if you do, the Master Document will no longer be able to find it. If you really want to rename or move one of these documents, do so from within the Master Document, like this:

1. **Open the subdocument using any of the methods described above, and choose File→Save As.**

2. **Type a new name for the subdocument and, if desired, choose a new location for it. Click Save or press Return.**

With these two steps, you've updated the Master Document's *link* to the subdocument. The next time you open the subdocument from within the Master Document, the one with the new name and location will open. (The subdocument with the old name and location is still there, sitting on your hard drive as an independent Word document. You can delete it, unless you have some further use for it.)

Splitting and combining subdocuments

Suppose you want to chop a long chapter into two shorter ones. Or perhaps two people who were collaborating on a report have had a big fight, requiring you to solve the problem by giving them individual assignments. Fortunately, the process of dividing a subdocument in two, which Word calls *splitting*, is comparatively painless.

To do so, expand the subdocuments in Master Document view. Click where you want your split-off document to begin, and then click the Split Subdocument button on the Master Document toolbar.

At other times, you may want your subdocuments to meld together. For instance, you may want to combine two short chapters into one longer one, without restarting the pagination. You could cut and paste text from one subdocument into another, but there's a more elegant way, which Word calls *merging*.

To perform this task, move the subdocuments that you intend to merge so that they're next to each other in your outline. Highlight them, and then click the Merge Subdocument button on the Master Document toolbar.

The new, merged subdocument carries the name of the *first* subdocument that you combined. The original, unmerged versions of the second (and other) subdocument files remain in their original folder locations on your hard drive, but they're no longer connected to the Master Document.

"Removing" a subdocument

The Remove Subdocument button on the Master Document toolbar doesn't actually delete it (for that, see below). Instead, this function brings the document's contents into the Master Document itself, so that it's no longer linked to an external file on your hard drive. For example, you might use it when, for formatting reasons, you want your introduction to be part of the Master Document, instead of giving it a subdocument of its own.

To do so, expand the subdocuments. Click the subdocument icon, and then click Remove Subdocument on the Master Document toolbar. The contents of that subdocument now appear in the body of the Master Document. (You can delete the old subdocument file, which is now orphaned on your hard drive—unless you want to keep it as a backup.)

Deleting Subdocuments

Deleting a subdocument from a Master Document is easy: With the subdocument expanded and unlocked (see page 212), click the subdocument icon to select it and then press Delete. (When you delete a subdocument, you only remove it from the Master Document; you don't actually delete its file. The original subdocument file is still in the same folder where you left it, and where it will stay until you Trash it.)

Master Documents and Formatting

Like all Word documents, every Master Document is based on a template (see page 226). Not surprisingly, all subdocuments have the same template as the Master Document.

What is surprising, and potentially confusing, is the fact that a subdocument can have its *own* template, independent of the Master Document—and yet it can still take on the Master Document template when you want it to.

In Master Document view, all subdocuments share the same Master Document template—its styles, headers, footers, and so on. When you print *from this view,* all subdocuments print in the styles of the master template, resulting in a very consistent look. But when you open a subdocument *in its own window,* the subdocument's own independent template applies—with its own type styles, headers, footers, and so on. All the template parts listed on page 227 can operate independently in the Master Document and its subdocuments.

Master Document Security

Master documents were designed for sharing. The fact that two different people can simultaneously work on subdocuments of the same Master Document makes collaboration easy. When the individual subdocuments are done, you can review and print the finished product in Master Document view, ensuring that the formatting is consistent throughout. An added challenge, however, is keeping people from messing with subdocuments that they shouldn't, whether or not they're doing it maliciously.

Locking and unlocking subdocuments

The simplest (and most easily foiled) way of keeping someone from tampering with a subdocument is to lock it, as described on page 212. When a subdocument is locked, you can open and read it, but you can't edit or change it.

Fortunately, anytime someone is working on a subdocument, it gets locked automatically when viewed by anyone else on the network. It remains locked until its editor finishes and closes it.

Assigning passwords

Locking a subdocument by using the Lock Subdocuments button is a good way to prevent others from making accidental changes to it, but it doesn't actually lock out those who know about the Lock Document button. For true security, Master Documents and subdocuments must be password-protected just like any other document. As always, you can password-protect either the Master Document or (if you've opened one into its own window) a subdocument; either way, the instructions on page 20 apply.

Sharing a Master Document on a Network

One of the most popular uses for Master Documents is file sharing. For instance, members of a public relations department can each work on a separate section of their company's annual report. The report is a Master Document, and each section is a subdocument.

Here are some tips for successful Master Document file sharing:

- Choose one person to be team leader. That person will format the Master Document, hold the passwords, and oversee the final proofreading and distribution of the completed document.

- To prevent accidental or mischievous tampering with the subdocuments, assign a password to each one, as described on page 20. Make sure the team leader keeps a record of them in a safe place.

- Make sure all Macs involved are networked and set up for file sharing. If any team members are not familiar with file sharing, a consultation with the network administrator is in order. To learn more about setting up file sharing, including the Owner and Group designations described below, choose Help→Mac Help in the Finder and search for *file sharing*, or consult *Mac OS X: The Missing Manual.*

Advanced Word Processing

Word is an almost immeasurably deep program. Most people use it to type letters, peck out recipes, design playoff brackets for March Madness, and little else. That's fine—Microsoft intended the program to be easy for even novices to use. But Word has much more to offer those willing to dive into its deep waters. There are footnotes and endnotes for the research minded, autosummaries and data merges for the time challenged, and captions, tables of contents, and indexes for those composing something meatier than a letter home to Mom.

This chapter takes you deep into the woods of Word's power-user features, well off the beaten path trod by millions of everyday, casual wordsmiths. The material you'll find here is at your disposal when you need to write a dissertation, full-length book, or another complex, structured document.

Headers and Footers

A header or footer is a special strip that can show the page number—as well as your book title, chapter title, name, date, and other information—at the top or the bottom of every printed page in your document (or one section of it).

Creating Headers and Footers

Word treats the header and footer as a special box at the top or bottom of the page. To view these special text areas, choose View→Header and Footer; dotted lines appear around the header and footer areas of your document, and the Header and Footer toolbar appears, as shown in Figure 7-1. Meanwhile, back in the document body, the rest of your text fades to gray. (If you find that faded representation of your body text distracting, hide it by clicking the Show/Hide Document Text icon on the Header and Footer toolbar.)

Tip: If you're working in Page Layout view, you don't have to bother with the View→Header and Footer command. Just move the cursor to the top or bottom of the page; when the cursor turns into this shape 🗏, double-click. The header and footer outlines appear.

Fill your header or footer by typing inside it and clicking icons in the Header and Footer toolbar. For your convenience, Word places a centered tab stop in the middle of the typing area, and a right-aligned tab stop at the right. You can choose View→ Ruler and adjust these tab stops, of course (see page 123), but they're especially handy when you want to produce a header like the one shown in Figure 7-1.

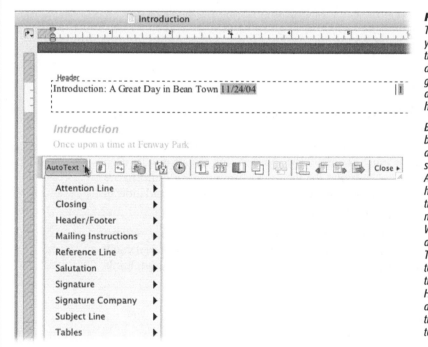

Figure 7-1:
Top: When you're editing your header or footer, the main part of your document appears in gray, and a dotted line appears around the header or footer area.

Bottom: The most useful buttons on the Header and Footer toolbar are shown here. To insert AutoText items into a header or footer, choose them from the AutoText menu on this toolbar; Word will keep them automatically updated. To return your document to its normal condition, choose View→ Header and Footer again, or click Close on the Header and Footer toolbar.

1. **Make sure the cursor is at the left margin. Type the chapter title.**

   After typing *Chapter 1: The Beginning,* you can highlight and format it; for example, italicize it by pressing ⌘-I.

2. **Press Tab.**

   The cursor jumps to the center-aligned tab in the middle of the header or footer.

3. **Insert the date.**

Click the Insert Date icon on the toolbar, as shown in Figure 7-1. (Word inserts the date as a *field*, which is continuously updated; whenever you open this document, the date will be current.)

4. Press Tab.

Now your cursor is aligned at the right margin.

5. Type *Page*, and a space; insert the page number by clicking the Insert Page Number icon on the toolbar (Figure 7-1); type *of*; insert the total number of pages by clicking the Insert Number of Pages icon.

(If you need help identifying an icon on this toolbar, point to it without clicking. As usual, in Office 2004, a screen tip appears to identify it.)

Word inserts placeholder fields (indicated by a nonprinting, gray background) into your header or footer, so that it says *Page 3 of 15*, for example. When you print or scroll through your document, you'll see that each page is correctly labeled in this way. (Of course, most people don't use the "Page X of Y" notation; if you want just the page number to appear, simply click the Insert Page Number icon and be done with it.)

Tip: If, at this point, you want more control over page numbering, click the Format Page Number button on the Header and Footer toolbar, as shown in Figure 7-1. In the dialog box that appears, you can specify how you'd like the page numbers to appear (*a, b, c,* or in Roman numerals, or with chapter numbers included). You can also indicate that you'd like them to begin with some number other than 1, which is ideal when your document is the *continuation* of a document you've already printed.

UP TO SPEED

Page Numbers: The Other Method

Page numbers are the most popular use of headers and footers. That's why Word provides buttons for adding and formatting them right on the Header and Footer toolbar (see Figure 7-1).

But there's an even easier way to number your pages in Word: Just choose Insert→Page Numbers. The Page Numbers dialog box opens, as shown here. Watch the Preview window change as you adjust the controls found here, such as Alignment (which includes Inside or Outside, for use when you're setting up bound-book pages); "Show number on first page" (turn it off if your document has a

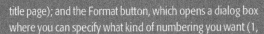
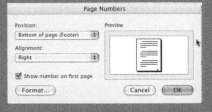

title page); and the Format button, which opens a dialog box where you can specify what kind of numbering you want (1, 2, 3; i, ii, iii; a, b, c; and so on).

When you turn on "Include chapter number," Word includes the chapter number along with the page number—in a "Chapter 1, Page 1" scheme. In the "Chapter starts with style" menu, choose the heading style that you used for the chapter number (you have to use one of Word's built-in headings—or a style based upon one of them—to make this numbering feature work). Then, choose a separator (a hyphen, dash, or whatever).

6. **Double-click the dimmed body portion of your document (or click the Close button on the toolbar) to exit the header/footer editing area.**

Tip: Headers and footers don't appear or print when you save your Word files as Web pages. But leave them in—they will appear and print (if you chose the "Save entire file into HTML" option) if you return to using the same file as a Word document.

Positioning headers and footers

By default, headers and footers extend from the left margin to the right margin. To make them wider than the text and extend them into the margins, give the header or footer a *hanging* or *negative indent* (see page 121).

To move a header or footer higher or lower on the page, click in it and choose Format→Document→Margins tab; adjust the numbers in the "From edge" boxes. (Higher numbers move the header or footer text closer to the middle of the page.) Alternatively, you can adjust it visually by clicking in the header or footer and then dragging its margin up or down in the vertical ruler at the left side of the page. This adjusts the distance between the header or footer and the body of the text. If the ruler isn't visible, click Word→Preferences→View→Window→Vertical Ruler.

Title pages

If your term paper has a title page (featuring the name of the paper centered on an otherwise blank page), it would look a little silly if the paper's title also appeared at the bottom.

Fortunately, you can give your first page a different header or footer—or none. To do so, go to the first page of your document. Choose Format→Document→Layout tab, click "Different first page," and click OK. (Alternatively, click the Different First Page button on the Header and Footer toolbar.)

Tip: The "first page" setting applies only to the *section* that contains your cursor (see page 132). In other words, you can control the header/footer's appearance independently for each section in your document.

Now you can edit and format the unique header and footer for your first page, or just leave them blank. (You can also apply this technique to the first page of each *section* of your document; see page 133) for more detail on sections.) If you haven't formatted the header and footer for the rest of the document, click the Show Next button on the Header and Footer toolbar; Word takes you to the second page, where you create the headers and footers for the rest of the pages.

Bound-book pages

If your document is going to be bound like a book, you'll probably want different headers and footers on odd and even pages, exactly like those on these book pages (book name on left-side pages, chapter name on right-side pages).

To create these mirror-image headers and footers, choose Format→Document→ Layout tab, click "Different odd and even," and click OK. (Alternatively, click the Different Odd and Even Pages icon on the Header and Footer toolbar.) Then edit the headers and footers for the odd and even pages in your document; when you edit *any single* odd or even page, Word applies the changes to *all* of them.

Different headers (and footers) for different sections

If you've divided your document into *sections* (see page 132), you can design different headers and footers for each section—a very common technique when you want to break your document into chapters.

By default, all headers and footers in a document are the same, even when you insert section breaks, so the trick is to *sever* the connection between the header and footer in consecutive sections. For instance, if you want a different header in each of your document's three sections, go to a page in the *second* section and choose View→ Header and Footer. Click in the header and click the Same as Previous icon on the Header and Footer toolbar. (This button breaks or rejoins the header/footer connection between each section and the one before it. You can use it to restore the header and footer connections if you change your mind, and once again make them uniform throughout the document.)

Repeat the process for the third section, and so on.

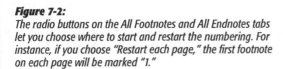

Figure 7-2:
The radio buttons on the All Footnotes and All Endnotes tabs let you choose where to start and restart the numbering. For instance, if you choose "Restart each page," the first footnote on each page will be marked "1."

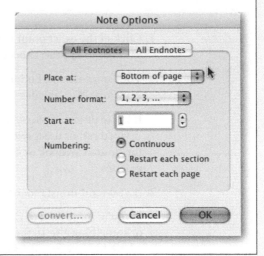

Footnotes and Endnotes

Footnotes, as any research scholar can tell you, are explanations or citations located at the bottom of each page, referred to by a small superscript number or symbol in the main text. (See Figure 7-3 for an example.) *Endnotes* are similar, except that they're listed together in a clump at the end of the document, instead of on each page. Word can handle each kind of annotation gracefully. Here's how to insert a footnote or endnote into your document:

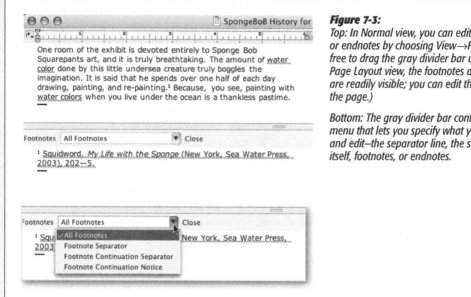

Figure 7-3:
Top: In Normal view, you can edit your footnotes or endnotes by choosing View→Footnotes; feel free to drag the gray divider bar up or down. (In Page Layout view, the footnotes and endnotes are readily visible; you can edit them directly on the page.)

Bottom: The gray divider bar contains a pop-up menu that lets you specify what you want to see and edit–the separator line, the separator text itself, footnotes, or endnotes.

1. **Click at the exact point in your document where you want the superscript note number to appear; choose Insert→Footnote or press Option-⌘-F.**

   The Footnote and Endnote dialog box appears, proposing a footnote. (Press the keystroke ⌘-E, or click Endnote, for an endnote instead.)

   If left to its own devices, Word will number your footnotes sequentially (1, 2, 3…). If you'd rather use a symbol (such as an asterisk), click "Custom mark" and type the desired symbol, or click the Symbol button and choose one from the various palettes.

2. **If you want nonstandard numbering, click Options.**

   If you're some kind of radical, you may prefer Roman numerals, letters, symbols, or something else. In the resulting dialog box (see Figure 7-2), you can also choose where to place footnotes and endnotes: at the bottom of the page or immediately after the text, for instance. Click OK to close the box.

3. **Click OK to close the Footnote and Endnote dialog box.**

   In Normal view, Word opens up a pane at the bottom of the document window, where you can type the actual text of the note. To toggle between displaying and hiding the note pane in Normal view, choose View→Footnotes; in Page Layout view, no such shenanigans are necessary—the notes simply appear at the bottom of the page, separated by the main text by a line. You can edit them directly.

Word usually draws a horizontal line, a third of the way across the page, above your footnotes, as you can see in Page Layout view. If you'd like to edit this line, however, you have to switch to Normal view, and then choose Footnote Separator or Endnote Separator from the Footnotes pop-up menu (in the bar at the top of the note pane). Now edit the text (or line) that you find there. You could even make the line a different color, for example, or delete it entirely by clicking it and pressing Delete.

4. **Type your footnote.**

A footnote is often a *citation*—a reference to a specific book or article that provided your information. One standard format for citations is called MLA (Modern Language Association) style, and it looks like this:

Watanna, Onoto, *A Japanese Nightingale* (New York, Harper & Brothers, 1901) 41.

The definitive guide to correct MLA-style footnotes is the *MLA Handbook for Writers of Research Papers* (for high school and undergraduate students) or the *MLA Style Manual and Guide to Scholarly Publishing* (for graduate students, scholars, and professional writers); for more information visit *www.mla.org*.

5. **Repeat from step 1 to add more footnotes, or click Close to move the Footnotes pane out of your way.**

Each footnote is marked in your text by a small number or symbol, as specified by you. At any time, you can jump back and forth between the footnote symbol (in the main window) and the Footnotes pane by pressing F6.

Tip: You can combine footnotes and endnotes in a single document. For example, footnotes might contain explanations and elaborations of text, while endnotes might contain citations.

Deleting Footnotes and Endnotes

To remove a footnote or endnote, select the superscript number or symbol in your text (not in the Footnote pane) and press the Delete key. The number and the entire note disappear, and Word renumbers the remaining notes as necessary. (Deleting the note number in the footnote or endnote itself, or in the Footnote pane, works no such magic. All you do is delete the little superscript number before the note. The rest of the note, and the number in your text, stay right where they are.)

Tip: You can convert footnotes to endnotes, or vice versa—a blessing for the indecisive. In Normal view, choose View→Footnotes, choose All Footnotes or All Endnotes from the pop-up menu in the gray divider bar, select the notes you want to convert, and Control-click the selection. Choose Convert to Endnotes or Convert to Footnotes from the shortcut menu.

Controlling Footnote Flow

If your footnotes are too long to fit on their "home" page, they flow into the footnote section of the next page. (Endnotes flow to the *top* of the following page.) As a courtesy

---

to your reader, you may want to add something to the separator line—"Continued on next page," for example. Word, being equally thoughtful, lets you do exactly that.

Open the note pane as shown in Figure 7-3 and choose Footnote (or Endnote) Continuation Notice from the Footnotes menu. Type your thoughtful text, ("See next page," or what have you), and click Close.

UP TO SPEED

Inserting Symbols

You can use hundreds of different symbols in Word 2004—both Unicode symbols like those you can get from Mac OS X's Character Palette and those in Word's own Symbol dialog box. The following terms, for example, all depend upon symbols for correctness and clarity: 98.6°, Oscar®, ¿Que pasa?, and so on. Larger symbols called dingbats let you do cool things like put a ☎ next to your phone number. High-tech dingbats, like those in Microsoft's Webdings font, come in handy on Web pages, such as + to indicate an email link.

To enter the wonderful world of symbols, choose Insert→Symbol. The Symbol dialog box appears, offering a palette of symbols in the Symbol font. Drag your cursor—now a magnifying glass—across them for a closer look.

If you don't see the symbol you're looking for, choose another symbol font from the Font menu. If you want a standard typographical symbol, such as © or ®, choose "Normal font" from this pop-up menu (or just click the Characters tab, where you'll find a cheat sheet of such common symbols and the keystrokes that produce them).

When you've finally highlighted the doohickey you're seeking, click Insert (or press Return) to place it into your document at the insertion point.

If there's a symbol you wind up using frequently—you're a Valentine's Day consultant, for example, and you use the ♥ symbol about 20 times a day—you can set it up for easier access in either of two ways.

First, you can assign a keyboard shortcut to it. To do so, click the ♥ in the Symbol dialog box (in the Zapf Dingbats font, for example), and then click Shortcut Key. In the resulting dialog box, press the keys you want to trigger this symbol (Control-H, for example). If you choose a key combination that's already assigned to another Word function—which is fairly likely—you'll just get an alert sound. Keep trying until you stumble onto an unassigned combination. (The keystroke will become part of the Normal template [see page 232], and so it'll work in all documents based upon it.)

But you may find it easier to use a word or letter combination to insert a symbol. For instance, if you want a to appear every time you type Apple, or your favorite dingbat (say ✿) to appear when you type a code like xq, click the symbol and then click AutoCorrect. The AutoCorrect dialog box opens, showing your chosen symbol in the Replace With box. Type the word or code you want to trigger the appearance of the symbol and then press Return twice.

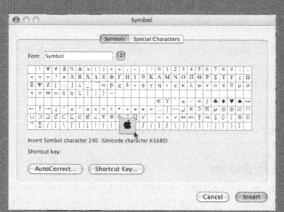

Insert Symbol character 240 (Unicode character 61680)

Tip: Word positions endnotes immediately after the document or section's text, according to your specification. To put them on a separate page for printing, click in front of the first endnote and choose Insert→ Break→Page Break. If you have numerous endnotes, you may want them to start on a new page so they're easier to check against your paper.

Line Numbers

If you're a lawyer, Bible scholar, or aspiring Hollywood scriptwriter, you're already familiar with *line numbering:* tiny numbers in the left margin every five or 10 lines (see Figure 7-4). But even in everyday business, they're occasionally useful; you could email a press release to your boss and ask, "Let me know if I come on too strong in lines 5–8," for instance.

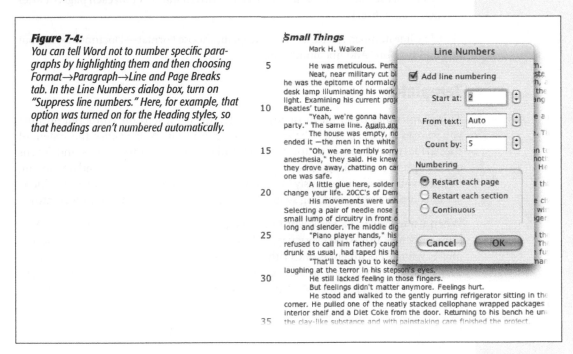

Figure 7-4:
You can tell Word not to number specific paragraphs by highlighting them and then choosing Format→Paragraph→Line and Page Breaks tab. In the Line Numbers dialog box, turn on "Suppress line numbers." Here, for example, that option was turned on for the Heading styles, so that headings aren't numbered automatically.

Line numbers show up only in Page Layout view (choose View→Page Layout or click the Page Layout button on the bottom left of the page). To add them to your document, select the text whose lines you want numbered. If it's a single section, for example, click anywhere in that section; if it's the whole document, choose Edit→ Select All or press ⌘-A. If you're at the start of a new document and want to start numbering immediately, read on.

Tip: By choosing Format→Paragraph→Line and Page Breaks tab and turning on "Suppress line numbers," you make Word skip over the selected paragraphs in its numbering. Keep this checkbox in mind when defining a style, too, since you can use it to ensure that your captions are *never* numbered, for example.

Choose Format→Document→Layout tab. If you've selected text as described above, choose "Selected text" from the "Apply to" menu at the right; click Line Numbers. Turn on "Add line numbering" and set the following:

- **Start at** tells Word what line to start counting with. Select 2, for instance, if you want Word *not* to include the heading at the top of the page.

- **From text** is the distance from the left margin of the text. Auto is a good start unless a certain distance has been specified.

- **Count by** tells Word: "Show numbers only on every ___th line." The most common settings are 5, 10, and 20.

- Numbering, when it's **continuous**, begins at the first line and goes all the way to the end of the document. You can also tell Word to start over on each page, or after each section break.

To delete line numbers, just select the text again, choose Format→Document→Layout tab, and turn off "Add line numbering."

Templates

This chapter may cover the most advanced features of Microsoft Word, but nothing you've read so far can touch the exasperating complexity of *templates*, the system of special files that Word uses to store your keystrokes, AutoText entries, styles, and dozens of other preference settings. There are two kinds of templates—global and document. Because you can simultaneously load more than one template, sometimes they interact in complex ways, including switching your text to radically different formatting.

When using Word as a basic word processor, you can safely ignore templates. Millions of people use Word every day, in fact, unaware that lurking behind the scenes of every single document is one critical global template called Normal. Every setting they change, every keystroke they redefine, every style they apply—everything gets stored in this template file. Most people, in other words, never need step into the piranha-infested Template River.

Learning about templates, however, can pay off for the ambitious and technically undauntable. For example:

- If you collaborate with other people, you can send them a template you've created that contains an officially sanctioned set of styles, so that all your documents will have a consistent look.

- Similarly, your boss or network administrator may give *you* a template file, filled with styles, so that your corporate correspondence will resemble everyone else's.

- Or maybe you plan to use your laptop, and want to ensure that all of the custom keystrokes, AutoText entries, and styles that you've carefully worked up on your desktop Mac are in place on the laptop.

The following pages take you through this insanely challenging topic with as few migraines as possible.

Document Templates

In any normal program, a template is simply a stationery pad, a locked icon in the Finder that, when opened, automatically generates a blank, untitled copy of the original. If you frequently (or even occasionally) need to create documents that incorporate certain standard elements, such as the top of your letterhead or boilerplate text on a contract, document templates can save you a lot of time.

Word offers something like this kind of template, too. You see dozens of these templates, called document templates, whenever you choose File→Project Gallery. These are regular Word documents—brochures, labels, newsletters, and so on—that have been saved in a special, self-duplicating format. You can read more about the Project Gallery in Chapter 18.

Creating a document template

It's very easy to create your own document template: Just prepare a Word document. Then dress it up with graphics, font selections, dummy text, tables, forms, whatever you like. It's very important to understand that you can also customize this document with Word's more advanced features, such as:

- Styles
- AutoText entries
- Macros
- Margins and tab settings
- Customized menus and toolbars
- Page layout (columns, for example)
- Headers and footers

Then choose File→Save As. You can, if you wish, choose Document Template from the Format pop-up menu, but it's not technically necessary; *any* Word document—even a normal one, which you save into the Applications→Microsoft Office 2004→Templates folder—behaves like a template in the Project Gallery. The primary advantage of choosing Format→Document Template is that Word jumps to that folder (or, rather, the Applications→Microsoft Office 2004→Templates→My Templates folder) automatically.

Name the file and then click Save.

Using a document template

From now on, whenever you'd like to peel off a copy of that template, choose File→ Project Gallery, click My Templates (or whatever folder you selected inside the Templates folder), and double-click the name of the corresponding template. It's just like opening a regular Word document, except that instead of appearing as a blank, stripped-down document, it comes complete with a number of predefined elements. The keystrokes you defined in the template, the styles you set up, the AutoText entries, dummy text, and so on will all be ready to use. All you need to do is save the new, untitled document and name it.

If you send a copy of this document template to another person or another machine, all of these preference settings will similarly be ready to use any time they open it. (If a Windows person might be the recipient, remember to add *.dot* to the end of the file's name; otherwise, Word for Windows won't recognize it.)

However, the settings, keystrokes, macros, toolbars, and so on, will not be available in any other Word document—only new ones "peeled off" from the document template will be available. You or your colleague may wind up longing for a method of making these customizations available universally, to any Word document, including existing ones. That's perfectly possible—and it's the purpose of *global* templates.

Global Templates

Every Word document, even a new blank one that you've just opened, is based on a template; that's why you see a list of styles available in the Formatting Palette of even a brand new file. Behind the scenes, every Word document is based, at the minimum, upon a template called Normal.

Normal is what Word calls a *global* template, meaning that it's available to all documents all the time (unless you intentionally *unload* it, as described on page 234). Exactly as with document templates, a global template determines which styles, macros, toolbars, page layout elements, AutoText entries, and other features are available when you use the document—but you don't have to go through the Project Gallery to open one, as you would with a document template.

Note: There's no technical difference between a document template and a global template–the same template file can serve as either one. The only difference is how you *load* it. If you use the Project Gallery, the template affects only a single document; if you use the Templates and Add-Ins command, as described on page 229, the template affects all documents.

Modifying a Template

No matter how hard you try to create a template the way you want it, the time comes when you have to go back and change it. You want to make your heading sizes smaller, or you have a new logo, and so on.

In a nutshell, you make such changes by opening the template file (choose File→ Open, navigate to the Applications→Microsoft Office 2004→Templates folder, and open the template you want to modify). Make whatever changes you want to the document—adjust the styles, margins, zoom level, default font, whatever—and then choose File→Save. From now on, all new documents you spin off from that template will reflect your changes.

Tip: When you modify a template, the changes don't automatically ripple through all *existing* documents you peeled off of it before the change. You can open each of those older files, however, and force them to update their styles, macros, keystrokes, and so on, to reflect the changed template. To do so, choose Tools→ Templates and Add-ins. Turn on "Automatically update document styles." Click OK.

Attaching a Document Template

It happens sometimes that 20 minutes into working on a new document, you realize that there's a template that would be just perfect for it. Fortunately, Word lets you *attach* a new template to a document, even if it began life as the offspring of a different document template. For instance, you begin a letter and decide that the Normal template looks a little too plain. You can look through the Project Gallery, find a letter template whose styles appeal to you, and attach it.

Here's how to attach a new document template:

1. **Choose Tools→Templates and Add-ins.**

   The Templates and Add-ins dialog box appears.

2. **Click Attach. In the Choose a File box, navigate to, and open, the template you'd like to attach, as shown in Figure 7-5.**

   The file name of the newly attached template appears in the "Document template" box of the Templates and Add-ins dialog box (see Figure 7-5).

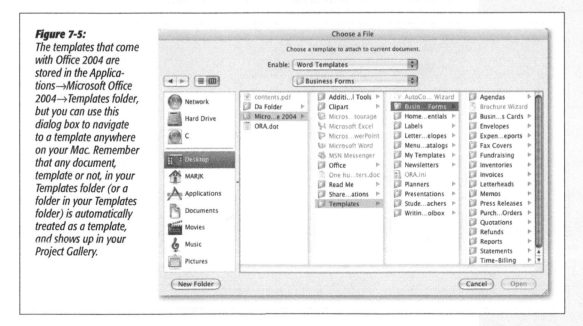

Figure 7-5:
The templates that come with Office 2004 are stored in the Applications→Microsoft Office 2004→Templates folder, but you can use this dialog box to navigate to a template anywhere on your Mac. Remember that any document, template or not, in your Templates folder (or a folder in your Templates folder) is automatically treated as a template, and shows up in your Project Gallery.

3. Click "Automatically update document styles"; click OK.

The Normal *style* in your document (which, confusingly, is unrelated to the Normal *template)*, along with other built-in styles (Heading 1, Heading 2, and so on), change to match those in the template you just attached. Moreover, your document now uses any macros, AutoText entries, custom toolbars, shortcut keys, and custom menus that were stored in the attached template. (If you want to use the macros and customizations without changing styles, do *not* click "Automatically update document styles" in step 3.)

> **Note:** Boilerplate text and graphics from the newly attached template don't suddenly appear in your document. Styles from the template don't appear either, unless the current document has styles whose names match. If you still want the new template's styles imported into your document, you must copy them into your document using the Organizer (see below) or the Format→Style dialog box.

Word only allows one document template to be attached at a time. When you attach a new one, the old one goes away. This is one of the ways that document templates are different from global templates, which you can gang up simultaneously.

The Organizer

Any style, AutoText entry, custom toolbar, or macro that you create and save to a document becomes part of a template (either the Normal template or a document template). Because of a little-known but very timesaving Word feature called the Organizer, you never have to create one of those custom items more than once. The Organizer, the great-great-grandchild of Apple's 1984 Font/DA Mover program, lets you transfer these items from file to file (see Figure 7-6).

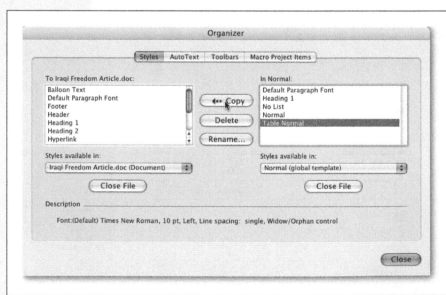

Figure 7-6:
When you click an item in either list box, the direction of the arrows on the Copy button changes accordingly. You can Shift-click to select a number of consecutive list items, or ⌘-click to select (or deselect) nonconsecutive items in the list.

To use the Organizer, proceed like this:

1. **Choose Tools→Templates and Add-ins; click Organizer.**

   You can also get to the Organizer by choosing Format→Styles and clicking Organizer, by choosing Tools→Macros and then clicking Organizer, and probably by tunneling underneath your kitchen floor. In any case, the Organizer dialog box opens, as shown in Figure 7-6.

2. **Inspect the file names above the two list boxes.**

   The left box represents the currently open document or document template if there is one; the right box represents the current global template. However, it doesn't matter which is which. You can move a style, AutoText entry, toolbar, or macro from any document or template to any other, in either direction.

3. **Set up the two lists so that the files you want to copy to and from are visible.**

   If you don't see the document or template that has what you want, click Close File below one of the boxes. When the button changes to Open File, click it again. The Choose a File dialog box opens; use it to navigate to, and open, the template or document that has the features you want.

Tip: To save frustration, note that the Show pop-up menu at the bottom of the Choose a File dialog box always defaults to *Word Templates*. In other words, if you're looking for a standard Word file that contains styles you like, it won't be activated in the Choose a File dialog box until you choose Show→All Word Documents.

If you began this exercise with the destination document (target document) open on the screen, it should already be listed on the left side of the Organizer. If not, however, it's easy enough to click its Close File/Open File button so that the correct destination file is also listed.

4. **Click the appropriate tab at the top of the Organizer dialog box, depending on the kinds of items you want to copy.**

   For example, suppose you created some terrific AutoText entries while working on a different Mac, and now you want to use them on your home-based Mac. So, you cleverly emailed yourself the file, sending those AutoText entries along for the ride.

   Now you've opened the Organizer; on the left side, you've opened the document that contains the AutoText entries. On the right side, you've opened the Normal template, so that Word will autocomplete those entries on *your* Mac all the time. Click the AutoText tab to see all the AutoText entries contained in the files on both sides.

5. **When you find an item you want to copy from one document or template to another, click it and then click Copy.**

   See Figure 7-6 for advice on selecting more than one entry. In any case, after you click Copy (or press ⌘-C), the selected items now appear in both lists. (If there's already an item of the same name in the target file, Word asks you to confirm that you want to replace it.) You can copy in both directions, as much as you like.

Tip: You can also use the Organizer to *rename* template items, such as styles and macros. Just click one and then click Rename. Enter the new name in the small dialog box that appears and click OK.

If you ever want to *delete* items—AutoText entries that pop up too often, or macros that you no longer need, for example—the Organizer is a good place to do that, too (although you may also go to Tools→AutoCorrect→ AutoText and delete them there too) Select the item in one of the list boxes and click Delete.

---

6. **Click Close.**

Word asks if you want to save the changes you made to your documents; click OK. You return to your document, where the changes you made in the Organizer are now in effect.

Normal and Global Templates

Every Word document is based on a global template. As noted earlier, 99 percent of all Word documents are based on the Normal global template, usually unbeknownst to their authors. In fact, the very first time you launch Word and click the icon for a blank document, you're using the Normal template.

The Normal template

Because Word documents are based on the Normal global template, the very first document you ever created (and probably most of them since that time) came set up to use certain default settings—the Normal font style (Times New Roman, 12 point), three heading styles, standard margins, and so on. Whenever you create new styles (as described on page 140), they wind up being saved as part of the Normal template, so that they'll appear in the Formatting Palette Style list of any other Word document you open.

But what if you want to change the default page margins, or change the Normal font to something a little less, well, normal?

The easiest way is simply to choose File→Open, navigate to the Home→Documents→ Microsoft User Data folder, and double-click the Normal template. Make whatever changes you want—to the Normal font style (choose Format→Style); to the paragraph containing the blinking insertion point, which all subsequent paragraphs will inherit (Format→Paragraph); to the document margins (Format→Document); and so on. Save and close the document. Your modified Normal template will now determine the specs of any subsequent documents you create.

Tip: The default setting that most of the world's Word users want to change is the *font;* experienced Word veterans–or most readers, for that matter–don't care if they ever see Times New Roman 12 again. For this reason, Microsoft provides a shortcut to modifying the default font in the Normal template–a method that protects the novice from even having to know about templates.

It's the Default button. Choose Format→Font, choose a typeface, and then click Default; click Yes to confirm. Any new documents you create using the File→New command automatically reflect your changes.

This useful Default button also appears when you're modifying your margins (Format→Document), page setup (File→Page Setup), proofing language (Tools→Language)–all of which represent the most popular default formatting changes. In this way, you can change the Normal template on the fly, without opening it.

Loading a template as global

Suppose someone has sent you a Word template containing macros, AutoText entries, custom toolbars, shortcut keys and custom menus that you'd like to use frequently. Instead of re-creating them, you can turn that person's document into a *global* template, and use those settings at will. To do so, open the document and proceed as follows:

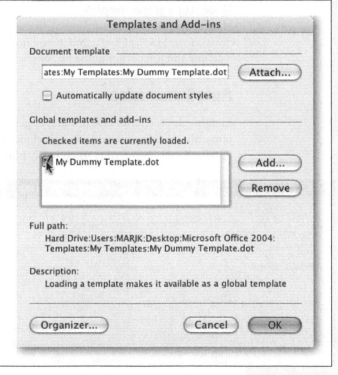

Figure 7-7:
You can make the custom items in any Word template available in every Word document by loading the template as a global template.

1. **Choose File→Save As. Navigate to the Microsoft Office 2004→Templates→My Templates folder. Click Save.**

   Word saves the document as a template.

2. **Open a new blank document. Choose Tools→Templates and Add-ins.**

   The Templates and Add-ins dialog box opens, as shown in Figure 7-7.

3. **Click Add. Navigate to the My Templates folder; open the template you just saved.**

   The template now appears in the list box as checked, (see Figure 7-7).

4. **Click OK.**

Loading a new global template has a similar effect to attaching a new document template (macros, AutoText, custom menus, and shortcut keys are transferred to your document), but because it's a *global* template, these items are available in all documents—until you either unload the template or quit Word, that is.

Note: You don't get a global template's *styles* when you attach it in this way. You can transfer them into your document using the Organizer, as described on page 230, or attach the same template as a document template.

Unloading a global template

Having several global templates open uses up memory, therefore slowing your Mac down. To unload a global template you no longer need, choose Tools→Templates and Add-ins and uncheck it in the list, or click Remove.

AutoSummarize

Imagine this scenario: Five minutes to get to the professor's office, and you suddenly remember that she wanted you to include an abstract (a summary) at the beginning of your thesis. Or this one: You proudly plunk your report on your boss's desk and he

---

POWER USERS' CLINIC

Using a Template as a Startup Item

Word automatically unloads any global templates you load (other than the Normal template) when you quit Word. When you open Word again, the Normal template is, by default, the only global template loaded.

If you want to make the AutoText entries, macros, and other attributes of another global template available all the time, you can pursue one of these two avenues:

- Copy them into the Normal template using the Organizer, as described on page 230.

- Turn the additional global template into a startup item.

To do the latter, navigate to the template on your Mac's hard drive; it's probably in the Microsoft Office 2004→ Templates folder. Click the template's document icon to select it and choose File→Duplicate. Drag the copied file to the Microsoft Office 2004→Office→Startup→Word folder (to make it available to everyone who uses your Mac), or to your Home→Documents→Microsoft User Data folder if you want this template to pertain only to your account.

From now on, this startup template is automatically loaded to every Word document you open. In other words, this global template is not automatically unloaded when you quit Word.

says, "I'm not reading all this. Give me the 15-minute version." Word's AutoSummarize feature comes to the rescue in situations just like these.

Unfortunately, Word doesn't actually read your document and then write a well-crafted summary. (Maybe in Word 2021.) What Word does is scan the document for frequently used words, then string what it believes to be the key sentences together into a summary. ("Key sentences" are those that include those most common words.)

In other words, you're best off setting fairly low expectations for this feature. Think of AutoSummarize as a glitzy feature for demos at trade shows, or perhaps as something that helps you come up with a *rough* summary; you can (and should) edit the summary later.

Creating an AutoSummary

Open the document you wish to summarize; choose Tools→AutoSummarize. Word immediately gets to work, compiling a list of key words in your document and flagging the sentences that contain them. Since it may take some time, especially in a long document, kick back and watch some TV. If nothing's on, you can press ⌘-period to cancel the process.

When Word's behind-the-scenes work is done, it presents you with a dialog box like the one in Figure 7-8.

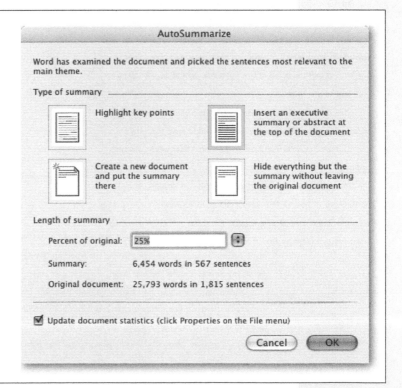

Figure 7-8:
If you've filled in the Keywords and Comments boxes on the File→Properties→Summary tab, uncheck the "Update document statistics" box here. Otherwise, Word will replace your keywords and comments with its own keywords and summary.

AutoSummarize

Word has examined the document and picked the sentences most relevant to the main theme.

Type of summary

Highlight key points

Insert an executive summary or abstract at the top of the document

Create a new document and put the summary there

Hide everything but the summary without leaving the original document

Length of summary

Percent of original: 25%

Summary: 6,454 words in 567 sentences

Original document: 25,793 words in 1,815 sentences

☑ Update document statistics (click Properties on the File menu)

Cancel   OK

Type of summary

The icons under the "Type of summary" heading let you choose how you want Word to display the summary it has generated:

- Click **Highlight key points** if you'd like to scroll through your document and see which sentences Word flagged as being key points for inclusion in the summary. This option is an effective way to see how Word has interpreted your document.

  When you click OK, your document appears with yellow highlighting on certain sentences. You also get a tiny toolbar containing a button for toggling between your original document and the highlighted version, as well as a slider for adjusting the length of summary percentage (see below). Click Close on this toolbar to return your document to its original condition.

- **Insert an executive summary** copies the sentences Word has chosen as representative and displays them at the *beginning* of the document as in Figure 7-9. If the

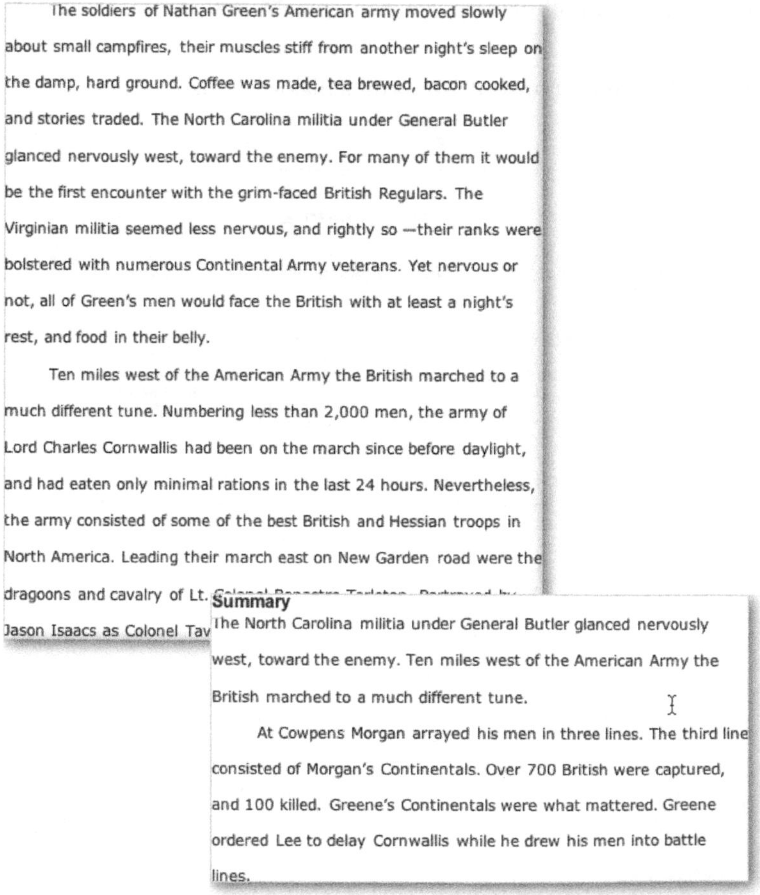

The soldiers of Nathan Green's American army moved slowly about small campfires, their muscles stiff from another night's sleep on the damp, hard ground. Coffee was made, tea brewed, bacon cooked, and stories traded. The North Carolina militia under General Butler glanced nervously west, toward the enemy. For many of them it would be the first encounter with the grim-faced British Regulars. The Virginian militia seemed less nervous, and rightly so —their ranks were bolstered with numerous Continental Army veterans. Yet nervous or not, all of Green's men would face the British with at least a night's rest, and food in their belly.

Ten miles west of the American Army the British marched to a much different tune. Numbering less than 2,000 men, the army of Lord Charles Cornwallis had been on the march since before daylight, and had eaten only minimal rations in the last 24 hours. Nevertheless, the army consisted of some of the best British and Hessian troops in North America. Leading their march east on New Garden road were the dragoons and cavalry of Lt. Colonel Banastre Tarleton. Portrayed by Jason Isaacs as Colonel Tav

Summary

The North Carolina militia under General Butler glanced nervously west, toward the enemy. Ten miles west of the American Army the British marched to a much different tune.

At Cowpens Morgan arrayed his men in three lines. The third line consisted of Morgan's Continentals. Over 700 British were captured, and 100 killed. Greene's Continentals were what mattered. Greene ordered Lee to delay Cornwallis while he drew his men into battle lines.

Figure 7-9:
Back: This narrative of an historical battle is a little hard to flight your way through.

Front: Word's Summarize feature helps you ferret out the highlights.

summary is either too long or too sketchy, press ⌘-Z to undo the AutoSummary. Now see "Length of summary" on page (Chapter 7).

- **Create a new document** opens a blank Word document and puts the summary there (instead of at the top of the document).

- **Hide everything** is the choice for those who can't commit. When you click OK, it shows you the summary, hiding the balance of the document without actually closing it. A small toolbar also opens, in which you can adjust the length of the summary (see below), and toggle between the summary and the full document.

- Under **Length of summary** at the bottom of the dialog box, Word shows you the length of the summary relative to the full document. The default is 25 percent, which means that the summary is exactly one-quarter the length of the document as a whole. When you change the percentage and then click OK, the AutoSummarize dialog box goes away, and Word recreates the summary according to your whims.

Fields

The concept of *temporary placeholders* is one of mankind's greatest inventions. When you change a tire, the jack acts as a stand-in for the tire, supporting the car until the new tire is in place. When technicians set up the lighting for a particular Hollywood movie scene, a low-paid extra models patiently, so the highly paid star doesn't have to while the technicians fiddle with shadows. When a magazine designer doesn't yet have the photo that will go on page 3, he'll simply place a box there in the correct size and label it FPO (for position only), with the intention of replacing it with the finished photograph when it's ready.

In Word, *fields* are temporary placeholders that stand in for information that may change or may come from another location on your hard drive—the current date, a page number, a place you've bookmarked, the name of a Word file, and so on. Fields, in fact, are the basis of some of Word's most powerful features. They let you:

- Create form letters and address labels, and merge them with your contact information (see page 263).

- Create indexes (page 256) and tables of contents (page 251).

- Create invoices that calculate their own totals (page 172).

- Create cross-references (page 248) and captions (page 244).

Inserting Fields

You can't *type* a field into a document. You must ask Word to create it in one of the following ways:

- Choose a command that creates a field. These are usually found on the Insert menu, such as Insert→Date and Time.

- Choose Insert→Field and choose one of the available field types from the Field dialog box (see Figure 7-10).

- Press ⌘-F9 and type the field *code*, if you know it. (The field code is a short piece of code, that tells Word what kind of information will go there.)

You may never have to create a field manually. Most of the time, fields are built right into a Word feature or another command. For instance, when you choose Insert→ Date and Time, Cross-reference, Bookmark, Footnote, or Caption, Word uses a field to define the location and content of these features.

Note: If you've used fields in Word before, you may be used to using the F9 and F11 keys to update and edit them. In Mac OS X 10.3, the Exposé feature has commandeered these two keys; however, in combination with the Option and ⌘ keys, they still have some field functions.

However, there are hundreds more fields at your disposal in Word, and inserting them is as easy as choosing them from a list in the Field dialog box.

Building fields in the Field dialog box

To place a field where the insertion point is located, choose Insert→Field to open the Field dialog box as shown in Figure 7-10. Because there are so many fields in Word, the program displays them in category groups. When you click a category in the left box, the list of fields in that category appears in the right box.

When you click a field name on the right side, the field code appears in the "Field code" box below (DATE in Figure 7-10 example). A more complete description ap-

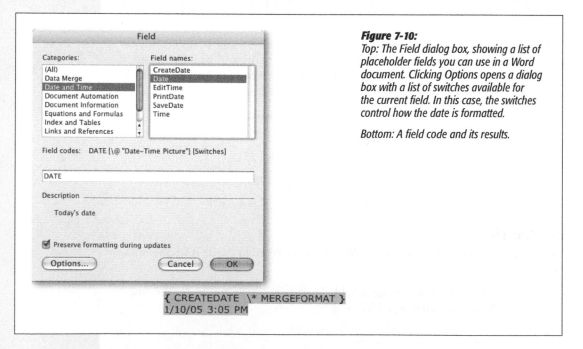

Figure 7-10:
Top: The Field dialog box, showing a list of placeholder fields you can use in a Word document. Clicking Options opens a dialog box with a list of switches available for the current field. In this case, the switches control how the date is formatted.

Bottom: A field code and its results.

pears in the Description panel near the bottom of the dialog box. You can learn a lot about fields just by clicking and reading the descriptions.

Modifying Fields with Switches

The Field dialog box has an Options button that lets you specify in more detail how you want a field to look and act. When you click it, the Field Options dialog box displays any applicable *switches* (software options), as shown in Figure 7-11. Like the Field dialog box, the Field Options dialog box has a Description panel below the "Field code" box; as you click each option, its description appears. You can read more about switches in the following tutorial.

As you build a field by adding switches or other options, you see the field code grow in the "Field code" box at the bottom of the Field dialog box. (Field veterans can type directly into this box, using the syntax shown above the box as a guide.)

Tip: If you know a thing or two about field codes, you can also edit them directly in the document. Just Control-click in the field code, choose Toggle Field Code, and edit away.

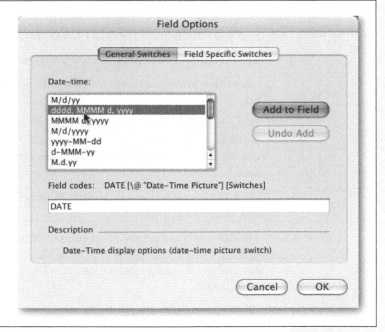

Figure 7-11:
Depending on the field you're modifying, the Field Options dialog box may show one Options tab, as shown here, or two Switches tabs. A switch is an instruction that modifies the field results. In this case, Date-Time switches tell Word how to display the current date and time.

When you've selected any options or switches, click OK (or press Return) to dismiss the Field and Field Options dialog boxes. Word returns you to your document with the newly placed field highlighted in dusky gray. The highlighting alerts you to the fact that you're looking at a field rather than normal Word text. (The highlighting doesn't show up when you print.)

Tip: If highlighted fields are just too obvious for you, then take the gray away. Choose Word→Preferences→ View tab. Choose When Selected or Never from the "Field shading" menu. Caution: If you choose Never, it will be much harder to tell where fields are. And since you can't edit field text as ordinary Word text, confusion may ensue.

What a Field Does

A field is a bit of computer code that, in one way or another, processes information. For instance, a Caption field remembers what number a caption is supposed to be, and displays that information (see page 244). The field code contains all the computerish instructions that tell Word how to figure out the Caption number and then format it. In another example, a Merge Field code (see page 263) tells Word what piece of information to grab from a database. Finally, a Date field retrieves the date from your Mac's System Preferences and places it in your document.

For example, suppose you're creating a fax cover sheet you plan on using every day. Since you keep forgetting to date your faxes, you want to create a document with a Date field in it. This way, when you fax your daily dispatch, it's automatically dated. Here's the process:

1. **Open a blank Word document and begin typing your fax cover sheet. Click wherever you want to place the date. Choose Insert→Field.**

   The Field dialog box opens, as shown in Figure 7-10.

2. **Click "Date and Time" in the Categories box (left) and "Date" in the Field Names box.**

   You actually have two options here. *CreateDate* inserts today's date, which is what you'll always see. *Date* updates automatically; it inserts the current date each time the document is printed. In this case, you obviously want the current date each time.

3. **Click Options. Choose your favorite Month/Day/Year combination from the list box, as shown in Figure 7-11.**

   The date codes are not exactly in common English, but there is a logic to them. In general, a single letter in one of these codes (M) stands for a number (*1* for January, and so on), and a repeated letter (MMMM) stands for a full version (*January* spelled out).

4. **Click Add to Field, then click OK twice.**

   The date appears in your document. When you click it, it appears highlighted in gray to indicate that it's a field, not a typed-in date.

5. **Save your document.**

   You could also save this document as a template. The Date field works either way.

Working with Fields in a Document

To change the text formatting for a field, select the entire field by dragging across it (either the field results or the field code, whichever is showing at the moment), and then use any of Word's formatting commands: press ⌘-I for italics, choose a font or font color from the Formatting Palette, and so on.

Tip: If you format fields this way, make sure that the "Preserve formatting during updates" box is turned on in the Field dialog box (see Figure 7-10). Otherwise, the field will revert to its original formatting whenever you *update* it (see below).

Displaying fields

When you look at a field in your document, you may see one of two things: the field code (which looks like intimidating gobbledygook) or the result of the field code. For example, when you insert the DATE field into a document, it might show up either as *{ CREATEDATE\@"m/D/YY"*MERGEFORMAT }* (the field code) or simply *6/20/05* (the result).

If you're seeing one of these but you'd rather see the other, Control-click the field and choose Toggle Field Codes from the shortcut menu (or click inside the field and then press Option-F9).

Or, to switch *all* fields in your document from field codes to their results, press Option-F9.

Updating fields

Because fields are just placeholders, the information that eventually fills them will change from time to time. The date changes, for example, or you may change your user information (which affects AUTHOR fields).

Word doesn't automatically update fields *while a document is open.* In other words, if you change your Mac's date in System Preferences, the date fields in your open documents don't reflect the change. However, if you change your Mac's date and then *open* a document with date fields, Word does update them upon opening. To update fields in open documents, press ⌘-A (selecting an entire document automatically selects all the fields in it) and press Shift-Option-⌘-U. A quick way to update a single field is to Control-click it and choose Update Field from the shortcut menu.

Tip: If you like, Word can update your fields automatically each time you print. The secret is to choose Word→Preferences→Print tab and turn on the "Update fields" box.

Locking, unlocking, and unlinking fields

There will be times, especially when you send someone else a copy of your document, when you really don't want anyone to change your carefully planned field codes. To protect a field from changes, click in it and press ⌘-F11. This keystroke *locks* the field, meaning that you can't update the field or edit its code. You can still format the field results, however. (To lock all fields in the document at once, press ⌘-A, then ⌘-F11.)

To unlock a field, thus enabling updating and editing again, select it and press Shift-⌘-F11.

If you *really* want closure on a field, you can freeze it in time forever with its current results. To do so, click in the field and press Shift-⌘-F9. Unlinked from its code, the field is now ordinary Word text; it's no longer a field, and will never be automatically updated.

Field printing options

Normally, you'll want to print your document with the field results; you want people to see a date, not { DATE MMMMd, yyyy * MERGEFORMAT }. However, it is possible to print out a copy that shows the field codes, so that a technical-type person can look them over, for instance. To do so, choose Word→Preferences→Print panel and turn on the "Field codes" box (under "Include with document").

Bookmarks

Bookmarks in Word are the digital equivalent of folding down the page or underlining a paragraph that you want to refer to later. You can use bookmarks in long documents as you write them, perhaps to mark places that need more work later. They're also useful in Word documents you get from others, to mark places that you have questions about, or pages that you're going to use most often. And because you give each digital bookmark a *name,* it's easy to jump to specific spots in a long (or even short) document.

Adding Bookmarks

Select the word, phrase, or paragraph that you want to bookmark, or just click in the text at the appropriate spot. Choose Insert→Bookmark (or press Shift-⌘-F5), and assign your bookmark a name in the "Bookmark name" box (see Figure 7-12). When creating a name, adhere to these parameters: Be descriptive and specific; use underlines instead of spaces (Word, in its ornery way, doesn't permit spaces in bookmark names); use numbers, if you like, but not as the first character; and do not exceed 40 characters.

Click Add or press Return when you're done.

Deleting Bookmarks

To delete one or more bookmarks, press Shift-⌘-F5 or choose Insert→Bookmark, click the name of the bookmark you want to discard, and click Delete. Of course, your other option is to delete the text or graphic object (if any) that the bookmark is attached to. When the text or image goes away, the bookmark goes with it.

Navigating by Bookmark

After you've scattered bookmarks throughout your document, you're ready for the fun part: leapfrogging from one bookmark to another, skipping all the extraneous stuff in between. Your choices are to take Word's word for it that you're at a bookmark, or make all bookmarks visible on the Preferences→View panel, as described above.

Note: What you see when you leap to a bookmark depends on what you did when you created it. If you had highlighted text or graphics before choosing Insert→Bookmark, that text or object is selected when you jump to it. If you had only clicked in some text *without* highlighting anything, you get a blinking insertion point at the bookmark when you jump to it—that's all.

- **Use the Bookmarks dialog box.** To go directly to a bookmarked location, press Shift-⌘-F5 or choose Insert→Bookmark; the Bookmark dialog box lists all the bookmarks you've created. Double-click the name of a bookmark. The insertion point moves to the selected bookmark; the Bookmark dialog box remains open so that you can repeat the process. Press Return or click Close to dismiss it.

- **Use the Go To command.** Another way to travel to a particular bookmark is to press F5, ⌘-G, or choose Edit→Go To. Each of these actions opens the Go To tab

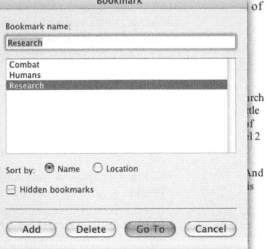

Figure 7-12:
Back: Bookmarks in a document are represented by heavy brackets.

Front: All bookmarks you've inserted appear in the Insert→Bookmark dialog box, which is also where you name new bookmarks. (If the Add button is grayed out, you've typed an invalid name; backspace and try again.)

Building the Perfect Beast – Research in *War of the Worlds*

If you are the [Humans], the Martian technology is overwhelming. You need to constantly have scientists researching weaponry and facilities to keep up with your nemesis. If you[...] of the Humans -- until, fina[...] spirit. Regardless of who[...]

The Second Arm[...]

Of course, [combat] is a pivot[...] is just as critical. Research, t[...] consistently and effectively [...] this world (pun intended) in [...] Ironclads, Level 2 Self-Prop[...]

[Research] affects combat. An[...] like combat, to research wel[...] chapter is all about -- whethe[...] perfect beast.

Bookmark

Bookmark name:
Research

Combat
Humans
Research

Sort by: ● Name ○ Location

☐ Hidden bookmarks

(Add) (Delete) (Go To) (Cancel)

Fgi0701.tif (Fighting Machines)

The Fighting Machines are tough customers... at least in the early game.

of the Find and Replace dialog box (see page 72). In the "Go to what" list box at left, click Bookmark and choose a bookmark name from the menu at right. Click Previous and Next to jump around by bookmark.

- **Use the Navigator buttons.** Start by using the Go To procedure described above to jump to the first bookmark. Now you can close the Find box and use the Navigator Buttons (see page 22) to move forward and backward through your bookmarks, or press the keyboard shortcuts, Shift-page down and Shift-page up, instead.

Tip: When using the Bookmark dialog box, checking the Hidden Bookmarks box adds cross-references (see page 248) to the bookmark list. Now you can use the Bookmark dialog box and the Go To feature to browse your cross-references.

Viewing Bookmarks

Bookmarks are invisible; even the Show/Hide (¶) button on the Standard toolbar or Formatting Palette doesn't uncover them. If you really want to see where they lie on your document, choose Word→Preferences→View tab; turn on the Bookmarks checkbox. (To hide them again, just turn off the box.)

When visible, text bookmarks are surrounded by thick brackets; location bookmarks appear as big, fat I-bars.

Captions

Captions are labels that identify illustrations, tables, equations created by Microsoft Equation Editor, and other objects by number (see Figure 7-13).

Most people type in captions manually, but Word's captioning feature has huge advantages over the manual method: It can number, renumber, and even insert captions automatically. Letting Word handle the captions not only saves you time, but could potentially save you from repeating a caption number, for instance, or leaving out a caption entirely.

Inserting Captions

To caption an item—table, picture, text box, or some other object—first select it, then choose Insert→Caption. Instead of typing a caption, you *build* it using the Caption dialog box, as shown in Figure 7-13.

- **Caption, Label.** You can't directly edit the words in the Caption box (such as "Figure"), which is how the caption will appear in the document. Instead, this box reflects whatever you select from the Label pop-up menu. If none of the three labels provided (Figure, Equation, Table) strikes your fancy, click New Label and type your own—*Illustration* or *Chart,* for instance—and hit Return.

- **Position.** This pop-up menu lets you choose one of the two most popular places for the location of your caption: above or below the captioned item.

- **Numbering.** Word numbers your captions automatically; this feature, after all, is the whole point of this exercise. Use the Numbering dialog box, as shown in Figure 7-13, to choose a number format (Roman numerals or whatever).

If you choose to include the chapter number in the captions (perhaps before the hyphen—"Figure 7-20," as in this book, for example), you need to tell Word how to *find* the chapter numbers. A couple of conditions apply: The chapters must all be within the same document, and you must use one of Word's built-in chapter-heading *styles* (see page 137) for the chapter headings.

Figure 7-13:
Top: Labels you add using the New Label button appear on the pop-up menu with the three preinstalled labels.

Middle: If hyphens don't do anything for you, choose a different separator such as a period, colon, or dash. If the chapter headings in your document use one of Word's built-in heading styles, you can make Word automatically number your figures 1-1, 1-2, 1-3, and so on.

Bottom: A caption in place. Note that if you're planning to import your Word document into a desktop publishing program, you'll probably lose your captions. The text of the captions may appear, but the numbering will be lost.

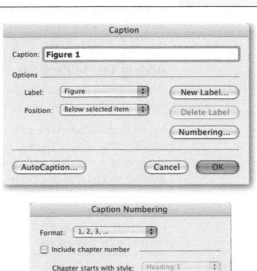

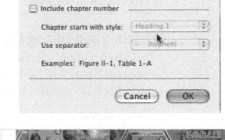

Figure **1** Jenson defends the village.

For instance, suppose you've formatted all your chapter headings using the Heading 1 style. Furthermore, suppose you've autonumbered them as described on page: you chose Format→Bullets and Numbering→Outline Numbered tab and selected one of the numbering styles with Heading 1, Heading 2, and so on.

Now, when you turn on the "Include chapter number" box (Figure 7-13) and choose Heading 1 from the pop-up menu, your captions include the correct chapter number. (And your chapter headings are automatically numbered, to boot.)

When you finish creating the caption, click OK. The caption (numbered 1) appears in a separate paragraph above or below the selected object. As you insert more captions, Word will number them in order. (*Deleting* or rearranging captions is another matter, however, as described below.)

Adding Text to Captions

If the caption for your bird picture reads "Figure 1," you can simply click after the 1 and type a description, such as *Blue-footed Booby*.

If you accidentally type over or delete the label or caption number, hit ⌘-Z (or choose Edit→Undo Typing) to restore order. If it's too late to Undo, then your only alternative is to delete and reinsert the caption. The document's captions may then need to be updated (see below).

Tip: A neat way to add supplementary text to captions is to click the caption and choose Insert→Caption; you can then type the extra text in the Caption window itself. This technique produces a caption that you can't edit in the document itself.

Deleting and Editing Captions

To delete a caption, select it and press Delete. To change a single caption—for example, to change Figure 1 to Table 1 and leave all the other Figure captions untouched—you must delete the caption and insert a new one as described above.

Word's captioning feature makes it exceptionally easy to change *all* captions of the same label at once. For example, if your document has a series of captions labeled Figure 1, Figure 2, and so on, you can easily change them to the more descriptive Photo 1.1, Photo 1.2, and so on. Just select any of the captions (be sure to select the *entire* caption) and choose Insert→Caption to open the Caption dialog box. Now you can choose a different label, create a new label, pick a different numbering system, and so on. Any changes you make will apply to *all* captions under the original Figure label.

Tip: Technically, captions are *fields,* which are described in full on page 237. So if you've used captions in your document, you may start to see strange-looking codes like { SEQ FIGURE *ROMAN } instead of the caption. Don't be alarmed—and don't delete them!

What you're seeing is Word's *field code*—its own, internal geek instructions for creating the caption. You need to tell Word to display the field *results*—the caption itself—instead. To do that, Control-click the field code and choose Toggle Field Codes from the shortcut menu.

Or, to return *all* caption field codes to normal, press ⌘-A (or choose Edit→Select All), Control-click any single field code, and *then* choose Toggle Field Codes. (Be sure to press Control *before* clicking, otherwise you'll undo the Select All.)

Updating Captions

When it comes to automatic caption numbering, Word's fairly good at counting—but not infallible. When you delete a caption or drag one out of sequence, the others don't get renumbered automatically. If you want your figures numbered sequentially, you must *update* the captions after making such a change.

To update a single caption, select it by selecting all of its text; then press Shift-Option-⌘-U. (Alternatively, Control-click the caption and choose Update Field from the shortcut menu.) Updating all captions in a document at once couldn't be easier: Just press ⌘-A (Select All), then Shift-Option-⌘-U.

AutoCaptioning

Inserting captions is easy enough, but you can make it downright effortless. Word's AutoCaptioning feature can automatically add a caption to any Clip Art, picture, or table whenever you add one to your document. Here's how it's done:

1. **Choose Insert→Caption; in the dialog box, click AutoCaption.**

   In the AutoCaption dialog box, you're presented with a list of checkboxes for the kinds of objects Word can automatically create captions for—a picture, a Microsoft Organization Chart, and so on.

Note: AutoShapes are *not* on the list. Captions for AutoShapes and other drawing objects must be inserted manually; fortunately, Word still numbers them correctly along with all those created automatically.

2. **Turn on the boxes—as many as you wish—for the kinds of graphics you want captioned.**

   You can have more than one kind of label in your document, and you can choose different object types for each one. For example, use "Table A" for tables and "Figure 1" for pictures and charts. To do so, turn on the "Microsoft Word Table" box and go on to step 3; choose "Table" for the labels. Then repeat the procedure, turning on the boxes for the items you want the "Figure" label applied to. You can have as many kinds of labels AutoCaptioned at once as you like, provided you can keep them all straight in your head!

3. **Using the pop-up menus, choose a label and a position for the captions.**

When you check a box as described in step 2, you may notice that the Label menu changes. Word is suggesting a label for that type of object. You can override it by making a different choice from the Label menu.

The label and position choices here work as described on page 244); as always, you can create new labels by clicking the New Label button.

4. **Choose a numbering style for the AutoCaptions.**

If you're using more than one type of caption label, each can have a different numbering style.

5. **Click OK.**

Now insert the pictures or tables in your document. The captions will appear automatically.

Turning AutoCaptions Off

To turn AutoCaptioning off, choose Insert→Caption, click AutoCaption, and uncheck the boxes for the captioned objects. Existing captions stay put, but no new ones will be added automatically.

Cross-References

Long, technical, or scholarly documents, frequently contain phrases like "see Chapter 12" or "see Figure 8 on page 100." These are *cross-references*—words that refer the reader to another place in the document. Of course, you can always type your own cross-references—but what a mess you'll have when you decide to cut a few pages from the first chapter, and all 1,424 of your cross-refs now point to the wrong page numbers!

Word stands ready to create smarter cross-references that update themselves no matter how you edit your document. What starts out saying "See page 24" will change automatically to say "See page 34" after you insert a 10-page introduction.

Remember these two principles as you start on the road to cross-reference nirvana:

1. **Word thinks of cross-references as pointing to *objects* in your document, not places.**

In other words, a cross-reference must be connected to a figure, a bookmark, or a heading.

2. **Cross-references can only refer to something within the same document.**

If you're creating a document with multiple chapters, you must combine them into one Master Document (see page 209) before working with cross-references.

Inserting Cross-References

When creating a cross-reference, start by typing appropriate lead-in text into your document: *See, Turn to, As shown in,* or whatever you like. Then it's time to get Word involved.

Here, for example, is how you might build a cross-reference that reads, "See Figure 1 below" (see Figure 7-14).

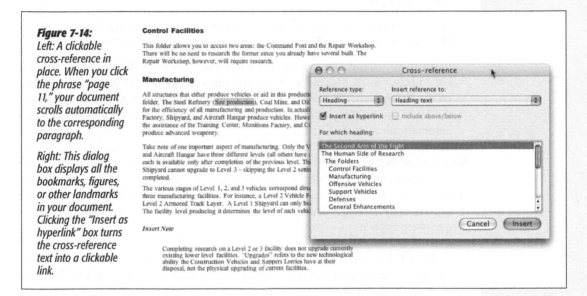

Figure 7-14:
Left: A clickable cross-reference in place. When you click the phrase "page 11," your document scrolls automatically to the corresponding paragraph.

Right: This dialog box displays all the bookmarks, figures, or other landmarks in your document. Clicking the "Insert as hyperlink" box turns the cross-reference text into a clickable link.

1. **Type *See Figure;* then choose Insert→Cross-reference.**

   The Cross-reference dialog box appears.

2. **Make a selection from the "Reference type" pop-up menu.**

   The list contains only the things that Word can recognize as a cross-reference: a figure (anything with a *caption,* as described in the previous section); a Word table; any text that's formatted with one of Word's built-in headings or numbered lists; an equation created with Microsoft Equation Editor; or a footnote, endnote, or bookmark.

Tip: If you don't use any of the above items in your document, but just want to refer to some text, you can always bookmark it (see page 242). For instance, if you want a cross-reference to read "See the discussion of komodo dragons on page 30," first go to page 30 and bookmark the paragraph where you talk about komodo dragons. Name the bookmark "komodo dragons." Now go to where you want the cross-reference positioned, choose Bookmark in the "Reference type" menu, and continue as described below.

---

3. **Choose the specific item you're cross-referencing in the "For which" list box.**

In Figure 7-20, "Bookmark" is the chosen reference type; the "For which" box lists all the numbered items in the document—an employee training manual in this case. If you had chosen "Numbered item," all the list items in your document would appear, and so on. From this list, choose the correct destination for this particular cross-reference.

4. **In the "Insert reference to" menu, specify what type of item you want the reference to point to.**

You have a choice of the actual text (of the caption or paragraph), the number (of the page, list item, or outline paragraph), or simply "above" or "below."

In other words, this is where you tell Word what you want the cross-reference to *say*. In Figure 7-14, the choice "Paragraph number" places the number "1" in the cross-reference after the typed word "See." If you were to go back and renumber the list in the training manual, the number in the cross-reference would change automatically.

Note to attorneys: Select the "Numbered item" reference in order to cross-reference numbered paragraphs in legal documents. The "Paragraph number (no context)" and "Paragraph number (full context)" options in the "Insert reference to" menu were created just for you. "Full context" names a cross-referenced paragraph by the entire string of outline numbers: 1. (a) (i), and so on. Use "no context" to refer to the same paragraph simply as (i).

If **above/below** is not one of the choices on the "Insert reference to" menu, turn on the "Include above/below box" to add "above" or "below" to the end of the cross-reference, as shown in Figure 7-14.

Thereafter, no matter where you move the referenced item—as long as it's within the same document—Word will change "above" to "below," or vice versa, as necessary.

5. **Click Insert or press Return when you're done creating the cross-reference.**

Modifying and Deleting Cross-References

To change a cross-reference (in case you've changed a figure or divided your document into two shorter ones), just select it, choose Insert→Cross-reference, and modify the settings. This way, you can change a cross-reference to Figure 2 instead of Figure 1, for example.

To delete a cross-reference, select it and press Delete. (When selecting a cross-reference, drag over only the shaded part, as shown in Figure 7-14; do not include any additional text you've typed.)

Note: You can't create a cross-reference to anything inside a *text box* (see page 151).

Like captions, cross-references are a type of *field* (see page 237), and also like captions, cross-references can sometimes spontaneously combust. Similarly, you fix them as you would broken captions. For example, if you see some cryptic characters like { REF_Ref372221765\r\p } instead of the cross-reference you were expecting, Control-click the shaded part of the cross-reference and select Toggle Field Codes from the shortcut menu.

Again like captions, Word sometimes misses a few—despite the fact that the program updates cross-references automatically when you move text in your document. Therefore, as part of the finishing touches on any document in which you've used cross-references, press ⌘-A and then press **Shift-Option-⌘-U**. You've just signaled Word to update all cross-references (and captions, for that matter).

Creating a Table of Contents

Word's Table of Contents (TOC) feature saves you time and helps organize your document. Once you've built a table of contents in Word, you can use it to navigate your document (just as you might with the Navigation Pane); you can custom format it to get just the look you want; you can save yourself the task of updating page numbers if you add or delete text from your document (which can be a major pain); and you can use it as a Web site map, because in Online and Page Layout views, a Word Table of Contents is automatically hyperlinked.

TOC the Easiest Way: Using Built-in Headings

If you have a well-organized document, and you've used Word's outliner or one of its built-in heading styles (Heading 1, Heading 2, and so on) to introduce each new topic, Word's TOC feature was made for you. Go directly to step 1 below.

If you wrote your document without headings, on the other hand, insert them before creating the table. (Use Word's built-in heading *styles,* as illustrated on page 137.) Be descriptive when you design the headings; instead of just "Chapter 10" or "Advanced Techniques," use "Chapter 10: Underwater Architecture" or "Advanced Card-Counting."

When you're ready to smack a TOC on the first page of your masterwork, proceed as follows:

1. **Click where you want the TOC to begin.**

   To put the TOC on the first page, click at the very beginning of the document. (You can also insert it after a title page or introduction.)

2. **Choose Insert→Index and Tables→Table of Contents tab.**

   You should now be staring at the Index and Tables dialog box shown in Figure 7-15.

3. **Choose a style in the Formats box, as described in Figure 7-15.**

If none of the format styles thrills you, choose "From template" and see "TOC the Harder Way: Using Other Styles" on page 253.

4. **Decide how many levels you want to show, using the "Show levels" control.**

For example, you may want your table of contents to show only chapter titles; in that case, choose 1 in the "Show levels" box. If you've divided your document into many levels of detail, each with its own heading level, you may want to show only the first two or three levels to keep the table from getting too long. (The table of contents in this book, for example, shows chapter titles and the first-level subject headings.)

5. **Format the page numbers.**

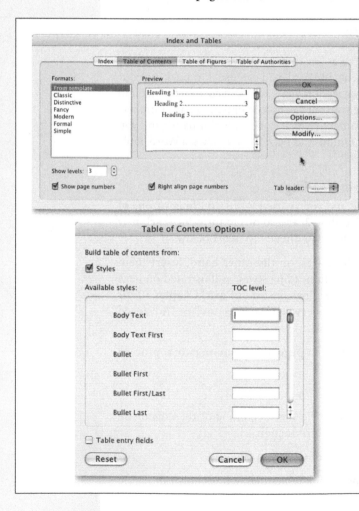

Figure 7-15:
Top: The "From template" format uses the styles in the current document template and results in a consistent appearance with the rest of your document. (See page 137 for more on styles.) Click on each one and look in the Preview window; choose the one that makes the best impression.

Bottom: The Options dialog box lets you build your table of contents from styles you've used in your document other than Heading 1, Heading 2, and so on. For instance, you can add the Bullet style to the list so that important list items will appear in the table of contents.

Most printed tables of contents include page numbers, of course, but if you're preparing a document for the Web where page numbering is irrelevant, then turn off "Show page numbers."

If you elect to use page numbering, you can also indicate whether you want them to be right-aligned (as in the Preview window in Figure 7-15) and what style of Tab leader you want (the dots, spaces, or lines that connect each title with its page number). The Preview window in Figure 7-15 shows a dotted line, but the "Tab leader" menu offers several other choices.

6. Click OK.

You now return to your document. If you switch into Page Layout view (View→ Page Layout), you'll see the table of contents, complete with page numbers (see Figure 7-16).

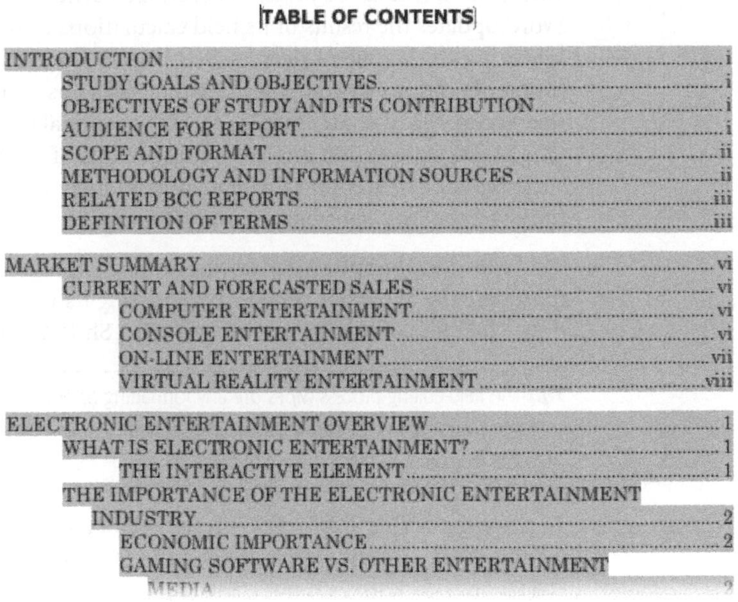

Figure 7-16:
A table of contents created from the headings in an actual Word document. The gray doesn't print; it simply informs you, the editor: "These are fields, and I, Microsoft Word, will be responsible for maintaining and updating them. Don't try editing anything here yourself."

TABLE OF CONTENTS

INTRODUCTION i
    STUDY GOALS AND OBJECTIVES i
    OBJECTIVES OF STUDY AND ITS CONTRIBUTION i
    AUDIENCE FOR REPORT i
    SCOPE AND FORMAT ii
    METHODOLOGY AND INFORMATION SOURCES ii
    RELATED BCC REPORTS iii
    DEFINITION OF TERMS iii

MARKET SUMMARY vi
    CURRENT AND FORECASTED SALES vi
        COMPUTER ENTERTAINMENT vi
        CONSOLE ENTERTAINMENT vi
        ON-LINE ENTERTAINMENT vii
        VIRTUAL REALITY ENTERTAINMENT viii

ELECTRONIC ENTERTAINMENT OVERVIEW 1
    WHAT IS ELECTRONIC ENTERTAINMENT? 1
        THE INTERACTIVE ELEMENT 1
    THE IMPORTANCE OF THE ELECTRONIC ENTERTAINMENT
        INDUSTRY 2
        ECONOMIC IMPORTANCE 2
        GAMING SOFTWARE VS. OTHER ENTERTAINMENT
        MEDIA 2

TOC the Harder Way: Using Other Styles

Life is easiest if you use Word's built-in heading styles (Heading 1, Heading 2...) when preparing your manuscript—but that's not your only option. If your document is delineated by other styles, whether built-in or ones you've created, you can use those as the basis for your table of contents headings instead.

To do so, chose Insert→Index and Tables→Table of Contents tab. Follow steps 1 through 5 on page 251, and then click Options.

In the Table of Contents Options dialog box, you see a scrolling list of all styles in your document (see Figure 7-15). If you scroll down, you'll see that Heading 1, 2, and

3 have been assigned to corresponding TOC levels. This is your opportunity: Delete the numbers from these heading styles and type new TOC level numbers (1, 2, and so on) into the boxes next to your own styles, exactly as shown in Figure 7-15.

Tip: You can even type each level number next to more than one style. For instance, if you want your captions to be listed in the table of contents under each main topic, like your Level 3 headings, just type 3 in the box next to Caption (as shown in Figure 7-15).

In fact, you don't even have to use different levels. If you make *every* heading style Level 1, every item in your Table of Contents will have equal weight—no indents or typeface changes.

Click OK and return to the Preview box to check your work.

Updating or Deleting a Table of Contents

Like many Word features, TOCs rely on self-updating, noneditable blocks of gray-background text called *fields,* as described earlier in this chapter. As you may recall, Word updates the results of its field calculations only when you *open* the document. If, during an evening of sleepless self-doubt, you decide to rewrite the names of the different sections in your thesis, it may come as something of a shock to discover that your table of contents still shows the original section names. And if you cut out that 31-page digression into the mating habits of the Venezuelan beaver, you may be surprised to discover that the table of contents page numbers haven't been updated to reflect the new, shorter status of your paper.

The solution is simple: After editing your document and before printing or sending it, update the Table of Contents by *updating* its fields. To do so, click at the left side of the first line of the TOC, and then press Shift-Option-⌘-U.

Tip: The field-editing process *wipes out* any formatting or editing you've done to the text in your table of contents—which is an excellent argument for formatting your TOC using the dialog boxes as described on page 251 instead of formatting them by hand.

To dispense with a TOC, click at the very beginning of the first line of the Table of Contents. Press Option-F9 to display the TOC field code against its gray background ({ **TOC\o"1-3"** }, for example). Select the entire field code, brackets and all, and press Delete. You've just vaporized all remnants of the Table of Contents.

POWER USERS' CLINIC

Custom Formatting the Table of Contents

You can change the typographical look of your TOC headings just as you would any style (see page 137 for more on styles). Just choose Format→Styles, click the TOC1 style name, click Modify, and proceed as described on page 143 . Click OK to return to the Style dialog box. Click the next TOC heading level, click Modify again, and repeat until you've designed a table of contents to call your very own.

Table of Figures and Table of Authorities

Creating a table of figures or table of authorities is very much like creating a table of contents. Word takes captions (for the Table of Figures) or citations (for the Table of Authorities) and compiles them into a table. You can custom design type styles just as in a TOC, and you can update and delete these tables exactly as described above. There are only a few differences.

Table of Figures

A table of figures is a list of captions, as opposed to headings. If you've inserted captions for pictures, tables, graphs, or equations in your document, Word can list them, along with their page numbers and tab leaders, just as in a table of contents. The steps for creating one are precisely the same as for creating a table of contents (page 251), except that you click the Table of Figures tab in step 2 instead of Table of Contents.

Table of Authorities

Lawyers, legal secretaries, and paralegals: This section is for you. In fact, nobody else is likely to know what a table of authorities *is*.

A table of authorities (TOA) doesn't automatically use existing document styles like headings or captions. You have to mark each citation (case, statute, or document) that you want the TOA to use. To create a table of authorities in Word, follow these steps:

1. **In your document, select a citation.**

   For example, you might highlight "Title 37, Code of Federal Regulations, Section 1.56(a)."

2. **Choose Insert→Index and Tables→Table of Authorities tab; click Mark Citation.**

   The keyboard shortcut, for the nimble-fingered, is Shift-Option-⌘-I.

3. **Select the current citation type in the Category menu.**

   If you want to use a category that's not shown, click one of the numbers (8 through 16) in the menu. Click Category; then type the new category name in the "Replace with" box. Click Replace, and then click OK.

4. **Edit the text of the citation in the "Selected text" box.**

   Do so only if you want the citation to appear differently in the Table of Authorities. For example, add boldface or underscores.

5. **Type an abbreviated version of the citation in the "Short citation" box.**

In the next step, Word is going to search for the next occurrence or occurrences of this citation. If you used a specific abbreviation in your document, use that here as well—"Title 37," for instance.

6. **Click Mark or Mark All.**

   If you want to go through your document and find citations individually, click Mark and then click Next Citation. To let Word find, and automatically mark, all long and short versions of the current citation, click Mark All. Word marks citations with TA *field codes* (see page 238).

7. **After marking all your citations, click Close.**

   The Mark citation box goes away.

   When you're done marking the citations, it's time to create the Table of Authorities itself.

8. **Click where you want the Table of Authorities to begin. Choose Insert→Index and Tables→Table of Authorities tab. Choose from the category menu.**

   You can make a table of authorities for All citations, or create a separate one for each category. If you formatted citations in the "Selected text" box (step 3 above), be sure to turn on the "Keep original formatting" box.

9. **Choose a design in the Formats box and continue formatting your Table of Authorities.**

   See the box on page 254 for more detail on formatting.

10. **Click OK.**

    If you add a new citation after completing the Table of Authorities, it's easy. Just select the new citation, press Shift-Option-⌘-I and follow steps 3 through 7 in the first set of instructions above.

    To update a Table of Authorities, click at the very beginning of the table and press F9. The same rules apply as described in "Updating or Deleting a Table of Contents," on page 254.

Indexing

Although Microsoft may hate to admit it, few people actually use Word to publish books. Most "real" books may be *written* in Word, but they're usually then poured into a proper page-layout program like Quark XPress or InDesign for the rest of the process.

That doesn't stop Microsoft from wishing its word processor were up to the challenge, though. As evidence, here's Microsoft's indexing feature, which can spew forth a professional-looking index for a document, complete with page numbers, subentries, and the works. (The operative word, however, is *can;* indexing involves considerable patience and tolerance on your part. As you'll soon find out, indexing often involves a descent into Word's sub-basement of field codes—a pseudo-programming language that's not intended for casual experimentation.)

Phase 1: Create Index Entries

As smart as Word 2004 is, it can't read your document and ascertain what the important topics are; you must tell it which concepts you want indexed.

You do so by reading over each page of your document. Each time you come to an important point that you want included in the index, perform the following steps:

1. **Select the word or phrase that you want to index.**

   For instance, in a book about birds, you might want to create an index entry for *eggs*. So you'd highlight the word *eggs* in the manuscript.

2. **Press Shift-Option-⌘-X.**

   You could also choose Insert→Index and Tables→Index tab and then click Mark Entry in the dialog box—but life's too short.

   Shift-Option-⌘-X is a keystroke well worth learning (or redefining to something easier—see page 677), since you'll be using it often. It opens the Mark Index Entry dialog box, shown in Figure 7-17.

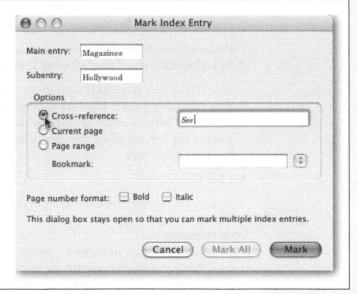

Figure 7-17:
The index entry for the term you high-lighted doesn't have to match the text you highlighted. If you'd rather have this index entry say Omelettes instead of Eggs, for example, feel free to type right over the proposed "Main entry" text here.

3. **Choose Bold or Italic for the page number, if you like.**

   Use this feature to make the principal mention of the indexed term boldface or italic. This will make it stand out from the rest of the page numbers for the same term—to indicate a page where an illustration appears, for example (Eggs, 9, 11–13, **34**, 51–52).

4. **Specify a subentry, if applicable.**

For instance, if the material on the current page is mainly about yellow-bellied nuthatch eggs, you may want the index to show "yellow-bellied nuthatch" as a subentry under "eggs" (see Figure 7-17). Type *yellow-bellied nuthatch* in the Subentry box. Word assumes that you want this particular phrase indexed as a subentry under "eggs" (or whatever your main entry was in step 1).

5. **Click Mark to create an index entry for your selected word or phrase.**

If you click Mark All instead, Word creates an index entry for *every* occurrence in the document of the word or phrase you selected in step 1. (The fact that it flags only the *first* occurrence in each paragraph is actually beneficial, since the entry may be repeated frequently in a paragraph. The purpose of the index is to direct the reader to the correct paragraph or page; to index each occurrence would create an overly long, cumbersome index.)

Note: Mark All is case-sensitive. In other words, Mark All will create entries for each occurrence of *eggs*, but not *Eggs*.

---

6. **Highlight the next entry in your document.**

The dialog box remains open even after you click Mark or Mark All. However, to move on to the next entry, you have to select another word or phrase and then press Shift-Option-⌘-X again.

7. **Proceed through your entire document, marking each entry you want in the index by highlighting it and then pressing Shift-Option-⌘-X.**

A *field code* (see page 238) appears in your document after each term you've indexed. Because these fields are formatted as *hidden text* (see page 112), Word automatically turns *on* the Show/Hide button on the Standard toolbar. That's why you see line breaks, paragraph breaks, and any other hidden text in addition to the index field codes.

8. **Click Close.**

Now you're ready to build the index as described on page 261.

Cross-references

A cross-reference in an index looks like this: "Eggs, *See reproduction.*" It tells your reader: "*You* may be looking under Eggs, but actually I've listed all of these entries under Reproduction." (Of course, if you create a cross-reference for "reproduction," you have to actually create index entries for that topic!)

To create a cross-reference, follow the steps above, but before clicking Mark Entry in step 3, type the cross-referenced term into the "Cross-reference" box. The word "See" already appears in the "Cross-reference" box; you can type text after it (or over it). For instance, you can change it to "See also" or just "also."

Page range entries

Occasionally, the information related to your index entry spans several pages, like this: "Eggs, 9–19." Unfortunately, Word requires that you *bookmark* the range of pages before creating the index entry. To do so:

1. **Select the entire block of text that you want indexed, even if it's many pages long. Choose Insert→Bookmark; name the bookmark in the "Bookmark name" box, then click Add.**

   You can name the bookmark anything, because this name doesn't affect the index entry name. If this is the first mention of eggs in the document, for example, you could call it Eggs1. After you click Add, the Bookmark dialog box closes. (See page 242 for more on bookmarking.)

2. **Back in your document, click at the end of the selected bookmark text.**

   This tells Word where to mark the index entry field. (If you don't see the bookmark brackets around the text, turn on Bookmarks on the Word→Preferences→ View panel.)

3. **Press Shift-Option-⌘-X.**

   The Mark Index Entry dialog box appears.

4. **Type the index entry, but then click "Page range." From the pop-up menu, choose the name of the bookmark you just created.**

   This menu contains all the bookmarks you've created so far in the document you're indexing.

5. **Click Mark and continue creating index entries, if you wish.**

When you later create the index, the range of pages you bookmarked will appear next to the index entry.

POWER USERS' CLINIC

Indexing on a Deadline

If time doesn't allow reading–or even skimming–your entire document for the topics you'd like to index, there's a quicker way. By typing the topics you want to index directly into the Mark Index Entry dialog box, you can create a quick, emergency index without having to do any re-reading. After all, if you wrote the document, you have a pretty good idea what the important points are.

Start by choosing Insert→Index and Tables→Index tab. Click Mark Entry to open the Mark Index Entry dialog box (see Figure 7-17).

Type the relevant word or phrase that you want to appear in the index in the "Main entry" box, then click Mark All; Word indexes all occurrences in your document of the word or phrase you typed. Type the next term you want indexed and click Mark All again; repeat this process until you've told Word about every important topic you can remember. Finally, click Close and proceed as described under "Building the Index" on page 261.

You can always redo or expand the index later, when time allows. Just select any word or phrase you want to add to the index, and proceed as described on page 257.

Phase 2: Editing Index Field Codes (Optional)

Like many Word features, Word's indexing feature relies on *fields* (invisible placehold-ers, as described on page 237). Because index entry fields are marked as hidden text (page 112), you can only see them when the Show/Hide (¶) button located on the Standard toolbar (or Formatting Palette) is on. At that point, the indexing codes show up, looking something like this: { XE "eggs" \r "eggs1" }.

In other words, if you'd like to see the field codes—so that you can delete them, edit them, or just see where they are—click ¶ on the Standard toolbar or the Document section of the Formatting Palette.

Once you've made your field codes visible, you can edit or delete them. To delete an index entry, select it by dragging over its field code (including the brackets), and then press Delete.

Unless you want to fool around with editing field codes, deleting an entry is also the easiest way to *edit* an entry; after deleting the faulty field codes, simply create a new replacement entry, as described on page 237.

If you're unafraid to edit field codes directly, however, here's how to edit the four kinds of index field codes:

- **Single page entry (eggs, 234).** The field code looks like { XE "eggs"\b }. If you mis-spelled the main entry, made an error in capitalization, or whatever, you can edit the word between the quotation marks. But be careful not to disturb any other part of the code, including the spaces. Also, in this example, the *b* after the backslash indicates boldface; an *i* here stands for italic. To change a boldface page number to plain text, for example, delete both the letter *b* and the backslash.

- **Cross-reference entry (eggs, *See* reproduction).** The field code looks like { XE "eggs" \t "*See* reproduction" }. In addition to editing the main entry, you can also change the cross-reference (reproduction) or the additional text (*See*). Again, be careful not to disturb any other part of the code.

- **Page range entry (eggs, 234-236).** The field code looks like { XE "eggs" \r "Eggs1" }. This one's tricky to edit, because in order to change the range bookmark name (see "Page range entries" on page 259), you have to type in the *exact* name of the bookmark. However, you can change this into a single-page entry by deleting the bookmark name with its quotes, the backslash, and the *r*. And, of course, you can edit the main entry name.

- **Subentries (eggs, robin's, 21).** The field code looks like { XE "eggs:robin's" }. The main entry is before the colon, the subentry is after. You can edit either one, and also create additional layers of subentries just by adding another colon followed by another subentry, and so on.

Phase 3: Building the Index

Once you've marked index entries in the document you're indexing, you can generate the index itself, as follows:

1. **If the field codes in your document are showing, turn off Show/Hide by clicking ¶ on the Standard toolbar to hide them.**

   This step ensures that your document is paginated correctly. When field codes are showing, they take up room just like extra words and throw off the page numbers.

   Most of the time, you'll want to insert a page break or section break just before the index, so that the index will begin at the top of a new page. Then:

2. **Click in your document where you want the index to begin. Choose Insert→Index and Tables→Index tab.**

   The Index and Tables dialog box opens, as shown in Figure 7-18.

   Choose a Type radio button to specify the layout of your subentries.

   If you click Indented, each subentry appears indented under the main entry. If you click Run-in, all entries in the index are flush left. (Watch the Preview window for an example of each.)

3. **Choose a Format from the Formats list.**

   If you choose "From template," Word uses (page 137) your current template's *styles*. To see what the other canned index designs look like (Classic, Modern, and so on), click each and view the results in the Preview window.

Figure 7-18:
Top: The Index and Tables dialog box previews the index you're about to create. If the Preview in your copy of Word—or, indeed, the final index itself—shows text that's cramped and hard to read, you need to click the Modify button and adjust the Index1, Index2, and Index3 predefined styles to clearer fonts and paragraph spacing.

Bottom: A sample index entry, with the "Tab leader" option turned on.

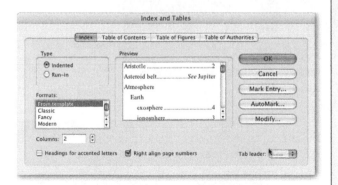

---

4. **Choose a number of columns in the Columns box by clicking the arrows or entering a number.**

You can choose one, two, three, or four columns per page. To save space, most indexes use a multiple-column format. If your document already *has* columns, choose Auto to make your index match the same number of columns.

5. **Turn on "Right align page numbers" to move the page number out to the right margin of the page or column.**

Turning this on affords you the option of using a *tab leader* (dots or dashes between the entry and its page number), as shown in Figure 7-18. Choose it from the small pop-up menu at the lower right.

6. **Click OK.**

Word creates an index. This will take a few minutes, especially if your document is long. You can stare at the watch icon or go get a snack.

POWER USERS' CLINIC

AutoMarking Long Documents

If your document is very long, reviewing it can be an exercise in tedium. Although the Mark All button helps, Word's AutoMark feature can accelerate the process even further. However, this feature is only worth using on very long documents—maybe 100 pages or more—because it entails an extra step that offers its own brand of tedium: creating a concordance file.

A concordance file is a Word document with a two-column table that you create yourself from a blank document. In the first (left) column, you type the text that you want Word to look for and mark in your document. In the right column, you type the index entry itself, which may not necessarily be the same term. (Using this technique, you can index, under printing, five pages of discussion about dot-matrix printers, laser printers, fonts, and ink cartridges; the actual word printing may never appear in the text.)

Another example: You could type egg, eggs, Egg, laying, reproduction in the left column (each in its own cell), and

egg	eggs
eggs	eggs
laying	eggs
reproduction	eggs
robin's eggs	eggs: robin's
hen's eggs	Eggs: chickens

eggs directly across from each in the right cell (as shown here). (To create a subentry, use a colon, also depicted in the illustration.) At the end of this exercise, Word will find each word in the left column and index it under the term you've specified in the right column—all of the sample terms shown here, for example, will be indexed under "eggs."

After logging each important term in your document this way, save and close the concordance file. Then open the manuscript document. Click at the end of the document, and then choose Insert→Index and Tables→Index tab.

In the resulting dialog box, click AutoMark. Navigate to your concordance file and open it. Now Word automatically places index entry fields in the document; you can see them highlighted as you scroll through it. If you missed any major topics, just create another concordance file and repeat the process.

Now build your index as described on page 261.

Phase 4: Cleaning Up the Index

Once Word has finished building the index, you can edit it as you would any text. You can also revisit it in any of these ways:

- **Reformat the index.** Click the index and choose Insert→Index and Tables; in the resulting dialog box, you can change any of the options on the Index tab, as described above. (Because you clicked the index first, any changes you make will apply to it, even though this dialog box normally creates a *new* index.)

- **Update the index (Shift-Option-⌘-U).** If, after sleepless nights of soul-searching, you decide to edit your document by inserting or deleting text, Word doesn't automatically update your index; all of its page numbering is now off. Similarly, if you decide to add, delete, or edit some index entries themselves, they won't be reflected in the index you've already generated.

  The solution, either way, is to click in your index and press **Shift-Option-⌘-U**. Word updates the index; as when you created the index, this will take some time.

- **Deleting an index.** To remove an index from your document, click it and press Option-F9 (it will be represented as a field code). Select and delete the entire field code to delete the index.

Tip: Deleting the index doesn't delete the index *entries* you've marked in your document. Usually, leaving them in place does no harm, since they're marked as hidden text and generally don't print or show up onscreen. But if you need a genuinely clean document, use the Replace command described on page 73. Using the Special pop-up menu, choose Field and replace it with nothing. Word will neatly extract them from your file.

Data Merges

If the term *data merge* is new to you, perhaps it's because "data merge" is a kinder, gentler euphemism for its result: *form letters*. A data merge grabs information from a database and uses that information to automatically fill in the blanks of a Word file ("Dear <<name>>, As a fellow <<city>> resident, I thought you might be interested in contributing <<income>> to our fundraiser"). In this example, a data merge can effectively churn out what seem to be personal, individually written letters. Merging data can also create labels, envelopes, or a catalog.

Having Office 2004 on your Mac puts you at a definite advantage: You get to use all the document-beautifying features of Word (see Chapter 3) to write the placeholder letter, and you have your choice of programs to organize the data. You can use an existing Excel file, your Entourage Address Book, a FileMaker Pro database, or a Word table to supply the data that you want plugged into the generic letter.

The placeholders Word uses when you write the letter are *fields* (see page 237). And because fields can process information like computer code, Word data merge documents are very powerful. For example, you can set them up to prompt you for information before proceeding with the merge ("What amount to ask for?").

To make these interactive functions easier to use, Office 2004 offers the Data Merge Manager. Just as the Formatting Palette consolidates dozens of different formatting features, so the Data Merge Manager also collects and automates the features you need for four of the most popular merges: form letters, labels, envelopes, and catalogs.

Preparing Data Sources

Before you begin your mail-merge experience, decide what computer document will contain the *source data*—the names and addresses for your form letters and envelopes, for example, or the items and prices in your inventory database that you'd like to merge into an attractive catalog.

The most common data source is a database of names, addresses, and other personal information. Office 2004 can grab data from Word tables, tab-delimited text files (such as ASCII), Excel files, the Entourage address book, or FileMaker Pro databases.

As you delve into merges, you'll need familiarity with two important pieces of database terminology: *records* and *fields*. A *field* is a single scrap of information: a phone number or a shoe size. (This *database* field isn't quite the same thing as the gray-text placeholder *Word* fields described earlier in this chapter—although the database kind of field will indeed be represented by a Word field in your form letter.) A *record* is the complete set of fields for one form letter, mailing label, or envelope—the name, address, phone number, and so on.

Tip: Whether you create a new database for your merge or use an existing one, make sure that each record is set up the same way. If you're using a database where the first and last names are in separate fields in some cases and together in others, you're going to have trouble getting the merge to work properly.

Creating a New Data Source

Let's say you have a bunch of application slips filled out by kids signing up for your hockey lessons, and you want to write each student a welcome letter. However, you don't have the database in electronic format yet.

The easiest way to start a data source file is to launch Word and choose Tools→Data Merge Manager. What you'll see is something like Figure 7-19.

The list of database fields you'll need depends on what you plan to say in the form letter. In the example in Figure 7-20, the coach realized that she'd need the date, first and last name, address, shoe size, school grade, the instructor name, and the entrance where the student's hockey class would gather for their first meeting. A few fields already in the database for other purposes—phone number, for example—won't be used in this letter; that's OK.

To create a data source for your project, proceed as follows:

1. **Open the main document.**

   "Main document" means the file that will contain the letter itself—the text that won't change from one printout to the next. Choose Tools→Data Merge Manager, if the palette shown in Figure 7-19 isn't already open.

2. On the Data Merge Manager, choose Create→Form Letters.

As you can see from the pop-up button, Word comes ready to access information from your Office (Entourage) Address Book or a FileMaker database—or to create a new list of data from scratch. That's what you'll be doing in this example.

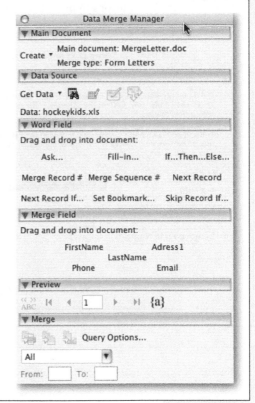

Figure 7-19:
The data-merge feature of Word isn't a shining example of simplicity. But the section structure of the Data Merge Manager palette, which looks a lot like the Formatting Palette, at least makes the steps sequential. The file name and main document type appear here—in this example, it's called MergeLetter (see it near the top?). So do the fields in the database you've selected (see them in the Merge Field section?). At the very bottom are the controls you use to actually perform the merge.

If you want to abandon the main document and start again, choose Create→Restore to Normal Word Document on the Data Merge Manager.

3. On the Data Merge Manager's Data Source section, choose Get Data→New Data Source.

The Create Data Source dialog box appears, as shown in Figure 7-20. It has a list of suggested fields for form letters. Edit the list of fields, also as shown in Figure 7-20.

4. Click OK. Name the database (*Hockey Kids,* for instance) and click Save.

You've just created a Word document with a table that will hold all your data.

Now you're confronted with a Data Form window like the one shown in Figure 7-21. It's time to play fill-in-the-blanks; use this dialog box to type in the information for each kid in your class.

5. **Enter the first kid's name, address, and other bits of information, pressing Tab or Return to jump from blank to blank. Click Add New to save the first record and clear the form for the next set of data.**

Click Delete to "backspace" over the record you just entered; click Restore to bring it back. The counter at the bottom reminds you where you are; use the navigation buttons to move backward and forward through the records.

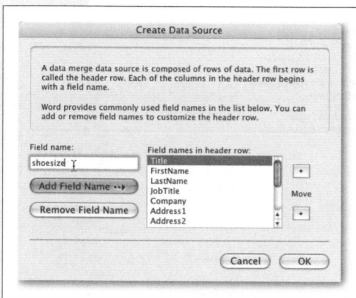

Figure 7-20:
Scroll through the "Field names in header row" box and click "Remove Field Name" for any you don't plan to use. To add fields you will need for your hockey letter (ShoeSize, for instance), type them in the "Field name" box and click Add Field Name. Note that Word does not permit spaces in the names of your fields.

Figure 7-21:
Top: You can click View Source at any time and see all your data in table form. The data source is a Word document that you can see anytime by choosing File→Open.

Bottom: You can return to the Data Form dialog box anytime by clicking Manage Fields on the Database toolbar.

6. **When you're finished typing in the data, click OK.**

A list of the fields you've created appears on the Data Merge Manager (see Figure 7-19).

To add more records to your data source at a later time, you have two alternatives. You can choose File→Open, open your Hockey Kids document, and add rows to the Word table you'll find there (see page 160 for full detail on working with tables). You can also choose Get Data→Open Data Source on the Data Merge Manager palette, and click the Edit Data Source button to pull up the Data Form shown in Figure 7-21. Once the data source is open, you can use the Database toolbar to sort and edit it. (If you don't see this toolbar, choose View→Toolbars→Database.)

You're ready to perform the merge; skip ahead to page 271.

Using an Existing Data Source

To merge an existing database into a form letter or envelopes, say in FileMaker Pro or Excel, you must first save the file. Then follow the steps below:

1. **Open your form letter (or create a new blank document).**

If the Data Merge Manager palette isn't already open, choose Tools→Data Merge Manager.

WORKAROUND WORKSHOP

Header Rows and Header Sources

To set up a data merge, you must insert fields from a database called the data source into the form letter or document. The data source usually takes the form of a table in which each column's name appears at the top (Name, Address, Phone, and so on). In fact, that's exactly what the steps described on page 264 do—they lead you through the construction of a correctly formatted Word table. (You could just as easily make your own Word table by hand, as long as the first row contains the field names and subsequent rows contain the records you want to merge.)

To know where to place what data, Word relies on the table's column names (like First, Last, and Phone), located in the header row. In other words, when Word comes to the FirstName field in the main document, it plugs in the next name from the FirstName column of the data source.

When creating a data source and main document from scratch, as described on page 264, your header row au-

tomatically matches the fields in your main document. If you're using an existing data source with a main document that already contains fields, you can change the top row or first record of the data source to match—usually.

But if you can't edit—or don't want to edit—the existing database, you can still make it match the fields in your main document by creating a separate header source.

To do so, choose Get Data→Header Source→New Header Source. Word opens a dialog box just like the Create Data Source box. The difference is, Word uses the field names you enter here as a substitute top row for your existing database. For example, if the first names are stored in the second field of your database, make FirstName the second field in the separate header source, even if the field is called something else in the database. The header source must have the same number of fields as the database, even if you don't plan to use them all in your merge.

---

2. **On the Data Merge Manager palette, choose Create→Form Letters (for this example).**

If you've already produced a main document with fields, then add to your existing database a first record (a header row) whose entry names match the fields in your main document (see "Header Rows and Header Sources" on page 267).

3. **On the Data Merge Manager, choose Get Data→Open Data Source.**

If the existing database is in FileMaker Pro or your Office Address Book in Entourage, choose the appropriate command from this pop-up button instead. (You need a copy of FileMaker on your Mac for that option to work.)

4. **Navigate to the file on your Mac and click Open.**

You're ready to proceed. If you haven't written your form letter yet, go to the next section. When both your form letter and data source are ready, go to page 270.

Creating the Main Document

When you're ready to write the actual form letter, you have a choice—like thousands of Publishers' Clearinghouse Sweepstakes form letter writers before you. You can either use an existing Word file as the body of the letter, or start from scratch.

To showcase the power of fields in a data merge document, here are the steps used to create the letter shown in Figure 7-22. In the Data Merge Manager, make sure the flippy triangle next to Merge Field is pointing downward, so that you can see the fields available in your data source. (If you haven't selected or created a data source,

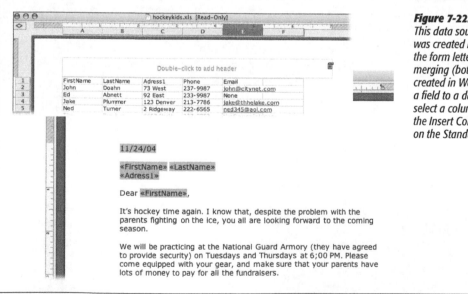

Figure 7-22:
This data source (top) was created in Excel, and the form letter, ready for merging (bottom), was created in Word. To add a field to a data source, select a column and click the Insert Columns icon on the Standard Toolbar.

see "Creating a new data source" on page 264 or "Using an existing data source" on page 267.)

1. **Open a new Word document. Type the date, if you like, and then press Return two or three times.**

   You're about to insert the first addressee's mailing address, as is customary in a standard business letter. But you don't want to have to *type* that information—that's *so* 1985. You want Word to fill it in for you, not just on this letter, but on every one of the 44 letters you're about to write and print.

2. **Drag-and-drop merge fields from the Data Merge Manager palette to place the mailing address into the letter, as shown in Figure 7-23.**

3. **Type *Dear* and a space, and then drag-and-drop the FirstName field.**

   Word represents the field (which, when you print, will be replaced by somebody's *actual* first name) using brackets. You should now see, in other words, *Dear <<FirstName>>*.

   If your data source contains a field for titles (such as Mr., Ms., or Dr.), you can insert it instead, and then drag the LastName field.

4. **Continue writing the letter, drag-and-dropping merge fields as appropriate (see Figure 7-23).**

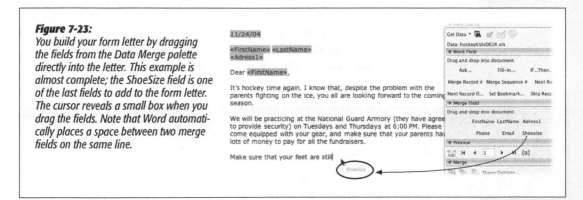

Figure 7-23:
You build your form letter by dragging the fields from the Data Merge palette directly into the letter. This example is almost complete; the ShoeSize field is one of the last fields to add to the form letter. The cursor reveals a small box when you drag the fields. Note that Word automatically places a space between two merge fields on the same line.

5. **Insert an Ask field to collect the instructor's name for the letter.**

   Our hapless hockey coach *still* doesn't know who the instructor will be. In fact, she won't know until it's almost time for the letters to go out. Therefore, she'll fill in the instructor's name during the merge itself.

   This is where the *Fill-in field* comes in. On the Word Field section of the Data Merge Manager palette, drag "Fill-in" to the point in the letter where the instructor's name should go. A dialog box appears; type *What's the instructor name?* or something else that will help you (or whoever's filling in the forms) remember what was supposed to go there.

This dialog box also gives you a chance to specify a fallback entry—default text that will appear in the letter in case you don't get the instructor list on time ("name to be determined," for example). If you turn on the "Ask once" box, Word will ask you once for the missing information, then merge it into *all* the letters.

Tip: You may be tempted to use the Fill-in field with abandon, so that Word will ask you, in the process of printing out the form letters, to fill in personalized information for each record. But you can't *see* the records *during* the merge, so you won't have any way of knowing which information should be filled in for each person's letter.

The way to customize the Fill-in field is with a *query* (page 271). For instance, filter the student database by grade and then conduct a separate pass for each, so that you can type a different instructor name for each batch of letters.

---

6. **Finish typing the letter and save the document as usual.**

Word has inserted field codes for all the merge fields you've just drag-and-dropped. To see them, choose Preview→View Field Codes ({a}) on the Data Merge Manager.

Previewing, Formatting, Preparing to Merge

After you've prepared a main document and inserted merge fields, you can see how the document will look with the actual data.

On the Preview section of the Data Merge Manager palette, click the View Merged Data button (identified as step 4 in Figure 7-23). Word shows you the first finished form letter, complete with *Dear Garfinkle* (or whatever the FirstName is in the first record from your data source). Click the arrows in the box on the Preview panel of the Data Merge Manager to browse the other merged records.

POWER USERS' CLINIC

Delimiting Numerous Fields

A Word table used for a data source can contain a maximum of 63 columns or fields. If you need more than that—if you're creating a catalog, for instance—you must turn the document into a tab-delimited text file (or an XL file, or a CSV file, if you happen to know what those terms mean) before using it as a data source.

A tab-delimited text file is a plain text document in which the information for each record (each person's mailing information, for example) appears on its own line, with a tab between each field (between Name and Address, for example).

You can create a tab-delimited text file in any database program, although the commands to do so vary slightly. In Excel, for instance, choose File→Save As; choose Text (tab delimited) from the Format pop-up menu. In AppleWorks, choose File→Save As and choose ASCII text from the File Type pop-up menu. And if you've built your data source as a Word table, turn the whole table into tab-delimited plain text using the instructions on page 171.

Before you use your tab-delimited file as a data source, inspect it in Word (choose File→Open to open it). Make sure that its very first row identifies the names of the columns (Name, Address, Phone, and so on).

In Preview mode, you can make formatting changes to the main document as well as to the merge fields. Just select text or fields in the usual way and use the Formatting Palette to add bold, italic, or other formatting. (When you reformat a field, the change applies to that *entire* field—for *all* documents in the merge.)

Once you've filled and prepared a data source, designed a main document, and outfitted it with merge fields, you're ready to merge. Check the Main Document and Data Source panels of your Data Merge Manager to ensure that the file names of your main and database documents appear correctly. Use the Preview feature as described above. Proofread your main document carefully, especially if you have numerous records in your database—you don't want a tiny mistake copied many times over!

When everything looks good, Word stands ready to merge your data and your form letter in any of three ways: sending it directly to the printer, merging into a new Word document, or merging into outgoing email messages.

Merging Straight to the Printer

If you've already previewed your merge, simply click the Print button (on the Standard toolbar) or Merge to Printer (an icon on the Data Merge Manager, shown in Figure 7-19). Specify the number of copies you need in the print dialog box and hit Return. Word prints the merged documents on your labels or paper.

Customizing merge printing

By default, the pop-up menu just below the Merge to Printer icon reads All, meaning that Word will print a merged document for *all* records in your chosen data source. The other choices are Current Record (to print just the record you're currently previewing in the document window) and Custom.

When you click Custom, you can use the From and To boxes below it to specify a range of records to merge. For example, if you have sticky laser labels that come 30 on a sheet, and you just want to print the first page of labels, enter *1* and *30*; Word will print only the first 30 records (that is, one page of labels). For the second page, enter *31* and *60*, and so on.

Query Options

If you want to print nonconsecutive records, use the Data Merge Manager's Query Options. This feature lets you *filter* your records before merging (choose only the records that meet certain criteria) or sort them.

With your main and data source documents chosen in the Data Merge Manager, click Query Options. The dialog box shown in Figure 7-24 appears. Let's say you want to send a special letter to clients in Denver, letting them know that you're going to be visiting their city next month. Your data source contains *all* your clients, even those in San Francisco, whom you obviously don't want to receive the same letter.

Since you're filtering by city, choose the City field on the Query Options→Filter tab and type *Denver* in the "Compare to" box. As you can see in Figure 7-24, there are lots of filtering options. You can even apply more than one.

For example, you can filter out the people who have a work phone number *and* who live in your state. You can filter out people who were born after a certain date *and* who are women. Click OK when you're done; now you can print the merged documents as described earlier.

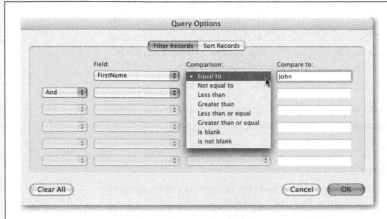

Figure 7-24:
Clicking the Sort Records tab lets you sort your data records as any Word table. (See page 160 for more detail on tables.) You can combine filtering and sorting. If the Office Address Book is your source, this dialog box looks a bit simpler, offering checkboxes that let you select only certain names and addresses for inclusion (or all names in certain categories).

Merging to a New Document

Instead of sending your form letters (or mailing labels) to a printer, it's often more useful to have Word generate a new Word document, looking exactly as though a tireless secretary had painstakingly typed up a copy of each form letter with the correct addresses inserted. This is the only way to go if, for example, you want to tweak the wording of each outgoing letter independently. You can always print the thing *after* looking it over and editing it.

Creating a new mass form-letter document is easy: After setting up your main document and data source, click the Merge to New Document icon on the Data Merge Manager palette. Word churns for a moment and then produces the document (with a page break automatically inserted after each copy of the letter).

Save the merge document to your hard drive. Edit, print, or duplicate it just as you would any Word document.

Merging to Email

You *know* it's the Internet age when your word processor comes with a feature that lets you send out form letters by email. Here's how this feature works:

1. **Create a form letter main document and a source document as described on the previous pages.**

   For best results, don't use complex formatting, since some people can only view email as plain text (see Chapter 9).

2. **Click the Merge to E-Mail icon on the Data Merge Manager palette.**

If the button is dimmed, it could be that Entourage isn't selected as your default email program. Open Apple's Mail program and choose Microsoft Entourage from the pop-up menu at the bottom of the window. Start again from step 1.

If all is well, however, the Mail Recipient dialog box opens, as shown in Figure 7-25.

3. **Using the To pop-up menu, choose the field that contains the email addresses. Complete the email message as you would any other.**

   For example, type a Subject line in the box.

4. **Using the bottom pop-up menu, specify whether to send the letter as text (in the body of the email) or as an attachment. Click Data Merge to Outbox.**

   The data merge proceeds as usual: Word asks you to type Fill-in fields, and so on. Entourage opens automatically, and you can watch the boldface digits next to its Outbox skyrocket as Word crams newly generated messages into it. There they wait until you click Send (or until a scheduled Send runs). There's no preview, but you can open any of the merged emails in the Outbox and look at them.

Figure 7-25:
If you choose to attach the letter as a file attachment, the name of your attachment will be the same as the file name of your main document. You may want to rename it for the benefit of your recipients, especially if you have a tendency to give documents unflattering names, like LettertoStupid.

Labels and Envelopes

Two of the most common Word data merges are automated for you: address labels and envelopes. Either way, this is an extremely powerful feature that lets you combine the database flexibility of your Entourage Address Book with the formatting smarts of Word. Whether you're the local Scout-troop master or an avid Christmas-card meister, letting Word prepare your mass mailings beats addressing envelopes by hand any day.

Prepare for one of these data merges as follows:

- Prepare a data source, as described on page 264.

- Know the size of the labels or envelopes you're going to use. Have some on hand as you begin the process. (You can buy sheets of self-adhesive labels at Staples or any other office supply store; Avery is one of the best-known names. These labels come in every conceivable size and shape; the 30-per-page version is the most popular.)

• Set aside some time for trial and error.

Merging onto labels

Make sure that the labels you buy will fit into your printer and feed smoothly—buy inkjet or laser labels, for example, to match your printer.

To create labels, open a new blank Word document and proceed as follows:

1. **Choose Tools→Data Merge Manager.**

   The Data Merge Manager palette appears.

2. **On the Data Merge Manager, choose Create→Labels.**

   The Label Options dialog box appears (see Figure 7-26, top). Unless you're that rare eccentric who uses a dot matrix (impact) printer, leave "laser and inkjet" selected.

3. **From the "Label products" pop-up menu, select the brand of labels you have.**

   Word lists every kind of label you've ever heard of, and many that you haven't.

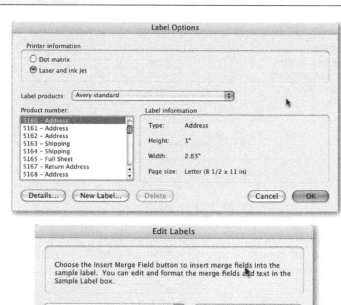

Figure 7-26:
Top: Avery 5160 is one of the most popular label products; it comes with 10 rows of three labels each.

Bottom: If you're assembling a bulk mailing and therefore need to bar code your own envelopes, click "Insert Postal Bar Code." Word asks you to select the name of the merge field where your Zip codes are, then prints the corresponding bar code on each envelope or label. Your mail is likely to reach its recipient faster if you use these bar codes.

Tip: If you've bought some oddball, no-name label brand not listed in Word's list, click New Label. Word gives you a dialog box, complete with a preview window, for specifying your own label dimensions.

4. **Inspect your label package to find out what label model number you have; select the matching product in the "Product number" list box. Click OK.**

The main document becomes an empty sheet of labels. It's time to start dragging field names from your source document.

5. **On the Data Merge Manager, use the Get Data pop-up button to select the database or file that contains your addresses.**

For example, to use your Entourage Address Book, choose Office Address Book from this menu. If your addresses are stored in an Excel spreadsheet or a tab-delimited text file, choose Open Data Source instead (then navigate to your database or data source file and open it).

If you haven't set up your database yet, choose New Data Source and follow the steps on page 264.

6. **In the Edit Labels dialog box that appears, choose field names from the "Insert Merge Field" pop-up menu to build your address.**

As illustrated at the bottom of Figure 7-26, use the Space bar and Return key as you go. For example, choose First_Name, insert a space, choose Last_Name, then press Return to start a new line. Choose City, type a comma if you like, and then choose State; add two spaces before choosing Zip code.

7. **Click OK.**

You return to your main document window, where placeholders for your labels now appear. (Click the <<abc>> icon on the Data Merge Manager's Preview panel to preview the actual names and addresses as they'll be printed.)

Now you can format the text using, for example, the Formatting Palette; you can change the font or size, add bold, italic, or color, and so on. Just select the text or the field placeholders to format them.

8. **Click Merge→Merge to Printer and print out one page of labels on a blank piece of paper.**

This way, you can check to see if the labels are properly aligned without wasting an expensive sheet of labels. Hold the paper printout over a label sheet and line them up in front of a window or light.

9. **If your labels need realigning, choose Create→Labels on the Data Merge Manager and click Details.**

A dialog box pops up, displaying the dimensions and specifications of your currently chosen label model, along with boxes and arrows for adjusting them. You can move the label text up, down, and side-to-side in order to better fit on the labels.

When everything's working properly, load the labels into your printer, and click Merge→Merge to Printer. Click Print.

Take advantage of the Merge→Custom box (see page 271) if you have a long mailing list. Some printers tend to jam if you try to print too many pages of labels at once.

Editing labels

You can edit a label document by opening it, just like any main document. But because of the unique problems involved in changing a sheet of labels, Word provides a couple of special tools. To make changes to an existing label document, proceed as follows:

1. **Open the label document.**

   Word opens the document and the Data Merge Manager. (If not, choose Tools→ Data Merge Manager.)

2. **Click the Edit Labels for Data Merge button.**

   It's the third icon in the Data Source section of the Data Merge Manager palette. The Edit Labels dialog box opens, as shown in Figure 7-26.

3. **Make changes to the label format.**

4. **Add or remove merge fields or change text formatting, for example, by selecting the merge fields and using the Formatting Palette. Click OK and proceed with the merge.**

Propagating labels

You can also edit labels right in the main document, which you may find easier than using the Edit Labels dialog box. The secret is in the Propagate Labels button on the Data Merge Manager (the rightmost icon in the Data Source section of the Data Merge Manager palette). Here's how to use this method of label editing:

1. **Open the label document; click the *first* label on the page.**

   Word opens the document and the Data Merge Manager. (If the Data Merge Manager is not open, choose Tools→Data Merge Manager.)

2. **Edit the label document.**

   For instance, you can drag merge fields from the Data Merge Manager, type additional text, and format the text or field placeholders (font, color, and so on). Remember, you're doing this only in the first label.

3. **Click the Propagate Label Document button on the Data Merge Manager.**

   Word changes all labels on the sheet so that they match the changes you just made in the first label.

   When you're done propagating, merge and print the labels as described on the previous pages.

Merging onto envelopes

Printing envelopes on computer printers has always been an iffy proposition; in essence, you're trying to ram two or three layers of paper through a machine designed to print on sheets only one-layer thick.

It's easier, however, if your printer is envelope-friendly. If your printer has guides for feeding envelopes, so much the better. Additionally, you may find that some brands of envelope fit your printer better than others.

When you're ready to begin, open a new blank document and follow these steps:

1. **Choose Tools→Data Merge Manager, then choose Create→Envelopes.**

   The Envelope dialog box opens, as shown in Figure 7-27. If you don't care for Helvetica, Arial, or whatever, click Font to call up a Font dialog box. You can use any of Word's fonts and effects.

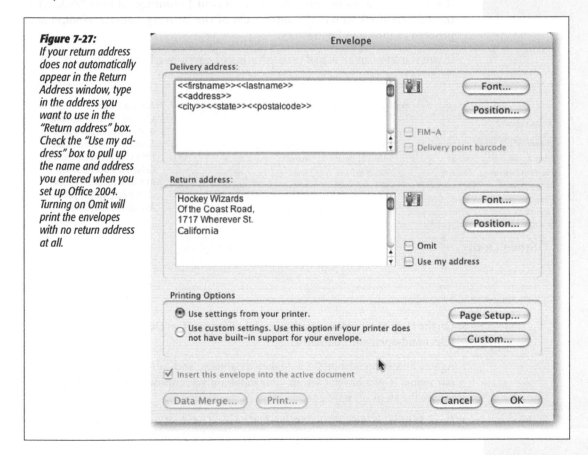

Figure 7-27:
If your return address does not automatically appear in the Return Address window, type in the address you want to use in the "Return address" box. Check the "Use my address" box to pull up the name and address you entered when you set up Office 2004. Turning on Omit will print the envelopes with no return address at all.

2. **Click Position. In the Address Position window, click the arrows to move the return and delivery addresses around on the envelope, if necessary.**

If the return address is too close to the envelope edges, for example, or the delivery address is too low, now's your chance to fix it.

3. **Click Page Setup.**

Word opens your printer's usual Page Setup dialog box. Choose the envelope size from the pop-up menu and click OK. (If you don't see the correct size, click Cancel; under Printing Options, click the "Use custom settings" button, then click Custom. In the Custom Page Options dialog box, choose an envelope size and tell Word how you plan to feed it into the printer.)

4. **Click OK, then OK again to dismiss the Envelope dialog box.**

Your chosen envelope format appears in the main document; it's time to "type in" the addresses you want to print.

5. **If you want to print just one address from your Entourage Address Book, click the Address Book icon at the upper right of the Delivery Address window, and proceed as shown in Figure 7-28.**

If you want to run an actual mass printing of envelopes, however, do this:

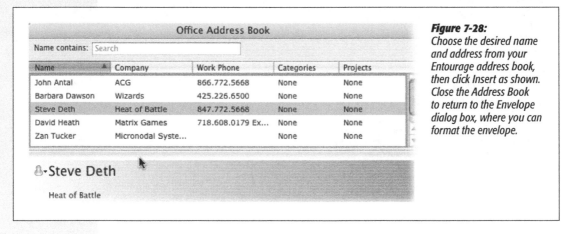

Figure 7-28:
Choose the desired name and address from your Entourage address book, then click Insert as shown. Close the Address Book to return to the Envelope dialog box, where you can format the envelope.

6. **On the Data Merge Manager, choose Data Source→Get Data→Open Data Source; select and open your database.**

Again, Excel spreadsheets, FileMaker databases, and tab-delimited text files are fair game. If you haven't set up your database yet, choose New Data Source and follow the steps on page 264.

7. **Drag field names from the Merge Field panel of the Data Merge Manager into the address box of the envelope in the main document.**

Add spaces and line breaks in the usual way, as shown in Figure 7-26.

8. **Prepare your printer's feed for envelopes; click Merge→Merge to Printer. Click Print.**

If the envelope gods are smiling, your printer now begins to print the envelopes perfectly. (If they're not, then you may discover that you'll have to rotate the envelopes in the paper slot, or worst case, remove the envelope with a pneumatic tool borrowed from your local garage). Depending on your printer model, you may have to print one envelope at a time—if so, choose Current Record from the drop-down menu at the bottom of the Data Merge Manager.

Macros

A *macro* is like a script: a step-by-step series of commands that Word performs, rapid-fire, each time the macro is run. Although they definitely qualify as a power-user feature, you should consider this feature any time you find yourself facing a repetitive, tedious editing task. For example:

- Changing three different character names in one pass (which is required for each chapter of the novel you just finished).

- Drawing a table with the months of the year automatically listed down the first column and the names of all salespeople across the top. (All you have to do to complete the daily sales report is fill in the figures.)

- Saving the table document above as a Word document in your Sales folder and saving an additional copy as a Web page (which you can now upload to the company intranet).

Office's macros are actually tiny programs written in a programming language called Visual Basic for Applications (VBA). People with programming skills and a lot of time on their hands can make VBA do astounding tricks; fortunately, you don't need to learn the language. You can generally get away with using Word's *macro recorder,* a "watch me" mode where Word writes the macro for you as you traverse the various steps once yourself. Once you've recorded the macro in this way, Word is ready to execute those actions automatically, like a software robot that's wired on caffeine.

Tip: A macro is saved into a document or a template. Thereafter, it works only when you've opened that same document (or a document based on that template). Macros in global templates are loaded whenever the template is loaded

To make a macro available in all Word documents, move it into the Normal template, as described under "The Organizer" on page 230. Fortunately, macros you create by recording are stored in the Normal template, so they're always available.

Creating a Macro

Even without knowing Visual Basic, you can create a macro for anything you know how to do in Word. Think of the macro recorder as a tape recorder that "listens" to what you do, and then replays it on command.

Note: The macro-recording feature in Word can't record mouse movements (other than menu selections and button clicks); so if your macro involves selecting text or moving the insertion point on the page, do it using keyboard shortcuts.

In this example, the company you work for has been sold, and you'd like to create a macro that goes through a document and replaces the old company name with the new one. Because you'll have to do this on dozens or hundreds of existing documents, you decide to store it as a macro that you can trigger at will.

1. **Open a document that needs your Find/Replace surgery. Choose Tools→Macro→ Record New Macro.**

   Alternatively, click to turn on the REC button on the bottom edge of your document window. The Record Macro dialog box opens, as shown at bottom in Figure 7-29.

2. **Type a name for the new macro.**

   If you find it a bit nerdy that you have to name the macro before you've even created it, just wait—Word's nerdiness is only warming up. For example, you're not allowed to use commas, periods, or even spaces in the name of your macro. In Figure 7-29, the macro has been named ReplaceCo.

Caution: If you assign a macro the same name as an existing macro, Word replaces the original one without so much as a by-your-leave. If you give your macro the same name as a preinstalled Word macro, for example, you'll lose the Word macro.

Type a description, too, so that later you'll remember what this macro was designed to do.

Again, before you've even created the macro, you must now tell Word how you intend to trigger this macro in the future. To do so, either press a key combination of your choice or click a button on a toolbar. (You can always change your mind, or choose both methods, later.)

3. **To create a button on one of your toolbars for this macro, click Toolbars.**

   The Customize dialog box appears, with a mutant version of your macro's name (such as Normal.NewMacros.ReplaceName) displayed on the right.

   Drag the macro's *name* from the Customize dialog box to the Standard toolbar or any open toolbar. (More on dragging to toolbars in Chapter 19.)

4. **If you want this macro to be available in only one document (as opposed to all Word documents), choose the name of the current document from the "Store macro in" pop-up menu.**

   Word assumes that the document you want to store the macro in is already open. If not, click Cancel, open the correct document, and start over.

5. To assign a keyboard shortcut to the new macro, click Keyboard.

The Customize Keyboard dialog box opens, with the cursor blinking in the "Press new shortcut key" box. Press a key combination on your keyboard (Control-R, say) that will be easy for you to remember.

The combination must include Control, ⌘, Control-⌘, or Shift-Control plus one or two other keys, such as letters and numbers. If the combination you press is already in use, you'll see the name of the conflicting command under "Currently assigned to"; see page 677 for more on changing Word keystrokes.

Click Assign, and then click Okay.

Figure 7-29:
The Macros dialog box, listing all macros you've created. Here's your opportunity to delete one or edit it, line by line. You can't rename one, however, except by entering the Visual Basic Editor described at the end of this chapter.

Bottom: All currently open documents appear in the "Store macro in" pop-up menu. If you store it in the Normal template, it will be available to you in all Word documents. You can click Pause while recording the macro if you need to leave the Mac for any reason.

Bottom inset: The Macro Recorder toolbar, short and sweet. The Pause button is on the right.

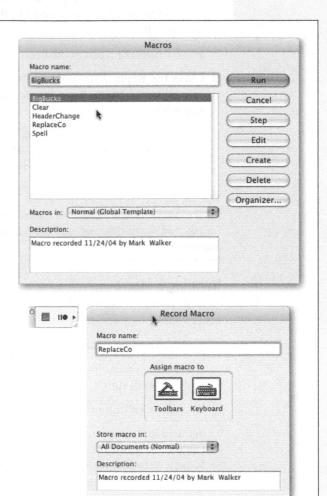

6. **Click OK to begin recording the macro.**

You now return to your document. Everything appears to be as it was, except for the presence of a tiny, two-button toolbar (Figure 7-29). (On the right: a Pause button, which you can click before and after you do something that you don't want recorded.) You'll also notice that the arrow cursor turns black when you pass it over text or over the edges of a window.

This is your opportunity to actually perform the steps that you want Word to reproduce later. In this example, you'll record a search-and-replace operation, thusly:

7. **Choose Edit→Replace. Type the old company name in the "Find what" box, press Tab, and then type the new name in the "Replace with" box (see page 72). Click Replace All.**

Word makes the replacement everywhere in the document.

8. **Close the Replace tile box, and then click the Stop button (the small blue square) on the Macro Recorder toolbar—or just click the REC indicator on your status bar.**

That's it—you've just recorded a macro. If you'd like to test it on the document that's still open before you, choose Edit→Undo Replace All (to undo the effects of your manual search-and-replace), and then trigger the macro as described below.

Tip: The macro doesn't become immortalized in your Normal template until you quit Word. If your Mac has a tendency to crash or freeze every now and then, you'd be wise to quit Word shortly after recording any important macros. Otherwise, you'll launch Word after a freeze or crash only to find that the macro has disappeared.

Running a Macro

As with so much else in Office, there are several ways to run a macro that you (or other people) have recorded. Here's a list:

- Press the keystroke that you assigned to the macro when you created it.

- Choose the macro in the Tools→Macro→Macros dialog box (Figure 7-29, top) and then click Run.

- Click the toolbar button that you assigned to the macro when you created it.

- Set up a macro to run automatically. To do this, give the macro one of these special names: **AutoExec** (runs when Word first launches), **AutoExit** (when you quit Word), **AutoOpen** (when you open an existing document), **AutoNew** (when you start a new document—very useful), or **AutoClose** (close a document).

You can also add your macro to any of the Word menus, as described on page 674.

The Macro Organizer

As with styles, AutoText, and toolbars, you can copy macros between documents or templates using Word's Organizer (see page 230 for complete instructions). Only these two subtleties make macro copying different:

- In the steps on page 231, click the Macro Projects tab instead of the Templates tab.

- You can't copy individual macros—only macro bundles called *macro projects*. (All of the macros *you* create wind up in a single macro project called NewMacros.)

Learning about Visual Basic

When you record a macro, Word automatically translates it into the Visual Basic programming language. To see how it looks, click a macro in the Macros dialog box (choose Tools→Macro→Macros) and click Edit. A supplementary program called Visual Basic Editor opens, displaying all the code for that macro. If you know anything about programming, you can learn quite a bit about Visual Basic just by examining the code.

Sometimes even the novice can make some sense of this code. For example, if you've recorded a macro that blows up your document window to 150 percent, you'll see a line of code that says *ActiveWindow.ActivePane.View.Zoom.Percentage = 150.* You don't have to be a rocket scientist to realize that you can edit the 150 if it turns out to be too much magnification. You could replace that number with *125* and then choose File→Close and Return to Microsoft Word, having successfully edited your macro. (The same trick works very well for modifying search-and-replace macros; it's very easy to change the phrases Word searches for and replaces with.)

Word also has help screens that describe the Visual Basic *objects* (commands) that you assemble to create a macro. Some commands are difficult or impossible to record in a macro. If you create lots of macros, or feel inclined to debug existing macros, the time may come when you need to delve into Visual Basic.

8

Word Meets Web

A s the Internet continues to play an ever larger role in human self-expression—
with things like personal blogs, online communities, and Web sites devoted to
every subject imaginable—it seems as though every piece of self-respecting
software, from databases to games, is replete with Web-ready features. Where would
you be if you couldn't convert, say, your recipe file into a Web page for the world to
see? Or keep a daily journal for your friends (and enemies) to read online?

Microsoft has no intention of being left out of all the fun, so all the key players in Office 2004 can convert your creations—like PowerPoint slideshows, Excel spreadsheets,
and Entourage calendars—into Web pages. But for traditional, hard-working Web
pages, Word is still the Web workhorse.

Figure 8-1:
*When you type a Web ad-
dress in the box in the Web
toolbar, Word launches Internet
Explorer (or whichever browser
is selected on the Web tab of
your Internet control panel) and
opens that Web page. No need
to type the "www" or ".com".*

Word as Web Browser

To be honest, Word isn't much of a Web browser. It does have a Web toolbar (choose View→Toolbars→Web), complete with Back, Forward, Stop, Refresh, and Home buttons (see Figure 8-1). There's even a Favorites menu, which you may be delighted to discover comes populated with the bookmarks in your Internet Explorer Favorites menu.

But this toolbar is only a remote control for Internet Explorer itself. Whenever you use one of its controls or type an address into its Address bar, your Web browser launches (if it isn't open already) and handles the actual task of displaying the Web page in question.

Opening Web Pages from the Web

That's not to say, however, that Word can't display Web pages in its own window, because it can. Just click the Open Web Page button on the Web Toolbar; a small dialog box appears, in which you can type the URL (Web address) of the Web page you want. When you click OK, Word connects to the Net and brings the specified page into its own window.

Note: In Word X you could also open a Web page by clicking File→Open Web Page. That, however, is no longer the case in Word 2004.

Unfortunately, Word is really only the strange preteen cousin of Internet Explorer; not only do Web pages take a long time to appear in Word windows, but they may also look peculiar, with a shuffled layout, enormous margins, unpredictable movie capabilities, and other anomalies. Still, this feature may be just the ticket when you want to grab some text out of a Web page article you just read. By bringing text into Word, you can copy, paste, reformat, and perform other editing tricks.

Tip: When you open any kind of Web-related document—a Web page, a Web template from the Project Gallery, a Word document you've saved as a Web page, or any other HTML file—in Word, it automatically opens in *Online Layout* view. If you ever find that you can't see images, background colors, or other Web features in your document, you've probably somehow gotten into the wrong view. Choose View→Online Layout.

Opening Web Pages from Your Hard Drive

Documents written using the HTML Web-design language aren't confined to the Internet anymore. Because they're relatively small, include formatting, and open with equal ease on Macs, Windows PCs, and every other kind of computer, HTML documents are now a common exchange format for Read Me files, software user manuals, and the like. (You know when you have one because its file name ends with *.htm* or *.html*.)

Word can open such documents directly: Just launch Word and choose File→Open, then navigate to the file on your Mac and click Open. The file opens into Word's

Online Layout view. Hyperlinks work, but otherwise the file acts more like a Word document than a Web page. For example:

- Scrolling text (see page 292) doesn't scroll.

- Animated GIFs, such as Active Graphics (see page 289) work, but only in Online Layout view.

- Movies designed to play automatically (and anything else requiring a Web-browser plug-in) don't work.

- Text flow and the positioning of images on your page may be different in Word than in a browser. Using a table for layout alignment (see page 294) results in more consistency between Word and browser views.

Note: Make sure that you have All Documents selected in the Enable pop-up menu in Word's Open dialogue box. If you don't, Word won't let you select and open HTML files.

Viewing HTML Code for a Web Page

When you open an HTML document, Word does its best to show you the images and text of that document just as though you're viewing it in a Web browser. In other words, you see the *results* of the HTML programming, not the HTML code itself.

If you're comfortable working in the HTML programming language, however, Word is only too happy to show you the underlying code:

1. **Open the Web page in Word. Choose View→HTML Source.**

   If that menu choice is grayed out, save the Web page document first. The Web page opens as a document full of HTML code. A tiny, one-button toolbar, ("Exit HTML Source") also opens.

2. **Edit the HTML in Word. Click Exit HTML Source when you're finished.**

   Word returns you to Online Layout view, where the changes you just made in HTML are reflected.

Creating a Web Page in Word

Most people who are serious about Web design use dedicated Web-design programs, such as Dreamweaver MX or Adobe GoLive.

But Word can convert any of its own documents into a Web page, ready to "hang" on the Internet. Make no mistake: Professional Web designers may sneer at your efforts, since Word fills the resulting behind-the-scenes HTML code with acres of unnecessary computer instructions that can make a Web page take longer to load into visitors' browsers. Furthermore, they can also render your design layout imprecisely. But when you need to create only the occasional Web page, or when simplicity and a short learning curve are more important to you than impressing professional Web designers, Word can suffice, and who cares about professional Web design geeks anyway?

Designing a Site Map

Before you start working on your Web page in Word, it's a good idea to have a plan of action. Take a blank piece of paper or Word document, draw a box for each page of your Web site, and label them to figure out how many Web pages your site will have, and how they'll be connected by navigational links. For instance, you might have a home page, an FAQ (frequently asked questions) page, a page of scanned photos, a long article on a page of its own, and a page with your contact information. Figure 8-2 shows an example sketch.

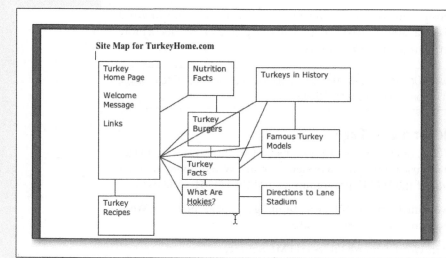

Figure 8-2:
You'll save yourself from temporary insanity if you begin your Web design with a site map. Draw arrows in all the directions that you're going to link the pages together, remembering that you'll want to link each page back to the home page, or at least to the page before it.

Basic Web-Page Layout

Once you've figured out which Web pages you'll need, create individual Word documents that represent those pages. You may need to use Word's advanced graphics and design tools—especially tables and hyperlinks—much more in a document that will ultimately become a Web page than, say, a run-of-the-mill memo. But otherwise, editing and designing a Web-bound Word document is similar to editing and designing any other Word file.

Tip: The following pages assume that you're interested in designing your Web pages essentially from scratch. The File→Project Gallery command, however, offers a Web Pages category filled with predesigned Web-page templates, such as a Frequently Asked Questions page, a Personal Web Page, and so on. If the Web page you have in mind is one of these basic types, by all means use the Project Gallery templates to save time. See page 657 for more on the templates.

Themes

Keep your site's graphic design simple. Although Word's Web tools let you use a riot of background and font colors, nothing looks cleaner and more readable on the Web than black type on a plain, light background.

Still, Word 2004 comes with a laundry list of canned color schemes for Web pages (and other documents), called Themes. Each theme incorporates professionally selected choices for font, bullet graphics, horizontal lines, headings, background colors, and other elements (see Figure 8-3).

To review your options, choose Format→Theme. The Theme dialog box opens. Click the various theme names for a preview of each. If you find one that appeals to you, click OK. Word applies the theme and returns you to your Word document, where you'll notice major differences only if you used Word's built-in heading styles, picture bullets, horizontal lines, and hyperlinks. (These are the elements a theme can affect.) If you've already saved the document as a Web page, or if you're in Online Layout View, you'll also get the full effect of the background pattern or color.

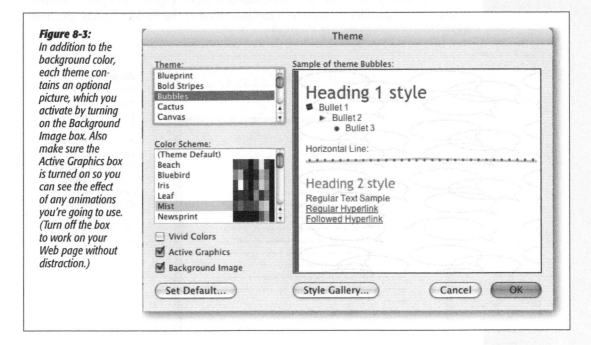

Figure 8-3:
In addition to the background color, each theme contains an optional picture, which you activate by turning on the Background Image box. Also make sure the Active Graphics box is turned on so you can see the effect of any animations you're going to use. (Turn off the box to work on your Web page without distraction.)

Here are more things you can do with Themes:

• Choose a different color scheme. Each theme has a default scheme, but you can substitute any of the 18 other color groupings listed in the **Color Scheme** box. Keep an eye on the Sample box (see Figure 8-3) until you find the colors that grab you.

• Once you've chosen a theme, turn on the **Vivid Colors** box and watch what happens to the colors; the background in particular changes to a brighter color. On the other hand, if your Web page contains lots of text, bear in mind that a dark or bright background can make it hard to read.

• Turning on **Active Graphics** *animates* the bullets and borders on the screen. Animated graphics blink, alternate between two different colors, or otherwise scream for your reader's attention. For the full effect, choose File→Web Page Preview to view your document in your Web browser.

- The **Background Image** checkbox turns on the default background pattern for each theme. If you find it detracts from your text, or if you prefer a plain background, simply turn it off.

- Finally, after applying the theme and returning to your document, you can tailor it to your liking. Just use the Formatting Palette and Word's other tools to change the background color, border style, and so on.

Style Gallery

The Style Gallery button in the Theme dialog box (see Figure 8-4) opens a window where you get another look at the templates listed in the Project Gallery (see page 657).

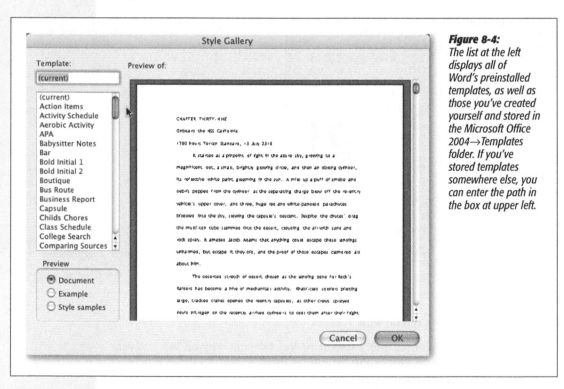

Figure 8-4:
The list at the left displays all of Word's preinstalled templates, as well as those you've created yourself and stored in the Microsoft Office 2004→Templates folder. If you've stored templates somewhere else, you can enter the path in the box at upper left.

As illustrated in Figure 8-4, the preview window (eventually) shows how your Web-page-in-progress will look in the selected template. (You might not notice much difference unless you've used Styles—especially Word's built-in Heading styles—in the document.) It's a good thing, too, because not all the templates work very well with all pages. For instance, the dark background of the Artsy theme, coupled with the dark print found in, say, the Mist color scheme may make your words difficult to read.

If you find one you like, click OK. As always, you can adjust the formatting once you've returned to your document.

Backgrounds

Although a white or very light background is your best bet for Web page legibility, Word lets you choose anything, from graceful to hideous, as the backdrop for your page. It can be a solid color background, a pattern or gradient, or a picture. (If you don't specify a background color, your visitors' Web browsers will use a default color, which is usually white or light gray.)

To choose a background color for your Web page, choose Format→Background; in the Background color palette, click one of the color blocks to make it the background color. You can choose a different color by clicking More Colors and using one of Word's color pickers as described on page 689. If you choose No Fill, your background will be the default color of your reader's Web browser.

Note: When you're adding a background color to a Web page template that already contains a background *pattern,* the color overrides the pattern. To remove the color and restore the pattern, click No Fill on the Background color palette.

You can also click Fill Effects on the Background palette; you'll be offered a wide range of fancy backdrops, from burlap to shimmering gradients. (See Chapter 20 for more on these options.) Most of them are much too busy for a Web page that you actually expect people to read. For the sake of humankind, please use background textures, patterns, pictures, and gradients sparingly—with only very light colors—or not at all. In Web page design, less is truly more.

When you choose a color, it appears instantly as the background of your Web page document. Word automatically switches into Online Layout view, if you weren't there already.

Font colors

You specify the color for the text of your Web page just as you would in any Word document—for example, using the Font Color button on the Formatting Palette.

POWER USERS' CLINIC

Automatic Color

When you open the Font Color section of the Formatting Palette, you'll notice that your first choice is Automatic Color. If you choose Automatic Color for text in a Web page, your reader will see it in whichever default color she's chosen for her Web browser. (In Internet Explorer, for example, you can specify your default text color by choosing Explorer→

Preferences. Click Web Browser→Web Content in the left pane and click the Text color block. Choose a color using one of Office's color pickers as described on page 689.)

Choosing No Fill for your background color and Automatic Color for your font is the ultimate in consideration for your reader. It does, however, limit your creativity.

When choosing a font color, the most important thing to remember is how it will show against your background. Remember, you want a lot of contrast between the background color and the font color. Black, blue, and red are good font color choices for light backgrounds.

White text on a black background sounds elegant, but it's not a good choice when working on a Web page in Word, since the black background shows up only in On-line Layout view. When you switch to Normal view, you'll get white text on a white background—the 21st century version of invisible ink without the whole lemon-on-paper-held-up-to-a-light thing. You lose the ability to print your page from Normal view for the same reason. (Furthermore, black backgrounds—solid color backgrounds of any kind, really—gulp down color ink from your Web site visitors' printers like it's Gatorade.)

Also, be aware that some people, in a vain attempt to load Web pages faster, turn off graphics in their Web browser. (In Internet Explorer, for instance, you do this by choosing Explorer→Preferences, then clicking Web Browser→Web Content in the left pane and turning off "Show pictures.") Because background pictures and patterns are, in fact, graphics, readers who've turned graphics off won't see them. Instead, they'll simply see your text against their browser's default background color, which is usually white or light gray—yet another reason why black, red, and dark blue are safe font colors for Web pages.

Other text effects

You can use any of Word's text formatting—such as different fonts, typefaces, and paragraph formatting—in documents you'll be saving as Web pages, but bear in mind that they may look different, or be lost completely, depending on your reader's browser. (See Chapter 3 for more detail on text formatting.)

Word also offers special effects for use on Web pages: animated text and scrolling text. Use them with caution—since flashing and animated text, as noted earlier, strikes many Web denizens as extremely annoying.

- **Animated Text.** To use Word's animated text effects, first select the text in your document. Then choose Format→Font; in the Font dialog box, click the Animation tab, as shown in Figure 8-5. Click each of the listed Animations and watch what happens in the Preview box. If you find one you like, click it and then click OK.

Note: Beware of the Default button in the Font dialog box. Clicking it applies the animation style to your Normal font, the one you see by default in every new Word document. Chances are you don't want Las Vegas Lights around everything you type in every Word document—or maybe you do. Either way, Word asks you before proceeding.

- **Scrolling Text.** Scrolling or marqueeing text is, unfortunately, a very popular text effect on Web pages. As shown in Figure 8-5, a single dialog box lets you determine all aspects of how the text looks and scrolls.

To open this box, highlight the text you want to scroll and then choose Insert→
HTML Object→Scrolling Text. Choose a font, size, and typestyle in the lower panel
of the dialog box, a different background color from the Background pop-up menu,
and an animation style from the Behavior, Direction, and Loop pop-up menus.

For example, *Scroll* makes the text roll across the screen just like the letters on
the marquee of a Broadway theater. (Use the Direction pop-up menu to specify
whether it starts from the left or the right.) It goes all the way across until it disappears, then reemerges at the opposite edge and starts over again. From the Loop
menu, choose the number of times you want the scrolling action to take place:
one through five times, or Infinite.

Slide scrolls the text to the opposite edge of the page, and then stops. *Alternate*
means that the text bounces back and forth across the screen as though in a slow-
motion game of Pong.

Figure 8-5:
*Top: The Las Vegas Lights and Sparkle Text ani-
mations feature multicolored speckles. Blinking
Background alternates a black background with
white or with the font color. You get the idea.*

*Bottom: The Font pop-up menu in the Insert→
HTML Object→Scrolling Text dialog box lets you
apply scrolling to text in any Word font. Scrolling
or "marqueeing" text rolls across the width of
your Web page from one side to the other.*

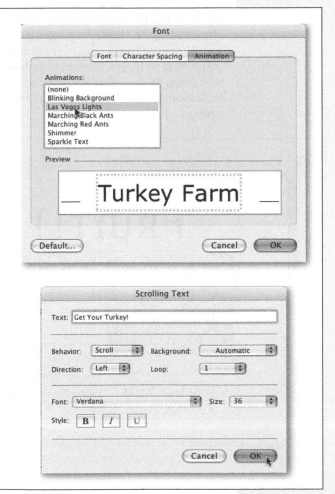

To edit your scrolling text, select the text and choose Insert→HTML Object→ Scrolling Text. Make any changes in the Scrolling Text dialog box. You won't see any text animation in Word; you have to save the result as a Web page and then open it in a Web browser.

Note: Use the scrolling text feature with caution. It's difficult to read, and often ads little to your page. People browse the Internet for information, not to exercise their eyes as they attempt to track scrolling text.

Tables in Web page layout

These days, it's a very rare Web page whose design is nothing but a single river of text running down the middle of the page. Most professional Web pages, including those at *www.macworld.com, www.nytimes.com,* and *www.missingmanuals.com,* are composed of several parallel columns. Each can contain an independent flow of text, as well as such standard elements as a graphic or navigation bar.

To create this effect in Word, use a Word *table,* as described in Chapter 4. Aligning objects using the HTML language alone is notoriously difficult. But if you compose your Web page with a table, you can use its rows and columns to align the text and graphics on your page. If you hide the borders, as described in Figure 8-6, your visitors won't even be aware that they're viewing a table. (You can still view the gray gridline indications in Word, but they won't show when the finished Web page is viewed in a browser.)

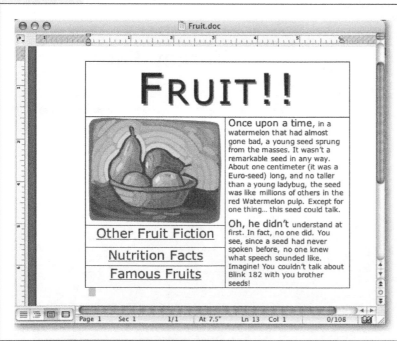

Figure 8-6:
A simple Web page laid out in a Word table. The table gridlines properly line up the text blocks, bullets, and links with each other. To make the black lines disappear, choose Table→Table Properties; click the Borders and Shading button; click None, OK, and OK. You can also select the entire table and choose No Border on the Borders and Shading panel of the Formatting Palette.

Tip: To ensure that as many people as possible can read your text—including people using older or text-only browsers—consider also designing a simple, table-free, text-only version of your Web page and link it to the front page of your Web site.

A single cell of your table can be extremely tall, if necessary. If yours is like a typical Web page, in fact, the entire page may be composed of a single row of the table, whose cells stretch the full height of the page. That's perfectly OK, and it's a clever way to get two or three parallel columns with independent text flows. (See page 159 for information on creating Word tables.)

Tip: Consider using *nested* tables for the smaller objects in your Web page. For example, create a table eight cells long by two cells wide to hold a list of links. Fill the table, then drag it into a large cell in your main table. The main table will help align the list relative to the rest of the page. (See the list of links in Figure 8-6, for example.)

Graphics, Sounds, and Movies

Both Word's Clip Art Gallery and the Web itself are brimming with images that you can use to adorn your Web pages. You can also use any of Word's drawing tools, such as AutoShapes and WordArt (see page 682), in the Web pages you create. When you save the Web page, Word saves the graphic in the Web page's folder as a GIF file (see the sidebar box on page 296).

Graphics do enhance your Web page's appearance. Keep in mind, however, that pictures take much longer to download than the text that surrounds them. Try to strike a balance, only using a couple pictures per page for the typical information-focused Web site. Remember, almost 50 percent of Web denizens are using dial-up, narrowband (56 kpbs) connections.

Downloading Graphics from the Web

When you see a picture you love on a Web site, you can download it and use it on your own Web site. (Of course, you'll do your best to avoid using a copyrighted image without permission.) Here are the easiest ways to download Web graphics:

• Right-click and *hold* the hand cursor on the image that you'd like to capture (or just Control-click it). From the shortcut menu, choose Download Image to Disk (Internet Explorer), Save Image (Netscape), Save Image As (Safari) or Image→"Save image to" (OmniWeb). In the resulting dialog box, select the folder on your hard drive where you like to keep downloaded images. Click Save.

• Drag the image itself right out of the browser window and onto your desktop or the folder where you're keeping downloaded images. Let go of the mouse button when the outline of the image appears on the desktop or when the destination folder appears highlighted.

Text wrapping and graphics

Wrapping text around images on Web pages works the same way as in other Word documents, as described on page 156. If you're using a table to lay out your Web page, you can even use text wrapping within a table cell.

The instructions for wrapping text around a graphic image are exactly as described on page 156—with one difference. In HTML, you can place graphics over text, behind text, with text above and below it, or wrapped around either side of it. What you can't do, however, is wrap text around *both* sides of a centered graphic. Thus, in Online Layout view, that option is grayed out on the Wrapping section of the Formatting Palette. To activate the choices on the "Wrap to" menu, drag the graphic to either side of the table cell or page.

Bullets and Dividers

Bullets and lines are very effective ways of "punctuating" your Web page and keeping its layout organized. Large, uninterrupted blocks of text make for difficult reading on the Web, so using these small graphic elements to break up your text helps prevent eyestrain—for both you and your readers.

Web bullets and divider graphics work just like other Word Clip Art, including the way they're inserted.

1. **Choose Insert→Picture→ClipArt.**

   The Clip Gallery appears. (See page 680 for more on this feature.)

UP TO SPEED

Graphics Formats on the Web

Like Internet Explorer, Netscape, and other modern Web browsers, Word lets you use for Web pages images in any of three formats: GIF, JPEG, and PNG. If you place any other kinds of images in your Web page, such as PICT or bitmap, Word converts and saves them in one of the three compatible formats listed above, based on the following criteria:

- Photographs are saved in JPEG format. (JPEG graphics use a compression system that's especially effective with photographs.)

- Clip art, drawing objects, and PICT files are saved as GIF files. (GIF images are limited to 256 colors, but download very quickly. In other words, they lend themselves to drawings and other simple images.)

- If you've chosen "Allow PNG as an output format" in Preferences (see below), Word saves all images in PNG—Portable Network Graphics format.

The newest of the major graphics compression formats, PNG is an improvement over both JPEG and GIF. PNG works equally well for both simple images and photographs. If you save all your Web page images as PNG, your Web page will load faster, take less storage space on your Mac, and work on all modern Web browsers.

To do so, choose Word→Preferences→General panel and click Web Options. Click the Picture tab and turn on "Allow PNG as on output format." Because PNG is gradually replacing GIF as the most popular Web graphics format, the only reason not to use it is that certain older browsers won't recognize such images.

---

2. **In the Category list in the Clip Gallery, scroll down to find the bullet that you desire.**

Each of these categories has several pages; click the "Next" icon at the bottom of the preview pane to see the next page.

3. **Click the image you want, and then click Insert.**

You return to your document, where the newly placed graphic appears.

Tip: Another quick way to open the Clip Gallery—and this is new in Word 2004—click the flippy triangle next to Add Objects on the Formatting Palette, and then click the Insert Clip Art button on the Graphics panel.

Horizontal Lines

Inserting a horizontal line between sections is another great way to break up the text on a Web page. If you started your Web page with a Word Web Page template or chose a theme, then Word has a line in a coordinating color and pattern already picked out for you. To insert one, proceed as follows:

1. **Choose View→Toolbars→Tables and Borders.**

The Tables and Borders toolbar opens.

2. **Click the arrow button next to the Borders button on the Tables and Borders toolbar. Choose Horizontal Line from the pop-up menu.**

Word inserts the line for your theme at the document's insertion point.

You can also insert a horizontal line in any Web page by choosing Insert→Picture→Horizontal Line. The Choose a Picture dialog box opens, showing you the contents of your Mac's Applications→Microsoft Office 2004→Clipart→Lines folder. Select a line (based on what you see in the preview window) and click Insert. Word places the line across your Web page document at the insertion point.

Note: The lines on the Add Objects panel's Lines tab (Formatting Palette) aren't the same as the horizontal line graphics described above.

Movies

Web pages created in Word can store and play digital movies in any of several formats: QuickTime, QuickTime VR, MPEG, and some AVI files. (Word converts AVI to QuickTime when you save the Web page.) You can use any such movie that you have on your Mac, whether you downloaded it or made it yourself, on a Web page you create in Word.

To use a movie from the Web in your Web page, you need to download it onto your Mac. If you just click a link to watch a movie, that doesn't necessarily download a copy for you. You have to Control-click the link and then, from the shortcut menu, choose either Download Link to Disk (Internet Explorer), Save Link As (Netscape and Safari), or Save Link To (OmniWeb). Either way, you'll get a chance to name the file and choose a folder location for it on your Mac, such as the desktop or your Documents folder.

Then:

1. **Choose Insert→Movie.**

   You must be in a Word document, not an .htm document, and you should be in Page Layout or Online Layout view. The Open File dialog box appears. (If you use the Insert→Movie command in Normal view, Word automatically switches to Page Layout view.)

Note: If you can't find the Movie command on your Insert menu, see the box on page 299 for a work-around.

---

2. **In the Insert Movie dialog box, navigate to the movie file on your hard drive and double-click it.**

   The movie appears on your page, where you can drag to place it anywhere on your Web page, wrap text around it, and resize it just like any Word picture—all using the Picture toolbar or Formatting Palette.

Giving a movie a poster frame

The *poster frame* is the still picture that you see when the movie is not playing. To give your movie a poster frame, click to select it and proceed as follows:

1. **Click the Play button on the Movie toolbar (see Figure 8-7).**

   As the movie plays, watch until you see an image that would make a great poster frame. If you've made the movie controls visible, you can also use it (or press the arrow keys) to locate just the right frame.

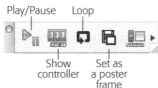

Play/Pause   Loop

Show controller   Set as a poster frame

Figure 8-7:
The Movie toolbar helps you find the "poster frame" that will represent the movie when it's not actually playing. Start by clicking the Show Movie Scroll Bar icon to make the standard movie controls appear at the bottom of your movie frame (bottom). Play the movie, or step through it one frame at a time by pressing the arrow keys.

2. **Click the Set as Poster Frame button on the Movie toolbar.**

   Repeat the process until you get the perfect poster frame.

3. **Click the Format Picture button on the Movie toolbar to open the Format Picture dialog box.**

The poster frame is like any Word picture. You can resize or crop the poster frame, apply a transparency to it, change its fill color, and so on, as described on page 687.

4. **Click OK.**

Removing a movie

Deleting a movie is easy: Click the icon or poster frame to select it and press the Delete key.

Tip: Your movie won't play on the Web unless each visitor to your page has installed the QuickTime plug-in. Not all Mac people have the most recent version, and Windows types may not have it at all. You can help them by giving them a link to the Web site where Apple gives downloads of a free version for both Windows and Mac. For example, you might add this text somewhere on your Web page: "You need the free QuickTime plug-in for Mac or Windows to view the movies on this Web page. Download it at *www.apple.com/quicktime.*" (See page 300 for more on inserting hyperlinks.)

Background Sounds

If your movies, background pictures, and animated text aren't enough multimedia to send your visitors' 56 K modems falling to their knees sobbing, don't give up; Word also comes with a library of sounds that play as your reader views your Web page. You can use one of them, or any sound you've downloaded in the WAV, AIFF, or MIDI format:

1. **Choose Insert→HTML Object→Background Sound.**

The Background Sound dialog box appears.

2. **Click Select; navigate to the sound file and double-click it.**

WORKAROUND WORKSHOP

The Crazy Movie Workaround

You can't put a movie on a Web page in Word when you're in a Web page. If you're working in a document that you've saved as a Web page, you can look on the Insert menu all you want; the command is just not there. Only in a standard Word document does the Insert→Movie command appear.

In Word 2001, you could see the Insert→Movie command in all documents and in all views, but you could only insert and view the movies in Page Layout view, Online Layout view, or a Web page document opened in Word.

In Word 2004, you must learn a whole different way of thinking. You'll have to design most of your Web page in a standard Word document, taking care to insert all your movies before saving the document as a Web page. You can play, reposition, format, and set a poster frame for movies after you've saved the document as a Web page, but you can no longer add new movies. (Your other alternative, of course, is to buy a copy of Dreamweaver MX or GoLive.)

The standard drag-and-drop installation of Office (see Appendix A on the "Missing CD" page at *www.missingmanuals.com*) offers a handsome set of sound effects in the Microsoft Office 2004→Office→Sounds.

3. **Choose the number of times you'd like the sound to play from the Loop menu, and then click OK.**

When your viewer opens the Web page, the background sound plays the number of times you chose to loop it.

To remove a sound, choose Insert→HTML Object→Background Sound. The name of the current background sound file is shown at the top of the dialog box. Click Clear to remove it from your Web page.

Hyperlinks

Hyperlinks—buttons, graphics, or text phrases that, when clicked, take you to a different document—are what Web sites are all about. In Word, you can make just about any kind of link you've ever dreamed of—links to Web pages, to other documents or pages you've created, to movies or sound files, or to a point in the same document or another document.

Tip: Hyperlinks are not just for creating Web pages. They work extremely well right on your own hard drive, where you can use them to create a living, clickable list of all the files—or even applications—that you open frequently. They also work as described here in Excel and PowerPoint.

The following examples show you how to create links to various locations on your hard drive or on the Web.

Linking to Another Place or Another Word Document

If your document is long, you may want links to help your reader navigate it. For instance, on a Web page (or even a senior thesis), you can place a link called "Back to top" at the bottom of your page, or a list of links at the top of the page that link to paragraphs farther down. Either way, this can save your reader lots of scrolling.

GEM IN THE ROUGH

Web Page Preview

As you build your Web page, you'll need to preview your work-in-progress from time to time. Yes, choosing View→ Online Layout shows what your document will look like in a Web page; but you won't be able to see your animated text and certain other browser-only features. Fortunately, the File→Web Page Preview command actually shows it in your Web browser, which provides a much more accurate preview.

The document name in the title bar may not match the file name that you gave the document when you saved it. That's because Word takes the Web-page name from the title box on the File→Properties→Summary tab. In other words, if you'd like to change the name that appears in the Web browser's title bar when opening your Word document as a Web page, simply choose File→Properties→Summary tab and change the title.

Hyperlinks can also jump from one *document* to another. This simple feature is the key to two dramatic Word features:

- For everyday Mac work, you can set up links to other Word files on your hard drive.

- When you're building a Web page, you can set up links to other Web pages you've created. For instance, you may have a Web site about birds, with a main page and a separate page for each bird.

Remember that you'll have to upload all such Web documents, in the same folder structure, to the Web along with the linking page; otherwise, the hyperlink won't work.

The easy way (copy and paste)

The routine goes like this:

1. **Copy some text in the document or paragraph you want to jump *to*.**

   A heading makes an especially handy target, but it can be anything at all, anywhere in the document.

2. **Switch to the document or paragraph where you want the link to appear; choose Edit→Paste as Hyperlink.**

   (If the command is dimmed, then you need to save the target document.)

   The copied material appears in your document; it should be blue, underlined, and ready to click. (You can change the text of the link itself as described later in this section.)

Tip: If you create these types of links frequently, use the ultimate link-creation shortcut. Set up both documents so that you can see their windows simultaneously. Highlight the "jump to here" text in the target document, then Option-⌘-drag it *out of its window* and into the document where the link will appear. When you release the mouse, a shortcut menu appears, offering commands like Move Here and Copy Here; click Create Hyperlink Here. You've just created a link to the text you highlighted.

The longer way (using bookmarks or headings)

You don't have to use the copy-and-paste routine. If you've used Word bookmarks (see page 242) or its built-in heading styles in the target document, you can use them as anchors—the targets—for your links, like this:

1. **Select the text ("Back to top," for example) or graphic that will be the hyperlink; choose Insert→Hyperlink.**

   The Insert Hyperlink dialog box opens, as shown in Figure 8-8. The text you selected in your Web page document appears in the Display box. If a graphic will serve as the link, then <<Selection in Document>> appears in the box.

Tip: Microsoft doesn't kid around about the Insert→Hyperlink command; it offers about 731 alternate methods of triggering it. For example, you can also Control-click the selected text or object and choose Hyperlink from the shortcut menu, or click the Insert Hyperlink button on the Standard toolbar, or press ⌘-K.

2. **Click the Document tab, then click Locate.**

   The Select Place in Document dialog box appears.

3. **Choose the bookmark or heading, click OK, then click OK.**

   If you haven't successfully created any bookmarks or used one of Word's built-in heading styles, Top of the Document is the only available choice. If you do have headings and bookmarks in the document, click the flippy triangles to view the entire list.

   After you click OK to close the Insert Hyperlink dialog box, the text you selected in step 2 turns into a blue, underlined hyperlink. To test it, just click the link; the document scrolls so that the heading or bookmark anchor jumps to the top of the screen.

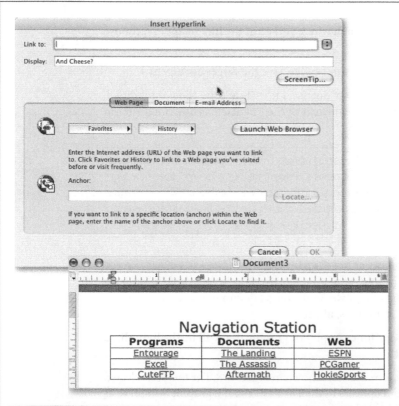

Figure 8-8:
Top: The Insert Hyperlink dialog box has a tab for each of the three types of Word hyperlinks. Click ScreenTip to edit the pop-up screen tip that appears when somebody points to your link without clicking.

Bottom: You don't have to think about links exclusively in the Internet context. A Word document can serve as a handy launch pad for all of the documents you use in a typical workday, and even certain programs—a miniature Dock without the icons.

Linking to an Application or Mac File

If you spend most of the day in Word, consider making yourself a launching pad document like the one shown in Figure 8-8, which serves as your "home page" for the entire computer. It works like this:

1. **Highlight the text or the image that will be the link "button"; choose Insert→ Hyperlink.**

   The Insert Hyperlink dialog box opens, as shown in Figure 8-8.

2. **Click the Document tab. Click Select.**

   Word opens the Choose a File dialog box.

3. **Navigate to the destination document or program on your Mac and select it; click OK.**

   You return to your document, where there now exists a living, working link to another file or program on your Mac.

Linking to Another Web Site

If you're designing a Web site, of course, the link you're probably most interested in creating jumps to *another* Web page. That's why Word provides so many different ways of creating a hyperlink to another page on the Web.

By typing a URL

As many an annoyed Mac fan can tell you, Word comes factory set to turn *any* Web address you type into a living hyperlink. When you're creating Web pages with Word is the one time you'll actually be grateful for this behavior. Just type the Web address into your Web page document, beginning with *www* and ending with *.com, .org,* or dot-whatever. Word automatically creates the hyperlink (unless you've turned off this feature in Word's Preferences, as described on page 100).

By dragging a URL

You don't have to memorize and type a URL in order to place a hyperlink in your document. All you have to do is find it on the Web; then you can drag and drop the Web address into your Web page.

To see how this works, open your Web browser and visit the Web page that you'd like to link to. Switch back to Word; drag the icon next to the Address window from the browser into your document, as shown in Figure 8-9.

When you let go of the mouse button, Word creates a hyperlink *field*. (If you see the field code [see page 238] instead of the title of the Web page, select the entire field code and press Option-F9.)

The text of the final hyperlink in your document will be the Web page's title (as seen in the title bar of your browser window), not the URL itself. If you want to see the underlying URL, point to the Web-page name without clicking to make the identifying yellow balloon appear.

If you'd like to use different text other than the Web page's real title for the hyperlink, edit the hyperlink as described on page 306. For example, if the Web page you're linking to is titled "Actor Bio 2," you might want to change it to the more descriptive "Brando: The Early Years."

Navigation Station		
Programs	**Documents**	**Web**
Entourage	The Landing	ESPN
Excel	The Assassin	PCGamer
CuteFTP	Aftermath	HokieSports
Dragoon	MM Chapter 7	MacCentral
Vampire: The Masquerade	Xbox Fan	Inside MacGames
Chess	PS2 Fan	

Figure 8-9:
You can make a Web link in a Word document just by dragging the @ sign out of the address bar in Internet Explorer–in this example, to make a "home page" of links you like to visit frequently.

By using a Favorite or History

If you have Internet Explorer on your Mac, the Favorites list in the Insert Hyperlink dialog box displays your Internet Explorer Favorites, while the History list displays the Web sites you've most recently visited in *Internet Explorer*. This pop-up menu can be a real timesaver; here's how to go about it:

1. **Insert your cursor where you wish to place the hyperlink and choose Insert→ Hyperlink.**

    The Insert Hyperlink dialog box opens, as shown in Figure 8-8.

WORKAROUND WORKSHOP

A Link to the Past

Way back when, in Word 2001, you could create a link to almost any application on your Mac. In Word 2004, many Mac OS X application icons in the Choose a File dialog box are grayed out when you're creating hyperlinks. The reason: Most Mac OS X program icons are actually packages—thinly disguised folders—each of which contains both the program itself and its supplementary software and files. Microsoft Office 2004's own programs (and other Mac OS X programs that haven't been turned into packages) are all you see in this list.

You can, however, still link to Classic applications in Word 2004. Thus, if you're using hyperlinks to create a launcher as

described on page 62, you're limited to three choices: documents, Classic applications, and Office 2004 applications.

If you're sneaky, however, you can work around this obstacle. Link to a document in a Mac OS X application—even a blank one. Word 2004 is perfectly happy to open a document, and therefore the program you're trying to launch opens automatically.

There is a drawback to this method: After doing some editing, you must remember to use Save As instead of Save for the first time, so that you don't commit your typing to the blank startup document.

---

2. **Click the Web page tab.**

Make sure the correct text for your hyperlink appears in the Display box; if not, change it.

3. **From the Favorites or History pop-up list, choose the Web site you want to link to.**

If the Web site you're looking for isn't in one of the lists, click Launch Web Browser to search the Web for it.

4. **Click OK.**

You've just added a link to the Web page you selected. The link's text/name will be the same as the Web page name (not necessarily the URL).

Note: Although there is an Anchor box on the Web Page tab in the Insert Hyperlink dialog box, it almost never works in Web sites. In order for this feature to work, the page must contain HTML anchor tags or Word bookmarks, as described in "To a specific location on another page."

Email Hyperlinks

An *email* hyperlink, also known as a *mailto* link, opens a new, preaddressed message in your default email program (or the program of whoever clicks the link). When you create a Web page, it's common practice to include an email hyperlink to yourself, so that your readers can contact you with questions, comments, or orders. To do so, just follow these steps:

1. **Type and select the text ("Contact me") that will become the email hyperlink.**

As with any other hyperlink, you can use a graphic, but you should also include some text to make clear what the link does.

2. **Choose Insert→Hyperlink. In the Hyperlink dialog box, click the Email Address tab. Type the email address you want the link to mail to in the To box.**

The Recent Addresses list contains a list of email addresses for which you've recently created hyperlinks (not necessarily ones you've actually used). To look up an address in your Entourage Address Book instead, click Launch Email Application. No matter what your default email program, Entourage launches. There's no further integration with Entourage, however, so you'll have to manually copy and paste the address you want out of its Address Book.

3. **Press Tab; type a subject line, if you wish.**

In other words, when your visitor clicks the "Contact me" link, his email program will automatically open. When it does, an outgoing blank email message will appear, preaddressed to you *and* with the Subject line already filled in. Including a subject line can help you keep track of emails that come from this particular Web page. However, not all Web browsers, or all email programs, work with the subject-line-in-an-email-hyperlink feature.

4. Click OK.

The email link is ready to click.

Note: If all you need is a simple Web or email hyperlink, just type it into Word. Word creates the hyperlink instantly (if, that is, you haven't turned off this feature in the Tools→AutoCorrect→AutoFormat As You Type dialog box). Later, should you want to change the link to read "Contact Me" or something more elegant-looking than your plain old email address, edit the link as described next.

Likewise, for simple addresses like *www.apple.com*, just type the URL into your document. You can always go back and change the text later, as described next.

Selecting and Editing Hyperlinks

When you click a hyperlink in Word, Word follows the link, even if that means launching your Web browser or opening some program or document on your Mac. But if clicking triggers the link, how are you supposed to *edit* the hyperlink text?

The easiest way is to Control-click the link and choose Hyperlink→Edit Hyperlink from the shortcut menu. The Edit Hyperlink dialog box opens; here you can change the URL, email address, display text, screen tip (see the box below), anchor, and so on.

POWER USERS' CLINIC

Hyperlink ScreenTips

When you browse the Web with Internet Explorer 4 or later (and who doesn't?), you can point to a hyperlink without clicking to summon a small, yellow, identifying ScreenTip (like a screen tip). The information shown in the ScreenTip depends on what kind of hyperlink you've created.

By default, Word creates Screen-Tips for each type of hyperlink automatically: the URL for a Web link, *mailto:myname@mac.com* (or whatever your address is) for an email link, or the full path and file name of the document on your Mac or other computer on your network.

You can change the ScreenTips to say whatever you like. For instance, say you have a picture of a house that links back to your home page. If your reader doesn't get it from the picture, the URL (which could be something like

http://www.geocities.com/~bobtheduck) may not be much help. You could change the ScreenTip so that when your reader passes the cursor over the house picture, "My Home Page" is the tip that pops up.

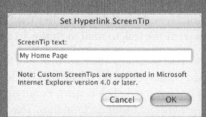

To write your own ScreenTip, Control-click the hyperlink and choose Hyperlink→Edit Hyperlink from the shortcut menu. In the Hyperlink dialog box, click ScreenTip.

The Set Hyperlink ScreenTip dialog box (shown here) opens; here you can type up to 254 characters of text for your ScreenTip. That's enough room to write a fairly long sentence, if you wish.

Click OK when you finish editing the ScreenTip. Click OK to close the Edit Hyperlink dialog box after making any other changes you like.

If the dog ate your Control key, you can also highlight the link by carefully dragging across it, then pressing ⌘-K (or choosing Insert→Hyperlink) to open the Insert Hyperlink dialog box. In fact, if all you want to edit is the display text for a hyperlink, just drag carefully across it (or Control-click it and choose Hyperlink→Select Hyperlink) and then retype—no overnight dialog box stay required.

Similarly, you can edit graphic links without triggering them; once again, the trick is to select the link without activating it—by Control-clicking it. After editing the image using the Formatting Palette or the Drawing or Picture toolbars, press Esc or click elsewhere to deselect the object and avoid inadvertently making further changes.

Hyperlink colors

In Word, text hyperlinks appear in blue type until they're clicked, whereupon they change to purple. You can change these default colors, if you like; the trick is to change the Hyperlink *style,* just as you'd change any Word style (see page 139 for instructions).

If you're *that* kind of person, you can even change the color that clicked hyperlinks change *into* after being clicked. Just modify Word's built-in Followed Hyperlink style.

These new hyperlink colors will override default hyperlink colors when the page is opened in Internet Explorer and Netscape Communicator. If your colors don't work, it's because your visitor has changed his browser preferences to override the color choices that have been programmed into Web pages.

Removing Hyperlinks

To remove a hyperlink you no longer want, you have two options:

- Drag over the hyperlink text and press Delete. Both the hyperlink and the display text or object are deleted.

- To cancel out the link while leaving the display text or object in place, Control-click the link and choose Hyperlink→Edit Hyperlink on the shortcut menu. Click Remove Link.

Web Forms

If you've ever searched a Web site, taken a poll, or made a purchase online, you've used a Web *form.* Web forms take the form of pop-up menus, checkboxes, and little text boxes. They're designed to collect information from the Web site visitor and save it on a server for processing.

You can build a Web form in Word, but you'll need the help of a Web programmer to write the necessary CGI scripts to make the form work. (CGI stands for *common gateway interface,* a software convention for transferring and processing data between Web pages and servers.)

To build a Web form, you must insert various *form controls* in your page—checkboxes, radio buttons, pop-up menus, buttons, and so on—that your visitors will use for submitting the information and resetting the form. You'll find them in the Insert→ HTML Object submenu. With the help of a programmer, select settings and values from the resulting dialog box.

Saving Web Pages

If you started your Web page from a Web-page template or a blank Web page, as described at the beginning of this section, all you have to do to save it is press ⌘-S or choose File→Save or Save As. You can also save a standard Word document or template as a Web page, like this:

1. Choose File→Save as Web Page.

The Save dialog box opens, as shown in Figure 8-10.

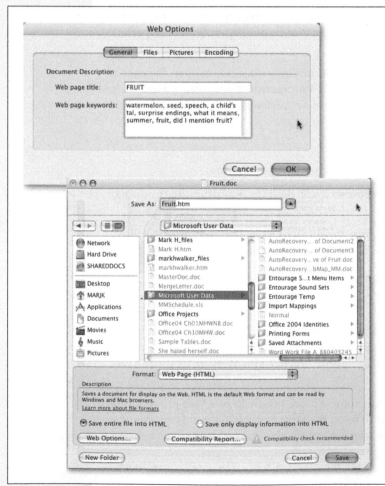

Figure 8-10:
Lower left: When you choose File→Save as Web Page, a Save dialog box opens, all set to save the document in HTML format. When you post the resulting files and folders online, be sure to preserve their folder structure on your Web server. For example, don't dump your HTML file into the folder containing your graphics. Create a matching folder online to hold the graphics.

Upper right: The Web Options dialog box is the same one that opens if you click Web Options on the Word→Preferences→General tab.

2. **Click one of the radio buttons depending on how you'd like to save the file.**

The **Save entire file into** HTML option creates a dual-purpose document. It stores the information *both* for display on the Web *and* for returning to it as a Word document. Such word processor–only elements as headers and footers, comments, page numbers, and page breaks will reappear when you open it again in Word.

Save only display information into HTML saves *only* the document attributes that work in a Web browser. Other information, such as page and section breaks, columns, and headers and footers will be lost. This option makes a smaller, more compact HTML file, which is a good thing if your Web service provider charges based upon how much server space you use.

Tip: If you choose this option, use Save As first to save a copy with all the normal Word elements intact; you may decide to use the document in Word again.

---

3. **Click Save.**

Word takes longer than usual to save the document. When it's finished, you can switch to Online Layout view (if you weren't already there) to see the Web page as it will appear online.

Web Options

When you click Web Options in the Save dialog box (see Figure 8-10), you can specify special Web features that would normally require mucking around in HTML code.

- The Web page *title* you enter on the **General Tab** appears in the title bar in a Web browser. The Web page *keywords* are the terms that search engines like Google and Yahoo spot when searching. (In HTML, these words are known as *meta tags*.)

- "Update links on Save" in the **Files** tab comes already turned on. If you've changed or moved any of your Web page's supporting files, such as bullets, graphics, or background patterns, Word updates the links so the page will work when you reopen it. The "Save only display information into HTML" checkbox turns on the corresponding radio button in the Save dialog box (see above).

- Checking "Allow PNG" on the **Pictures** tab saves all the images in your Web page in Portable Network Graphics format, as described on page 296. The "Screen size" pop-up menu shows just about every screen size and resolution combination your Web page visitors are likely to have. 1024 x 768—standard on iBooks and iMacs, for example—is the smallest screen most people use today, and therefore a pretty safe bet.

In the "Pixels per inch" box, 72 is the best setting for Mac monitors; your text will look gigantic on Windows PC screens. If you're creating a page that's going to be viewed primarily on Windows PCs, change this setting to 96; unfortunately, your text will look tiny when viewed by Mac monitors. (You're witnessing the unfortunate side effect of competing Mac/Windows standards. There's no simple solution, other than encouraging your Mac friends to use Internet Explorer 5.0 or later for its automatic text-enlargement feature.)

- The menu on the **Encoding** tab displays all the foreign languages and browser formats Word can use for saving your Web page. If your page contains text in a different alphabet system (such as Cyrillic or Japanese), choose it from this menu.

Tip: As you complete your Web page, consider testing it in different Web browsers. Text may wrap differently, colors and graphics may look different, and movies and marquees may not operate the same way, if at all, in different browsers.

If you have a copy of the America Online program, for example, open your page using its File→Open command. Try the same experiment in Netscape Navigator (available free at *www.netscape.com*). You would do well to also check the increasingly popular browsers, OmniWeb (*www.omnigroup.com*) and Opera (*www. opera.com*).

Lost in the Translation

Despite all its Web-savvy trappings, Word, when you get right down to it, isn't actually an HTML editor. The Web pages it creates capture the spirit of the original Word document you prepared, but not the letter, since you lose quite a bit of its look in the conversion to a Web page. Among the casualties: text boxes; fancy text effects like embossed type, shadow, and strikethrough; drop caps; page numbering; margin settings and page borders; headers and footers; multiple columns; and styles. All of these Word features drop out when the document is converted to HTML. Fields (see page 237) *sort of* carry through; the resulting Web page shows the field information (such as the date), but it's no longer self-updating. Tabs aren't reliable, either, since Word

---

POWER USERS' CLINIC

HTML Text Styles

The HTML styles in the Format→Style dialog box let you transform a saved Web page into an attractive Word document. For example, suppose that someone at your company created an online training manual, but no one made a paper version. Or maybe you want to download an article from the Web and create a printed version (with permission, of course).

These Web pages are HTML documents, and the text in them is formatted using HTML codes. For instance, one HTML code creates a first-level heading, another denotes an address or citation, and another creates hyperlinks. These labels are listed in the Styles list box in the Format→Style dialog box; except for Hyperlink and Followed Hyperlink, their style names all begin with the letters HTML.

You can format and redefine these styles as you would any Word styles; when you do, Word will use them for HTML-formatted text whenever you open a Web page in Word. You may want to make all hyperlinks match your Normal style, for example. (Headings in HTML are automatically changed into your Word heading styles.)

To convert a Web site into a Word document, open the Web page in your browser. Choose File→Save or Save As; save the page onto your Mac in HTML format. Open the page in Word by choosing File→Open and navigating to the Web-page file. You will see the text in the document, but not the images (they don't get saved along with the rest of the page).

---

converts them into HTML tabs, which, in some Web browsers, turn into spaces. (Use tables wherever you're inclined to use tabs.) Footnotes, on the other hand, perform beautifully. The superscript numbers turn into hyperlinks that scroll to the notes at the bottom of the page.

Posting Your Web Site Online

Creating HTML documents is only the first step in establishing a Web presence. The final step is uploading them to a *Web file server*—a computer that's always on and connected to the Internet. You have several options:

- **Use your own Mac.** If you have a full-time connection (cable modem or DSL), you can use the built-in Web Sharing feature of Mac OS 9 or Mac OS X to make your Web site available to the Internet at large. Your Web address won't be very memorable (along the lines of *http://192.168.34.2*), the speed won't be great, and not very many people can visit your site at once, but the price ($0) is right. The Mac's online help and *Mac OS X: The Missing Manual* contain instructions.

- **Use your ISP.** Most Internet service providers (ISPs), as well as America Online, offer somewhere between 5 and 10 megs of free space to hold your Web pages as part of your monthly fee. Into that space, you can upload your Web pages directly, making them available for public browsing. Your ISP takes care of keeping its computer up, running, and connected to the Internet.

- **Use the Apple HomePage feature.** Apple offers every Mac fan 100 MB of Web space, for a $100 yearly fee, in the form of the Sites folder on your iDisk—a virtual hard drive. (Visit *www.mac.com* for details.) Just put the HTML documents you've created—name your home page *index.html* for best results—and graphics into the Sites folder of your iDisk. (Don't bother using the .Mac HomePage-building tools; Web pages you've designed using Word don't show up. But if you just drag them into your iDisk's Sites folder, they're instantly available to the Internet.)

UP TO SPEED

Naming and Nesting Folders

If you've had experience creating Web pages using a real HTML editing program, you know about the headache of creating sets of folders to organize all the pages and picture files that compose your Web site. If the various HTML documents (the individual Web pages) and their graphics (your picture bullets, background patterns, and so on) aren't on your hard drive and on the Internet in precisely matching folder hierarchies, you'll get dead links, missing graphics, and worse. You also need to save the graphics files (for picture bullets, background patterns, and so on) in folders.

When you save a Word document as a Web page, you create one document (whose name ends in .htm) containing the text, and an accompanying folder that contains all of the graphics, sounds, and movies. All you have to do is post them online in the same relative folders.

If you're making a large Web site with many pages, you may want to nest folders within one larger folder to help keep things organized.

Part Two: Entourage

Chapter 9: Entourage Email and Newsgroups

Chapter 10: Calendar, Tasks, and Projects

Chapter 11: Address Book and Notes

Chapter 12: Advanced Entourage

2

Entourage Email and Newsgroups

Entourage is Office's answer to people who need a personal assistant—named Mac. Much more than an email program, Entourage can help you schedule meetings, track tasks, and scope out your daily, monthly, and even yearly calendars. Since Office 2001, Entourage has sought to be a person's personal information manager (PIM) and email program all in one, as well as being a vehicle to tie together all the individual programs. The Project Center, described in Chapter 10, is the next logical step toward that goal. You could always take notes in Entourage, but now they're more accessible. You could always flag Word documents for follow up and have Entourage remind you about them, and you could always use Entourage to manage projects, but now the tools for doing that are easier to access, and you get an attractive new screen to view your project as a whole.

In addition to its organizational capabilities, Entourage is still a first rate email program. Entourage handles email and newsgroups with the ease that it schedules your tasks and coordinates your projects. And since every Inbox in the world gets more incoming messages every day, Entourage 2004 includes a new Groups feature to help keep track of them all.

The Big Picture

The Entourage main window is divided into three main areas: buttons for Entourage's main functions at top left, a list of "file folders" for your email at bottom left, and a big viewing area for your actual messages, calendars, tasks, and so on, on the right. Like changing stations on a car radio, you can switch among Entourage functions by clicking their buttons.

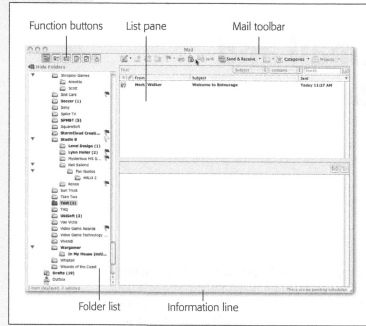

Function buttons   List pane   Mail toolbar

Figure 9-1:
In addition to the Folder list and an email-specific toolbar, Entourage has a List pane that lists all of the messages in a particular folder. There's also an information bar at the bottom of the screen that shows how many messages are in a given folder, how many are selected, and what schedules (if any) Entourage has on deck. Don't miss the Fonts tab in Entourage→General Preferences, where you can specify the type size and style you prefer for reading your email and other Entourage components.

Folder list   Information line

Entourage Functions

When you first launch Entourage (Figure 9-1) and complete the Setup wizard (described in a moment), the Mail button at the upper left is already selected. But mail is only one of Entourage's functions. This chapter and those that follow cover all of them in depth, but here's a quick overview to let you know what you're in for. The six big icons at the upper-left corner of the Entourage screen correspond to the following features:

- **Mail.** This, of course, is the big workhorse feature: email. This chapter covers the Mail feature in detail.

- **Address Book.** Your electronic "little black book"—home to not just the email addresses in your social entourage, but also phone numbers, home addresses, and so on. The Address Book also features predefined Address Book *Views* that let you find subsets of your data—every member of your family, for example. See Chapter 11 for complete details on the Address Book.

- **Calendar.** Plan your day, your week, your month…if you dare, plan your year! You can manage your schedule and track important events using the Entourage Calendar. Once again, a set of Views can quickly show you only work- or family-related events, recurring appointments, or whatever. See Chapter 10 for details.

- **Tasks.** Your to-do list. When you click this button, the right side of the screen shows the list of tasks you've set up for yourself. See Chapter 10 to read everything about Tasks.

- **Notes.** Memo-pad-like musings that you can attach to names in your address book, tasks in your to-do list, and so on. See Chapter 11 for details.

- **Project Center.** Calls up the Project Center from which you may track the email messages, documents, notes, pictures, tasks, and calendars associated with your

---

POWER USERS' CLINIC

The Mighty Morphing Interface

You don't have to be content with the factory-installed design of the Entourage screen. You can control which Entourage panes are visible, how big they are, and which columns show up in list views.

Some people like to read email messages in separate windows, while others like to use the Preview pane at the right side of the window, which displays the current message right in the main Mail window. To turn on Entourage's Preview pane, choose View→Preview Pane and gratefully select either On Right, Below, or None. (Before Entourage 2004, Below was your only option.)

Another way you can individualize your Entourage experience is by organizing your email and newsgroup message using *groups*. This new 2004 feature lets you divide and conquer your messages in the list window according to project, subject, sender, priority, and more, something you couldn't dream of doing in Entourage X. (See the box on page 337 for full detail.)

You can also hide or show the toolbar or the Folder list using the View menu. For example, to hide the toolbar, choose View→Toolbars.

To change the size of a pane, drag its border, as shown here. You can drag any border that features two parallel lines in the center. (You don't have to drag right on those lines, though.)

Entourage also lets you decide what columns appear in Mail's List pane. If you don't care about seeing the Categories column for your email, for example, you can hide it, leaving more space for Subject and Date. To switch columns on or off, choose from the View→Columns submenu.

You can also rearrange the columns, which can be handy if you'd rather see the Subject column first instead of the Sender, for example.

Just drag the column's header horizontally; release when the vertical dotted line is where you'll want the column to wind up. To make a column wider or narrower, drag the short black divider line between column names horizontally.

You can't resize the skinny icon columns on the far left, but you can move any of them except the first two.

---

current projects and begin new ones. It's your one-stop project organizing center (see page 410 for details).

Tip: When you launch Entourage the first time, it's set to display each major function (Mail, Address Book, Calendar, and so on) in the main window when you click on the appropriate icon in the top left corner. (For more viewing room in the leftmost column, you can make those icons smaller if you wish, in the Entourage→ Preferences→General panel.) Whichever feature you choose takes over the main Entourage window and hides the others. But what if you want to see your calendar and your email at the same time?

You can—by opening them into separate windows. To do that, Control-click any of the six major function buttons, and choose the Open in New Window command from the shortcut menu. Now you can see two views simultaneously, such as your Calendar and Notes, two Mail windows, your Address Book and Tasks, and so on.

The Toolbar

Entourage has only one toolbar (see Figure 9-2), which changes to reflect your current activity. For example, if you've clicked an email folder, the toolbar's buttons all pertain to email functions; if you click the Calendar button, the toolbar gains calendar-appropriate commands. You'll encounter these commands in the context of the email, newsgroup, calendar, address book, notes, and task discussions in this and the following chapters.

Figure 9-2:
Entourage's toolbar commands change to match the Entourage function you're using, as in the email toolbar shown here.

Setting Up Entourage

When you first launch Entourage (or when you create a new *identity,* as described on page 451), the Entourage Setup Assistant presents itself. The Setup Assistant presents a long series of question-and-answer screens that give you the opportunity to set up your email accounts, import your address book information from whatever mail program you used to use, and so on.

Any email program requires a number of technical details that define your particular email account. If you have another email program that's been working fine (Apple Mail, Outlook Express, Netscape Communicator (4.6x-4.8) or Eudora, for example), Entourage can usually import all the details from the older program (and from the settings in the Internet pane of your Mac's System Preferences program).

If you've never used your Mac for email before, however, or if you're using a Mac that doesn't have a functioning email program, you'll need to type these email settings into Entourage directly. Unless you're quite a technical person, your sole source of this information is the help line (or Getting Started booklet) of your *ISP* (Internet Service Provider), the company to whom you pay a monthly fee for Internet access. You need the account information your ISP gave you in order to receive or send email, so have this info on hand as you set about getting Entourage ready.

Note: Entourage can't check America Online mail.

Then let the Setup Assistant take you by the hand like this:

1. **By clicking Yes or No, indicate whether or not you want Entourage to be your** *default* **email program.**

UP TO SPEED

POP, IMAP, and Web-based Mail

When it comes to email, there are three flavors of accounts (not counting America Online mail, which is a mutant breed, or Exchange Server, which is mainly used by larger businesses): POP (also known as Post Office Protocol or POP3), IMAP (also known as IMAP4), and Web-based. Although the lines between them are often blurry, each has its own distinct nature, with different strengths and weaknesses.

POP accounts are the most common kind. This type of account usually transfers your incoming mail to your hard drive before you read it, which works fine as long as you're using only one computer to access your email.

If you want to take your Entourage email world along with you on the road, you have to copy the Documents folder on your desktop Mac's hard drive—or, at the very least, the Documents→Microsoft User Data folder—into the corresponding location on your laptop's hard drive. Then, when you run Entourage on the laptop, you'll find your messages and attachments already in place.

(Another travelers' tip: Entourage can leave your POP mail on the server, so that you can read it while on the road, but still find it waiting on your home Mac when you return. See page 331.)

IMAP accounts are most often found among educational institutions and corporations. Unlike POP, where your mail is stored on your hard drive, IMAP keeps your mail on the remote server, downloading it only when you want to read or act on a message. Thus, you can access the same mail regardless of the computer you use. IMAP servers remember which messages you've read and sent, too.

The downside to this approach, of course, is that you can't work with your email except when you're online, because all of your mail is on an Internet server, not on your hard drive.

Web-based servers are similar to IMAP servers, in that they store your mail on the Internet; you use a Web browser on any computer to read and send messages. (As a Microsoft service, Hotmail.com offers a twist on Web-based accounts: you can check your Hotmail email with Entourage instead of having to use a Web browser. This service, which started out as a free bonus, will soon cost $20 per year—it may already as you read this. Keep in mind, however, the Hotmail account is free, it's the ability to check it from Entourage that costs.)

Although Web-based accounts are convenient, they're also slower and more cumbersome to use. Most also put ads in your email, and you'll usually find it awkward to compose and manage messages using a Web browser.

POP and IMAP accounts offer the quickest service and greatest reliability. The only downside is that if you switch ISPs, you have to switch your email address as well. To prevent this problem, you can try a free service like mail.com, pobox.com, bigfoot.com), or Apple's mac.com, which give you a permanent email address. If your "real" email address changes, these services simply forward your mail to whatever new address you specify. That way, you'll never have to send out a change-of-email-address again.

The very first thing you see the first time you run Entourage is a question: "Would you like Microsoft Entourage to be your default email program?" If you answer in the affirmative, Entourage will open whenever you click an email link (on a Web page or in a program's online help, for example).

Tip: If you decide later that you'd prefer a different email program, open Apple's own Mail program using any of the usual methods, choose Mail→Preferences, and then select your default mail reader. In fact, this procedure is the same even if you don't want to end up using Mail.

After you've made your choice, the Setup Assistant asks for your name.

2. **Enter your first and last name.**

   Entourage will use this information in the From field of all outgoing mail. Most people, having nothing to hide, provide this information, but you can type anything you want (or nothing) here, depending on how courteous an Internet citizen you want to be (see "Email Netiquette" on page 368). Click the right arrow button (or press Enter) to continue.

3. **Enter your home information.**

   Entourage asks you for your street address, city, state, Zip code, country, and telephone number. If you'll be using Entourage mostly from home, also turn on "This is my default address."

   You've just specified the address that Office 2004 will use whenever it needs your home address; for example, this is the address Word proposes printing on envelopes as your return address. If you're nervous about the Microsoft Evil Empire collecting your data for its own nefarious purposes, you can leave these blanks empty.

Tip: The information you specify here is the same information you can access in Word by choosing Word→Preferences→User Information panel. It also creates a special entry in your Entourage Address Book, marked with a lowercase *i* icon, denoting it as your own information "card."

As in any Office 2004 dialog box, you can advance from one field (text box) to the next by pressing the Tab key. Once you've specified your home address (or decided not to do so), click the right arrow button or press Enter.

4. **Enter your work address.**

   Entourage gives you the option of making *this* address Office's default address for you. Click the right arrow to continue.

5. **Import your calendar, address book information, and email from your older programs, if you like.**

   As part of Entourage's campaign to serve as the only communication and organization program you'll ever need, the Setup Assistant now offers to import email and address book information from (almost) any email program, calendar program, or address book program that you *used* to use before the great day of Entourage's arrival.

This feature saves you astronomical amounts of time. Since all of your familiar data is instantly available, you can get comfortable with your new email/calendar/address book program in record time.

The assistant now offers five choices: to import nothing at all; or to import information from an earlier version of Entourage, from another email program, from a calendar/address book program, or from *both* your email program and a calendar/address book program.

If you choose to import email, the Setup Assistant presents you with a list of email programs from which it can import information: Outlook Express 5, Entourage 2001, Qualcomm Eudora (4.0) Apple Mail, Netscape Communicator (4.6x – 4.8 only), or Claris (2.0v3). You can also tell Entourage that your email program isn't listed, at which point it does its level best to import the information anyway. In addition to the email messages themselves, Entourage can sometimes import email filters (rules), email filing folders, and other bits of information that you've created in your former email program. (For some unfathomable reason, Microsoft Entourage is especially good at importing information from Microsoft Outlook Express.)

If you choose to import data from another PIM (personal information manager—that is, calendar/address book), you'll be presented with a choice of software whose information Entourage understands: Claris Organizer, Palm Desktop, Now Contact, and Now Up-To-Date. Select the program that currently contains your addresses and calendar, and then click the right arrow to continue. (The older program needs to be still installed on your Mac for this to work.)

Finally, you'll be presented with a list of individual items to import: your mail messages, addresses, account information, filters, signatures, calendar items, tasks, and notes. Once you've selected the items to import, click the right arrow to start the process, which can take a long time. (Better go grab a snack.)

When the importing is complete, click Finish. If you didn't previously indicate that you wanted Entourage to be your default email program, the Setup Assistant will ask you again. Tell this eager-beaver software Yes or No.

If you successfully imported your email account's settings, you're ready to start using Entourage. Skip to the next section.

If you didn't import settings from an existing email program, however, or if the importing didn't go smoothly, you may now have to type in the email settings for your account.

6. **Enter the name with which you'll want to "sign" your email and newsgroup messages.**

You've now moved into the account setup portion of the Entourage Setup Assistant. The text box already contains the name that you entered in step 2, but you can put any name you like here—*Queen of the Universe,* if you like. (Again, though, read up on etiquette on page 368.)

7. **Tell Entourage your email address.**

In this step, either you can set up an account for an existing email address, or you can sign up for a Hotmail/MSN account (see the box on page 319).

If you do, in fact, have an Internet account, it came with an email account as part of the package, so the first option is the one most people choose. Enter your email address in the text box. Click the right arrow to continue.

If you'd prefer to set up a Hotmail account, click the Hotmail button and then the right arrow. On the next screen, you'll be given the option to open your Web browser and go online to the .NET Passport sign-up page, where you can get a Hotmail email address and password.

Once you have an account set up, you can return to Entourage and enter your ID and password to finish setting up your Hotmail account.

8. **Tell Entourage what kind of incoming mail server you'll be using, and type in your incoming and outgoing *mail server addresses.***

As noted above, you need to consult the account information your ISP gave you when you signed up (or ask your network administrator, if you're on a corporate network) to figure out what settings to use on this screen.

Click the right arrow button.

9. **Enter your account ID and password.**

In this step, you'll need to enter your *email account ID* (the portion of your email address that comes before the @ symbol) and the password for your account.

Entourage is willing to store your password in the Mac OS *Keychain* (a handy Mac OS X feature that memorizes all of your email and file-sharing passwords for you). Turn off the "Save password" box only if you want to have to type your password every time Entourage checks your email.

The buttons "Click Here for Advanced Receiving Options" and "Click Here for Advanced Sending Options" open dialog boxes where you specify security options and alternative ports for mail services. Your network administrator or ISP help desk will tell you if you need to use these options. (For example, you may have to turn on *authentication* in the sending options in order to send email if you travel or access the Internet using another ISP.)

Click the right arrow button to continue.

10. **Name your account.**

Entourage needs a name for your brand new account, such as *Earthlink Account* or *Hotmail account*.

A word about the other checkbox here: The Entourage toolbar contains a button called Send & Receive All. If you have more than one email account, a click on this single button can check *all* your email accounts. Turn off the "Include this account in my Send & Receive All schedule" option on this screen if you *don't* want this account to be checked automatically.

Note: On the other hand, you may also select which account you wish to send and receive email from the pop-up menu beside the Send & Receive button.

---

11. **Click Finish to wrap things up.**

Entourage now has all the basic information it needs to start work. If you haven't already selected Entourage as your default email program, it will ask you yet again whether you want Entourage as your default program; even though you've long-since made up your mind on this issue, again click Yes or No.

GEM IN THE ROUGH

Using Your Mac.com Address with Your ISP

If you're looking for an email address with a little Macintosh flair, or if the address your ISP has given you is hopelessly hard to remember, check out Apple's mac.com email service.

Mac.com can forward mail from your mac.com address to your ISP, but you can also send and receive mail directly via your mac.com address. This can avoid confusion: your correspondents simply use your mac.com address, and your messages appear to come from your mac.com address rather than a hard-to-remember ISP address. No one needs to know about your ISP. In fact, as noted earlier, you can change ISPs and continue using your mac.com mail without anyone having to update their address books.

Here's how to do it: Choose Tools→Accounts. In the window that pops up, click the Mail tab. Double-click the mac.com account that you just created. In that window, click the Account Settings tab and enter your mac.com email address in the "E-mail address" field. Enter your ISP's mail server address (its SMTP server) in the "Sending mail" section.

Now, mail sent using your mac.com address will appear to come from your mac.com account; that is, your recipients will see the mac.com address as your return address.

If you get an error when you try to send mail from your mac.com address, return to the account settings, click "Click here for advanced sending options," turn on "SMTP server requires authentication," and enter the account ID and password for your ISP email account (*not* your .Mac account).

Apple's .Mac site also offers instructions for sending and receiving mail via mac.com, which might help if you still have problems and your ISP can't help.

All this fun isn't, however, for free. In order to get your nifty email address, you must sign up for the whole .Mac package, which costs $100 a year—really not so bad considering you get a bunch of other features like Web server space and some free software. Nevertheless, the subversive among you can get a mac.com email address (without any of the other .Mac features) with a much smaller price tag. It only costs $10 a year to add additional email addresses to an existing .Mac account, so you'll need a friend with a .Mac account, and then you'll need to talk him into adding you to their account. Just tell the friend the address you want to use, give him $10, and ask them to sign you up. From then on, you can use the mac.com address independently (and please, remember to pay your friend back every year).

Setting Up a Second Email Account

The Account Setup Assistant just described offers a relatively painless procedure for setting up your main email account. But if you have additional accounts to set up, you can return to the Setup Assistant like this:

1. **With Entourage open, choose Tools→Accounts.**

   This brings up the Accounts window, the central point for dealing with email, Usenet news, and directory services accounts in Entourage.

2. **With the Mail tab selected, click the New button.**

   Entourage's Account Setup Assistant reappears. Continue with step 6 of the previous instructions.

Note: If you have more than one email account set up in Entourage, one of these accounts is the *default account*. The default account is the one that's used to send and receive mail unless you specify otherwise. To specify the default account, choose Tools→Accounts and click the Mail tab in the resulting window. The current default account is shown in bold. Select the account that you want to make the default, click Make Default, and close the window.

Configuring Your Account Manually

If you've got all the necessary settings for a new account on a slip of paper in front of you, then the screen-by-screen assistant may seem unnecessarily slow. Here's how to create a new email account without any Setup Assistant help .

Choose Tools→Accounts to open the Accounts window. Then, with the Mail tab selected, click New. When the Account Setup Assistant appears, click Configure Account Manually. Entourage now asks what kind of account you want to set up: POP, IMAP, or Hotmail/MSN. Choose the account flavor you want from the pop-up menu, and click OK. A window opens displaying two tabs in which you can enter all of your relevant information.

Note: Setting up an account manually has another payoff: It offers advanced control over how Entourage sends and receives mail. (Hotmail accounts aren't included.) These are options most people can and should ignore (unless your ISP requires them).

Under the Account Settings tab (see Figure 9-3), click "Click here for advanced receiving options." You get a window in which you can specify a secure connection, choose a different port for your POP or IMAP connections, or force Entourage to use a secure password.

If you click the Options tab, you can specify the default *signature* for this account (page 368), additional *headers* you want added (for geeks only), and whether you want to limit message sizes (page 333).

If you have an IMAP account, you're also offered some additional options, which are described on page 326.

Sending and Receiving Mail

All of the setup leads up to this: telling Entourage to check for incoming mail and send any outgoing mail. The basic process is easy, but several subtleties can make your email experience more satisfying.

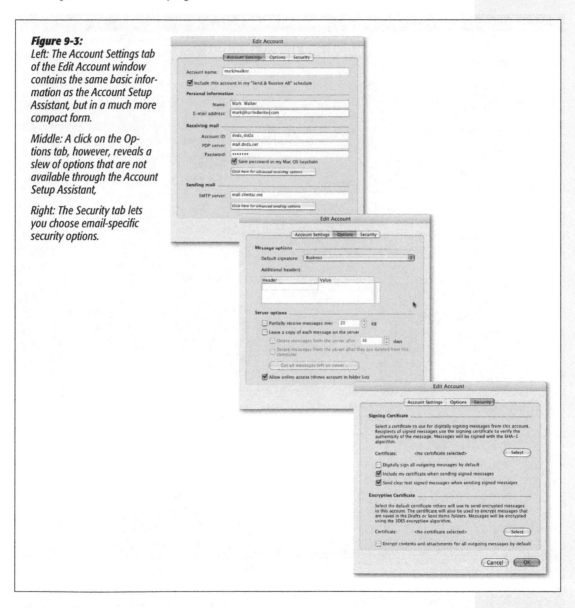

Figure 9-3:
Left: The Account Settings tab of the Edit Account window contains the same basic information as the Account Setup Assistant, but in a much more compact form.

Middle: A click on the Options tab, however, reveals a slew of options that are not available through the Account Setup Assistant,

Right: The Security tab lets you choose email-specific security options.

Send and Receive All

When Entourage opens for the first time, you've got mail; the Inbox contains a message for you from Microsoft. It wasn't actually transmitted over the Internet, though—it's a starter message built into Entourage just to tease you. Fortunately, all your future mail will come via the Internet.

You get new mail and send mail you've written using the Send & Receive command. You can trigger it in any of several ways:

POWER USERS' CLINIC

Configuring IMAP Options

IMAP accounts offer lots of flexibility—but as usual in the software world, that means that they also offer lots of complexity. To find Entourage's staggering array of email options, choose Tools→Accounts; double-click the name of your IMAP account; and click the Options tab. Here you'll find special options, in addition to those described at the end of this chapter:

- **Download complete messages in Inbox.** Normally, when you connect to an IMAP account, Entourage grabs only the message's headers—its size, subject line, sender's name, and date. The body of the message stays on the server until you click the message's name in your message list, at which time Entourage retrieves the whole thing. If you turn on this box, however, Entourage downloads both the headers and the message contents to your Inbox, making them instantly available. This option, in other words, makes your IMAP account behave a lot like a POP account.

- **Root folder.** If you haven't heard from your IMAP account administrator that this is something you need to fill in, ignore it.

- **Live Sync.** These options let you choose how Entourage manages its connection to IMAP servers—for example, whether it tries for a connection as soon as Entourage is launched, how long it should stay connected, and whether it should connect to all of your mail folders or just the Inbox.

- **Check for unread messages in subscribed folders.** If you've subscribed to IMAP folders, turning on this option makes Entourage check them for new mail automatically. Turning it off

means you'll have to look inside the folders yourself.

If you're an especially technical IMAP user, you can also tweak the Advanced tab in the Edit Account window. There, you'll be able to fine-tune two sets of preferences:

- **Special folders.** Ordinarily, an IMAP account stores your incoming, deleted, and filed messages on an Internet server. Messages you've sent or haven't yet sent (because they're in your Drafts folder), however, remain on your hard drive. If you turn on "Store special folders on IMAP server" and then turn on the corresponding folder checkboxes, Entourage stores the contents of the Sent Items and Drafts folders on the server, too, so that you'll have access to them from anywhere. (You'll need to specify a server's folder path for these items, should they be named anything but "Sent Items" and "Drafts.") You can also choose a folder to collect the junk mail that hits your IMAP account, as determined by Entourage's junk mail filter. (If you disagree, click on the "junked" message and click the Junk button in the Entourage toolbar—which now changes to Not Junk.)

- **Delete options.** This feature has nothing to do with wiping out stock holdings. Instead, it has to do with how your IMAP Internet server processes a message that you delete: It can either delete it outright or move it to its own Deleted Items folder. You can also indicate here when deleted messages are actually deleted—when you quit Entourage, after messages reach a certain age, or when you close an IMAP folder.

- Click the Send & Receive button in the toolbar.

- Choose Tools→Send & Receive→Send & Receive All (or choose from the submenu *which* account you wish to send and receive email from).

- Press ⌘-K. (If you're used to ⌘-M from Office 2001, note this change. Microsoft had to avoid ⌘-M, which is the Minimize command in Mac OS X.)

Tip: You can also set up Entourage to check your email accounts automatically according to a schedule, as described on page 328.

Now Entourage contacts the mail servers listed in the account list, retrieving new messages and downloading any files attached to those messages. It also sends any outgoing messages and their attachments.

Tip: After it's done, Entourage tries to communicate its success or failure by playing a cheerful chime—one for "You've got mail," a different one for "You've got no mail," and so on. You can change these sounds, opt to have Entourage flash the menu bar instead, elect to have Entourage bring itself in front of your other open Mac programs when there's new mail, or even choose a completely different sound *set.* All of this fun awaits in the Entourage→General Preferences→Notification tab.

In the list on the right side of your screen, the names of new messages appear in bold type. Folders *containing* new messages show up in bold type, too (in the Folder list at the left side of the screen). The boldface number in parentheses after the word "Inbox" lets you know how many of its messages you haven't yet read.

Finally, after messages are downloaded, Entourage applies its filters—what it calls *Rules*—to all new messages, putting mail from mailing lists into specific folders, for example. More on rules on page 353.

The Progress window

While it's connecting to the Internet and transferring messages, Entourage displays brief details of its activity at the bottom of the main window. If you'd like more detail,

Figure 9-4:
Top: The progress window first appears as a small window with a flippy triangle on the left side.

Bottom: When you click it, the window shows you all of the details when it makes a network connection: what server has been checked, the number of messages left to be downloaded, where they're coming from and how much of each message is left to be downloaded.

open Entourage's Progress window, as shown in Figure 9-4, by choosing Window→
Progress or pressing ⌘-7.

Checking a specific email account

You don't have to check *all* of your email accounts whenever you want to get mail.
Suppose, for example, that you want to send a message to *yourself*, from your work
account to your home account. In that case, you'd want to send/receive mail only
from your office account; if, later in the day, Entourage also downloaded messages
from your home account, you'd wind up with the same message in your office Mac's
copy of Entourage, defeating the whole purpose.

You can exclude an account (or several accounts) from the "Send & Receive All" routine easily enough. Open the Accounts window (Tools→Accounts), double-click the
account's name, turn off "Include this account in my 'Send & Receive All' schedule,"
click OK, and close the Accounts window.

But suppose you *usually* want to check all accounts, but *occasionally* want to check
only one of them. On such an occasion, choose that account's name from the Send &
Receive pop-up button menu on the main Entourage window. (Alternatively, choose
the account name from the Tools→Send & Receive submenu.)

Advanced Mail-Getting Features

Hundreds of thousands of people are perfectly content to use Entourage for email
just as it comes out of the box. But if you're willing to slog through some technical
options, you can unleash some awesome variations on the "Click a button to download mail" routine.

Automatic checking on a schedule

Stop pressing a button to check your email. You can set up Entourage to check your
email according to a regular schedule. To be sure, this is an advanced feature, which
may force you to think, just for a moment, like you're a computer. But there's no debating the convenience of checking Entourage in the morning to find that, for example,
it has fetched all your new mail automatically during the night. (On the other hand,
some folks enjoy sipping coffee while the morning email pours in.)

To create a schedule, choose Tools→Schedules to bring up the Schedules window
(Figure 9-5, left). Click the New button in the window's toolbar, which brings up the
Edit Schedule window with an untitled schedule (Figure 9-5, right). (If you want to
edit an existing schedule, double-click it in the Schedules window.)

In this window, you can set three options: the schedule's name, when it happens, and
what happens. To give the schedule a name, just type it in the Name field at the top
of the window.

The *When* portion of this window lets you determine when a schedule runs, using
a pop-up menu:

- **Manually.** Nothing will happen automatically. To run the schedule, you'll have to
  choose its name from the Tools→Run Schedule submenu.

- **At Startup.** Entourage will run the schedule whenever you launch the program.

- **On Quit.** Entourage will run the schedule when you *quit* the program.

- **Timed Schedule.** You can set specific times and days for schedules to execute. That is, you can set a schedule to run every Thursday and Sunday at 12:27 p.m., if you like.

- **Repeating Schedule.** Unlike with a timed schedule, you can set a schedule to run at regular intervals, such as every 30 minutes or every three days.

- **Recurring.** This option lets you use a recurring schedule to run in a recurring pattern over a defined period of time—such as monthly on the 21st day of each month for a period of three months, starting two months from today.

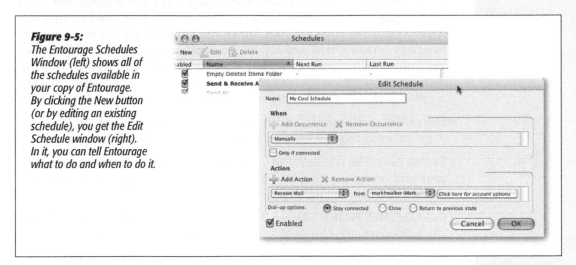

Figure 9-5:
The Entourage Schedules Window (left) shows all of the schedules available in your copy of Entourage. By clicking the New button (or by editing an existing schedule), you get the Edit Schedule window (right). In it, you can tell Entourage what to do and when to do it.

For Timed and Repeating schedules, you can set the particulars by clicking the button next to the pop-up menu, which opens a window in which you can set exact days, hours, and minutes for schedules to run.

By clicking the Add Occurrence button, you can add up to three "triggers" for this automated action. For example, you might set up a Timed Schedule, an At Startup action, and an On Quit event, so that, for example, your email gets checked once when Entourage is launched, then every hour, and once again when Entourage quits.

Tip: If you turn on "Only if connected," you can prevent Entourage from trying to connect to the Internet when the schedule is run (dialing furiously and seizing command of your Mac over and over again). Instead, Entourage will trot off to the Internet only if your Mac is already connected.

Now that you have specified *when* your schedules are to be run, you need to determine *what happens* when a schedule is run; Entourage can do much more on a timetable than check your mail. You do this in the Action section of the Edit Schedule window. The pop-up menu offers seven options:

- **Receive Mail.** Entourage will connect to a mail server and download any waiting mail. This is an ideal action to schedule at startup.

- **Receive News.** If you want to download the latest newsgroup postings, you can tell Entourage to download that information—another one that's useful in a startup schedule.

- **Send All.** This action sends all waiting mail—a useful one to schedule for when you quit Entourage. That way, you can make sure that all of your outgoing mail goes out before you walk away from your Mac.

- **Run AppleScript.** AppleScript scripts can be made to do just about anything—they're especially good for integrating functions of several programs, not just email (for additional details see Chapter 21). For instance, you could tell Entourage to run a script that backs up your Documents folder onto a different hard drive when you quit Entourage. (AppleScript is a programming language—an easy one to master, but still a programming language. Information and links to online resources are also available at Apple's AppleScript Web site, *www.apple.com/applescript.* You can also read all about it in *AppleScript: The Missing Manual* by Adam Goldstein.)

- **Delete Mail.** Entourage will delete mail from your Deleted Items folder, which might be something that you want to do whenever you quit the program.

- **Launch Alias.** This schedule item opens an alias to any document or program on your hard drive—powerful stuff if you want to launch, say, your Web browser whenever you launch Entourage.

- **Excel Auto Web Publish.** This item has to do with Excel's Save As Web Page feature, which lets you publish an Excel workbook as a Web page automatically.

  So why is an Excel option showing up in an Entourage dialog box? When you set a workbook to publish on the Web on a recurring basis, Excel hands the task off to Entourage's scheduling feature, where it appears as a schedule. Once it's in Entourage, you can further customize *when* the automatic publishing of that workbook takes place. When Entourage executes an Auto Web Publish schedule, it opens the workbook in Excel and saves it as a Web page. (This option is not available unless you've already created an autopublishing workbook in Excel.)

Once you've selected one of these options, you can also select parameters for it. For example, if you choose Receive News, you can specify which subscribed newsgroups (see page 370) you want to read.

You can add dozens of actions to take place in a single schedule. To add an action, click the Add Action button. A new pop-up menu appears. (To delete one, too, click its "block" in the dialog box and then click the Remove Action button.)

Entourage comes with three prefab schedules that you can edit to meet your own evil ends: Empty Deleted Items Folder, which deletes all messages in the Deleted Items folder; Send & Receive All, which sends all outgoing mail and receives any waiting mail for all the accounts you've set up; and Send All, which sends all outgoing mail without checking for *incoming* mail. You can run these schedules, as well as any you've set up yourself, by choosing from the Tools→Run Schedule submenu.

The hotel-room feature: online accounts

As noted earlier in this chapter, the world's most common email account types are POP (in which your messages are transferred from the Internet to your hard drive) and IMAP (in which your messages always remain on your mail server rather than your computer). The kind of account you have depends on your ISP.

But like other hip email programs, Entourage can let you use POP accounts almost as if they *were* IMAP accounts—that is, you can grab your messages without removing them from your Internet server. Better yet, the program can download only the *headers* of the messages, which takes but an instant, even over a slow (or expensive) connection. Once you have the headers, you can survey the subject lines or the names of the senders, and choose which messages you want to download in their entirety.

This feature is ideal for use when you're in a hotel room, dialing your Internet account over a slow modem connection, for two reasons. First, you're spared the tedium of downloading a bunch of messages and attachments you don't really need while on the road. Second, the mail stays on the server until you delete it manually; it'll still be there when you return home, when you can again download the messages, this time onto your main Mac.

Note: Most Internet service providers allow you to accumulate only 5 or 10 megabytes' worth of mail. Beyond that limit, incoming messages get "bounced" back to their senders. In other words, you can't delay downloading your messages indefinitely, and attachments can easily consume a lot of your quota. Unfortunately, there's no way within Entourage to see how much space your mail is using on your ISP's server.

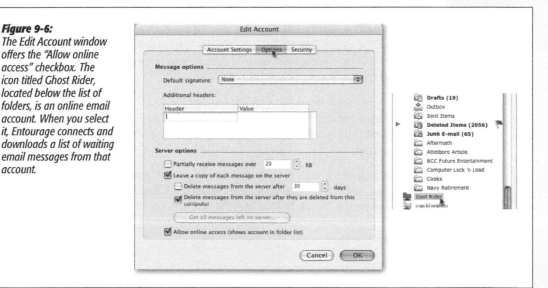

Figure 9-6:
The Edit Account window offers the "Allow online access" checkbox. The icon titled Ghost Rider, located below the list of folders, is an online email account. When you select it, Entourage connects and downloads a list of waiting email messages from that account.

Microsoft calls this feature *online access,* by which it means that you will be accessing mail in this account only via the Internet, rather than downloading it to your hard drive. To set up your account this way, choose Tools→Accounts, which brings up the Accounts window. Double-click the account that you want to make available for online access.

In the resulting Edit Account window, click the Options tab and turn on "Allow online access," as shown in Figure 9-6. You wind up with a new icon in the Folder Items pane: the online representation of your account, bearing the same name.

Setting up an account for online access doesn't remove its mail or folders from your hard drive. It just sets up a different way of accessing the account, as represented by a new icon in the Folder List for that account. (Yes, this is confusing.)

Tip: When you set up an account for online access, it's usually a good idea to turn off Entourage's Preview pane (View→Preview Pane). You'll see why in a moment.

To make Entourage check the Internet for new messages sent to this account, click this icon in the Folder Items list—just one click. Entourage starts by downloading only the *header information* of the waiting messages: subject lines, sender names, date and time the message was sent, and so on. It doesn't download the messages themselves.

If you see a message whose subject line or sender looks promising, click it. If Entourage's Preview pane is showing, Entourage downloads the message and shows it there. If not, double-click the message to make Entourage download it and display it in the message window.

Either way, the message also remains on the Internet email server—that's the big difference between using the online access feature and using the Send & Receive command for that account.

To delete mail from an online account, select the messages that you want to delete, and then press the Delete key. (Now you see why it's a good idea to turn off the Preview pane—when you click a message to delete it, you simultaneously tell Entourage to *download* it if the Preview pane is on the screen.)

The message doesn't move, but a "deleted online message" icon appears in the message's Online Status column (see Figure 9-7). When you next connect to that account in online mode, Entourage deletes the message from the server, if you're still connected to the Internet.

On the other hand, if you change your mind and want to *keep* a message you've marked for deletion, click the deleted online message icon. From the pop-up menu, choose Leave Message on Server, so that the "deleted online message" icon disappears. The message will be there waiting for you when you check your email account in one of the "normal" ways.

Tip: Advertisers—and spammers—are increasingly using *Web bugs,* which are references to tiny, 1-by-1 pixel graphics that come embedded in HTML-formatted email messages. Web bugs exist purely for tracking purposes: If your email program downloads a Web bug, a corresponding entry appears in the advertisers (or spammer's) Web server log. Now they know where and when someone viewed the message.

There's no way to tell if an HTML-formatted message contains a Web bug (at least not without examining the HTML source). But if you tell Entourage not to "Display complex HTML in messages" (choose Entourage→ Preferences→Security, and turn off the appropriate checkbox), you preserve a little more privacy. Even with this setting turned on, Entourage doesn't download pictures, which, after all, could be Web bugs, until you click the "Download Pictures" link at the top of the preview window. If you're the happy medium type, on the same panel, turn on the checkbox that automatically downloads HTML images only from senders in your Address Book (whom, presumably, you trust).

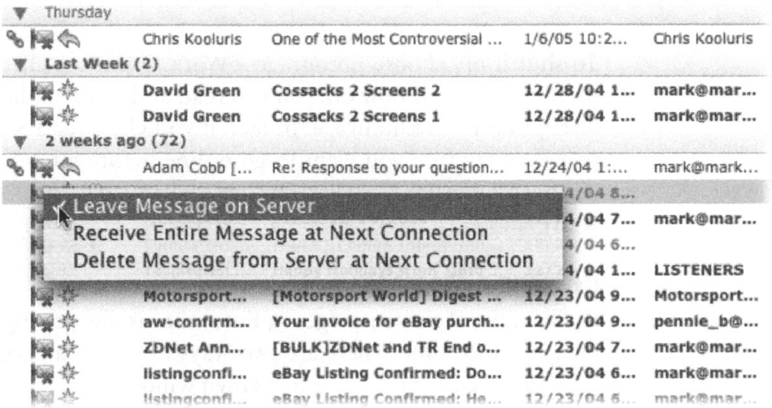

Figure 9-7:
Online messages that have been deleted still show up in the message list, bearing an icon that looks like an envelope with a red X. The next time that you connect to an online account, any messages that are marked for deletion will be shown the door. If you change your mind, you can click the deleted online message icon and choose Leave Message on Server.

Restricting download sizes

For road warriors stuck with slow modem connections, you can tell Entourage to grab only the first portion of a message, so that you don't have to sit through an hour-long modem connection to download that "You Want It When?" cartoon that your friend thought was just *so* funny.

To do this, select Tools→Accounts and then open the account for which you want to limit the size of downloaded messages. Click the Options tab at the top of that window, and then turn on "Partially retrieve messages over ___ KB." You can set how much of a message you want to grab (see Figure 9-6). If you decide that you want to download the entire message, click the broken-envelope icon; choose Receive Entire Message at next Connect from the menu that pops up.

Note: It's crucial to remember to turn this option *off* once you get home, or you'll be wondering why Entourage keeps chopping off your messages and giving you half-downloaded, inoperable attachments.

Offline access

When you're in the plane or bus terminal, you probably don't have an Internet connection. In such situations, you may want to read and write replies to your email—but you may find it annoying that, every 15 minutes or so, Entourage tries vainly to get online, triggering an avalanche of error messages.

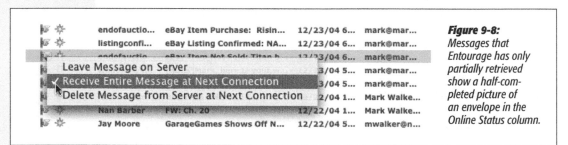

Figure 9-8:
Messages that Entourage has only partially retrieved show a half-completed picture of an envelope in the Online Status column.

To shut it up, choose Entourage→Work Offline. A checkmark appears next to the menu item. From now on, you can read and write replies to your email without interruption from Entourage. In fact, if you click Send & Receive, Entourage will ask you if you're sure you want to go online before attempting to make a connection. (Choose Entourage→Work Offline again to return to the normal "connect when ready" mode.)

Reading a Message

Seeing a list of new messages in Entourage is like getting wrapped presents; the best part is yet to come. There are two ways to read a message: using the preview pane, and opening the message into its own window.

To preview a message, first make sure the preview pane is showing. (If not, choose View→Preview Pane and choose whether you want the Preview Pane to the right of your message list (⌘-\) or below it (Shift-⌘-\).) The Entourage main window splits in half and the Preview Pane opens either to the right of the message list or below it. When you click a message's name in the message list, the body of the message appears in the preview pane. Don't forget that you can adjust the relative sizes of the List and Preview panes by dragging the gray border between them.

POWER USERS' CLINIC

Where Are the Headers?

As a favor to you, and to make Internet email look less intimidating, Entourage normally hides the blobs of technical-looking text known as Internet headers. This information shows all the email servers a message has visited on its way to your Inbox, along with dates, times, and other data.

Sometimes this information can be enlightening or helpful in troubleshooting or reporting a problem to an ISP. To view the header information, open a message into its own window and then choose View→Internet Headers (Shift-⌘-H).

To open a message into a window of its own, double-click its name in the List pane. An open message has its own toolbar, along with Previous Message and Next Message arrows in the left corner. These are pop-up menu buttons; they offer commands that let you move to another read or unread message, delete the current message, and so on.

Tip: Entourage tries to condense the lettering of messages in list views, if necessary, to show you their entire names. This tightened letter spacing isn't particularly attractive, but may make the difference between your being able to read the subject line of a message and seeing it chopped off.

You can, if you like, resize Entourage's columns to make more room for the text: just drag the border between the columns. You can also point to a particular bit of condensed text without clicking. A small, yellow pop-up balloon appears, revealing the entire, non-condensed message name.

Regardless of your viewing preference, any attached pictures, sounds, or movies *also* appear in the body of the message. You can even play those sounds and movies in the email message itself. (Entourage displays and plays any kind of file that QuickTime can understand—JPEG, GIF, PICT, Photoshop files, and so on—and can also call on Mac OS X's graphics smarts to preview Acrobat PDF documents.)

Tip: If the text of a message is too small to read, click the Increase Font Size button on the message's toolbar at the far right of Entourage's Preview pane (it looks like an "A"). If a message's text is too *big* (for a narrow window or a laptop screen, say), Option-click the Increase Font Size button to make Entourage decrease the size of the text.

Figure 9-9:
When you open an email message by double-clicking its name, you may see several things in addition to the text of the message: the attachments and the attachment control buttons, basic information (such as who sent the message, when it was sent, and what its subject is), and an email toolbar, complete with Previous and Next Message buttons (circled).

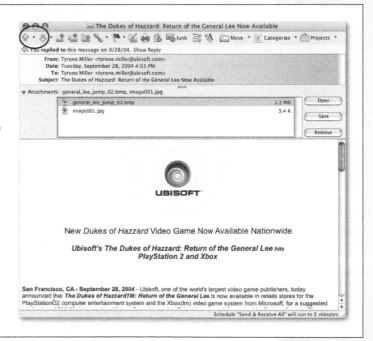

Once you've read a message, you can view the next one in the list either by pressing ⌘-] or by clicking its name in the List pane. (If you're using the preview mode, and haven't opened a message into its own window, you can also press the up or down arrow keys to move from one message to the next.)

Tip: To mark a message that you've read as an *unread* message, so that its name remains bolded, choose Message→Mark as Unread (Shift-⌘-T), Control-click (Windows refugees can right-click) the message's name and choose Mark as Unread from the shortcut menu.

Here's another timesaver: You can *hide* all the messages you've already read. Just choose View→Unread Only (Shift-⌘-O). To bring the hidden messages back, choose View→Unread Only again.

Icons in the message list

After you've received some messages in Entourage, you'll notice that some of those messages have icons at the left side of their list-view lines. These badges or flags give you useful information about the messages:

- **Links.** A chain-link icon here (🔗) indicates that a message has been *linked* to another message, calendar event, task, note, or the like. (See page 347 for more on linking.)

- **Online Status.** An icon that looks like an emaciated folder (📁) indicates that a message has only been partially retrieved—a dead giveaway that you've turned on the "Partially download" option described on page 333. A folder with a red X through it (📁) indicates that the message has been deleted from the server in an *online account* (page 331). Finally, an icon with a red, downward-pointing arrow indicates that the message will be fully downloaded the next time that you connect.

- **Status.** The status column shows the status of particular messages. A blue star (✦) means that the message has been received but not yet read. A curved arrow facing left (↩) denotes a message that you've answered. A purple, angular arrow facing right (↪), on the other hand, indicates that you've *redirected* the message (see page 343). A green, curved arrow facing right (↪) denotes mail that you've forwarded to someone else.

Note: Unfortunately, Entourage displays these last three icons only after your replies, forwards, and redirects have actually been sent, rather than when you write the reply, or choose to forward or redirect a message. As a result, it can be difficult to determine whether or not you've processed a message if you don't happen to be connected to the Internet and checking mail every 30 seconds.

If you modify the subject or text of a message you've received (see page 341), the status column shows a pencil (✏️) to let you know. If a message is associated with a calendar event (or invites you to an event—see page 395, the message status icon offers a small calendar (📅). (Caution: the calendar status overrides things like the symbols for forwards and replies.)

- **Priority.** This column's icons indicate a message's priority: a red exclamation point (❗)for highest priority; an orange one for high priority; a dark blue downward arrow (⬇) for low priority; and a pale blue downward arrow for lowest priority. No icon means normal priority.

Note: You see a priority icon only when your correspondents used their email program's priority-labeling feature, or if you change the priority of a message once you've received it. After all, what Bob at the office thinks is wildly important may not even be a blip on your radar.

- **Attachments.** If a message has one or more files attached (see page 349), a paper-clip icon (📎) appears in this column.

- **Groups.** If you're using Entourage's new groups view of email or newsgroup messages (see the box below), the group title bar displays a flippy triangle (▶) at the left: click the triangle to expand or collapse the list of messages in the group.

How to Process a Message

After you've set up your Entourage email account, and received your first batch of messages, the fun really begins. Here are the many things you can do with a message:

Deleting messages

Sometimes it's junk mail, sometimes you're just done with it. Either way, it's a snap to delete a message that's before you on the screen: just press the Delete key. Alternatively, you can:

- Press the forward-delete key, if your keyboard has one.

GEM IN THE ROUGH

Where are My Threads?

Entourage Email and Newsgroups used to be all about the threads. For the uninitiated, threads were strings of related emails, usually with the same subject. Utilizing threads made it very easy to track all the messages relating to, say The Red Claw episode in Shogo. But alas, the threads are no longer in Entourage 2004. But fear not, Entourage 2004's new groups are an able substitute.

Entourage's standard view is actually a grouped view: messages are organized into groups by the date received (for example, Today, Yesterday, or Last Week). You can, however, change this to suit your needs. To do so, select View→Arrange By→Show in Groups and then choose your poison.

For instance, if you View→Arrange By→Subject, your

messages group by subject. For example, all the Red Claw messages will cling together under the Red Claw title bar, and so on. You can scroll through the message list to find the subject you're looking for, and all the messages and replies with that subject line.

Or perhaps you want to track who sent the message. This works great for folks who can remember who wrote something, but can't remember when they wrote it or what the subject of the message was. Just choose View→Arrange By→From, and Entourage groups the messages in the active folder by the sender's name. Every person who has sent you email gets a header bar, with all her messages listed underneath it.

- Click the Delete (trash can) button on the toolbar.

- Choose Edit→Delete Message.

- Press ⌘-Delete.

You can also delete a batch of messages at once by highlighting them and then using a delete button, menu command, or keystroke.

Tip: If you want to delete a message and move to the next in one easy step, press Option-⌘-]: that's the same as the key command for moving to the next message (⌘-]) plus the Option key. If you want to delete the current message and move to the *previous* message, press Option-⌘-[instead.

Either way, the message or messages don't actually disappear, just as moving a file icon to the Macintosh Trash doesn't actually delete it. Instead, these commands move the messages to the Deleted Items folder. If you like, you can click this icon to view a list of the messages you've deleted. You can even rescue messages by dragging them into any other mail folder (such as right back into the Inbox, as illustrated in Figure 9-10).

Entourage doesn't truly vaporize messages in the Deleted Items folder until you "empty the trash." You can empty it in any of several ways:

- Control-click the Deleted Items folder. Choose "Empty 'Deleted Items'" from the shortcut menu.

Figure 9-10:
By dragging an item out of the Deleted Items folder, you can save it from certain doom. You can also delete messages by dragging them into the Deleted Items folder.

UP TO SPEED

Selecting Messages

When you want to process a group of messages simultaneously—to delete, move, or forward them, for example—you need to master the art of multiple message selection.

To select two or more messages that appear consecutively in your message list, click the first message, then Shift-click the last. This trick selects every message between the two that you clicked.

To select two or more messages that aren't adjacent in the list (that is, skipping a few messages between selected ones), ⌘-click the messages you want. Only the messages you click get selected—no filling in of messages in between.

After using either technique, you can also deselect messages you've managed to highlight—just ⌘-click them again.

- Click a message, or a folder, within the Deleted Items Folder list and then click the Delete icon on the toolbar (or press ⌘-Delete). You'll be asked to confirm its *permanent* deletion.

- Choose Tools→Run Schedule→Empty Deleted Items Folder.

- Set up a schedule to empty the folder automatically when you quit Entourage, for example, or to delete only messages that are older than, say, 60 days. See page 328 for instructions.

Replying to messages

To reply to a message, click the Reply button in the toolbar, choose Message→Reply, or press ⌘-R. Entourage creates a new, outgoing email message, preaddressed to the sender's return address.

To save you additional time, Entourage pastes the entire original message at the top of your reply, complete with the > brackets that serve as Internet quoting marks (Entourage indents quoted text in HTML messages). (It's also a feature you can turn off; choose Entourage→Mail & News Preferences, click the Reply & Forward tab, and turn off "Include entire message in reply.") Entourage also tacks *Re:* ("regarding") onto the front of the subject line, a long-standing convention of Internet email, and prefixes the quoted message with a one-line label indicating who originally wrote it, and when it was written.

TROUBLESHOOTING MOMENT

Fixing the Entourage Database

Entourage keeps all of its messages in a single, gigantic database file on your hard drive. It's called Database, and it sits in the Documents→Microsoft User Data→Office 2004 Identities→Main Identity folder in your Home folder (in the Finder, choose Go→Home).

As you add and delete hundreds of messages from this database over time, some digital sawdust gets left behind, resulting in peculiarities when addressing messages, or general Entourage sluggishness. You also wind up with massive Entourage files, which can consume hundreds of megabytes of disk space. That's a particular bummer if you like to copy your message database to your laptop when you go on a trip, or if you back up your data every day.

Fortunately, it's easy enough to rebuild the database, a procedure that cleanses, repairs, organizes, and purges your message files. You wind up with a much more compact and healthy database.

To rebuild the Entourage database, quit any other Office 2004 applications you're running. Then hold down the Option key when launching Entourage. After the logo screen pops up, you'll be given two choices: Typical Rebuild or Advanced Rebuild. Most of the time, a typical rebuild does the trick, taking several minutes to repair and compact your database.

If you're still having problems, launch Entourage again with the Option key held down, and this time choose Advanced Rebuild. This should clear up any problems you may be having, but it also requires you to redownload folder lists and messages for your Hotmail or IMAP accounts, and replace any pictures of contacts in your Address Book.

In either case, you'll now find two sets of database files in your Microsoft User Data folder—one set bears the prefix "Old." You can throw the "Old" files away after the rebuild is finished, and you've confirmed that the new ones work fine.

Tip: If you need to quote only *part* of a message in your reply, select the text you want to quote, then hold down the Shift key as you choose Message→Reply (or simply press Shift-⌘-R). Entourage creates a reply that includes only the text you selected as the "quotation." See page 368 to find out why keeping your quoted material brief is a thoughtful gesture for your correspondents.

Meanwhile, if you want to include text you've copied from some other source—a Word file, for example—as a quotation, click in your message where you'd like the text to appear, and choose Edit→Paste Special→ Paste As Quotation (or press Shift-⌘-V). Entourage inserts the text in the clipboard as it would any other quoted material in your email message.

Your cursor appears at the bottom of the message area, below any quoted text; you can begin typing your reply. You can also:

- Add recipients to the message by adding email addresses in any of the recipient fields (To, Cc, or Bcc).

- Remove one or more recipients (by clicking their names and then clicking the Remove button in the window that appears, or pressing the Delete key).

- Edit the Subject line or the original message.

- Use the Return key to create blank lines within the bracketed original message in order to place your own text within it. Using this method, you can splice your own comments into the paragraphs of the original message, replying point by point. The brackets preceding each line of the original message help your correspondent keep straight what's yours and what's not.

- Attach a file (see page 364).

Note: If the original message came with an attached file, Entourage doesn't fasten the attachment to the reply.

There are two kinds of replies, each represented by a different icon on the toolbar:

- A **standard reply** (click the Reply button) goes only to the sender of the message. If that sender is a mailing list (see the box on the facing page), then the message may be sent to the *entire* mailing list, which could get you in trouble. Check the To address to make sure you're sending a message to the right place!

- **Reply To Sender** creates a reply that goes to the person who wrote the original message (or posted the message to a newsgroup; see page 370). Use this option if you'd like to reply privately to a message posted to a mailing list or a newsgroup, avoiding sending the message to the entire mailing list or group. (If you use this command on a message that *didn't* come from a mailing list or a newsgroup, Entourage treats it as a standard reply.)

- The **Reply To All** button addresses a message to *all* recipients of the original message, including any Cc recipients. This is the button to use if you're participating in a group discussion; all six of you can carry on an email correspondence, always sending each response to the other five. (Reply To All doesn't send the reply to anyone who may have been in the secret Bcc field, as described on page 357.)

Tip: Entourage starts out placing the insertion point at the bottom of any quoted text in a reply. If you're the kind of person who likes to put your response *above* the quotation, choose Entourage→Mail & News Preferences, select the Reply & Forward tab, and turn on "Place insertion point before quoted text."

Editing messages

Entourage lets you edit a message somebody *else* wrote. For once in your life, you can edit down some long-winded person without hurting his feelings.

Just double-click a message to open it into a window, and then choose Message→Edit Message or, new in Office 2004, click the Edit Message icon in the Message toolbar. (If it's HTML formatted, you'll be warned that the note is about to become a plain-text message.) Feel free to delete or rewrite the text. When you close the window, Entourage asks if you want your changes preserved. After you click Save, a notepad icon appears next to the message's name, a reminder of your meddling.

Reformatting messages

Some messages are forwarded and replied to about a million times. With each round, more brackets get added at the beginning of each line. Sooner or later, these messages become almost illegible (see Figure 9-11).

Fortunately, Entourage can usually clean up a message's text. It can, for example, make a message's text all uppercase or all lowercase, increase or decrease its quoting levels (those multiple brackets >>>), or even straighten out curly quotes (which often arrive at the other end of Internet email as gobbledygook).

The most useful of these tools is Rewrap Paragraphs. When you have a badly wrapped message, the Edit→Auto Text Cleanup→Rewrap Paragraphs command (or click the

---

UP TO SPEED

About Mailing Lists

During your email experiments, you're likely to come across something called a mailing list. Mailing lists come in two general forms: discussion lists in which members of the mailing list contribute to a group discussion via email, and broadcast-only lists that transmit messages to subscribers. For example, a group of Celtic music fans might have an email discussion list in which members write about anything they like, but a particular Celtic artist might have a broadcast list to announce concerts and albums to fans who've signed up for updates. By searching Yahoo (*www.yahoo.com*) or

similar Web directories, you can turn up mailing lists covering just about every conceivable topic.

Many Internet discussion lists are unmoderated, which means you can send a message to all members of the group by sending a message to a single address—the list's address. That's why you have to be careful when you just want to reply to one person in the discussion group; if you accidentally reply to the list address and not to a specific person, your message may be distributed to everyone on the mailing list—sometimes with embarrassing or disastrous consequences.

Rewrap Text icon) does its best to remove all those funky line breaks so that the message is clean and legible once again.

Tip: When you use the Rewrap Paragraphs command on a message you've received, Entourage asks if you want your changes to the original made permanent. Sometimes that's just fine, but other times you may want to keep the original (bad) formatting around, just in case Rewrap Paragraphs messed up a chart or specially formatted text like pop-song lyrics.

No biggie: You can have *both* the original and the cleaned-up version. Just make a duplicate of the message (select the message, choose Edit→Duplicate Message), and then use Entourage's reformatting tools on the copy.

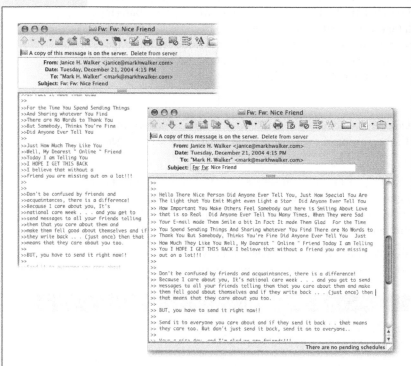

Figure 9-11:
Back Left: You can see how badly text gets mangled when it has been forwarded a few times.

Front Right: After using the Remove Quoting and Rewrap Paragraph commands, the message's lines are neat and tidy. (An open message also offers a Rewrap Paragraphs button right on the toolbar.)

Forwarding messages

Instead of replying to the person who sent you a message, you may sometimes want to *forward* the message—pass it on—to a third person. You can do that in one of two ways: pass the message along as is, or package it up in an attachment to a new message (a new twist in Entourage 2004).

To send a message off just as it came, click the Forward button in the toolbar, choose Message→Forward, or press ⌘-J. A new message opens, looking a lot like the one that appears when you reply. Once again, before forwarding the message, you can edit the subject line or the message itself. (For example, you may wish to precede the original message with a comment of your own, along the lines of: "Frank: I thought you'd be interested in this joke about Congress.") Entourage inserts one-line labels indicating what part of your message is the forwarded content, which helps eliminate confusion.

When you forward a message this way, Entourage puts the insertion point at the top of the message, and inserts labels—"Forwarded message" and "End of Forwarded Message"—to indicate where the forwarded message starts and stops. You can also tell Entourage to use Internet-style quote characters (">") before the forwarded text: choose Entourage→Mail & News Preferences, select the Reply & Forward pane, and check "Use quoting characters when forwarding." (You can also change the starting position of the insertion point from this panel.)

If you have a long message that's like a document in itself, you might want to keep it separate from the text you're adding, so you can have Entourage turn the mail into an attachment. This method also keeps the material safe from prying eyes until your recipient chooses to open the attachment. To do so, click Message→Forward as an Attachment, and take it from there.

All that remains for you to do is to specify who gets the forwarded message. Just address it as you would any outgoing piece of mail.

Note: If the original message contained an attachment, this time, Entourage *does* keep the attachment attached (unless you delete it first).

Redirecting messages

A *redirected* message is similar to a forwarded message, with one extremely useful difference: when you forward a message, your recipient sees that it came from *you*—just as if you'd written the whole thing yourself. But when you *redirect* a message, your recipient sees the *original* sender's name as the sender; the message bears almost no trace of your involvement. In other words, a redirected message uses you as a low-profile relay station between two other people.

Treasure this Entourage feature; plenty of email programs, including Microsoft's own Outlook and Outlook Express for Windows, don't offer a Redirect command at all. You can use it to transfer messages from one of your own accounts to another, or to pass along a message that came to you by mistake. You might use it when, for example, you, a graphic designer, receive a question from a customer about the sales tax on his bill. You could redirect it to someone in the accounting department, who could respond to it directly just by clicking Reply. You'd then be mercifully insulated from *any* ensuing discussion of sales tax.

To redirect a selected message, choose Message→Redirect, or press Option-⌘-J. Entourage presents an outgoing copy of the message for you to address. You'll notice that unlike a forwarded message, this one lacks quoting brackets. You can't edit a redirected message; the whole idea is that it ends up at its destination unaltered. If you need to make a comment to the new recipient, use Forward instead.

Note: When you redirect a message, you do leave some electronic fingerprints on it. If the recipients look at the Internet *headers* of a message you've redirected, they'll see information Entourage inserted indicating who resent the message, and there may be other clues. Entourage inserts these details both to help avoid confusion and to prevent abuse.

Printing messages

To print a message, click the Print button in the toolbar, choose File→Print, or press ⌘-P; the Entourage Print window appears. Once you've changed any necessary settings and clicked OK, the standard Print dialog box pops up, so that you can specify how many copies you want, what range of pages, and so on. Finally, click Print.

Tip: If you know you just want one copy of a message using the default print settings, choose File→Print One Copy, or press Option-⌘-P. Entourage will zap a single copy of the current message to your printer, with no need for any additional dialog boxes.

Filing messages

Entourage lets you create new folders in the Folder list. Then, by dragging messages from your Inbox onto one of these folder icons, you can file away your messages into appropriate storage cubbies. You might create one folder for important messages, another for order confirmations when shopping on the Web, and so on. In fact, you can even create folders *inside* these folders, a feature beloved by the hopelessly organized: your Family folder might have subfolders for each of your siblings.

To create a new folder, choose File→New→Folder, press Shift-⌘-N, or choose New Folder from the New pop-up button on the Entourage toolbar. A new folder appears

---

GEM IN THE ROUGH

The Entourage Email "Paper Trail"

As a sensational convenience to you, Entourage keeps track of what you've done with a message—replied, forwarded, or redirected. It displays your message's history in a yellow

Only the most recent action you've taken on a message fits in the yellow banner, however. If you want to look at the entire history of actions performed on a message, click the History

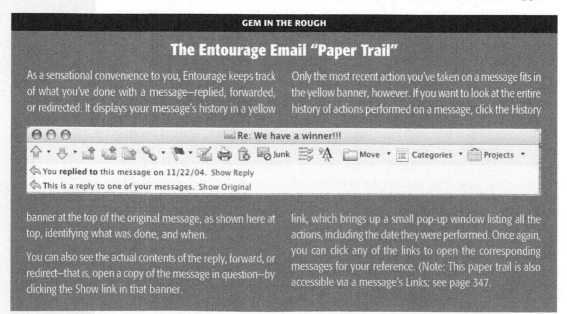

banner at the top of the original message, as shown here at top, identifying what was done, and when.

You can also see the actual contents of the reply, forward, or redirect—that is, open a copy of the message in question—by clicking the Show link in that banner.

link, which brings up a small pop-up window listing all the actions, including the date they were performed. Once again, you can click any of the links to open the corresponding messages for your reference. (Note: This paper trail is also accessible via a message's Links; see page 347.)

---

in the Folder list, with the imaginative name "untitled folder." Just type a new name and then press Return.

Tip: To rename a folder you've created, click it once to select it, and then click its name. Now rename the folder as you would any Macintosh icon. You can't rename Entourage's built-in folders (Inbox, Drafts, Sent Items, and so on), but your own folders are up for grabs.

You can move a message into a folder in any of three ways:

- Drag it out of the List pane onto the folder icon. You can use any part of a message's "row" in the list as a handle. You can also drag a bunch at once.

Tip: If you *Option*-drag a message into a folder, you make a copy of the message in that folder, leaving the original message where it was.

- Highlight a message in the List pane, or several, and then choose Message→Move To→Move To Folder (or press Shift-⌘-M). A window appears, listing all folders in the Folder list. Highlight the folder you want (by clicking or typing the first couple letters of its name). Then press Enter or Return (or click Move).

- Control-click a message (or one of several that you've highlighted); from the resulting shortcut menu, choose Move To Folder. Once again, the Folder list appears; select the one you want, then press Return.

POWER USERS' CLINIC

Exporting and Archiving Email

Believe it or not, at some point you'll probably want to get some email out of Entourage. Perhaps you'd like to give a collection of messages to someone who uses a different email program (without forwarding them all), or perhaps you'd like to keep years-old correspondence around for posterity's sake, but would prefer not to keep it forever in Entourage's ever-growing, monolithic database. Or maybe you just want to back up some of your email separately from Entourage.

Fortunately, Entourage makes it easy to extract a bunch of messages for storage or transfer: just collect (or copy) the messages you wish to export into a single mail folder, and then drag that folder to the Mac OS X desktop. Entourage saves all the messages in a standard, text-only .mbox format. Virtually every email program (including Entourage) for any

Mac, Unix, or Windows machine, can open and import these files, making them ideal for transferring messages between programs. Note that Entourage doesn't include subfolders in these exports—if you want to export a group of folders, you must do so one at a time and then reorganize them when you bring them back into Entourage or another email program.

If the messages you export have attachments, Entourage includes encoded versions of those attachments in the .mbox file. You may not want to include attachments in your exports, and other email programs or computers may not be able to understand some of the attachments—for instance, a Mac has little use for an MS-DOS batch file. If you don't want to include attachments in your export, delete them from messages before you export them.

Tip: When you click a flippy triangle in the Folder list (or highlight a folder and press ⌘-right arrow), you get to see any folders within that folder, exactly as in the Finder's List view. You can drag folders inside other folders, nesting them to create a nice hierarchical folder structure. (You can drag a nested folder back into the list of "main" folders—just drag it to the "On My Computer" item at the top of the Folder list.)

You can also drag messages between folders. Just drag one from the message list onto the desired folder at the left side of the screen.

This can be a useful trick when applied to a message in your Outbox. If you decide to postpone sending it, drag it into any other folder (like Drafts). Entourage won't send it until you drag it *back* into the Outbox.

Flagging messages

Sometimes you'll receive an email message that prompts you to some sort of action, but you may not have the time (or the fortitude) to face the task at the moment. ("Hi there…it's me, your accountant. Would you mind rounding up your expenses for 1993 through 2001 and sending me a list by email?")

That's why Entourage lets you *flag* a message, summoning one little red flag in the Status column next to a message's name *and* next to the folder that contains it in the Folder list. There are two commands for flagging messages: Flag and Flag for Follow-Up.

- **Flag.** The little red flags are simply visual indicators that you place for your own convenience, meaning whatever you want them to mean. You can hide all the messages that *aren't* flagged by choosing View→Flagged Only (Option-⌘-O).

  To flag a message in this way, select the message (or several messages) and click the Flag button in the toolbar, choose Message→Flag, or Control-click the message's name in the list and choose Flag from the shortcut menu.

- **Flag for Follow-Up.** Flag for Follow-Up shows one of the benefits of integrating an email program with a calendar. This command lets you attach a reminder to an email message. That reminder will pop up at a specified later date to remind you to do something about the message. These reminders are actually Entourage Tasks; you can read more about them in Chapter 10.

  To flag a message for follow-up, click the message and then choose Message→Flag for Follow-Up. (Alternatively, choose Flag for Follow Up from the Flag toolbar pop-up button.)

  Now a follow-up window appears, as shown in Figure 9-12; here you can specify when you want the reminder to pop up.

You can clear a flag from a message by selecting the message and then choosing Message→Clear Flag, by using the Flag pop-up button in the toolbar, or by Control-clicking the message in the list and choosing Clear Flag from the shortcut menu. Note that clearing a flag does *not* delete any follow-up reminder you may have set up for the message. To do that, you need to delete the task itself (see Chapter 10).

Linking messages

Email messages can be much more valuable when they're linked to other bits of Entourage information, such as other messages, calendar events, notes, and so on—yet another payoff of having an email program with built-in calendar and address book info. For example, you can link a message to a calendar event; thereafter, you'll be able to click the link in the appropriate calendar square to consult the original message (because it contained directions, for example).

Entourage creates some links for you automatically: for instance, when you reply to a message (or forward or redirect it), Entourage automatically creates a link between the original message and your response. That's how the message history feature works (see Figure 9-12). When flagging a message for follow-up (see above), you create a reminder that links to the original message.

Figure 9-12:
When you select a message and choose Flag for Follow-Up from the Flag button's pop-up menu, you can set a reminder that pops up at the appointed time to give you a gentle nudge.

Chapter 13 offers full details on links. In the meantime, here's a summary that's specific to email:

In addition to responding to messages, you can link messages in three ways: by opening the links menu, creating a link to an existing item, and creating a link to a new item.

- **Open Links.** To open the Links window, choose Tools→Open Links or click the Link button in the toolbar. In the Links window for the selected message, you can create or remove links to existing or new items. You can also open the item on the other end of a link.

- **Link to Existing Item.** You can create a link to one of seven kinds of existing Entourage info-bits: another (email) Message, a Calendar Event, a Task, a Note, a Contact (address book entry), a Group, or even a File on your hard drive. (This last feature can be extremely handy. You might link a message about the date of your Macworld Expo talk to, for example, the Word document that contains your outline.)

  To link to an existing item, choose the kind of link you want to make from the Tools→Link to Existing Item submenu, then select the item to which you want to link. You can also create such a link from the Links window.

- **Link to New Item.** You can also link a message to a Message, Calendar Event, Task, Note, Contact, or Group that you're *about* to create—that is, you can simultaneously create a link *and* the item it's linked to. This is handy when you suddenly get the inspiration to create a link, but you haven't yet created the item on the other end of that link. If a message makes you think, "Ooh, I need to remember to bring a dish to Phoebe's potluck next week!" you can create a link from that message to a new calendar item, then create the event using Entourage's calendar feature.

To create a link to a new item, choose the kind of link (and new item) that you want to create from the Tools→Link to New Item submenu. Once you've created a link, a small chain-link icon appears in the Links column in the message list.

To remove a link, open the Links window (choose Tools→Open Links, choose Open Links from the Link pop-up button in the toolbar, or click the link column next to

---

POWER USERS' CLINIC

Custom Arrangements

Custom arrangements enable you to design your own, custom manner of displaying the messages. Think about it. How much time do you spend every day ordering your email alphabetically by the From column to find a friend's name, then clicking the Sent column to bring the most recent messages back up to the top? Do you find that you arrange your Mail window quite differently when you have 4,365 unread messages and need to ferret out the most important work-related ones than when you're keeping up with everyday correspondence?

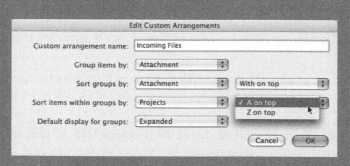

3. Choose the options you want from the four pop-up menus. The various options let you decide exactly how you wish to display and order the messages. For example, if you group the items by Subject and then sort the groups by Sent, all the messages with the same subject will be sub-divided into groups based on who sent the message. You can also decide whether you wish to alphabetize from A to Z or Z to A. By the same token, your chronological order can begin with the most recent or the oldest.

Entourage's Custom Arrangements feature was made for you. Once you set up one of these complex email-management schemes, which are based on the Groups feature (see the box on page 337), you can recreate it anytime just by choosing its name from the View→Arrange By submenu.

Don't waste another minute. Choose View→Arrange By→ Edit Custom Arrangement and follow these steps:

1. Click New.

2. In the Custom arrangement name box, type a name.

4. After you're finished, click OK.

You can also duplicate an arrangement, to create a new but similar one. To do so, select the arrangement in the list, and then click Duplicate. Entourage whisks you away to the Edit Custom Arrangement dialog box, where you can rename or otherwise alter the custom arrangement. To clear away old, unused arrangements from the menu, choose View→ Arrange By→Edit Custom Arrangement, select the arrangement and click Delete.

---

the message in question). Once the Links window is open, select the link, and then click the Remove Link button at the top of the window.

Prioritizing messages

You can set one of five priority levels for messages that you've received: Highest, High, Normal, Low, and Lowest. Once you've assigned priorities to your messages, Entourage can sort them so that the most important messages appear at the top.

To set a message's priority, highlight its name in the List pane and then choose from the Message→Priority menu. To sort messages by priority, click the Priority column header (the exclamation-point icon at the left side of the List pane). The first time you click, Entourage sorts your mail from lowest priority to highest; the second time, it lists them from highest to lowest importance.

Note: You're not the only one who can set a message's priority. Sometimes incoming messages have their priority already set—invariably to Highest (for those who think their messages are vital) or Lowest (for those considerate about sending out genuinely unimportant mail). You can change a message's priority once you've received it by choosing from the Message→Priority submenu.

Opening Attachments

Sending little text messages is fine, but it's not much help when somebody wants to send you a photograph, a sound recording, a Word or Excel document, and so on. Fortunately, enclosing such items as *file attachments* is one of the world's most popular email features.

When you receive an email message with an attachment, you'll notice that it often takes much longer than usual to download from the Internet. That's because attached files are typically much larger than email messages. (For more information on attaching files to send to others, see page 364.

When you've received a message with an attachment, a small paper-clip icon appears in the attachments column at the far left of the List pane.

Unlike, say, America Online or Eudora, Entourage doesn't store downloaded files as normal file icons on your hard drive. Instead, they're stored in the Entourage database—a big, specially encoded file on your hard drive. To extract an attached file from this mass of data, you must first open the message (either in the Preview pane or by opening the message into its own window). Now you'll see a new section in the window labeled Attachments, as shown in Figure 9-13, listing any files that came along with the message.

If you expand the flippy triangle to the left of the word Attachments, you see a list of the files, complete with their icons, plus three buttons: Open, Save, and Remove. At this point, you can proceed in any of several ways:

- Click one of the file icons (or Shift-click to select several, or click one and then press ⌘-A to highlight them all), and then click Save. The Save File dialog box appears, so that you can specify the folder in which you want to save the files on your hard drive.

- Drag a file icon (or several selected ones) clear out of the message window and onto any visible portion of your desktop, as shown in Figure 9-13.

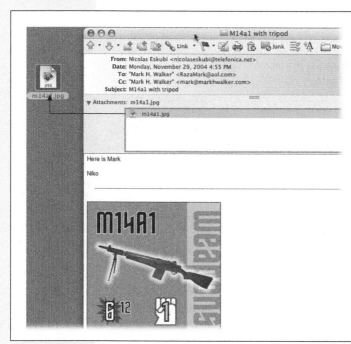

Figure 9-13:
When you receive an attachment via email, you see it represented just above the message text. You can click the open, save, or remove the attachment, respectively. But dragging an attachment's icon onto your desktop takes the file out of the Entourage world and into your Macintosh world, where you can file it, trash it, open it, or manipulate it as you would any file.

- Double-click the attachment's icon in the message (or highlight it and click Open). If you were sent a document—a photo, Word file, or Excel file, for example—it now opens in the corresponding program (Photoshop, Word, Excel, or whatever).

Warning: *After the attachment is open, if you make any changes to it, use the File→Save As command to save the file into a folder of your choice. Otherwise, your changes evaporate immediately.*

- Highlight an icon (or several) and click Remove. You've just detached, and discarded, the file, reclaiming space on your hard drive.

Tip: *It's easy to set up Entourage to save all incoming file attachments into a particular folder on your hard drive—or onto your desktop for easy retrieval—saving you the step of manually saving or dragging them. (This arrangement should sound familiar to America Online, Eudora, and Claris Emailer fans.)*

The trick is to use the message rules described in the next section. One of them offers an option to save all file attachments (or only those from certain senders) automatically into a folder you specify.

When attachments don't open

Several factors may be at work if you're unable to open a file attachment. For starters, your correspondent's email program may have *compressed* or *encoded* the file to make it take less time to send. If you're having trouble getting a file to open, therefore, your first step should be to drag the attachment's icon onto that of StuffIt Expander, the free program that comes on every Macintosh hard drive. (Look in the Applications→ Utilities folder.)

StuffIt Expander can gracefully decode and decompress just about any geeky Internet file, including those with file name suffixes like .sit, .cpt, .hqx, .gz, .z, .arc, .uu, and .zip.

Note: Of course, Mac OS X generally hides these extensions, but you can always see a file's hidden extension by highlighting it, choosing File→Show Info, and choosing Name & Extension from the pop-up menu.

If the file still won't open, even after being decompressed, then you may be dealing with a file from a Windows PC. Some you can open; some require more work. Many, for example, open in the Mac OS X program called Preview, which you'll find in your Applications→Utilities folder.

The best clue is the three-letter *file name extension* on the file's name. For example:

- **.doc, .xls,** and **.ppt.** These extensions identify Microsoft Office documents: .doc is for Microsoft Word, .xls is for Excel, and .ppt is for PowerPoint. You should be able to open these documents with Office 2004 by double-clicking them, but there

---

FREQUENTLY ASKED QUESTION

Viruses by Email

I'm scared of attachments. Won't I get a virus?

Newspaper and television reporters periodically get breathless and wide-eyed about new viruses and worms (programs that have been deliberately written to gum up a computer), such as the "Melissa" and "I Love You" viruses. These little programs often come attached to, or masquerade as, ordinary files or messages sent to you—sometimes inadvertently by people you know.

When you try to open or save an attachment, Entourage warns you of the possibility of viruses and gives you an opportunity to chicken out. (Entourage doesn't warn you if you drag the attachment out of the message to your desktop.)

Where viruses are concerned, using a Mac is a good thing; most viruses affect only Windows PCs. Of the very few viruses

that run in Mac OS X, one called "Opener"—which can disable OS X's built-in firewall, steal personal information, and destroy data—is the most notorious.

It's a good idea to delete all attachments, without opening them, from people you don't know. If you receive unexpected attachments from people you do know, check with them before opening any files, particularly if the message is brief or out of character, or if that person uses Windows.

Then there are macro viruses, written with Office's own programming language and embedded into Word and Excel documents. Here again, most such viruses do nothing on a Macintosh—but if you ever open an attached file and encounter a big, stern-sounding dialog box, click the Disable Macros button to play it safe. You've just shut down any macros that were embedded in the file, viruses or not.

---

may be times when you have to drag the document to the icon of the appropriate Office program.

- **.mpg.** You've been sent an MPEG movie. You can generally play these using Quick-Time Player.

- **.wmf.** You've been sent a file encoded in Windows Media Format—a Microsoft media format similar to QuickTime. You can play WMF files using the ironically named Windows Media Player for Macintosh.

- **.mp3.** MP3 files are compact, great-sounding music files. They're what Apple's iTunes and iPod are all about. If an MP3 file doesn't play when you double-click it, drag it onto the iTunes icon. (Ditto for audio files like .wav and .aif.)

- **.ra, .rm,** or **.ram.** This file is an audio, video, or streaming media item for RealPlayer. Neither QuickTime nor Windows Media Player can play these items. You can get a copy of RealPlayer at *www.real.com.*

- **.bmp.** This is a Windows Bitmap file. You should be able to open this type of graphic using Mac OS X's Preview program, or Word 2004.

- **.tif** or **.tiff.** TIFF graphics files are common in desktop publishing. (The graphics in this book, for example, are TIFF files.) If you can't open it by double-clicking, the Mac OS X Preview program can show it to you. Word can also open TIFF images.

- **.psd.** A Photoshop document. You can view these in Preview if you don't have Photoshop.

- **.exe.** This extension denotes an *executable* file for Windows—like a program on a Mac. By itself, your Mac can't run Windows programs, just as Windows computers can't run Macintosh programs. You need a program like VirtualPC from *www.connectix.com* (which also comes with the Pro version of Office) to run Windows programs on a Mac.

- **.bat, .pif, .scr,** or **.com.** These are other kinds of Windows programs, which you can't run on the Mac without VirtualPC. They're also, unfortunately, often associated with email-based worms and viruses. They can't harm a Mac, but delete them anyway, so that you don't pass them along accidentally to a Windows-using friend.

- **.jpg** or **.gif.** You can open these graphics files in Word, PowerPoint, Preview, or Internet Explorer. In fact, you often see these images or photographs right in the body of the email messages that brought them to you.

- **.pdf.** This downloaded item is probably a manual or brochure. It came to you as a portable document format file, better known as an Adobe Acrobat file. Entourage generally shows you a preview of the PDF file right in the email message, but you can also open the document with either Preview or the free Acrobat Reader that comes with every Mac.

- **.html or .htm.** A file whose name ends in .html or .htm is a Web page. In the beginning, Web pages hung out only on the Internet. These days, however, you're increasingly likely to find that you've downloaded one to your Mac's hard drive (it may be a software manual for some shareware, for example). To open the Web page, double-click in the attachment area of the message to open it in your Web browser, or drag the document to the visible area of a Web browser window, if you already have one running.

- **.vcf.** You've got yourself an electronic "business card," called a vCard, containing contact information for the sender. See page 431.

- **.rtf.** RTF stands for Rich Text Format, and indicates a formatted word processing document as described on page 60. Word 2004 opens this kind of file with ease.

- **.wps.** This file was created using Microsoft Works, an all-in-one software suite that's something like AppleWorks. Unfortunately, Office 2004 can't read these files; ask your correspondent to export the file as RTF, plain text, or another format if possible. For a greater feeling of self-reliance, buy a file-conversion program like MacLinkPlus (*www.dataviz.com*).

- **.wpd.** This suffix denotes a WordPerfect document. Several years ago, WordPerfect was the dominant word processing program for PCs. (The file name extension *.doc* "belonged" to WordPerfect files, in fact, until Microsoft co-opted it for use with Microsoft Word—one of many actions that caught the Justice Department's attention over the years.) Office 2004 can't open WordPerfect files directly. Here again, ask your correspondent to export the document as RTF, HTML, or plain text.

- **.fp5 and .fp7.** These are FileMaker Pro databases (*www.filemaker.com*).

If you were sent a file with a three-letter code not listed here, you may well have yourself a Windows file that can be opened only by a Windows program that you don't actually own. You might consider asking your correspondent to resend it in one of the more universal formats described above.

Using Message Rules

Once you know how to create folders, the next step in managing your email is to set up a series of *message rules* (or *filters*) that file, answer, or delete incoming messages *automatically* based on their contents, such as subject, address, or size. Message rules require you to think like the distant relative of a programmer, but the mental effort can reward you many times over; message rules turn Entourage into a surprisingly smart and efficient secretary.

Setting up message rules

Here's how to set one up:

1. **Choose Tools→Rules.**

The Rules dialog box appears, as shown in Figure 9-14. As you can see, the tabs here let you set up different rules for each kind of email account (POP, IMAP, Hotmail), plus separate rules for newsgroups (page 370), and outgoing messages.

2. **Click the tab you want to work with, and then click New.**

The Edit Rules dialog box appears.

3. **Use the top options to specify how Entourage should select messages to process.**

For example, if you'd like Entourage to watch out for messages from a particular person, you would set up the first two pop-up menus to say "From" and "Contains," respectively.

To flag messages containing *loan, $$$$, XXX, !!!!,* and so on, set the pop-up menus to say "Subject" and "Contains."

If you click Add Criterion, you can set up another condition for this message rule. For example, you can set up the first criterion to find messages *from* your uncle, and a second that watches for messages whose subject line contains "humor." This way, only jokes passed on from your uncle get placed automatically into, say, the Deleted Items folder.

If you've set up more than one criterion, use the "Execute" pop-up menu to indicate whether the message rule should apply if *all* the conditions are true, or if *any* of them are true.

You can also set up catch-all rules that do their thing *unless* any or all criteria are met. For instance, if you're using an account purely for internal email at your company, you can set up a rule for that account that files away (or deletes) all mail *except* messages from an address containing your company's ".com" name.

4. **Specify *which* words or people you want the message rule to watch out for.**

After you've used the two pop-up menus, a text box appears. Into this box, type the word, name, or phrase you want Entourage to watch out for—a person's name, or *XXX*, in the previous examples.

GEM IN THE ROUGH

Using the Junk Mail Filter

The Entourage Junk Mail Filter scans your incoming messages for some telltale signs of spam (junk email), and then moves suspect mail to a folder called Junk Mail, thus keeping your Inbox relatively clean of worthless come-ons.

To use the Junk Mail Filter, choose Tools→Junk E-Mail Protection, and then, in the dialog box that opens, choose the level of protection that you desire. By clicking on the Domain tab, and typing in domain names in the space provided, you can specify certain domains (companies or entities, as indicated by everything after the @ sign in the email addresses) to exclude from the filter—such as stuff arriving from your work domain. Messages from addresses in your Address book are never identified as junk, and the Junk Mail Filter never targets mailing lists you're managing using the Tools→Mailing List Manager feature.

---

5. **In the lower half of the box, specify what you want to happen to messages that
match the criteria.**

If, in steps 1 and 2, you've told your rule to watch for junk mail containing *$$$$*
in the Subject line, here's where you can tell Entourage to delete it or move it into,
say, a Spam folder.

With a little imagination, you'll see how the options in this pop-up menu can
do absolutely amazing things with your incoming email. Entourage can delete,
move, or print messages; forward or redirect them to somebody; automatically
save attachments into a Downloads folder that you've set up; or when you receive
messages from some important person, play a sound, animate the Entourage icon
in the Dock, or display a dialog box.

6. **In the very top box, name your mail rule. Click OK.**

Now the Rules dialog box appears (Figure 9-14, top). Here, you can manage the
rules you've created, choose a sequence for them (those at the top get applied first),
and apply them to existing messages.

Tip: Entourage applies rules as they appear, from top to bottom, in the Rules window. If a rule doesn't seem
to be working properly, it may be that an earlier rule is intercepting and processing the message before the
"broken" rule even sees it.

To fix this problem, try moving the rule up or down in the list by selecting it and then clicking the Move Up
or Move Down buttons. You can also drag the rule to a higher or lower place in the list, or selectively turn
preceding rules on or off.

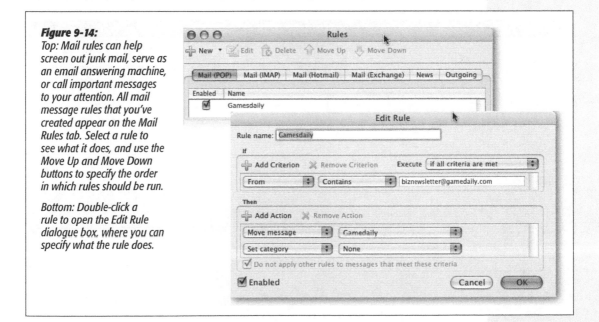

Figure 9-14:
*Top: Mail rules can help
screen out junk mail, serve as
an email answering machine,
or call important messages
to your attention. All mail
message rules that you've
created appear on the Mail
Rules tab. Select a rule to
see what it does, and use the
Move Up and Move Down
buttons to specify the order
in which rules should be run.*

*Bottom: Double-click a
rule to open the Edit Rule
dialogue box, where you can
specify what the rule does.*

Two sneaky message-rule tricks

You can use message rules for many different purposes. But here are two of the best:

- **Create a spam filter.** When spammers send junk mail, your address often doesn't appear in the To or Cc lines—it's as if they Bcc'd you on their message (see page 357). If you don't receive much mail on which you're *legitimately* Bcc'd, just make a rule that messages in which "Any recipient" "Does not contain" your email address, and have Entourage move the message to a "Possible Spam" folder. (You probably

Figure 9-15:
In this example, if Entourage receives an email message with a specified subject and address—from you, for example—it launches an AppleScript script. A script can update your Web site, look up something in a FileMaker database and send you the results via email, or tell iTunes to play loud music to make sure that your cat isn't sleeping on your keyboard—you name it.

POWER USERS' CLINIC

Using Directory Services

You're all set to send someone an email message, when it hits you: You don't know his address.

Fortunately, several Web services (such as Bigfoot and four11) serve as "email phone books." To capitalize on this feature, choose Tools→Directory Services to bring up the Directory Services window, choose one of the listed Web sites (servers), enter a name or email address, and then click the Find button. If you're lucky, the person's information appears in the list below. More likely, you'll get either no results, or a huge list of possible matches. Unfortunately, the accuracy of Internet-wide directories is limited, and many people avoid being listed in them to prevent their information from being "harvested" by spammers.

This feature is of far more value if you work in a company that provides its own email directory (via an electronic phone book known as an LDAP server). In that event, choose Tools→Accounts, click the Directory Service tab, and then click the New button in the window's toolbar. The Account Setup assistant now walks you through a two-step process of entering your server's information. (Get it from your network administrator.)

While you're in the Edit Account window, you can choose which LDAP account you'd like to be your main directory by selecting the account's name and then clicking the Make Default button in the toolbar. Entourage displays your default service in bold.

OFFICE 2004 FOR MACINTOSH: THE MISSING MANUAL

want to set these filtered messages aside rather than delete them outright; there are times it's perfectly legitimate to be Bcc'd on a message.)

You can then glance through the Possible Spam folder once in a while and see if there's anything there you need to read, then delete any unwanted messages. Make this one of the *last* rules in the Rules window, so that any rules for friends, work, family, and other special cases are handled *before* this rule is applied.

- **The email answering machine.** If you're going to be on vacation, turn on "Is not from a mailing list" and "Is not junk mail" in step 3 above, and then "Reply with message" in step 5. In other words, you can turn Entourage into an email answering machine that automatically sends a canned "I'm away until the 15th" message to everyone who writes you, except mailing lists and junk mailers. That is, as long as you have an "always on" Internet connection, and you leave Entourage running, with orders to periodically check email.

Writing a Message

To create an email message in Entourage, use one of these tactics:

- Choose File→New→Mail Message.

- Press ⌘-N. (If you're using an Entourage function that has nothing to do with email—the Calendar or Tasks, for example—press Option-⌘-N instead.)

- Choose Mail Message from the New pop-up button on the toolbar.

In each case, an empty email message window appears, filled with email composition tools.

Step 1: Addressing the message

The first thing you'll see when you create a new email message is the address pane, a pop-up window with four buttons and three sections (see Figure 9-16). The fields here are labeled To, Cc, and Bcc, each of which has its own purpose:

- **To.** Most of the time, you'll type your correspondent's email address here. If the recipient's email address resides in your address book, Entourage can autocomplete it for you after the first couple of letters. Just scroll through the suggestions until you find the correct address, and double-click or press Enter.

- **Cc.** Cc stands for *carbon copy;* the name is a reference to the days with typewriters, when creating a copy of a document required inserting carbon paper between two sheets of typing paper. In email terms, putting someone's email address in the Cc area means, "No reply required; just thought you'd want to see this." People listed in the Cc field receive a copy of the message, but aren't the primary recipients.

- **Bcc.** A *blind carbon copy* is a secret copy. This feature lets you send a copy of a message to somebody secretly, without any of the other recipients knowing that you did so. The names in the To and Cc fields appear at the top of the message for all recipients to see, but nobody can see the names you type into the Bcc box.

You can use the Bcc field to quietly signal a third party that a message has been sent. For example, if you send your co-worker a message that says, "Chris, it bothers me that you've been cheating the customers," you could Bcc your boss or supervisor to clue her in without getting into trouble with Chris.

The Bcc box is useful in other ways, too. Many people send email messages (containing jokes, for example) to a long list of recipients. You, the recipient, have to scroll through a very long list of names in the To or Cc field.

But if the sender used the Bcc field to hold all the recipients' email addresses, you, the recipient, won't see any of those names at the top of the email.

Tip: After addressing a message, you can drag the addresses back and forth among these three blanks: from the To box into the Cc line, for example.

If you want to send a message to more than one person, click the Add button and type in a second (or third, or fourth) email address, or just click in an empty area of an addressing box and start typing. As in most dialog boxes, you can jump from blank to blank in this window by pressing the Tab key (to proceed from the To field to the Cc field, for example).

You don't have to remember and type out all those email addresses, either. As you type, Entourage compares what you're typing with the names in your Address Book. If it finds a match—that is, if you've typed *zar* and your Address Book contains the name *Ed Zarynski*, for example, Entourage sprouts a list of that and any other matches. Entourage also remembers the last 200 addresses you've used that *aren't* in your address book, which can be handy when you think of something you'd like to add to a

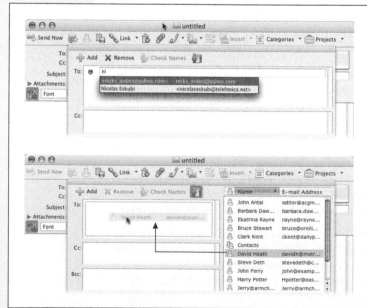

Figure 9-16:
Top: As you type an address, a pop-up menu of matching names from your address book appears. Click the one that you want, or press the down arrow key to highlight it and then press Enter or Return.

Bottom: To use the address book pane, find the recipient in the list (either by scrolling or by typing the first few letters of the name). Then add this person's name to the list by double-clicking (or by dragging it into the address area). You can repeat this process to add other names.

recent exchange. (You can turn this feature off in the Compose tab in Entourage→
Mail & News Preferences if it bothers you.)

You can choose from this list of proposed addressees either by clicking a name, or by
pressing the down arrow key to highlight a name, and then pressing Enter to select
it. If none of Entourage's guesses are correct, just keep typing; Entourage quietly
withdraws its suggestions.

Alternatively, you can access your address book just by clicking the Address Book
button just above the To field (see Figure 9-16).

Tip: The tiny icon that appears in front of each email address that you've entered indicates Entourage's
understanding of the address. If you see a tiny human figure, (similar to the MSN Messenger icon) you've
input an address that's in the Address Book; if you see a blue circle/button symbol, you've typed an address
that's not in your Address Book. (Of course, you can always add one of these addresses to your Address
Book just by Control-clicking it and choosing Add to Address Book from the shortcut menu.)

A green question mark indicates Entourage doesn't understand the address, probably because it isn't a correctly formed email address and no matching names appear in your Address Book.

Across the top of the address window are a few handy buttons. **Add** opens up a new
empty row in the current addressing field, in which you can specify an additional address. The **Remove** button removes a selected recipient's row. **Check Names** is handy
if you don't know somebody's email address; after typing her name into the Address
box, click this button to consult an Internet email directory (see page 356) in hopes
of turning up the email address.

Tip: You can use the Tab key to move between address fields, subject line, and the message's body text.

If you have more than one account set up in Entourage, a From pop-up menu appears above the message's addressees. Use it to choose which account you want to
use from that pop-up menu.

Step 2: The Subject line

Some people, especially in the business world, get bombarded with email. That's
why it's courteous to put some thought into the Subject line (use "Change in plans
for next week" instead of "Hi," for example). Press the Tab key to make your cursor
jump into the large message-body area. Don't make your subject too long: remember,
most people will see it in a list with other information like your name and the date
and time you sent the message, and the subject may get compressed or truncated.
If you try to send a message without a subject, Entourage will warn you this isn't a
good idea, but it's not a fatal one either. You can go ahead and send it. Entourage will
automatically insert "<no subject>" as a subject line. And your recipient's spam filter
will probably delete it.

Step 3: Composing the body

After you've addressed your message and given it a subject, it's time to fill in the message's body text. To do this, just click (or Tab into) the message area and start typing. You can use all the standard editing techniques, including selection, drag-and-drop, and the Cut, Copy, and Paste commands, to rearrange the text as you write it.

As you type, Entourage does something rather wonderful (or alarming, depending on your point of view): it checks your spelling as you go, using a red squiggly underline to mark questionable spelling. To check for possible alternative spellings for a suspect word, Control-click the red-squiggled word; a list of suggestions appears in a shortcut menu. Choose the word you really intended, or choose Add to add the word to the Office 2004 dictionary.

If you want to spell check a message all at once, choose Tools→Spelling (or press Option-⌘-L) after composing it. (To turn off automatic spell checking, choose Entourage→General Preferences, click the Spelling tab, and then turn off "Check spelling as you type.")

Tip: You can use the same keyboard shortcuts in Entourage that you use in Word (such as ⌘-right arrow to move the cursor one word to the right)—a great timesaver. Just choose Entourage→General Preferences, click the General tab, and make sure that "Use Microsoft Office keyboard shortcuts for editing text" is turned on.

That same preference tab lets you make Entourage resemble Word in other ways, too. It lets you turn on automatic whole-word selection, "smart cut and paste" (spaces are automatically added or removed as necessary when you insert or delete text), and a Font menu that shows fonts in their own typefaces. Similarly, the Spelling tab in the General Preferences dialog box offers the same control over spell-checking options that Word does.

All of this should sound familiar; it's precisely the same basic mechanism that Word 2004 employs when it looks for spelling mistakes on the fly, as described on page 79.

Tip: If you're composing a long email message, or it's one you don't want to send until later, click the Save as Draft button (⌘-S) or choose File→Save to save the message in your Drafts folder. To reopen a saved draft, click the Drafts folder in the Folder list, and then open the draft that you want to work on from the list on the right.

Step 4: Choosing a format (HTML or plain text)

When it comes to formatting a message's text, you have two choices: *plain text* or *HTML* (hypertext markup language).

Plain text means that you can't format your text with bold type, color, specified font sizes, and so on. HTML, on the other hand, lets you use formatting commands such as font sizes and bold text.

But there's a catch: some email programs can't read HTML-formatted email, and email programs that *can* handle HTML don't always handle it the same way. An HTML message that looks fine for you may be incomprehensible for someone using another email program. HTML messages can also be much larger (and therefore slower to download) than plain-text messages, especially if you include pictures, sounds, or other multimedia elements.

So which should you choose? Plain text lends a more professional, old-hand feeling to your messages—but, more important, it's the most compatible. Whether your recipient uses a high-end workstation, a Web browser, a cell phone, or a 20-year-old terminal in a dusty university basement, a plain-text message almost *always* gets through intact. (There are some exceptions: accented characters and language encodings may complicate the issue.)

HTML-formatted messages, on the other hand, may not arrive intact. Your recipient may see a plain-text version of the message, which Entourage includes as a courtesy, but some email programs can't even display *that* neatly. Furthermore, since a lot of junk mail is formatted with HTML, using HTML formatting may route your message into some people's Junk Mail folders.

In general, you're better off using plain text for most of your messages, and sending HTML only when you're sure your recipients can see it.

To specify which format Entourage uses for all outgoing messages (plain text or HTML), choose Entourage→Preferences, click the Compose tab (under Mail & News Preferences), and select a format from the "Mail format" pop-up menu.

You can also change formats on a message-by-message basis. For example, if you generally like to send plain-text messages, you can switch one particular message into HTML mode by clicking the Use HTML button to the left and just above the body text area (see Figure 9-17), or choose Format→HTML. Either action activates the HTML toolbar, which you can use to add pizzazz to your messages. This toolbar is broken up into six sections:

- **Fonts.** The two controls in this section let you choose a font and font size for your email.

Note: If your message's recipient doesn't have the font you specify in this toolbar section, her email program substitutes some other font. To avoid such problems, stick to common fonts like Arial, Courier, Times New Roman, or Verdana.

- **Styles.** Just as you'd expect in a word processor, you can choose Bold, Italic, Underline, or Teletype (which puts the selected text into a fixed-width font) styles for your messages.

- **Alignment.** Lets you choose left, center, or right paragraph alignment for your text.

- **Bullets and Indents.** Lets you put the selected text in a bulleted or numbered list. It also lets you set the indent level of the selected text for some good organizational formatting.

- **Color.** These two controls let you choose a text color and a background color for your email messages. You can choose from one of 16 prefab colors, or you can mix your own (see page 689).

- **Rules.** There's only one button here, the Horizontal Line button, which puts a horizontal rule (in other words, a line) at the insertion point.

Remember: less is more. If you go hog-wild formatting your email, you may make the message hard to read, especially for people using email programs that interpret the HTML codes differently than Entourage does.

Tip: All of the HTML toolbar's commands are also accessible in the Format menu.

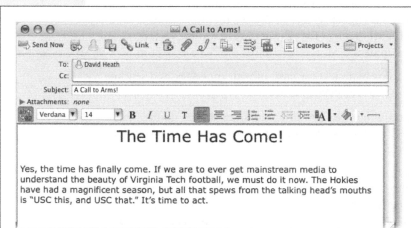

Figure 9-17:
HTML-based email lets you exercise some control over the layout of your email messages, including font, color, and text alignment. The HTML toolbar, shown just above the message body, is similar to what exists in many word processing programs. With it, you can turn plain text into an HTML-formatted masterpiece.

WORKAROUND WORKSHOP

The Lowdown on "Complex" Markup

If you've created Web pages using the HTML language, you're probably scratching your head as you read about Entourage HTML email features. Where are tables? Where are forms? Where is JavaScript? Heck, how do you even embed a link into text instead of spelling it out as an ugly URL?

The short answer is: You don't. Entourage's HTML features are meant to enhance typical email communication, not to produce sophisticated Web pages.

Fortunately, you can call on another Office 2004 program for assistance. Open Word, type the email of your dreams, including links, pictures, tables, or whatever. When you're finished, choose File→Send To→"Mail Recipient (as HTML)". Doing so opens Entourage and imports the document into an email message. Just address the message, give it a subject, and set it free. Entourage doesn't interpret the HTML perfectly—sometimes your pictures and tables may be sloshed about a bit—but hey, it's better than nothing.

Since you're probably not going to all this trouble for a casual message, be sure to send it to yourself as a test (and maybe also to some friends who use a variety of email programs) before setting your message loose on the world. You'll find that creating HTML that works in email programs is a different art from creating HTML for a Web site.

You can also insert pictures, sounds, or movies into HTML email messages. Type your message, place the insertion point where you'd like the item to appear, and then choose the appropriate command from the Insert pop-up button on your message's toolbar. Entourage asks you to locate and double-click the file you want to insert.

Tip: You can also drag the icons of graphics and movies right into the window of an outgoing HTML email message, where they appear at the insertion point. For sounds and background graphics, on the other hand, you must use the Insert button on the toolbar.

Note that Entourage automatically converts TIFF and PICT images into JPEG format when you add them to HTML messages. If you need your recipient to receive these files unaltered, send them as standard file attachments instead of inserting them or dragging them into the window.

Once you've inserted a media item into a message, you can't move it around except by inserting Returns and spaces in front of it. To delete a picture, sound, or movie, backspace over it, or select it and then press the Delete key. (There's no way to remove a background image once you've inserted it.)

Tip: Just as file attachments can make an email message enormous, images, sounds, and movies can mean that your message will be measured in megabytes. That's fine if all your recipients have fast connections like cable modems. But if one of them is trying to check email on the road using a modem, your ultra-cool inline images, movies, and sounds will become a giant headache.

UP TO SPEED

Sig and Ye Shall Find!

As cool as signatures are, don't go overboard. Few things are more annoying than downloading a two-line message followed by a full-screen signature. On mailing lists and newsgroups, a big signature is likely to get you drummed out of town. When making signatures, follow these guidelines:

- Keep signatures to four lines of text or less, focusing on essential information.

- Consider including a hyperlink to a Web page where people can find out more about who you are and what you do.

- Avoid potentially offensive material or blatantly commercial come-ons (although a brief pointer is OK, particularly if it's to something you're personally involved with).

- Protect your privacy: consider not including email addresses, phone numbers, postal addresses, and other personal data, especially when sending messages to public forums like mailing lists and newsgroups. There's no telling where that information may go or who may get their hands on it. (See "Canning Spam" on page 366.)

- If you really like flamboyant signatures for your email to your regular correspondents, great! But also create a simple, bare-bones sig just for mailing lists, newsgroups, and people outside your circle of friends.

Step 5: Adding a signature

Signatures (or "sigs") are bits of text stamped at the bottom of your email or newsgroup messages. Signatures began as a way to provide contact information without having to type it out in every message. But as online culture evolved, signatures became personal statements. A signature may contain a name, a postal or email address, a memorable quote, or even art composed of typed characters.

To create a signature, choose Tools→Signatures, which brings up the Signatures window. In it, you'll see something called the Standard signature. You can edit this signature by double-clicking it, or you can create any number of new signatures by clicking the New button. Either way, you get an editing window in which you can type your new signature. (Your signature can be either plain text or HTML-based, as described in the previous section.)

Note: If you format your signature with HTML, Entourage automatically converts it to plain text when you write a plain-text message. Be sure your signature looks good in either format!

Once you've created one or more signatures, you can tack them onto your outgoing mail either always or on a message-by-message basis:

- **Always append a signature.** Choose Tools→Accounts. In the Accounts window, double-click the account in question. (You can have a different standard signature for each account.)

  In the resulting window, click the Options tab to reveal a pop-up menu of signatures. Select the signature that you'd like to have at the bottom of every email message created using that account. (You can always override this choice on a message-by-message basis.)

Tip: If you turn on the Random checkbox, Entourage will randomly select one of these gems to grace the bottom of every email message that you send. This is the way to rotate your pithy quotes from, say, *Monty Python* without seeming repetitive to your correspondents. (Select Tools→Signatures, and then click the Random tab to turn on this feature.)

- **Message by message.** After writing your message, choose the signature you want from the Signature pop-up button (the little pen) in your message's toolbar. Entourage pastes the signature at the location of your insertion point.

Step 6: Add any file attachments

You read about *receiving* attachments earlier in this chapter; *sending* them sometimes involves a little extra brainwork.

To attach a file or files to an outgoing email message, Microsoft, in its usual fashion, offers several different methods:

- **Drag-and-drop.** If you can see the appropriate Finder window or item on the desktop behind the Entourage window, you can drag file or folder icons directly off the desktop and anywhere into the outgoing email message window, or to Entourage's icon on the Dock.

Tip: If you drag the *alias* of a file or folder, Entourage is considerate enough to ask you whether you mean to send the alias file itself (which will probably be worthless to your correspondent) or the file that opens when you double-click the alias.

- **Add button.** Click the Add Attachments button in the message's toolbar, or click the Add button in the Attachments section of the outgoing email window. Either way, the Open File dialog box appears. Navigate to, and highlight, the file or folder you want to send, and then click Choose.

- **Use a menu.** Choose Message→Add Attachments (or press ⌘-E) to do the same thing.

Once you've attached files, their names appear in the message's Attachments section, seen in Figure 9-18.

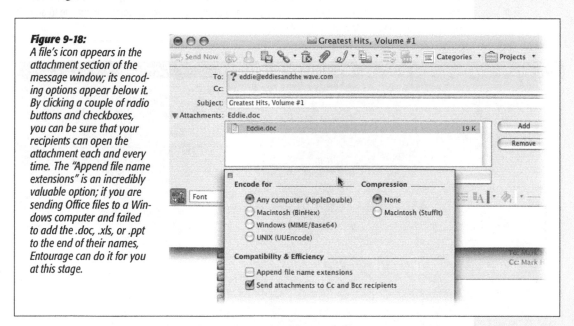

Figure 9-18:
A file's icon appears in the attachment section of the message window; its encoding options appear below it. By clicking a couple of radio buttons and checkboxes, you can be sure that your recipients can open the attachment each and every time. The "Append file name extensions" is an incredibly valuable option; if you are sending Office files to a Windows computer and failed to add the .doc, .xls, or .ppt to the end of their names, Entourage can do it for you at this stage.

Attaching files is the easy part; knowing how to *encode* those files can be tricky. Not all computers (including the Internet computers that transmit messages) can understand Macintosh files. Furthermore, some email servers still mangle anything that isn't a plain-text message. Encoding your attachments is the solution to both problems.

Unfortunately, different computers recognize different file-encoding schemes. If this encoding is done improperly, the file turns into gibberish and can't be opened on the other end.

To make matters even more complicated, files can also be *compressed* (as StuffIt or Zip archives, for example) to make them smaller and reduce the amount of time it takes to send and receive them.

Fortunately, Entourage uses an encoding scheme called *AppleDouble*, which both Macs and Windows PCs can reconstitute. And it compresses your files only if you attach an entire folder (not individual files). It uses StuffIt compression in that case, which other Macs can decompress with no trouble.

There may be times, however, when you want to change these options. For example, you may want to turn on the StuffIt compression for a single large file. Or you may have trouble sending files to someone using the factory settings, so you want to try different settings.

Tip: However you choose to encode your file, be considerate of the recipient's time. Over half of the email users in the United States still connect to their email servers with a dial-up connection. Sending attachments larger than 1.5 MB takes those users quite a while to download. If you have a large file to send, it's best to check with the recipient before sending. If they can't accept the size, consider uploading the file to an FTP site or placing it on a ROM and snail-mailing it.

FREQUENTLY ASKED QUESTION

Canning Spam

Help! I'm awash in junk email! How do I get out of this mess?

Spam is a much-hated form of advertising that involves sending unsolicited email messages to thousands of people. While there's no instant cure for spam, you can take certain steps to protect yourself from it.

1. Don't publicize your email address on the Internet—don't put it on your Web page or in your signatures, and don't allow it to be listed in any public place—like a newsgroup. Spammers have automated software robots called trawlers that scour every public Internet message and Web page, automatically collecting email addresses they find, and then sending spam to those addresses or selling them to other spammers.

2. Get a second email address you can use for Web sites, software registration, and mailing lists. At least if this address "leaks" to spammers, your primary address hasn't been compromised.

3. When filling out forms or registering products online, always look for checkboxes requesting permission for the company to send you email or share your email address with its "partners." Just say no. If the company doesn't explicitly post its privacy policy on the Web site, assume no information you provide will be kept private.

4. Use the Entourage Junk Mail Filter (page 354) .

5. Create message rules to filter out messages containing words and phrases most often found in spam (such as casino, search engine placement, herbal Viagra, and so forth. (You'll find instructions on page 353 in this chapter.)

Consider using a mail filtering service like SpamCop (*www.spamcop.net*), or asking your ISP if they can use DNS blacklists to prevent known spam sites from sending you junk. (Your ISP may be doing this already.)

If you really have a spam problem, get a new email address. Give it to people you trust. Use the old address only for junk mail, and check it for messages only infrequently.

To change encoding and compression options, click the gray encoding-summary bar just below the Attachments window (see Figure 9-18). A little pop-up window appears, where you can change both encoding and compression options:

- **Any computer (AppleDouble).** This encoding scheme flattens a Mac file into something that other kinds of computers can read, including mail servers and Windows machines.

- **Macintosh (BinHex).** This encoding method is for Mac-to-Mac transfers only. Use it only when you've tried sending a file to another Mac user using the AppleDouble setting and had no luck.

- **Windows (MIME/Base64).** This encoding method is for sending files to Windows and some Unix computers. Again, use it only when you've had no luck using AppleDouble.

- **Unix (UUEncode).** UUEncode (which stands for Unix-to-Unix Encode) is the best thing for sending to a Unix or Linux user. (It's also useful when you don't know *what* email program or operating system your recipient is using and AppleDouble doesn't work; UUEncode has been around so long that almost any email program can open UUEncoded messages.)

- **Compression: None/Macintosh (StuffIt).** As noted earlier, Entourage automatically compresses your attachments when they're included in a *folder*. Only Macintosh email programs will be able to open them and turn them back into a folder on the other end; Windows users can do it, but only if they're willing to download and install the free Expander for Windows program from *www.aladdinsys.com*.

Tip: When sending a file to a Windows PC, Entourage has the potential to end your "they can't open my files" headaches forever. Just remember to follow three steps in the Encoding window shown in Figure 9-18: Use no compression; use AppleDouble encoding; and turn on the "Append file name extensions" checkbox. Of course, you still have to send your Windows-using friend a file his system can actually *open*—for instance, most Windows machines can't open AppleWorks documents, no matter what encoding you use.

To remove an attachment, select its icon in the expanded Attachments window (Figure 9-18) and press the Delete key (or click Remove). (*Dragging* an attachment out of the Attachments window doesn't remove it from the message. Instead, it makes a copy of the file where you drag it—unless you drag it to the Trash can in the Dock.) You can also remove all attachments in one fell swoop by choosing Message→Remove All Attachments.

Step 7: Send your email on its way
Once your message is put together properly, you can send it in any of several ways:

- Click the Send Now button in the message's toolbar.
- Choose Message→Send Message Now.
- Press ⌘-K.

- If you want to wait until the next time Entourage is connected before sending the message, choose Message→Send Message Later, press Shift-⌘-K, or click the Send Later button in the message's toolbar.

Once the message has been sent, it disappears from your Outbox, but a copy appears in the Sent Items folder for your reference. (If you're a person of steely nerve and impeccable memory, you can turn off this feature; choose Entourage→Mail & News Preferences, click the Compose tab, and turn off "Save copies of sent messages in the Sent Items folder.")

Email Netiquette

Different companies, organizations, and groups have different email cultures, so email norms might vary from place to place. But over the years, general rules of Internet etiquette—that is, netiquette—have evolved. Knowing a little netiquette not only saves you embarrassment in public forums like mailing lists, but also makes your messages more understandable.

Most of these items apply to newsgroup postings as well as ordinary email, but a few points of netiquette apply strictly to newsgroups:

- **Use your real name.** Entourage lets you enter anything you like for your name when you set up an account (see page 318). But using your real name gives you more credibility and lets your friends and correspondents more easily manage mail from you.

Note: An exception to this rule would be a newsgroup or mailing list where the privacy of participants is very important, such as online support groups. For these cases, consider using another email address managed via a separate Entourage account. The account can use whatever pseudonym (and signature) you like. (See page 324 for information on setting up multiple accounts.)

- **Write clearly.** Since email is a written medium, good writing can make you look *really* good. You don't have to be Shakespeare or even sound like a professional author. But do make sure your message includes all information your correspondent may need, check your grammar, and use Entourage's spell checker. Also, make allowances for people whose writing seems awkward or difficult to understand: English may be the most common language on the Internet, but it's not the primary language for millions of Internet users.

- **Be civil.** Some people write things in email that they would never dare say to your face. No matter how offended you might be, responding in kind just makes things worse. The best response to rude email is no response at all.

- **Quote sparingly.** When quoting another message, only quote enough material so your correspondent knows what you're talking about. Quoting the entire message makes it harder for your correspondent to understand what you're saying. You can also put your responses in between bits of quoted text, which makes it obvious what you're replying to.

- **Use blank lines.** Insert blank lines between paragraphs and quoted material in your message.

- **Put angle brackets around URLs.** If you put a Web address (URL) in a message, surrounding it with angle brackets <like this> turns it into a live, double-clickable link in a wide range of email programs.

- **Avoid all caps.** Capital letters are difficult to read on computer screens and MAKE YOU LOOK LIKE YOU'RE SHOUTING.

- **Write specific subjects.** Remember that the subject of a message is one of the few things (besides your name) that your correspondents see in a typical mailbox listing. Make your messages easy to find later by using specific subjects. "Lunch at Little John's Monday at 12:30?" is a better subject line than simply "Psst! You hungry?"

Mailing List Etiquette

The following points are particularly relevant to mailing lists:

- **Don't use HTML formatting.** There's bound to be someone—or a lot of someones—on a mailing list who can't handle, or can't abide, HTML-formatted messages. Furthermore, many mailing lists are available as *digests* where all the messages each day are sent as one large message late at night, rather than as individual messages throughout the day. HTML-formatted messages often don't come across in digests at all.

- **Don't send file attachments.** It's almost always wrong to send a file attachment to a mailing list, even if it's small. If you *must* make a file available to a mailing list, put it up on a Web or FTP site for interested members to download (Apple's .Mac service is perfect for this sort of thing). Then all you have to do is put a URL in your message.

- **Keep your sig short!** Your signature (page 363) should be four lines or less.

- **Stay on topic.** Most mailing lists are devoted to a particular subject, and your messages should be reasonably "on topic" for that list. It wouldn't be appropriate to discuss sports cars on a mailing list dedicated to acoustic guitars, or ask questions about Apple's latest Mac models on a mailing list devoted to 1970s television sitcoms. On the other hand, there's probably an appropriate mailing list for almost anything you want to discuss!

- **Keep private conversations off lists.** Sometimes it's more appropriate to reply to a particular list member privately rather than the entire list. In those cases, just write a private email to the person.

- **Trim the quoting down to the essential.** When you send a reply to somebody's posting, trim out all of the >quoted >portion except the part in question. Nobody needs to read the entire treatise again.

Finally, as tempting as it may be to send out flurries of advertising about your products or business using the Internet, it's a bad idea. Spam is not only illegal in many jurisdictions (meaning you can be sued), it's guaranteed to get your Internet account shut down without notice. It's fine to keep in contact with current customers via email if they've given you permission, but quite another to use the Internet as a means to harass others.

Newsgroups

Newsgroups don't necessarily contain news; in fact, they're Internet bulletin boards collectively referred to as *Usenet*. There are well over 60,000 newsgroups on every conceivable topic: pop culture, computers, politics, and every other special (and *very* special) interest. More than 100 of them are just about the Macintosh. Fortunately, in addition to being an email and calendar program, Entourage is also a *newsreader*. You can use Entourage to read and reply to newsgroup messages almost exactly as though they were email messages.

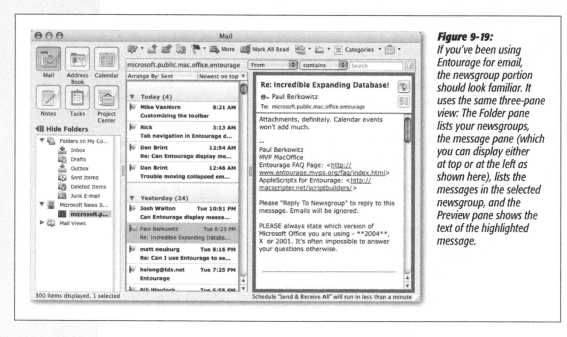

Figure 9-19:
If you've been using Entourage for email, the newsgroup portion should look familiar. It uses the same three-pane view: The Folder pane lists your newsgroups, the message pane (which you can display either at top or at the left as shown here), lists the messages in the selected newsgroup, and the Preview pane shows the text of the highlighted message.

In fact, Entourage lets you use multiple *news servers* (bulletin-board distribution computers), subscribe to individual newsgroups, filter messages in your newsgroups using Rules, and post and read messages (complete with attachments, if needed). See Figure 9-19.

Tip: Be wary of arachnids when posting to newsgroups. Email retrieval robots called *spiders* comb the Usenet for email addresses and gather them up by the thousands. The spider's owner then slaps the addresses on a CD and sells them to spammers. Does that mean you shouldn't use newsgroups? No, but it does mean you should exercise caution when posting. One method to avoid unwanted spam is to create a Web-based Hotmail or Yahoo email account and use it only for newsgroups. Spiders can still retrieve this address, but at least you aren't handing them the email the address that goes to your computer. Additionally, both Hotmail and Yahoo have sophisticated spam filters, capable of filtering most of the junk the spammers send.

Setting Up an Account

Setting up a new news account is similar to setting up a new email account; the adventure begins by contacting your Internet service provider and finding out its *news server address.* Depending on how your ISP runs its news service, you may also need your user name and password.

Next, choose Tools→Accounts. Choose News from the New pop-up button in the resulting Accounts window.

You can either enter news server information manually, or click the Assist Me button to have the Account Setup Assistant step you through the process of creating a news account like this:

1. **With the Account Setup Assistant open, select the email account you want to use and enter your organization.**

    Entourage needs an email address because every newsgroup posting has an email address associated with it.

UP TO SPEED

Newsgroups Explained

Newsgroups (also known as Usenet) began as a way for people to have discussions via a bulletin-board-like system, in which a message gets posted for all to see, and anyone can reply to that posted message. These public discussions are divided into categories called newsgroups, which cover the gamut from miscellaneous photographic techniques to naval aviation.

These days, newsgroups have a certain reputation as a place to exchange photos of scantily clad pets, cartoon characters, and even humans, not to mention pirated software and MP3 files that carry doubtful copyright pedigrees or even viruses.

Even so, there are tens of thousands of interesting, informative discussions going on, and newsgroups are great places to get help with troubleshooting, exchange recipes, or just see what's on the minds of your fellow Internet jockeys.

Although using newsgroups is like using email in Entourage, it's important to remember that anything you see or post in a newsgroup is public, and will probably remain so for years to come. (Sites like Google maintain searchable newsgroup archives going back to the mid-1980s, complete with email addresses!) Think before you post, especially if you have aspirations to run for Congress someday.

Tip: As noted previously, spammers use software robots to trawl newsgroup postings for "fresh" email addresses. Any email address you enter here will be targeted by junk mail.

The best way to avoid this torrent is to create a special account in Entourage just for newsgroups, making sure the email address used for that account is undeliverable. If you want your audience to be able to contact you privately for some reason, you *can* use your real email address, but insert something like NOSPAM, IHATESPAM, or REMOVETHIS somewhere into it to confuse the junk-mail address-hunting robots. That tactic isn't foolproof, but it's better than nothing.

Or use the domain *mouse-potato.com* in your bogus address—*chris@mouse-potato.com*, for example. The mouse-potato.com domain not only is unreachable, but has a delicious payoff: spammers trying to send mail to such addresses get their *own* machines pummeled with spam mail!

2. **Click the right arrow. Enter your news server address, and indicate whether that server requires you to log on with name and password.**

   In this step, you'll need to enter the address of your news server. Sometimes you get newsgroup access (and the necessary settings) from your ISP. If your ISP doesn't provide newsgroup access, you'll have to subscribe to a news service. They run about $10 a month, and they're generally more reliable than news servers run by ISPs. Visit *www.easynews.com, www.supernews.com,* or *www.newsguy.com* for a directory of such services.

   If you're directed to do so by your ISP, turn on Authentication and enter your user name and password.

3. **Click the right arrow. Enter your account ID and password.**

   If you told Entourage that you needed to log into your news server, you'll have to provide the details in this step. The password is optional—if you want Entourage to save it, turn on "Save password in my Mac OS keychain." If you don't enter it here, you'll have to type it every time you connect to your news server.

4. **Click the right arrow. Give your account a name.**

   You can give it any name you want, such as *Earthlink Newsgroups.*

5. **Click Finish.**

   An icon for your new account shows up in the Folder list.

Note: If you prefer to enter all of the news server particulars in one step, rather than using the multiscreen assistant, you can skip the assistant entirely, or bail out of it at any time by clicking the "Configure account manually" button in the lower part of the assistant window.

Download the List of Newsgroups

When you first click a news server icon, Entourage asks you if you want to download a list of newsgroups. Click Yes.

Entourage goes to work downloading the list, which can be quite long—tens of thousands of entries, in many cases—and takes several minutes if you connect to the Internet with a dial-up modem. Once that's done, though, you don't have to do it again. You should occasionally update the list, however, by selecting the server's icon in the Folder list and clicking the Update List button (or choosing View→Get New Newsgroups). New newsgroups appear on a more-or-less constant basis, and unused newsgroups sometimes even disappear.

The number (and nature) of newsgroups available on a particular server is up to its operators. For example, Entourage comes preconfigured to connect to the Microsoft News Server. Instead of carrying tens of thousands of newsgroups on every conceivable topic, the Microsoft News Server carries about 2,000 newsgroups, all related—surprise!—to Microsoft products. (Incidentally, these aren't bad places to learn about Office 2004 programs: check out the newsgroup called *microsoft.public. mac.office.entourage.*)

Even the big ISPs rarely carry *every* available Usenet group. Furthermore, they may not keep individual newsgroup postings around for very long, since the storage required to do so is enormous, and the number of people who actually want to read many of these newsgroups can be very small. (Honestly, do you think you'll be a regular contributor to *alt.alien.vampire.flonk.flonk.flonk*?)

Figure 9-20:
Top: After you create a newsgroup account, Entourage offers to fetch the list of every newsgroup on the server.

Bottom: Enter the text that you want to look for in the newsgroup's title (such as arabic*). If you turn up an appealing sounding topic in the gigantic list beneath, select the group and click the Subscribe button in the Entourage toolbar, to subscribe to it so that Entourage will download the latest messages on that topic every time you connect.*

Furthermore, many ISPs refuse to carry newsgroups that carry stolen software, music, video, and other materials. In fact, your ISP may simply deny access to the *alt.* hierarchy, which is where the most free-wheeling (and most dubious) activities take place. That's not to say *alt.** newsgroups are fundamentally bad, but if there's one you want to read (say, *alt.guitar.beginner*), you might have to ask your ISP to specifically enable it.

Caution: Like certain Web sites, plenty of newsgroups are not appropriate for children. Similarly, because newsgroups are public, spammers tend to litter newsgroups with their cheesy schemes and material many would find offensive. No one regulates newsgroups, and no one has complete control over what can and cannot be posted there.

Finding Newsgroups and Messages

If you're looking for a particular topic—guitars, for example—you can view a list of those discussions by typing a phrase into the "Display groups containing" field at the top of the window. Entourage hides any newsgroups that don't match that text (see Figure 9-20).

Try different criteria—typing in *mac* will show you many Macintosh-related newsgroups, but will also turn up newsgroups devoted to Fleetwood Mac, macho trucks, and GNU emacs. Typing in *garden* shows a number of newsgroups related to gardening, but may also show newsgroups devoted to the band Soundgarden.

Reading Messages

Once Entourage has downloaded a list of available newsgroups, it's up to you to sift through them and select the discussions you want to keep up with.

Fortunately, Entourage makes it easy to follow the raging Internet discussions with a feature called *subscriptions*. To subscribe to a newsgroup, select its name in the list, and then click the Subscribe button in the toolbar. An icon for that newsgroup now appears under the server's name in the Folder list, where it will act like a nested folder.

The next time you connect to the Internet, Entourage downloads all of the messages in the discussions to which you've subscribed. (There may be just a few messages, or several hundred. They may go back only a few days or a couple of weeks, depending on how much "traffic" there is in each discussion and how long your news server keeps messages available.)

Tip: Entourage keeps copies of newsgroup messages in your Entourage database. Over time, you'll realize that most newsgroup messages are ephemeral things you don't necessarily want taking up space on your hard drive. To clean out Entourage's local cache of newsgroup messages, Control-click the name of your news server in your Folder list and choose "Clear Cache" from the shortcut menu. Entourage purges its local cache of newsgroup messages. Afterward, you might want to compact the Entourage database to reclaim unused space; see page 339.

To read the actual messages in a newsgroup, either double-click its icon in the Folder list (which opens its list of messages in a new window), or click its name once in the

Folder list to the left (which reveals the list of messages in the right pane of the window). Either way, Entourage downloads a list of articles in that newsgroup.

You read messages in a newsgroup exactly as you read email messages. Since you're probably reading the newsgroup to expand your knowledge of a certain topic, you may want to choose View→Arrange By→Show in Groups and choose Subject from the same submenu to gather the messages into groups according to their subject lines. (As discussed in the box on page 337, Entourage 2004's groups provide a multitude of ways to organize your messages. All in all, there are 13 groups, from Subject to Sender.)

As with normal email messages, newsgroup messages that come with file attachments appear in an Attachments section inside the message; you can save those attachments just as you would email attachments. (Exercise extreme caution with any attachment downloaded from a newsgroup.) Some particularly large attachments in newsgroups get automatically divided into multiple segments. If you're having trouble saving a multipart attachment to your hard drive, make sure that you've selected the message that contains the *first* part. Even then, you may find that joining multipart newsgroup messages isn't one of Entourage's strongest features.

Tip: To help sift through the spam that clogs newsgroups, you can set up *news rules* by choosing Tools→ Rules, clicking the News tab, and then clicking the New button. Exactly as with the message rules described on page 353 you can set up rules that screen out messages from certain people, messages with certain phrases in their Subject line, and so on.

Composing, Forwarding, and Replying to Messages

Working with newsgroup messages is very similar to working with email messages. You reply to them, forward them, or compose them exactly as described earlier in this chapter (see Figure 9-21). As with email, you can use either plain text or HTML formatting, attach files, and clean up text that may have been wrapped badly somewhere along the way.

Usenet Netiquette

Although newsgroups are anarchic places, they also have traditions and general norms. Many of the points in "Email Netiquette" (see page 368) apply to composing messages for Usenet, but newsgroups have a few considerations of their own:

- **Lurk before you post.** When you read a newsgroup but don't post messages to it, you're considered a "lurker." There's no shame in lurking. In fact, you *should* lurk in a newsgroup for at least a few days, to get a sense of what topics are commonly discussed and who the most active participants are. Many newsgroups have cultures of their own—newcomers are always welcome, but it's best to avoid stepping on anyone's toes.

- **Read the FAQ and search the archive.** Many newsgroups have a FAQ ("frequently asked questions") document available on a Web site or posted periodically to the newsgroup. These documents contain the questions most often asked by newcomers to the group—and, even better, answers to those questions! Before posing a question you suspect may have come up before, check to see if the newsgroup has a FAQ, or search a Usenet news archive (like *http://groups.google.com*) to see if the topic has been covered recently.

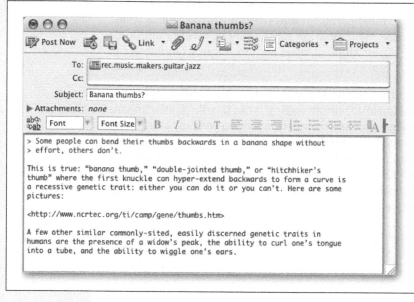

Figure 9-21:
A full-blown message ready for posting features a news-group address, a subject line, and a message text. This one also links to an image readers can view in a Web browser if they're interested. The message will be uploaded to the news server when you click the Post Now button. (If you click Post Later, Entourage waits until the next connection to post the message.)

- **Newsgroups are not billboards.** Do not post advertising to newsgroups. If you're an established member of a newsgroup, a brief announcement of something relevant to the group is fine—for instance, if you're a regular in a guitar-oriented newsgroup, you might mention that your little brother just released his first finger-style guitar CD. Similarly, a pointer in your signature to your company or your products is fine. But anything above that scale is likely to incite derisive comments or even result in abuse reports to your ISP.

- **Avoid extensive cross-posting.** Posting a message to more than one newsgroup is called *cross-posting*. It's OK to post to a handful of newsgroups if you genuinely aren't sure where your question or message is most appropriate. But widely cross-posting a message isn't much different than spamming, and so your message will be treated much like spam: derided, ignored, or even reported to your ISP.

- **Avoid HTML formatting.** Millions of people access newsgroups using old computers, old software, and slow connections. HTML-formatted newsgroup messages are frowned upon because they take longer to download and don't look good in a wide variety of newsreaders. If the major participants in a particular group all use HTML and no one objects when they do it, then posting HTML-formatted messages is probably fine. Otherwise, always use plain text.

- **Avoid "me-too" messages.** As a general rule, don't respond to messages if you're only going to agree with or restate what has just been said. (If you absolutely *must* say "I second that!" at least refrain from quoting the entire previous message in your response.)

- **Neither a troll nor a flamer be.** Tossing out provocative or insulting statements just to stir up other newsgroup participants is called *trolling,* and it's frowned upon. On the other hand, don't respond to abusive or deliberately provocative messages. You may incite a *flame war,* in which a newsgroup degenerates into increasingly vitriolic exchanges and insults. When a flame war erupts, reasonable people tend to abandon the newsgroup, sometimes never to return. If a particular person in a newsgroup always pushes your buttons, create a rule (see page 353) so you never see newsgroup messages from that person.

Tip: Although Entourage is an OK newsgroup reader, some of its newsgroup features are limited and awkward. If you find yourself participating in Usenet newsgroups regularly, consider a separate newsreader program that offers more comprehensive features—full threading, message scoring, FAQ retrieval, and more. A good newsreader can vastly improve your Usenet experience.

You can find good lists of Mac newsreaders at *www.newsgroups.com* and *www.macorchard.com/usenet. html*—in particular, check out Thoth or one of the numerous descendents of NewsWatcher.

Mail and News Preferences

Entourage keeps track of two sets of preference settings: one covering how email and newsgroups are handled, and one handling Entourage's general behavior. The following section details the email and newsgroup options.

You can view the mail and news preferences by choosing Entourage→Preferences→ Mail & News Preferences. The Mail & News Preferences section, shown in Figure 9-22, is divided into four panels: Read, Compose, Reply & Forward, and View.

Read panel

The controls under this section govern what happens when you read your email, and they're divided into three parts: Messages, Languages, and IMAP. As you'll soon discover, some of them are intended exclusively for the technically minded.

- **Messages** governs what happens to open messages that you delete or file (such as whether Entourage closes the message window or opens the next message in line). You can also specify how many seconds must elapse, with a message open in front of you, before Entourage considers it as having been read, and therefore no longer displays its name in boldface type. For example, if you've set the "Mark message as read after displaying for ___ seconds" option to 3, Entourage waits three seconds before considering an open message as having been read. This feature can be useful if you like to skim through your messages, glancing for just a few seconds at each, without changing their unread status.

- **Languages** lets you select a *character set* (including non-Roman alphabet sets like Cyrillic, Greek, or Korean) for messages that arrive without a specified character set. Set this option to the character set that you read most often—usually your primary language group.

- **IMAP.** If this box is checked, deleted IMAP messages don't show up in your message lists. If this box *isn't* checked, IMAP messages marked for deletion will still be visible in their respective folders.

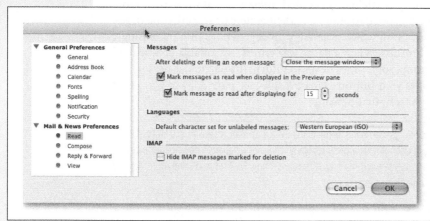

Figure 9-22:
In the Read section, you can specify how many seconds must elapse when a message is opened before Entourage considers it read (and therefore no longer displays its name in boldface type. This can be useful if you like to skim through your messages without changing their unread status.

Compose panel

This set of preferences controls what happens when you're writing messages. It's divided into three parts: General, Attachments, and Recent Addresses.

- The **General** checkboxes govern whether Entourage checks the names of your addressees against your default directory service (which is generally only useful if your company organization runs its own; see page 356) and whether or not you like to keep copies of sent messages in the Sent Items folder.

  You can also govern whether the HTML Formatting toolbar is visible when you're composing mail, and you can specify your preferred format for mail and news messages—plain text or HTML.

- **Attachments** lets you set up how Entourage processes file attachments—how you want such files to be compressed and encoded, and whether or not you want Windows file name suffixes added automatically.

  This dialog box also controls whether or not Entourage sends file attachments to addressees in the Cc and Bcc fields, on the assumption that you may sometimes want to send the *file* only to the primary recipients, but send the *message* to a long list of other people (whose addresses are in the Cc or Bcc fields)—the most common way of doing business.

- **Recent Addresses** controls whether Entourage offers to autocomplete the last 200 email addresses you've used (ones that *aren't* in your Address Book) when you're addressing messages. Some people find this feature annoying and turn it off, but others find it useful to be able to quickly re-enter email addresses without first having to create an address book entry for them.

Reply & Forward panel

These controls govern replies and forwarded messages:

- **Include entire message in reply.** When you reply, this option adds the text of the original message, for your recipient's reference. Unless the original message is short, you'll want to edit down the original as you compose your reply.

- **Use quoting characters when forwarding.** This option adds quoting characters to each forwarded message's text. The > symbols are an Internet convention used to make it clear that *you* didn't write the bracketed text. If you turn off this box, Entourage will instead insert tags above and below the message to indicate where quoted text starts and stops.

- **Reply to messages in the format in which they were sent.** If this box is turned on, Entourage chooses the message format (HTML or plain text) according to the formatting of the *original* message. Uncheck this box to use the format you've specified on the Compose tab of the Mail & News Preferences dialog box.

- **Reply using the default account.** If this box is turned on and you have more than one email account, Entourage always uses your *default* (primary) account to send replies—even if the original message was sent to a different account.

- **Mail Attribution.** If you like, Entourage can tack on some stock text that introduces a message you're answering. As you can see in the edit box, Entourage can even incorporate the sender's name and/or email address, or the date the original message was sent into this boilerplate text. As with signatures, some people get clever with these lines, coming up with introductory lines like this: "On [DATE], [NAME] is thought to have uttered:"

- **Place insertion point before quoted text.** This little checkbox puts the cursor at the *top* of the email message when you create a reply or a forwarded message. Turn this option *on* if you like your reply to appear *above* the original message text, and *off* if you like to type your reply *below* the quoted text.

Tip: On the Internet, the most accepted practice is to put replies *below* any quoted material. In the business world, however, an email culture has arisen in which replies go *above* any quoted material—thanks to the predominance of Microsoft Outlook, which comes set to do it that way.

- **News Attribution.** Like the Mail Attribution option, the News Attribution option automatically fills in some basic information when you reply to a newsgroup message. This attribution can display the message's author, the date, the time, and the article ID of the message to which you're replying.

View panel

These controls manage how Entourage displays messages, subscriptions, and quotes:

- **Show unread messages as bold.** This checkbox is responsible for displaying the names of unread messages in bold type in the message list.

- **Show messages using these colors.** Lets you choose colors (instead of—or in addition to—bold text) to indicate which messages have been read. After turning on this box, click the color swatch next to the words "Unread and Read" to choose from a menu of 16 different colors. (Or choose the 17th option, Other, which opens the Mac OS X color picker for an infinite variety of color choices.)

- **Show Internet headers.** Turn on this box if you want to see a message's Internet *headers*—technical-looking text that details which servers the message passed through on its way to you, what attachments and encoding schemes were involved, and so on. (Even if this option is off, you can always see the headers for a particular message by choosing View→Internet Headers when you're reading it.)

- **Show attached pictures and movies in messages.** Entourage generally displays picture or movie attachments right in the message window, saving you the trouble of opening them. This option can, however, make such messages take longer to appear on the screen.

- **Toggle open threads that contain flagged messages.** If messages in a *thread* (a set of newsgroup messages on the same subject, marked by a flippy triangle) are flagged—perhaps by a Rule you've created—this option make sure that the thread is "expanded," so that you don't miss seeing the flags it contains.

- **Show newsgroups and IMAP folders using these colors.** When turned on, this option lets you color-code the names of newsgroups and IMAP mail folders to which you've subscribed or have not subscribed to.

POWER USERS' CLINIC

Exchange Server

Microsoft's Exchange Server is like a virtual file box that people on all the computers in a corporation have access to. Among a vast number of other talents, it lets everyone store (and share) email messages, contacts, calendar items, tasks, and notes. People using Outlook on Windows world have been using Exchange Server for years (whether they know it or not), but only now can Entourage mavens join the party.

Entourage 2004 lets Mac fans "talk" to their Windows brethren on a common Exchange server. You use the Account Setup Assistant to hook up with your company's Exchange server. If everything goes as smoothly as Microsoft envisioned, you need only type in your account ID, password, and domain, and Entourage does the rest. (If not, it's time to call in the system administrator.) After setup, you'll be able to:

- Send and receive Exchange-based email messages.

- Address messages by using the Global Address List that is housed on the common server.

- Share your contacts and calendar information.

- See whether other folks using the server are on "free" or "busy" status.

- View and share information through public folders—a feature of Exchange Server that provides an effective way to collect, organize, and share information with others in an organization.

Unfortunately, it's not always so easy, and covering the Microsoft Exchange Server details is beyond the scope of this book. You can, however, find more details in the Office Resource Kit at *www.microsoft.com/mac/*.

- **Color Quoting.** In this multihued box, you can change the color given to various levels of text quoting—levels one through four, at least.

For example, suppose you write to your boss: "How does it look?" She writes back to you, "How does WHAT look?"—and you see your own original query bracketed (>) and in blue type. When you reply to her, your original question now appears with *double* brackets (>>) and in the second-level color you choose here. This color-coding can make it simpler to follow a protracted discussion taking place via email or a newsgroup.

Anything higher than level-four quoted text takes on the same color as level-four quoting. To change a color, click one of the text strings in the box and select a new color from the menu that pops up.

Calendar, Tasks, and the Project Center

Computers are supposed to be ultra-efficient timesaving devices, so why is everyone more pressed for time than ever? There are reports to be written, bosses to be appeased, shopping to be done, and kids to be taken to soccer. Although Entourage can't get your kids to practice, it can help you take control of your precious time. It gives you a new tool for keeping track of the million things you need to do and the information you need to do them—the Project Center.

Entourage has perhaps changed more than any other program in Office 2004. Sure, much of its email setup is familiar (Chapter 9), and the Calendar and Tasks have been around for a while, but the Project Center is radically new. It gives you one-stop-shopping access to all the email messages, appointments, to-do items, Word documents, Excel spreadsheets, and other files connected to a certain project. A project can be a major work-related goal, but it can also represent your volunteer work, holiday festivities, kids' activities, financial planning, or any life pursuit. All you have to do is create a project and tell Entourage which items to "file" under it. From then on, everything you need for that project is at your mousetip.

This chapter shows you how to use all of Entourage's organizational goodies, starting with the Calendar and Tasks features, then how to pull them all together under the Project Center.

The Calendar

You can open the Entourage calendar either by clicking the Calendar icon in the upper left of the Entourage main window, choosing View→Go To→Calendar, or pressing ⌘-3. No matter how you open it, your calendar shows up with all scheduled events listed on the appropriate days at the appropriate times (see Figure 10-1). In fact, it can display anything from a single day to six weeks on a single screen.

Actually, you get two different calendars. In addition to the main one, there's a miniature overview calendar in the lower-left corner. (Drag the divider bar above the overview calendar to dictate the number of months it shows.)

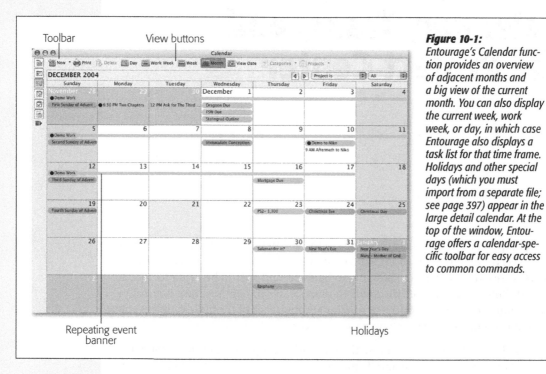

Toolbar   View buttons

Repeating event banner   Holidays

Figure 10-1:
Entourage's Calendar function provides an overview of adjacent months and a big view of the current month. You can also display the current week, work week, or day, in which case Entourage also displays a task list for that time frame. Holidays and other special days (which you must import from a separate file; see page 397) appear in the large detail calendar. At the top of the window, Entourage offers a calendar-specific toolbar for easy access to common commands.

Working with Views

Entourage offers two kinds of views: a *month view,* which looks like every wall calendar you've ever seen (see Figure 10-2), and a *column view,* which displays up to seven days' worth of events as vertical time lines (look ahead to Figure 10-3).

Displaying days, weeks, and months

To control what the main calendar window shows, use the following buttons on the Entourage toolbar or commands on the Calendar menu:

- **Day** shows the appointments for a single day in the main calendar area, broken down by time slot.

- **Work Week** depicts five columns, representing the workdays of the current week.

- **Week** fills the main display area with seven columns, reflecting the current week (including Saturday and Sunday).

Tip: If you enjoy an eccentric work schedule, you can redefine which days constitute your work "week" by choosing Entourage→General Preferences, selecting the Calendar tab, then changing the days-of-the-week checkboxes. When you choose "Work week" using the toolbar or the Calendar menu, Entourage will be happy to display columns for only Tuesday, Thursday, and Friday (or whichever days you work).

- **Month** shows the current month in its entirety.

- **List,** unlike the other views, doesn't offer a vertical grid of time slots. Instead, it creates a list of the events that you were looking at in the view you just switched from. For example, if you were perusing Day view, then List view shows that same day's events—in List format. These are the events scheduled for the current day (or days), as shown at top in Figure 10-3. Unlike the other views, List view isn't available via the toolbar, but you can choose it from the Calendar menu or by Control-clicking anywhere in the detail calendar area and choosing List from the resulting shortcut menu.

- **View Date** allows you to choose a specific date to examine. The chosen date is displayed onscreen in Day view, and highlighted in Work Week, Week, or Month view.

You can also determine which days appear in the detail calendar by selecting them in the overview calendar at the lower left of the Entourage main window. For example, to make the calendar show nothing but an important three-day stretch, simply drag the cursor across those three calendar squares in the mini-calendar at lower left (Figure 10-3). You can even drag across up to six weeks to maximize the number of days you can see in month view and get the big picture.

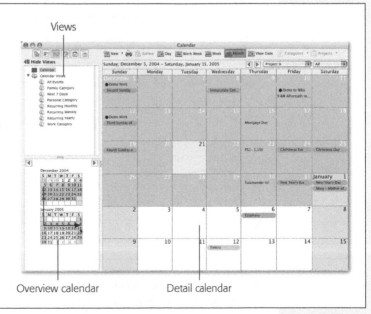

Figure 10-2:
When you drag the cursor across a set of dates in the overview calendar, the main calendar shows nothing but those days. You can select as many as six weeks worth using this method. Just drag from the first date to the last date you want to see—you can even drag across months. Boldface numbers in the overview calendar indicate dates on which you have something scheduled.

Views

Overview calendar   Detail calendar

Tip: Entourage provides a quick way to access the current day's date: Choose Calendar→Go to Today, or press ⌘-T. If you're in month view, the command displays the current month with today's date selected; otherwise, Go to Today displays information for only the current date, regardless of the view you were using.

Recording Events

Most of Entourage's calendar is intuitive. After all, with the exception of one unfortunate Gregorian incident, we've been using calendars successfully for centuries.

In many ways, Entourage's calendar is not so different from those analog versions we leave hanging on our walls for months past their natural life span. But Entourage offers several advantages over paper calendars. For example:

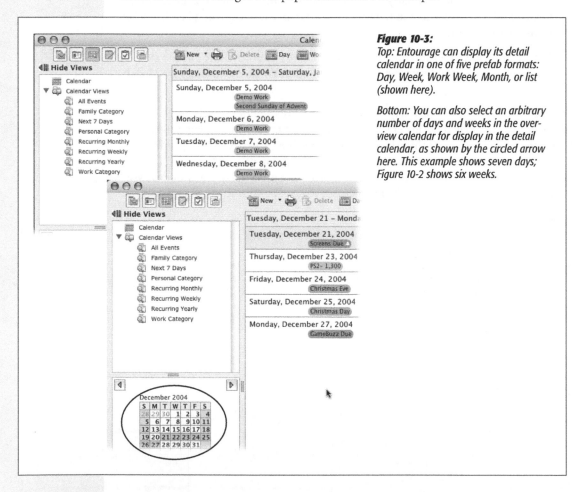

Figure 10-3:
Top: Entourage can display its detail calendar in one of five prefab formats: Day, Week, Work Week, Month, or list (shown here).

Bottom: You can also select an arbitrary number of days and weeks in the overview calendar for display in the detail calendar, as shown by the circled arrow here. This example shows seven days; Figure 10-2 shows six weeks.

• Entourage can automate the process of entering repeating events, such as weekly staff meetings or gym workout dates.

- Entourage can give you a gentle nudge (with a reminder in a pop-up dialog box) when an important date is approaching.

- Entourage can automatically send email to other people to let them know about important meetings. (Let's see one of those "Hunks of the Midwest Police Stations" calendars do *that!*)

- Entourage's calendar integrates with the new Project Center by placing important project—or email follow-up, or task—dates on your calendar

You can record an appointment using any of several methods, listed here in order of decreasing efficiency:

- When viewing a column view, such as a day, week, or work week, drag vertically through the time slots that represent the appointment's duration, and then double-click within the highlighted area (see Figure 10-4).

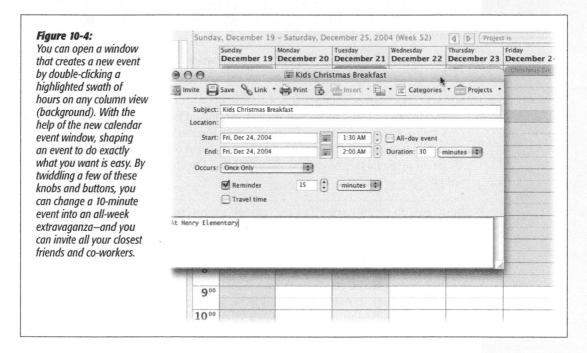

Figure 10-4:
You can open a window that creates a new event by double-clicking a highlighted swath of hours on any column view (background). With the help of the new calendar event window, shaping an event to do exactly what you want is easy. By twiddling a few of these knobs and buttons, you can change a 10-minute event into an all-week extravaganza—and you can invite all your closest friends and co-workers.

- Using either of the month views (large or mini), double-click the appropriate date.

- Click the New toolbar button and choose Calendar Event.

- Choose File→New→Calendar Event (or press ⌘-N).

In each case, Entourage brings up an untitled new calendar event window, depicted in Figure 10-4. Here's an unusually elaborate example of how you might enter an appointment:

1. **Type a name for this appointment into the Subject line.**

For example, you might type *United States Grand Prix*.

2. **Press Tab to jump to the Location field. Specify where this event is to take place. For example,** *Indianapolis.*

This field makes a lot of sense; if you think about it, almost everyone needs to record where a meeting is to take place. You might type a reminder for yourself like *My place*, a specific address like *212 East 23*, or some other helpful information like a contact phone number or flight number.

You can also leave this field empty if it's not important to you.

3. **Press Tab. Specify the starting date, if necessary.**

If you began this entire exercise by double-clicking a date in Entourage's month view, or by dragging through time slots on one of the Entourage calendar displays, then skip this step, since Entourage has automatically filled in the date you indicated. Isn't it a nice program?

Otherwise, you can change the date here in two ways. First, you can edit the date displayed here, using almost any format—12/12/02, 4-4-03, or Nov 14—to specify the date. (If you omit the year, Entourage assumes you mean this year.)

Or you can prefer to click the tiny calendar button next to the Starting Date field. A mini-calendar window appears; move to the month you want by clicking the arrows at the top, and then click the date you want (or the Today button) to close the mini-calendar. You've successfully filled in the Starting Date and Ending Date fields.

Tip: When editing a date, pressing the + key moves the date one day forward, and pressing – moves the date one day backward. The + and – keys on the numeric keypad work great for this.

---

4. **Press Tab. Specify the ending date.**

Most events, thank goodness (unless it's a weekend excursion to a Virginia Tech football game), start and end on the same day. Entourage saves you time by making that assumption, and setting both Starting and Ending dates to match. (The only time you have to type the ending date manually is if it's later than the starting date.) Entourage lets you type an ending date earlier than the starting date for an event, but complains only when you actually try to save the event.

5. **Turn off the "All day event" checkbox, if necessary, and then specify the starting and ending times.**

If you opened this dialog box by dragging through time slots on the Entourage calendar, then skip this step. Entourage has already filled in the starting and ending times for you. It is truly a prince among software.

Otherwise, turn off "All day event" (unless, of course, this event really will last all day; we've all had meetings like that). Doing so prompts the starting- and ending-time boxes to appear for the first time. You can adjust the times shown here by typing, clicking buttons, or a combination. For example, start by clicking the hour, then increase or decrease this number by clicking either of the arrow buttons or by pressing your up and down arrow keys. (Of course, you can also type a number; you might need to preface numbers less than 10 with a zero.) Press Tab to highlight the minutes, and repeat the arrow buttons-or-keys business. Finally, press Tab to highlight the AM/PM indicator, and type either *A* or *P* to change it, if necessary. (You can also press the up or down arrow keys or the Space bar to toggle between AM and PM.)

Continue pressing Tab to highlight the ending-time field.

By now, you're probably exhausted just reading the steps required to set up, say, a lunch meeting. That's why it's usually quicker to begin the appointment-entering process by dragging vertically through an Entourage calendar column display; it spares you from having to specify the date and time.

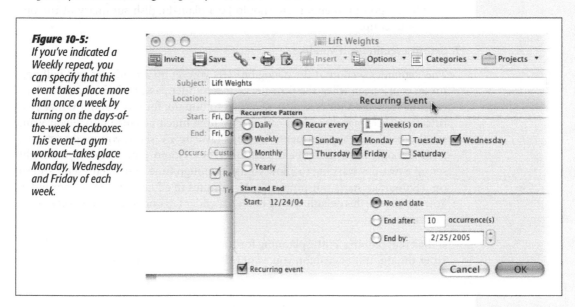

Figure 10-5:
If you've indicated a Weekly repeat, you can specify that this event takes place more than once a week by turning on the days-of-the-week checkboxes. This event—a gym workout—takes place Monday, Wednesday, and Friday of each week.

6. **Use the Occurs pop-up menu if an event will recur according to a predictable schedule.**

The Occurs pop-up menu contains common options for recurring events: once a week, on a particular day of every month, on a particular day each year, every day, or every weekday. You can select any of these items, or move immediately to the Custom option, which opens the Recurring Event window (Figure 10-5). Use the Recurring Event window to indicate how often the event recurs (daily, weekly, monthly, or yearly). Once you've clicked the appropriate button, an additional set of controls appears, offering such plain-English variations as "Every January 14," "The second Tuesday of January," "The third Tuesday of every __ months," and so on.

Tip: Unfortunately, there's a bug in scheduling recurring reminders and events. If you set the event to "Last day of month," it repeats *every day!* Until Microsoft fixes it, there's a workaround. Instead of "Last day," set it to the 31st of every month. When you save, you see a message box stating that in months shorter than 31 days, your reminder or event will occur on last day of the month—which is exactly what you want.

The bottom part of the box lets you indicate how long this event will keep repeating. If you click "No end date," you'll be stuck with seeing this event repeating on your calendar until the end of time (a good choice for recording, say, your anniversary—especially if your spouse consults the same calendar). You can also turn on "End after ___ occurrences," a useful option for car payments provided you know how many more you have to make. You can also turn on "End by", and specify a date that will cut off the repetitions; use this option to indicate the last day of school, for example.

Click OK when you've finished setting up how events will repeat. To the right of the Occurs pop-up menu, there should be a plain-English summary of the options you set up.

7. **Set up a reminder, if you like.**

The Reminder section of the dialog box lets you set up a reminder that will pop up on your screen when the time for your reminder passes. (Office Notifications must be turned on for reminder windows to pop up; for more about Office Notifications, see page 406.) You can specify how much advance notice you want for this particular appointment. For your favorite TV show, you might set up a reminder only five minutes before air time; for an important birthday, you might set up a two-day warning to allow yourself enough time to buy a present; and so on. (Entourage starts out proposing 15 minutes in advance for every reminder. You can change this default setting in the Calendar tab under Entourage→General Preferences.)

If the event requires a little planning for travel, turn on "Add travel time" and then enter the amount of cushion you want to leave yourself for traffic and the like.

Figure 10-6:
The Office Notifications program, which comes with Office 2004, handles reminders for events and tasks. When a reminder comes due, Office Notification pops a reminder window in front of whatever else is on your screen. You can then choose to deal with the matter immediately (Open), or later (Snooze)...or never.

8. **Press Tab. In the white, empty Notes area, type or paste any helpful text.**

Here's your chance to customize your calendar event. You can add any text that you like in the notes area—driving directions, contact phone numbers, a call history, or whatever. Several pages' worth of information can fit here.

If you choose to use the invitation feature described on page 395, the text you place here will be included in the email invitations you send out.

9. **Specify a category or project for this appointment, using the pop-up menu at the right end of the toolbar.**

See page 458 to read more about categories. For now, it's enough to note that Entourage's color-coded categories are helpful in distinguishing your calendar events at a glance. Family events might show up in blue, for example, and work events in red.

For more information on the Project Center, see page 410. Assigning an event or appointment to a project displays the appointment with the project, and color-codes the appointment with a circle in the color you assigned to the project.

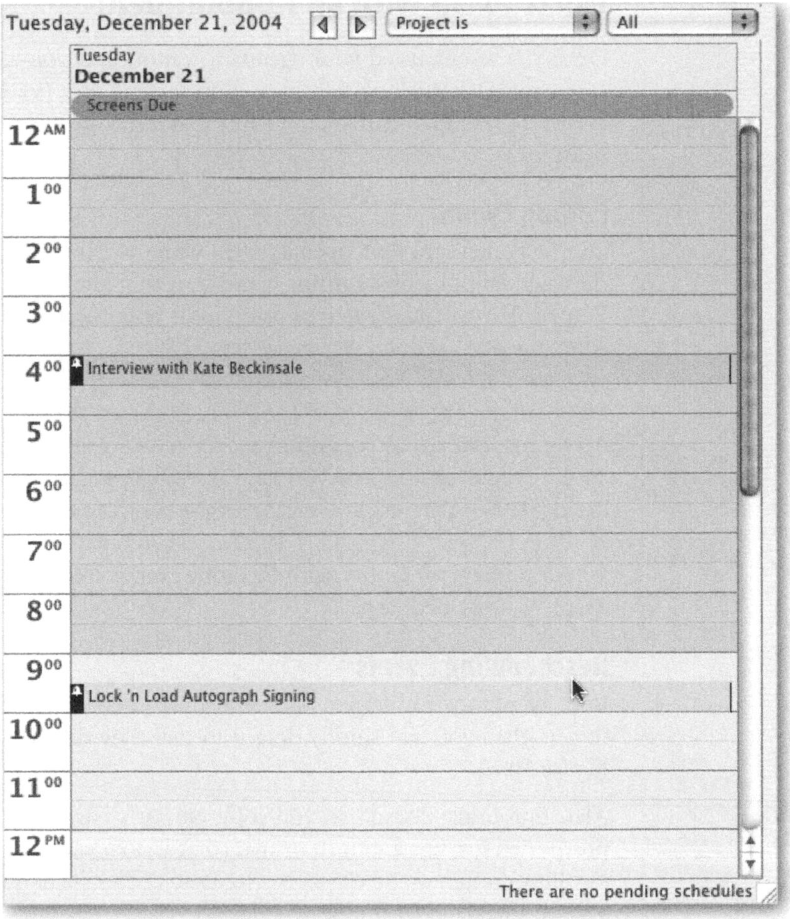

Figure 10-7:
After you've created your event, it dutifully appears in your daily calendar nestled among your other calendar events. This column view shows all-day events (or banner events) at the top of the calendar, above the start of your day. Then, each event shows up as a colored rectangle in the column. If an event has a reminder, a small alarm clock icon appears in the box; if the event is recurring, it shows two arrows in a yin-yang arrangement.

Tuesday, December 21, 2004 ◄ ► Project is ▾ All ▾

Tuesday
December 21
Screens Due

12 AM

1 00

2 00

3 00

4 00 ⏰ Interview with Kate Beckinsale

5 00

6 00

7 00

8 00

9 00 ⏰ Lock 'n Load Autograph Signing

10 00

11 00

12 PM

There are no pending schedules

Note: The date book program on Palm handhelds doesn't offer a Category feature, so the categories you assign in Entourage won't appear on your handheld.

10. **Click Save (or press ⌘-S), then close the event window (by pressing ⌘-W, for example).**

    Your newly scheduled event now shows up on the calendar, complete with the color coding that corresponds to the category you've assigned. (In month views, the text of the event itself reveals the color; in column views, the block of time occupied by the event reflects its category color.) Appointments that last longer than one day (such as vacations) appear as category-colored banners that stretch across squares on the month view; in column views, they appear just beneath the date at the top of the column (see Figure 10-7).

What to Do with an Appointment

Once you've entrusted your agenda to Entourage, you can start putting it to work. Microsoft Office is only too pleased to remind you (via pop-up messages) of your events, to reschedule them, to print them out, and so on. Here are a few of the possibilities.

Editing Events

To edit a calendar event, open its event window either by double-clicking its name on the calendar or by highlighting it and choosing File→Open Event (⌘-O) or pressing Return. The calendar event pops up in its window, exactly as shown in Figure 10-4. Alter any of its settings as you see fit.

Tip: When changing only an appointment's category, bypass the event dialog box. Instead, just Control-click the appointment's block or its name, and choose Categories from the resulting shortcut menu. Click a category to assign the event to that category. Note that it's perfectly OK for an event to have more than one category. And you can unassign an existing category by clicking it again.

You don't have to bother with this, however, if all you want to do is reschedule an event, as described next.

Rescheduling Events

If an event in your life gets rescheduled to a new date that's currently visible on the screen, then you can simply drag it to that new date to officially reschedule it (see Figure 10-8).

Alas, Entourage doesn't let you copy, cut, or paste calendar events. If something is postponed for, say, a month or two (that is, to a calendar "page" that would require scrolling), you have no choice but to double-click its name and then edit the Starting and Ending dates or times.

Note: When rescheduling a recurring event, Entourage applies the change *only* to the event you've moved, leaving the rest of the recurring events intact. If you want to change the time or date of the whole series, open the event for editing. Only then does Entourage ask whether you want changes applied to just the event you opened, or all the recurring events.

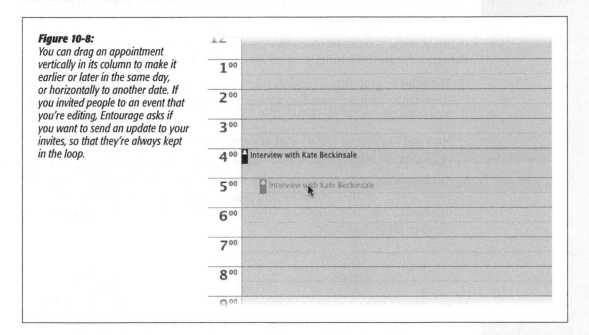

Figure 10-8:
You can drag an appointment vertically in its column to make it earlier or later in the same day, or horizontally to another date. If you invited people to an event that you're editing, Entourage asks if you want to send an update to your invites, so that they're always kept in the loop.

Lengthening or Shortening Events

If a scheduled meeting becomes shorter or your lunch hour becomes a lunch hour-and-a-half (in your dreams!), changing the length of the representative calendar event is as easy as dragging the top or bottom border of its block in any column view (see Figure 10-9).

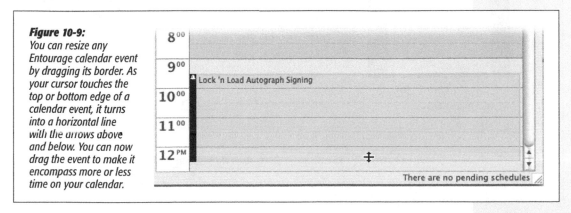

Figure 10-9:
You can resize any Entourage calendar event by dragging its border. As your cursor touches the top or bottom edge of a calendar event, it turns into a horizontal line with the arrows above and below. You can now drag the event to make it encompass more or less time on your calendar.

Printing Events

Entourage has a user-friendly way of committing your calendars to paper. To get there, click the Print toolbar button, choose File→Print, or press ⌘-P. The first thing that Office X aficionados will notice is the new print box. Microsoft has done away with the intermediate print dialog box, that displayed when printing an Entourage task or calendar. Office 2004 incorporates the same features in the OS X print dialog box.

In this window, you can exercise control over how Entourage prints your calendar by changing the control settings: Print, Start and End dates, Layout, and Form:

- The **Print** pop-up menu presents four options regarding what to print: a Daily Calendar, a Calendar Event List, a Weekly Calendar, and a Monthly Calendar (see Figure 10-10).

- **Start** and **End** let you specify start and end dates for the printout.

- **Layout** lets you choose which portions of the calendar to print: Events, Tasks, or All-day events. It also lets you specify whether *cutting lines* (for trimming your pages to fit a day planner), notes, and page numbers are printed. You can also opt to have "punch holes here" indicators printed on each sheet, for use with daily planners (described next).

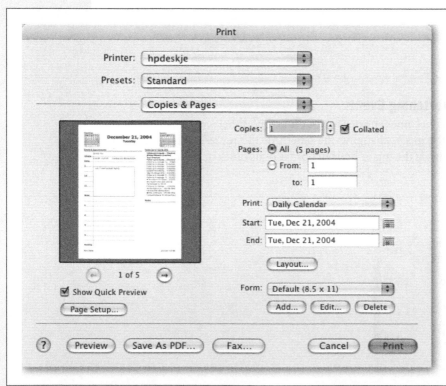

Figure 10-10:
In this window you may set the printing options for Entourage calendars. You can even shape them to fit paper planners, as shown here. If your planner brand isn't listed in the form section, click Add Form to set the margins so that they fit your printer.

- **Form.** If you use a paper-based, binder-style day planner (such as a FranklinCovey, Day-Timer, or Day Runner), you're in luck. Entourage lists canned layouts for the most popular formats in the Forms pop-up menu.

- **Standard Print Options** The other potions are identical to those presented in Chapter 1. You may choose your printer, presets, number of copies, and the page setup. Then you can preview the print job, save it as a PDF, or fax it.

Deleting Events

To delete an appointment, first select it, then either click the Delete button in the toolbar, choose Edit→Delete, press ⌘-Delete, or simply press the Delete key. In the confirmation dialog box, click Delete (or press Enter).

Tip: If you delete a recurring event (like a weekly meeting), Entourage asks if you want to delete just that particular instance of the event or the whole series.

Sending Invitations

At last it's time for you to harness the power of your combined calendar/email/address-book program. If you click the Invite button in an event window (see Figure 10-4), Entourage sprouts an Invite field. Use it like the "To:" field in an email message, as described in Chapter 9; that is, specify the email addresses of anyone that you'd like to invite to the event. If they're already in Entourage's address book (Chapter 11), you save a lot of time, thanks to the pop-up menu of addresses that match the few letters you've typed.

To compose the actual invitation, use the blank white notes area at the bottom of the Event dialog box (see Figure 10-4); this is the message your invitees will see.

Sending the invitation

Once an invitation becomes part of an appointment, the toolbar sports these three new buttons:

- **Send Now** sends an email message to everyone on the guest list (complete with the subject, location, and any notes).

- **Send Later** adds outgoing email messages to your Outbox without actually sending them. They won't get broadcast until you use the Send & Receive command, as described in Chapter 8.

- **Cancel Invitation** deletes any invitations in your Outbox that you haven't sent yet. It also sends cancellation messages via email to attendees you've already invited.

Receiving an invitation

If you're on the receiving end of one of these meeting summonses, but you don't use Entourage (or another *iCalendar-aware* email program) as your email program, you get a note like the one shown in Figure 10-11.

Caution: Even among iCalendar-aware programs, invitations don't always work perfectly. With other people using Entourage or folks using Outlook on the same Exchange server (page 380), you'll probably have good luck. In other cases, you may just get an attachment with an .ics extension. If you open an .ics file in Entourage, you'll see the event appear in your calendar, but you won't get the Accept and Decline options (page 397), and there may even be errors in the time and date. You've been warned.

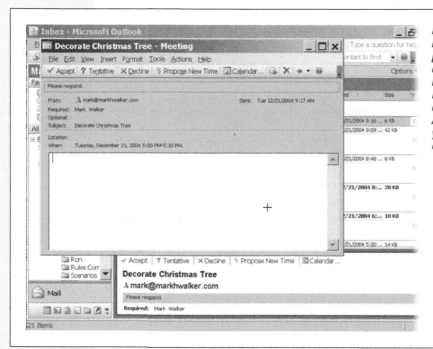

Figure 10-11:
In non-Entourage email programs like Eudora or Microsoft outlook, invitations sent from Entourage look like ordinary email messages. As in this example, even your Windows friends can view them.

But if you're using Entourage as your email program, a special thrill awaits: The invitation inserts *itself* into your calendar, complete with times and reminders (Figure 10-12). You even get a yellow banner in the email message window that lets you respond to the invitation by clicking either the Accept, Decline, or Accept Tentatively button in the toolbar. (Links with the same functions also appear in the yellow banner at the top of the email message.)

Clicking any of these links sends an email message *back* to the sender, whose copy of Entourage now offers even more surprises.

Receiving RSVPs for your invitation

Now suppose you're the person who sent the original invitation. As your invitees reply to your note, one of two things might happen:

- If you sent the invitation to somebody who doesn't use Entourage, you'll simply receive an uninspired email message that says, for example, "OK, I'll be there."

After reading this reply, double-click the event on your calendar that represents the get-together. In the event window, you'll see a yellow banner across the top of the message indicating that you've sent invitations. It also contains a "View Attendee Status" link. When you click the link, a floating window appears that lists all the people you invited, complete with a pop-up menu that lets you track their responses: No Response, Accepted, Tentative, or Decline (see Figure 10-12). Use the pop-up menu to update the list, according to the reply you just received.

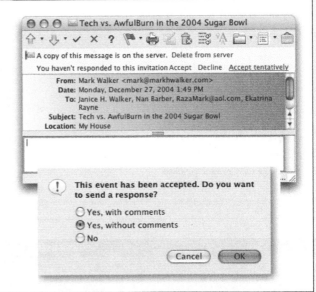

Figure 10-12:
Top: When receiving an invitation in Entourage that's from Entourage, you get Accept, Decline, and Accept Tentatively buttons at the top of the message, along with an automatic link to your own calendar.

Bottom: If you accept an invitation, Entourage asks whether you want to send a response with or without comments, or not send any response at all.

- If you sent the invitation to somebody who *does* use Entourage, life is sweet indeed. The program *automatically* updates the Attendee Status window, based on the button that your prospective guest clicked (Tentative, Accept, or Decline) upon receiving the invitation.

Whenever you change the specifics of a calendar appointment about which you've sent invitations (such as its date), Entourage offers to send an updated email message to the guests. The buttons in the upper-left corner of the event dialog box now read Send Update and Send Later.

Adding Holidays

Your Entourage calendar doesn't come with any holidays listed. In marketing a customizable calendar that can reflect the holidays of different countries, cultures, or religious beliefs, Microsoft didn't presume to know which canned events you'd want to add. Fortunately, it's easy to tell Entourage what you want.

To import a set of holidays into Entourage's calendar, choose File→Import. Entourage's Import assistant opens, and asks whether you want to import information from a program, import information from a text file, or import holidays. Choose "Import holidays" and click the right arrow.

Now Entourage presents a list of more than 40 countries and religions for which you can import holidays (see Figure 10-13). Turn on the checkboxes next to the countries or religions whose holidays you want imported, and click OK. Those holidays now appear in your Entourage calendar.

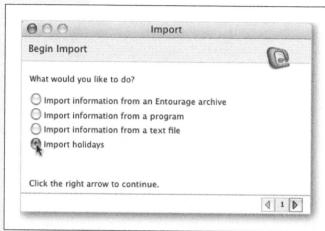

Figure 10-13:
To add holidays to your Entourage calendar, just turn on the checkboxes next to the countries or religious holidays that you want to import, and then click OK. Entourage takes care of the rest. You can import, one, some, or all of these holidays, if you like. As a convenience, Entourage labels them with the category called, as you might expect, Holidays.

POWER USERS' CLINIC

Your Very Own Holidays

The Holidays file isn't massively difficult to decipher. If you visit your Applications→Microsoft Office 2004→Office folder, you'll see a SimpleText file called Holidays. If you open it in a text editor or Word, you'll discover that it's just a simple list of holidays in this format:

Father's Day,2000/6/18

Father's Day,2001/6/17

Father's Day,2002/6/16

Father's Day,2003/6/15

Each country, region, or religion is preceded by a bracketed title and a number indicating the number of entries for the category. In other words, it's easy enough to create Holiday files of your own.

First, make a copy of the Holidays file in the Finder, and rename it something like "My Holidays." Then open your file in Word 2004; delete the existing text; type the name of each holiday, followed by a comma, no space, then the date (in year/month/day format); press Return and type the next holiday the same way.

When you're finished, type a category name and the total count at the top of the file (use the default Holidays file as an example), and then save it as a text-only file. Finally, choose File→Import, select Import Holidays, and open your customized Holiday category just as you would any other.

You can use this trick to set up a file containing any number of occasions—corporate events for the year, a softball league game schedule, church social meetings, the birthdays of your favorite rock stars, etc.—so that your colleagues can import them into their own calendars.

Note: The holiday data that Entourage imports might contain significant days that aren't technically holidays. For example, if you import United States holidays, "Tax Day" (April 15) winds up on your calendar—an example of a special day that you can observe, but probably don't *celebrate*.

Saving Calendars as Web Pages

One of the calendar module's best features is its capability to save your calendar as a Web page. You can make your calendar available to a select few (perhaps via Mac OS X's built-in Web Sharing), or you can post the result on the Internet for all to see. For example, you might use this feature to post the meeting schedule for a group or club that you manage, or to make clear the agenda for a series of upcoming financial meetings that all of your co-workers will need to consult.

Note: There's no way to include only certain categories on a Web-published calendar, so that only your corporate appointments are publicized but not your private ones. You can, of course, maintain a separate calendar under a different Entourage *identity* (see page 450 for this purpose).

Begin by choosing File→Save as Web Page. The Save as Web Page window appears (Figure 10-14). Here, you customize how your saved calendar is going to look and work. For example, you can specify:

- **Start and End dates.** This option prevents you from saving an entire century's calendar in HTML form.

- **Include event details.** Use this option if you want your Web page to include the notes that you've entered in a calendar event's Notes area.

- **Use background graphic.** Turn on this box if you want your Web-page calendar superimposed on a picture. Then click the Choose button to the right. You'll then be asked to select a graphics file from your hard drive.

Tip: To avoid the ridicule and wrath of your audience, use the graphics feature with caution. Choose only an extremely light, low-contrast image, so that the text of the calendar is still legible when superimposed over it. If possible, choose a graphic image that's roughly the same size as the calendar, too, so Entourage doesn't stretch out of shape. Also remember that downloading an enormous background image over a modem is no one's idea of a good time.

- **Web page title.** The text you enter in this box will appear as the Web page's title.

- **Open saved Web page in browser.** If this box is turned on, Entourage will open the newly saved calendar in your Web browser just after saving it, so that you can make sure it wound up the way you intended.

Once you've set your options, click Save.

Next, in the Save dialog box, name the calendar file (suppose it's *Summer Schedule*). Select a folder location on your hard drive, then click Save. Entourage creates two new icons on your hard drive—an HTML file called Summer Schedule.htm, and a folder called Summer Schedule. The folder contains a bevy of graphics and HTML files that comprise your calendar.

When you press Enter, your Web browser connects to your own Mac to call up the calendar. (If you don't get your calendar, go through the steps again to verify that everything works.)

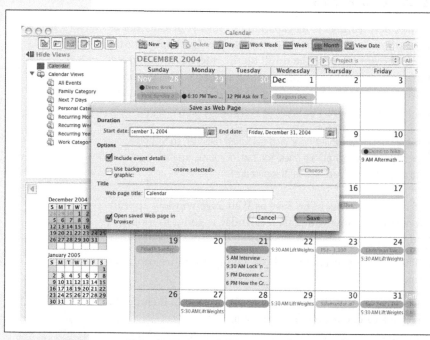

Figure 10-14:
When you save your calendar as a Web page, you can control what dates are saved for the Web and what information is included. You're welcome to give your Web page a title more imaginative than Calendar.

POWER USERS' CLINIC

Your Mac as Web Server

If you have a full-time Web connection, such as a cable modem or DSL service, you can use the Mac's own Web Sharing feature to post your calendar for the entire online world to see. A complete discussion of this feature awaits in *Mac OS X: The Missing Manual*, but here's a summary.

Open the Mac OS X System Preferences, select the Sharing pane, click the Services tab, and turn on the Personal Web Sharing box. Make a note of the IP address displayed in the lower part of the File & Web tab: It might be a name (like *mymac.example.com*) or a series of numbers (like *127.0.0.1*).

Next, return to the Finder and open your Home folder (Option-⌘-H). Once there, you'll find a folder called Sites. Drag your calendar file and folder into it.

To view your calendar, open a Web browser and enter a URL in this form:

<http://192.168.1.11/~chris/SummerSchedule.htm>

Of course, for 192.168.1.11, substitute the actual address you noted in the Services tab, replace Chris with your Mac OS X account name (preceded by a ~), and replace SummerSchedule.htm with the name of the calendar file Entourage created.

If you chose "Open saved Web page in browser" (Figure 10-14), your newly saved calendar now appears. Review it for accuracy, and marvel that it offers live links; clicking an item brings up details about it in the right-hand frame of the Web page (Figure 10-15).

Note: The Web pages created by Entourage exploit such advanced Web-browser features as frames, style sheets, and JavaScript. Not surprisingly, they tend to behave best using Microsoft's Internet Explorer browser.

If the file looks good, the final step is to upload the Web page to a Web server so others see it. Of course, this step requires that you have a Web site. You can contact your Internet service provider to find out how much Web space your account grants you and what steps are required to post new Web pages there. There's also Apple's annual $100 .Mac service, which includes up to 250 MB on the Web, along with email and other perks.

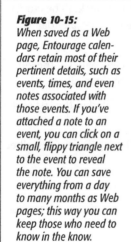

Figure 10-15:
When saved as a Web page, Entourage calendars retain most of their pertinent details, such as events, times, and even notes associated with those events. If you've attached a note to an event, you can click on a small, flippy triangle next to the event to reveal the note. You can save everything from a day to many months as Web pages; this way you can keep those who need to know in the know.

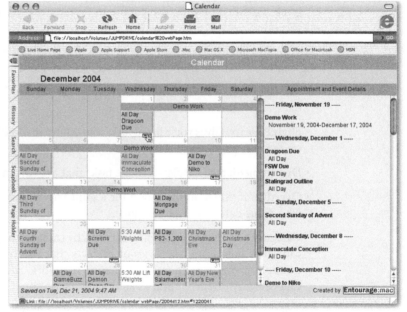

Tasks

Entourage's Tasks feature lets you make a To Do list, all the while helping you along with gentle reminders, if you so desire. And, like just about every other item in Entourage, Tasks can be linked to email messages, calendar events, the new Project Center, and even to other tasks.

You can put Entourage into Task mode either by clicking the Tasks icon at the upper left, choosing View→Go To→Tasks, or pressing ⌘-5. You get a simple list of tasks, complete with due dates and categories (see Figure 10-16).

Changing Your Views

When you first enter the Tasks module, Entourage shows you a simple list of all tasks you've entered or imported—a view which you can alter to suit your preferences. To do so, cruise over to the View menu and select one of the following:

- **All Tasks.** This screen shows all the tasks in your busy life; it's the view Entourage shows you unless you choose otherwise. It even displays the tasks you have completed—something that makes most people feel a little better.

- **Incomplete Tasks.** Displays everything that you have yet to do. In most cases this is more useful, and less cluttered, than displaying All Tasks.

- **Due Today.** Focuses on the present; this option shows just what's due today.

- **Due This Week.** Displays everything that's due in the current week. (The current week is defined by what you choose in Preferences→Calendar→Calendar Work Week.)

You can also filter the tasks with the options displayed in the View panel at the left of the window. Click the flippy triangle next to Tasks Views to see them all:

- **Changed in Last Seven Days.** Shows every task that you've edited in the last seven days.

- **High Priority.** Gives you a list of tasks that you've marked high priority (described on the next page).

- **Due Immediately.** Displays just the tasks that are currently due.

- **Overdue.** If you're in the mood for a guilt trip, you can view incomplete tasks whose due date has come and gone.

- **Category** and **Project.** You can view tasks by category or project. In this case, you can select only from categories or projects that you have assigned to tasks. For example, if you have no tasks assigned to the Work category (an ideal situation), that category doesn't appear as an organizing option.

No matter what view you select, there are five columns to the left of the tasks' names:

- **Links** (indicated by a tiny chain-link icon) shows if the task is linked to any other item, such as a message or a calendar event (see page 456).

- **Status** (indicated by a tiny checkmark icon) shows a checkbox, which you can turn on when the task is complete (or sooner, if you just need a bright spot in your day).

- **Priority** (indicated by a tiny exclamation point) is the same as the priority column found in Mail—Highest, High, Normal, Low, and Lowest. It helps you prioritize what you really *should* be working on.

- **Recurring** (indicated by a double arrow) shows, at a glance, whether the task is a one-time deal or something you must contend with on a continuing basis.

- **Reminder** (indicated by a tiny alarm clock) shows a similar alarm clock icon if you've set a reminder for a particular task—in other words, it's a reminder of your reminder.

- You specify the **Task** name, **Due Date,** and **Categories**—and new in Entourage 2004, **Project**—when you type in your to-do list, described next.

Note: If you've used the Flag for Follow Up feature (in Word, Excel, PowerPoint, or Entourage's Mail) to remind you to return to a document or message, those follow-ups appear as items in Entourage's Task list. You can edit and manage them as you would any other task.

Creating Tasks

To create a new Entourage Task , take your pick of the usual array of options:

- Choose File→New→Task.

- If the Tasks icon is selected in the upper left of the Entourage widow, press ⌘-N.

- Click the New toolbar button. (If you're not already viewing your to-do list, choose Task from the New pop-up button.)

Figure 10-16:
Entourage's Tasks toolbar includes common Entourage commands, listed across the top, and a filter box so you can quickly isolate the tasks you want to see.

The new task window appears (Figure 10-17). Conduct your task-recording business like this:

1. **Type a name for the task.**

    This will be the title that appears in your task list. You can probably come up with something more illuminating than "untitled."

2. **Change its priority, if you like.**

If you take a moment to categorize your tasks this way, you'll be able to sort your task list by priority.

3. Specify a due date for this item, if you like.

Turn on "Due date" and enter a deadline date. Feel free to use any of the same date-setting tricks described on page 388.

There's only one difference between a dated to-do item and one that doesn't have a due date: When the specified date goes by, an incomplete to-do item shows up in boldface in the Tasks window. If you double-click it, you'll see Overdue next to an attention-getting light bulb icon at the top of the task's description window.

4. If this to-do item reflects a recurring headache, such as a weekly staff meeting, use the options in the Occurs pop-up menu.

You'll be able to specify a duty that recurs daily, weekly, monthly, or yearly. The Occurs options here work much like those described for events on page 389.

Tip: If you set your task to reoccur, a new Edit button pops to the right of the Occurs pop-up menu. You can click this button to further refine the reoccurrence. However, if you turn on the "After task is complete, create a new task due in ___", then once you check off the task, the next one resets to one day (or week, month, or year) from when you got it done, not the original recurrence date. This is perfect if you have to submit a report, say, every 30 days, but not on the same day every month.

---

5. Turn on the Reminder checkbox, and set a date and time for the reminder to get in your face—in the form of a pop-up dialog box displayed by the Office Notifications program. (See page 406 for more on reminders.)

6. Make notes for more information.

Tab to the Note box to type, or paste, text that helps describe your task.

7. Assign it to a project, if you like.

If you've created any projects in Entourage's Project Center, they're listed under the Projects button.

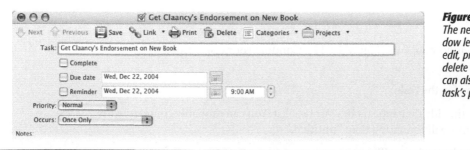

Figure 10-17:
The new task window lets you create, edit, print and delete tasks; you can also set all of a task's particulars.

If you're finished entering tasks, you can close the window (press ⌘-W). Otherwise, change the text and options in the dialog box to create another to-do list, starting over at step 1.

Other Task Tricks

Once you've recorded some to-do items, you can manipulate them in ways that should be familiar if you've used the Entourage calendar.

Editing a task

Change a task's name by selecting the task, clicking the task's name, and then waiting about one second for the editing box to appear. Type a new name and then press Enter or Return. Similarly, you can change its category by clicking in the Categories column; a pop-up menu of your categories appears.

You can change a task's priority, repeat status, and so on, by double-clicking its name in the Tasks window (or by highlighting it and pressing ⌘-O, or choosing File→Open Task). The dialog box shown in Figure 10-17 reappears, allowing you to change any aspect of a task and save it again.

Checking off a task

After finishing a task, you can celebrate by turning on its checkbox in your list. Once you do so, Entourage puts a line through the task to give you the satisfaction of crossing it off your list. If a task's window is open, you can also turn on the Complete checkbox and then close the window. (When you check off a reoccurring task, Entourage only marks that specific instance complete. The next recurrence will still rear its ugly head when due.)

Deleting a task

To delete a task, click it in the task list and then either click the Delete button, press ⌘-Delete or the Delete key, or choose Edit→Delete Task. (You'll be asked to confirm the deletion. And that's fortunate, because no Undo command is available, and the deleted task doesn't go into the Deleted Items folder; instead, it's gone forever.)

Tip: You can select multiple tasks (in preparation for deleting them en masse, for example) just as you would email messages: using either the Shift-clicking or ⌘-clicking tricks described in the box on page 338.

Printing tasks

It's easy enough to print out a list of your to-dos. To print only some of them, start by highlighting the ones you want (see the preceding Tip).

Now click the Print button in the toolbar, or choose File→Print (⌘-P). This triggers the custom Entourage Print window, which lets you choose which tasks to print (all tasks, selected tasks, tasks due today or this week, and so on), what style you want to use for printing them, and whether you want to print those pages on standard paper or special FranklinCovey, Day-Timer, or Day Runner paper.

When you finally click OK, your printer's standard Print dialog box appears. You're on your way to a hard copy reminder of the errands and chores that await you.

Linking tasks

Linking tasks to other Entourage items is a great use of the Links function (see Chapter 12), since it lets you draw connections between tasks that you're working on and any email messages, calendar events, or contacts that might be related to the task. When you have a task's window open, you can create a link with the click of a Links button, which opens the Links window. If you use the Links button as a menu, your choices let you link that task either to an existing Entourage item or to a new one that's created on the spot.

Office Notifications

After you've set up a reminder for an appointment or task in Entourage (or via the Flag for Follow Up feature in any Office 2004 program), Office 2004 will display handy onscreen alerts when your items come due. You can instruct these alerts to go away or to return later, or you can use them for quick access to appropriate appointments, documents, or messages.

Office 2004 uses a small add-on program called Office Notifications to perform the alerting. (It's in the Microsoft Office 2004→Office folder, if you're curious.) When an alert comes due, Office Notifications appears as a separate item in the Mac OS X Dock. When you've dealt with any pending items, Office Notifications vanishes, reappearing when it's time for the next reminder or follow-up.

It might sound complicated to deal with yet another program to handle alerts and notifications, but Office Notifications is straightforward. First, you can manage everything about alerts and notifications within Entourage, so you don't really feel like you're using a separate program. Second, using a separate tiny program to handle alerts and notifications means these alerts work *all the time*, even when no Office 2004 programs are running. This is a big improvement over Office 2001, where your reminders popped up only when an Office program was running. (Of course, you can turn off Office Notifications at any time, so you won't be interrupted during an air guitar solo. Choose Office Notifications→Turn Off Office Notifications, or within Entourage choose Entourage→Turn Off Office Notifications.)

Tip: If you use Microsoft's MSN Messenger and Passport services, Office Notifications can also tie in Microsoft's .NET Alerts. For instance, a shipping company might use .NET Alerts to provide status updates on a package, a bank might notify you of deposits to your account, or an auction site might let you know that an item you've always coveted is up for sale.

You can't manage .NET Alerts within Entourage. Typically, you sign up for (and configure) .NET services via a service provider's Web site and set your contact preferences using Microsoft Passport. However, you do *not* need MSN Messenger or a Passport to use Office Notifications, as described here.

The Notifications Window

When a reminder, task, or item you've flagged for follow-up comes due, the Office Notifications window appears in front of any other programs, a sound plays, and the name of the item appears. If more than one item is due, the Office Notifications window lists them all, but have to either scroll or drag the window larger to see them all. Figure 10-18 shows three different kinds of notifications: an event reminder, a Microsoft Word document flagged for follow-up, and a task set up in Entourage. The Office Notifications window also has three buttons across the bottom: Open Item, Snooze, and Dismiss. Snooze and Dismiss also act as pop-up menus; their options are covered below.

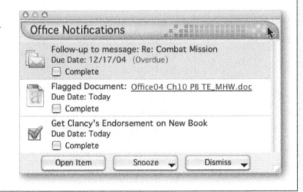

Figure 10-18:
Here Office Notifications shows three items: a reminder of an email message that's overdue for follow-up, a Microsoft Word document that's flagged for follow-up, and a completed item on Entourage's Task list.

Alerts show three basic items:

- **Icon.** An alert's icon indicates where the alert came from. For example, a reminder about an appointment displays a calendar icon (like the top item in Figure 10-18), and a flagged Microsoft Word document appears with a Word document icon (Figure 10-18, middle).

- **Title.** The Alert's title is the subject of the appointment or task you set up, or it indicates the title of the document or message you flagged.

  Flagged documents also have a blue, underlined link, which you can click to open the flagged document immediately. Opening a flagged document or message does not dismiss or snooze the alert in Office Notifications (see next page); it just brings the flagged item front and center for you to act on, so you don't first have to hunt around your mail folders (or your hard drive).

- **Due date.** Office Notifications also shows the item's due date or, for reminders of pending calendar items, how much time remains until the event. If an item is past due (like the first item in Figure 10-18), Office Notifications shows "(Overdue)" in red next to the due date.

Tasks and flagged documents also have a checkbox you can use to mark an item as complete. This checkbox actually performs two functions in one easy step: It indicates that you're finished with an item *and* dismisses the alert box.

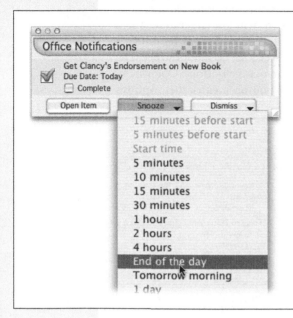

Figure 10-19:
Use the Snooze pop-up menu to specify when you'd like an alert to reappear. Some of the choices are obvious—come back in 10 minutes, two hours, three days, and so on—but some choices (like "15 minutes before start" and "End of the day") are nicely flexible.

Acting on Notifications

When a notification appears, it can be processed in one of three ways: by opening it, snoozing it, or dismissing it.

- **Open Item.** Double-clicking an item opens the corresponding task, calendar entry, or mail message in Entourage. (If an item is already highlighted, you can also click the Open Item button.)

  The Open Item button does *not* open any documents you can have flagged for follow-up. Instead, it opens the Entourage *task* that marks the follow-up, so that you can change the time, category, or other information associated with the task.

Tip: You can select multiple items in the Office Notifications window just by Shift-clicking to select a range of items, or ⌘-clicking to choose nonadjacent items in the list—exactly as in the Finder or in the Entourage email module. At that point, the Open Item button opens *all* the corresponding calendar items or tasks in Entourage, letting you see, edit, or dispose of a bunch of related items all at once.

- **Snooze.** Use the Snooze button to make an alert go away—for now. The selected item will reappear in five minutes to nag you again. If you want items to Snooze for a different amount of time (say, until tomorrow morning), use the Snooze pop-up menu (see Figure 10-19).

- **Dismiss.** Click Dismiss to make a selected alert go away, never to be seen again.

  If you want to dismiss all the items shown by Office Notifications, choose Dismiss All from the Dismiss pop-up button. All the current alerts are dismissed (although no documents or tasks get marked as completed).

- **Mark as Complete.** Use the Complete checkbox on tasks and flagged items to indicate you're finished with the task or item you flagged. Unlike other elements appearing with individual alert items, turning on the Complete checkbox both marks the task as completed *and* dismisses the alert, so that the item disappears from Office Notifications.

Note: Watch out—the program doesn't allow enough time to *un*check the box if you make a mistake. If you turn on the Complete checkbox on an item that you really *aren't* done with, you must return to Entourage's Task list, where the item appears with a line through its name. To "uncomplete" an item, turn off the Complete checkbox in the Status column (and set up another reminder, if you like).

Configuring Office Notifications

Office Notifications is a simple program, generally keeping out of sight until the moment when you want to be reminded about something. You can change only two settings: whether the program is enabled or disabled and whether or not an alert sound plays when an item comes due.

Turn Office Notifications on or off

Sometimes you might not want Office Notifications to display alerts onscreen, even if something comes due. For instance, you can be using your Macintosh to give a demo or presentation to clients—or to save the planet from extraterrestrial insect hordes. (We all have our priorities.)

Here are the two ways to turn off Office Notifications:

- In Entourage, choose Entourage→Turn Off Office Notifications.

- If Office Notifications is already on your screen, click its window once to ensure it's the frontmost program, and then choose Office Notifications→Turn Off Office Notifications.

Turning Office Notifications back on again is almost identical:

- In Entourage, choose Entourage→Turn On Office Notifications

- If Office Notifications is on your screen, click its window once to make it the frontmost program, and then choose Office Notifications→Turn On Office Notifications.

Turn Office Notifications sounds on or off

Office Notifications generally plays a sound when an alert appears. If you don't want to hear these sounds, turn them off by choosing Office Notifications→Turn Off Sounds. Alternatively, choose Entourage→General Preferences, select the Notification tab, and

---

then turn off the checkbox next to "Reminder sound." To turn the sound back on, just turn the "Reminder sound" checkbox back on.

Project Center

Entourage's Project Center is hidden behind one of Entourage's view buttons, but it's one of the most revolutionary features of Office 2004. Using Project Center, you can organize projects large and small, such as a Super Bowl party or a regional sales meeting, and track all the documents, files, and emails associated with the event in one convenient location.

Starting a Project

Before delving into the deep secrets of projects, it helps to have some experience creating your own. There's no doubt that the easiest way to create a project is with the New Project Wizard. Here's how:

1. **From the Entourage toolbar, select New→Project.**

   The New Project Wizard appears. Fill in the blanks as shown in Figure 10-20, and then click Next.

2. **On the next screen you can set your project's *watch folder* location and import items. In other words, you tell Entourage where to keep the documents you're**

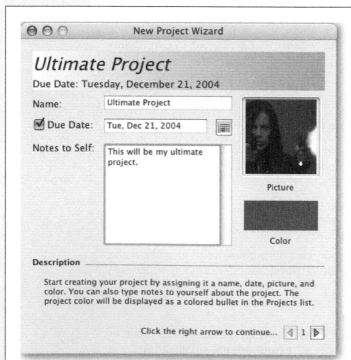

Figure 10-20:
The initial window of the New Project Wizard lets you customize your project. Drag whatever image you have pertaining to the project into the image window. (Perhaps one of your boss would look nice? Maybe not.) Choose a color by clicking in the appropriate box, and set an overall due date (you can change this later). You can also type notes to yourself about the project. You know, helpful stuff like, "When I'm done with this I can go to Jamaica."

going to use for this project and which existing items (if any) to keep with this project from now on.

If you choose to automatically create a project watch folder, Entourage creates a folder that matches your project's name. But maybe you've already accumulated some files on your Mac. You can manually set the project's watch folder: Browse to the location of the folder that you wish to set, and do so yourself. You can also set a folder within Entourage to store the project's email messages. (Something with a name similar to the project is a good idea.)

If you have an existing Entourage category or Project that you want to become this *new* project, choose it from the Category or Project menu. (If you choose a category, Entourage imports *everything* under that category—contacts, tasks, calendar events, and so on.) After you're finished, click the right arrow to continue.

3. **On the third screen, you set the rules for the project, and also decide if you want a project folder alias on the desktop.**

    Associate Email from Project Contacts. Perhaps there are contacts in your address book that are intricately involved in the project. If the project is writing a cookbook with your sisters, for example, you'll want to keep track of all email correspondences from your sisters regarding this project. Once you add your sisters to your Project (see the Tip below), all email from them gets associated with the project, too.

Tip: You can also associate contacts with the project from the Contacts tab in the Project Center at any time. Here's how it goes: Click the Contacts tab, then click the Add button on the bottom of the tab. This springs open a list of your contacts; choose your sister's name, and then click Add. Presto—she's added to your project contacts.

    Associate email with the following subjects. By the same token, you'll want to associate any emails with subjects that include the words *Cookbook* or *Recipe* to your cookbook project. Type in the email subjects you choose here.

    Don't apply other rules to these messages. It's not a good idea to apply other Entourage rules (see page 353) to project messages. Doing so can lead to some strange and unexpected filings including placing project email in non-project watch folders.

    Apply rules to existing messages. This, on the other hand, is a good idea. Clicking this box applies the new rules you just created (associating contacts and subjects with your project) to messages that you've already received. It's a nifty way to get your project off to an organized start.

    Add Project Watch Folder alias to the Desktop. Why not? It makes it easy to find and drag files to.

4. **Read the summary on the final wizard screen and check to make sure that the location of your project watch folder, as listed on this screen, is correct.**

This final page also has some helpful hints for adding items to your project, and sharing it. Click the right arrow to complete your project's construction.

The Project Center Window

To start working in a project, click the Project Center button, or choose View→ GoTo→Project Center, or press ⌘-6. The Project Center slides onto the screen, as shown in Figure 10-21.

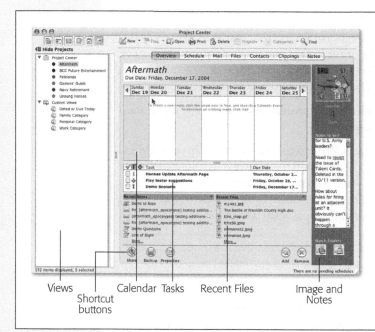

Figure 10-21:
The Project Center window provides access to all the important Project Center functions. From here you may browse an overview of your projects, check out recent emails, and open the files associated with the project, to name but a few of the feats you can accomplish.

Views   Calendar Tasks   Recent Files   Image and Notes

Shortcut buttons

The Project Center initially displays two panes beneath a familiar set of Entourage toolbar icons. The six buttons on the left of the Entourage toolbar are the same as those displayed in all other Entourage toolbars, in that they can transport you back to the Mail Center, Address Book, Calendar, Notes, or Tasks modules.

To the right of these icons is the New button, which you can click to begin your new project adventure, or to create a new whatever (email, task, contact, and so on) from the pop-up menu. You can also click the Open icon to open a highlighted project in a new window, or delete it with the Delete icon. The Find button on the right lets you search for whatever you like.

Note: The Project Center toolbar changes to complement your selection. For example, after you open a project, the toolbar provides additional options, such as flagging, printing, project, and category assignment.

Project Views

On the left side of the Project Center screen rests the view panel that lets you choose what you view in the larger viewing pane on the right. The view panel displays a Project Center and Custom Views icons. If you have several ongoing projects, the Project Center icon has a little flippy triangle adjacent to it. Click the triangle to view your projects and then click the project name to display it in the viewing window.

Click the flippy triangle adjacent to Custom Views to display the custom views options. You can choose to view all the project material dated today, or material that fits into any category that you've established in Entourage. (Unlike the other views that only show one type of material, like Mail or Contacts, these custom views contain a mixture of all of the above.) You can hide the projects panel—and get more viewing space—by clicking the Hide Projects icon.

The Project Center's right window really displays the meat of the matter. When you first open the Project Center, the window lists your current projects. Click any of the listed projects and then click Open to fill the view window with it; mouse aficionados can just double-click the project. Either way, your selected project jumps into the viewing window and you're ready to get to work.

Getting Around the Project Center

The Project Center truly shoehorns an amazing amount of information into a relatively small space, as shown in Figure 10-21.

The main Project Center view window displays the project du jour. You can customize this display to suit your viewing pleasure by selecting one of the seven tabs at the top of the window. Their descriptions follow:

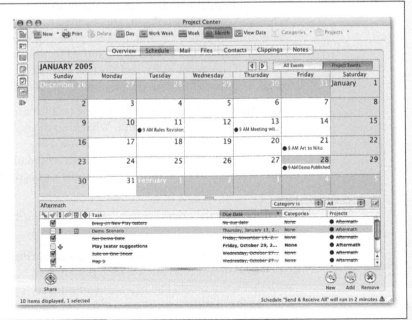

Figure 10-22:
Each of the tabs in the Project Center, like the Schedule tab shown here, gives you a window specially tailored for working on a particular aspect of your project. If you've used Entourage before, parts of the Project Center will look familiar. The Schedule tab, for example, borrows heavily from Entourage's Calendar view. The beauty of the Project Center is the way it combines Entourage's disparate features into compact views. In addition to Calendar events, the Schedule tab lets you access tasks related to the same project.

Overview

The Overview tab provides the overall project information. This is the Project Center window Entourage shows you first, and where you'll want to go to get a general feeling of the status of your project. It's extremely useful, for example, if you've been away for a long weekend and want to get reacquainted with the project. From the Overview display you can access the disparate elements of your project.

- **Calendar.** A seven-day calendar runs across the top of the Overview display. Click the arrows on either end of it to page through previous or subsequent weeks. The calendar shows events and tasks that you've set for the project. It's a great way to double-check what you really should be working on this week. Right-click any day and choose New Calendar Event to add one. Menu surfers can click the arrow beside the New button and choose Calendar Event from the pop-up menu.

Tip: Keep the names for your calendar events short, like *Dinner at Hal's.* Doing so lets the entire event header to display on the calendar. (Of course, pausing your cursor over long-winded calendar events also displays their entire heading.)

- **Tasks.** Below the seven-day calendar resides a Tasks pane. Double click a task to see more details or edit it. You can organize the tasks by any of the columns by clicking on the column header. More often than not, you'll organize them by date, unless, obviously, you have a boss who likes you to turn in your assignments in alphabetical order.

  Three columns line up to the left of the task's name: Status, Priority, and Shared. When you complete a task—or are just tired of messing with it—place a check in the box in the Status column. A task's priority shows up in the Priority column. You can double-click a task's name and set its priority in the pop-up menu (page 403). Or, if you prefer, right-click the task and select the priority from the shortcut menu. The Shared column denotes a task's shared status (page 420).

- **Recent Items and Files.** Listed below the task list are two columns worth of stuff that you've recently worked with. What kind of stuff? That's up to you: Click the title bar in either column to choose what you'd like to display. Items include Recent Items, Due this Week, Past Due, New and Recent Mail, Important Contacts, Recent Notes, and Recent Files. You can also choose a category to see all the items covered by it.

At the bottom of the Overview window are five icons that control what you can do with the project.

- **Share.** Organizing an endeavor—like co-authoring a cookbook with your sisters—as a project is a fantastic idea. But an even better one is to share the work with them. You can do that by *sharing* your project, and this button is the key that unlocks the sharing door. Sharing files and projects allows several people to share all the files and project information. Entourage creates a shared folder on a file server (like a common LAN server), an Internet FTP site, or an iDisk and moves any shared files to that shared folder. Shared files are accessible only when you're connected to the file server.

When you're working in a shared project, you must have permission to access both the shared project file and the location where it is stored. Not all files can be shared, but notes most certainly can. For more details see page 421. You'll find this button at the bottom of each view in the Project Center.

- **Backup.** Afraid that lightning might strike or that someone *will* actually invent a virus that wipes your Mac's hard drive slick? If so, you might want to back up your project and all its pertinent files. Click the back up button to open a dialog box where you can create an Entourage archive file (see page 435).

- **Properties.** Click the Properties icon to access the Project Properties dialog box as shown in Figure 10-23. Think of this as a mini-overview, one from which you can massage your project, as discussed in the box on page 416.

- **Add.** Click the small triangle to display a shortcut menu for adding anything from a task to an email to the current project. Simply choose what type of Entourage item you wish to add, scroll to it in the list box that appears, and click Add. You'll find this button at the bottom of each view in the Project Center.

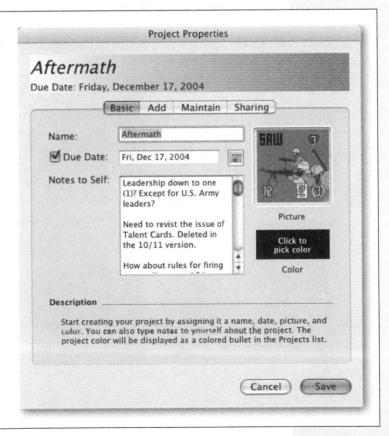

Figure 10-23:
You can change the project's picture by dragging a new picture into the picture box. By the same token, you can personalize your project with its own color. Just click the color box and do so.

Note: When using this method to add Tasks, Contacts, Messages, or Notes, you can click on the column header in the list box to sort the items you're adding by that column. But not for Events—for inexplicable reasons, your many commitments are listed by the date you created them, and clicking the headers does nothing. You're forced to scroll through them all to find the one you want!

- **Remove.** Highlight the item that you wish to remove, and then click the Remove button to do so. You'll find this button at the bottom of each view in the Project Center.

Schedule

The Schedule tab displays just about what you would imagine—a schedule of events related to your topic. From here you can look at what you need to do, and see how soon it needs to be done. The Schedule tab displays the following bevy of information:

- **Calendar.** The calendar displays the amount of time selected in the toolbar above it. The options are Day, Work Week, Week, or Month. You may also jump to any date that you wish—Super Bowl Sunday, for example—by clicking the View Date icon and filling in the information.

  Two arrows directly above the calendar let you page back and forth. One click on an arrow moves the calendar one increment (depending on the view selected

---

POWER USERS' CLINIC

Project Properties at a Glance

A very close relative of the New Project Wizard, the Project Properties box can modify basic project parameters, add folders and items, and much more. Four tabs divide the box: Basic, Add, Maintain, and Sharing.

Basic. The Basic tab lets you rename the project (in case, perhaps, your boss doesn't like the name you chose). You can also select a new due date by either typing it into the window or choosing it from the mini-calendar adjacent to the window. (If your project seems to go on forever, you can remove the checkmark beside the due date). The Notes to Self box is the place for quick jottings. (When displaying the Project Palette, you can type the notes right into the notes window—a convenient way to type short reminders or fleeting flashes of brilliance.)

Add. In this section, you can choose what folders to associate with the project, if they've changed since you first set up the project. Files in these folders show up in the list of recently used files on the Overview page and under the Files tab in

the Project Center. You can change the location of this folder by clicking on the Change button and browsing to your new folder location. To associate an Entourage email folder (and all the messages that you place in it) with your project, place a checkmark beside Entourage, and then select the folder by clicking Change and browsing to the location. Import items from other categories and projects by choosing them in the Import Items section.

Maintain. In addition to associating email messages from a particular folder, you can also associate mail from specific contacts, and with particular subjects. Using the same techniques as when setting up your project (see page 411), tell Entourage which email messages to bring into the project now or edit your original rules.

Sharing. You may have tried to go it alone, but now you need to call in some help. If you didn't share your project when you first created it (page 420), you can do so now from the Project Properties box.

---

above). You may also choose to display All Events or Project Events by clicking on the buttons to the right of the arrows.

- **Tasks.** The Tasks pane provides a list of tasks associated with the project. Double-click any of the tasks to open it. The task will open in the familiar Entourage task window. The task window also has columns that indicate special attributes of each task, including Links (a link appears if the Task includes links), Status, Priority, whether the task is recurring, Reminder, and Shared.

  The **Task Contains** pop-up menu lets you filter the tasks by their allegiance to a project or category. Choose whether to filter by project or category, and then in the adjacent pop-up menu, choose the category or project you're interested in. (You can add or remove any of the status columns to the left of the task title by right-clicking on them and choosing from the pop-up menu, depending on your level of clutter-tolerance.)

Note: At the bottom of the Schedule view are four buttons: Share, New, Add, and Remove. They do the same things as the buttons at the bottom of the Overview tab.

Mail

Clicking the Mail tab displays all of the email messages pertaining to the current project in the left-hand pane. Click the "Arrange by" title bar to see the pop-up menu from which you can choose the order to display the messages; click "Newest on Top" to alter the chronological order that the messages are displayed. Most of the choices on the "Arrange by" pop-up menu are familiar, but Show in Groups (see the box on page 337) and Edit Custom Arrangements (see page 348) are unique to Entourage's approach to organizing email.

If you double-click a message in the left panel, Entourage opens it in a garden-variety message window, and you can work with it as you normally would (Reply, Forward, and so on). When you single-click a message, it appears in the right panel. In this case, you can use the toolbar buttons to work with these messages, but some features—such as Link and Resend—aren't available.

Feel free to adjust the relative size of the panels in this Mail view. To do so, pass your mouse over the adjustment bars in the center of the panel divider. When the curser changes to a double-sided arrow, click and drag the divider. Choose View→Columns or Control-click (right-click) anywhere in the column headers to see the full list of columns available.

Tip: You can also right-click any message in the right pane, and chose from a myriad of message options, including Reply, Forward, Redirect, and so on.

At the bottom of the Email view are four icons. Share, Add, and Remove are the same icons as the ones at the bottom of the Overview tab (page 414). The fourth one, New, starts a new email message.

Files

Clicking the Files tab displays a list of files associated with your project. Specifically these are the files stored in the folder and location designated when you birthed your project. You can change the location of this folder by returning to the Overview tab, clicking the properties icon at the bottom of the window, and selecting the Add tab in the Project Properties dialog box. Under Project Watch Folders, click Change, and then browse to the folder you wish to include. Highlight the folder and click Choose.

Tip: You can see where these files are located without opening the Project Properties box. The secret: Add a Path column to the Files list. Simply right-click any of the column headers and choose Path. The other secret: You can use this trick to customize the columns in any of the Project Center's tabs.

You can open any of the files or folders in the Files window just as you would in any Finder window. Perhaps you want to send one of your project files to a friend. Well, you can do that too, as shown in Figure 10-24.

At the bottom of the Files view are four buttons, which operate much like the ones on the Overview panel (page 414), but with the following twists:

- **Share.** Click here if you wish to share this project or the highlighted file. Not all files can be shared, but most can; see the Tip on page 420.

Caution: Sharing a file *moves* it from its original location to the project's watch folder. If you're used to accessing it from somewhere else, like your Documents folder, place an alias of the file in the Documents folder (or wherever). (In the Finder, open the project's watch folder, click the file and press ⌘-L. Then drag the alias anywhere you like.) This way, you can share the document as part of your project and still have a convenient way to access it.

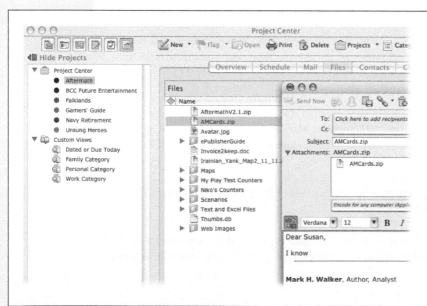

Figure 10-24:
Emailing a file to a friend (or enemy) is easy from the Project Center. First, highlight the file. Next, click the Send icon at the bottom of the window and choose whether to send the file as an email attachment or directly to an MSN contact. If you send the file as an attachment, a shiny new email opens with the file attached. Fill out the email and send it as you normally would.

- **Send**. Send a file to a friend, as described in Figure 10-24.

- **Add.** If you've previously written a file that you wish to add to the project, you can click the Add button. The Add File window slides onto the screen. Click the file that you wish to add, and then click Add.

- **Remove**. Select a file in the window and click the Remove button to remove it. This doesn't delete the file, just disassociates it with the project.

Contacts

The Contacts tab displays a list of Entourage Address Book items you've associated with the currently viewed project. Highlight a contact in the top pane to display a detailed list of their contact information in the bottom pane. You can also right-click a contact in the top pane to send the person an email, assign the contact to another project or category, copy or delete the contact, or print the contact information.

If you're looking for one particular contact, you can search the list using the pop-up menus at the top of the window. For example, if you know the company a salesperson works for, but can't remember his name, you can narrow the search to Company Contains. Just type in the first three or four letters of the company—say "Micr" for Microsoft—and you're off to the searching races.

At the bottom of the Contact view are five icons. Share, Add, and Remove work much like the ones in the Overview panel (page 414), except that Add takes you straight to a list of everyone in your Entourage Address Book. New opens Entourage's standard New→Contact window, and MSN Messenger is a quick way to launch the MSN Messenger program that Office 2004 installed on your Mac. From here, you can sign into an existing MSN account or start a new one. If any of your project contacts are also on MSN Messenger, you can communicate with them this way.

Clippings

The Clippings view displays all the *clippings* (that is, chunks of text and graphics that you've saved in the Office Scrapbook) associated with the current project. Clicking on a clipping pops its preview in the preview window, and its keywords in the key-words window, just like in the Scrapbook (page 663). If your project involves lots of clippings—perhaps a catalog containing lots of pictures, logos, and paragraphs of boilerplate text—you'll be grateful for those keywords, and you can use the pop-up menu near the top of the window to help winnow your way through the list.

At the bottom of the Clippings view are three icons: Share, Add, and Remove. Share and Remove work just like in the Overview panel (page 414). The Add button opens a small window listing those clippings you've created recently by dragging text or images to the Scrapbook. Click the one that you wish to add, and then click OK.

Notes

Perhaps you're a note-taker who enjoys using Entourage's Notes feature to copy research from the Internet or jot reminders to yourself. If you assign those notes to a project (by clicking the Projects icon in the Notes window), you'll see them listed here. The display lists the note's title, when it was created and last modified, categories and projects the note belongs to, and whether it's linked or shared.

As in other Project Center views, you can order your list of notes according to any of the column headings. If you're just interested in the most recent additions to your chest of notes, click the Date Modified column until the triangle points down. Your most recent note is listed first, and all the stuff that's old news is at the bottom of the list.

You can search the notes, as described in the previous sections, by using the pop-up menu to narrow your search. Your three narrowing options are Title Contains, Category, and Project. If you select Title Contains, you must then type all, or a portion, of the title you're looking for. Choosing category or project activates a list of categories and projects. Choose the one that you want to sort by.

At the bottom of the Note view are four now-familiar icons: Share, New, Add, and Remove. They basically work the same as the buttons in the Overview tab (page 414), except that New only lets you create a new note, and Share lets you share either the entire project or just the selected note.

Sharing

Your mother told you it was good to share, and she may just be right. Sharing projects places the project—or pieces of the project—on a common server that all project members can access. That can be anything from an individual or networked computer to an Exchange server for a huge corporation. Sharing makes collaboration easier than ever. For example, if you're performing an aerodynamic and structural analysis of adding a bathroom to a passenger jet, you might have people providing input from throughout your large design and production plant. Sharing the project lets all the people involved contribute and view files, and browse the schedule—to name but a few of the advantages.

Sharing a project

To share a project, do the following:

1. **Open the Project Center by clicking on its button on the Entourage window. Once there, open the project you want to share.**

2. **Click the Share button near the bottom of the window, and then choose Start Sharing Project.**

   Entourage launches the Project Sharing Assistant, which begins with an information screen. After reading this brief introduction to sharing, click the right arrow to move to the next screen.

3. **Pick the name of the project you want to share.**

   The pop-up menu on this screen lists all the projects that aren't shared yet.

   Now it's time to choose a location to store your shared project data. Click the right arrow to move on.

4. **Click Choose, then browse to a folder to store the shared project.**

   You can choose an Appleshare file server, an HTTP DAV server, or an iDisk. Note that you may also save the data on a hard drive on your Local Area Network—even your own Mac, if you're so inclined and your project buddies have access to it. Click the right arrow when done.

5. **Choose whether to store current project data or begin storing from this point on.**

   More often that not, it's the best idea to store current project data, so that everyone working on the project has the same information. Be aware, however, that if you do decide to share, Entourage immediately moves your files to the shared server. You may want to make yourself a backup copy first. Again, click the right arrow when you're finished.

6. **Choose whether to share new items as they're added.**

   If you choose No, you give yourself a chance to decide later whether you want to share a certain new document or note that you add to the project. If you choose Yes, anything you add to the project gets shared immediately.

Note: You can decide to share or stop sharing any project item at any time. Just click the Share button at the bottom of most Project Center panels and choose Share Item or Do Not Share item.

---

7. **Click the right arrow one last time.**

   Entourage shows you a summary screen, explaining where the project is located, and providing a couple of tips. For instance, you can identify shared items by the yellow diamond icon, and adjust your sharing policies later in Project Properties (page 416). Click Close when you're done reading.

Tip: Some items are unsharable. For example, you can't share Address Book groups, email messages, notes containing multimedia elements, or Scrapbook clips.

Sharing the shared project

Of course, what's the point of a shared project that isn't shared? And to share the project, you're going to need to tell folks about it. Well, you could walk across the hall and tell your fellow workers, but wouldn't an email be better? Here's how to notify potential new members by email.

1. **In the Project Center, select a shared project.**

2. **On the Overview tab, click on the Share button at the bottom of the window, and select "Invite people to join the project."**

3. **Click "Create email invitation."**

4. **A minty-fresh email swims onto your monitor, with your invitation written in the body and a link to click in order to join the shared project. Now just address and send it... and you're done.**

Tip: If you save your shared project to a shared folder on your computer, you won't be able to send email invitations to others. They will have to subscribe to the project manually by clicking Subscribe on the File menu.

Accessing Projects from Other Office Programs

Entourage is the place to set up your projects, but it's not the only Office program that can access and modify projects. You can view your projects from Word, Excel, and PowerPoint as well. Here are the ways:

- **Project Gallery.** You can access projects from the Project Gallery (which opens when you launch Word, Excel, or PowerPoint). Click the Project tab, select your project and click Open. You can also double-click any of the project files displayed in the Projects Gallery, or select the file and then click Open. If the Project Gallery isn't visible, choose File→Project Gallery.

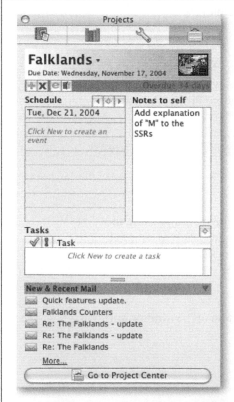

Figure 10-25:
You can also open the Project Center from the other programs in Office 2004. To do so just click Tools→Project Palette, or, if the Tool-box is open, click the briefcase button at its upper right. This panel provides a capsule view of the items in your project that you're most likely to need at your fingertips, like today's schedule, currently due tasks, and recent email messages. (For more detail, see page 667.) The Projects Palette can show only one project at a time; choose from the pop-up menu at the top to choose among them. Here, the project is called "Falklands."

Clicking the Go to Project Center button at the bottom of the Projects Palette opens the main Project Center window shown in Figure 10-21.

- **Tools menu.** Choosing Tools→Projects Palette in Word, Excel, and PowerPoint opens Projects pane of the Toolbox (page 663). Click the arrow next to the currently displayed project to view a pop-up menu with a list of all your projects. Click on the project that you wish to display.

- **Toolbox.** Click the red toolbox icon on the Standard Toolbar in Word, Excel, and PowerPoint to open the Toolbox, then click the briefcase icon to display the Projects Palette (Figure 10-25). You can get a quick overview from this panel, or for full detail click the Go to Project Center button at the panel's bottom.

Address Book and Notes

E ven if you're still living under the delusion that Entourage is only good for email, you can benefit from its built-in Rolodex function that saves all your email addresses and also full contact information, such as name, address, phone number, and photo.

But make no mistake: The names and accompanying information don't just stay locked away in storage. No, they're a hardworking lot that often offer their services as you work in Office's other programs. For example, once your Address Book contains a few names, Entourage offers to automatically complete addresses as you start typing in the To field of email messages. It can also fetch the phone numbers of people you're inviting to events that you schedule in Entourage's calendar. You can also easily include address book information in Word, Excel, or PowerPoint. You can also assign your contacts to Entourage projects (see Chapter 10). Hence, when you open up the new Projects palette anywhere in Office, you'll see all the contacts that have anything to do with the project listed there.

This chapter will show you the quickest and best ways to use Entourage to keep track of all the people in your life. It also covers one of the program's handiest but most overlooked features—the Notes module.

Address Book

The Address Book isn't a separate application that you double-click when you want to look up something; it's just one module of Entourage. You view it by clicking the Address Book icon in the upper left of Entourage's main window, by choosing View→ Go To→Address Book, by pressing ⌘-2 (and probably in dozens of other ways).

Tip: As with email in Entourage, you can opt to view your address book either as a single pane of the Entourage screen, as shown in Figure 11-1, or in a window of its own. To do the latter, Control-click the Address Book icon in the Entourage main window and choose Open Address Book in New Window from the shortcut menu that appears.

A Tour of Address Book World

The Address Book interface parallels Entourage's email view, which shows a list of messages above, the body of the highlighted message below. In the Address Book, when you click someone's name in the list above, you get a detailed view beneath. Sometimes you'll have recorded only a name; sometimes you'll have gone whole-hog, recording that person's mailing addresses, anniversary, astrological sign, and so on.

You also manipulate the Address Book list view exactly as you do with email. For example, you navigate the list and highlight selected names exactly the same way (see page 338). And you manipulate the various columns of address information just as you would with email messages. The columns give you at-a-glance information about your acquaintances—whether they have any links or flags, the person's name, company, phone numbers, email address, and category.

Tip: Entourage can show you more than 40 columns of information about each person in your address book. Unless you have either (a) a 70-inch monitor, or (b) some kind of weird obsession with detail, you can probably get by with a subset of these. To specify which columns show up in the list view, select them from the View→Columns submenu.

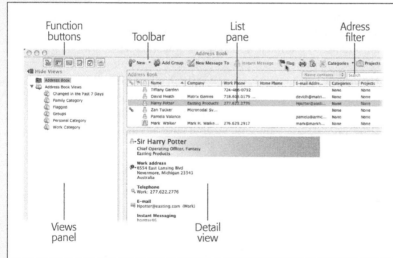

Function buttons — Toolbar — List pane — Adress filter

Views panel — Detail view

Figure 11-1:
Much like the Entourage Mail module, the Address Book window has a Preview pane showing a list up top, detailed information down below. It reveals the last time you sent a message to—or received a message from—the person whose name is highlighted, along with a plethora of other information. Like the Mail and News modules, the Address Book module has a quick-find filter in the upper-right corner. To find a certain person's information quickly, type a few letters of his name into this box.

Creating Contacts

Suppose you're already looking at your Address Book list. To open a new "Rolodex card" for somebody you know—a new *contact,* in Address Book lingo—click the New button or press ⌘-N. (If you're *not* already in Address Book view, choose File→New→ Contact, or choose Contact from the New pop-up button.)

Entourage presents the Create Contact window (Figure 11-2). You can use this window to enter basic data about new contacts, such as names, addresses, email addresses, and phone numbers.

Tip: If someone has sent you contact information via email using a vCard (usually appearing as an email attachment with a ".vcf" extension), you can drag the vCard directly to Entourage's address list. Entourage creates a new contact record for you automatically. See page 431 for more details.

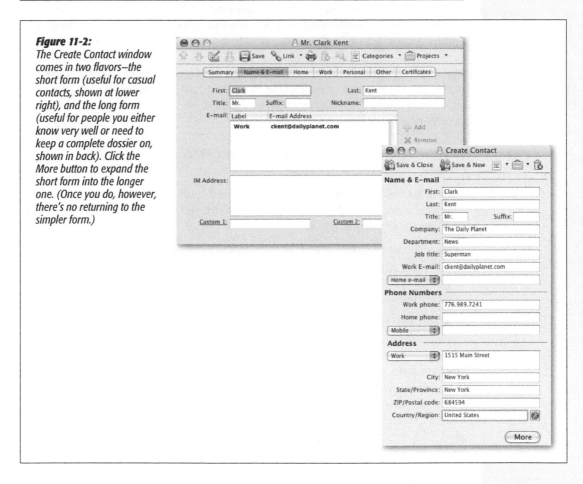

Figure 11-2:
The Create Contact window comes in two flavors—the short form (useful for casual contacts, shown at lower right), and the long form (useful for people you either know very well or need to keep a complete dossier on, shown in back). Click the More button to expand the short form into the longer one. (Once you do, however, there's no returning to the simpler form.)

Three of the fields—email, the address field, and one of the phone fields—have pop-up menus next to them for labeling the information you've recorded. You can use these to specify whether the address or email address you've just typed in is home or work, or whether a phone number is mobile, fax, or whatever.

It's not necessary to click inside each field before typing into it. As in any dialog box, you can press Tab to move the cursor to the next field (from the First Name to Last Name field, for example), or Shift-Tab to jump back to the *previous* field.

Tip: Don't bother with parentheses and hyphens in phone numbers—Entourage adds them for you. You'll find the controls for turning this feature on and off (and specifying the punctuation you prefer) by choosing Entourage→General Preferences and clicking the Address Book tab.

In an unusual, uncharacteristic Microsoftian feature lapse, Entourage doesn't automatically capitalize names. Nor is there any way to use information in a previously created contact as a starting point for a new contact. In other words, if you know 30 people who work for Microsoft and you want to enter their contact information in Entourage, you'll have to type (or paste) *Microsoft* 30 times.

Tip: Although Entourage lacks some built-in timesaving features, it is *scriptable.* If you're familiar with AppleScript, you can create a simple script that handles such repetitive tasks automatically. Easier yet: If you're familiar with the Web, you can download some excellent, ready-to-run Entourage scripts from *www. macscripter.net/scriptbuilders/.*

Once you've filled out the information in this window, you can click any of three buttons:

- **Save & Close.** Entourage stores your info, nods politely, and takes you back to the master Address Book screen. (*Keyboard shortcuts:* ⌘-S saves your new contact; ⌘-W closes the box.)

- **Save & New.** Entourage adds the person's info to its database, and then empties all of the fields in the dialog box, making them ready for you to enter the next person's contact specifics. (*Keyboard shortcuts:* ⌘-S saves your new contact; ⌘-N clears the box.)

- **More.** This button expands the form into the long form (Figure 11-2), which has places for more exhaustive information on your contacts.

The long form

If you click the More button at the bottom of the window, you've moved into *long-form* country, where the detail-oriented and information-obsessive roam (sung to the tune of "Home on the Range"). While the short-form window is great when all you need in a contact is a person's name, address, email address, and phone number, the long form turns Entourage into a giant personal information database, in which you can enter a contact's birthday, astrological sign, and even a photo.

Tip: You open the expanded version of the Contact dialog box whenever you double-click an existing contact in your address book. You can also reach the expanded form by highlighting a name and pressing ⌘-O or choosing File→Open Contact.

The long form has its own toolbar with many familiar commands (Save, Print, Delete, and so on), but a few deserve special mention:

- **New Message To.** Creates a new email message addressed to the currently open contact.

- **Instant Message.** New in Office 2004 is the Instant Message command. If you have the MSN instant messenger program installed on your Mac, clicking here opens an instant message window with the current addressee.

- **Find Related.** With one click, this button has Entourage round up all email messages that you've sent to or received from this person (and haven't yet deleted).

- **Categories.** Lets you choose a category for the currently open contact (see page 426).

- **Projects.** Lets you assign the current contact to a project, which means you'll see it in the Contacts tab of your project in the Project Center. (See page 410 for more details on projects.)

This long form window also sports six tabs along the top that you can use to enter and view more information about the currently open contact:

- **Summary tab.** Shows all of the information that you've entered about the person. If you haven't entered any contact information yet, this window is blank. The bottom of the Summary tab also displays when you last sent or received a message from the contact.

- **Name & E-mail tab.** Lets you enter complete naming information about your contact, including a title, nickname, and suffix, if any. It also lets you enter a slew of email and MSN messenger addresses.

Note: Curiously, Entourage doesn't directly offer a place for middle names or initials. You'll just have to enter them as part of the First Name. (Just watch out if you use your Address Book to fuel a mail merge!)

This window also offers *custom fields*—Custom 1 and Custom 2—where you can store other kinds of information about this contact's name and email addresses, such as what email address a person prefers to use while on vacation.

Tip: If you use one of this person's email addresses most of the time, select it and click the Make Default button to the right of the E-mail field. From now on, when you type that person's email address in a new message, Entourage will suggest that address alone as the primary address.

- **Home tab.** Shows the person's home address, Web page, and telephone numbers, along with two more custom fields—Custom 3 and Custom 4—where you can enter your own kinds of data (perhaps the person's garage color or favorite lawn fertilizer).

If you turn on the Default Address checkbox in this window, this address becomes the *default* address for that contact, the one that Entourage goes to first when you don't have a choice of addresses—for example, when you choose Contact→Map Address.

- **Work tab.** Shows the contact's work address, employer's Web page, and work telephone numbers. It also includes the contact's company, job title, and department. Once again, you get a couple of custom fields—Custom 5 and Custom 6—to handle any extra information.

- **Personal tab.** Here, you can enter your contact's birthday. It's worth typing in a couple of friends' birthdays, if only to see the raw power of Microsoft software at work: Entourage automatically calculates the astrological sign and age for your pal, saving you the math.

There's also room here for recording a spouse's name, the names of any children, your contact's anniversary, and any interests of note.

You can probably guess the function of the "Drag and drop image here" box. Yes, it's a place to paste in, or drag in, a graphics file that depicts this person for handy visual reference.

Tip: The tiny calendar icon to the right of the Birthday and Anniversary fields is a pop-up menu. It offers commands that summon a pop-up calendar for easier date selection, inserting today's date, or adding a birthday or anniversary to your Entourage calendar so that you don't forget to buy a gift.

- **Other tab.** Lets you enter notes about your contact, and provides still more custom fields—Custom 7 and Custom 8, plus Custom Date 1 and Custom Date 2—to provide places for any data that Microsoft may have missed.

- **Certificate.** Click here to choose the encryption certificate that you wish to use when sending an email to this contact. If you don't have one, you can obtain one from a digitally encrypted message sent by this contact, or by importing their encryption certificate. (This new Entourage 2004 security feature lets you send and receive emails that only you and the recipient can open and read. The certificate acts as the "key" to unlocking these digitally safety-sealed messages.)

Tip: To change the name of a custom field, click it and type in a new field name in the window that results. Click OK or press Enter—but note that you're changing this field's label for *all* "cards" in your Address Book.

GEM IN THE ROUGH

The Illustrated Rolodex

If you have a digital photo of one of your contacts, you can drag the graphics file right out of a Finder window or a Web browser and into the well at the Personal tab's right edge. Entourage accepts most standard graphics formats—even Photoshop files.

You can use any size picture, but keeping it small is wise from a disk-space and memory perspective. After all, does your address book really need an 8 x 10 image of your boss?

When you finish entering all of this information about your contact, you'll have quite an impressive dossier. Click Save (or press ⌘-S) to commit it to your hard drive When you first try to close without saving, Entourage asks you if you want to save automatically in the future when closing. If you click No, you'll be seeing this message a lot in the future. If you click Yes, Entourage saves all contacts without bugging you first. (If you should ever want to get this and similar warning messages back again, turn on the "Reset Confirmation Dialogs" button in Entourage→Notification→ Preferences panel.)

Tip: When you're processing email, you can add someone's email address to your Address Book without having to bother with all of the dialog-box shenanigans described in this section. Whenever you're looking at an open email message—or even a closed one in a list of messages—Control-click the sender's email address and choose Add to Address Book from the shortcut menu. Entourage instantly creates a new Address Book entry for that person, featuring the email address and the person's name (if they supplied it with the email message). Adding the other details is up to you.

To add information from a *directory service* search (see page 356), select the address in the search results window and click the Add to Address Book button.

POWER USERS' CLINIC

Working with vCards

You've probably received plenty of email messages that come with strange little files attached whose names end in .vcf—but unless you pay very close attention to Internet standards, you may not know what they are.

They're vCards, which were invented as a way of exchanging business-card information via email, sweeping away the drudgery of manual input forever. Although they sound like a good idea, vCards haven't really caught on; primarily because they're typically incomplete and poorly implemented (most people don't enter all of the pertinent information). Furthermore, they litter your hard drive with annoying attachments. Entourage is one of the few Mac programs that can understand vCards at all.

To pull the information out of a vCard and into the Entourage Address Book, drag the .vcf attachment onto your open Address Book. The contact information nestles itself nicely among your other contacts. If the .vcf file is on your hard drive (rather than attached to an email message), drag it into your Address Book window instead.

To send contact information as a vCard (which could be either your own electronic business card or any of your contacts'), drag a name from your open Address Book (or an entire row in a list view) anywhere onto a waiting email message. (Alternatively, highlight a name in your Address Book and then choose Contact→Forward as vCard.) Either way, your outgoing message now displays the .vcf file attached. If you want to create individual vCard files, just drag contacts from your Address Book to the Mac OS X desktop.

When using vCards, remember there's no way to choose what information Entourage includes in a vCard: nearly everything goes in, including birthdays, notes, complete home and work contact info, and even a photo if you've entered one. (A photo can make the vCard enormous, and in any case is only likely to get through to other Entourage users.) So before you send a person's vCard to someone else, be certain it's appropriate to send along everything you have recorded about the contact.

Your correspondent will be able to incorporate that Address Book "card" into her own address book, and will appreciate your timesaving gesture—if she's even heard of vCards, that is.

Opening, editing, and deleting contacts

To edit a contact you've already entered into Entourage, double-click the appropriate row of the Address Book list, or click once and then choose File→Open Contact (⌘-O). Entourage presents the Summary window shown in Figure 11-3. Click the appropriate tab to edit the details on it, just as you did to begin with.

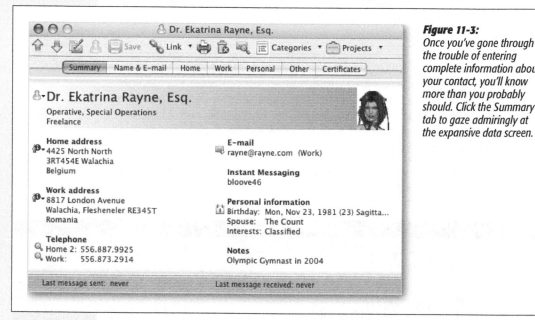

Figure 11-3:
Once you've gone through the trouble of entering complete information about your contact, you'll know more than you probably should. Click the Summary tab to gaze admiringly at the expansive data screen.

If someone is no longer part of your life—or you wish it were so—click the Delete button in the toolbar, choose File→Delete Contact (⌘-Delete), or just press the Delete key if the contact is selected in the list view. Entourage asks if you're sure you know what you're doing (there's no way to undo such a deletion).

Creating groups

As you might expect, collections of contacts fill *groups*. They make it easy to send an email message to everyone in a group in one fell swoop—just address it to the group instead of entering a bunch of single email addresses.

Here are three fascinating tidbits about groups:

• You can enter an email address into a group without having to enter it first as an independent Address Book card.

This feature may come back to haunt you, however. You may one day start to address an email message by typing *McGi*, frustrated that Entourage refuses to complete *McGillicuddy*, even though you're certain you entered Bob McGillicuddy into the Address Book. What's probably happened is that you entered old Bob into a group without first creating an independent address book card for him. (People whose names exist only in a group aren't eligible for Entourage's AutoComplete feature.)

• Someone can be a member of more than one group.

• A group can nest in another group.

To create a new group when you're viewing the Address Book, choose New Group from the pop-up menu beside New. (In other views, choose File→New→Group, or choose Group from the New pop-up button.)

Now the Group window appears. Once you've typed in a name *(Design Dept., Newsletter List,* or *Pass Jokes On,* for example), creating a group is easy. You can add people's names to the group by dragging them in from the Address Book window (Figure 11-4).

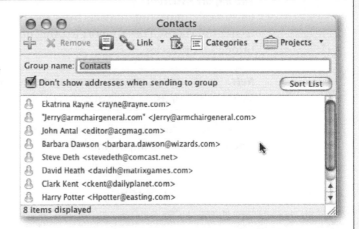

Figure 11-4:
By dragging addresses to a group window, you can quickly create a group. Turn on "Don't show addresses when sending to a group" to protect the privacy of members of that group. That way, the individual email addresses won't show on the message; however, your group's name and your own address will appear on both the From and To lines of the message. This configuration, unfortunately, makes the message vulnerable to certain spam filters, including, ironically, Entourage's own Junk Mail Filter.

If you'd rather type than drag, you can type an email address from your Address Book (which Entourage automatically completes for you), or you can enter a completely new email address as part of the group. Simply click the Add button on the toolbar, which adds a blank space in the group, ready for you to type in an email address.

Tip: You can also ⌘-click or Shift-click any number of contacts in the Address Book, and then click the Add Group button to create a new group populated with those contacts.

Importing Contacts

If you haven't used Entourage before, there's a good chance that, if you keep your addresses on the Mac at all, it's in another program, such as Now Contact, Palm Desktop, Claris Organizer, or even Netscape Communicator. "No problem," says the ever-confident Microsoft. Entourage can import contact information from these programs and several more.

Furthermore, if your little black book resides in something like a FileMaker Pro database, an Excel spreadsheet, or some obscure off-brand address software, Entourage can grab contact information from a *tab-* or *comma-delimited text file*. Most databases, and many address book programs, can save their contents in these intermediary formats, precisely to make it easier for you to transfer your life from one such program to another. If you were to open up one of these files in a word processor, you'd see that a press of the Tab key (Bob→Smith→23 Main Street→Chicago, and so on) or a comma separates each piece of information, and that a press of the Return key separates each "card's" information.

It's in Microsoft's best interest to make sure that Entourage can import as many formats as possible, because switching over to a new email or contact management program is not a trivial endeavour.

The Import Assistant

Fortunately, importing contacts from another program into Entourage *is* relatively trivial. Just choose File→Import to bring up the Import Assistant, which walks you through the process.

Note: The File→Import command begins the importing contacts, mail messages, *and* calendar events process, so you may see some references to those other data types on the Import Assistant's screens.

In the first window, choose "Import information from a program." Next, you're asked whether you want to import information from one of ten programs—Entourage 2001,

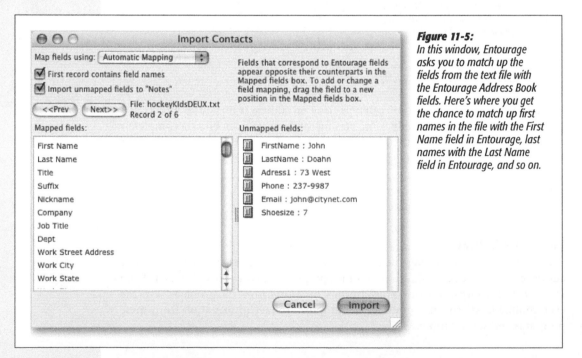

Figure 11-5:
In this window, Entourage asks you to match up the fields from the text file with the Entourage Address Book fields. Here's where you get the chance to match up first names in the file with the First Name field in Entourage, last names with the Last Name field in Entourage, and so on.

Entourage X, Outlook Express 5, Qualcomm Eudora (4.0 or higher), Apple Mail, Netscape Communicator (4.6x-4.8), Claris Emailer (2.0v3 only), Now Contact, Now Up-To-Date, Claris Organizer, This process may feel familiar; it's the same Import Assistant you saw when setting up Entourage for the first time.

Note: At the initial import window, you may also choose to import information from a text file (see below). This procedure replaces the option to import text information formally offered with the above ten programs.

If you choose to import information from one of these ten programs, Entourage asks you what information you would like to grab—such as contacts or calendar events—and then proceeds to inhale that information.

If, on the other hand, you choose to import contacts from a text file, Entourage asks you for the location of that text file. Then it opens the Import Contacts window (see Figure 11-5).

To align the fields in the list so that they match up with the corresponding tidbits of address info, drag them up or down, using the ribbed rectangular handle that appears on each line. If there are *unmapped* fields—fields from your older address book software that Entourage isn't sure *what* to do with—you can drag them from the "Unmapped fields" section into the proper place on the left side of the window.

Once you've lined up all the fields correctly, click Import (or press Enter) to bring your social circle into its new software home.

Exporting Contacts and Archives

Entourage lets you export contacts in either the time-honored tab-delimited text file or—new in Entourage 2004—to an Entourage Archive, which you can subsequently save, store, and import into another copy of Entourage (like the one on your

---

WORKAROUND WORKSHOP

Cross-platform Contact Imports

If you're moving an address book from a Windows-based program to Entourage, you won't encounter much trouble. Just export the contact list as a tab-delimited text file, which you can transfer to the Mac via network, email attachment, or disk. Then, in Entourage, choose File→Import and proceed exactly as described on these pages.

To move contacts in the opposite direction—from Entourage to a PC—export your contacts as a tab-delimited file, and then hand them off to your PC. Don't forget to append the required Windows suffix .txt to the end of your file's name. Also, when naming the file, use standard letters and

numbers; Windows doesn't accept such wacky characters as the vertical bar (|) or the asterisk (*).

Finally, note that the invisible character that ends each line in a text file is different in Mac OS 9, Mac OS X (and other Unix operating systems), and Windows. If a Windows program doesn't understand your text file, you may have better luck if you send it to the Windows machine via email (which should convert the line endings), or switch the file to Windows line endings using a program like the free BBEdit Lite (*www.barebones.com*) or the text-processing utilities you can find at *www.versiontracker.com*.

PowerBook). What makes the Entourage Archives so cool is that they can encompass so much more than tab files—not just contacts, but also emails, tasks, notes, and even calendar events.

If you want to export your contacts to a tab-delimited file—for example, to use in Excel—choose File→Export Contacts and then turn on "Export contacts to a tab-delimited text file." As you proceed through the Assistant, choose a folder location for the file, and then click Save.

If you wish to create an Entourage archive, choose File→Export Contacts and turn on "Export contacts to an Entourage archive." Then, under the archive header, choose either contacts or any other Entourage items (those in a specific project, in a category, or all items) that you wish to export by clicking on the radio buttons. If you choose items in a project or category, a pop-up menu allows you to choose *which* project or category.

You can also choose what Entourage items (tasks, email messages, and so on) you wish to archive by turning off or on the checkboxes next to the item type. For example, you may only want your contact list in order to mail greeting cards. If so, remove the checkmark from beside the other categories.

After you make your archiving decisions, Entourage asks if you wish to keep the archived items in Entourage or delete them after archiving. Err on the side of caution and keep a backup in Entourage. Next, choose a directory in which to save the items, and click Save.

Using Contacts

Once your Address Book is brimming with people, it's time to actually *do* something with all that data. Besides providing email addresses for Entourage mail, you can put all those names and numbers to work in Word, Excel, or PowerPoint, or you may assign them to projects, where they will show up along with your project in the Project Center. Here are a few of the ways you can reap the benefits of your Address Book:

Sending email to someone

Chapter 9 covers the various ways you can address a piece of outgoing email from within the email portion of Entourage. But you can also summon a preaddressed piece of outgoing email from within the Address Book itself. For example:

- Click a name in the Address Book and choose Contact→New Message To.

- Control-click someone's name and then choose New Message To from the shortcut menu that pops up.

Either way, Entourage whips open a new email message addressed to that lucky individual.

Flagging a contact

It's useful to flag someone's name in a number of different situations. For example, flagged contacts bubble up to the top of a list when you sort it accordingly (by clicking the Flag column in the Address Book list); this makes flags an excellent way to denote important contacts. And when you print your contacts, you can print just the flagged ones.

To plant that little red flag to the left of a contact, select the contact and choose Contact→Flag.

To get rid of flags, select the corresponding rows of the Address Book and then choose Contact→Clear Flag.

Using contacts in Word

Suppose you're writing a letter to someone listed in your Address Book. As you start to type the person's name in Word, a floating yellow AutoText balloon appears, as shown in Figure 11-6, showing the contact's full name. If Word has correctly guessed what you're trying to do, press the Return key while the autotext balloon is showing. Word obligingly completes the person's name for you.

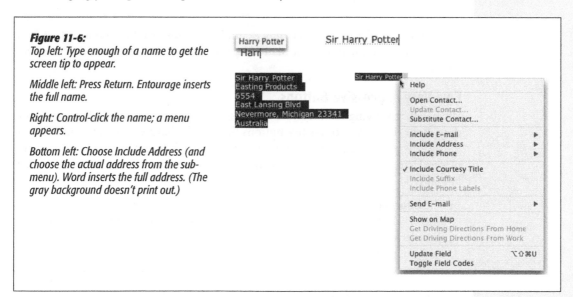

Figure 11-6:
Top left: Type enough of a name to get the screen tip to appear.

Middle left: Press Return. Entourage inserts the full name.

Right: Control-click the name; a menu appears.

Bottom left: Choose Include Address (and choose the actual address from the submenu). Word inserts the full address. (The gray background doesn't print out.)

If you *don't* intend to type a name—that is, if you've typed *will,* but Word's autotext balloon proposes William Shakespeare (a name it found in your Address Book), just continue typing without pressing Return. The box goes away. (This behavior springs from Word's AutoCorrect feature, described on page 91.)

As Figure 11-6 points out, you can Control-click an inserted person's name if you'd like to add her phone number, mailing address, and so on. The resulting shortcut menu gives you several choices:

- **Open Contact.** Opens the contact into its own window, where you can get more information or even edit the contact info, without having to launch Entourage.

- **Update Contact.** You'd use this command when editing a Word document you wrote some time ago. The command consults the Entourage Address Book and updates the name, number, or address (if it's been changed in Entourage since you first created the Word document).

- **Substitute Contact.** Brings up your contact list, so that you can substitute a different person's information. You might use this command when, for example, sending an existing letter out to a different person.

- **Include E-mail, Include Address, Include Phone.** Pastes the contact's email address, postal address, or phone number into the document. These commands are only available if, in fact, you've specified that information in Entourage. If the contact has several emails—perhaps one for work, one for home—you get to choose which to paste.

Note: Office applications only draw contact information from the currently active Entourage *identity* (more on identities in Chapter 12).

This auto-insert feature isn't the only example of Entourage/Word integration. You also encounter it when doing a Mail Merge in a Word document, as described on page 265.

Five Very Impressive Buttons

When you're viewing the expanded address book screen for somebody in your Address Book, Entourage offers five buttons that let you harness the data you've input in clever ways. These five icons appear in the contact's Summary tab, among other places. Here's a look at what they do, in the order in which you see them illustrated in Figure 11-7:

- The **information** icon sits to the left of every street address. It hides a menu that, when clicked, offers to consult the Internet for a map of, or driving directions to, the selected address (or, less glamorously, to copy the address to the Clipboard, ready for pasting into a letter you're writing in a word processor). Not surprisingly, Entourage only uses mapping services from Expedia, a Microsoft Web site.

- The globe-like **Web page** icon appears next to any URLs (Web addresses) you've entered onto somebody's "card." When you click this button, your Web browser opens the associated Web page.

- When you want to dial a contact's telephone number, click the small **magnifying glass** icon to the left of it. Doing so doesn't *dial* the phone for you. It does, however, magnify that telephone number so that it's big enough to see from several feet away (Figure 11-7).

- The **message** icon sits next to the contact's email address. When you click it, Entourage creates a new email message addressed to that contact.

- The **calendar** icon appears to the left of the Birthday and Anniversary fields. Clicking it adds a recurring event to your Entourage calendar—handy insurance against missing important birthdays or anniversaries.

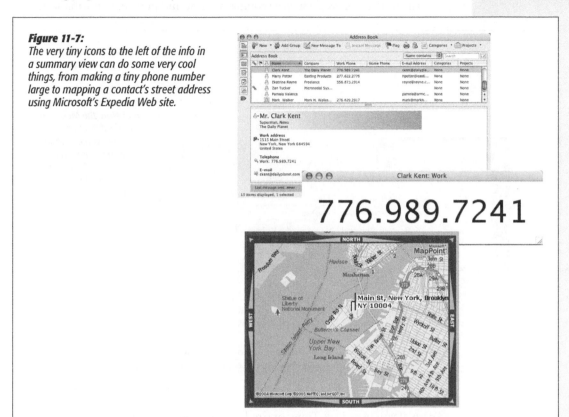

Figure 11-7:
The very tiny icons to the left of the info in a summary view can do some very cool things, from making a tiny phone number large to mapping a contact's street address using Microsoft's Expedia Web site.

Printing the Address Book

Thanks to some fine attention to detail by the Entourage programmers, you can print the Address Book in a variety of formats, specifying just the details you want to have on paper.

Start by clicking the Address Book icon at the upper left of the Entourage main window. Then choose File→Print, which brings up the Print window (Figure 11-8). In addition to a print preview, it offers four small sections:

- **Print.** This pop-up menu lets you select what to print: All Contacts, Flagged Contacts, or Selected Contacts (that is, names you've highlighted by clicking, Shift-clicking, or ⌘-clicking, as described on page 338).

- **Style.** This pop-up menu lets you choose whether you want to print a full address book (with lots of contact information per page) or a simple phone number list.

- **Layout.** The Layout button opens the Print Layout window, in which you can specify how contacts are sorted, whether first names or last names are printed first, whether cut lines and punch holes are printed, and what other bits of contact information are printed (such as company name and personal information).

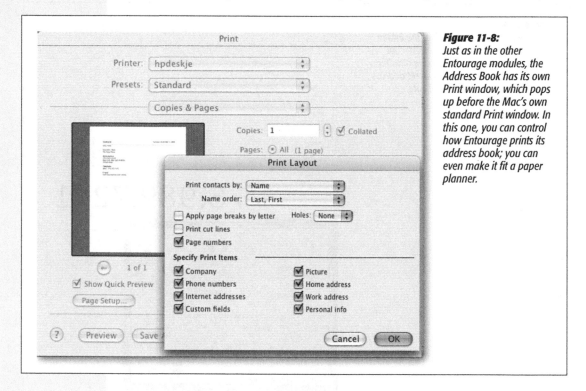

Figure 11-8:
Just as in the other Entourage modules, the Address Book has its own Print window, which pops up before the Mac's own standard Print window. In this one, you can control how Entourage prints its address book; you can even make it fit a paper planner.

- **Form.** If you use a Day-Timer or similar paper planner, you can choose a template from this pop-up menu, corresponding to the most popular precut paper types that are available at office-supply stores. You can also use the Add, Edit, and Delete buttons to create and delete your own paper designs.

The Note Pad

The oft-ignored Notes section can store random thoughts and odd things that you want to write down. You can attach a note to any other Entourage element, making it ideal for tasks like these:

- Typing in the driving directions to an event you've added to your calendar.

- Adding a record of a follow-up phone call you had with a contact to an email message.

- Adding phone-call details, physical descriptions, or Web site address to somebody's card in your Address Book.

Notes are incredibly flexible and satisfy numerous textual needs.

Notes Mode

To put Entourage into Notes mode, click the Notes icon in the upper left of the Entourage main window, or choose View→Go To→Notes (⌘-4). The right side of the Entourage main window switches over to the Notes feature, as shown in Figure 11-9.

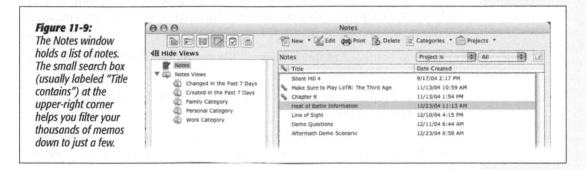

Figure 11-9:
The Notes window holds a list of notes. The small search box (usually labeled "Title contains") at the upper-right corner helps you filter your thousands of memos down to just a few.

Creating Notes

To create a new note once you're viewing the Notes list, click the New button or press ⌘-N. (If you're not already in Notes view, choose File→New→Note, or choose Note from the New pop-up button.)

You get the untitled note window shown in Figure 11-10. Type a title for the note, press Tab, and then type the body of the note into the lower, larger box (driving directions, an order number, or whatever).

As you go, don't miss the formatting toolbar that lets you add colors, fonts, and other visual spice to a note. These formatting controls offer the same HTML capabilities

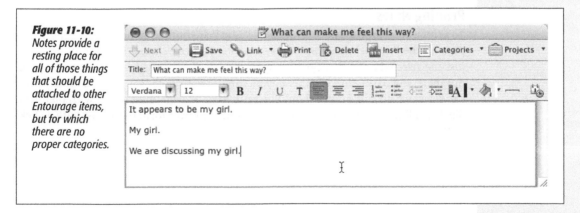

Figure 11-10:
Notes provide a resting place for all of those things that should be attached to other Entourage items, but for which there are no proper categories.

as email messages, which means that you can paste a formatted note into an email message when the day comes where you'd find that necessary. You can also paste—or drag—formatted text from another application (say, a Word document) into a note and have the text retain much of its formatting. Notes can also contain hyperlinks, pictures, sounds, movies, background images, and so on. Although Notes are mostly intended to help organize small bits of text and information, they frequently grow quite large, holding hundreds of kilobytes of text if necessary.

Once you've typed your note (or pasted text into it), just close the window, or click Save, or choose File→Save, or press ⌘-S. Your note's title now shows up in the Notes list (if you don't see it, click the Notes button or press ⌘-4). But, as John Madden would say, "Wait a minute." Now that you've got yourself a note, here are some of the cool things you can do with it:

- Link it to another Entourage element like an appointment or contact (page 456).

- Save it as a separate file (Control-click the note in the list and choose Execute Script→Save Selection.)

- Give it a Category (page 458), so that you can keep all your family-related notes together, for example. (Control-click the note and choose from the Category submenu.)

- Assign it to a Project, as described in Chapter 10. (Control-click the note and choose from the Projects submenu.) This way, every time you open the Project Center or Projects palette (page 410), all your notes taken-on-the-fly will be in one place, along with email and everything else you need for that project.

To delete a note, highlight its name in the list and then click the Delete button in the toolbar, or choose Edit→Delete, or press ⌘-delete.

Tip: Notes like linking to other Entourage elements (calendar appointments, for example). Don't miss the discussion of Links that begins on page 456.

Printing Notes

To print a note, choose File→Print, or click the Print button in the toolbar. Entourage puts up the Print window for Notes, in which you can choose to print all notes or just the selected ones. You can also specify those notes are laid out (cut lines, page numbers, and so on) and whether any pictures in your notes get printed. Finally, you can select whether the notes should be printed in a format that works with planners like FranklinCovey or Day-Timer, or even add your own form to that list with a click of the "Add form" button.

Advanced Entourage

S ince its introduction in Office 2001, Entourage has grown into a superhero among time management and communications programs. Although the last three chapters have plumbed the depths of Entourage's colossal primary modules, this vast program has even more power up its software sleeve. This chapter shows you a few more ways to harness the program's seething mass of muscle, including:

- **Palm Synchronization.** How to synchronize the data on your Palm (or other handheld) with your Mac.

- **Searching.** How to find a particular scrap of information in the Entourage haystack of events, messages, and contacts.

- **Linking.** How to link bits of data to each other, forming a useful web of interrelated events.

- **Categorizing.** Placing your Entourage messages in categories.

- **Apple Scripting.** Running Apple Scripts to enhance your Entourage experience.

Palm Synchronization

For those who believe that organization is the key to life—those who believe if they can just get all those meetings, reports, and schedules into one, all-encompassing database—Entourage offers synchronization with Palm and its descendants (Handspring, Sony, and so on). For everyone else, there are notepads available at your local grocery store. But seriously folks, one of the most exciting aspects of Entourage is its ability to synchronize the information in its Categories, Address Book, Notes, Calendar, and Task modules with the Palm's corresponding programs, so that you can carry the

Mac-based details of your life around in your pocket. Every time you make a change to this information, either on the handheld or Mac, the next HotSync (synchronization) session updates both machines so that they contain the identical information.

In fact, if you've decided to entrust your calendar, address book, and other databases to Entourage (instead of that grocery store notepad), you can safely retire Palm Desktop, the software that normally stores your Palm's data on the Mac.

Note: Unfortunately, although most Palm-compatible models include a little email program called Palm Mail or VersaMail, Entourage can't synchronize your email messages with it. You'll have to be content with sending your Entourage calendar, addresses, notes, and to-do lists to your palm.

About Conduits

Conduits are small programs that sit in the Library→Application Support→Palm HotSync→Conduits folder. Each translates a different kind of data between the Palm and your Mac. For example, your Palm came with one conduit apiece for the Date Book, Address Book, Memo Pad, and To Do programs, each designed to shuttle information into the Palm Desktop program.

Note: You'll need Palm Desktop 4.0 or later for Entourage's Handheld Synchronization to work. Although you don't have to use or even open Palm Desktop, you do need it installed on your Mac. If your handheld doesn't get along with that program, you can't sync with Entourage either. Sorry.

But these aren't the only conduits available, as you're about to find out. Various software companies have introduced new kinds of conduits that let more kinds of Palm data talk to more Mac programs. (There are conduits for FileMaker Pro, Quicken, and Apple's iCal program for example.)

When an installer puts a new conduit in the Conduits folder (as Entourage is about to do), the HotSync software will have a new way of moving information to and from your Mac and Palm. Fortunately, Entourage is clever enough to move the existing conduits out of its own way, into a folder called Disabled Conduits, to avoid confusing your Mac. Otherwise, you might wind up with, say, two side-by-side Address Book conduits—one designed to send the Palm's data to Entourage, and the older one designed to send it to Palm Desktop.

Tip: If you're lucky enough to own an Apple iPod music player, you don't need a Palm organizer just to carry your little black book around in your pocket. You can transfer your contact list right to the iPod, where you can scroll through it using the new Contacts menu (latest iPod software update required). All you need is the AppleScript program called Entourage to iPod. It's a free download from the Apple Web site or from *www.missingmanuals.com*.

Installing the Software

Once upon a time, Office required you to download the Handheld Sync Installer from an obscure Microsoft Web page, but such is no longer true. The installer lives happily on your Mac inside the Applications→Microsoft Office 2004→Additional Tools folder.

Running the installer

To install the Entourage conduits, double-click the Handheld Sync Installer icon and follow the instructions on the screen. Several things happen during this installation process. First, Entourage creates a folder called Disabled Conduits inside the Library→Application Support→Palm HotSync folder and moves the original Address, Datebook, Memo, and To Do conduits into that folder. Then it installs Entourage Conduit into the Conduits folder. From now on, whenever you press the HotSync button on your palm's cradle or cable, Palm Desktop won't "hear" anything that goes on; Entourage is the new Mac home for your Palm's data.

Tip: If you decide that Entourage isn't for you, you can always return to Palm Desktop. To do so, you'll have to uninstall the Entourage conduits. Do that by moving the Entourage Conduit file out of the Palm→ Conduits folder (into, say, the Disabled Conduits folder). Then move your handheld's original conduits (now in the Disabled Conduits folder) back into the Palm→Conduits folder. Your Palm will once again HotSync to the Palm Desktop software.

Conduit Settings

Now that the Entourage conduits are in their proper places, it's time to set them up to perform as you want them to when you hit the HotSync button. To do this, open the HotSync Manager program.

You can get to it in either of two ways. You can click and hold the Palm Desktop icon in the Dock and choose HotSync→Conduit Settings, or you can simply find the HotSync Manager program in your Applications→Palm folder. Either way, the Conduit Settings window appears.

With the Conduit Settings window open, double-click the Entourage Conduit entry (see Figure 12-1). You'll be faced with the Entourage Conduit Settings window, in which you can edit the HotSync settings for the Address Book, Calendar, Notes, and Tasks. The idea behind synchronization is to combine two different sets of data (such as the notes in Entourage and the notes on your Palm) so that they match. Most of the time, a HotSync does just this. But every now and then, you may want one of these other options:

- **Synchronize.** Entourage will compare its data with the Palm's data and merge the two together. Any new or edited items on either side of the cable show up in both places after a HotSync; your Mac and Palm are now mutually up to date.

- **Entourage overwrites handheld.** You may occasionally prefer this option—such as when you've made a mess of the data on your Palm, for example. When you HotSync, your Entourage data will wipe out, and replace, your Palm's data.

- **Handheld overwrites Entourage.** On the other hand, suppose you want your Palm's data to replace what's on the Mac (after a hard drive crash or sale of your old Mac, for example). This choice is the opposite of "Entourage overwrites Handheld." It copies your Palm's data to Entourage, overwriting the data in Entourage in the process.

- **Do Nothing.** If you'd rather not wait for your Entourage addresses and appointments to be transferred—perhaps because you want to update only your FileMaker data or only one Entourage module—then select this option. Your Palm's data and Entourage's data won't intermingle at all.

These four choices appear in a pop-up menu next to the Address Book, Notes, Calendar, and Tasks labels (Figure 12-1), letting you choose one of these synchronization types for each module.

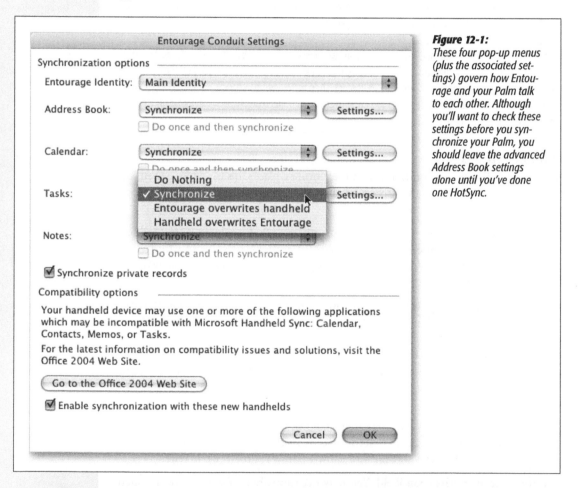

Figure 12-1:
These four pop-up menus (plus the associated settings) govern how Entourage and your Palm talk to each other. Although you'll want to check these settings before you synchronize your Palm, you should leave the advanced Address Book settings alone until you've done one HotSync.

Below each pop-up menu is a "Do once then synchronize" checkbox. If you turn on this box, then whatever setting you've just made in the pop-up menu will take effect only for one HotSync cycle—the next one. After that, the pop-up menu will automatically reset itself to Synchronize mode. That's a useful arrangement if, for example, you want to have the data in your Palm overwrite the data in your Entourage right now, but synchronize thereafter.

Private records

The checkbox at the bottom of the dialog box pertains to addresses, notes, to-dos, and appointments that, on your Palm, you've designated as private. (Preference settings on the Palm let you mask or completely hide records you've marked this way until a password is correctly entered.) Entourage offers no equivalent feature; if private records are moved into Entourage when you HotSync, they're no longer private. If the security of such records on your Mac is a concern, turn on "Don't synchronize private records" and they'll simply remain on your Palm, hidden as always.

Special settings

The Settings button (to the right of the Address Book, Calendar, and Tasks pop-up menus) opens a second settings window; Figure 12-2 shows an example.

Note: Microsoft suggests synchronizing your Palm at least once before changing the settings here. The reason: After you change the conduit settings, Entourage's data will *overwrite and replace* the current copy of your Palm's data. In other words, if Entourage hasn't already been brought up to date with your Palm, you might lose data in your Palm's address list, to-do items, or calendar.

These options vary by Palm module. Each lets you limit the syncing to just one category, and also lets you govern the syncing in other ways:

- **Address Book.** In this Settings box, you can specify which Entourage address (Home or Work) you want transferred to the Palm, for example (see Figure 12-2).

- **Calendar.** Because memory is precious, and Palm memory especially so, Entourage can automatically delete old events from its calendar—a change that will keep your Palm similarly cleansed and updated. That's the purpose of the "Synchronize calendar events in this date range only" controls; after all, how often do you look up appointments you had last year?

- **Tasks.** The "Synchronize incomplete tasks" option tells your Palm to delete tasks from its To Do list once you've marked them as having been completed, which saves you space in your handheld's limited memory. (The items stay in Entourage as completed Tasks until you delete them.)

Doing the HotSync

After establishing your conduit settings, press the HotSync button on the front of your Palm cradle (or on your HotSync cable). It should connect to your Mac and start synchronizing its information with Entourage.

Alas, the complexity doesn't end there. Although Entourage and Palm have similar groups of data, they don't correspond precisely—and that can cause problems.

How the data differs

Because Entourage data and Palm data differ slightly in some key areas, you might experience some oddities when you synchronize the two. Here's a look at the shared data and how it differs.

- **Categories.** The category names you create on your Palm come across to Entourage, but not all of the ones you create in Entourage move across to your Palm. Only categories attached to records (names, appointments, tasks, and so on) get transferred. If it's very important that the categories on your Palm and Entourage match, create and edit them on your Palm first, and then synchronize the two.

  Furthermore, although Entourage can handle an unlimited number of categories, your Palm can only handle 15 for each program (Address Book, Memo Pad, and so on). Therefore, if you have 37 categories assigned in Entourage, all of which you're using in your Address Book, you're bound to lose a few categories when transferring to your Palm. Remember, too, that Palm category names can only be 15 characters long. (Entourage category names can be nearly endless.)

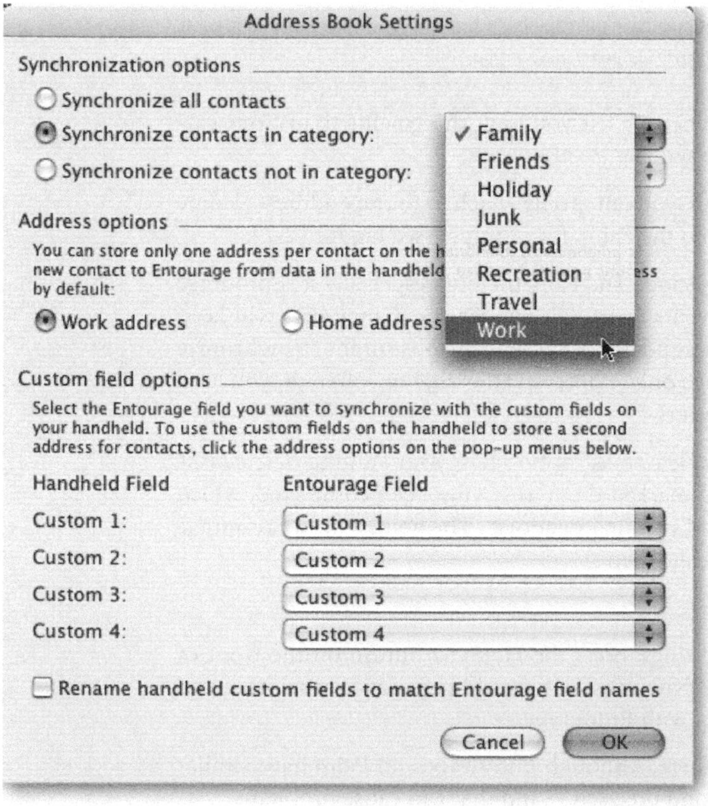

Figure 12-2:
Here you can tell Entourage and your Palm how to match custom fields and exactly which address—work or home—to use when synchronizing. (The Palm offers room for only one address.) You can also opt to place custom fields from your Palm's Address module into one of the four custom fields in Entourage.

Another anomaly: An Entourage item can have more than one category at a time, but a Palm item cannot. When an item with multiple categories gets transferred, the Palm keeps the Entourage item's primary category.

Finally, the Palm Date Book doesn't offer a categories feature at all, so Entourage calendar events with categories attached may lose their category flags on the Palm.

Tip: In the Settings box, you can limit syncing a certain kind of data to all records in just one category, or all records that aren't in a certain category.

- **Address Book.** Your Palm offers four custom fields in your Address Book; you can label them Birthday, Spouse Name, Latest Hair Color, or whatever you desire. Entourage, on the other hand, can handle 10 custom fields. To specify which custom fields you want synced to the Palm, open the Settings box shown in Figure 12-2.

  Furthermore, Entourage can handle two addresses per person in your Address Book, whereas the Palm only offers a single address listing. As a result, you'll need to tell the Entourage conduit which address to use when synchronizing with your Palm. Here again, you specify which address you want synced using the Settings box illustrated in Figure 12-2.

- **Calendar/Date Book.** Entourage can store more data about a calendar event than your Palm can. As a result, such Entourage items as the event's location, invitees, travel time, and its category don't migrate to your Palm.

  And, although your Palm can handle recurring calendar events, be warned: If you change one event in a recurring series on the Palm, your Palm turns it into a separate event that's no longer connected to the series. Each individual appointment still finds its way into Entourage, but Entourage no longer treats it as a single repeating event.

  Finally, the Palm doesn't treat multi-day events (which appear as a banner across the Entourage calendar) the same way Entourage does. Instead, the Palm treats

---

TROUBLESHOOTING MOMENT

Troubleshooting Sync Problems

Even after all those notes and precautions, the HotSync process is a fragile one. After all, it consists of getting two vastly different computers to exchange information without you doing much at all—almost wishful thinking in the world of high technology.

If synchronization fails miserably, it's unlikely that the Entourage conduit itself has anything to do with the problem. Unfortunately, HotSynching in general has a reputation for flakiness on the Mac.

If your HotSync never gets started or never finishes up, check to make sure that all the cables are plugged in solidly. Be sure that you're using the latest version of Palm Desktop for Mac OS X. If you're using a USB Palm cradle (or USB adapters), unplug the connector and refinish it after the Mac has finished starting up; doing so often forces the Mac to reload the Palm USB driver software. If you're still having trouble, contact your palm's tech support number.

---

such an event as a one-day thing that repeats daily until the "banner" ends. But when you sync your Entourage calendar, such an appointment appears only on the first day of the "banner" when transferred to the Palm. You're supposed to tap it, tap Details, and turn it into a daily-repeating event manually, which makes the whole notepad from the neighborhood grocery look much more attractive.

- **Tasks/To Do List.** Priorities on your Palm's To Do list and Entourage's Tasks are different: Entourage offers priority labels called Highest to Lowest, while your Palm ranks priorities from one to five.

  Also, although you can set up alarms (reminders) for your Entourage task list, the Palm doesn't offer alarms for To Do items. Don't expect alarms that you've associated with "Turn in IRS tax forms" on the Mac to make your Palm start beeping at the appropriate time.

  Finally, although you can set up Entourage To Do items to repeat at regular intervals, the Palm's To Do program doesn't offer this feature. When you sync your Palm with Entourage, only the first occurrence of a recurring task makes it to your Palm.

- **Notes/Memo Pad.** Each "page" of the Palm Memo Pad program can only contain 4 K of text (about a page-and-a-half of writing). Entourage notes, on the other hand, can be much longer. When you sync your Entourage data, therefore, any Entourage note larger than 4 K gets chopped off when it makes it over to your Palm. (Furthermore, if you've used HTML formatting in your Entourage notes, the formatting disappears in the move to the Palm.)

Note: Be careful editing such memos on the handheld; when you perform your next HotSync operation, the truncated memo replaces the full-length one in Entourage. That's because, during the synchronization process, Entourage sees the version on your Palm that's been edited after the item in Entourage, so it assumes that the truncated version is the latest, and thus the one to keep.

Multiple Identities

Trying to master every last feature of Office 2004 could drive almost anyone into schizophrenia.

When Microsoft refers to multiple identities, however, it's talking about an Entourage feature that lets several members of a family, school, or work circle use the same program on the same Mac—but maintain independent calendars, email accounts, mailing list info, rules, messages, preferences, signatures, to do lists, address books, and so on.

You'll find reference to these *identities* throughout the Office 2004 suite. For example, the currently selected Entourage identity is the source of names for the AutoText feature in Word, as described on page 93. (That's also why you can't edit or switch identities while Word, Excel, or PowerPoint are open. They depend on the currently active Entourage identity for some information.)

To some extent, of course, Mac OS X makes the Identities feature obsolete. After all, everyone who shares a Mac OS X machine generally signs in with a name and password as it is—and therefore each person's mail, calendar, and other information is *already* separate. Still, there's nothing to stop you from using Identities on Macs where the user-accounts feature isn't turned on (because it's just you and a spouse, say, with no secrets from each other), or when you want to create different identities for *yourself* (a Work and a Home collection of email, for example). For more detail on handling multiple users and identities, see the box on page 452.

Creating a New Identity

When you first set up Entourage, you get a single identity. (Of course, you can have multiple email *accounts* within that identity.) To create a new identity, proceed like this:

1. **Quit all Microsoft Office programs except Entourage. In Entourage, choose Entourage→Switch Identity (Option-⌘-Q).**

    (Just be careful not to hit *Shift*-⌘-Q, which logs you off your Mac!)

    Entourage asks you if you really want to switch identities.

2. **Click Switch.**

    The identity management window opens (Figure 12-3). In this window, you can create, rename, or delete a selected identity (or quit Entourage). Be careful before you delete an identity. Once an identity's gone, you can't retrieve any of its information.

Tip: If you turn on "Show this list at startup," Entourage will offer a tidy list of identities each time you start up the program, making it easy to specify which identity to use for that session.

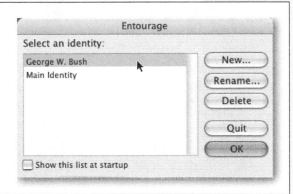

Figure 12-3:
Any identities that you create in Entourage show up in this window. Use the three buttons along the right-hand side to create, edit, or delete those identities.

3. **Click New.**

    The small New Identity window pops up.

4. **Type a name for your new identity.**

Choose a descriptive name for the new identity.

5. **Follow the Setup Assistant.**

Once you've chosen a name for your new identity, Entourage asks you if you want it to be your default email program. Your reply here actually changes a system-wide setting in Mac OS X, so this choice will apply to *all* your Entourage identities.

After you choose Yes or No, Entourage walks you through the Setup Assistant to create your new identity—a process identical to what you did when you first set up Entourage (see Chapter 9). When you're done, Entourage opens its main window, displaying that familiar "Welcome to Entourage" mail message in your new Inbox.

Finding Messages

In a short time—shorter than you might think—you'll collect a lot of email messages, contacts, and other Entourage items. Trying to find a particular morsel of information just by browsing becomes impractical. ("I remember reading something about a good deal on Mac memory in some mailing-list posting just last week. Now where the heck did I file it?…")

Fortunately, Entourage includes a powerful search feature that can help you find what you're looking for. Even better, you can save these searches as Custom views so you

UP TO SPEED

Identities vs. Multiple Users in Mac OS X

Identities are for convenience, not security–that is, they're not guarded by passwords. Anyone sitting in front of your Mac can switch among your Entourage identities at will, read your email, modify or delete your contacts, calendar items, or even delete your identity altogether.

To protect your data with a password, you should set up individual accounts for each person who uses your Mac, instead of using Entourage identities. At its core, Mac OS X is a multiuser operating system, and each account holder has his own desktop, Documents folder, programs, bookmarks, music and picture collections, and more–all of which can be protected from other people who use the same machine. You set up user accounts in the →System Preferences→Users panel. See your Mac OS X Help program for more details.

If you've already set up identities in Entourage before you've created Mac OS X user accounts, more work is involved. Each

identity that you've created is represented by its own folder in the Home→Documents→Microsoft User Data→Office 2004 Identities folder of whomever first set up Mac OS X.

To straighten out your folder setup, you can move the identities to other Mac OS X users. First, log in as the Mac OS X user who has the Entourage identities you want to move. Find the appropriate identity folders within your Office 2004 Identities folder, and then drag (or copy) them to your Home→Public folder.

Next, have other account holders log in. Once they've done so, they can navigate to your Public folder and copy the appropriate identity folders to their own Home→Documents→Microsoft User Data→Office 2004 Identities folders. The next time each person opens Entourage, the copied identity will be in place, revealing only that person's email, calendar, and so on.

can use them again later—a handy timesaver if you find yourself often performing similar searches.

The Find Window

To conduct a basic search, choose Edit→Find (⌘-F) to display the Find window (Figure 12-4). Although the basic Find window is small, it offers a wealth of search features. For example:

• In the Find box, type the word or phrase that you're searching for.

• Click "Current item" to search for the specified phrase within the currently selected item (such as a message or note).

• Use the pop-up menu to search for the phrase within just one facet of Entourage: Messages (your email), Contacts (your addresses), Calendar Events, Tasks, or Notes. If you can't even remember which of these features contains the elusive message, you can choose All Items—but be prepared to rent a video during the time Entourage will take to search its entire multi-megabyte database.

Figure 12-4:
The basic Find function in Entourage is a simple window with a single text field and a couple of controls to help you narrow your search. Use this feature when you're searching for a single item that you're pretty sure is in a specific message or location.

UP TO SPEED

A Quicker Find

Entourage's Find window is a simple tool to use, but for quick searches, Entourage has included something that's even quicker. Located in the upper right of the Entourage window is a quick and dirty find function that let's you rapidly search, the message's From, To, or Subject field. Look through messages related to a specific project or category, or ask the search engine to search for matches that either contain or begin with the letters you've typed. This is a handy tool,

| Inbox (Search Results) | Subject | contains | peace of mind |

for example, the email folder you're currently working in.

To do so, just type your search in the search window and press Enter (or wait two seconds after typing for Entourage to begin the search). You can use the two pop-up menus to the left of the search window to restrict your search to

especially if you can't remember if the message came from Mr. Jones or Mr. Mones.

Other Entourage views (Notes, Tasks, Address Book, and Calendar) have a search field in the same place, with various pop-up menus that let you tailor your search accordingly.

- If you turn on "Search subjects, titles, and names only," Entourage restricts its search to just those things, *greatly* speeding up the search. Now, instead of having to "read" every word of every message, address, and set of driving directions, for example, Entourage can just skim their titles.

- Click More Options to open the Advanced Find window, described next.

After specifying how and where you want to search, click Find or press Return. Entourage begins its quest.

Once the search is wrapped up, the results appear in a Search Results window. It looks very much like an email folder window, with a small set of columns indicating an item's type and status; columns for Title, Date, and Category; plus a standard Entourage toolbar along the top of the window. If your search turns up lots of results, you can sort the found items by any of these criteria, just as you'd sort your Inbox window.

Advanced Find

Suppose you want to search for a message containing the term "Rosebud" from your friend *c_kane@example.com*—a message that came with an attached file. Performing such a pinpoint, multiple-criteria search would be impossible using the Find methods described so far.

The Advanced Find dialog box, on the other hand, lets you build complex searches like this one with just a few pop-up menus.

To use Advanced Find, choose Edit→Advanced Find, press ⌘-F, or click More Options in the Find window. As shown in Figure 12-5, the resulting mega-Find dialog box is divided into three sections:

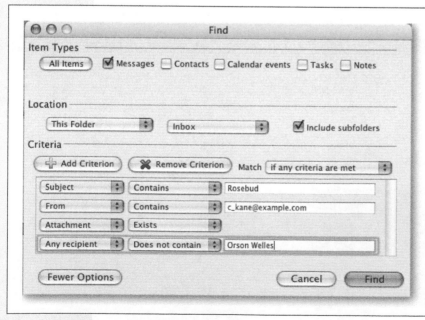

Figure 12-5:
If you happen to be looking for messages with the subject of Rosebud sent from c_kane@example.com, but you want only the ones with attachments that weren't sent to that busybody Orson Welles, then Entourage's Find window can handle what you want.

- **Item Types.** Use the checkboxes in this section to select any combination of Messages, Contacts, Calendar events, Tasks, or Notes to search. If you've got time to burn, you can click All Items to turn them all on.

- **Location.** This section lets you confine the search to the email folder listed in the "Only in this folder" pop-up menu—a huge timesaver. If you turn on "Search subfolders," Entourage also searches through the folders *within* the selected folder, if any. (These options apply only to mail and newsgroup messages, not calendar items, tasks, and so on.)

- **Criteria.** This is the heart of Advanced Find's power, where you specify exactly what you are—or are not—looking for. Using the pop-up menus, you can choose any of 25 different characteristics for the email message or other Entourage tidbit you're looking for: who it's from, whether there was an attachment, whether it's junk mail, its category or status, and so on.

Once you've selected a criterion from the first pop-up menu at the left, use the second pop-up menu to tell Entourage what it is about that criterion that you're looking for, such as a subject that does not end with "izza." (Figure 12-5 shows an example.)

As if these controls didn't let you be specific enough, you can layer on additional criteria by clicking the Add Criterion button. Each time you do so, you get a new row of pop-up menus to further refine your search. See Figure 12-5 for an example.

POWER USERS' CLINIC

Custom Views

After you've performed a search, the results appear in a Search Results window. If you save the search results window as a custom view, you in effect save the search itself, enabling you to repeat the same search over and over without the work of opening the Find window.

For example, you could set up a custom view that rounds up only the messages that are less than a week old, from your boss, with a subject line pertaining to your current project.

To save a custom view, perform a search using either Find or Advanced Find, and then choose File→Save As Custom View (or click the Save As Custom View button in the search results window toolbar). This brings up a window that looks like the Advanced Find window, except that it has room for you to name your search. Give it a name ("Baxter Project Emails," for example) and click OK. Your search now appears with its own icon in a section of Entourage's Custom Views function, as shown here.

Entourage comes with dozens of prefab custom views, sorted into categories based on their search criteria: Mail Views, Address Book Views, Calendar Views, and so on. A special category called Combined Views (Project Center) contains searches that span more than one Entourage function, like one that hunts through both tasks and calendar items. The canned views look for contacts in certain categories, for messages received today, and so on.

To perform one of the searches described by a custom view, just click its name; Entourage automatically shows the matching items on the right side of the main window, temporarily hiding all others. Custom views you create yourself (such as "Budapest" or "Anniversary Msgs & Events" illustrated here) appear in categories related to what they search. If your custom view searches email and newsgroup messages, it'll appear under Mail Views, and so on.

If you're into logic puzzles, you can also use the Match pop-up menu to indicate whether you want to see search results that match any of your criteria, all criteria, or none of the criteria.

Find Related

Entourage has another way of searching for items—the Find Related command. It lets you find all email messages to or from an individual person in one fell swoop—a handy technique when there are hundreds or thousands of messages in your message list, and you're trying to find the messages that constituted a particular correspondence.

To use this feature, open your address book. Click the name of a person listed, and then choose Edit→Find Related. Entourage searches for any messages sent to or received from that person. The results appear in a Search Results window, which you can save as a custom view, if you like.

Links

The Link command lets you weave your own web of connections between Entourage items. You might use it to connect, for example, someone in your address book to a specific calendar event *and* to all of the messages sent to and from that person *regarding* that calendar event, for example.

Once you've set up such a link, you can use it to quickly open the event to which it's linked. When you've linked an item, a small link icon appears in the item's listing in Entourage's main window. To open a link, click the link icon and select a linked item from the menu that pops up (see Figure 12-6).

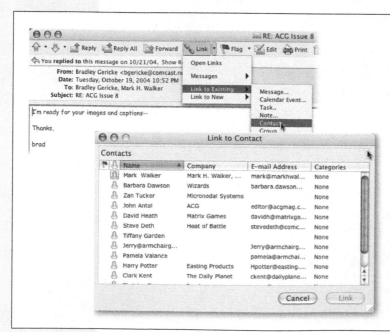

Figure 12-6:
Top: To create a link, choose from the Links pop-up button on the toolbar.

Bottom: After you've created a link, you can use the Link button as a menu, or click it to open a separate window showing all linked items. The submenus list the different categories of linked items you've set up. In this example, you can jump directly from the Links window to the contact window of any of the four people who'll be coming to the meeting, as well as the messages and notes linked to the meeting.

You create a link like this:

1. **Select the item that you want to create a link for.**

   For example, click the name of an email message, click an item on your calendar, or highlight the name of one of your to-do items.

2. **Choose from the Tools→Link to Existing submenu to create a connection with a piece of information already in Entourage.**

Tip: You can also click the link in the Links column (if the Link column isn't visible, right-click on the header bars and select Links), which displays the Links pop-up menu. From the pop-up menu, you can surf over to linked messages or link to new or existing messages, calendar events, tasks, notes, contacts, or groups.

In the good old days (that is, in Office X) a Link Maker window opened, but no more in 2004. Now, when you choose Link to Existing, you must also choose what you want to link to (message, task, or whatever). After doing so, the "Link to" window opens, where you can browse to the Entourage item you want to link to, highlight it, and click the Link button as shown in Figure 12-6. Presto-chango! You're linked. If, instead, you want to link to an empty, brand new Mail Message, News Message, Calendar Event, Task, Note, Contact, or Group, choose from the Tools→Link to New submenu. (Here again, you can also use the Link pop-up button on the Entourage toolbar to produce the Link to New submenu.)

Entourage creates the corresponding tidbit (email message, calendar event, or whatever) right away and lets you fill in the details on the fly. When you save the new item, Entourage automatically forges the link. For example, if you link somebody's address book card to a new mail message, Entourage creates a new mail message for you to address and fill out.

Using Links

A tiny chain-link icon appears next to linked Entourage items. In Office 2004 you can click the link symbol and choose Open Links to open the Links window. Click on a linked item in the Links window to instantly (well, actually semi-instantly…you know how computers are) open that item.

To view the Link window, use one of these techniques:

- Click the chain-link icon that appears next to a linked item and select Open Links.

- Open an item that displays the chain-link icon, and then use the Link pop-up button on the Entourage toolbar as a menu, as in Figure 12-6.

- Highlight an icon that shows the chain-link icon and then choose Tools→Open Links.

The Links window, lets you go beyond simply opening link items. Its toolbar buttons—Open, Remove Link, Link to Existing Item, or Link to New Item—let you open the item to which the link leads, remove a link, or create a link to new or existing items, respectively.

Categories

Categories are labels that you can apply to just about any Entourage item. They're designed to let you apply an organizational scheme to a group of items that don't have much in common.

For example, you can define a category related to a trip that you're taking, or to a certain work project, and apply that category to dissimilar Entourage information bits (calendar, email, and to-do items, for example). Each category can have its own color, making it easy to identify at a glance. Categories, in other words, are a convenient, easy-to-use means of helping you organize and keep track of your Entourage information. In pre-Project Center days, you may have used Categories to associate related items in Entourage. Now you can import those categories directly into a project (see page 410).

Setting Up Categories

Entourage comes with eight prefab categories—Family, Friends, Holiday, Junk, Personal, Recreation, Travel, and Work. If you import holidays into Entourage—see page 397—they show up in a category of their own.

Note: Don't confuse Categories with Entourage 2004's brand-spanking-new Projects feature. Although both are methods for organizing information, the projects do much more than merely assign an organizational label to an item. See Chapter 10 for details.

You can also create new categories, of course. To do so, choose Edit Categories from the Categories pop-up button on the toolbar, or choose Edit→Categories→Edit Cat-

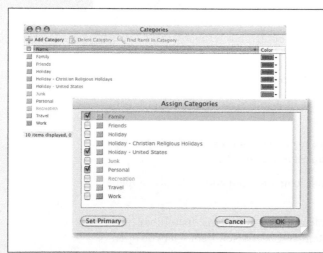

Figure 12-7:
Top: Entourage lets you create any number of your own categories, which you can then apply to Entourage items of any kind—including folders in your email box.

Bottom: To assign multiple categories to an item, open the Assign Categories window and then turn on the checkboxes next to the categories you want to assign. Once you've done so, click OK; Entourage assigns all checked categories to the selected items.

egories. Either way, you now face the Edit Categories window (Figure 12-7). To create a new category, click New and type the name you want. Entourage assigns a color to your new category, but you can choose any of the 13 colors listed on the pop-up menu, or choose Other to mix your own color.

You can also delete a category, by clicking its name and then clicking Delete.

Tip: The Categories window has one other nifty feature: the Find Items in Category button. Select a category for which you'd like to search for items, and then click this button. Entourage shows you a tidy listing all of the items in your Entourage world—messages, tasks, and so on—that have been assigned to that category.

Assigning a Category

To assign a category to an Entourage item—an email message, calendar event, task, note, news message, contact, or even an item in the email Folder list—simply highlight it. (You can also highlight several at once, if that's what you want to do.) Use the Categories pop-up button in the toolbar or the Edit→Categories submenu to choose a category. Entourage assigns the category to the selected item for you and changes its color accordingly.

Tip: The main window for certain kinds of Entourage information, including email messages, tasks, notes, and the Address Book, includes a column called Categories. One of the easiest ways to apply a category to an item is to click in this column, if it's showing; a pop-up menu of your categories appears.

You can even place an individual Entourage item into more than one category. To do so, click the Categories button (or press ⌘-comma) to bring up the Assign Categories window (Figure 12-7), in which you can assign as many categories as you want by turning on the appropriate checkboxes. For instance, a note with flight information might pertain to both the Travel and Work categories. (You can do the same thing by choosing Edit→Categories→Assign Categories.)

Tip: You can assign more than one category to an item. Only the primary (first) category determines the color of the item.

Checking Your Spelling

In parts of Entourage that involve lots of text (such as notes and mail messages), you can ask Entourage to check your spelling for you. Although Entourage can do this on the fly by marking suspect words with a red squiggly underline, it also has a more traditional spell checker at its disposal.

To use Entourage's spell checker, open the note or message that you want to check and then choose Tools→Spelling (Option-L). The procedure works like it does in Word (see Figure 12-8), and in fact relies on the same spelling dictionaries.

The Script Menu

There's no more conspicuous badge indicating that Microsoft has gotten Macintosh religion than its embrace of AppleScript, the Macintosh-only programming language. As a happy result, even advanced-beginner programmers can automate the Office programs with custom features.

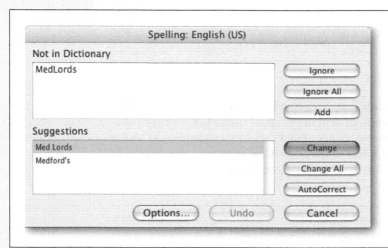

Figure 12-8:
Entourage's Spelling window flags questionable words; you click the buttons on the right to ignore, add, or correct those words. The Options button at the bottom is a direct link to the Spelling preferences, in which you can control aspects of how spell checks are conducted.

Like its sibling Outlook Express, Entourage has some impressive AppleScript capabilities. (In fact, Entourage is the only Office program that *doesn't* exploit Microsoft's own programming language, Visual Basic for Applications.) It even has a Script menu that houses several AppleScript scripts, which add useful features like:

- **Create Event from Message.** When you highlight an email message and choose this command, Entourage creates a new calendar event based on the message. All you have to do is fill in a few details. Even better, the event is automatically linked to the original message.

POWER USERS' CLINIC

Adding a Shortcut Key to Script Menu Items

You can add a keyboard shortcut for any script in the Entourage Script Menu Items folder.

First, locate the file's icon in the Finder. (You'll find it in your Home→Documents→Microsoft User Data folder→ Entourage Script Menu Items folder.) Onto the end of its file name, just tack a backslash (\), the letter c, and then the modifying key that you'd like to use. For example, to add

the shortcut key equivalent to an archive email script, add the following text to the end of its file name: \cA. (That first character is a backslash.)

The next time you pull down the Script menu in Entourage, you'll see your key combo (represented by the ^ symbol, which designates the Control key, and the key that you chose) next to the script's name.

- **Insert Text File.** When you choose this command, Entourage opens the Choose a File dialog box, so that you can locate a text file to insert into the body of a message. This feature can be handy when you want to send quick, canned responses from time to time.

- **Save Selection.** Here's a great way to save some critical information that's been emailed to you into its own text file on your desktop. Highlight some text, choose Script→Save Selection, and then provide a file name and location when Entourage asks for it.

The best thing about this menu, however, is that you can add your own scripts to it. (Of course, writing such scripts requires some familiarity with programming AppleScript.) Save such scripts as compiled scripts (not text files or applets), and then drop them into your Home→Documents→Microsoft User Data folder→Entourage Script Menu Items folder. They'll show up in the Entourage Scripts menu the next time you run the program.

If you aren't an AppleScript programmer, you can still capitalize on this feature by downloading scripts that other people have written. For example:

- *www.macscripter.net/scriptbuilders* is Apple's own page on script editing, offering helpful instruction.

- You can find a hearty collection of Paul Berkowitz's Entourage scripts at *www.applescriptcentral.com.*

- *www.webmastermac.com/article.php/20040117014023822* is an awesome collection of AppleScript links. For more information about AppleScripts in Office 2004, please see Chapter 21.

Part Three:
Excel

3

Chapter 13: Basic Excel

Chapter 14: Formatting and Charts

Chapter 15: Advanced Spreadsheeting

Basic Excel

The best ad Microsoft ever ran for Excel went like this: "99% of spreadsheet users use Microsoft Excel. What are we doing wrong?" It was good because it was true; Excel is the biggest thing going when it comes to hard-core business programs. But Microsoft still seems determined to keep finding ways to make it better, warming the hearts of accountants and statisticians the world over.

Excel 2004 sneaks in a few subtle new features like Smart Buttons—they look familiar 'cause you've seen 'em in Word. Also new is the Page Layout view, which displays your spreadsheet on the monitor exactly as it will look when printed (Windex streaks excepted). Charts in Excel 2004 have also been vastly improved, as have the means to edit and check your work.

Spreadsheet Basics

You use Excel, of course, to make a *spreadsheet*—an electronic ledger book composed of rectangles, known as *cells*, laid out in a grid (see Figure 13-1). As you type numbers into the rectangular cells, the program can automatically perform any number of calculations on them.

Opening a Spreadsheet

A new Excel document, called a *workbook,* is made up of several pages called *worksheets.* (More on the workbook/worksheet distinction in Chapter 15.) Each worksheet looks a great deal like a traditional spreadsheet, with lettered columns and numbered rows. The letters and numbers provide a quick way to refer to the cells in the grid—it's a lot like the game Battleship. (In fact, with a lot of time and some sophisticated programming skills, you could even *play* Battleship using Excel.)

You can create a plain-Jane Excel workbook by selecting File→New Workbook (⌘-N), or you can use the Office Project Gallery (File→Project Gallery). The Project Gallery lists preformatted spreadsheets, complete with formulas already inserted. If you happen to find a template that fits what you're trying to do, such as planning a budget, the Gallery can be a real timesaver. (See page 657 for more on the Project Gallery.)

Tip: You can also open an existing document by choosing from the list of recent files at the bottom of the File menu. If you'd rather Excel not keep track, you'll find the "Recently used file list" control by choosing Excel→Preferences→General panel. This is also the place to change how *many* recent files show up in the File menu.

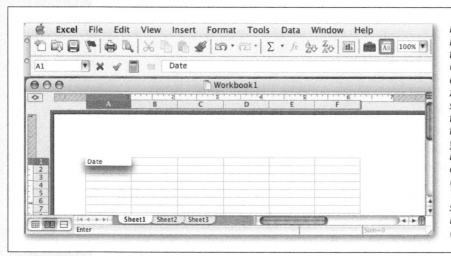

Figure 13-1:
Excel 2004 has all the usual Mac OS X doodads, like close, minimize, and zoom buttons and a status bar. In the status area at the bottom left, Excel tells you what it thinks is happening–in this case, the active cell (A1) is being edited. This window also shows Excel's new Page Layout view (page 467).

Each worksheet can grow to huge proportions—256 columns wide (labeled A, B, C… AA, AB, AC…all the way to IV), and 65,536 rows tall (see Figure 13-2). Furthermore, you can get at even more cells by using other worksheets in the workbook—switch to them by clicking the tabs at the bottom left. You can add many more sheets to a

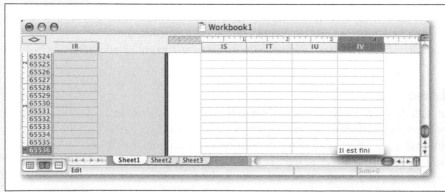

Figure 13-2:
You can't scroll all the way to cell IV65536 in a new spreadsheet, but you can leap to the lower-right corner by entering IV65536 in the Name box on the left side of the Formula bar.

workbook, too, if you need them, by choosing Insert→Worksheet. (This command inserts a new worksheet *before* the currently active worksheet.)

In total, you can have billions of cells in a single Excel document. The only company that needs more space than *that* for its accounting is Microsoft.

Tip: To rename a worksheet, double-click the sheet's name (it's on the tab on the bottom) and type in a new one. Sheet names can be as long as 31 characters.

Each cell acts as a container for one of two things: data or a formula. *Data* can be text, a number, a date, or just about anything else you can type. A *formula*, on the other hand, does something with the data in *other* cells—such as adding together the numbers in them. (More on formulas later in this chapter.)

Excel refers to cells by their coordinates, such as B23 (column B, row 23). A new spreadsheet has cell A1 selected (surrounded by a thick border)—it's the *active* cell. When you start typing, the cell pops up slightly, apparently hovering a quarter-inch above your screen's surface, with a slight shadow behind it. Whatever you type appears in both the active cell and the Edit box on the right side of the Formula bar (see Figure 13-1). When you finish typing, you can do any of the following to make the active cell's new contents stick:

- Press Return, Tab, Enter, or an arrow key.
- Click another cell.
- Click the Enter button in the Formula bar.

Tip: If you keep landing in this "in-cell editing" mode accidentally, choose Excel→Preferences→Edit panel, turn off "Edit directly in cell," and click OK. Now you can edit cell contents only in the Edit box on the Formula bar.

UP TO SPEED

A New View to Thrill

As mentioned previously, the Page Layout view is new to Excel 2004. Its benefit is obvious—you can now see how your printed page will look without looking at a print preview of your work. In fact, some people will want to work in this view from the get-go, so they can design their spreadsheet to fit on whatever size paper they'll eventually print it on. No longer must you construct a spreadsheet, print it, and then be surprised by the results. Working in Page Layout view provides gloriously instantaneous feedback on how your numerical creation will look when it goes hard copy.

On the downside, in Page Layout view, you get to see less of that creation on the screen, but what better excuse to invest in a new 21" monitor?

To open the Page Layout view, select View→Page Layout. Your worksheet instantaneously (well, almost) morphs into a fresh, new Page Layout view, ready for you to input data (or, less intimidatingly, type some numbers). Mousers can click the Page Layout view icon at the bottom left of the screen.

Data Entry

Working in an Excel sheet is simple, at its heart: You enter data or a formula into a cell, move to the next cell, enter more information, and so on. But before entering data in a cell, you must first *select* the cell. Clicking is the easiest method; after you click a cell, the cell border thickens and the cell does that popping-up thing.

Figure 13-3:
When you enter by pasting, you'll immediately notice one of Excel 2004's new features—Smart Buttons. A Smart Button appears just after you paste data into a cell. Click its arrow to display a small pop-up menu from which you can choose to retain the Source Formatting (so that the text will retain the formatting it had in its original location or document) or match the destination formatting (in which Excel automatically adjusts the text to the formatting in the current workbook). Since Excel isn't psychic, the Smart Button gives you a chance to tell it whether you had the old or new formatting in mind.

To select a cell far away from the current active cell, enter the cell's *address* (the column letter followed by the row number) in the Name box on the Formula bar (see Figure 13-2). Or choose Edit→Go To, which brings up a dialog box in which you can enter the address of the lucky cell in the Reference field.

But the fastest means of getting from cell to cell is to use the keyboard. Excel is loaded with keyboard shortcuts that make it easy to plow through an entire sheet's worth of cells without having to touch the mouse. Here are the navigation keystrokes that make data input easier:

Keypress	What Happens
Arrow key	Selects a different cell—the next one above, below, to the left, or to the right of the current one.
Shift-arrow key	Selects the current cell and the one above, below, to the left, or to the right. Hold the Shift key down and press the arrow key more than once to extend the selection.
Option-left arrow, -right arrow	Makes the previous or next sheet in the workbook active.
Control-arrow key	Moves the active cell to the next non-empty cell in the direction indicated by the arrow key.
Return	Accepts the entry and moves the active cell down one row.
Shift-Return	Accepts the entry and moves the active cell up one row.
Tab	Accepts the entry and moves the active cell right one column (or to the first cell in the next row in a multiple-cell selection).

Shift-Tab	Accepts the entry and moves the active cell left one column.
Control-Option-Return	Starts a new line within the same cell.
Control-Return	Fills each selected cell with the same entry. (First select the cell range, type the data that you want repeated in each cell, and then hit Control-Return to fill all of the cells.)
Esc	Cancels an entry.
Control-D	Fills the active cell with the contents of the cell directly above it.
Control-R	Fills the active cell with the contents of the cell directly to the left of it.
Control-'	Fills the active cell with the formula in the cell directly above it.
Control-;	Enters the current date.
Control-Shift-:	Enters the current time (to the nearest minute).

UP TO SPEED

Window Tricks

Because spreadsheets can be wide, sprawling affairs, Excel is filled with window-manipulation tools that let you control how the program uses your precious screen real estate.

For example, when you need to see a few more rows and columns, choose View→Full Screen. Excel hides all of its toolbars, status bars, and other nonessential detritus. Your cells fill your monitor. Choose View→Full Screen again (or click Close Full Screen on the tiny, one-button toolbar) to bring back the bars.

Another example: As shown here, Excel's scroll bars offer vertical and horizontal split boxes, which you can double-click or drag to split a sheet into independently scrolling sections, as shown here. (Note the discontinuity in the lettering and num-

bering of rows and columns in this illustration; these panes have been independently scrolled.) To remove the split, just double-click the split box or the split bar that separates the panes. (Or choose Window→Remove Split.)

You don't have to split the window if all you want to do is keep the row and column names in view while scrolling the rest of the document, however. Excel offers a much more streamlined means of locking the column and row labels: Click in the cell just below and to the right of the row/column label intersection, and then choose Window→ Freeze Panes. Now scrolling affects only the body of the spreadsheet; the row and column labels remain visible.

CHAPTER 13: BASIC EXCEL   **469**

Tip: Return doesn't have to select the next cell down; it can select any of the four neighboring cells, or do nothing at all. You change what the Return key does in the Excel→Preferences→Edit panel.

A quick glance at that table should confirm the bad news to Excel users who haven't upgraded in a while. Back in Excel 2001, Microsoft changed the Excel 98 keystrokes for some of the most important editing commands as part of an effort to make all Office programs use more consistent keystrokes, and those changes are still present in Excel 2004. Combinations that used to involve the ⌘ key, such as ⌘-D for Fill Down and ⌘-I for Insert Cells, now require the Control key instead.

In Excel 2004, fortunately, you're allowed to change the program's keystrokes back to their old assignments—or anything you like. See page 677.

Kinds of Data

You can enter four kinds of data into an Excel spreadsheet (not including formulas, which are described beginning on page 484: numbers, text, dates, or times. Most of the time, entering data is as straightforward as typing, but there are exceptions.

Numbers

- There are only 21 characters that Excel considers numbers: 1 2 3 4 5 6 7 8 9 0 . , ( ) + - / $ % e and E. Anything else is treated as text, which is ineligible for performing most calculations. For example, if Excel sees *three point one four* in a cell, it "sees" a bunch of typed words with no numerical value; when it sees *3.14,* it sees a number.

- Depending on the formatting of the cell in which you're entering numbers, Excel might try to do some work for you. For example, if you've applied *currency formatting* to a cell (see page 520), Excel turns *3/2* into $1.50. But if you've formatted the same cell as a date, Excel turns *3/2* into a date—March 2 of the current year.

- When the cell is formatted to accept General input, and the number you've entered is longer than 11 digits (such as *12345678901112*), Excel converts it to scientific notation (*1.23457E+13*).

Text

- Text can be any combination of characters: numbers, letters, or other symbols.

- To make Excel look at a number as if it were a string of text (rather than a number with which it can do all kinds of mathematical wizardry), you must format the cell as a text-based cell or precede the number with an apostrophe. To format the cell, just select the cell and choose Format→Cells (or right-click the cell and choose Format Cells from the shortcut menu). Click the Number tab and then select Text from the Category list. Click OK.

Dates

- You can perform math on dates, just as though they were numbers. The trick is to type an equal sign (=) into the cell that will contain the answer; then enclose the dates in quotation marks and put the operator (like + or *) between them. For example, if you click a cell, type =*"4/1/2002" -"3/2/1965"*, and then press Enter, Excel will fill the cell with 13544, the number of days between the two dates.

  This math is made possible by the fact that dates in Excel *are* numbers. Behind the scenes, Excel converts any date you type into a special date serial number, which is composed of a number to the left side of a decimal point (the number of days since January 1, 1904) and a number on the right (the fraction of a day).

- When entering dates, you can use either a slash or a hyphen to separate months, days, and years.

Warning: Usually it's OK to format date and time numbering at any time. However, you might avoid the occasional obscure problem by applying date or time formatting *before* you enter the data in the cell.

Times

- Excel also treats *times* as numbers—specifically, as the fractional part of a date serial number, which is a number representing the number of days since midnight on January 1, 1904.

- Excel bases times on the 24-hour clock, or military time. To enter a time using the 12-hour clock, follow the number with an *a* or *p*. For example, to Excel, *9:34* always means 9:34 a.m., but *9:34 p* means 9:34 p.m. (*21:34* also means 9:34 p.m., but it appears in the spreadsheet the way you typed it—as 21:34.)

WORKAROUND WORKSHOP

When Excel Formats Numbers as Dates

If you enter what looks like a date to Excel (say, May 3, 1999), and then later, in the process of revising your spreadsheet, enter a number containing a decimal (such as 23.25), Excel converts your decimal into a date. (23 becomes January 24, 1904).

What's going on?

All cells start out with a generic format. But when you enter what Excel interprets as a date or time, Excel automatically applies date or time formatting. In this example, when Excel interpreted the first entry as a date, it applied date formatting to the cell.

Later, when the first entry was replaced with a decimal number, Excel retained the date formatting—and merrily displayed the number as a date. You don't have to let Excel guess at what format you want, though. Take charge! Select the cells in question and choose Format→Cells (or right-click the cells and choose Format Cell from the shortcut menu). Use the Number tab to select the appropriate format, and your troubles are over.

Similarly, to keep Excel from turning two numbers separated by a forward slash into a date, and keep it as a fraction instead, put a 0 and a space in front of the fraction (enter 0 1/4). Excel now understands that you intended to enter a fraction.

- As with dates, you can perform calculations on times by entering an equal sign and then enclosing the times in quotation marks and typing the separator in the middle. For example, =*"9:34"-"2:43"* gives you 0.285416667, the decimal fraction of a day between 2:43 a.m. and 9:34 a.m. (If you format the cell with time formatting, as described on page 471, you instead get 6:51, or six hours and 51 minutes' difference.)

Tedium Savings 1: AutoComplete

Excel 2004 is teeming with features designed to save you typing. The first, *AutoComplete,* comes into play when you enter repetitive data down a column. Find out more in Figure 13-4.

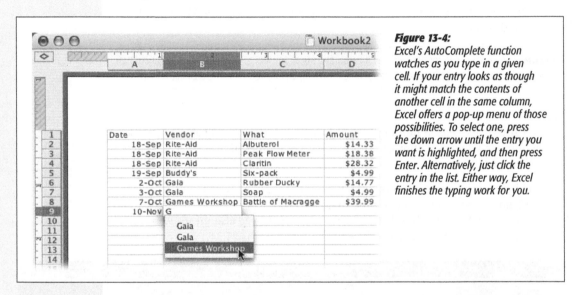

Figure 13-4:
Excel's AutoComplete function watches as you type in a given cell. If your entry looks as though it might match the contents of another cell in the same column, Excel offers a pop-up menu of those possibilities. To select one, press the down arrow until the entry you want is highlighted, and then press Enter. Alternatively, just click the entry in the list. Either way, Excel finishes the typing work for you.

Tedium Savings 2: AutoFill

Excel's AutoFill feature can save you hours of tedious typing, thanks to its ingenious ability to fill miles of cells with data automatically. The Edit→Fill submenu is especially useful when you're duplicating data or typing items in a series (such as days of the week, months of the year, or even sequential apartment numbers). It has seven options: Down, Right, Up, Left, Across Worksheets, Series, and Justify.

Here's how they work. In each case, suppose you've started the process by typing data into a cell and then highlighting a block of cells beginning with that cell:

- **Down, Up.** Fills the selected block of cells with whatever's in the top or bottom cell of the selected block. You might use one of these commands when setting up a series of formulas in a column that adds a row of cells.

- **Right, Left.** Fills the selected range of cells with whatever's in the leftmost or rightmost cell. For example, you'd use this feature when you need to put the same total calculation at the bottom of 23 different columns.

- **Across Worksheets.** Fills the cells in other sheets in the same workbook with the contents of the selected cells. For example, suppose you want to set up worksheets that track inventory and pricing over different months in different locations, and you want to use a different worksheet for each location. You can fill in all of the general column and row headings (such as part numbers and months) across worksheets with this command.

To make this work, start by selecting the cells whose contents you wish to copy. Then select the sheets you want to fill by Shift-⌘-clicking the sheet tabs at the

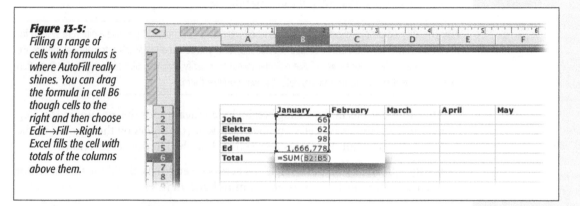

Figure 13-5:
Filling a range of cells with formulas is where AutoFill really shines. You can drag the formula in cell B6 though cells to the right and then choose Edit→Fill→Right. Excel fills the cell with totals of the columns above them.

bottom of the window. (If you can't see all the tabs easily, drag the slider between the tabs and the horizontal scroll bar. When you drag it to the right, the scroll bar shrinks, leaving more room for the tabs.)

Choose Edit→Fill→Across Worksheet. A small dialog box (see Figure 13-6) asks whether you want to copy data, formulas, or both across the selected worksheets. Make your choice by clicking one of the radio buttons, and then click OK.

Figure 13-6:
You can copy into other worksheets: All (both the formulas and data), Contents (just the data information in the worksheet), or Formats (just the formulas in the worksheet).

- **Series.** Fills the selected cells with a *series* of increasing or decreasing values based on the contents of the topmost cell (if the selected cells are in a column) or the leftmost cell (if the cells are in a row).

For example, suppose you're about to type in the daily statistics for the number of dot-com startups that went out of business during the first two weeks of 2002. Instead of having to type 14 dates into a row of cells, you can let Excel do the grunt work for you.

Enter *1/1/2002* in a cell. Then highlight that cell and the next 13 cells to its right. Now choose Edit→Fill→Series. The Series window appears, in which you specify how the fill takes place. You could make the cell labels increase by months, years, every other day, or whatever. Click OK; Excel fills the cells with the date series 1/1/2002, 1/2/2002, 1/3/2002, and so on.

Tip: The above example reflects the way Americans write dates, of course. If you use a different system for writing dates (perhaps you live in Europe or Australia), and you've used the Mac's International preference pane (in the Finder, choose →System Preferences) to specify that you like January 14, 2002 written *14/1/2002,* Excel automatically formats dates the way you like them.

The other options in this dialog box include Linear (adds the amount in the Step field to each successive cell's number), Growth (*multiplies* by the number in the Step field), and AutoFill (relies on the lists described in the next section).

- **Justify.** Spreads the text in a single cell across several cells. You'd use this function to create a heading that spans the columns beneath it.

If the cells are in a row, this command spreads the text in the leftmost cell across the selected row of cells. If the cells are in a column, it breaks up the text so that one word goes into each cell.

Using the Fill handle

You don't have to use the Edit→Fill submenu to harness the power of Excel's AutoFill feature. As a timesaving gesture, Microsoft also offers you the *fill handle* (see Figure 13-7), a small square in the lower right of a selection rectangle. It lets you fill adjacent cells with data, exactly like the Fill commands—but without a trip to a menu and a dialog box.

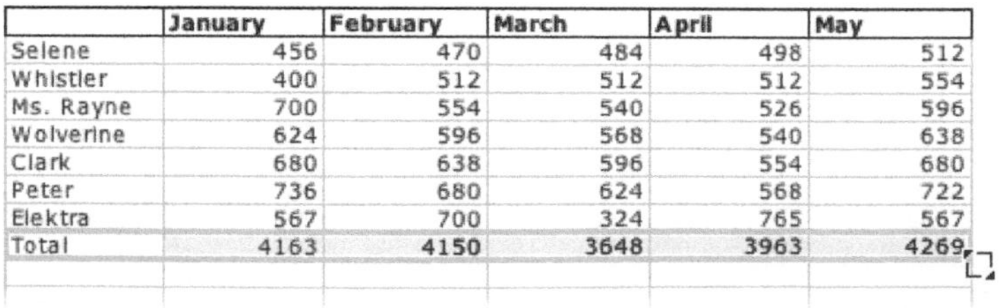

	January	February	March	April	May
Selene	456	470	484	498	512
Whistler	400	512	512	512	554
Ms. Rayne	700	554	540	526	596
Wolverine	624	596	568	540	638
Clark	680	638	596	554	680
Peter	736	680	624	568	722
Elektra	567	700	324	765	567
Total	4163	4150	3648	3963	4269

Figure 13-7:
To use the fill handle, select the cell containing the formula or values you want to replicate and drag the tiny fill handle at the lower-right corner of the selection across the cells you want to fill..

To use it, select the cells that contain the data you want to duplicate or extend, then drag the tiny fill handle across the cells where you want the data to be, as shown in Figure 13-7. Excel then fills the cells, just as though you'd used the Fill Down, Right, Up, or Left command. (To fill a series, Control-click the handle and choose an option from the shortcut menu.)

Tip: Excel can perform some dramatic and complex fill operations for you if you highlight *more than one* cell before dragging the fill handle.

Suppose, for example, that you want to create a list of *every third* house on your street. Enter *201 Elm St.* in the first cell, then *204 Elm St.* in the next one down. Highlight both of them, then drag the fill handle at the lower-right corner of the second cell downward.

Excel cleverly fills the previously empty cells with *207 Elm St., 210 Elm St., 213 Elm St.,* and so on.

What's more, the fill handle can do *smart filling* that you won't find on the Edit→Fill submenu. For example, if you type *January* into a cell and then drag the fill handle across the next bunch of cells, Excel fills them with February, March, and so on; ditto for days of the week. In fact, if you type January, March, and then drag across subsequent cells, Excel will fill them in with May, July, etc. That's so cool.

What's more, you can teach Excel about any other sequential lists you use regularly in your line of work (NY Office, Cleveland Office, San Diego Office, and so on). Just choose Excel→Preferences→Custom Lists panel; click Add and then type the series of items in order, each on its own line. Click OK; the AutoFill list is now ready to use.

Tip: You can also type the list in a column of cells, select the cells, and then choose Preferences→Custom Lists→Add.

FREQUENTLY ASKED QUESTION

Invasion of the ######s

A few of my numbers have been replaced by ##### symbols. Do I have a virus?

A string of number signs in a cell means, "The cell isn't wide enough to show whatever text or number is supposed to be here. Widen the column—or use a smaller font—if you ever hope to see your numbers again."

As noted later in this chapter, the quickest way to fix the problem is to double-click the divider line between the gray column-letter headings—the one to the right of the column

containing the ######s. Excel instantly makes the column wide enough to show all the numbers inside of it.

That's not the only error notation you might see in a cell, by the way. Excel might also react to faulty formulas by showing, for example, #DIV/0! (your formula is attempting to divide a number by zero, which is a mathematical no-no); #VALUE! (you've used unavailable data in a formula, by referring to an empty cell, for example); #REF (a bogus cell reference); and so on. For a complete table of these error codes, choose Help→Search Excel Help and search for *error values*.

Selecting Cells (and Cell Ranges)

Selecting a single cell in Excel is easy. Just click the cell to select it. Often, though, you'll want to select more than one cell—in readiness for copying and pasting, making a chart, applying boldface, or using the Fill command, for example. Figure 13-8 depicts all you need to know for your selection needs.

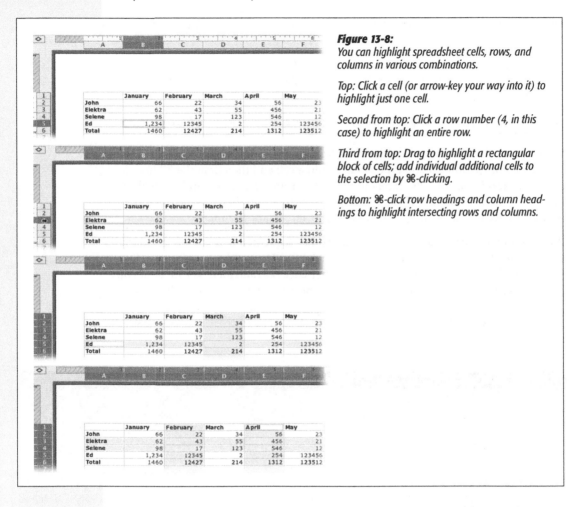

Figure 13-8:
You can highlight spreadsheet cells, rows, and columns in various combinations.

Top: Click a cell (or arrow-key your way into it) to highlight just one cell.

Second from top: Click a row number (4, in this case) to highlight an entire row.

Third from top: Drag to highlight a rectangular block of cells; add individual additional cells to the selection by ⌘-clicking.

Bottom: ⌘-click row headings and column headings to highlight intersecting rows and columns.

- **Select a single cell.** To select a single cell, click it or enter its address in the Name Box (which is shown in Figure 13-1).

- **Select a block of cells.** To select a rectangle of cells, just drag diagonally across them. You highlight all of the cells within the boundaries of the imaginary rectangle you're drawing. (Or click the cell in one corner of the block and then Shift-click the cell diagonally opposite.)

- **Select a noncontiguous group of cells.** To select cells that aren't touching, ⌘-click (to add individual independent cells to the selection) or ⌘-drag across cells (to add a block of them to the selection). Repeat as many times as you like; Excel is perfectly happy to highlight random cells, or blocks of cells, in various corners of the spreadsheet simultaneously.

- **Select a row or column.** Click a row or column *heading* (the gray label of the row or column).

- **Select several rows or columns.** To select more than one row or column, *drag through* the gray row numbers or column letters. (You can also click the first one, then Shift-click the last one. Excel highlights everything in between.)

- **Select noncontiguous rows or columns.** To select two or more rows or columns that aren't touching, ⌘-click, or ⌘-drag through, the corresponding gray row numbers. You can even combine these techniques, by highlighting first rows, and then columns. This forms intersecting swaths of highlighting.

- **Select all cells.** Press ⌘-A to select every cell on the sheet—or just click the gray, far upper-left rectangle with the diamond in it.

Tip: To select within the *contents* of a cell, double-click the cell and then use the I-beam selection tool to select the text that you want.

Moving Things Around

Once you've selected some cells, you can move their contents around in various ways—a handy fact, since few people type everything in exactly the right place the first time.

Cutting, copying, and pasting

Just as in any other Mac application, you can use the Edit menu commands—Cut (⌘-X), Copy (⌘-C), and Paste (⌘-V)—to move cell contents around the spreadsheet—or to a different sheet or workbook altogether.

But unlike other Mac applications, Excel doesn't appear to cut your selection immediately. Instead, the cut area sprouts a dotted, *moving border,* but otherwise remains unaffected. It isn't until you select a destination cell or cells and select Edit→Paste that the cut takes place (and the shimmering stops).

Tip: Press the Esc key to make the animated dotted lines stop moving, without otherwise affecting your copy or cut operation. One more piece of advice: Check the status bar at the bottom of the window to find out what Excel thinks is happening ("Select destination and press ENTER or choose Paste," for example).

Paste Special

The Edit→Paste Special command summons a dialog box that inquires about *how* and *what* to paste. For example, you might decide to paste the formulas contained in the material you copied so that they continue to do automatic math—or only the *values* (the results of the calculations as they appear in the copied material).

Tip: This dialog box also contains the mighty Transpose checkbox, a tiny option that can save your bacon. It lets you swap rows-for-columns in the act of pasting, so that data you input in columns winds up in rows, and vice versa.

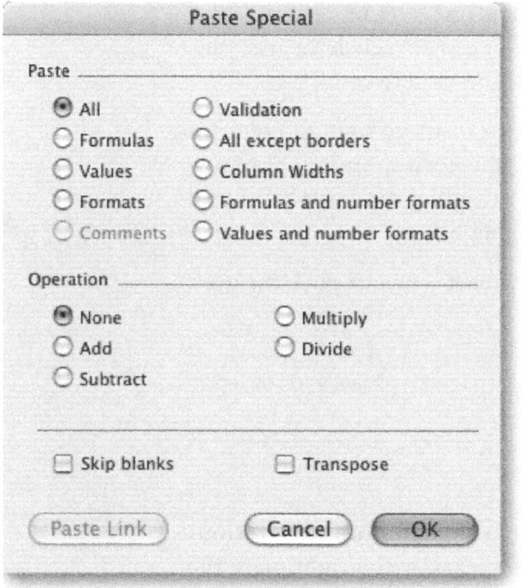

Figure 13-9:
The Paste Special command lets you paste formulas, comments, and formatting independently. The Operations options let you perform a mathematical operation as you paste, such as adding what you've copied to the contents of the cells you're pasting over.

Drag-and-drop

Excel also lets you grab a selected range of cells and drag the contents to a new location. To do this, select the cells you want to move, then point to the thick border on the edge of the selection, so that the cursor changes into a little hand that grabs the

POWER USERS' CLINIC

The Difference Between Cut and Copy

When you use the Cut command on formulas, you paste relative cell references; when you copy a formula, you paste absolute references. Page 495 defines these concepts.

For example, if the formula in cell A1 was =SUM(B1:B4) when you copied it, the pasted formula in cell A10 changes to say =SUM(B10:B13). The cell references have been offset nine cells down, to reflect the distance between the formula's original cell and its copy. Because you're placing a copy of the formula in a new place, the cells to which the formula refers should be offset by the same amount—which is handy

for filling in a spreadsheet that has lots of similar formulas in different locations.

To avoid this shift in pasted formulas, you can make the cell references absolute by putting a dollar sign in front of each cell address that you don't want to change.

In the example above, if you always want a SUM function to refer to cells B1 through B4, even after it's been copied and pasted, change the formula to read =SUM($B$1:$B$4). That'll make sure that everything stays in place.

cells. You can now drag the selected cells to another spot on the spreadsheet. When you release the mouse button, Excel moves the data to the new location, exactly as though you'd used Cut and Paste.

There are a few keys that, if held down, modify how dragging and dropping items in Excel works:

- **Option**. If you hold down the Option key, Excel *copies* the contents to the new location, leaving the originals in place.

- **Shift**. Normally, if you drag cells into a spreadsheet area that you've already filled in, Excel asks if you're sure you want to wipe out the cell contents that were already there. If you Shift-drag cells, however, Excel creates enough new cells to make room for the dragged contents, shoving aside (or down) whatever cell contents were already there to make room.

- **Option and Shift**. Holding down both the Option *and* Shift keys as you drag copies the data *and* inserts new cells for it.

- **Control**. Control-dragging yields a menu of 11 options when you drop the cells. This menu lets you choose whether you want to move the cells, copy them, copy just the values or formulas, create a link or hyperlink, or shift cells around. It even lets you cancel the drag.

Inserting and Removing Cells

Suppose you've just completed your spreadsheet cataloging the rainfall patterns of the Pacific Northwest, county by county, and then it hits you: You forgot Coos County in Oregon. Besides the question of how you could possibly forget Coos County, the larger question remains: What do you do about it in your spreadsheet? Delete the whole thing and start over?

Fortunately, Excel lets you insert blank cells, rows, or columns into existing sheets through the Insert menu. Here's how each works.

- **Cells**. The Insert→Cells command summons the Insert dialog box. It lets you insert new, blank cells into your spreadsheet, and lets you specify what happens to the cells that are already in place—whether they get shifted right or down. See Figure 13-10.

Tip: Longtime Excel fans should note that the keystroke for Insert Cells is now Control-I, not ⌘-I.

- **Rows**. If you choose Insert→Rows, Excel inserts a new, blank row above the active cell.

Tip: If you select some cells before using the Insert→Cells command, Excel inserts the number of rows equal to the number of rows selected in the range. That's a handy way to control how many rows get added—to add six blank rows, highlight six rows, regardless of what's in them at the moment.

- **Columns.** If you choose Insert→Columns, Excel inserts a new blank column to the left of the active cell. If you've selected a range of cells, Excel inserts the number of columns equal to the number of columns selected in the range.

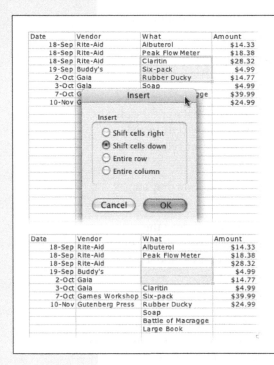

Figure 13-10:
When you select cells and then choose Insert→Cells, Excel asks where you want to put the new cells (top). The two buttons at the bottom let you insert entire rows or columns. Excel will then insert the same number of cells as you've selected in the location selected, and will move the previous residents of those cells in the direction that you specify (bottom).

Find and Replace

Exactly as in Word, Excel offers both a Find function, which helps you locate a specific spot in a big workbook, and a Replace feature that's ideal for those moments when your company gets incorporated into a larger one, requiring its name to be changed in 34 places throughout a workbook. The routine goes like this:

1. **Highlight the cells you want to search.**

   This step is crucial. By limiting the search range, you ensure that your search-and-destroy operation won't run rampant through your spreadsheet, changing things you never suspect are being changed.

2. **Choose Edit→Find. In the resulting dialog box, specify what you want to search for, and in which direction (see Figure 13-11).**

   You can use a question mark (?) as a stand-in for a single character, or an asterisk (*) to represent more than one character. In other words, typing *P*ts* will find cells containing "Profits," "Prophets," and "Parakeets."

   The "Find entire cells only" checkbox means that Excel will consider a cell a match for your search term only if its entire contents match; a cell that says "Annual profits" isn't considered a match for the search term "Profits."

3. **If you intend to** *replace* **the cell contents (instead of just finding them), click Replace; type the replacement text into the "Replace with" box. Click Find Next (or press Return).**

Each time you click Find Next, Excel highlights the next cell it finds that matches your search phrase. If you click Replace, you replace the text with the "Replace with" text. If you click Replace All, of course, you replace *every* matching occurrence in the selected cells. Use caution.

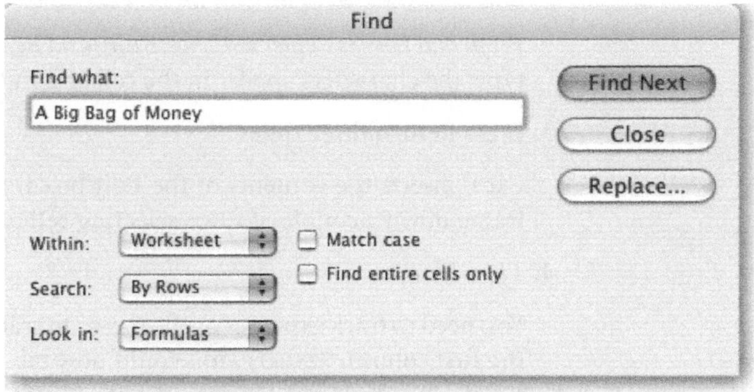

Figure 13-11:
Using the Search pop-up menu, you can specify whether Excel searches the highlighted cells from left to right of each row ("By Rows") or down each column ("By Columns"). Use the "Look in" pop-up menu to specify which cell components are fair game for the search: formulas, values (that is, the results of those formulas, and other data you've typed into the cells), or comments.

Erasing Cells

"Erase," as any Enron staff member can attest, is a relative term. In Excel, the Edit→ Clear submenu lets you strip away various kinds of information without necessarily emptying the cell completely. For example:

- **Edit→Clear→All** truly empties the selected cells, restoring them to their new-spreadsheet, unformatted condition. (Control-B does the same thing.)

- **Edit→Clear→Formats** leaves the contents, but strips away formatting (including both text and number formatting).

- **Edit→Clear→Contents** empties the cell, but leaves the formatting in place. If you then type new numbers into the cell, they take on whatever cell formatting you had applied (bold, blue, Currency, and so on).

- **Edit→Clear→Comments** deletes only electronic yellow sticky notes (see page 591).

None of these is the same as Edit→Delete, which actually chops cells out of your spreadsheet and makes others slide upward or leftward to fill the gap. (Excel asks you which way you want existing cells to slide.)

Tutorial 1: Entering Data

If you've never used a spreadsheet before, the concepts described in the previous pages may not make sense until you've applied them in practice. This tutorial, which continues in a second lesson on page 491, can help.

Suppose that you, former billionaire CEO of a dot-com startup, have just gone bankrupt. As the vulture-like office equipment repossession guys begin to pack up your desks and chairs, you whip out Excel to see if you can figure out how it all went wrong.

1. **Create a new spreadsheet document by choosing File→New (⌘-N).**

    Excel fills your screen with the spreadsheet grid; the first cell, A1, is selected as the active cell.

2. **Begin by typing the title of your spreadsheet in cell A1.**

    Profit and Loss Statement: Riches, Ruin, and Recovery might be a good choice. As you type, the characters appear in the cell and in the Edit box in the Formula bar.

3. **Press Return three times.**

    Excel inserts the contents of the Edit box into cell A1 and moves the active cell frame down a couple of rows, selecting cell A4.

4. **Type *January.***

    You need to track expenses over time, so to track the project by calendar year, name the first column *January.* You could now tab to the next cell, enter *February,* and work your way down the spreadsheet—but there's an easier way.

    As noted earlier, Excel can create a series of months automatically for you, saving you the effort of typing *February, March,* and so on—you just have to start it off with the first entry or two.

5. **Click once outside cell A4 to get out of entry mode, and then click cell A4 again to select it.**

6. **Carefully click the tiny square at the lower-right corner of the highlighted cell; drag directly downward through 11 more cells.**

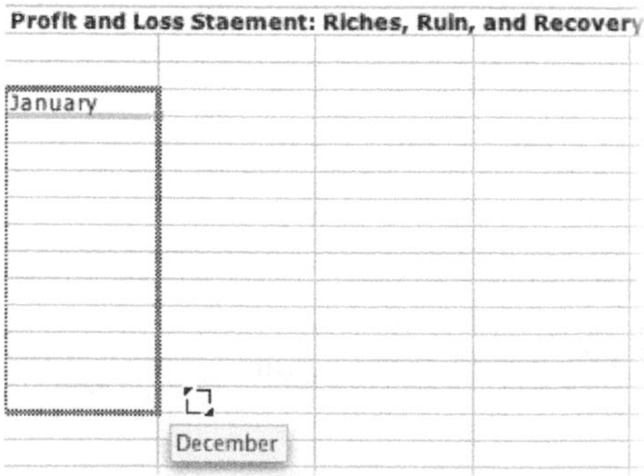

Profit and Loss Staement: Riches, Ruin, and Recovery		
January		

Figure 13-12:
Drag the lower-right corner handle of a cell to autofill a sequence of months, dates, or times. (In this example, if January is in row 4, December will end up in row 15.)

Pop-out yellow screen tips reveal what Excel is autofilling into the cells you're dragging through. They let you know when you've gone too far; when the screen tip says *December,* stop.

Excel highlights the cells you dragged through. Figure 13-12 illustrates this step.

Now it's time to add the year headings across the top.

7. **Click cell B3 to select it. Type** *1999.* **Press Tab, type** *2000,* **then press Enter.**

You'll use the same AutoFill mechanism to type in the names of the next four years. But just dragging the tiny square AutoFill handle on the 1998 cell wouldn't work this time, because Excel wouldn't know whether you want to fill *every* cell with "1999" or to add successive years. So, you've given it the first *two* years as a hint.

8. **Drag through the 1999 and 2000 cells. Carefully click the tiny square at the lower-right corner of the 2000 cell; drag directly to the right through three more cells.**

Excel automatically fills in *2001, 2002,* and *2003,* using the data in the first two cells to establish the pattern.

If you like, you can now highlight the year row, the month column, or both, and then press ⌘-B to make them boldface (see Figure 13-13). Chapter 14 offers much more detail on formatting your spreadsheets.

Now that the basic framework of the spreadsheet is in place, you can begin typing in actual numbers.

Figure 13-13:
You can make the headings stand out from the data you'll soon put in the cells by changing the font style and alignment (see Chapter 14). In this example, you've finished typing in the numbers, as described in steps 9 through 12.

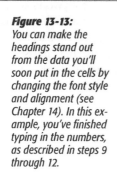
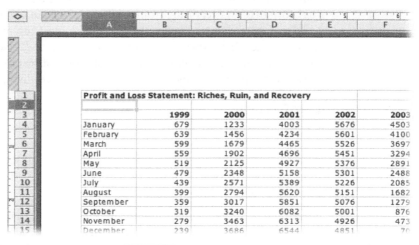

	1999	2000	2001	2002	2003
Profit and Loss Statement: Riches, Ruin, and Recovery					
January	679	1233	4003	5676	4503
February	639	1456	4234	5601	4100
March	599	1679	4465	5526	3697
April	559	1902	4696	5451	3294
May	519	2125	4927	5376	2891
June	479	2348	5158	5301	2488
July	439	2571	5389	5226	2085
August	399	2794	5620	5151	1682
September	359	3017	5851	5076	1279
October	319	3240	6082	5001	876
November	279	3463	6313	4926	473
December	239	3686	6544	4851	7C

9. **Click cell B4, January 1999. Enter a figure for your January income.**

You didn't make much money in January, and the first year was slow, so you were living off credit cards at the time; $250 might be about right. Leave off the dollar sign—just type *250.*

10. **Press Return (or the down arrow key).**

    Excel moves the active cell frame to the next row down.

11. **Type another number to represent your income for February; press Return. Repeat steps 9 and 10 until you get to the bottom of the 1999 column.**

    For this experiment, the exact numbers to type don't much matter, but Figure 13-13 shows one suggestion.

12. **Click in the January 2000 column (C4); fill in the numbers for each month, pressing Return after each entry. Repeat with the other years.**

    Remember to type extremely high numbers in the 2000 and 2001 columns (when venture capitalists poured money into your company), and equally huge negative numbers (each preceded by a minus sign) for the 2002 column, as the technology recession hit. Increase the numbers again in 2003, since business picked up once your advertisers realized that you weren't going down with the dot-com ship—not yet anyway.

    You've successfully populated your spreadsheet with data; choose File→Save to preserve and name the document. You'll return to it later in this chapter—after you've read about what Excel can *do* with all of these numbers.

Formula Fundamentals

Without *formulas*, Excel would be just glorified graph paper. With them, Excel becomes a number-crunching powerhouse worthy of its own high-powered Hollywood agent. Excel formulas do everything from basic arithmetic to complex financial analysis. And Excel 2004 can do it better than ever. The most recent version of Excel adds new error-checking features, smart buttons, and easier ways to construct charts. You can even use formulas to switch the capitalization of text, remove all nonprintable characters from a text string, and probably vacuum the living room.

Basic Calculations

A *formula* in a cell can perform calculations on other cells' contents. For example, if cell A1 contains the number of hours in a day, and cell A2 contains the number of days in a year, then you could type =A1*A2 into cell B3 to find out how many hours there are in a year. (In spreadsheet lingo, you'd say that this formula *returns* the number 8670.)

After typing the formula and pressing Enter, you'd see only the mathematical answer in cell B3; the formula itself is hidden, though you can see it in the Formula bar if you click the cell again.

Formulas do math on *values*. A value is any number, date, time, text, or cell address that you feed into a formula. The math depends on the *operators* in the formula—symbols like + for addition, – for subtraction, / for division, * for multiplication, and so on.

Tip: Your formulas don't have to remain invisible until clicked. To reveal formulas on a given sheet, press Control-` (the key in the upper-left corner of most keyboards). This command toggles the spreadsheet cells so that they show formulas instead of results. (Excel widens your columns considerably, as necessary, to show the formulas.) To return things to the way they were, press Control-` again.

You can consider that keystroke a shortcut for the official way to bring formulas into view: Excel→Preferences→View panel. Under Window options, click Formulas; click OK. Repeat the procedure to restore the results-only view.

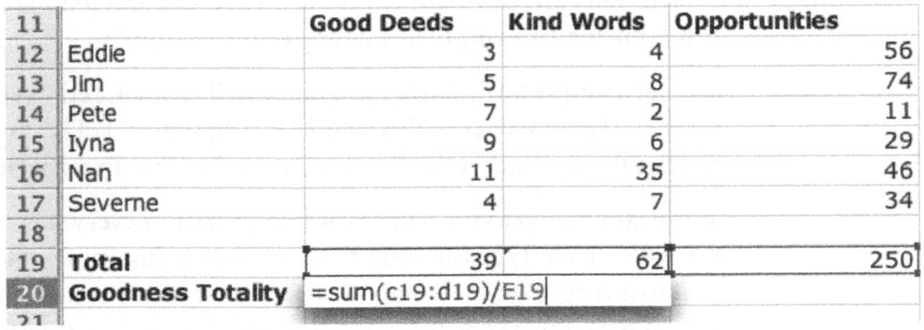

Figure 13-14:
The Rangefinder highlights each cell that's included in the formula you're currently typing. Furthermore, the color of the outline around the cell matches the typed cell reference.

11		Good Deeds	Kind Words	Opportunities
12	Eddie	3	4	56
13	Jim	5	8	74
14	Pete	7	2	11
15	Iyna	9	6	29
16	Nan	11	35	46
17	Severne	4	7	34
18				
19	Total	39	62	250
20	Goodness Totality	=sum(c19:d19)/E19		
21				

Error checking

If you make a mistake when you're typing in a formula, Excel 2004's new error-checking buttons attempt to return you to the straight and narrow. For example, if you type *suum E3-E6*, Excel displays "#Name?" in the cell. Click the cell to display the error-checking button, as shown in Figure 13-15. Clicking the tiny arrow on the right of the button displays several options and bits of information, like the following:

- **Error Name.** The name of the error heads the list. Fortunately, it's a descriptive name of the error, like Invalid Name Error.

- **Help on this Error.** Click here to view the Excel Help screen on this particular error. This information may help you understand where you went wrong.

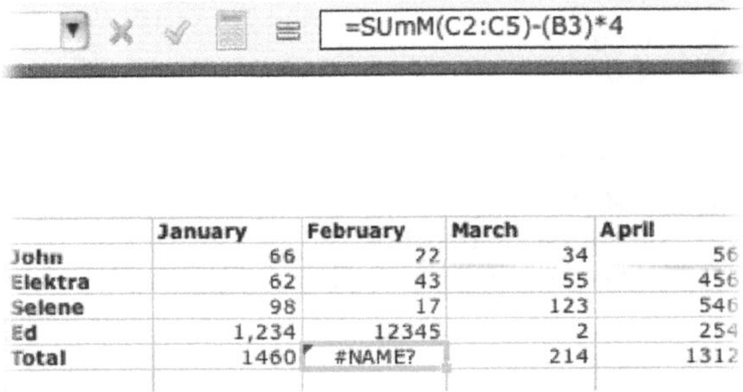

Figure 13-15:
If you choose to edit the formula in the Formula bar, the alleged formula becomes active in the Formula bar. There you can edit it, and with any luck fix the problem. Note that when presented in the Formula bar, the formula's arguments are color coded to indicate which color-coded cell they apply to.

`=SUmM(C2:C5)-(B3)*4`

	January	February	March	April
John	66	72	34	56
Elektra	62	43	55	456
Selene	98	17	123	546
Ed	1,234	12345	2	254
Total	1460	#NAME?	214	1312

- **Trace Error.** Draws lines to the cells that might be causing the errors. Examine the cells in question to determine what you might have done incorrectly.

- **Ignore Error.** The computing equivalent of saying "never mind." Choosing this item tells Excel to leave the formula as you entered it. (Excel obeys you, but there's no guarantee that the formula will work.)

- **Edit in Formula Bar.** This option lets you edit the formula in the Formula bar as described in Figure 13-15.

- **Error Checking Options.** Opens the Excel→Preferences→Error Checking tab. Here you can turn error checking on and off, and tell Excel which kinds of errors to look for, like empty or missing cells in formulas.

To enter a simple formula that you know well, just select the cell and then click the Edit box in the Formula bar, which is shown in Figure 13-1. The cursor appears simultaneously in the cell and in the Edit box, signaling that Excel awaits your next move.

Your next move is to type an equal sign (=), since every formula starts with one (see page 488). Then type the rest of the formula using values and operators. When you want to incorporate a reference to a particular cell in your formula, you don't actually have to type out *B12* or whatever—just *click* the cell in question.

Tip: If you mess up while entering a formula and want to start fresh, click the Cancel button on the Formula bar. (It looks like an X.)

To complete a formula, click the Enter button on the Formula bar (it looks like a checkmark) or press Enter. Pressing Return or Tab also works.

Functions

When you tire of typing formulas (or, let's be honest, when you can't figure out what to type), you can let Excel do the brainwork by using *functions*. In addition to time-honored features like the AutoSum button and the Calculator (page 489), Excel 2004 gives you Function screen tips, which display the correct format for over 140 functions. They make sure that your functions function, just like you want. Every time.

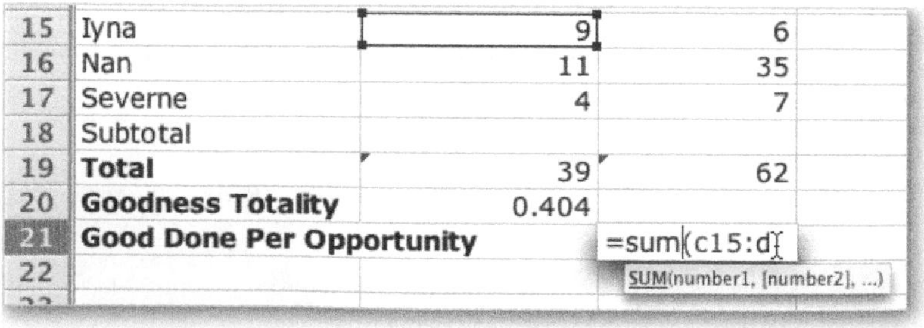

Figure 13-16:
Excel's Function screen tips make an educated guess at what you're trying to do—usually a pretty darn good one—and provide the correct syntax for doing it. Here the Function screen tip explains how to add a column of numbers.

Function screen tips

Screen tips for function help are new in Excel 2004, and they're a real boon to spread-sheeting neophytes and dataheads alike. As you type a function into a cell, a screen tip displays the syntax of the function in a pale yellow box just below where you're typing. Not only does the screen tip show you how to correctly type the function it believes you have in mind, but you can also use the screen tip in other ways. For example, you can drag the screen tip to reposition it (to get a better look at your worksheet), click a piece of the tip to select it, or click the function to open up its Help topic in a separate window.

Tip: If you want to turn off function screen tips, choose Excel→Preferences and select the View tab. Remove the checkmark next to Function ScreenTips.

The AutoSum button

You don't need access to Microsoft's reams of focus-group studies to realize that the most commonly used spreadsheet function is *adding things up*. That's why Excel comes equipped with a toolbar button that does nothing but add up the values in the column directly above, or the row to the left of, the active cell; Figure 13-17 illustrates the idea. (The tutorial that resumes on page 491 also shows why AutoSum is one of the most important buttons in Excel.)

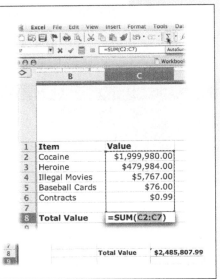

Figure 13-17:
Top: The powerful AutoSum button on the Standard toolbar (shown by the cursor) is the key to quickly pasting functions in cells. A click of the button puts a SUM function in the selected cell, which assumes that you want to add up the cells above it. Note that it doesn't write out C3+C4+C5+C6+C7+C8+C9; it sets up a range of numbers using the shorthand notation C3:C9.

Bottom: When you press Enter, you see only the result, not the formula.

The flippy triangle to the right of the AutoSum button reveals a menu with a few other extremely common options, such as:

- **AVERAGE.** Calculates the average (the arithmetic mean) of the numbers in the column above the active cell. For example, if you fill a cell with *=AVERAGE(2,4,4,5)* and press Enter, you'll get the answer 3.75.

- **COUNT.** Tells you *how many* cells in a selected cell range contain numbers. It can also tell you how many times a specific number appears in a selected set of cells.

- **MAX** and **MIN.** Shows the highest or lowest value of any of the numbers referred to in the function. If you enter *=MAX(34,23,95,34)*, you'll get 95.

A sixth pop-up menu command reads More Functions. When selected, More Functions brings up the Paste Function dialog box, described shortly.

Tip: After you click the AutoSum button (or use one of its pop-up menu commands), Excel assumes that you intend to compute using the numbers in the cells just *above* or *to the left of* the highlighted cell. It indicates, with a moving border, which cells it intends to include in its calculation.

But if it guesses wrong, simply grab your mouse and drag through the numbers you *do* want computed. Excel redraws its border and updates its formula. Press Enter to complete the formula.

Looking up functions

Whipping up the sum or average of some cells is only the beginning. Excel is also capable of performing the kinds of advanced number crunching that can calculate interest rates, find the cosine of an arc, and so on. There are probably only two or three people who have most of these functions memorized.

Fortunately, you don't have to remember how to write each function; save that brainpower for figuring out what to have for lunch. Instead, you can use Excel's Paste Function dialog box to look up the exact function that you need. To call up the Paste Function dialog box, choose Insert→Function, or click the Paste Function button on the Standard toolbar.

UP TO SPEED

The Anatomy of a Function in a Formula

Like Web-page addresses, formulas have a regular form. If you understand that anatomy, you'll find working with formulas much easier.

The first element in a formula is the equal sign (=), which signals to Excel that what follows is a formula, not plain old data. Next comes the function name, like SUM. After the function name comes a left parenthesis, which tells Excel that the function's arguments are coming next.

Arguments in this case have nothing to do with cranky accountants, and everything to do with telling the function what values to process. Some functions have one argument;

others have more. To use more than one argument, separate them with commas. Finally, finish the function with a closing parenthesis.

For example, the formula =SUM(B2,B4:B8,20) adds the contents of cells B2,B4, B5, B6, B7, and B8, and then adds 20.

Given the many functions and operators Excel provides, you can do more number crunching in an hour with Excel than you probably did in your entire grade-school experience. (Unless, of course, you used a computer during grade school, in which case you may have already programmed Excel to play Battleship.)

Note: When the Paste Function dialog box appears, the Office Assistant—if it's visible—offers to help with any function you select. (See Appendix B for more on this little animated Help character.) You can safely ignore the Assistant, since it hides its offer and goes away when you click OK or Cancel.

In the Paste Function dialog box, you'll see two panels: the left panel lists the function *categories* (nine of them, plus two special categories at the top of the list); the right panel lists the individual functions in the selected category (see Figure 13-18).

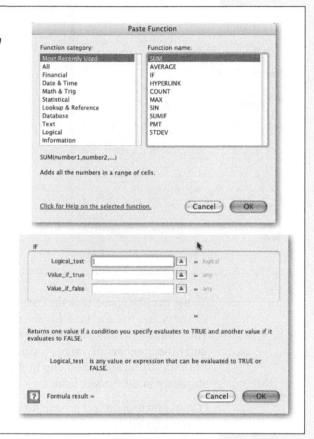

Figure 13-18:
Top: First, select a category in the left panel, and then pick a function from the right panel. Excel describes the selected function in the space below the panels. Once you have the right function (such as the Average function when you're building a grade book), click OK; Excel pastes the function into the selected cell.

Bottom: Next, Excel pops up the Formula palette, in which you can fine-tune your function's arguments—the values that the function uses to do its calculations.

Using the Calculator to assemble formulas

What with all the operators, parentheses, cell addresses, functions and such, all of which must be entered in exactly the correct order, assembling a formula can be a painstaking business.

Fortunately, the Calculator centralizes formula creation. It has a lot of the standard buttons that you might find on a pocket calculator, plus parentheses buttons, an IF button (to insert an IF statement), and a SUM button (to insert a SUM function). As shown in Figure 13-19, the window also has three fields: a large one up top that displays the current formula (and also lets you type your own formula, if you're so inclined) and two smaller ones below it, which show the answer to the formula and the cell where the formula is located.

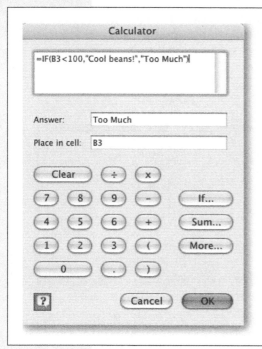

Figure 13-19:
The Calculator lets you build a formula with just a few button clicks—in this case, an IF statement that presents different messages depending on the value of B3. Once the formula is perfected, click OK to insert it into the spreadsheet.

To use the Calculator, click the Calculator button in the Formula bar (just to the right of the X and the checkmark). To create a formula, click the calculator's buttons as you would on a real calculator. If you prefer clacking on your keyboard, you can also enter the numbers that way. As you build your formula with the various calculator buttons, the formula shows up in the top window, and the result of the calculation shows up in the Answer field.

If you want to access other functions (besides the IF and SUM functions), click More. This brings up the Paste Function dialog box (Figure 13-18), which gives you access to almost every one of Excel's functions.

Once you've built your formula, click OK to paste it into the spreadsheet. (And don't let your friends who use Excel for Windows see this, as they don't have this feature.)

Tip: If you need a little help with a balky formula that you've already entered (perhaps you haven't gotten its syntax just right), select the cell and then click the Edit Formula button in the Formula toolbar. This brings up the Formula palette (a relative of the Calculator), which shows the formula's possible arguments and lets you know how they should be used. It's like having a friendly Excel nerd in your Mac.

Order of Calculation

Anyone who managed to stay awake in algebra knows that you get different answers to an equation depending on how its elements are ordered. So it's important for *you*, the purveyor of fine Excel formulas, to understand the order in which Excel calculates its values.

If a formula is spitting out results that don't jibe with what you think ought to be the answer, consult the following table. Excel calculates the operations at the top of the table first, working its way down until it hits bottom. For example, Excel computes cell references before it tackles multiplication, and it does multiplication before it works on a "less than" operation.

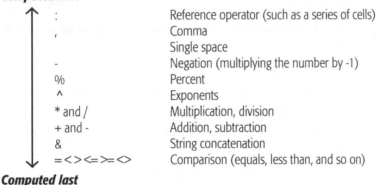

Excel's Calculation Order
Computed first

:	Reference operator (such as a series of cells)
,	Comma
	Single space
-	Negation (multiplying the number by -1)
%	Percent
^	Exponents
* and /	Multiplication, division
+ and -	Addition, subtraction
&	String concatenation
= < > <= >= <>	Comparison (equals, less than, and so on)

Computed last

For example, Excel's answer to =2+3*4 is not 20. It's 14, because Excel performs multiplication and division within the formula *before* doing addition and subtraction.

You can exercise some control over the processing order by using parentheses. Excel calculates expressions within ( ) symbols before bringing the parenthetical items together for calculation. For example, the formula *=C12*(C3-C6)* subtracts the value in C6 from the value in C3 and multiplies the result by the value in C12. Without the parenthesis, the formula would read *=(C12*C3-C6)*, and Excel would multiply C12 by C3 and *then* subtract C6—a different formula entirely.

Tip: Excel does its best to alert you to mistakes you make when entering formulas manually. For example, if you leave off a closing parenthesis (after using an open parenthesis), Excel pops up a dialog box suggesting a fix.

Tutorial 2: Yearly Totals

Suppose you've entered a few numbers into a spreadsheet, as described in the tutorial earlier in this chapter. Now it's time to put these numbers to work. Open the document shown in Figure 13-13.

Now that it has some data to work with, Excel can do a little work. Start with one of the most common spreadsheet calculations: totaling a column of numbers. First create a row for totals.

1. **Click cell A17 (leaving a blank row beneath the month list). Type** *Total.*

   This row will contain totals for each year column.

2. **Click cell B17, in the Total row for 1999. Click the AutoSum button on the Standard toolbar.**

   In cell B17, Excel automatically proposes a *formula* for totaling the column of numbers. (It's =*SUM(B3:B16),* meaning "add up the cells from B3 through B16.") The moving border shows that Excel is prepared to add up *all* of the numbers in this column—including the year label *1999!* Clearly, that's not what you want, so don't press Enter yet.

3. **Drag through the numbers you** *do* **want added: from cell B4 down to B15. Then press Enter.**

   Excel adds up the column.

   Now comes the real magic of spreadsheeting: If one of the numbers in the column *changes,* the total changes automatically. Try it:

4. **Click one of the numbers in column B, type a much bigger number, and then press Enter.**

   Excel instantly updates 1999's total to reflect the change.

Tip: The AutoSum feature doesn't have to add up numbers *above* the selected cell; it can also add up a *row* of cells. In fact, you can even click the AutoSum button and then drag through a *block* of cells to make Excel add up all of *those* numbers.

You *could* continue selecting the Total cells for each year and using AutoSum to create your totals. Instead, you can avoid repetition by using the Fill command described earlier in this chapter. You can tell Excel to create a calculation similar to the 1999 total for the rest of the columns in the spreadsheet.

5. **Starting with the cell containing the 1999 total (B17), drag to the right, all the way over to the 2003 column (F17).**

   You've highlighted the range of cells for column totals, as shown in Figure 13-20.

6. **Choose Edit→Fill→Right.**

   You could have bypassed steps 5 and 6 simply by dragging the lower-right corner handle of cell B17, using the AutoFill process described on page 472.

   Either way, Excel copies the contents of the first cell and pastes it into every other cell in the selection. In this example, the first cell contains a *formula,* not just a total you typed yourself. But, instead of pasting the exact same formula, which would place the 1999 total into each column, Excel understands that you want to total each column, and therefore enters the appropriate formula in each cell of your selection. The result is yearly totals calculated right across the page.

Finally, to make the yearly totals in the tutorial example more meaningful—and see just how much money you actually made—calculate an overall total for the spreadsheet.

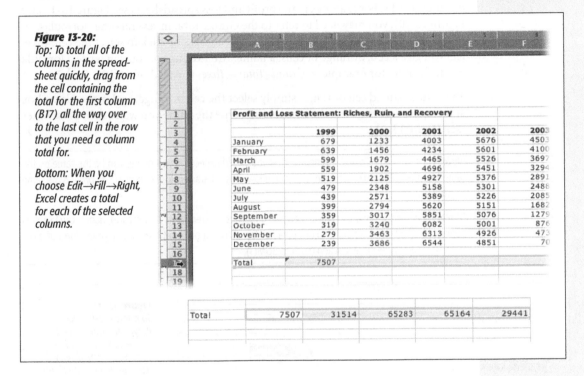

Figure 13-20:
Top: To total all of the columns in the spreadsheet quickly, drag from the cell containing the total for the first column (B17) all the way over to the last cell in the row that you need a column total for.

Bottom: When you choose Edit→Fill→Right, Excel creates a total for each of the selected columns.

Profit and Loss Statement: Riches, Ruin, and Recovery

	1999	2000	2001	2002	2003
January	679	1233	4003	5676	4503
February	639	1456	4234	5601	4100
March	599	1679	4465	5526	3697
April	559	1902	4696	5451	3294
May	519	2125	4927	5376	2891
June	479	2348	5158	5301	2488
July	439	2571	5389	5226	2085
August	399	2794	5620	5151	1682
September	359	3017	5851	5076	1279
October	319	3240	6082	5001	876
November	279	3463	6313	4926	473
December	239	3686	6544	4851	70
Total	7507				

Total	7507	31514	65283	65164	29441

7. **Click cell E19 and type** *Grand Total*. **Press Tab twice.**

   Excel moves the active cell to G19.

   To calculate a lifetime total for the spreadsheet, you need to tell Excel to add together all the yearly totals.

8. **Click the AutoSum button on the Standard toolbar.**

   In this case, the cells to be added aren't lined up with the Grand Total cell, so the AutoSum button doesn't work quite right; it says only *=SUM( )*, with nothing in the parentheses. You need to tell Excel what to put into those parentheses.

9. **Drag across the yearly totals (from B17 through F17).**

   As you drag across the cells, Excel inserts the cell range within the parentheses. In this example, the function now reads, =SUM(B17:F17)—in other words, "add up the contents of the cells B17 through F17, and display the result."

10. Press Enter.

Excel performs the calculation and displays the result in cell G19, the grand total for the life of your startup.

Named ranges

As you create formulas, you may find yourself referring over and over to the same cell or range of cells. For example, in the profit and loss spreadsheet (see Figure 13-13 and Figure 13-20), you may need to refer to the Grand Total in several other formulas. So that you don't have to repeatedly type the cell address or click to select the cell, Excel lets you give a cell, or range of cells, a name. After doing so, you can write a formula in the form of, for example, = *Grand_Total – Taxes* (instead of =*G19 – F27*).

To create a named cell or range, simply select the cell or range, and in the Name box at the upper-left corner of the Formula bar, type the name you want, then press Enter (see Figure 13-21).

Note: No spaces are allowed. Furthermore, as you would expect, no two names can be the same on the same worksheet, and Excel considers upper- and lowercase characters to be the same, so *profit* is the same as *PROFIT*.

Other requirements. The first character of a name must be a letter (or an underscore), names can't contain punctuation marks (except periods) or operators (+, =, and so on), and they can't take the form of a cell reference (such as B5) or a function (such as SUM()).

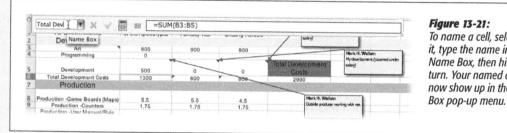

Figure 13-21:
To name a cell, select it, type the name in the Name Box, then hit Return. Your named cell will now show up in the Name Box pop-up menu.

From now on, the cell's or range's name appears in the Name Box pop-up menu. The next time you want to go to that cell or range or use it in a formula, you need only select it from this pop-up menu. Excel displays the name instead of the cell address whenever you create a formula that refers to a named cell.

If you need to change or remove a name, choose Insert→Names→Define to display the Define Names dialog box. From there, you'll find it easy to delete, create, or apply names.

Tip: You can use named cells as a quick way to navigate a large spreadsheet. By naming cells at key points in the spreadsheet, you can select them from the Name Box pop-up menu and jump to the corresponding cells.

References: absolute and relative

When you create a formula by typing the addresses of cells or by clicking a cell, you've created a *cell reference*. Excel generally considers cell references in a *relative* way—it remembers those cell coordinates by position relative to the selected cell, not as, for example, "B12." For example, a relative reference thinks of another cell in the spreadsheet as "three rows above and two columns to the left of this cell" (see Figure 13-22).

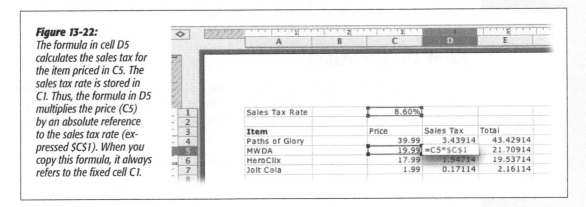

Figure 13-22:
The formula in cell D5 calculates the sales tax for the item priced in C5. The sales tax rate is stored in C1. Thus, the formula in D5 multiplies the price (C5) by an absolute reference to the sales tax rate (expressed $C$1). When you copy this formula, it always refers to the fixed cell C1.

Relative cell references make it possible for you to insert a new row or column into your spreadsheet without throwing off all of the formulas you've already stored. They make the Fill Right command possible, too. They also make formulas portable: When you paste a formula that adds up the two cells above it into a different spot, the pasted cell adds up the two cells above *it* (in its new location).

The yearly totals in Figure 13-20 work this way. When you "filled" the Total formula across to the other cells, Excel pasted *relative* cell references into all those cells that say, in effect, "display the total of the numbers in the cells *above this cell*." This way, each column's subtotal applies to the figures in that column. (If Excel instead pasted absolute references, then all the cells in the subtotal row would show the sum of the first-year column.)

Absolute references, on the other hand, refer to a specific cell, no matter where the formula appears in the spreadsheet. They can be useful when you need to refer to a particular cell in the spreadsheet—the one containing the sales tax rate, for example—for a formula that repeats over several columns. Figure 13-22 gives an example.

You designate an absolute cell reference by including a $ in front of the column and/or row reference. (For the first time in its life, the $ symbol has nothing to do with money.) For example, $A$7 is an absolute reference for cell A7.

You can also create a *mixed reference* in order to lock the reference to *either* the row or column—for example, G$8, in which the column reference is relative and the row is absolute. You might use this unusual arrangement when, for example, your column A contains discount rates for the customers whose names appear in column B. In writing the formula for a customer's final price (in column D, for example), you'd use a *relative* reference to a row number (different for every customer), but an *absolute* reference to the column (always A).

Tip: There's a handy shortcut that can save you some hand-eye coordination when you want to turn an absolute cell reference into a relative one, or vice versa. First, select the cell that contains the formula. In the Formula bar, highlight only the cell name you'd like to change. Then press ⌘-T. This keystroke makes the highlighted cell name cycle through different *stages* of absoluteness—for example, it changes the cell reference B4 first to $B$4, then to B$4, then to $B4, and so on.

Excel, the List Maker

After spending years loading up Excel with advanced number-crunchy features like pivot tables, database queries, and nested formulas, in 1999 Microsoft decided to step back and conduct some studies to see how its customers were enjoying their NASA-caliber spreadsheet program.

And what were 60 percent of Excel users doing with all this power?

Making lists.

That's right—most people use the software that drives uncounted businesses and statistical analyses for nothing more than building lists of phone numbers, CD collections, and so on.

That's why Microsoft, which never met a feature it didn't like, added to Excel 2001 the Macintosh-only List Manager, which simplifies building and manipulating lists (Figure 13-23). Excel does this by creating something called a *list object*, which is

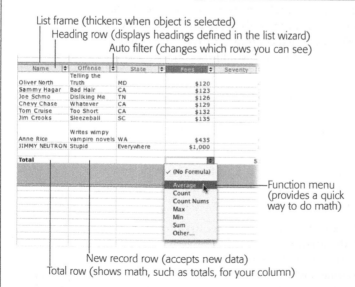

List frame (thickens when object is selected)
Heading row (displays headings defined in the list wizard)
Auto filter (changes which rows you can see)

New record row (accepts new data)
Total row (shows math, such as totals, for your column)

Function menu
(provides a quick
way to do math)

Figure 13-23:
List objects are among Excel's best features. These self-contained mini-databases can fold and spindle a list in record time. The top row has in-cell buttons for popping up the AutoFilter menu. This menu lets you sort your list and temporarily hide any unwanted data. In the optional total row at the bottom, you can quickly insert formulas via in-cell buttons that pop up the Function menu.

nothing more than a simple database. It's made up of rows (which are the same as database *records*—that is, the individual "Rolodex cards" of an address database) and columns (which are like the *fields* in a database record—that is, the address, city, zip code, and other bits of information). These rows and columns are contained inside a list frame.

The List Manager offers a number of features that improve upon using regular spreadsheet cells to store your lists (and upon Excel *databases,* as they were called in some previous versions):

- The list frame, a special border that appears when you click a list object, clearly outlines your data. You don't have to wonder which cells are meant to be part of the list.

- Excel keeps the column headings of a list completely separate from the data beneath them. As a result, they won't disappear or get sorted into the rows of the list itself, as might have happened outside a list object.

- You always get an empty record row at the bottom of the list, making it easy to add a new record; just click in the row and type.

- Lists have pop-up AutoFilter menus that make it simple to sort their rows or even *filter* them (so that only certain rows remain visible).

- Unlike Excel databases of old, you can have more than one list per spreadsheet.

The List Manager feature, in other words, is ideal for tasks like these:

- Build a list of all of the DVDs in your vast collection and sort them by genre, rating, number of stars in reviews, whether discs have director's commentaries—the possibilities are endless.

- Create a restaurant list for every city you visit, complete with names, categories, comments, and telephone numbers. When leaving for a trip to Detroit, you can filter that list so that it shows only the names of eateries in Detroit.

- Make an inventory list, with prices, part numbers, and warehouse location; you can later add a column to that list when you remember that you should have included something to indicate availability. Plus, you can format your list with alternating row colors that still alternate properly when you add a new column.

Just try *any* of these tricks with a plain spreadsheet and you'll soon be sobbing in frustration.

Building Your List with the List Wizard

Excel's List Wizard walks you through building a list. Here's how to build a new list from scratch—in this example, an enemies list in the style of former president Nixon.

Tip: To build a list object out of an existing list, first select all of the cells that make up your existing list, and then choose select Insert→List. The List Wizard walks you through turning your ersatz list into the real deal.

---

1. **In a new spreadsheet, click where you want the list to be.**

   You can always move it later.

2. **Choose Insert→List.**

   Excel presents the List Wizard (see Figure 13-24). The first screen asks you for the location of the data for your list and where you want the list to appear. Leave the data location radio button set to None (in this example, you'll be typing in the data *after* setting up the table), and leave the list location radio button set to "On existing worksheet."

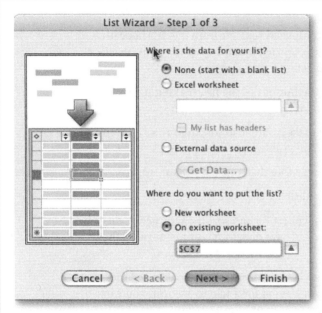

Figure 13-24:
The first step in the List Wizard has three options for data sources for your lists: none (meaning you'll enter the data as you go along), Excel worksheet (use this to convert a selection into a list), and External data source (which lets you access a database via Microsoft Query for Excel 2004 and ODBC—more on page 567). As for where the list goes, you can specify a location in the worksheet currently open, or you can tell Excel to create a whole new sheet for your list to call home.

3. **Click Next.**

   Now the List Wizard wants you to specify the columns for your list. If you've ever used FileMaker Pro or another database program, you should be familiar with this process—it's very similar to the one used to create fields for a database file.

   The enemies list will include four columns: Name, Offense, State Where Incident Occurred, and Rating.

4. **Type *Name* into the Column name field.**

   The List Wizard lets you classify each column as one of 10 data types, such as numbers, text, or dates. It even lets you set a column to be *another* list or a calculated value, which lets you bring formulas into your lists.

5. **From the "Data type" pop-up menu, choose Text; click Add.**

Excel adds the Name column to its list.

6. **Type *Offense*, then click Add; type *State Where Incident Occurred*, then click Add.**

The "Data type" pop-up menu remains set to the correct setting—*Text*—throughout this column-building procedure. The last column, however, will be a number.

Figure 13-25:
The second step of the List Wizard looks like a database field definition dialog box, and for good reason—Excel lists are databases, at heart. In this step, you can create as many or as few columns as your list needs and specify settings for each column.

> **List Wizard – Step 2 of 3**
>
> Columns
>
> | | |
> |---|---|
> | Name | Text |
> | Offense | Text |
> | State of Offense | Text |
> | Rating | Whole number |
>
> (Add) (Modify) (Delete) (Settings...)
>
> Column name: Rating
>
> Data type: Whole number ⬍
>
> (Cancel) (< Back) (Next >) (Finish)

7. **Type *Rating*; change the "Data type" pop-up menu to read Whole Number. Click Add.**

Once you've created a column, you can click its name and then click the Settings button to bring up the Column Settings dialog box. Here, you can change the settings for the column (including its name and data type). You can also specify a *default* value for it—that is, each time you add a new row to your list, Excel will fill in a canned entry for this row automatically. If most of your CDs are jazz recordings, for example, your CD-database list might contain a Category column with *Jazz* set up to be the default value for each new recording you add to your list. (For the CDs in different categories, you could always type in something different.)

Column Settings also offers a checkbox called "Unique values only." If you use this option, Excel requires that whatever you type into this list column is *unique* (not duplicated in the list)—for example, a serial number.

Suppose you turn this on for the Title field in a CD list, for example. When somebody tries to enter the name of a CD that has already been cataloged, Excel will beep, alert them that this column is supposed to contain unique values, and refuse to budge until the entry is changed.

You can also format cells using two handy buttons. By clicking the Formatting button, you bring up Excel's Format Cells dialog box, in which you can set up this column's type and formatting characteristics: number formatting; text alignment, rotation, and indentation; font size, style, and color; cell borders; fill patterns and colors; and whether a cell is locked or hidden. (The first half of Chapter 14 offers much more on these possibilities.)

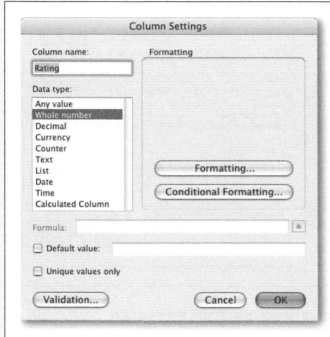

Figure 13-26:
The Column Settings dialog box contains much of the power behind Excel's lists. Here you can set a column's data type, whether the data entered in a column has to be a specific kind of data, and how that data is formatted. The Conditional Formatting button is the key to some of the graphic power of lists, letting you specify changes in appearance depending on how the data in the column changes.

The Conditional Formatting button, on the other hand, brings up the Conditional Formatting dialog box, in which you can set a series of rules to change a cell's formatting *automatically,* depending on what's happening in the cell. This feature can do things like make positive numbers in your Profits column appear in green, and losses in red. (More on conditional formatting in Chapter 14.)

Finally, Column Settings offers a Validation button. It summons a powerful window called Data Validation, where you can specify limits for the text or numbers typed into each cell in this column—and what happens if somebody disregards the limits. Figure 13-27 shows the procedure.

When you're finished with the Column Settings dialog box—if, indeed, you opened it at all—click OK. You return to the wizard.

8. **Click Next to continue.**

Finally, step 3 of 3 (at least according to the List Wizard). In this near-final step, you name the list, choose to show the totals row, and control whether the list's visuals—its display of pop-up menu controls and such, that is—appear.

Of particular interest here is the "Autoformat list after editing" checkbox. If you turn it on and then click AutoFormat, you're offered a list of 16 preset formats (color and accent schemes) for the list, as shown in Figure 13-28.

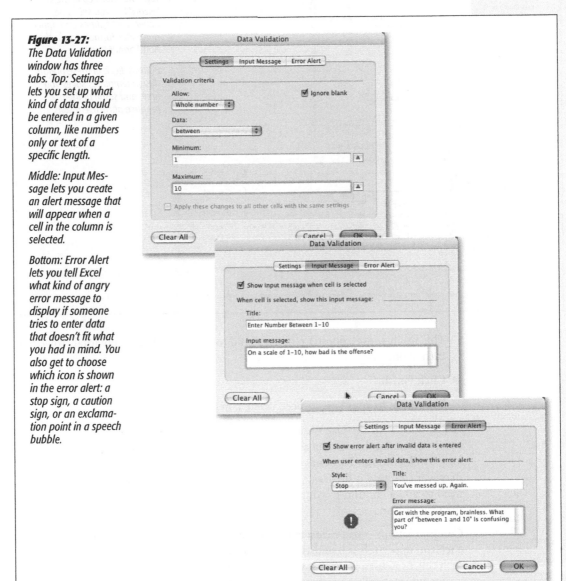

Figure 13-27:
The Data Validation window has three tabs. Top: Settings lets you set up what kind of data should be entered in a given column, like numbers only or text of a specific length.

Middle: Input Message lets you create an alert message that will appear when a cell in the column is selected.

Bottom: Error Alert lets you tell Excel what kind of angry error message to display if someone tries to enter data that doesn't fit what you had in mind. You also get to choose which icon is shown in the error alert: a stop sign, a caution sign, or an exclamation point in a speech bubble.

If you turn on "Show totals row," Excel will add a row at the bottom of your list that automatically keeps a running total (or count, or average) of the numbers above it; see page 505 for details.

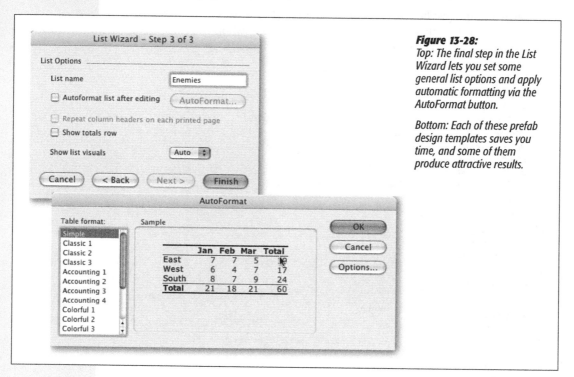

Figure 13-28:
Top: The final step in the List Wizard lets you set some general list options and apply automatic formatting via the AutoFormat button.

Bottom: Each of these prefab design templates saves you time, and some of them produce attractive results.

This list, however, doesn't require a total row, so leave the "Show totals row" box turned off.

9. Click Finish.

You return to your spreadsheet, where a newborn list appears.

You're done with the List Wizard, but not with the list; it still needs some touching up. By widening the columns, you can make room for column entries that are extra long. And although Excel has thoughtfully provided a place for a new column, you may want to hide it by dragging its right edge to the left. (If, by some chance, you need to add a column to your list later, you can click the Insert Column button in the List toolbar.)

Congratulations—you've just made an enemies list! To populate it with information, click the upper-left cell and type the first person's name. Press Tab after you fill in each cell, or Return whenever you want to jump down to the next row. The list frame grows automatically to accommodate your growing stack of rows.

As you go, you may note that AutoComplete works in list objects as well as in regular worksheets. In fact, Excel may sprout a pop-up list as you enter information into a cell. The list consists of entries you've added to the column that begin with the same characters you've typed in the cell. If a sprouted list contains an entry you want to reuse, just click the entry (or press the down arrow until you highlight the desired entry and then press Enter); Excel fills in the cell you were editing, saving you some typing.

Note: Excel offers a list of entries you've used in the column *even* if you've turned on the "Unique values only" option for the column. It just goes to show you: Even smart software can be pretty simpleminded.

What to Do with a List

An Excel list is a dynamic, living object that has more in common with a database than it does with a regular pencil-and-paper list. What follows are some basic things that you can do with a list, just to get you on the road to your personal list-making nirvana. For many of these tricks, you'll need the List toolbar. It generally opens when you click a list so that its frame appears; if you don't see it, choose View→Toolbars→List.

Add a row or column

To add a row to a list, select a cell or cells in the row *below* where you want the new row to appear, then click the Insert Row button on the List toolbar. To insert a column in a list, select a cell or cells *to the right* of where you want the new column to appear, then click the Insert Column button. The new column appears to the left of the selected cell or cells. You can also get to either of these insert commands by choosing Insert→ Row or Insert→Column from the List pop-up button in the List toolbar.

Note: Excel calls inserting a row in a list *inserting a row* (or a *record*), and it calls inserting a column in a list *inserting a field*.

Delete a row or column

To delete a row or column, select a cell or cells in the row or column you want to delete, and then choose Delete→Row or Delete→Column from the List pop-up button in the List toolbar.

When you delete a column or row in a list that you've formatted with an alternating colored-row scheme using AutoFormat, Excel automatically reshades all of the rows and columns so that they're still alternating—something that you'd have to do by hand if you tried this in a spreadsheet without the list feature.

Rearrange a row or column

To move an entire row to a new location, select it by moving the cursor over the list border to the left, and then click to select the row (as shown in Figure 13-29). Now move the row by dragging it by one of its borders, as if it were a range of cells (the cursor should look like a hand). Moving an entire column works the same way: Select it by moving the cursor over the list border until it changes shape (Figure 13-29), and then click to select the column. You can now move the column by dragging one of its borders.

Sort and filter the list

You can pop up the AutoFilter menu on the right side of each column heading to *sort* your list (change the order of your records) and *filter* it (choose which records to show and which to conceal). Figure 13-23 shows the menu.

Note: If the in-cell buttons for the AutoFilter menu don't appear in the top row when you click the list, check the List toolbar and turn on Visuals and AutoFilters.

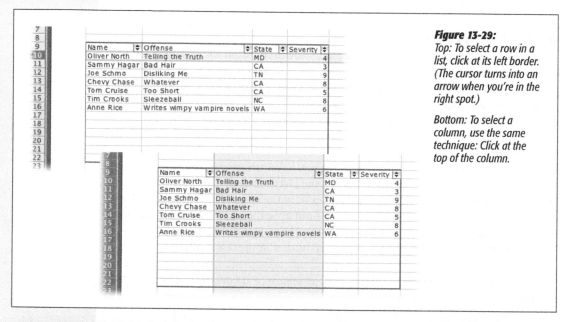

Figure 13-29:
Top: To select a row in a list, click at its left border. (The cursor turns into an arrow when you're in the right spot.)

Bottom: To select a column, use the same technique: Click at the top of the column.

POWER USERS' CLINIC

Building a Custom List Filter

By selecting Custom Filter from the pop-up AutoFilter menu, you open up the Custom AutoFilter dialog box, where you can build your own filter. In it, you can set up a rule for what data is shown with some simple operations and logical statements.

For example, you can show all data that's greater than a certain value or contains the word "blue." The Custom AutoFilter

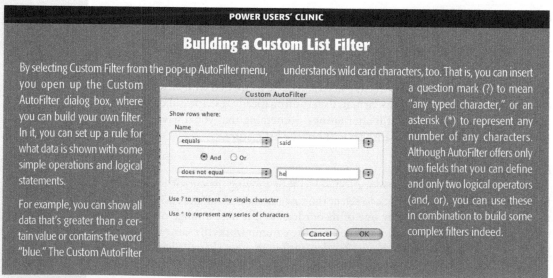

understands wild card characters, too. That is, you can insert a question mark (?) to mean "any typed character," or an asterisk (*) to represent any number of any characters. Although AutoFilter offers only two fields that you can define and only two logical operators (and, or), you can use these in combination to build some complex filters indeed.

Slicing and dicing your list is easy with the three-part AutoFilter menu. Choose commands from the top part to sort the list based on the entries in that column in ascending or descending order. The middle part lets you filter the list using three different commands: Show All reveals all items in the list, Show Top 10 shows the top 10 items or percent (for numerical items only), and Custom Filter lets you build your own filter. The bottom part lists the unique entries in the column; if there are duplicate entries, Excel shows only one of each.

Tip: For more advanced sorting, select Sort from the List pop-up button in the List toolbar. The Sort dialog box lets you choose three criteria by which to sort your list, much as you might do with a database.

Use the total row

A great feature in Excel's List Manager is the total row—which you can use by turning on the "Show totals row" checkbox in step 3 of 3 in the List Wizard. (You can also hide or show it by clicking the Total Row button in the List toolbar.)

The total row appears at the bottom of the list. If the rightmost column of your list contains number fields, Excel automatically adds up its contents and displays the result in the rightmost total row cell. If not, Excel counts the number of occupied rows appearing in your list and shows that result in the cell instead. (You can change this function using the pop-up Function menu that becomes available when you click the rightmost cell in the total row.)

But you're not limited to placing a formula beneath the rightmost column. Using the Function pop-up menu in each cell of the total row, you can summon a variety of functions (see Figure 13-30). If you'd rather, you can choose Other and then work in the Paste Function dialog box to concoct your own, even more complex formula. (You can even enter any formula you like using the Formula bar, and that formula needn't have *anything* to do with the items in the list.)

Figure 13-30:
To quickly add a formula to a cell in the total row, click the cell to activate its pop-up menu. Choose a function from the menu, or choose Other to bring up the Paste Function dialog box, where you can noodle over Excel's entire function collection.

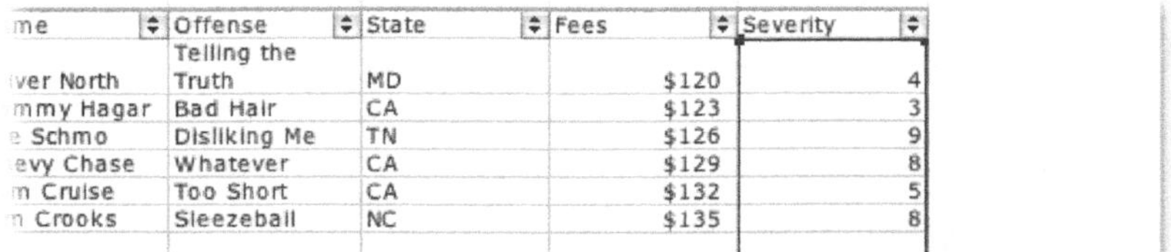

me	Offense	State	Fees	Severity
	Telling the			
ver North	Truth	MD	$120	4
mmy Hagar	Bad Hair	CA	$123	3
e Schmo	Disliking Me	TN	$126	9
evy Chase	Whatever	CA	$129	8
m Cruise	Too Short	CA	$132	5
n Crooks	Sleezeball	NC	$135	8
	Writes wimpy			
ne Rice	vampire novels	WA	$435	6
MY NEUTROI	Stupid	Everywhere	$1,000	8
tal				=SUBTOTAL(9, E10:E17)
				SUBTOTAL(function_num, ref1, [ref2]

Move or delete the whole list object

You must first select a list object to move or delete it. To perform this surprisingly delicate operation, click the list to make its frame appear. Then position the cursor carefully over the upper-left corner of the frame until the cursor turns into a hand. With the hand cursor, click the upper-left corner to select the entire list object. Now you can:

- Delete the list by choosing Edit→Clear→All.

- Move the list by choosing Edit→Cut. Then click where you want the upper-left cell of the list to move to, and choose Edit→Paste. Excel moves the list to the new location. (You can move the list elsewhere on its worksheet, or switch to a different sheet in the workbook by clicking a tab at the bottom of the window.)

Caution: Microsoft recommends that a list object containing more than 50 rows should go on its own worksheet all by itself. A worksheet holding nothing but a list object is called a *listsheet.*

The List Menu

The List toolbar gives you access to some of Excel's most powerful list-related features. Most of its buttons relate to features you already encountered during your list construction.

But take special note of the List pop-up button, which is rife with useful commands. Some of them (Insert, Delete, Clear Contents) are self-explanatory. A few others could stand clarification:

- **Sort.** Opens the advanced Sort dialog box, in which you can sort your list by up to three criteria (by Company, for example, and then alphabetically within each company group).

- **Filter.** AutoFilters are the canned filtering options that appear when you open the pop-up menu atop any column (such as Ascending, Descending, Top 10, and so on). Using this Filter command, however, you can choose AutoFilter to turn *off* the pop-up menu controls, thus removing your option to use those canned filters. (The other commands in this submenu apply to old-style Excel databases, not to list objects.)

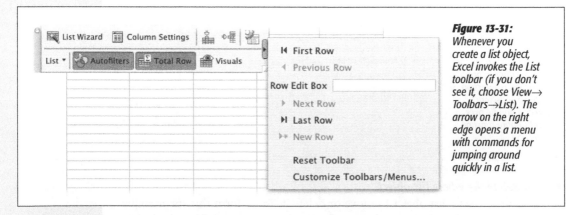

Figure 13-31:
Whenever you create a list object, Excel invokes the List toolbar (if you don't see it, choose View→ Toolbars→List). The arrow on the right edge opens a menu with commands for jumping around quickly in a list.

- **Form.** Calls up the Data Form, which lets you work with your list in a database-like environment.

- **Chart.** Turns your list into a chart, as described in Chapter 13.

- **PivotTable Report.** Opens the PivotTable Wizard to help you turn your list into a PivotTable (see Chapter 14).

- **Remove List Manager.** Converts the list back into a block of ordinary cells.

- **Refresh Data.** Grabs fresh data from the list's external data source, if it has one (see page 567).

Formatting and Charts

W hen you enter information in an Excel spreadsheet, your text appears in crisp, 10-point Verdana type. Very nice…at least initially. But too much of any font on a background resembling graph paper can look drab, so Excel comes packed with formatting tools that take spreadsheets from blah to brilliant.

For starters, Excel offers a broad selection of fonts, colors, and borders to make your sheets stand out. Excel can also import pictures and movies (either clip art provided by Microsoft or images of your own), and you can even use Excel's drawing tools to create your own works of art.

Excel is also expert, of course, at turning your dull numbers into lively charts and graphs—for many people, that's the whole point of typing in all those numbers in the first place. And Excel 2004 does an even better job than previous iterations of the program. Excel 2004's charts include professionally designed color schemes that change at the click of a button, as well as the convenience of controlling a chart's look from the Formatting Palette.

This chapter covers all of these visual aspects of Excel, including the payoff moment of printing out your beautifully formatted spreadsheets.

Formatting Worksheets

When it comes to spreadsheets, the term *formatting* covers a lot of ground. It refers to the size of the cell, how its borders look, what color fills it, how the contents of the cell are formatted (with or without dollar signs, for example)—anything that affects how the cell looks.

There are two ways to add formatting to your spreadsheet: by using Excel's automatic formatting capabilities or by doing the work yourself. Odds are, you'll be using both methods.

FREQUENTLY ASKED QUESTION

Changing the Default Fonts

How do I change the default font and other formats?

Ah, you've been reading Microsoft's Top Ten Tech Calls list, haven't you?

Whether you want a funky new font to lighten up your serious number crunching, or you want to switch back to the Geneva 9-point font of Office versions gone by, a quick trip to the Edit→Preferences→General panel will solve your problem. After you change the standard font and size (the controls are right in the middle of the General panel) and click OK, Excel displays a warning message, noting that you must quit and restart Excel before the new formatting takes effect in new worksheets. Even better, if you save the file as a template named *Workbook* in the Microsoft Office 2004→Office→Start→Excel folder, all new workbooks started by pressing ⌘-N will be based on that file. Similarly a one-worksheet template named *Sheet* in the same location will be used when you choose Insert→Worksheet.

To apply the changes to old worksheets, press ⌘-A to select the entire sheet, and then change the formatting in the Format→Cells→Font tab (shown here). Or click the Font title bar in the Formatting Palette and change it there.

To make broader changes, you can modify the Normal style (page 524) or create a template—a generic document that can be used over and over to start new worksheets. Because a template can hold formatting and text, it's a great base for a worksheet that you redo regularly (such as a monthly report).

To create a template, use a new worksheet or a copy of one that already looks the way you like it. You can select the entire sheet or specific sections of it, apply formats (as described in this chapter); and even include text (column headings you'll always need, for example). When you finish formatting the sheet, choose File→Save As. In the Save dialog box, enter a name for the template in the "Save As" field, and then choose Template from the Format menu. Excel gives your file an .xlt extension and switches the Where pop-up menu to "My Templates." Click Save.

Back in Excel, close the template worksheet.

Thereafter, whenever you'd like to open a copy of the template, choose File→Project Gallery. Click the My Templates category, click your template, and click OK.

Automatic Formatting

If you're not interested in hand-formatting your spreadsheets—or you just don't have the time—Excel's AutoFormat tool is a quick way to apply formatting to your sheets. It instructs Excel to study the layout and contents of your spreadsheet and then apply colors, shading, font styles, and other formatting attributes to make the sheet look professional.

Note: AutoFormat is best suited for fairly boring layouts: column headings across the top, row labels at the left side, totals at the bottom, and so on. If your spreadsheet uses a more eccentric layout, AutoFormat may make quirky design choices.

To use the AutoFormat feature, select the cells you want formatted, and then choose Format→AutoFormat. The AutoFormat dialog box appears, complete with a list of formats on the left. By clicking each one in turn, you'll see (in the center of the dialog box) that each one is actually a predesigned formatting scheme for a table-like makeover of the selected cells (see Figure 14-1).

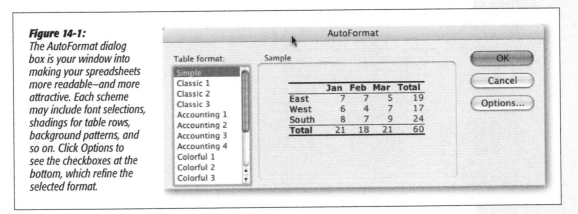

Figure 14-1:
The AutoFormat dialog box is your window into making your spreadsheets more readable—and more attractive. Each scheme may include font selections, shadings for table rows, background patterns, and so on. Click Options to see the checkboxes at the bottom, which refine the selected format.

On the right is a button labeled Options, which lets you control the formatting elements that will be applied to the selected cells.

Once you've selected an AutoFormat option (and made any tweaks to the applied formats), click OK. Excel goes to work on the selected cells. If you don't care for the results, you can always undo them with a quick ⌘-Z.

The Format Painter

Another way to quickly apply formatting to a group of cells is the Format Painter. Suppose you've painstakingly applied formatting—colors, cell borders, fonts, text alignment, and the like—to a certain patch of cells. Using the Format Painter, you can copy the formatting to any other cells.

To start, select the cell(s) that you want to use as an example of good formatting. Then click the Format Painter button (the little paintbrush) on the Standard toolbar.

Now move the cursor over the spreadsheet so that it changes to look like a + sign and a paintbrush.

Next, drag the cursor over the cells you'd like to change to match the first group. Excel applies the formatting—borders, shading, font settings, and the like—to the new cells (Figure 14-2).

Tip: To format discontinuous areas without going back to the paintbrush, double-click the paintbrush control. Now you can apply the format multiple times. To stop, click the paintbrush control again.

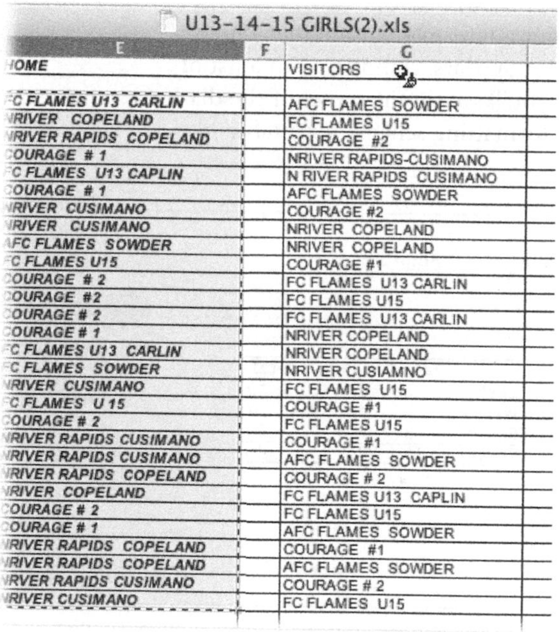

Figure 14-2:
The Format Painter can take everything but the data from the cells on the left, and apply it to the cells on the right.

Formatting Cells by Hand

If the AutoFormat feature is a bit too canned for your purposes, you can always format the look of your spreadsheet manually.

When formatting cells manually, it's helpful to divide the task up into two concepts—formatting the cells themselves (borders and backgrounds), and formatting the *contents* of those cells (what you've typed).

Changing cell size

When you open an Excel worksheet, all the cells are the same size. Specifically, they're 1.04 inches wide (the factory-set width of an Excel column) and 0.18 inches tall (the height of an Excel column). The good news is that there are several ways to set a cell's height and width. Here's a rundown:

Note: If you use the Metric system, you can change to centimeters or millimeters on the Excel→Preferences→General tab. Choose from the "Measurement units" pop-up menu. Unfortunately, 4.59 millimeters is just as hard to remember as 0.18 inches.

- **Dragging the borders.** Obviously, you can't enlarge a single cell without enlarging its entire row or column; Excel has this funny way of insisting that your cells remain aligned with each other. Therefore, you can't resize a single cell independently—you can only enlarge its entire row or column.

  To adjust the width of a column, drag the divider line that separates its *column heading* from the one to its right, as shown in Figure 14-3; to change the height of a row, drag the divider line between its row and the one below it. In either case, the trick is to drag *in the row numbers or column letters.* Your cursor will look like a double-headed arrow if you drag in the right place.

Note: Excel adjusts row heights automatically if you enlarge the font or wrap your text.

POWER USERS' CLINIC

Conditional Formatting

Cell formatting doesn't have to be static. With Conditional Formatting, you can turn your cells into veritable chameleons, changing colors or typography on their own, based on their own contents.

By far the most common example is setting up income-related numbers to turn bright red when they go negative, as is common in corporate financial statements. Another common example is using this feature to highlight in bold the sales figures for the highest-earning salesperson listed in a column.

To use conditional formatting, select the cell(s) that you want to change on their own, and then choose Format→Conditional Formatting. In the Conditional Formatting dialog box, set up the conditions that trigger the desired formatting changes.

For example, to set up a column of numbers so they'll turn red when negative, use the first pop-up menu to choose "Cell Value Is" and the second to choose "less than." Finally,

type 0 into the text field, as shown here. Then click Format to specify the typographical, border, and pattern changes you want to see if a highlighted cell's contents fall below zero. For example, in the Font tab, choose red from the Color pop-up menu and Bold from the Font Style list. Click OK.

By clicking the Add button at this point, you can even add a second set of conditions to your cells. For example, you might want your monthly income spreadsheet to show numbers over $10,000 with yellow cell shading.

You can apply up to three conditions to the same selection, but if more than one condition applies, Excel uses only the first one.

The dialog box previews how your cells will look if a condition is met. If everything looks right, click OK. You return to the spreadsheet, where numbers that meet your conditions now display their special formatting.

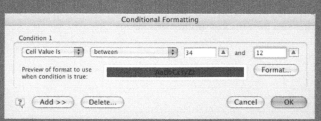

- **Menu commands.** For more exact control over height and width adjustments, choose Format→Row→Height, or Format→Column→Width. Either command pops up a dialog box in which you can enter the row height or column width by typing numbers on your Mac's keyboard.

- **Autosizing.** For the tidiest spreadsheet possible, highlight some cells and then choose Format→Row→AutoFit, or Format→Column→AutoFit Selection. Excel readjusts the selected columns or rows so they're exactly as wide and tall as necessary to contain their contents, but no larger. That is, each column expands or shrinks just enough to fit its longest entry.

Tip: You don't have to use the AutoFit command to perform this kind of tidy adjustment. You can also, at any time, make an individual row or column precisely as large as necessary by double-clicking the divider line between the row numbers or the column letters. (The column to the *left* of your double-click, or the row *above* your double-click, gets resized.) When using this method, there's no need to highlight anything first.

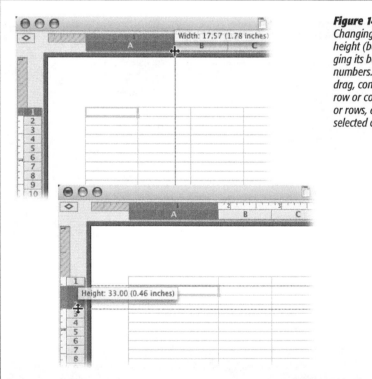

Figure 14-3:
Changing the width (top) of a column or height (bottom) of a row is as simple as dragging its border in the column letters or row numbers. A small yellow box pops up as you drag, continually updating the exact size of the row or column. If you select multiple columns or rows, dragging a border changes all of the selected columns or rows.

Cell borders and colors 1: The Format Cells window

The light gray lines that form the graph-paper grid of an Excel spreadsheet are an optical illusion. They exist only to help you understand where one column or row ends and the next begins, but they don't print out (unless you want them to; see page 549).

If you'd like to add solid, printable borders to certain rows, columns, or cells, Excel offers three different methods: the old, slightly stale Format Cells dialog box, the whiz-bang Borders and Shading section of the Formatting Palette, and the very similar Border Drawing *toolbar*. All techniques let you control how lines are added to the cell's edges, but only the Formatting Palette and the toolbar let you change borders and shading without first opening a dialog box to make the changes.

Hiding and showing rows and columns

There are any number of reasons why you may want to hide or show certain columns or rows in your spreadsheet. Maybe the numbers in a particular column are used in calculations elsewhere in the spreadsheet, but you don't need them taking up screen space. Maybe you want to preserve several previous years' worth of data, but don't want to scroll through them. Or maybe the IRS is coming for a visit.

In any case, it's easy enough to hide certain rows or columns. Start by highlighting the rows or columns in question. (Remember: To highlight an entire row, click its gray row number; to highlight several consecutive rows, drag vertically through the row numbers; to highlight nonadjacent rows, ⌘-click their row numbers. To highlight certain columns, use the gray column letters at the top of the spreadsheet in the same way.)

Next, choose Format→Row→Hide, or Format→Column→Hide. That's all there is to it: The column or row disappears completely, leaving a gap in the numbering or letter sequence at the left or top edge of the spreadsheet. The row numbers or column letters surrounding the hidden area turn blue.

Making them reappear is a bit trickier, since you can't exactly highlight an invisible row or column. To perform this minor miracle, use the blue-colored row numbers or column headers as clues. Select cells on either side of the hidden row or column. Then choose Format→Row→Unhide, or Format→Column→Unhide.

Alternatively, you can also select a hidden cell (such as B5) by typing its address in the Name box on the Formula bar, and then choosing Format→Row→Unhide, or Format→Column→Unhide.

To add cell borders using the time-honored Format Cells command, highlight some cells and then choose Format→Cells (or press ⌘-1). The Format Cells dialog box appears; now click the Border tab to show the border controls. In this tab, you'll see three sections: Presets, Border, and Line (see Figure 14-4).

1. **If you don't want to use the default line style and color, choose new ones in the Line section.**

   Excel loads your cursor with your desired style and color.

2. **If one of the preset options appeals to you, click it. To border all cells in your selection, click Outline and Inside.**

If you change your mind, click None to remove the option. Excel previews your work in the Border section.

3. **To apply custom borders, use the buttons that surround the preview in the Border section, or click directly between the guides in the preview.**

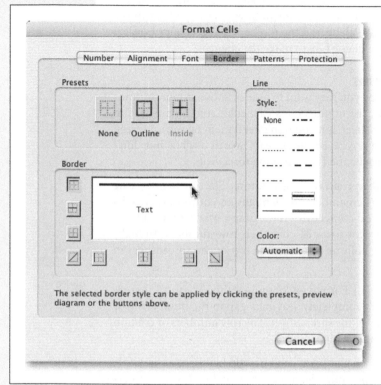

Figure 14-4:
Clicking in the preview area inside the Border section allows you to place borders where you want them. First, select the style of line on the right side, and then click in the preview area to place the line—if you do it the other way around, you'll get the line style that was selected for the last line drawn. If the preview makes you dizzy, use the Presets buttons above or try the eight buttons around the left and bottom edges of the preview area to draw your horizontal, vertical, and diagonal borders.

To change a line style, reload the cursor with a new style from the Line section and then click the borders in the preview area you wish to change.

If you mess up, click None in the Presets area to start again.

4. **Once the borders look the way you'd like, click OK.**

Excel applies the borders to the selection in your spreadsheet.

Cell borders and colors 2: The Formatting Palette
To use Excel's Formatting Palette to draw borders, select the cells you want to work with, and then open the Borders and Shading portion of the palette by clicking on the Borders and Shading Title Bar.

In this section of the palette, you'll see six controls that help you box in your cells and apply colors and patterns (Figure 14-5).

Here's what each control does.

- **Type.** The button itself indicates the kind of border you've already applied to the selected cells; if you haven't applied a border, the icon on the button is a faint, dotted-line square. In any case, click it to open a pop-out palette of 18 different border styles, covering most conceivable border needs. The first 12 borders are standard fare, mostly outlines and single lines. The last six styles show more variety; some put borders on two sides of a selection or include thicker borders on one side. (If you point to one of these border styles without clicking, a yellow pop-up screen tip offers a plain-English description of its function.)

Figure 14-5:
The Formatting Palette is one of the best things to come to Excel in a long time—and the Borders and Shading section makes adding borders to your spreadsheet painless. Click the flippy triangle to the left of "Borders and Shading" (or anywhere on that bar) to show or hide the controls.

If you don't see the Formatting Palette, choose its name from the View menu or click the palette button in the toolbar (next to the Toolbox icon).

This pop-up palette should be your first stop. Some of the other palettes described here aren't even available until you've first selected a border type.

- **Style.** Choose a line style, including dotted lines and thick lines.

- **Color.** This button lets you choose from one of 40 preset line colors. Note that you can also leave the line color set to Automatic (which usually means black) if you choose, but you can't mix your own line color.

- **Pattern.** Instead of changing the style of *line* that surrounds the selected cells, this button offers patterns with which to fill the selected cells' *backgrounds*. (The bottom half of this menu specifies the color that Excel will use to draw the black areas of the displayed patterns. You'll probably find that most of the patterns make your cell contents illegible, unless you also select a very light color for the fill.)

  "Automatic," by the way, means "no pattern."

- **Fill color.** Clicking this button reveals options for 40 preset fill colors for your cell backgrounds. Here again, use this option with caution; unless you also change the text color to something bright, you should use only very light colors for filling the cell backgrounds. (To change which colors appear here, choose Excel→Preferences→Color panel and then click Modify.)

- **Draw borders by hand.** Clicking Draw by Hand brings up the Border Drawing toolbar, a mosquito of a toolbar with five unlabeled buttons. (Point to each without clicking to reveal its pop-up yellow label.)

  The first one, Draw Border, pops up so you can choose between two modes: Draw Border and Draw Border Grid. The Draw Border tool lets you create a border that encloses an otherwise unaffected block of cells just by dragging diagonally in your spreadsheet; the border takes on the line characteristics you've specified using the other tools in the toolbar. The Draw Border Grid tool works similarly, except that it doesn't draw one master rectangle. Instead, it adds borders to every cell *within* the rectangle that you create by dragging diagonally, "painting" all four walls of every cell inside.

POWER USERS' CLINIC

Protecting the Spreadsheet Cells

Excel's Format Cells dialog box is a real workhorse when it comes to applying a bunch of formatting changes to a sheet. The first five of its tabs—Number, Alignment, Font, Border, and Patterns—let you exercise pinpoint control over how your spreadsheet—both cells and text—looks and feels, as described in this chapter.

The last tab—Protection—is the exception to the formatting rule. The Protection tab has only two options, presented as checkboxes: Locked and Hidden. These two options let you protect selected cells from changes or hide formulas from view.

But be warned: Neither of these options takes effect unless you also protect the sheet through the Protection feature, which is nestled in the Tools menu.

To erase borders from the spreadsheet, click Erase Border and then drag across any unwanted borders (or those painted in by mistake). Press Esc to cancel the eraser cursor. (The middle button, Merge Cells, is described on page 525).)

Tip: You can tear palettes off the Formatting Palette, which makes for easy access if you need to get to their functions frequently. To do so, click the Font Color button, for example, and then click the double-dotted line at the top of the pop-out. The Font Color palette "tears off" and becomes a palette unto itself.

Changing How Text Looks

Borders and fills aren't the only things that you can change to make your sheets look their best; Excel gives you a great deal of control over how your text looks, as well. The text controls in Excel are divided into three major categories: number formatting, font control, and text alignment.

Adding number formats

Number formats in Excel add symbols, such as dollar signs, decimal points, or zeros, to whatever raw characters you've typed—usually numbers, but certain kinds of text are eligible, too. For example, if you apply Currency formatting to a cell containing *35.4*, it appears in the spreadsheet as $35.40; if you apply Percentage formatting, it becomes 3540.00%.

What may strike you as odd, especially at first, is that this kind of formatting doesn't actually change a cell's contents. If you double-click the aforementioned cell that says $35.40, the trappings of currency disappear instantly, leaving behind only the *35.4* that you originally entered. All number formatting does is put the niceties in numbers to make them easier to read. (The exception: dates and times. Date and time formatting may change the actual contents of these cells, as described on page 471.)

To apply a number format, select the cells on which you want to work your magic, and then select the formatting that you want to apply. Excel comes prepared to format numbers using eleven broad categories of canned formatting. You get at them in any of three ways:

- The Format pop-up menu in the Number section of the Formatting Palette (better known as "the easy way"), as shown in Figure 14-6.

- The Format Cells dialog box that appears when you choose Format→Cells (or Control-click some cells and choose Format Cells from the shortcut menu).

- The old Formatting toolbar (choose View→Toolbars→Formatting). The new Formatting Palette is light-years more flexible, so if you have the screen space for it, you can safely ignore the Formatting toolbar. (Unless you, as a diehard Excel 98 fan, have a raging antipathy toward change, that is.)

Each method offers the same broad categories of formatting; however, options in the Formatting Palette are far fewer. Instead, they apply the most popular choice (for example, $ signs when you choose the currency formatting) without asking your opinion. The Format Cells dialog box, on the other hand, offers more control over each format, along with a little preview of the result.

The following descriptions identify which additional controls are available in the Format Cells dialog box:

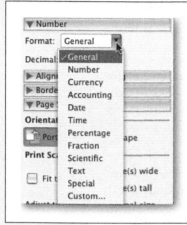

Figure 14-6:
The Number section of the Formatting Palette provides quick access to common number formatting options via the Format pop-up menu. It also lets you increase or decrease the number of decimal places shown by clicking the Increase Decimal or Decrease Decimal buttons.

- **General.** This option means "no formatting." Whatever you type into cells formatted this way remains exactly as is.

- **Number.** This control formats the contents as a generic number, automatically adding commas and two decimal places.

  Format Cells dialog box extras: You have the option to specify exactly how you want negative numbers to appear, how many decimal places you want to see, and whether or not a comma should appear in the thousands place.

- **Currency.** A specific kind of number format, the Currency format adds dollar signs, commas, decimal points, and two decimal places to numbers entered in the selected cells.

  Format Cells dialog box extras: You can specify how many decimal places you want to see. You also get a Currency Symbol pop-up menu that offers a list of hundreds of international currency symbols, including the euro. You can also set how Excel should display negative numbers.

Tip: The Currency setting in the Formatting Palette applies dollar formatting only if that's the currency you've typed in the Numbers tab of the International panel of the Mac's System Preferences program.

- **Accounting.** A specific kind of *currency* format, the Accounting format adds basic currency formatting—a $ sign, commas in the thousands place, and two decimal places. It also left-aligns the $ sign and encloses negative numbers in parentheses.

Format Cells dialog box extras: You can opt to use a different currency symbol and indicate how many decimal places you'd like to see.

• **Date.** Internally, Excel converts the number in the cell to a date and time *serial number* (see page 471) and then converts it to a readable date format, such as 11/2.

Format Cells dialog box extras: You can specify what date format you want applied, such as 11/2/02, November-02, or 14-Nov-2002.

• **Time.** Once again, Excel converts the number to a special serial number and then formats it in a readable time format, such as 1:32.

Format Cells dialog box extras: The dialog box presents a long list of time-formatting options, some of which include both the time and date.

• **Percentage.** This displays two decimal places for numbers and then adds percent symbols. The number 1.2, for example, becomes 120%.

Format Cells dialog box extras: You can indicate how many decimal places you want to see.

• **Fraction.** This option converts the decimal portion of a number into a fraction. (People who still aren't familiar with stock market statistics represented in decimal form will especially appreciate this one.)

Format Cells dialog box extras: You can choose from one of nine fraction types, some of which round the decimal to the nearest half, quarter, or tenth.

• **Scientific.** The Scientific option converts the number in the cell to scientific notation, such as 3.54E+04 (which means 3.54 times 10 to the fourth power, or 35,400).

Format Cells dialog box extras: You can specify the number of decimal places.

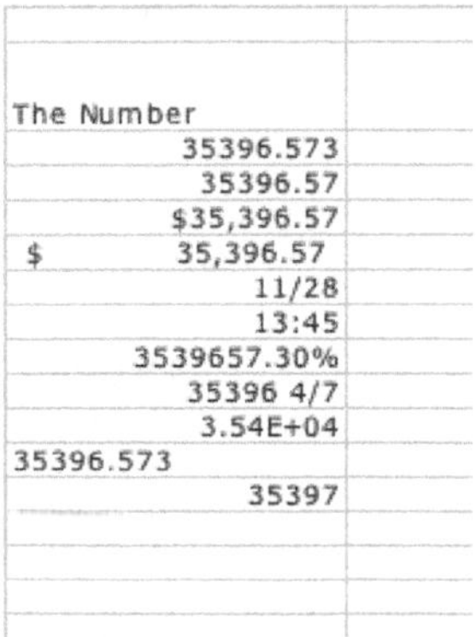

Figure 14-7:
Here's how the 11 different number formats make the number 35396.573 look. Some of the differences are subtle, but important. The contents of Text formatted cells are left-justified, for example, and the Number format lets you specify how many decimal places you want to see. Date and Time formats treat any number you specify as date and time serial numbers—more a convenience for Excel than for you.

The Number	
	35396.573
	35396.57
	$35,396.57
$	35,396.57
	11/28
	13:45
	3539657.30%
	35396 4/7
	3.54E+04
35396.573	
	35397

- **Text.** This control treats the entry in the cell as text, even when the entry is a number. The contents are displayed exactly as you entered them. The most immediate change you'll discover is that the contents of your cells are left-justified, rather than right-aligned as usual. (No special options are available in the Format Cells dialog box.)

- **Special.** This option formats the numbers in your selected cells as postal Zip codes. If there are fewer than five digits in the number, Excel adds enough zeros to the beginning of the number. If there's a decimal involved, Excel rounds to the nearest whole number. And if there are more than five digits, Excel leaves the additional numbers alone.

  Format Cells dialog box extras: In addition to Zip code format, you can choose from several other canned number patterns: Zip Code + 4, Phone Number, and Social Security Number. In each case, Excel automatically adds parentheses or hyphens as necessary.

- **Custom.** The Custom option brings up the Format Cells dialog box, where you can create your own number formatting, either starting with one of 39 preset formats or writing a format from scratch using a small set of codes. For example, custom formatting can be written to display every number as a fraction of 1000—something not available in the Fraction formatting.

Add or remove decimal places

To add or remove decimal places, turning *34* and *125* into *34.00* and *125.00,* for example, click the Decimal buttons in the Formatting Palette, as shown in Figure 14-6. Each click on the Increase Decimal button (on the left) adds decimal places; each click on the Decrease Decimal button (on the right) decreases the level of displayed precision by one decimal place.

Changing fonts

Excel lets you control the fonts used in its sheets via the Font portion of the Formatting Palette. As always, the Macintosh instructions are (1) highlight what you want to format, and (2) apply the formatting, in this case using the Formatting Palette.

Of course, you can highlight the cell(s) you want to format using any of the techniques described on page 476. But when it comes to character formatting, there are additional options; Excel actually lets you apply different fonts and font styles *within* a single cell. The trick is to double-click the cell and then use the I-beam cursor—carefully—to select just the characters in the cell that you want to work with. As a result, any changes you make in the Formatting Palette affect only the selected characters.

Once you've highlighted the cells or text you want to change, open the Fonts section of the Formatting Palette (Figure 14-8) to reveal its four main controls:

- The **Name** pop-up menu lets you apply any installed font on your Mac to the highlighted cell(s).

Tip: If your Mac has numerous fonts installed, you may find it faster to specify your desired font by typing its name in the Name field rather than using the pop-up menu. (Unfortunately, you must type the entire font name before pressing Return; you can't type simply *pal* to indicate Palatino, as you can in Word.)

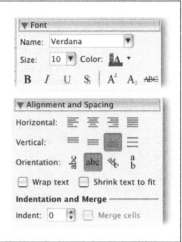

Figure 14-8:
Top: By tweaking the controls in the Font section of the Formatting Palette, you can quickly create your own custom text look.

Bottom: The Alignment and Spacing section of the Formatting Palette provides precise control over how text fills a cell; it can even be used to join cells together.

- The **Size** pop-up menu lets you choose from nine commonly used font sizes (9 point, 18 point, and so on). If the size you want isn't listed, type a number into the Size field and then press Enter or Return. (Excel accommodates only whole- and half-number point sizes. If you type in any other fractional font size, such as 12.2, Excel rounds it to the nearest half-point.)

- The **font style** item offers buttons for applying bold, italic, underline, or strikethrough (or any combination thereof).

Tip: You can apply or remove these font styles to selected characters or cells without even visiting the Formatting Palette; just press ⌘-B for bold, ⌘-I for italic, ⌘-U for underline, or Shift-⌘-hyphen for strikethrough. In fact, you can use keyboard shortcuts to apply shadow and outline styles, which don't even appear in the Formatting Palette (probably because they look terrible). Try Shift-⌘-W for shadowed text, and Shift-⌘-D for outlined text.

- Finally, the **font color** control lets you choose from one of 40 different text colors for the selected text, cell, or cells.

Aligning text

Ordinarily, Excel automatically slides a number to the right end of its cell, and text to the left end of its cell. That is, it right-justifies numbers, and left-justifies text. (*Number formatting* may override these settings.)

But the Formatting Palette offers far more control over how the text in a cell is placed. In the Text Alignment section of the palette (Figure 14-8, bottom), you'll find enough controls to make even a hard-core typographer happy:

- **Horizontal** affects the left-to-right positioning of the text within its cell. Click one of the four buttons to specify left alignment, centered text, right alignment, or full justification. You probably won't see any difference between the full justification and left-alignment settings unless there's more than one line of text within the cell. (And speaking of full justification, note that it wraps text within the cell, if necessary, even if you haven't turned on the text-wrapping option.)

- **Indent** controls how far text should be indented from the left edge of its cell. Each time you click the up arrow button, Excel slides the text approximately two character widths to the right. You can also click in the Indent field and type a number, followed by Enter or Return.

  It's especially important to use this control when you're tempted to indent by typing spaces or pressing the Tab key. Those techniques can result in misaligned cell contents, or worse.

- **Vertical** aligns text with the top, middle, or bottom of a cell. If the cell contains more than one line of text, you can even specify full vertical *justification*, which means that the lines of text will be spread out vertically enough to fill the entire cell.

POWER USERS' CLINIC

Making Your Own Styles

If you format spreadsheet cells in the same ways over and over again, you can save a lot of time and tedium by defining a particular set of formatting attributes as a style.

Exactly as in Word (see page 137), a style is a canned set of formatting characteristics, which you can apply to a selection with just a couple of clicks, saving time and ensuring consistency. Excel comes with a few preset styles, but there's room for more.

To create your own style the quick way, apply any of the formatting characteristics described in this chapter to a selected cell or block of cells. Now choose Format→Style, which calls up the Style dialog box. Enter a new style name. You'll see that Excel has already recorded the formatting exhibited by the selected cells: the number format, the text alignment, the font, the border, the cell pattern, and the cell protection. If you're happy with the formatting, click the Add button on the right.

Or, if you want to further change any of the settings, click

Modify to summon the Format Cells dialog box. In fact, if you failed to highlight some already-formatted cells before choosing Format→Style, this is how you would define your style characteristics from scratch.

To apply a style to selected cells in the spreadsheet, choose Format→Style. In the Style dialog box that appears, select the style name you want to apply, and then click OK. You'll see your canned formatting applied to the selected cells.

Excel doesn't offer nearly as many ways to apply styles as Word does; style sheets simply aren't as critical in spreadsheet formatting as they are in word processing. For example, you can't associate a particular keystroke with a certain style, unless you create a macro for the task (see page 592).

Still, there is a Style pop-up menu, which is easier to use than burrowing into the Format→Style dialog box. However, you have to add it to one of your toolbars manually, using the Tools→Customize command as described on page 671.

- **Orientation** rotates text within its cell. That is, you can make text run "up the wall" (rotated 90 degrees), slant at a 45-degree angle, or form a column of right-side-up letters that flow downward. You might want to use this feature to label a vertical stack of cells, for example.

- **Wrap text** affects text that's too wide to fit in its cell. If you turn it on, the text will wrap onto multiple lines to fit inside the cell. (In that case, the cell grows taller to make room.) When the checkbox is turned off, the text simply gets chopped off at the right cell border (if there's something in the next cell to the right), or it overflows into the next cell to the right (if the next cell is empty).

- **Shrink to fit** attempts to shrink the text to fit within its cell, no matter how narrow it is. If you've never seen 1-point type before, this may be your opportunity!

- **Merge cells** causes two or more selected cells to be merged into one large cell (described next).

Merging cells

Every now and then, a single cell isn't wide enough to hold the text you want placed inside—the title of a spreadsheet, perhaps, or some other heading. For example, the title may span several columns, but you'd rather not widen a column just to accommodate the title.

The answer is to *merge cells* into a single übercell. This function removes the borders between cells, allowing whatever you put in the cell to luxuriate in the new space. You can merge cells across rows, across columns, or both.

To merge two or more cells, select the cells you want to merge, verify that the Text Alignment portion of the Formatting Palette is open, and then turn on the Merge Cells checkbox, shown in Figure 14-8.

Warning: Merging two or more cells containing data discards *all* of the data except whatever's in the upper-left cell.

Figure 14-9:
Because Excel treats merged cells as one big cell, you can align the contents of that cell any way you'd like; you don't have to stick to the grid system imposed by a sheet's cells. One typical use for this is centering a title over a series of columns. Without using merged cells, centering doesn't do the job at all. When you merge those cells together and apply center alignment, the title is happily centered over the table.

Enemies of the Empire

Name	Offense	State	Fees	Severity
	Telling the			
Oliver North	Truth	MD	$120	4
Sammy Hagar	Bad Hair	CA	$123	3
Joe Schmo	Disliking Me	TN	$126	9
Chevy Chase	Whatever	CA	$129	8
Tom Cruise	Too Short	CA	$132	5
Tim Crooks	Sleezeball	NC	$135	8
	Writes wimpy			
Anne Rice	vampire novels	WA	$435	6
JIMMY NEUTROI	Stupid	Everywhere	$1,000	8
Total				**51**

To unmerge merged cells, select the cells and turn off the Merge Cells checkbox; the missing cell walls return. Note, however, that although the combined space returns to its original status as independent cells, whatever data was discarded during the merge process doesn't return.

You can also merge and unmerge cells by using the Format Cells dialog box. To do this, select the cells to merge, then choose Format→Cells (or Control-click the cells and choose Format Cells from the contextual menu). In the Format Cells dialog box, click the Alignment tab, and then turn on (or turn off) the Merge cells item in the Text control section.

Adding Pictures and Movies

Although you probably won't want to use Excel as a substitute for Photoshop (and if you do, you need licensed help), you *can* add graphics and even movies to your sheets and charts. Plus, if you're artistically inclined (or unwilling to heed the warnings of your high school art teacher), you can use Excel's drawing tools to create your own art.

When using Excel for your own internal purposes—analyzing family expenditures, listing CDs, and so on—the value of all this graphics power may not be immediately apparent. But in the business world, you may appreciate the ability to add clip art, fancy legends, or cell coloring (for handouts at meetings, for example). You can even add short videos explaining how to use certain features of your spreadsheet.

Excel offers two ways of embellishing your spreadsheets with graphic elements of all kinds, the Insert→Picture submenu, and the Add Objects panel of the Formatting Palette. (Speaking of embellishments, this panel is a new Excel 2004 addition.)

Inserting by the Picture submenu

To summon the Picture toolbar, use the Insert→Picture submenu, which has six options. Here's a summary:

- **Clip Art.** This command brings up the Microsoft Clip Gallery, a database containing hundreds of images in over 40 categories. You can also search for specific images using the built-in search feature.

- **From File.** Using this option, you can import into your sheet any graphic file format that QuickTime understands, including EPS, GIF, JPEG, PICT, TIFF, or Photoshop.

- **AutoShapes.** Choose this command to summon the AutoShapes toolbar, from which you can insert many different automatically generated shapes—arrows, boxes, stars and banners, and so on.

- **Organization Chart.** When you choose this menu item, Excel launches the MS Organization Chart application, which lets you create a corporate-style organizational chart with ease. (This kind of chart, which resembles a top-down flowchart, is generally used to indicate the hierarchy of employees in an organization. But it's also an effective way to draft the structure of a Web site.)

- **WordArt.** Using the WordArt menu command, you can apply some wild effects to type, including 3-D effects, gradients, shadows, or any combination.

- **From Scanner or Camera.** Excel can use Photoshop or TWAIN drivers to access images directly from a scanner or camera. Choosing this option leads you through a series of steps that help you import images. (Of course, most Mac OS X fans have set up iPhoto or Image Capture to open automatically when a camera is plugged in, thus getting to your pictures before Excel can.)

Inserting by the Add Objects palette

The Insert menu works splendidly, but it's a little slow and stodgy. In Excel 2004 you can add all of the above objects and more with a quick click on the Formatting Palette. To access them, click the Add Objects title bar on the Formatting Palette. The section is divided into two sections—an objects section and a graphics section. The object section includes:

- **Charts.** This button, which looks like a chart, is a shortcut to the Insert→Chart command (page 530). If you already know what you want your chart to look like, clicking it in this palette is the fastest way to go.

- **Symbols.** Adds the © (copyright) symbol and 50 other possibilities (yeah, someone counted), saving you a trip to the Insert→Symbol dialog box.

- **Autoshapes.** This palette lets you add any of Office's AutoShapes (page 682).

- **Lines.** This button does the same thing as the Line tool on the Drawing toolbar (page 684)—gives you a way to draw arrows, curves, and other types of lines right on your worksheet.

- **Text Shapes.** Text Shapes consist of not only WordArt (page 683), but also text boxes. You can add a free-floating block of text to your worksheet, and work with it just like text boxes in Word (page 151).

At the bottom of the Add Objects panel are four buttons that are simply shortcuts to features on the Insert Menu.

- **Clip Art** and **From File** do the same thing as choosing the Insert→Picture→Clip Art and Insert→Picture→From File commands described earlier.

- **From Scanner or Camera** lets you import images just like the Insert→Picture→ From Scanner or Camera command.

- **Insert Movie** opens the Insert Movie dialog box (page 298) from which you can locate any QuickTime movie on your Mac that you'd like to make part of your worksheet. Select it, and then click Choose. The movie appears in the selected cell; double-click the cinematic masterpiece to play it. (For more detail on working with movies, see page 299.)

Each of these graphics types is described more completely in Chapter 20.

Charts

To paraphrase the old saying, "a graph is worth a thousand numbers." Fortunately, Excel can easily turn a spreadsheet full of data into a beautiful, colorful graphic, revealing patterns and trends in the data that otherwise might be difficult or impossible to see.

In Excel 2004, you have two ways of bringing a chart to life. If you're new to charting, step through the Chart Wizard, which helps you build all the elements your chart needs. If you're an experienced charter, simply select the data you want to chart, click the appropriate chart type in the Add Objects panel, and edit your chart (page 536) if necessary.

The keys to making an effective chart are to design your spreadsheet from the beginning of charthood, and then to choose the right chart type for the data (see Figure 14-10).

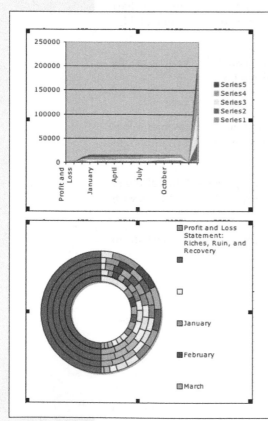

Figure 14-10:
Here's an example of the importance of choosing the right chart to match your data. Both charts use the same set of data, but the area chart on the top is appropriate for the kind of data presented. Conversely, the doughnut chart below is the wrong way to present this information. All you get is a rainbow of colors that fails to communicate any useful information.

Step 1: Select the Data

The first step is to select the data that you want to chartify. You select these cells exactly the way you'd select cells for any other purpose (see page 476).

Although it sounds simple, knowing which cells to select in order to produce a certain charted result can be difficult—almost as difficult as designing the sheet to be charted in the first place. Think about what you want to emphasize when you're charting, and then design your spreadsheet to meet that need.

Note: If you've done this a few (or a few hundred) times before, you can skip the Chart Wizard entirely. After you select your data as described on these pages, click the Add Objects title bar in the Formatting Palette and choose the chart type you have in mind. (And if you don't know what the chart types are, then you're not ready for this shortcut. Read ahead to the next page.)

Excel places the new chart on your spreadsheet. Skip directly to step 7 on page 536 for an overview of ways you can edit your chart.

Here are a few tips for designing and selecting spreadsheet cells for charting:

- When you're dragging through your cells, include the labels you've given to your rows and columns. These labels will be incorporated into the chart.

- Don't select total cells unless you want them as part of your chart.

- Give each part of the vital data its own column or row. For example, if you want to chart regional sales revenue over time, create a row for each region, and a column for each unit of time (month or quarter, for example).

- It's usually easier to put the *data series* (see the sidebar box on the next page) into columns rather than rows, since we tend to see a list of data as a column. Furthermore, the numbers are closer together.

UP TO SPEED

Understanding Data Series

To master Excel charts, you'll have to first master the concept of a data series. Put simply, a data series is a group of numbers or data points that encompasses a single row or column of numbers from a spreadsheet (such as monthly revenues). In a simple bar or column chart, Excel turns each data series into its own set of bars or columns and assigns a different color to each.

For example, suppose you have a chart with two data series—that is, the numbers begin life as two spreadsheet columns, as shown here with Revenue and Profit columns.

When you create the chart, each month's revenue might show up as a blue bar, and each month's expenses as a green bar. Each set of like-colored bars came from the same data series.

One more tip: When you make a chart from a selection of cells, whichever there is fewer of—rows or columns—becomes the data series. You can always switch this arrangement, swapping the horizontal and vertical axes of your chart, once the chart is born.

- Keep your data to a minimum. If you're charting more than 12 bars in a bar chart, consider merging some of that data to produce fewer bars. For example, consolidating a year's worth of monthly sales data into quarterly data uses four bars instead of 12.

- Keep the number of data series to a minimum. If you're charting more than one set of data (such as gross revenues, expenses, and profits), avoid trying to fit six different data series on the same chart. Use no more than three to avoid hysterical spreadsheet confusion. (A pie chart can't have more than *one* data series.)

- Keep related numbers next to each other. For example, when creating an XY chart, use two columns of data, one with the X data and one with the Y data.

- You can create a chart from the data in nonadjacent cells. To select the cells, hold down the ⌘ key while clicking or dragging through the cells to highlight them, as described on page 476. When you finally choose Insert→Chart (or click the Chart Wizard button in the Standard toolbar), Excel knows exactly what to do.

Step 2: Choose a Chart Style

When you choose Insert→Chart, the first screen of the Chart Wizard appears (Figure 14-11). Your first challenge is to choose the kind of chart that's appropriate for the data at hand. Don't use a pie or doughnut chart to show, say, a company's stock price over time (unless it's a bakery).

Here are your options, each of which may offer several variations. Note that the illustrations accompanying these descriptions reveal which cells were highlighted to produce the charted results shown.

Tip: This chart choosing is no doubt useful—even productive. Be aware, though, that you can shortcut this process in Excel 2004 by choosing a chart from the Add Objects tab on the Formatting Palette. Once you choose a chart type, Excel instantly formats it and plops it into your spreadsheet.

- **Column** charts are ideal for illustrating the data that changes over time—each column might represent, for example, sales for a particular month. As you'll see in the dialog box when you click Column, Excel offers seven variations of this chart type. Some are two-dimensional, some are three-dimensional, some are stacked, and so on. (Stacked-column charts reveal totals for subcategories each month. That is, the different colors in each column might show the sales for a particular region, while 3-D charts can impart even more information—sales over time plotted against sales region, for example.)

- **3-D Column** charts let you compare two sets of data. You can apply a transparent fill applied to the front data series to make it easier to see the ones behind it.

- **Bar** charts, which resemble column charts rotated 90 degrees clockwise, are as good as column charts for showing comparisons among individual items—but bar charts generally aren't used to show data that changes over time. Again, you can choose (in the right side of the dialog box) stacked or 3-D bar chart variations.

- **Line** charts help depict trends over time or among categories. The Line sub-type has seven variations; some express the individual points that have been plotted, some show only the line between these points, and so on.

- **Pie** charts are ideal for showing how parts contribute to a whole, especially when there aren't very many of these parts. For example, a pie chart is extremely useful in showing how each dollar of your taxes is spent on various government programs, or how much of your diet is composed of, say, pie. The Pie subtype has six variations, including "exploded" views and 3-D ones.

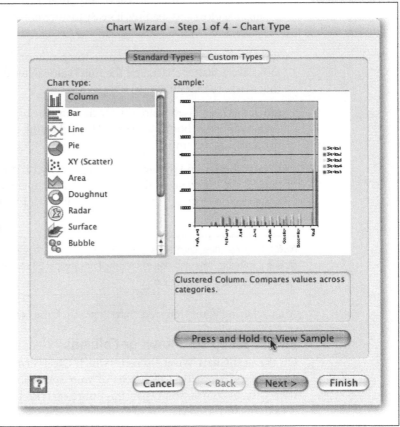

Figure 14-11:
When you click the "Press and Hold to View Sample" button without releasing the mouse button, Excel displays, in the area originally occupied by all the little example graphs, a miniature version of the actual graph you're about to create, using your own data. It's important to use this button to make sure that the chart type you've chosen is the right one for what you're doing. In most cases, you can tell immediately if the graph Excel is about to produce looks anything like the one you envisioned.

- **XY (Scatter)** charts are common in the scientific community; they plot clusters of data points, revealing relationships among points from more than one set of data.

- **Area** charts are useful for showing both trends over time or across categories *and* how parts contribute to a whole. **3-D area** charts, of course, are even better when you want to compare *several* data series, especially if you apply a transparent fill to reduce the problem of one series blocking another.

- **Doughnut** charts function like pie charts, in that they reveal the relationships of parts to the whole. The difference is that the various rings of the doughnut can represent different data sets (data from different years, for example).

- **Radar** charts exist for very scientific and technical problems. A radar chart features an axis rotated around the center, polar-coordinates style, in order to connect the values of the same data series.

- **Surface** charts act like complicated versions of the Line chart. It's helpful when you need to spot the ideal combination of different sets of data—the precise spot where time, temperature, and flexibility are at their ideal relationships, for example. Thanks to colors and shading, it's easy to differentiate areas within the same ranges of values.

- **Bubble** charts are used to compare three values: the first two values form what looks like a scatter chart, and the third value determines the size of the "bubble" that marks each point.

- **Stock** charts are used primarily for showing the highs and lows of a stock price on each trading day, but it's also useful for indicating other daily ranges (temperature or rainfall, for example).

- **Cone, cylinder, and pyramid** charts are simply variations on basic column and bar charts. The difference is that, instead of a rectangular block, either a long, skinny cone, narrow cylinder, or a triangular spike (pyramid) represents each column or bar.

Note: *If none of these chart types is exactly what you're looking for, Excel isn't finished with you yet. By clicking the Custom Types tab, you can choose from another 20 chart types, or even define your own. This tab is described in the next section.*

After selecting your preferred chart type, click the Next button to continue.

Step 3: Set up Your Rows or Columns

On the next Chart Wizard screen (which Excel terms "Step 2 of 4 – Chart Source Data"), specify exactly which cells of your spreadsheet you want to graph. If you were wise, of course, you began this entire exercise by highlighting the appropriate cells in the spreadsheet.

But if you forgot, or you're some kind of iconoclast, you can do it now. One way is to edit the contents of the "Data range" field, where the spreadsheet, starting cell, and ending cell are represented with absolute cell references (see page 495).

The easier way to do it is to click the cell-selection triangle icon to the right of the "Data range" field. This icon, wherever it appears in Excel, always means, "Collapse this dialog box and get it out of my way, so that I can see my spreadsheet and make a selection." (Figure 14-12 illustrates the procedure.)

Tip: You don't have to collapse the Chart Wizard in order to change the data range. Any clicking or dragging in the spreadsheet will be reflected in the Data range field, whether the dialog box is collapsed or not.

This is also your opportunity to swap the horizontal and vertical axes of your chart, if necessary. (The preview on the first Chart Wizard screen should have provided an early warning that you might have your X and Y axes mixed up.)

If that preview looked all wrong, swap the horizontal and vertical dimensions of your chart by clicking the Rows or Columns radio button, whichever contains the data series.

Step 4: Add More Series

The other tab here is the Series tab, which you can use to tweak the data series included in your chart (see Figure 14-13). If things look good, click Next to continue.

Figure 14-12:
Top: The cell-selection icon (circled) pops up in dozens of Excel dialog boxes.

Middle: When you click it, Excel collapses the dialog box, permitting access to your spreadsheet. Now you can select a range by dragging.

Bottom: Clicking the cell-selection triangle again returns you to the dialog box, which uncollapses and displays, in Excel's particular numeric notation, the range you specified.

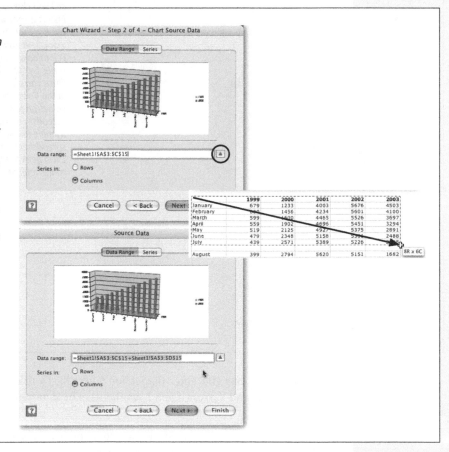

Step 5: Design the Chart

When it comes to customizing your chart, this Chart Wizard screen ("Step 3 of 4 – Chart Options") is the big one (Figure 14-14). Its six tabs let you change the look of every conceivable chart element, including the chart and axes titles, how gridlines are displayed, where the legend is placed, how data is labeled, and whether the spreadsheet cells used to make the chart are displayed. For example:

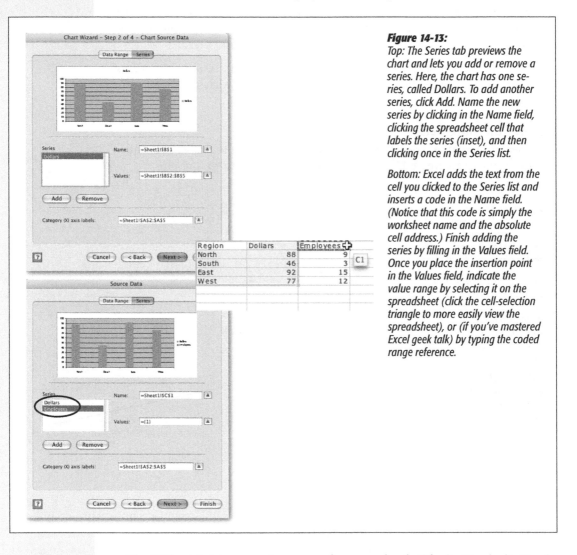

Figure 14-13:
Top: The Series tab previews the chart and lets you add or remove a series. Here, the chart has one series, called Dollars. To add another series, click Add. Name the new series by clicking in the Name field, clicking the spreadsheet cell that labels the series (inset), and then clicking once in the Series list.

Bottom: Excel adds the text from the cell you clicked to the Series list and inserts a code in the Name field. (Notice that this code is simply the worksheet name and the absolute cell address.) Finish adding the series by filling in the Values field. Once you place the insertion point in the Values field, indicate the value range by selecting it on the spreadsheet (click the cell-selection triangle to more easily view the spreadsheet), or (if you've mastered Excel geek talk) by typing the coded range reference.

- The **Titles** tab lets you enter names for your chart's title, its X axis, its Y axis, and second X and Y axes (if you have them). These names appear as parts of the chart.

- The **Axes** tab allows you to specify whether the X axis is a *category* axis (that is, whether it displays the label you've assigned each group of data series in the chart), or whether it's a time scale, depicting change over time.

- The **Data Table** tab lets you choose whether your chart shows the actual data that was used to build your chart, along with the chart itself. If you answer in the affirmative, this data appears in a series of cells below the chart itself. Check "show legend keys" to make Excel reveal how each data series appears on the chart. You can see this helpful option in the preview on the Data Table tab.

Figure 14-14:
This big tabbed screen holds a lot of the controls that you can use to customize your chart. Each tab area controls a different aspect of the chart's look.

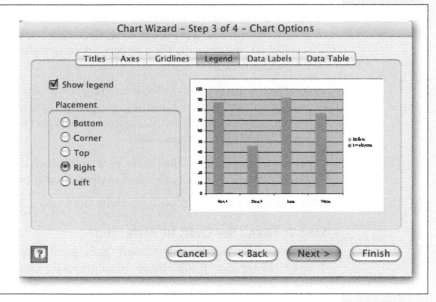

Figure 14-15:
Here's how a typical line chart breaks down into its parts. The X axis represents the dates in column A, and the Y axis represents the value of the numbers in columns B and C in dollars—in other words, columns B and C are each a data series. The text headers at the top of columns B and C are the series names, which Excel uses in the legend.

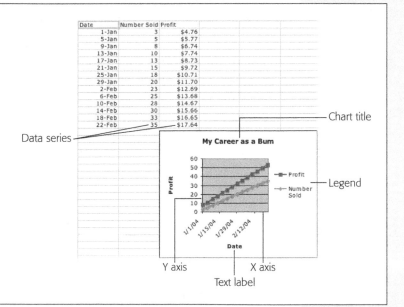

Keep an eye on the preview on the right side of the wizard to see how your chart is shaping up. Once you've made settings to your heart's content, click the Next button to continue.

Step 6: Tell Excel Where to Put It

The final Chart Wizard screen asks where you want the chart to wind up:

- **As new sheet.** Your chart will occupy a new worksheet, called a chart sheet, in the current workbook document. Use this option when what you really wanted all along was a chart, and plugging the numbers into a spreadsheet was just a scratchpad for the chart's benefit.

- **As object in.** You will create an embedded chart—a chart floating as a graphic object right in your spreadsheet. (Use the pop-up menu to identify which worksheet you want the chart to appear in.) Use an embedded chart when you want your flashy graphics next to their data source.

Either way, charts remain linked to the data from which they were created, so if you change the data in those cells, the chart updates itself appropriately.

After making your selection, click the Finish button to make Excel place your chart.

Step 7: Tweak the Chart to Perfection

As is so often the case, the wizard is only the beginning. Once the chart has appeared onscreen, hundreds of flexible formatting options are now available to you.

Before redesigning the various pieces of your chart, however, it may be worthwhile to learn their anatomical names:

- **Legend.** The *legend* is the key that tells you what the chart's elements represent—its lines, pie slices, or dots. It's just like the legend on a map.

- **Axes.** An *axis* is the "ruler," either horizontal or vertical, against which Excel charts your data. The horizontal line that forms the floor of the chart is called the X axis; the vertical one that forms the "left wall" is the Y axis.

- **Axis labels.** This term may refer either to the tick mark labels ("January, February, March…") or to the overall label of the horizontal or vertical scale of your chart ("Income, in millions" or "Months since inception," for example).

When modifying your chart, start with the most urgent matters:

- **Move the chart** by dragging it around on a sheet.

- **Delete some element of the chart** (such as the legend) by clicking it and then pressing the Delete key.

- **Resize the chart** by dragging any of the black square handles at its corners and edges. (If you don't see them, the chart is no longer selected. Click any blank white area inside the chart to select it.)

- **Reposition individual elements in the chart** (the text labels or legend, for example) by dragging them.

- **Convert a chart sheet into an embedded chart (or vice versa)** by selecting the chart and then choosing Chart→Location and making the appropriate choice in the resulting dialog box.

- **Rotate a 3-D chart** by clicking inside the actual graph to produce its corner handles, and then dragging one of those corner handles vertically or horizontally. As shown in Figure 14-16, you see a wireframe representation of the chart while you're dragging. When you release the mouse, the chart redraws itself at the new angle that you specified.

Figure 14-16:
Top: Rotating a 3-D chart is one of the flashiest Excel features; more practically, it lets you put your chart in the best possible light. To rotate a chart, drag a corner square (a tiny square visible in an active chart).

Middle: The chart rotates as a wire-frame cube. You can press ⌘ at any time to see wireframes of the series objects inside the chart.

Bottom: When you release the mouse button, the chart appears, once again fleshed out, in its newly rotated position.

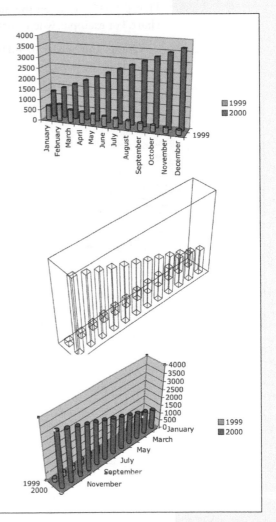

Or, for a less free-form approach to chart rotation, choose Chart→3-D View and enter numbers in the various configuration fields, or click the various buttons to step through different views. (If you're rotating a chart in order to reveal a hidden data series, you can also format the blocking data series with a partially transparent fill. Learn more in the following section.)

- **Move series in a 3-D chart** to put smaller series in front of larger ones. Start by double-clicking any data series to open the Format Data Series dialog box, and then click the Series Order tab. Watch the preview in the dialog box as you click Move Up or Move Down.

Many different specialized Format dialog boxes await your investigation, too (see Figure 14-17). To open the dialog box, just double-click the pertinent piece of the chart. For example, when working with a simple bar chart:

- **Change the border or interior color** of the chart by double-clicking within the body of the chart.

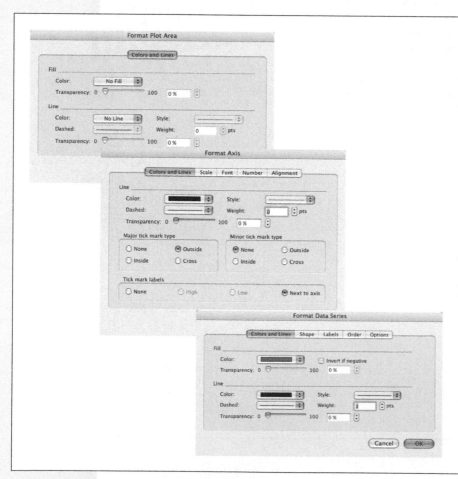

Figure 14-17:
By double-clicking the individual elements in a chart, you open a dialog box that lets you change every conceivable aspect of them. Top: The dialog box that appears when you double-click a chart background. Middle: The choices that appear when you double-click an axis. Bottom: Additional choices that appear when you double-click a chart bar.

- **Change the font, color, or position of the legend** by double-clicking it.

- **Change the scale, tick marks, label font, or label rotation of the axes** by double-clicking on their edges or slightly outside their edges.

- **Change the border, color, fill effect, bar separation, and data label options of an individual bar** by double-clicking it. You can even make bars partially transparent, revealing hidden series at the rear, as described in the next section.

You'll also notice that when a chart is selected, the Formatting Palette offers specialized formatting controls borrowed from the Chart Wizard. Using the palette, you can change the chart type, gridline appearance, legend placement, and so on. And if you still haven't found your preferred method of formatting a finished chart, you can use the Chart toolbar (View→Toolbars→Chart). It offers a pop-up menu listing the various chart components that you can edit by double-clicking (such as Corners, Floor, Legend, and Series Axis).

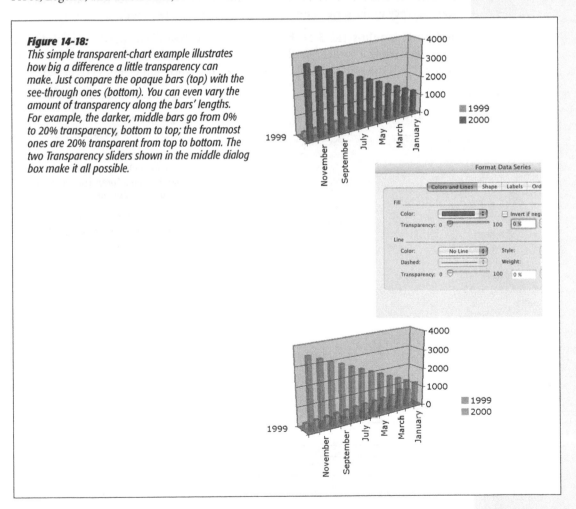

Figure 14-18:
This simple transparent-chart example illustrates how big a difference a little transparency can make. Just compare the opaque bars (top) with the see-through ones (bottom). You can even vary the amount of transparency along the bars' lengths. For example, the darker, middle bars go from 0% to 20% transparency, bottom to top; the frontmost ones are 20% transparent from top to bottom. The two Transparency sliders shown in the middle dialog box make it all possible.

Tip: You can copy a selected chart into another program either by dragging it or by using the Copy and Paste commands in the Edit menu.

Transparent Bars

Individual bars of a chart can be partially or completely see-through, making it much easier to display 3-D graphs where the frontmost bars previously would have obscured the back ones.

You can apply transparent fills to most chart types, but their see-through nature makes the most sense in charts with at least two data series, where the front series blocks a good view of the rear (Figure 14-18, top).

Begin applying a transparent fill to a data series by double-clicking the series (the bar or column, for example). In the resulting Format Data Series dialog box, click the Patterns tab and then click Fill Effects. Now, in the Gradient tab, you can adjust the transparency of the series using the sliders (Figure 14-18, middle).

To format a multi-series 3-D chart for maximum "Wow" factor, you may also wish to rotate it (drag a corner handle to spin the chart, or choose Chart→3-D View) or change the series order (double-click a series and work in the Series Order tab).

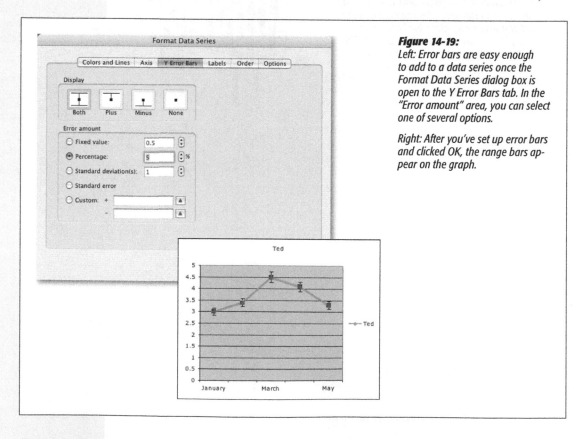

Figure 14-19:
Left: Error bars are easy enough to add to a data series once the Format Data Series dialog box is open to the Y Error Bars tab. In the "Error amount" area, you can select one of several options.

Right: After you've set up error bars and clicked OK, the range bars appear on the graph.

Advanced Charting

The Chart Wizard suffices for almost every conceivable kind of standard graph. But every now and then, you may have special graphing requirements; fortunately, Excel can meet almost any charting challenge that you put before it—if you know how to ask.

Error bars

On some charts—such as those that graph stocks and opinion polls—it's helpful to graph not only the data, but also the range of movement or margin of error that surrounds the data. And that's where *error bars* come in. Error bars let you specify a range around each data point displayed in the graph, such as a poll's margin of error (Figure 14-19).

To add error bars to a chart, first select the data series (usually a line or bar in the chart) to which you want to add error bars. Choose Format→Selected Data Series (or double-click the selected line or bar) to bring up the Format Data Series dialog box. To add error bars along the Y axis—the usual arrangement—click the Y Error Bars tab; then choose display and error amounts for your bars. Click the OK button to add the error bars to your data series. If you want to remove them later, open the Format Data Series dialog box and set the Display to None.

Figure 14-20:
Top: The Add Trendline dialog box gives you six trend lines from which to choose. If the trend line allows for it, you can also set the trend line's parameters in the Options tab.

Bottom: Once you've applied a trend line, it appears on top of your chart. You can also predict how the data might change in the future by setting the forecast values in the Options tab. If you set your trend line to display the R-squared value (also under the Options tab), Excel displays this value for you below the line. In this case, you have an R-squared value of 0.9166, which is very close to 1—a good fit.

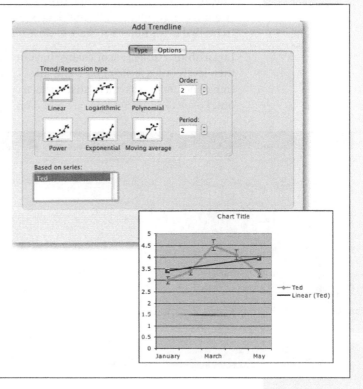

Note: You can add error bars to 2-D area charts, bar charts, bubble charts, column charts, line charts, and scatter charts. In fact, X-axis error bars can even be added to scatter charts. (You'll see this additional tab in the Format Data Series dialog box.)

Trend lines

Graphs excel at revealing trends—how data is changing over time, how data probably changed over time before you started tracking it, and how it's likely to change in the future. To help with such predictions, Excel can add *trend lines* to its charts (Figure 14-20). Trend lines use a mathematical model to help accentuate patterns in current data and to help predict future patterns.

Note: You can use trend lines only in unstacked 2-D area charts, bar charts, bubble charts, column charts, line charts, scatter charts, and stock charts.

To add a trend line to your chart, click to select one of the data series in the chart—typically a line or a bar—and then choose Chart→Add Trendline. This opens the Add Trendline dialog box, which has the tabs Type and Options.

The Type tab lets you choose one of these trend-line types:

- **Linear.** This kind of trend line works well with a graph that looks like a line, as you might have guessed. If your data is going up or down at a steady rate, a linear trend line is your best bet, since it closely resembles a simple straight line.

- **Logarithmic.** If the rate of change in your data increases or decreases rapidly and then levels out, a *logarithmic* trend line is probably your best choice. Logarithmic trend lines tend to have a relatively sharp curve at one end and then gradually level out. Logarithmic trend lines are based on logarithms, a mathematical function.

POWER USERS' CLINIC

The One-Step Chart

If you want an insta-chart without having to fumble around with the Chart Wizard, there's an incredibly easy way to do it. Just select the data, and click the desired chart in the Add Objects pane of the Formatting Palette.

You can also select the data you want in the chart and then press F11. Excel instantly creates a standard chart, in its own document window, made from that data. (There's a toolbar button for this command, but it isn't on the Standard toolbar. To add it to one of your toolbars, follow the instructions on page 671. Excel uses a default chart type to create this insta-chart, so you get less flexibility than using the Add Objects panel.)

However, if you end up making the same kind of chart, all the time, it's helpful to know how to change that default (and from then on just press F11 instead of making a detour to the Formatting Palette). To do so, first select a chart, choose Chart→Chart Type, and then, in the Chart Type dialog box, click the "Set as Default Chart" button. When Excel asks if you really want to do this, click Yes. Then click OK to finish up.

- **Polynomial.** A *polynomial* trend line is great when graphed data features hills and valleys, perhaps representing data that rises or falls in a somewhat rhythmic manner. Polynomial trend lines can also have a single curve that looks like a camel's hump (or an upside-down camel's hump, depending on your data). These trend lines are based on polynomial expressions, familiar to those who've spent some time in a high school algebra class.

- **Power.** If the graphed data changes at a steady rate, as in an acceleration curve, a *power* trend line is the way to go. Power trend lines tend to curve smoothly upward.

- **Exponential.** If, on the other hand, the graphed data changes at an ever-increasing or decreasing rate, then you're better off with an *exponential* trend line, which also looks like a smoothly curving line.

- **Moving Average.** A *moving average* trend line attempts to smooth out fluctuations in data, in order to reveal trends that might otherwise be hidden. Moving averages, as the name suggests, can come in all kinds of shapes. No matter what the shape, though, they all help spot cycles in what might otherwise look like random data.

The Options tab, on the other hand, lets you name your trend line, extend it beyond the data set to forecast trends, and even display the R-squared value on the chart. (The R-squared value is a way of calculating how accurately the trend line fits the data; you statisticians know who you are.)

Incidentally, remember that trend lines are just models. As any weather forecaster, stockbroker, or computer-company CEO can tell you, trend lines don't necessarily predict *anything* with accuracy.

Printing Worksheets

Now that you've gone through the trouble of making your sheets look their best with killer formatting and awe-inspiring charts, the next logical step is printing them out.

Print Preview (Microsoft's)

Excel comes with a print-preview function that can save you frustration and time, as well as an old-growth forest that would otherwise be harvested for the sake of your botched spreadsheet printouts. What's a little strange is that Mac OS X, of course, comes with its *own* print-preview function with slightly different features. Ah, well—if one is good, two must be better.

To use Excel's print preview, choose File→Print Preview, which puts Excel into Print Preview mode (Figure 14-21). In this specialized view of the currently selected sheet, you can see how your data will look when divided up onto several sheets of paper. Use the Print Preview toolbar to tweak how your sheet prints. Here's a quick look at the toolbar buttons.

- **Setup.** This button opens the Page Setup dialog box, as described on page 545.

• **Print.** This button opens up the Print dialog box, where you can set your print options and send your sheet to the printer.

• **Zoom.** Click the Zoom button to magnify or reduce the preview, giving you a closer look at the cell contents that may be chopped off at the edge of the page. The Zoom button provides quick toggle action for reducing and enlarging the overall page; to enlarge a particular area, click the area with the cursor instead.

• **Prev, Next.** If your spreadsheet is too big for a single sheet of paper, these buttons show you the previous page, or next page, of the preview.

• **Margins.** Click this button to reveal or hide dotted lines and little black handles, representing the margins of your page. You can drag them to adjust the sizes of your margins. For example, if your spreadsheet is only slightly too big to fit on a page, shrinking the margins might make just enough room to accommodate the whole thing.

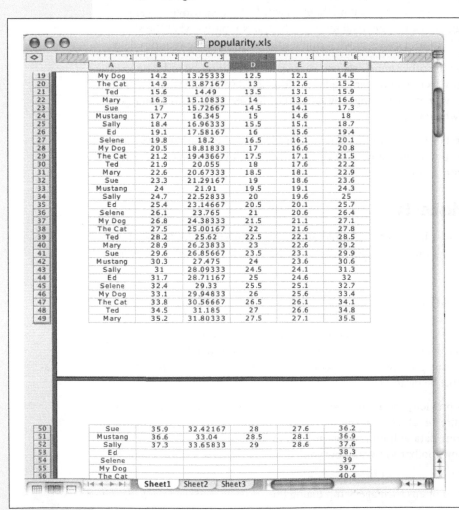

Figure 14-21:
A disaster waiting to print. This printout will be chopped off in mid-chart. Fortunately, by choosing File→Print Preview before actually printing the spreadsheet, you get a chance to see how it's going to spill over onto two sheets—and you get the chance to correct it by using the print-preview controls.

- **Page Break Preview.** Microsoft is justifiably proud of this feature. When you click this button, you enter Page Break Preview mode, where thick blue-dotted lines indicate how Excel plans to divide your spreadsheet onto multiple pages (Figure 14-21).

Tip: To check out your page-break preview without doing a print preview first, just choose View→Page Break Preview or click the Page Break Preview control at the bottom-left of the Excel window.

Suppose you've resigned yourself to the fact that your spreadsheet is too big for a single sheet—but Excel is cutting it off at a really bad place, such as just before the December sales-figure column. The beauty of Page Break Preview is that you can drag the blue-dotted lines up, down, left, or right to redefine where the page breaks fall. After each drag, Excel automatically shrinks or enlarges the contents of the affected pages to accommodate your page-break preferences. (All things in moderation, however; with this feature it's possible to force Excel to shrink the numbers in your cells to the size of atoms.)

To exit Page Break Preview mode, choose View→Normal.

- **Close.** This button closes the Print Preview window and returns you to your regularly scheduled spreadsheet.

- **Help (?) icon.** The question-mark button opens Microsoft Office Help to the topic of Print Preview.

Tip: To print just a certain portion of your spreadsheet, select the cells that you want to print and then choose File→Print Area→Set Print Area. This tells Excel to print only the selected cells. To clear a custom print area, select File→Print Area→Clear Print Area.

Print Preview (Apple's)

As in any Mac OS X–compatible program, you turn a document into a print-preview file by choosing File→Print and then, in the Print dialog box, clicking the Preview button at the bottom. Your Mac fires up the Preview program, where you see the printout-to-be as a graphic. Use the commands in the Display menu to zoom in, zoom out, scroll, and so on.

The best part, though, is the File→Save As PDF command. It turns your printout into an electronic document—a PDF or Acrobat file—that you can send to almost anyone with a computer, so they can open, read, search, and print your handiwork. (The software they need is the free Acrobat Reader program.)

Page Setup

Excel's Page Setup dialog box (Figure 14-22) is far more comprehensive than the Page Setup that appears when you choose File→Page Setup in TextEdit, for example. In it, you can control how pages are oriented, how spreadsheets fit on a page, the print quality, the margins, how headers and footers are printed, and the order in which pages are printed.

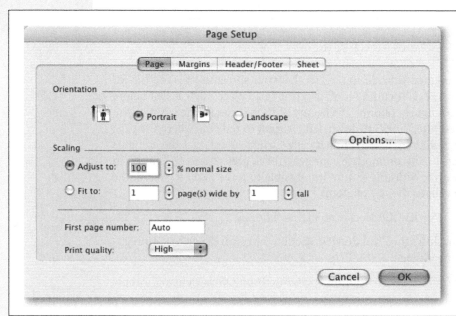

Figure 14-22:
The Page tab of the Page Setup dialog box is where to start if you want a spreadsheet to print on one page. A click in the "Fit to" radio button (in the Scaling area) automatically adjusts your spreadsheet's print size to fit on a sheet of paper. If you want it to fit on more than one sheet, adjust the numbers in the "Fit to" area.

Page tab

In the Page tab, you can change the orientation of each page (Portrait for the usual up-and-down style or Landscape for a sideways style), reduce or enlarge the printout by a certain percent, or—using the "Fit to" radio button—force the spreadsheet to fit onto a certain number of printed pages. (Using this control, of course, affects the printout's type size.) If you don't want the pages of your spreadsheet numbered 1, 2, and so on, then type a different number into the "First page number" field. This is how you force Excel to number the pages beginning with, say, 5 on the first printed sheet.

Tip: Setting the starting page number in the Page tab won't make page numbers appear on your sheets; you must also initiate page numbering in the Header/Footer tab. The easiest technique is to choose a page number option from the Header or Footer pop-up menu.

An Options button on the right brings up the more familiar Page Setup dialog box for your printer, in which you can set more of your printer's options (such as paper size).

Margins tab

The Margins tab (Figure 14-23, top) lets you specify the page margins for your printout (and for the header and footer areas). You can also tell Excel to center the printout on the page horizontally, vertically, or both. The Options button, once again, summons the standard Page Setup dialog box for your printer.

Header/Footer tab

If you want something printed on the top or bottom of every page (such as a title, copyright notice, or date), it's time to visit the Header/Footer tab (Figure 14-23, bottom).

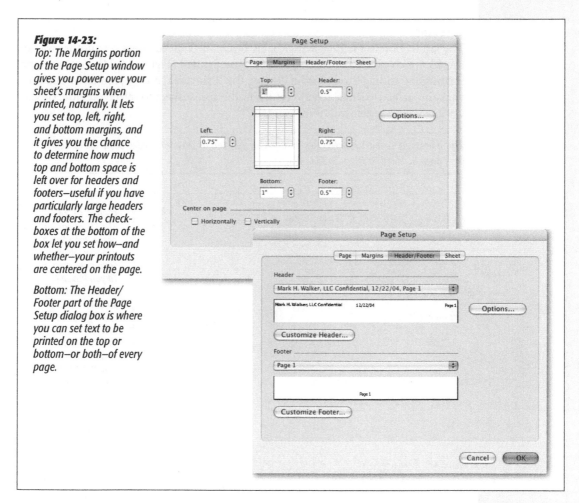

Figure 14-23:
Top: The Margins portion of the Page Setup window gives you power over your sheet's margins when printed, naturally. It lets you set top, left, right, and bottom margins, and it gives you the chance to determine how much top and bottom space is left over for headers and footers—useful if you have particularly large headers and footers. The check-boxes at the bottom of the box let you set how—and whether—your printouts are centered on the page.

Bottom: The Header/ Footer part of the Page Setup dialog box is where you can set text to be printed on the top or bottom—or both—of every page.

Here, you can use the Header or Footer pop-up menu to choose from a selection of prepared headers and footers—"Page 1 of 7," "Confidential," and so on.

If the header or footer message you want isn't there, click the Custom Header or Custom Footer buttons to bring up a customization dialog box. In it you can enter your own header or footer text; click the Font button to format the text; and use the remaining buttons to insert placeholder codes for the current page number, the total number of pages, the current date, the current time, the file name, and the tab name.

You can combine these codes with text that you type yourself. For example, in the "Center section" box, you could type, *CD Collection Status as of,* and then click the fourth icon. Excel inserts the code *&[Date};.* Now whenever you print this document, you'll find, across the top of every page, "CD Collection Status as of 9/15/02," or whatever the current date is.

Sheet tab

The last section of the Page Setup dialog box, called Sheet, offers yet another way to specify which portions of the sheet are to be printed (Figure 14-24). You can type starting and ending Excel coordinates into the "Print area" box (separated by a colon), click the striped-triangle icon to return to the spreadsheet to select a region, or you can highlight the cells you want printed.

Tip: If fields are dim in the Sheets tab, they can be accessed by closing the Page Setup dialog box, closing print preview, and then choosing File→Page Setup.

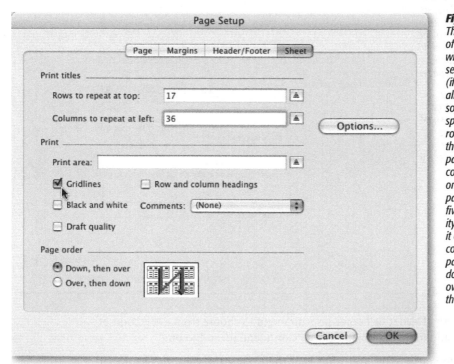

Figure 14-24:
The Sheet portion of the Page Setup window lets you set a print area (if you haven't already done so). You can also specify that certain rows repeat at the top of each page and/or columns repeat on the left of each page. It gives you five print-quality options, and it enables you to control whether pages are printed down and then over, or over and then down.

You'll also find the following in the Sheet tab:

- **Rows to repeat at top, Columns to repeat at left.** If you've carefully typed the months of the year across the top of your spreadsheet, or product numbers down the left side, you'll have a real mess on your hands if the spreadsheet spills over onto two or more pages. Anyone trying to read the spreadsheet will have to refer all the way back to page 1 just to see the labels for each row or column.

  Excel neatly avoids this problem by offering to reprint the column or row labels at the top or left side of *each* printed page. To indicate which row or column contains these labels, click in the appropriate "Print titles" field, and then click the desired row number or column heading directly in the spreadsheet. Or click the triangle icon just to the right of each field; this more effectively shrinks the dialog box and more easily selects the repeating cell range.

- **Grid lines, Row and column headings.** It's too bad that the answer to one of the world's most frequently asked spreadsheet questions—"How do I get the gridlines to print?"—is buried in the fourth tab of a buried dialog box.

  In any case, this tab should clarify everything. Excel never prints gridlines or the gray row and column headings unless you turn on their corresponding checkboxes here.

- **Black and white, Draft quality.** Use these two checkboxes when you're in a real hurry. Draft quality speeds up printing by omitting graphics and some formatting. "Black and white" means that your printer won't bother with time-consuming color, even if color appears in the spreadsheet.

- **Comments.** Use this pop-up menu to specify where *comments* (see page 591) appear on the printout—on its last page, or right where you put them in the spreadsheet itself.

- **Page order.** Use this to control whether Excel prints a multiple-page spreadsheet column by column (of pages), or row by row.

Advanced Spreadsheeting

Congratulations, you've mastered enough of Excel to input numbers, perform calculations, create charts and graphs, and log your CD collection using the List Manager. In fact—you already have far more spreadsheet ability than most people.

If, on the other hand, you're the kind of person who uses Excel for more than a word processor, whose business depends on the flow of numbers, projections, and calculations, there's still more to learn. This chapter covers the eerie realms of power Excel, where several people can work on the same spreadsheet simultaneously over the network, files can connect to databases or even the Web for their information, and Excel can be programmed to function by itself.

Workbooks and Worksheets

A *workbook* is an individual Excel file that you save on your hard drive. Each workbook is made up of one or more *worksheets*, which let you organize your data in lots of complex and interesting ways. Try thinking of a workbook as a bound ledger with multiple paper worksheets. Although most of the work you do is probably in an individual sheet, it's often useful to store several spreadsheets in a single workbook document—for the convenience of linking multiple Excel worksheets.

Working with Multiple Worksheets
Although it doesn't offer quite the heart-pounding excitement of, say, the List Manager, managing the worksheets in a workbook is an important part of mastering Excel. Here's what you should know to get the most out of your sheets.

Tip: Several of the techniques described here involve selecting more than one worksheet. To do so, ⌘-click the tabs of the individual sheets you want—or click the first in a consecutive series, then Shift-click the last.

- **Adding sheets.** Every Excel workbook starts out with three sheets, bearing the inspired names Sheet1, Sheet2, and Sheet3. (You can set the number of sheets in a new workbook in Excel→Preferences→General panel.)

  To add a new sheet to your workbook, choose Insert→Worksheet, or Control-click one of the tabs at the bottom of the worksheet and choose Insert from the contextual menu. A new sheet appears *to the left* of the currently selected sheet, and it's named Sheet4 (or Sheet5, Sheet6, and so on).

Tip: To insert multiple sheets in one swift move, select the same number of sheet tabs that you want to insert and *then* choose Insert→Worksheet. For example, to insert two new sheets, select Sheet1 and Sheet2 by ⌘-clicking both tabs, and then choose Insert→Worksheet. Excel then inserts Sheet4 and Sheet5 (yes, to the *left* of Sheet1).

- **Deleting sheets.** To delete a sheet, click the doomed sheet's tab (or select several tabs) at the bottom of the window, and then choose Edit→Delete Sheet. (Alternatively, Control-click the sheet tab and choose Delete from the contextual menu.)

Warning: You can't bring back a deleted sheet. The Undo command (Edit→Undo) doesn't work in this context.

- **Hiding and showing sheets.** Instead of deleting a worksheet forever, you may find it helpful to simply hide one (or several), keeping your peripheral vision free of distractions while you focus on the remaining ones. To hide a sheet or sheets,

---

POWER USERS' CLINIC

Adding Background Pictures to Sheets

Every now and then, it's easy to feel sorry for Microsoft programmers; after umpteen revisions, what possible features can they add to Excel? They must rack their brains, lying awake at night, trying to figure out what else they can invent.

Surely, the ability to add a graphics file as a background image behind your cell grid is an idea that sprang from just such a late-night idea session.

Start by choosing Format→Sheet→Background. An Open dialog box pops up, in which you can choose the graphics file (JPEG, GIF, Photoshop, and so on) that you want to use as a background. Once you've selected it and clicked Insert, the image loads as the spreadsheet's background. If the image isn't large enough to fill the entire worksheet, Excel automatically tiles it, placing copies side by side until every centimeter of the window is filled.

Clearly, if this feature is ever successful in improving a worksheet, it's when the background image is extremely light in color and low in contrast. Most other images succeed only in rendering your numbers and text illegible.

If, after adding an image to a sheet, you decide that it makes things much, much worse, choose Format→Sheet→Delete Background. Your normal white Excel sheet background returns. By the way, the background doesn't print. It's a screen-only thing.

select the corresponding worksheet tabs at the bottom of the window, then choose Format→Sheet→Hide. To show (or *unhide*, as Excel calls it) sheets that have been hidden, choose Format→Sheet→Unhide; this brings up a list of sheets to show. Choose the sheet that you want to reappear, and click OK.

Note: You can unhide only one sheet at a time.

- **Renaming sheets.** The easiest way to rename a sheet is to double-click its tab to highlight its name, and then type the new text (up to 31 characters long). Alternatively, you can select the tab of the sheet you want to rename and then choose Format→Sheet→Rename. You can also Control-click the sheet tab and choose Rename from the contextual menu.

- **Moving and copying sheets.** To move a sheet (so that, for example, Sheet1 comes after Sheet3), just drag its tab horizontally. A tiny black triangle indicates where the sheet will wind up, relative to the others, when you release the mouse. Using this technique, you can even drag a copy of a worksheet into a different Excel document.

Tip: Pressing Option while you drag produces a copy of the worksheet. (The exception is when you drag a sheet's tab into a different workbook; in that case, Excel copies the sheet regardless of whether the Option key is held down.)

As usual, there are other ways to perform this task. For example, you can also select a sheet's tab and then choose Edit→Move or Copy Sheet, or Control-click the sheet tab and choose Move or Copy from the contextual menu. In either case, the Move or Copy dialog box pops up. In it, you can specify which open workbook the sheet should be moved to, whether the sheet is copied or moved, and where you want to place the sheet relative to the others.

Figure 15-1:
From left to right, the four sheet scrolling buttons perform the following functions: scroll the tabs to the leftmost tab, scroll the tabs to the left by one tab, scroll the tabs to the right by one tab, and scroll the tabs all the way to the right.

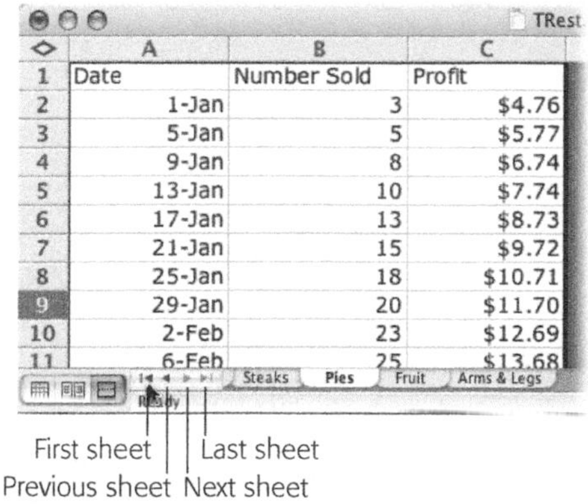

- **Scrolling through sheet tabs.** If you have more sheet tabs than Excel can display in the bottom portion of the window, you can use the four tab scrolling buttons to scoot between the various sheets (see Figure 15-1). Another method is to Control-click any tab-scrolling button and then choose a sheet's name from the contextual menu.

- **Showing more or fewer sheet tabs.** The area reserved for Sheet tabs must share space with the horizontal scroll bar. Fortunately, you can change how much area is devoted to showing sheet tabs by dragging the small, gray, vertical tab split bar that sits between the tabs and the scroll bar. Drag it to the left to expand the scroll bar area (and hide worksheet tabs if necessary); drag it to the right to reveal more tabs.

Sharing a Workbook

With a little preparation, several Excel users on the same network can work on a single worksheet at the same time. (If you want to share a workbook, but prevent others from accessing it, read about protection on page 555 first. Bear in mind, some protection commands must be applied *before* you turn on sharing.) To share a workbook, choose Tools→Share Workbook, which brings up the Share Workbook dialog box. On the Editing tab (Figure 15-2), turn on "Allow changes by more than one user at the same time." Click the Advanced tab for the following options:

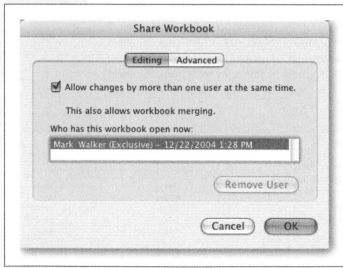

Figure 15-2:
The Share Workbook dialog box reveals exactly who else is using a shared workbook. If you worry that one of your fellow network citizens is about to make ill-advised changes, click her name and then click Remove User. Your comrade is now ejected from the spreadsheet party. If she tries to save changes to the file, she'll get an error message explaining the situation. You should also note that there's little security in shared workbooks. As you can see, the same user is logged in and able to make changes from two different Macs at the same time. Of course, if you password-protect the sheet before sharing it, you'll achieve a basic, keeping-honest-people-honest level of security.

- **Track changes.** This section lets you set a time limit on what changes are tracked (see "Tracking Changes" on page 557). If you don't care what was changed 61 days ago, you can limit the tracked changes to 60 days. You can also tell Excel not to keep a change history at all.

- **Update changes.** Here, you specify when your view of the shared workbook gets updated to reflect changes that others have made. You can set it to display the changes that have been made every time you save the file, or you can command it to update at a specified time interval.

If you choose to have the changes updated automatically after a time interval, you can set the workbook to save automatically (thus sending your changes out to co-workers sharing the workbook) and to display others' changes (thus receiving changes from your co-workers' saves). Or you can set it not to save your changes, and just to show changes that others have made.

- **Conflicting changes between users.** This section governs whose changes "win" when two or more people make changes to the same workbook cell. You can set it so that you're asked to referee (which can be a *lot* of work), or so that the most recent changes saved are the ones that win (which can be risky). Clearly, neither option is perfect. Since each person can establish settings independently, it might be worth working out a unified collaboration policy with your co-workers.

- **Include in personal view.** These two checkboxes—Print settings and Filter settings—let you retain printing and filtering changes that are independent of the workbook. They can be set independently by anyone who opens the workbook.

When you click OK, Excel prompts you to save the workbook—if you haven't already. Save it on a networked disk where others can see it. Now, anyone who opens the workbook from across the network opens it as a shared book.

Shared workbooks have some limitations, detailed in the online help topic, "Limitations of shared workbooks." Here's a summary of things that you *can't* do with a shared workbook:

- Assign, change, or delete a password that protects a worksheet.

- Create, edit, view, or assign *macros* (see page 592).

- Insert charts, hyperlinks, objects, or pictures.

- Make or change PivotTables, or make or refresh data tables (page 576).

- Merge, insert, or delete blocks of cells; delete worksheets.

- Use automatic subtotals or drawing tools.

- Use or create conditional formats or data validation.

- View or edit *scenarios* (page 579).

Protecting the spreadsheet

Fortunately, there's no need to give everyone on the network unfettered access to your carefully designed spreadsheet. You can protect your spreadsheet in several ways, as described here, and your colleagues can't turn off these protections without choosing Tools→Unprotect Sheet (or Unprotect Workbook)—and *that* requires a password (if you've set one up).

- **Protect a workbook from changes.** Choose Tools→Protection→Protect Work-book, which brings up the Protect Workbook dialog box. By turning on Structure and/or Windows, you can protect the workbook's *structure* (which keeps its sheets from being deleted, changed, hidden, or renamed) and its windows (which keeps the workbook's windows from being moved, resized, or hidden). Both of these safeguards are especially important in a spreadsheet you've carefully set up for onscreen reviewing. You can also assign a password to the workbook so that if a user wants to turn *off* its protection, he must know the password.

- **Protect a sheet from changes.** Choose Tools→Protection→Protect Sheet to bring up the Protect Sheet dialog box. Turn on the Contents checkbox to protect all *locked* cells in a worksheet (described next), as well as formats in a chartsheet. Turn on Objects to prevent changes to graphic objects on a worksheet, including formats of all charts and comments. Finally, turn on the Scenarios checkbox to keep *scenario* definitions (page 579) from being changed.

  The bottom of the dialog box lets you assign a password to the worksheet; this password will be required from anyone who attempts to turn off the protections you've established.

- **Protect individual cells from changes.** Excel automatically formats all cells in a new worksheet as locked, so if you protect the contents of a sheet you've been working in, all the cells will be rendered unchangeable. If you want *some* cells in a protected sheet to be editable, you must unlock them while the sheet is unprotected. Unlock selected cells by choosing Format→Cells. In the resulting dialog box, click the Protection tab, turn off the Locked checkbox, and then click OK.

- **Require a password to open a workbook.** Open the workbook you want to protect and choose File→Save As (or, if you've never saved this workbook before, choose File→Save). In the Save dialog box, click Options. In the resulting dialog box (Figure 15-3), enter one password to allow the opening of the file and another to allow file modification.

Figure 15-3:
Entering a password in the top text box prevents others from open-ing your workbook without the password. If you specify only the second password, people can open the file, but can't make changes without the password.

Warning: Remember these passwords. If you forget them, you've locked yourself out of your own workbook. There's no way to recover them unless you buy a separate password-cracking program to break back in.

- **Hide rows, columns, or sheets.** Once you've hidden some rows, columns, or sheets (page 515), you can prevent people from making them reappear by choosing Tools→Protection→Protect Workbook. Turn on Structure and then click OK.

- **Allow selection of only certain parts of a worksheet.** If you're a programmer with serious knowledge of macros and Visual Basic, you can use the EnableSelection property to keep specific cells from being selected by other people. Although you can play with changing this property from NoRestriction to UnlockedCells in the Visual Basic Editor (which keeps you from selecting cells that are locked), to actually *implement* this change into a worksheet requires writing code in Visual Basic.

- **Protecting a shared workbook.** To protect a shared workbook, choose Tools→ Protection→Protect Shared Workbook, which brings up the Protect Shared Workbook window. This window presents you with two protection choices. If you turn on "Sharing with track changes" and enter a password, you prevent others from turning off change tracking—a way of looking at who makes what changes to your workbook. Turning on this checkbox *also* shares the workbook, as detailed previously.

Tracking Changes

When people make changes to your spreadsheet over the network, you aren't necessarily condemned to a life of frustration and chaos, even though numbers that you input originally may be changed beyond recognition. Exactly as in Word, Excel offers a *change tracking* feature that lets you see exactly which of your co-workers made what changes to your spreadsheet and, on a case-by-case basis, approve or eliminate them. (The changes, not the co-workers.)

To see who's been tip-toeing through your workbook, choose Tools→Track Changes→ Highlight Changes, which brings up the Highlight Changes dialog box (Figure 15-4). In it, you can choose how changes are highlighted: by time or by the person making the changes. To limit the revision tracking to a specific area on the worksheet, click the triangle icon at the right of the Where field, select the area, and then click the triangle again.

As life goes on with this spreadsheet on your network, changes made by your co-workers appear as a triangular flag at the upper-left corner of a cell or block of cells (Figure 15-4, middle).

Once you've reviewed the changes, you may decide that the original figures were superior to those in the changed version. At this point, Excel offers you the opportunity to analyze each change. If you think the change was an improvement, you can accept it, making it part of the spreadsheet from now on. If not, you can reject the change, restoring the cell contents to whatever was there before your network comrades got ambitious.

To perform this accept/reject routine, choose Tools→Track Changes→Accept or Reject Changes. In the Select Changes to Accept or Reject dialog box, you can set up the reviewing process by specifying which changes you want to review (according to when they were made, who made them, and where they're located in the worksheet). When you click OK, the reviewing process begins (Figure 15-4, bottom).

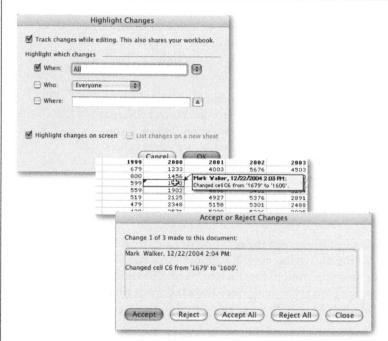

Figure 15-4:
Top: This dialog box lets you turn on change tracking and specify whose changes are highlighted. By turning on Where, clicking the tiny triangle icon next to the box, and dragging in your worksheet, you can also limit the tracking feature to a specific area of the worksheet.

Middle: The shaded triangle in the upper-left corner of a cell indicates that somebody changed its contents. A comment balloon lets you know exactly what the change was.

Bottom: Using this dialog box, you can walk through all the changes in a spreadsheet one at a time, giving each changed cell your approval or restoring it to its original value.

Merging Workbooks

In many work situations, you may find it useful to distribute copies of a workbook to several people for their perusal and then incorporate their changes into a single workbook.

Performing this feat, however, requires some preparation—namely, creating a shared workbook (see the previous section), and then configuring the workbook's *change history*. You'll find this option by choosing Tools→Share Workbook and then clicking the Advanced tab (Figure 15-5). The number that you specify in the "Keep change history for" box determines how old changes can be before they become irrelevant. The theory behind this feature contends that you'll stop caring about changes that are older than the number of days that you set. (Tracking changes forever can bloat a file's size, too.)

Once you've prepared your workbook, distribute it via email or network. Ask your colleagues to make comments and changes and then return their spreadsheet copies to you (within the time limit you specified, as described in the previous paragraph). Collect all of the copies into one place. (You may need to rename the workbooks to avoid replacing one with another, since they can't occupy the same folder if they have the same names.)

Now open a copy of the shared workbook and choose Tools→Merge Workbooks, which brings up an Open dialog box. Choose the file you want to merge into the open workbook, and then click OK. This process must be repeated for every workbook you want to merge.

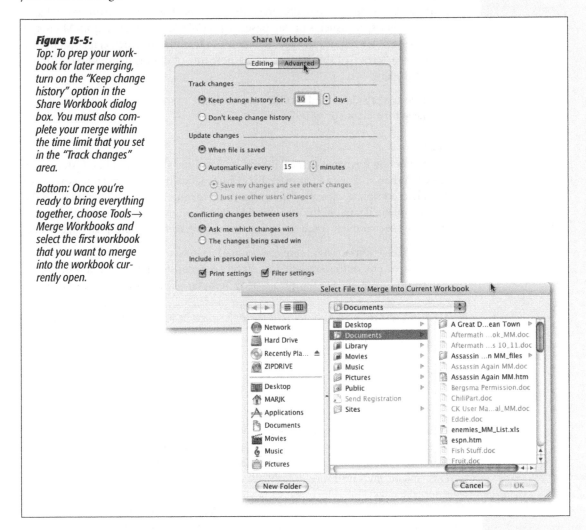

Figure 15-5:
Top: To prep your workbook for later merging, turn on the "Keep change history" option in the Share Workbook dialog box. You must also complete your merge within the time limit that you set in the "Track changes" area.

Bottom: Once you're ready to bring everything together, choose Tools→ Merge Workbooks and select the first workbook that you want to merge into the workbook currently open.

Exporting Files

Every now and then, it can be useful to send your Excel data to a different program—a database program, for example, or AppleWorks (if you're collaborating with somebody who doesn't have Office). Fortunately, Microsoft engineers have built in many different file formats for your Excel conversion pleasure.

To save your Excel file in another file format, choose File→Save As; then select the file format you want from the Format pop-up menu. Here are a few of the most useful options in that pop-up menu.

Text (tab delimited)

The *tab-delimited* file format provides an often-used way of getting your Excel sheets into other spreadsheets or databases (AppleWorks, FileMaker, non-Microsoft word processors, and so on). It saves the data as a text file, in which cell contents are separated by a "press" of the Tab key, and a new row of data is denoted by a "press" of the Return key.

Saving a file as a tab-delimited text file saves only the currently active worksheet, and doesn't keep formatting or graphics.

Template

The Template file format is a special kind of Excel file that works like a stationery document: When you open a template, Excel automatically creates and opens a *copy* of the template, complete with all of the formatting, formulas, and data that were in the original template. If you use the same kind of document over and over, templates are a great way to save yourself some time. (For more on Excel templates, see page 510.)

To save an Excel workbook as a template, choose File→Save As and then select Template in the pop-up menu of the Save window. Excel proposes storing your new template in the Microsoft Office 2004→Templates→My Templates folder on your hard drive.

Note: Any templates created this way appear in the My Templates portion of the Project Gallery (see page 510).

Web page

Where would a modern software program be without the ability to turn its files into Web pages?

Sure enough, Excel can save workbooks as Web pages, complete with charts, and with all sheets intact. In the process, Excel generates the necessary HTML and XML files and converts your graphics into Web-friendly file formats (such as GIF). All you have to do is upload the saved files to a Web server to make them available to the entire Internet (see page 311). Once you've posted them on the Internet, others can look through your worksheets with nothing but a Web browser, ideal for posting your numbers for others to review. That's the *only* thing they can do, in fact, since the cells in your worksheet aren't editable.

To save a workbook as a Web page, choose File→Save As, and then choose Format→ Web Page. At this point, the bottom of the Save window offers some powerful options that control the Web-page creation process:

- **Workbook, Sheet, Selection.** Using these buttons, specify how much of your workbook should be saved as a Web page—the whole workbook, the currently active sheet, or just the selected cells. (If you choose Workbook, all of the sheets in your workbook will be saved as linked HTML files; there'll be a series of links along the bottom that look just like your sheet tabs in Excel. Here again, though, these features won't work smoothly for everyone, because not all Web browsers understand JavaScript and frames, which these bottom-of-the-window tabs require.)

- **Automate.** This button brings up the Automate window, which lets you turn on a remarkable and powerful feature: Every time you save changes to your Excel document, or according to a complex schedule that you specify, Excel can save changes to the Web-based version automatically. Of course, you'll still be responsible for posting the HTML and graphics files to your Web server.

  To set up a schedule, click "According to a set schedule" and then click Set Schedule. In the Recurring Schedule window, set the Web version to be updated daily, weekly, monthly, or yearly. You can also specify the day of the week, as well as a start and end date for automatic updating.

- **Web Options.** The Web Options dialog box lets you assign appropriate titles and keywords to your Web pages. (The title appears in the title bar of your visitors' browser windows and in search results from search engines like Yahoo and Google; search engines also sometimes reference these keywords.)

  On the Pictures tab, you can also turn on *PNG* (Portable Network Graphics) *graphics,* which makes smaller graphics that download more quickly. Unfortunately, not all Web browsers can display this relatively new graphics format, so leave this option unchecked unless you're *sure* that all of the Web browsers used to view your Web-based spreadsheet are PNG-savvy. (Most recent browsers are.)

  Finally, these controls can be used to specify the *target monitor size;* that is, what's the smallest monitor size your visitors will be using? Your answer to this question is important, because it will determine the width of Excel's finished Web pages. If you spew out Web pages with broad dimensions, your visitors must do a lot of scrolling; if you set the dimensions too small, Excel will do its best to cram the graphics and text into the smaller area. If necessary, Excel can spread out a spreadsheet's contents to maintain the same layout as the original, even if you've asked it to keep pages small.

Tip: You can test the workbook-saved-as-Web-page feature by dropping the HTML file on your Web browser's icon. If you prefer, you may also choose File→Web Page Preview to view the Web page.

Spreadsheet properties

Excel gives you the chance to attach additional information to your files through something called *properties*. To call up the Properties dialog box for a worksheet, select File→Properties. In the resulting dialog box, you'll see five tabbed subject areas with all kinds of information about your file.

- **General.** This subject area tells you the document type, its location, size, when it was created and last modified, and whether it's read-only or hidden.

- **Summary.** This feature lets you enter a title, subject, author, manager, company, category, keywords, comments, and a hyperlink base for your document.

- **Statistics.** This tab shows when a document was created, modified, and last printed, as well as who last saved it. It also displays a revision number and the total editing time on the document.

- **Contents.** Here, you'll see the workbook's contents—mostly, the worksheets embedded in it.

- **Custom.** Finally, this tabbed area lets you enter any number of other properties to your workbook by giving the property a name, type, and value. You can enter just about anything here.

Advanced Formula Magic

Chapter 13 covers the fundamentals of formulas—entering them manually, using the Calculator, and so on. The following section dives deeper into the heart of Excel's power—its formulas.

Note: There's a difference between formulas and *functions*. A *formula* is a calculation that uses an arithmetic operator (such as *=A1+A2+A3+A4+A5*), while a *function* is a canned formula that saves you the work of creating a formula yourself (such as *=SUM(A1:A5)*).

Because there's no difference in how you *use* them, this chapter uses the terms interchangeably.

Nested Formulas

A *nested* formula is a formula that's used as an argument to another formula. For example, in the formula *=ABS(SUM(A1:A3))*, the formula *SUM(A1:A3)* is nested within an absolute-value formula. When interpreting this formula, Excel first adds the contents of cells A1 through A3, and then finds the absolute value of that result—that's the number you'll see in the cell.

Nested formulas keep you from having to use other cells as placeholders; they're also essential for writing compact formulas. In some cases (such as with the IF function), nesting lets you add real sophistication to your Excel spreadsheets by having Excel make decisions based on formula results.

The Formula Palette

The Formula Palette is a quick way of building powerful mathematical models in your spreadsheets. When activated, the Formula Palette shows every imaginable aspect of a formula: the value of the cells used in it, a description of what the formula does, a description of the arguments used in the formula, and the result of the formula.

To use the Formula Palette, click the Edit Formula button (which looks like a bold = sign) in the Formula bar. When the Formula Palette pops up (Figure 15-6), it shows one of two things:

- If the currently active cell doesn't contain a function, the Formula Palette turns into a small pane displaying the formula result. The result updates itself as you create or edit the formula.

- If the currently active cell contains a function, or if you type a function into your formula, the Formula Palette opens fully and tries to help you with the function.

Once the Formula Palette appears, you can use it to construct your formula. It provides a text box for each function parameter. Typing the parameter in the text box effectively inserts it into its proper place in the formula. You can also click the small cell-selection triangle by each parameter box for easy cell-dragging, as described on page 533.

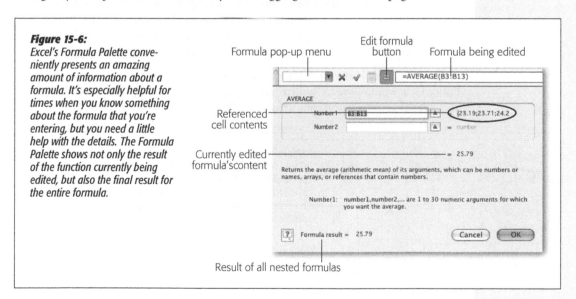

Figure 15-6:
Excel's Formula Palette conveniently presents an amazing amount of information about a formula. It's especially helpful for times when you know something about the formula that you're entering, but you need a little help with the details. The Formula Palette shows not only the result of the function currently being edited, but also the final result for the entire formula.

As you fill out the formula in the Formula Palette, the formula's result appears in the bottom of the palette. When you're done creating the formula in the Formula Palette, click OK to paste it into the cell.

Although the Formula Palette might seem like overkill when it comes to simple formulas (such as a SUM), it's a big help when you're dealing with more complex formulas. It outlines the parameters that the formula is expecting and gives you places to plug in those parameters. The rangefinder feature (page 485) also makes it easier to track your calculations. The rangefinder highlights each cell cited in the calculation with the same color used to denote the cell in the calculation. It's a sharp way to keep track of what you're doing, and which cells you're doing it with.

Circular References

If you create a formula that, directly or indirectly, refers to the cell *containing* it, beware of the *circular reference*. This is the spreadsheet version of a Mexican standoff: The formula in each cell depends on the other, so neither formula can make the first move.

For example, suppose you type into cell A1, the formula *=SUM(A1:A6)*. This formula asks Excel to add cells A1 through A6 and put the result in cell A1—but since A1 is included in the range of cells for Excel to add, things quickly get confusing. To make matters worse, a few specialized formulas actually *require* that you use formulas with circular references. Now, imagine how difficult it can be to disentangle a circular reference that's *inside* a nested formula that *refers* to formulas in other cells—it's enough to make your teeth hurt. Fortunately, Excel can help.

For example, when you enter a formula containing a circular reference, Excel immediately interrupts your work with a dialog box that explains what's happening. You may enter a formula that doesn't itself contain a circular reference, but instead completes a circular reference involving a group of cells. Or the formulas in two different cells might refer to each other in a circular fashion, as shown in Figure 15-7.

To leave the formula as is, click Cancel. For help, click OK, which brings up a Microsoft Office Help window loaded with directions and the Circular Reference toolbar. (Excel also overlays circles and skinny arrows on the cells of your spreadsheet.)

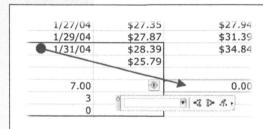

Figure 15-7:
Double-click the skinny arrow to jump to the next cell involved in the circular reference, or click the buttons on the toolbar. With these tools, Excel reveals the various cells involved in the circular reference; eventually, you should be able to understand the problem (and correct it, if necessary).

Iterations

On the other hand, certain functions (mostly scientific and engineering) *need* circular references to work properly. For example, if you're doing a bit of goal-seeking (page 577), you can use circular references to plug numbers into a formula until the formula is equal to a set value.

In these cases, Excel must calculate formulas with circular references repeatedly, because it uses the results of a first set of calculations as the basis for a second calculation. Each such cycle is known as an *iteration*. For example, suppose you want to figure out what value, when plugged into a formula, will produce a result of 125. If your first guess of 10 gives you a result of 137 when plugged into the formula, a circular reference can use that result to *adjust* your guess (say, reducing it to 9.5), then make a second pass at evaluating the formula. This second pass is a second iteration. If 9.5 doesn't do the trick, Excel can make a third iteration to get even closer, and so on, until it reaches a level of accuracy that's close enough.

To turn iteration on (and set some of its parameters), choose Excel→Preferences; click Calculation. In the Calculation panel, turn on Iteration, and change the number of iterations and a maximum change value, if you like. By default, Excel stops after 100 iterations, or when the difference between iterations is smaller than 0.001. If you make the maximum number of iterations larger or the maximum change between iterations smaller, Excel produces more accurate results. Accordingly, it also needs more time to calculate those results.

TROUBLESHOOTING MOMENT

Keeping Track of References

The problem with referring to other workbooks in formulas is that things change—and cause confusion. Suppose, for example, that one Excel workbook, Document A, contains a formula reference to a cell in Document B. But if somebody renames Document B, renames the disk it's on, or moves the file to a different folder, Excel can't find Document B. The link to the external workbook is broken.

of the external file on your hard drive. The first phrase after the left parenthesis and single quote is the name of the hard drive (Lindy, in this illustration). Then come a series of folder names separated by colons; in this illustration, the file is in the tonya user directory, in the Documents folder, and then in a folder called Information. Finally, you'll find the file's name (ReportInfo, in this example) inside the brackets.

When you try to update those references, Excel will tell you that it can't find the sheet that contains the data it needs. It'll also put up an Open dialog box, asking you to locate the missing data. Now all you need to do is navigate to Document B—even if it has a new name or it's on a new hard drive—and click OK. Excel fixes the reference so that everything works normally.

For the curious (or masochistic), there's a manual way to fix such a broken link, too. Click the cell with the external reference; the formula—complete with the external reference—appears in the Formula bar. Inside the formula, there's a series of names with colons and brackets, as shown in the illustration here.

Think of this path notation as a street map to the location

The phrase to the right of the right bracket identifies one worksheet name inside the file (Sheet1). After that, there's another single quote and an exclamation point, which marks the end of the external reference. Then, finally, there's the name of the cell (expressed as absolute cell references with $ signs, as described on page 495) used in the formula.

Armed with this information, you can repair a broken external cell reference. If you renamed the hard drive, correct the problem by changing the first name in the list to match the new hard drive name. If you've changed the folder location of Document B, you can correct the situation here by typing the proper folder path. If you've renamed Document B, simply enter the new file name in the space between the brackets.

Connecting to Other Workbooks

Formulas don't have to be confined to data in their own "home" worksheet; they can be linked to cells in other worksheets in the same workbook, or even to cells in other Excel documents. That's a handy feature when, for example, you want to run an analysis on a budget worksheet with your own set of Excel tools, but you don't want to re-enter the data in your workbook or alter the original workbook.

To link a formula to another sheet in the same workbook, start typing your formula as you normally would. When you reach the part of the formula where you want to refer to the cells in another worksheet, click the sheet's tab to bring it to the front. Then select the cells that you want to appear in the formula, just as you normally would when building a formula. When you press Enter after clicking or dragging through cells, Excel instantly returns you to the sheet where you were building the formula. In the cell, you'll find a special notation that indicates a reference to a cell on another sheet. For example, if a formula on Sheet 3 takes the sum of I1 through I6 on Sheet 1, the formula looks like this: *=SUM(Sheet1!I1:I6)*.

To link a formula in Document A to cells in another workbook (Document B), the process is almost identical. Start typing the formula in Document A. Then, when it's time to specify the cells to be used in the formula, open Document B. Select the cells you want to use by clicking or dragging; when you press Enter, they appear in the formula. Excel returns you to the original document, where you'll see the Document B cells written out in a *path notation* (see the Tip below).

Once you've set up such a cell reference, Excel will automatically update Document A each time you open it with Document B already open. And if Document B is closed, Excel asks if you want to update the data. If you say yes, Excel looks into Document B and grabs whatever data it needs. If somebody has changed Document B since the last time Document A was opened, Excel recalculates the worksheet based on the new numbers.

Tip: If you want Document A updated automatically whenever you open it (and don't want to be interrupted with Excel's request to do so), choose Excel→Preferences, click Edit, and then *turn off* "Ask to update automatic links." Excel now automatically updates the link with the data from the last saved version of Document B.

Auditing

Every now and then, you'll find a formula whose cell references are amiss. If the formula references another formula, tracing down the source of your problems can be a real pain. Excel's Auditing tools can help you access the root of formula errors by showing you the cells that a given formula references and the formulas that reference a given cell. Brightly colored *tracer arrows* (these won't appear in an Excel workbook saved as an HTML file) appear between cells to indicate how they all relate to each other.

The key to correcting formula errors is the Tools→Auditing menu item, which has five submenu choices:

- **Trace Precedents** draws arrows from the currently selected cell to any cells that provide values for its formula.

- **Trace Dependents** draws arrows from the currently selected cell, showing which *other* formulas refer to it.

- **Trace Error** draws an arrow from an active cell containing a "broken" formula to the cell or cells that caused the error.

- **Remove All Arrows** hides all the auditing arrows.

- **Show Auditing Toolbar** hides or shows the Auditing Toolbar. This toolbar's buttons turn on (and off) the kinds of arrows described in the previous paragraphs, all in an effort to help you trace how formulas and cells relate with each other.

Working with Databases

Excel has much in common with database programs. Both kinds of software keep track of a list of *records* (like cards in a card catalog—or rows of a spreadsheet), and let you browse through those records and even perform some calculations on them. No wonder Excel is so adept at incorporating database files into its spreadsheets; Excel 2004 can access data in Web pages and FileMaker Pro databases, and may be able to use *open database connectivity* to access data from additional databases. Open database connectivity, usually called ODBC (pronounced "oh-dee-bee-see"), is a standard set of rules for transferring information among databases, even if the databases are in different programs from different companies.

GEM IN THE ROUGH

Open Database Connectivity (ODBC)

Previous versions of Excel could access data from ODBC databases, which are standard in many corporations—but Excel 2004 can't. Although Microsoft updated (Carbonized) most of Office for the most recent version of Mac OS X, a few components didn't make the shipping deadline, including the ODBC-related components. (This discussion applies to non-FileMaker databases. Excel-to-FileMaker links work just fine (as long as they refer to File Maker Pro 6.0 or earlier files) in every version of Office 2004.)

First, since you can't create new queries in Excel 2004, you must make them in a different version of Excel, such as Excel 2001 (or, since queries are just text files, you can create them in TextEdit), and then open the query-containing worksheet in Excel 2004.

Second, to make those queries work, you must install a driver

for the database you want to query. Microsoft doesn't supply drivers to Office 2004 customers; instead, you must purchase a driver from another company, such as OpenLink Software (*www.openlinksw.com*).

Excel 2004 also comes equipped with the necessary smarts to use Microsoft Query for Excel 2004—software that puts a graphical user interface on the task of creating queries. With this program, you can finally create and modify queries in Excel 2004—if you have the driver installed, that is. Look for it in the Applications→Microsoft Office 2004→Office folder.

Once you've rounded up and installed all the required ODBC software, you can get started with ODBC by investigating the commands listed on the Data→Get External Data submenu and playing with the External Data toolbar (View→Toolbars→External Data).

Fetching FileMaker Pro Data

Excel can import data from FileMaker Pro databases directly into its worksheets—no muss, no fuss, no messy translation workarounds.

Here's how to go about it.

Note: Excel can only work with FileMaker databases if you actually *have* FileMaker on your Mac.

Step 1: Import the database

A FileMaker Pro database can be imported in either of two ways. First, you can bring the data into Excel once, where you continue to work on it (this is called a *one-time* import). Second, the data can remain connected to FileMaker, and updates itself in Excel when it's updated in FileMaker (this is called an *updating* import).

- **For a one-time import,** which puts data into Excel as a *list sheet* (a sheet containing nothing except a list object, as described on page 496), choose File→Open, then navigate to, and double-click, the FileMaker file's icon in the Open dialog box.

  Alternatively, in the Finder, simply drag the icon of your FileMaker file onto the Excel icon. (Try this procedure twice if it doesn't work completely on the first attempt.) Either way, if you make changes in FileMaker and want the changed data to come into Excel, you must reimport the entire database.

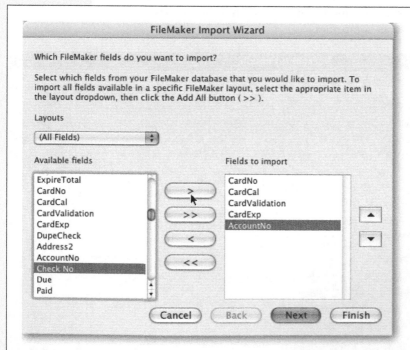

Figure 15-8:
If one of the FileMaker file's layouts contains the fields you want, select its name from the Layouts pop-up menu; otherwise, leave the pop-up menu set to All Fields. Next, choose the fields you want by double-clicking each in the "Available fields" pane on the left. (Move all fields at once by clicking the >> button between the two panes.) This action adds each selected field to the pane on the right. You can also rearrange the order of the fields in the right-hand list by clicking one and then clicking the up and down arrow buttons on the right.

- **For an updating import,** which places data in an Excel worksheet and lets you control how often cells update to reflect changes made in FileMaker, choose Data→ Get External Data→Import from FileMaker Pro. (You must have a workbook open in Excel for this menu option to be available.)

In either case, an amazing thing happens: Excel now triggers FileMaker Pro to launch automatically, opening the specified database.

Then the FileMaker Import Wizard window appears. On the first screen, specify which of the FileMaker file's fields you want to import (Name, Address, Phone, or whatever). You can also specify the fields and layout you want, as shown in Figure 15-8.

Click Next to continue.

Step 2: Choose only the data you want

The next screen in the FileMaker Import Wizard offers to *filter* (screen out) the records that you import into your Excel workbook (see Figure 15-9). The wizard lets you specify three criteria to help eliminate unwanted data from the import process. (If you want *all* of the data, skip this step by clicking Finish.)

Click Finish to continue. Excel commences importing the data from your FileMaker file.

Note: This process may take a long time (depending, in part, on how much data you're importing). Because there's no progress bar, spinning cursor, or any other sign that Excel is working, you might assume that the program has crashed. Be patient and don't switch out of Excel; the program is communicating with the database and constructing the spreadsheet.

Figure 15-9:
Suppose you want to import only the records for contacts who have donated more than $500 and have active member status, so that you can focus on the people with the big bucks. Set the Criteria 1 pop-up menu to Donor-Total, set the middle pop-up menu to >, and type 500 into the final field. After filling in Criteria 1, you can set up additional requirements in the Criteria 2 and Criteria 3 rows.

If you began this process by choosing File→Open, you're all set; Excel produces a new listsheet, a worksheet with the database's contents embedded in it as a list object. Listsheets also display the List toolbar.

If, on the other hand, you chose Data→Get External Data→Import from FileMaker Pro, Excel now asks you exactly where you'd like the imported data to be placed. You can specify a cell or opt to create a new worksheet (Figure 15-10).

Figure 15-10:
The last step in bringing in FileMaker Pro data is choosing where the data goes (top). It can be delivered into the worksheet currently open or into a new worksheet with the click of a radio button. Clicking Properties brings up the External Data Range Properties dialog box (bottom), whose options include "Refresh data on file open" (sets whether Excel receives fresh data every time the file opens) and "Use List Manager" (puts data into a list object). The list object offers easy sorting and filtering. But to use the data layout controls in the dialog box, you must first turn off "Use List Manager" and forgo the extra features that it provides. (See page 496 for List Manager info.)

After telling Excel where and how to place the data, click Finish. Excel imports the data and shows the External Data toolbar, and if you turned on the "Use List Manager" checkbox in the properties section of the FileMaker Import Wizard, it also shows the List toolbar. The External Data toolbar lets you quickly change options on incoming database information, set special query criteria, and refresh data from a database.

Grabbing Data from the Web

If pulling data from a database isn't exciting enough, Excel can also grab data from certain Web sites (and FTP, Gopher, or intranet sites).

Excel comes with three canned Web queries that help demonstrate the power of this little-known feature:

- **MSN MoneyCentral Currencies.** This query grabs the current currency value for more than 50 countries on an open exchange. Check it before you head out on an

---

Figure 15-11:
Using the saved MSN MoneyCentral Major Indices Web query, you can call up current information on a number of major stock market indices directly in your Excel worksheet. Now all you need is some serious cash to be an international tycoon.

Stock Quotes Provided by MSN Money
Click here to visit MSN Money

			Last	Previous Close
DOW JONES INDUSTRIAL AVERAGE	Chart	News	10803.92	10759.43
DOW JONES COMPOSITE INDEX	Chart	News	3400.33	3391.6
DOW JONES TRANSPORTATION	Chart	News	3796.45	3792.09
DOW JONES UTILITIES INDEX	Chart	News	335.78	335.57
Frankfurt DAX	Chart	News	4241.28	4214.39
FTSE 100	Chart	News	4777.4	4733
Hong Kong Hang Seng	Chart	News	14151.08	14180.79
AMEX INTERACTIVE WEEK INTERNET	Chart	News	171.85	171.78
NASDAQ COMPOSITE INDEX	Chart	News	2155.92	2150.91
$NI225 (Invalid symbol)	???	???	???	???
Paris CAC 40	Chart	News	3806.15	3770.03
PHLX SEMICONDUCTOR SECTOR	Chart	News	424.4	424.4
RUSSELL 2000 STOCK INDEX	Chart	News	648.41	646.2
S&P 100 INDEX	Chart	News	574.83	573.36
S&P 500 INDEX	Chart	News	1208.62	1205.45
Singapore Straits Times	Chart	News	2055.77	2063.59
Sydney All Ordinaries Index	Chart	News	4037.4	4018.3
$TI300 (Invalid symbol)	???	???	???	???

Symbol Lookup	MSN Money Home
Find stocks, mutual funds, options, indices, and currencies.	Discover MSN Money's tools, columns, and more!

Terms of Use. © 2002 Microsoft Corporation and/or its suppliers. All rights reserv
Quotes supplied by Standard & Poor's ComStock, Inc. and are delayed at least 20 minutes. NY
Fund data provided by Morningstar, Inc. © 2002. All rights reserved.
Canadian investment fund pricing (c) 2002 CANNEX Financial Exchanges Limited

TROUBLESHOOTING MOMENT

"Microsoft Office is not able to run FileMaker Pro at this time."

You may encounter this error message when attempting to open a FileMaker database into Excel. Of course, there are many reasons why Office might not be able to run FileMaker—it's not installed, it's compressed, or it's out on a lunch break. You can solve the problem, though, by launching FileMaker on your own. (You can launch FileMaker by double-clicking its icon in the Finder.)

If you don't have FileMaker 5.5 or later, your Macintosh will first launch the Classic environment (Mac OS X's "Mac OS 9 simulator") and then open FileMaker in Classic mode. After launching FileMaker, try to open the database again from Excel.

---

international trip, so you'll know how much you're being gouged at the currency-exchange counter.

- **MSN MoneyCentral Major Indices.** This query grabs data for around 20 stock exchanges, including the Dow, S&P 500, FTSE 100, and NASDAQ.

- **MSN MoneyCentral Stock Quotes.** This query looks up data including last value, close value, volume, and change for a stock symbol you specify. (If you're among the thousands of people who use Excel to track your stock market holdings, behold the dawn of a new era—you no longer need to type in the latest stock prices. Your software can do it automatically.)

To use one of these predesigned Web queries, choose Data→Get External Data→Run Saved Query, which brings up an Open dialog box. Double-click one of the queries listed here. (You can find the saved queries in the Microsoft Office 2004→Office→Queries folder.)

Excel then asks you where in the spreadsheet you want to put the information that it downloads from the Web. (This modest dialog box calls itself Returning External Data to Microsoft Excel.) After you select a location and click OK, Excel connects to the Internet, downloads the information, and inserts it into the spreadsheet.

Note: Excel may ask you if you want to accept *cookies* while importing Web-based data. (Cookies are small text files that Web sites place on your hard drive as preference files.) Excel, Entourage, and Internet Explorer all share a common cookies file. Excel is simply obeying the cookie-alert messages you've set up using the preferences settings in Internet Explorer.

Importing Data from a Text File

Databases and the World Wide Web both make effective data sources, but sometimes you just want to pull some information out of a text file and into your Excel worksheet. Here's how to do it.

Choose Data→Get External Data→Import Text File; in the resulting Open dialog box, navigate to, and double-click, the text file that you want to import. The Text Import Wizard walks you through a three-step process to bring the data from the text file into the currently open worksheet.

Opening the Excel Toolbox

Like a good piece of Swiss Army Software, Excel provides tools that go beyond the basics. Using features like PivotTables, Scenarios, and Goal Seeking, Excel lets you look at your data in new and interesting ways.

Making a PivotTable

A *PivotTable* is a special spreadsheet entity that helps summarize data into an easy-to-read table. You can rotate the table's rows and columns (thus the name PivotTable) to achieve different views on your data. PivotTables let you quickly plug different sets of numbers into a table; Excel does the heavy lifting of arranging the data for you.

PivotTables are useful when you want to see how different but related totals compare, such as how a retail store's sales per department, category of product, and salesperson relate. They let you build complicated tables on the fly by dragging various categories of data into a premade template. PivotTables are especially useful when you have a large amount of data to wade through, partially because Excel takes care of subtotals and totals for you.

Here's how to create a PivotTable from data in an Excel sheet.

Step 1: Choose the data source

Suppose, for example, that you're a TV advertiser trying to decide which cable TV cult-hit show should be the beneficiary of your advertising dollars. You have a spreadsheet that shows three days' worth of data on five different shows (such as each show's ranking, number of viewers for the day, and ad revenues). But you can't yet see the trends that identify which shows reach the largest number of people for the least dollars while achieving the highest ranking in the ratings. A PivotTable, you realize, would make the answer crystal clear.

Select a cell in the data range from which you want to create a PivotTable. Choose Data→PivotTable Report, which brings up the PivotTable Wizard. This will walk you through the process of creating a PivotTable in three steps.

In the first step, locate the data from which you want to create a PivotTable. Your choices include an Excel list, multiple consolidation ranges (which use ranges from one or more worksheets), and another PivotTable. If you've installed the necessary ODBC-related software (see page 567), you can also use data from an external data source.

In this example, you want to create a PivotTable from existing data in an Excel sheet. Choose "Microsoft Excel list or database"; click Next to continue.

Step 2: Choose the cells

This PivotTable Wizard asks for the cell range that you want to use in your PivotTable. Excel—bless its digital heart—takes its best guess, based on the active cell when the wizard was invoked. If that range is *not* correct, type the range you want in the Range field or use the cell-selection triangle (see page 533) to select the range yourself. Click Next to continue.

Step 3: Direct the PivotTable

Finally, Excel asks where you want to place your new PivotTable. You can put it either in a new worksheet or in an existing worksheet at a specific location. Because this table is relatively small, place it in the same worksheet as the source data.

This last screen offers two additional buttons for your customization pleasure:

- The **Layout** button opens the Layout window, in which you can exercise some control over how the PivotTable is laid out.

• The **Options** button opens the Options window, in which you can choose to include grand totals, to preserve cell formatting, and how you want data sources handled.

To finish your PivotTable, click Finish.

Step 4: Pivot

At this point, Excel has dropped a blank PivotTable into the specified location, but there's still no data in it. To help with the data-insertion process, Excel opens the PivotTable toolbar, which you can use to add elements to your blank slate.

The bottom of the PivotTable toolbar shows a few names that coincide with the column names in your original data (Figure 15-12); these are called *field names*. To complete your PivotTable, you need to drop these field names onto the row axis (the column on the left), the column axis (the row across the top), or the data field (the big empty space in the center). A different table will form, depending on which data fields you drop on which axes.

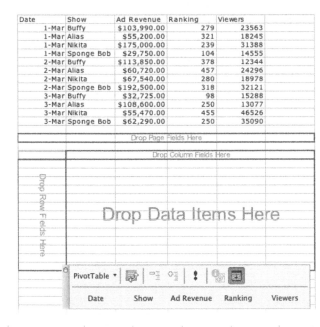

Figure 15-12:
Top: To finish your PivotTable, fill in the blank table with field items from the PivotTable toolbar. Drag these items onto the column to the left, the row across the top, or the data field in the middle to complete your PivotTable.

Bottom: This table results from dragging field names from the PivotTable toolbar onto the waiting PivotTable.

Step 5: Build the table

As the advertising buyer, suppose you want to build a table that shows how much ad revenue each show took in on each of three days. Drag the Date field name onto the Row Field area, the Show field name onto the Column Field area, and the Ad Revenue field name onto the data area.

As depicted in Figure 15-12, Excel builds a table that displays how much ad revenue each show took in, and adds the totals for each show at the bottom and for each day at the right.

Step 6: Massage the data

Now that you've created your simple PivotTable, you can quickly rearrange it by dragging field names to different areas in the PivotTable, or you can add a new dimension by dragging yet another field name (in the case of the ad buyer, the number of viewers) onto the table. If you add a new field to the data area, Excel divides each row into

Figure 15-13:
These three PivotTables were created using the same data source—the only difference is that the fields from the PivotTable toolbar were dragged to different areas on the blank PivotTable. In the case of the complicated PivotTable (bottom), two different fields were dragged to the same axis. Exercise this option with caution, since dragging multiple fields to the same axis can quickly render a PivotTable unreadable.

Sum of Ad Revenue	Show				
Date	Alias	Buffy	Nikita	Sponge Bob	Grand Total
1-Mar	55200	76521	33879	29750	195350
2-Mar	60720	25621	67540	74360	228241
3-Mar	68910	32725	55470	42030	199135
Grand Total	184830	134867	156889	146140	622726

Sum of Ad Revenue	Viewers							
Ranking	12344	13077	14555	15288	18245	18978	23563	24296
98				32725				
104			29750					
239								
250		68910						
279							76521	
280						67540		
318								
321					55200			
378	25621							
455								
457								60720
660								
Grand Total	25621	68910	29750	32725	55200	67540	76521	60720

		Viewers				
Ranking	Data	12344	13077	14555	15288	18245
98	Sum of Ad Revenue				32725	
	Count of Show				1	
104	Sum of Ad Revenue			29750		
	Count of Show			1		
239	Sum of Ad Revenue					
	Count of Show					
250	Sum of Ad Revenue		68910			
	Count of Show		1			
279	Sum of Ad Revenue					
	Count of Show					
280	Sum of Ad Revenue					
	Count of Show					
318	Sum of Ad Revenue					
	Count of Show					
321	Sum of Ad Revenue					55200
	Count of Show					1
378	Sum of Ad Revenue	25621				
	Count of Show	1				
455	Sum of Ad Revenue					
	Count of Show					
457	Sum of Ad Revenue					
	Count of Show					
660	Sum of Ad Revenue					
	Count of Show					
Total Sum of Ad Revenue		25621	68910	29750	32725	55200
Total Count of Show		1	1	1	1	1

two, showing how the data for each date interrelate. The more field names you drag into the data area, the more complex your table becomes, but the more chance you'll have to spot any trends. Field names can also be added to the row and column axes for an entirely different kind of table.

Analyzing Your Data

PivotTables aren't the only way to analyze your Excel data. In fact, if you're the type who loves to pose "what if" questions, then Excel has a few tools for you: *data tables, goal seek, scenarios,* and the *Solver.*

Data tables

Data tables let you plug several different values into a formula to see how they change its results. They're especially useful, for example, when you want to understand how a few different interest rates might affect the size of a payment over the life of a five-year loan.

Data tables come in two flavors: one-variable tables (in which you can change one factor to see how data is affected) and two-variable tables (in which you can change two factors). The hardest part about using a data table is setting it up. You'll need to insert the formula, the data to substitute into the formula, and an *input cell* that will serve as a placeholder for data being substituted into the formula.

To create a one-variable table, arrange the data in your cells so that the items you want plugged into your calculation (the interest rate, for example) are in a continuous row or column; then proceed as shown in Figure 15-14. If you choose a row, type the

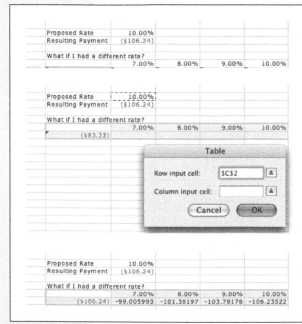

Figure 15-14:
Get ready to set up your data table by determining your question. In this case (top), you're considering a 10% loan (C2) (with interest calculated monthly), to be paid over 60 months, for $5,000. After calculating your resulting monthly payment (C3), you may want to determine how your payment would change with a lower interest rate. To do so, set up some different interest rates that you want to substitute into a formula in a contiguous row or column. Now type in a formula below and to the left of the substituting data (cell B3 here), using C2 has your input cell. (You can use any cell outside the data table area as an input cell.) elect the cells that contain the substitute data and the cells where the resulting monthly payments will be plugged in (middle). Choose Data→Table; in the Table dialog box, enter the address of the row input cell (since the variable data is in a row). If your data is arranged in a column, choose the column input cell instead. When you click OK, Excel builds the table, calculating the payment for each interest rate (bottom).

formula you want used in your table in the cell that's *one column to the left* of that range of values, and one row below it. If you choose a column, type the formula in the row above the range of values, and *one row to the right* of it. Think of the values as row or column heads, and the formula's location as the heading of an actual row or column in your soon-to-be-formed table. You'll also need to decide on the location of your input cell; it should be outside this table.

If you use Excel to do the same table, be sure to tell it to compute the size of a payment based on different interest rates *and* a different number of total payments. This is called a two-variable data table, and it's created in much the same way as a single-variable data table.

To create a two-variable table, enter a formula in your worksheet that refers to the *two* sets of values plugged into the formula. Now proceed as shown in Figure 15-15.

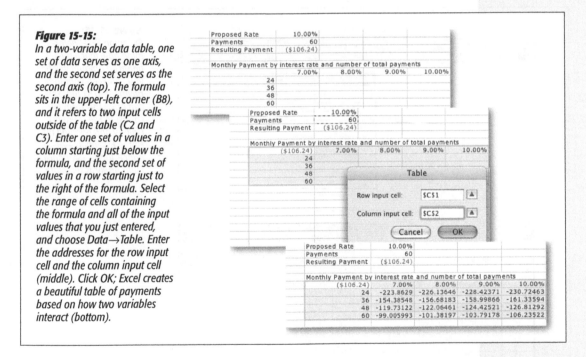

Figure 15-15:
In a two-variable data table, one set of data serves as one axis, and the second set serves as the second axis (top). The formula sits in the upper-left corner (B8), and it refers to two input cells outside of the table (C2 and C3). Enter one set of values in a column starting just below the formula, and the second set of values in a row starting just to the right of the formula. Select the range of cells containing the formula and all of the input values that you just entered, and choose Data→Table. Enter the addresses for the row input cell and the column input cell (middle). Click OK; Excel creates a beautiful table of payments based on how two variables interact (bottom).

Goal seek

When you know the answer that you want a formula to produce but you don't know the values to plug into the formula to *get* that answer, then it's time for Excel's *goal seek* feature.

To use it, choose Tools→Goal Seek. In the resulting dialog box (Figure 15-16), fill in the following three fields:

- **Set cell.** Specifies which cell to start from—the cell containing the formula you're using to seek your goal. For example, Figure 15-16 illustrates a mortgage calculation. The Set cell (the upper-right cell), which shows the amount of the monthly payment, would be I10. The purpose of this exercise is to find the amount you can mortgage if the most you can pay each month is $1,100.

- **To value.** Specifies the value that you want to see in that cell. In the example of Figure 15-16, the To value is $1,100.

- **By changing cell.** Tells Excel which cell it can tinker with to make that happen. The key cell in Figure 15-16 is I5, the amount financed. You want to know how much you can spend on a house with a $1,100 mortgage payment.

Click OK to turn Excel loose on the problem. It reports its progress in a Goal Seek Status dialog box, which lets you step Excel through the process of working toward your goal. There are a couple of caveats: You can select only single cells, not ranges, and the cell you're tweaking must contain a value, not a formula.

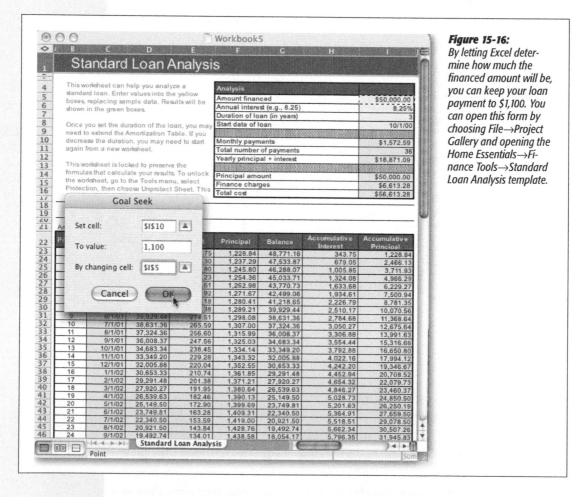

Figure 15-16:
By letting Excel determine how much the financed amount will be, you can keep your loan payment to $1,100. You can open this form by choosing File→Project Gallery and opening the Home Essentials→Finance Tools→Standard Loan Analysis template.

Tip: Another way to conduct a little goal-seeking is to fiddle with a chart. First, set up a chart of the data, and then link a couple of cells with the Tools→Goal Seek function. That way, when you resize an element (such as a bar in a bar chart), the value in the cell represented by that element changes automatically. The Goal Seek dialog box pops up, giving you the opportunity to seek the new value.

Scenarios

Scenarios are like little snapshots, each containing a different set of "what if" data plugged into your formulas. Because Excel can memorize each set and recall it instantly, scenarios help you understand how your worksheet model is likely to turn out given different situations. (You still have to enter the data and formulas into your spreadsheet before you play with scenarios, though.) In a way, scenarios are like saving several different copies of the same spreadsheet, each with variations in the data. Being able to quickly switch between scenarios lets you run through different situations without retyping any numbers.

To create a scenario, choose Tools→Scenarios to bring up the Scenarios Manager, in which you can add, delete, edit, and merge different scenarios, as shown in Figure 15-17.

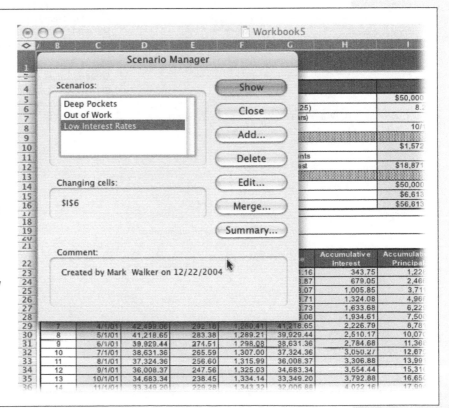

Figure 15-17:
In the Scenario Manager dialog box, you can switch between saved scenarios, add new ones, edit existing ones, merge scenarios from other worksheets into the Scenarios list, and even summarize your scenarios to a standard summary or PivotTable. The Scenarios list displays all of the scenarios that you've created and saved, and by selecting a scenario and clicking a button, you can do wonderful things with it (upper left).

The list box on the left side displays all of the scenarios that you've saved. By selecting a scenario and then clicking a button on the right, you can display your scenarios in your spreadsheet, or even make a summary. Here's what each does:

- **Show.** The Show button lets you switch between scenarios; just select the scenario you want to view, and then click Show. Excel changes the spreadsheet to reflect the selected scenario.

- **Close.** This button simply closes the Scenario Manager.

- **Add.** Click this button to design a new scenario, courtesy of the Add Scenario dialog box (Figure 15-18). It lets you name your scenario and specify the cells you want to change (either enter the cell references or select them with the mouse). Excel inserts a comment regarding when the scenario was created. This comment can be edited to say anything you like, making it a terrific place to note exactly what the scenario affects in the spreadsheet.

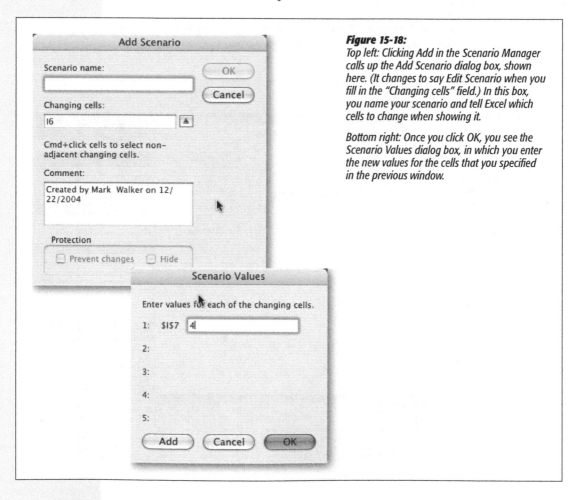

Figure 15-18:
Top left: Clicking Add in the Scenario Manager calls up the Add Scenario dialog box, shown here. (It changes to say Edit Scenario when you fill in the "Changing cells" field.) In this box, you name your scenario and tell Excel which cells to change when showing it.

Bottom right: Once you click OK, you see the Scenario Values dialog box, in which you enter the new values for the cells that you specified in the previous window.

After clicking OK, you're taken to the Scenario Values dialog box, in which you enter new values for the cells you specified in the previous window. Once you're done entering your new values, click OK. The new scenario appears in the Scenario Manager.

- **Delete.** This button deletes the currently selected scenario.

- **Edit.** The Edit button opens the Edit Scenario dialog box, which looks just like the Add Scenario box. Use this box to adjust a previously saved scenario.

- **Merge.** This command merges scenarios from other worksheets into the Scenario list for the current worksheet. To merge scenarios, open all of the workbooks that contain scenarios that you want to merge, and then switch to the worksheet where you want the merged scenarios to appear. This is your destination worksheet for the merge.

Open the Scenario Manager (Tools→Scenarios) and click Merge; proceed as shown in Figure 15-19.

Tip: When you're merging scenarios, make sure that your destination worksheet is the same as all of the scenarios. Otherwise, merged data will still appear in the proper cells, but if those cells aren't properly placed or formatted, it'll look strange.

Figure 15-19:
Top: A summary report shows all of the scenarios in your worksheet. Click the + and – buttons in the margins to expand and contract rows.

Bottom: To merge several scenarios into one worksheet, click Merge in the Scenario Manager, select the workbook that has the scenarios to merge, then select the sheet that contains the actual scenarios.

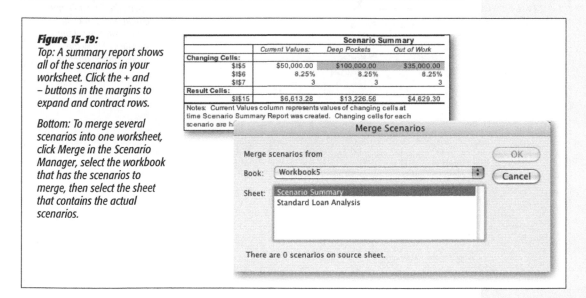

- **Summary.** When you click the Summary button, the Scenario Summary dialog box appears. It has two radio buttons: one for a standard summary (which creates a table) and one for a PivotTable summary (a PivotTable of your changes *really* lets you tweak the numbers). Figure 15-19 demonstrates a standard summary, complete with buttons for expanding and contracting the information.

Solver

Excel's Solver builds a spreadsheet model that works by adjusting the values of some of the sheet's cells; it's a great tool for such tasks as balancing a complicated budget. In practice, it's similar to goal-seeking, only more powerful.

To use the Solver, choose Tools→Solver. In the Solver Parameters dialog box (Figure 15-20), you can tell the Solver what its target solution is, what cells it can change, and some rules to adhere to while it's working toward its solution. By entering the right cell references and clicking the buttons, you can have Excel tweak your worksheet to reflect a reality that you hope (or fear) will come true. Here are the functions of each field; go through the first few fields from top to bottom to enter your information.

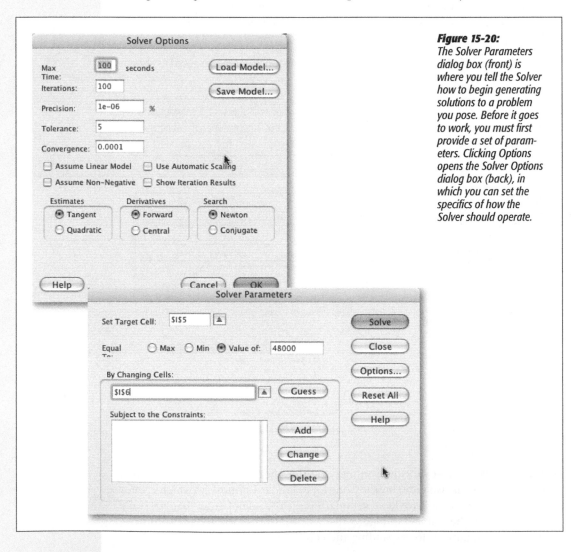

Figure 15-20:
The Solver Parameters dialog box (front) is where you tell the Solver how to begin generating solutions to a problem you pose. Before it goes to work, you must first provide a set of parameters. Clicking Options opens the Solver Options dialog box (back), in which you can set the specifics of how the Solver should operate.

- **Set Target Cell.** This cell contains the value that you want to solve for. Type in the cell reference, or click it to enter it automatically.

- **Equal To.** These three radio buttons set the goal for the Solver. This is the value that you want in the target cell after the Solver has done its work.

- **By Changing Cells.** This is where you tell Excel which cells are fair game to change while looking for a solution. You can also click Guess, which will tell Excel to examine the spreadsheet and take its best guess as to which cells to change. This rarely provides the definitive solution, but it's a good starting place.

- **Subject to the Constraints.** This field, with Add, Change, and Delete buttons, lets you enter conditions that the Solver has to follow when coming up with a solution. When you click Add, a dialog box appears in which you can tell Solver to keep certain cells within a certain value range. This is important because without adding constraints, Solver could use values that theoretically solve the problem but don't work in the real world. You can use the Change button to edit an existing constraint, or select a constraint and hit Delete to get rid of it.

Once you enter a constraint (or several), you can use the five buttons on the right—Solve, Close, Options, Reset All, and Help—to further refine or continue your work.

- **Solve.** This is the Go button. When you click it, Solver goes to work on your problem.

- **Close** closes Solver Parameters without looking for a solution.

- **Options** opens the Solver Options dialog box, in which you can get very specific about how Solver goes about its task. You can set a time limit, an iteration limit, and tell it how precise to be, plus you can load and save these Solver models for use later. This window also lets you control the intricacies inherent in the Solver, such as whether it uses a linear model for its changes, and how it handles estimates, derivatives, and searches. (Don't miss the Help button. You may need it.)

- **Reset All.** This resets the items in the Solver Parameters window so you can start over.

- **Help.** This button opens Excel's help system to the entry for the Solver Parameters dialog box.

Once you click Solve, Solver will go about its business, plugging new numbers into the spreadsheet. It will then put up a Solver Results dialog box, which lets you change your spreadsheet back to the way it was or keep the Solver results. You can also save the Solver's changes as a scenario in your worksheet, if you like.

Tapping the Data menu

Granted, PivotTables and databases are some of the most powerful elements found in the Data menu, but they're not the only ones. A few other commands in the Data menu let you perform additional tricks with your data.

• **Sort.** This powerful menu command lets you sort selected data alphabetically or numerically. You can perform several levels of sorting, just as you can when sorting database items—for example, sort by year, then by month *within* each year. As shown in Figure 15-21, the beauty of the Sort command is that it sorts entire *rows*, not just the one column you specified for sorting.

Tip: Clicking "Header row" avoids sorting the top-row column labels into the data—a common problem with other spreadsheet software. Excel leaves the top row where it is, as shown in Figure 15-21.

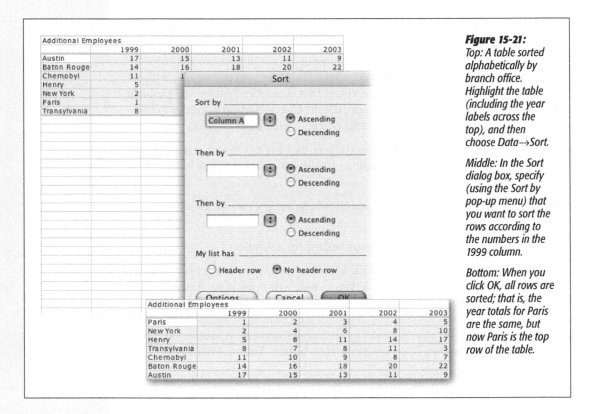

Figure 15-21:
Top: A table sorted alphabetically by branch office. Highlight the table (including the year labels across the top), and then choose Data→Sort.

Middle: In the Sort dialog box, specify (using the Sort by pop-up menu) that you want to sort the rows according to the numbers in the 1999 column.

Bottom: When you click OK, all rows are sorted; that is, the year totals for Paris are the same, but now Paris is the top row of the table.

• **Filter.** When you choose AutoFilter from this submenu, you get pop-up menus at the top of each column in your selection (Figure 15-22). You can use them to hide or show certain rows or columns, exactly like the filters found in list objects (see page 496). AutoFilter pop-up menus can be applied to only one selection at a time in a worksheet. Also on the Filter submenu, Show All displays items that you hid using the AutoFilter pop-up menus, and Advanced Filter lets you build your own filter. (Consult the online help if you want to build an advanced filter.)

• **Subtotals.** This command automatically puts subtotal formulas in a column (or columns). The columns must have headings that label them (Figure 15-23 illustrates an example).

To use this feature, select the relevant columns, including their headings, and then choose Data→Subtotals. In the Subtotal dialog box that pops up, you can tell Excel which function to use (your choices include Sum, Count, StdDev, and Average,

Figure 15-22:
You can quickly and easily sort the rows of selected data by choosing Data→ Filter→AutoFilter, then choosing from the pop-up menus that appear. For example, this command shows only the highest 10 values within this column; all other rows of the table are temporarily hidden.

Additional Employees		
	1999	2000
Paris		2
New York		4
Henry	Sort Ascending	8
Transylvania	Sort Descending	7
Chernobyl		10
Baton Rouge	✓ (Show All)	16
Austin	(Show Top 10...)	15
	(Custom Filter...)	
	2	
	5	
	8	
	11	
	14	
	17	

Figure 15-23:
Top left: Select a set of data that could stand some subtotals. Middle: When you choose Data→Subtotals, the Subtotal dialog box appears. In this box, you can choose the column that determines where subtotals go (in this case, at each change in the date), which function is used, and in which columns the subtotal appears.

Bottom right: When you click OK, the subtotals appear in your data, grouped appropriately according to the column you selected in the Subtotal dialog box. (Excel uses its outlining notation, as described on page 589, making it easy to collapse the result to show subtotals only.)

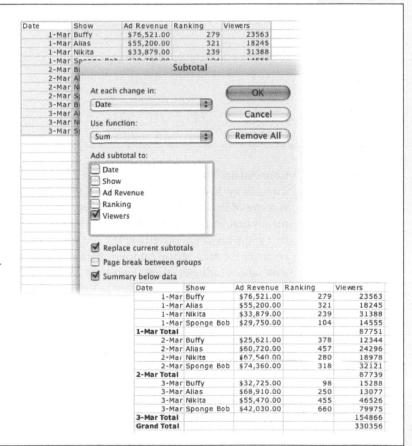

Date	Show	Ad Revenue	Ranking	Viewers
1-Mar	Buffy	$76,521.00	279	23563
1-Mar	Alias	$55,200.00	321	18245
1-Mar	Nikita	$33,879.00	239	31388
1-Mar	Sponge Bob	$29,750.00	104	14555
1-Mar Total				87751
2-Mar	Buffy	$25,621.00	378	12344
2-Mar	Alias	$60,720.00	457	24296
2-Mar	Nikita	$67,540.00	280	18978
2-Mar	Sponge Bob	$74,360.00	318	32121
2-Mar Total				87739
3-Mar	Buffy	$32,725.00	98	15288
3-Mar	Alias	$68,910.00	250	13077
3-Mar	Nikita	$55,470.00	455	46524
3-Mar	Sponge Bob	$42,030.00	660	79975
3-Mar Total				154866
Grand Total				330356

among others). If you've selected more than one column, you can add the selected function to whichever column or columns you choose.

- **Text to Columns.** Suppose you've pasted a phrase into a single cell, and now you'd like to split each word into a separate column. Or maybe a cell contains several cells' worth of text, each separated by a nonstandard delimiter (such as a semicolon) that you'd like to split in a similar fashion. Text to Columns is the solution, as shown in Figure 15-24.

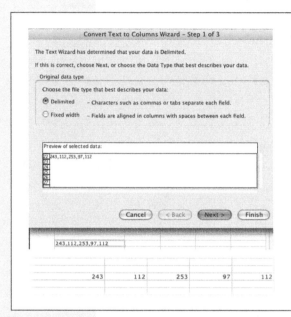

Figure 15-24:
Top: To split delimited text into several columns, select the cell and choose Data→Text to Columns.

Middle: The three-step Convert Text to Columns Wizard appears. You'll be asked what kind of split you'd like to perform, what punctuation serves as the delimiter, and what the data and cell formatting looks like.

Bottom: Excel splits the data into columns.

- **Consolidate.** The Consolidate command joins data from several different worksheets or workbooks into the same area, turning it into a kind of summary. In older versions of Excel, this command was important; in Excel 2004, Microsoft recommends that you not use it and instead simply type the references and operators that you wish to use directly in the consolidation area. For example, if you track revenues for each region on four different worksheets, you can consolidate that data onto a fifth worksheet. Figure 15-25 shows the procedure. (To learn more, read the "Consolidate data" entry in Excel's online help.)

Data form

A spreadsheet is certainly a compact and tidy way to view information. But for the novice, it's not exactly self-explanatory. If you plan to turn some data-entry tasks over to an assistant who's not completely at home with the row-and-column scheme, you might consider setting up a *data form* for him—a little dialog box that displays a single spreadsheet row as individual blanks that must be filled in (see Figure 15-26). Data forms also offer a great way to search for data or delete it one row (that is, one record) at a time.

To set up a data form, start with a series of columns with column headers at the top—a list does nicely. These headers serve as categories for the data form. Then, with the cursor in the list, choose Data→Form, which brings up the data form window for that particular list (Figure 15-26).

Figure 15-25:
Top: A workbook holds similar worksheets for each region in your company, broken down by product. You want to analyze and view all this information in one place.

Middle: You can set up formulas that use data from different worksheets in a new worksheet. In this case, cell B2 shows the sum of Basic Cruise revenue from all four regions.

Bottom left: Fill the rest of the table quickly using the AutoFill techniques described on page 472.

Bottom right: The completed table summarizes the results from all worksheets.

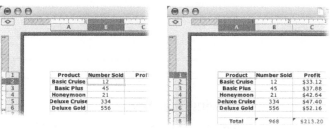

POWER USERS' CLINIC

Validating Data

To ensure that the right kind of data is entered in a cell or cells, use a built-in Excel feature called Data Validation. This feature makes sure that dates, for example, don't end up in cells meant for currency.

To set up data validation for a cell or cells, select them and then choose Data→Validation, which brings up the Data Validation dialog box. This box has three tabs: Settings, Input Message, and Error Alert.

In the Settings tab, you can choose which data types are allowed to be entered (such as whole numbers, decimals, or lists). In the Input Message tab, you can enter a message that will pop up when you (or whoever uses this spreadsheet) select the cell in question. The Error Alert tab, meanwhile, lets you specify which error message Excel should display when someone enters the wrong kind of data.

When the form appears, the text boxes show the first row of data in the list. You can scroll through the rows (or records) using the scroll bar. On the right, eight buttons let you perform the following functions: add a new record (or row) of data at the bottom, delete the currently selected row, click Criteria to enter search criteria in the text boxes next to the field names, and then search for that information using Find Prev and Find Next. Finally, the Close button closes the window.

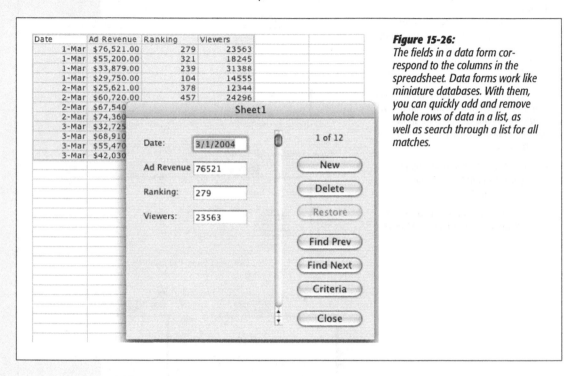

Figure 15-26:
The fields in a data form correspond to the columns in the spreadsheet. Data forms work like miniature databases. With them, you can quickly add and remove whole rows of data in a list, as well as search through a list for all matches.

Viewing Your Data

Excel worksheets can grow very quickly. Fortunately, Excel has some convenient tools to help you look at just the data you want.

Custom views

Excel can memorize everything about a workbook's window: its size and position, any splits or frozen panes, which sheets are active and which cells are selected, and even your printer settings—in a *custom view*. Custom views are snapshots of your view options at the time that the view is saved. Using custom views, you can quickly switch from your certain-columns-hidden view to your everything-exposed view, or from your split-window view to your full-window view.

To create a custom view, choose View→Custom Views, which brings up the Custom Views dialog box. To make Excel memorize your current window arrangement, click Add (and type a name for the current setup); switch between custom views by clicking a view's name in the list and then clicking Show.

Reports

Reports combine sheets, views, and scenarios into a convenient printable format. They're great when you have a sprawling spreadsheet from which you want to print only a few key cells. For example, if you want to create a report with just the capital expenditures sheet of a huge yearly budget, the Report Manger can do the trick

To create a report, choose View→Report Manager. In the Report Manager, you can create, edit, print, and delete reports by clicking the buttons on the right.

For example, to create a new report, click Add; in the Add Report dialog box, name the new report, then create a report section—choose a sheet, an optional view, an optional scenario, and click Add. Note that you can create multiple sections, too. When you've created all your sections, click OK, which returns you to the Report Manager window. You should see your newly minted report in the Reports list. Print it by selecting it and then clicking Print.

Outlining

In Excel, *outlines* help to summarize many rows of data, hiding or showing levels of detail in lists so that only the summaries are visible (see Figure 15-27). Because they let you switch between overview and detail views in a single step, outlines are useful for worksheets that teem with subtotals and details. (If you're unfamiliar with the concept of outlining software, consult page 200, which describes the very similar feature in Microsoft Word.)

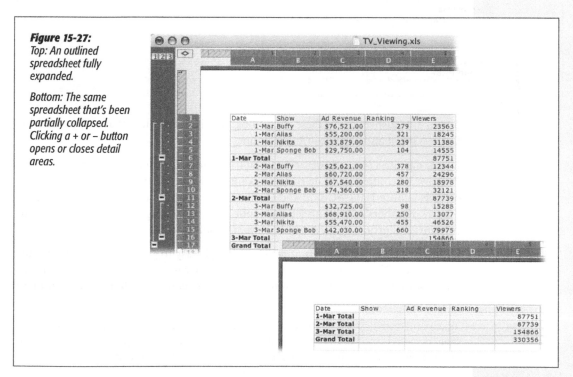

Figure 15-27:
Top: An outlined spreadsheet fully expanded.

Bottom: The same spreadsheet that's been partially collapsed. Clicking a + or – button opens or closes detail areas.

You can create an outline in one of two ways: automatically or manually. The automatic method works only if your worksheet is properly formatted, as follows:

- Summary *columns* must be to the right or left of the data they summarize. In Figure 15-28 at top, the D column is a summary column, located to the right of the data it summarizes.

- Summary *rows* must be immediately above or below the cells that they summarize. For example, in Figure 15-28 at bottom, each subtotal is directly below the cells that it adds together.

	East	West	Subtotal
April	3435	55567	59002
May	4356	35356	39712
June	5277	15145	20422
July	6198	35353	41551
August	7119	353556	360675

Date	Show	Ad Revenue	Ranking	Viewers
1-Mar	Buffy	$76,521.00	279	23563
1-Mar	Alias	$55,200.00	321	18245
1-Mar	Nikita	$33,879.00	239	31388
1-Mar	Sponge Bob	$29,750.00	104	14555
1-Mar Total				87751
2-Mar	Buffy	$25,621.00	378	12344
2-Mar	Alias	$60,720.00	457	24296
2-Mar	Nikita	$67,540.00	280	18978
2-Mar	Sponge Bob	$74,360.00	318	32121
2-Mar Total				87739
3-Mar	Buffy	$32,725.00	98	15288
3-Mar	Alias	$68,910.00	250	13077
3-Mar	Nikita	$55,470.00	455	46526
3-Mar	Sponge Bob	$42,030.00	660	79975
3-Mar Total				154866
Grand Total				330356

Figure 15-28:
Top: Because the column of subtotals (column D) is to the right of the data to which it refers, this spreadsheet can be automatically outlined.

Bottom: Each subtotal is beneath the cells that it summarizes, making this spreadsheet, too, a fine candidate for automatic outlining.

If your spreadsheet meets these conditions, creating an outline is as easy as selecting Data→Group and Outline→Auto Outline.

If your data isn't so neatly organized, you'll have to create an outline manually. Select the rows or columns of data that you want to group together into one level of the outline; choose Data→Group and Outline→Group. A bracket line appears outside the row numbers or column letters, connecting that group. Keep selecting rows or columns and grouping them until you've manually created your outline.

Outlines can have eight levels of detail, making it easy to go from general to specific very quickly. Thick brackets connect the summary row or column to the set of cells that it summarizes; a + or – button appears at the end of the line by the summary row or column.

To expand or collapse a single "branch" of the outline, click a + or – button; if you see several nested brackets, click the outer + or – buttons to collapse greater chunks of the outline. Also, the tiny, numbered buttons at the upper left hide and show outline levels and correspond to Level 1, Level 2, and so on, much like the Show Heading buttons on the Outlining toolbar in Word (see page 208).

Tip: Although outlines were originally designed to hide or reveal detail, you can use them to hide *any* rows or columns that you like.

Flag for Follow-Up

Sometimes, when you're presenting the contents of a workbook to someone else—or when you're up battling a bout of insomnia by going through your old Excel workbooks—you come across something in a spreadsheet that needs updating, research, explanation, or some other kind of follow-up. Excel's *flag for follow-up* feature lets you attach a reminder to a file, which you can program to appear (as a reminder box on your screen) at a specified time. See Figure 15-29 for details, or page 406 for more on Office 2004 reminders.

Adding a Comment

Here's another way to get your own attention (or somebody else's): Add a *comment* to a cell—a great way to annotate a spreadsheet. A note might say, for example, "This estimate seems way too high—call me," or "If you hadn't noticed, the dot-com era is over, pal." See Figure 15-30 for details.

To edit a comment that already exists, select the cell and then choose Insert→Edit Comment. To *delete* a comment, select the cell with the comment and choose Edit→ Clear→Comments. You can also reveal all comments on a worksheet at once by choosing View→Comments.

Tip: Like the Stickies program on every Mac, Excel comment boxes lack scroll bars. If you have a lot to say, keep typing past the bottom boundary of the box; Excel expands the note automatically. You can press the up and down arrow keys to walk your insertion point through the text, in the absence of scroll bars.

(Alternatively, drag one of the white handles to make the box bigger.)

POWER USERS' CLINIC

Proofing Tools

A spelling error can ruin the credibility of an otherwise brilliant spreadsheet, especially when you've gone through the trouble of getting it to look just right. Running a spell check on your spreadsheet before you show it to others can prevent just such an embarrassing mishap. Fortunately, Excel is part of a larger office suite—one that includes spelling tools.

To run a spell check on your spreadsheet, choose Tools→ Spelling. Excel scans the text in your spreadsheet; if it comes across a suspect word, the Spelling dialog box appears. It works much like the Word spell checker described on page 79, and, in fact, relies on the same spelling dictionaries. There's probably not much call for a definitions dictionary in spreadsheets these days, but if you run across a term in a spreadsheet that you don't know (profit, for example), you can access Office's definitions dictionary by choosing Tools→ Dictionary and typing in the word you'd like defined.

Macros: Making Excel Work for You

A *macro* is a recorded series of actions that Excel can play back automatically, at high speed and with perfect accuracy. Macros are useful for automating tedious processes, such as formatting or data entry tasks.

For example, if you're constantly getting malformed expense reports because someone in sales insists on changing the formatting in mileage cells to Currency instead

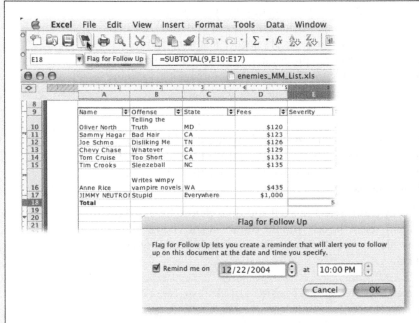

Figure 15-29:
To flag a file for follow-up, click the Flag for Follow Up button in the Standard toolbar (top), which brings up the Flag for Follow Up dialog box (bottom). In this box, you can set a time and date to be reminded that you need to attend to your worksheet. (Press Tab if you have trouble moving the insertion point around in the dialog box.) Once the date is set, click OK and save the document. Excel creates a task in Entourage; the reminder will pop up at the specified time, provided an Office 2004 program is running at the time.

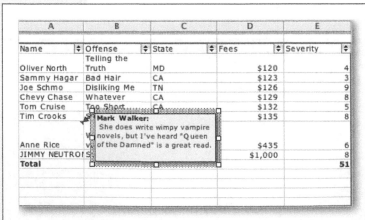

Figure 15-30:
To add a note to a cell, click the cell and then choose Insert→Comment. A nice yellow "sticky note" opens with your user name on the top (as it appears in the Excel→Preferences→General tab). Type your comment in the window. When you click elsewhere, the note disappears, leaving only a small triangle in the upper-right corner of the cell. To make the comment reappear, let the cursor hover over the triangle.

of Number, you can write a macro that selects the mileage column and reformats it as Number in the blink of an eye.

But that's just the beginning. People who develop high-level macro-writing skills can use it as a full-on programming language. Their macros can throw dialog boxes onto the screen to ask users for information, plug the provided responses into appropriate cells in a spreadsheet, massage it with formulas, and format it for beautiful printing. Such a macro, in other words, can ask for five stock symbols and their closing prices over a week, and then produce a neatly formatted percentage-of-change table for you.

You can record your own macros or run macros you find embedded in a worksheet that came from somebody else.

Recording a Macro

To record a macro, choose Tools→Macro→Record New Macro. The Record Macro box appears (Figure 15-31), giving you the chance to name your new macro (and provide a description).

At this point, you can also specify where you want to store the macro. Using the "Store macro in:" pop-up menu, you can choose to store it:

- **In the currently open workbook.** It will ride along with the data that was used when you created it, but you won't be able to use the macro without opening the workbook that contains it.

- **In a brand new workbook created to store the macro.** This option is useful when you don't want to sully the workbook that you're working on with a macro, but still want to use a macro with it.

- **In your Personal Macro Workbook.** The Personal Macro Workbook is a special workbook that stays with the copy of Excel where the macro is created. Think of it as a library where you can store all kinds of macros for use in any workbook. It's the perfect place for macros that you'll be attaching to menu items or buttons (see page 671 for details).

When you click OK, Excel puts up the macro toolbar (complete with a Stop button) and begins to watch and memorize your every move; each click, drag, and menu command becomes a part of the macro. Excel macros are surprisingly versatile: Besides just data entry and formatting, they can drag data around, resize and move chart elements, and execute menu commands that involve dialog boxes.

Like anything that sounds too good to be true, though, there are some limitations. Macros don't understand what the data actually means. If you alter the landscape of a spreadsheet by moving some of its data and formulas around (without modifying the macro to notice the new locations), the macro assumes that everything is in its old place. Therefore, when it runs, it'll move the wrong things around.

Tip: When you record a macro, you can use the Relative Reference button on the macro toolbar to ensure that the macro refers to relative cell coordinates, which helps alleviate the problem of altering the wrong data with a macro. To solve the problem completely, you must keep your worksheets largely untouched after you've recorded a macro.

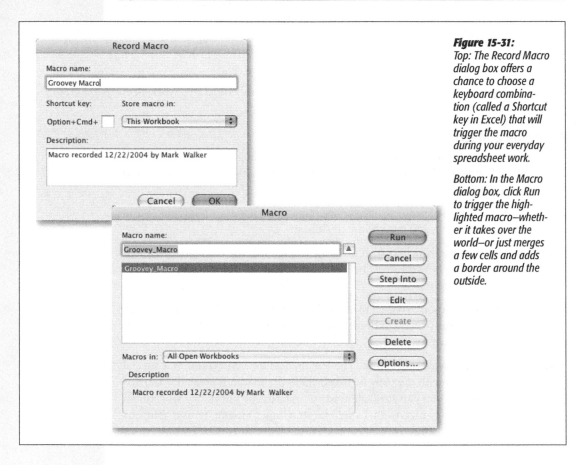

Figure 15-31:
Top: The Record Macro dialog box offers a chance to choose a keyboard combination (called a Shortcut key in Excel) that will trigger the macro during your everyday spreadsheet work.

Bottom: In the Macro dialog box, click Run to trigger the highlighted macro—whether it takes over the world—or just merges a few cells and adds a border around the outside.

Once you've done everything that you want the macro to do, click the Stop button on the toolbar. You've just created a macro.

Playing a Macro

To play a macro that you've recorded (or that someone has embedded in the currently open workbook), choose Tools→Macro→Macros. This brings up the Macro dialog box. In it, double-click the name of the macro you want to play (or click it once and click Run).

Tip: If you've specified a key combination for your macro, just press the key combination to run it, bypassing the visit to the Macro box.

Excel now plays back the macro, doing everything that you specified when you recorded it—but at very high speed and with computerish precision.

Using Macros in Menus and Toolbars

You don't have to use the Macro dialog box to trigger a macro you've recorded; you can assign it to an Excel toolbar or even a menu, putting its power only a click away.

To assign a macro to a toolbar button, choose Tools→ Customize→Commands tab. In the categories list, select Macros; drag a Custom Button to the toolbar where you want the macro button to appear. Click OK, then click the new custom button. This brings up the Assign Macro dialog box, in which you choose the macro to link to the button. Once you've done so, click OK. Now, every time you click the toolbar button, the macro attached to it runs.

You can turn a macro into a menu command, too. Choose Tools→Customize →Commands tab. Select Macros in the Categories list, and then drag the Custom Menu Item in the Commands list to the menu where you want it to appear.

(See page 674 for more on customizing menus.) Once it's in the menu, double-click the menu item to open the Command Properties dialog box; now you can change its name to something recognizable. Click OK, then OK again to dismiss the Customize box.

Now click your new menu command, which brings up the Assign Macro dialog box. Select the macro that you want to assign to the menu command; click OK. From now on, when you choose the new menu command from the menu, Excel will run the macro you assigned.

Note: These macros must be saved in your Personal Macro Workbook. Otherwise, you'll need to open the workbook that contains the macro every time you want to use the button or menu command.

The Trouble with Macros

Although they seem simple on the surface, macros represent a messy, controversial subject (for Excel, PowerPoint, and Word veterans) , thanks to the fact that they're an ideal carrier of viruses. It's perfectly possible for some maladjusted social deviant to write a destructive little program that, say, erases your entire spreadsheet.

Fortunately, most macro viruses are written so that they work only on Windows PCs. Furthermore, the Office 2004 programs themselves help guard against macro viruses. When you open a document containing an embedded macro, for example, Office shows you a warning message that offers to disable any macros attached to the document (thus rendering them harmless). If you're still worried about macro viruses, you can buy antivirus software (and keep it up-to-date); modern antivirus programs can scan for macro viruses in Office documents.

Macros are also a messy, controversial subject, because, behind the scenes, they're written in a programming language called Visual Basic for Applications. If you aspire to writing or editing macros by hand, then take a peek at the VBA code by choosing Tools→Macro→Macros, clicking a macro name, and then clicking the Step Into button. This catapults you into Microsoft's VBA editor, where the macro's source code is visible.

If you're convinced that perhaps you don't want to become a programmer after all, click the Excel button in the editor's Standard toolbar to get rid of the VBA editor. On the other hand, if you're interested in editing your macro by changing the code (or perhaps learning how to code these things by hand), this source code is an excellent place to begin your studies. A book or Web site on VBA programming (like *Writing Excel Macros* from O'Reilly) is another good idea.

Sharing Macros

To share a macro with someone else, save your macro in a workbook when you create it, and then hand the workbook off to your macro tradee. When that person opens the workbook, your macro is available in the Macro dialog box.

Part Four: PowerPoint

4

Chapter 16: Basic PowerPoint

Chapter 17: Advanced PowerPoint

Basic PowerPoint

Whether you're teaching geography to a class of third-graders or pitching an ad campaign to a Fortune 500 CEO, nothing beats a slideshow to get your point across fast. With a bit of know-how, PowerPoint lets you blend words, graphics, movies, sounds, and animations to create dazzling presentations that grab and hold your audience's attention.

Triple View

PowerPoint presentations are made up of *slides*, a holdover term from the days of 35 mm film transparencies. (PowerPoint still has a setting for 35mm slides, but nowadays most people use a video projector to display their presentations.) PowerPoint's three-pane Normal view lets you concentrate on one slide at a time. The largest pane displays everything that's on the current frame—apart from animations and other special effects, it shows you exactly what your audience will see (see Figure 16-1). The pane on the left gives you an overview of the entire presentation in outline format. The third pane, below the slide, lets you enter speaker notes that you can refer to while you're talking. Although the slide area is the biggest by default, you can resize the panes by dragging the dividers that separate them. You can also hide the outline and notes panes by clicking on the Slide View icon at the bottom left of the window.

Step 1: Specify a Design

Even though your slides may display different kinds of information—text, charts, tables, and pictures, for example—it's usually best if they follow a consistent plan that uses the same fonts, background graphics, color scheme, and so on. The design sets the overall tone for the presentation, so choosing one that suits the topic and audience is critical.

Thankfully, Microsoft makes life easier for presentation newbies by providing an assortment of prefab designs. They let you start building your slideshow without having to waste a lot of time on the design elements—or even placing the text on the slides. As soon as you launch PowerPoint, the first thing you see is the Project Gallery, which should look familiar if you've used Word 2004 or Excel 2004. (See page 657 for full detail on the Project Gallery.)

Tip: If you don't want to see the Project Gallery every time you launch PowerPoint, uncheck Show Project Gallery at startup in PowerPoint→Preferences→View panel. You can always summon the gallery with File→ Project Gallery.

When project deadlines are looming and there are a million things that need to be done (including creating a presentation), you'll welcome these timesaving features.

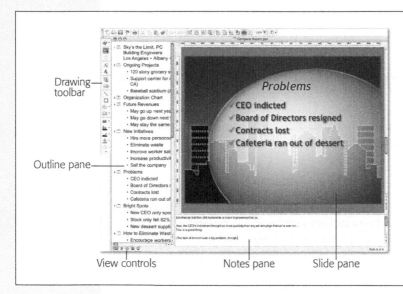

Drawing toolbar

Outline pane

View controls   Notes pane   Slide pane

Figure 16-1:
PowerPoint's three-paned Normal view includes an area for the slideshow's outline, a smaller area for notes, and an area in which you actually build the slide. Controls in the lower-left corner offer additional view options.

Canned Design Templates

In the Project Gallery Groups List, open the Presentations group by clicking the triangle to its left, then click Designs to reveal a selection of design templates (see Figure 16-2). (PowerPoint displays the templates in thumbnail or list form, depending on which view control you highlight at the right of the Groups List.) The names of the templates in the Designs group (Hearts, Ocean, Wood, and so on) are supposed to evoke their appearance, although some are more fanciful than others.

If one of these templates looks like it will work for you, double-click it. The New Slide dialog box appears, as described on page 604.

Tip: When choosing a design template, consider how you're going to present the final product. All the included designs look terrific when projected from the Mac itself (using a portable projector, for example). On the other hand, if you plan to *print* the various slides (as handouts, for example), avoid designs with solid colors in the background. Not only will they take forever to print (and consume a lot of ink or toner), but the blended background on some of these designs may not look as smooth as it did onscreen.

Complete Slideshows, Including Prewritten Text

True to its name, the Content group includes a different selection of presentation templates that are tailored for specific purposes. These templates include both a design theme (complete with backgrounds, font choices, and standing graphics) and an outline befitting the situation.

For example, if you choose the Communicating Bad News template, you get a seven-slide outline to help you through the process of telling your colleagues about rocky times ahead, complete with a positive spin (and a placeholder for morale-building information bits). Such *content templates,* in other words, provide a canned but thoughtful structure for your presentation.

To survey a list of these ready-made shows, click Presentations in the Groups list (of the Project Gallery window) and then click Content. You'll see a long list of ready-to-use slideshows, such as Communicating Bad News, Training, or Brainstorming Session (see Figure 16-2).

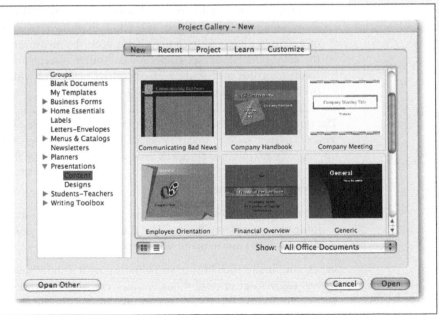

Figure 16-2:
PowerPoint provides a collection of templates for your presentation needs, including a template for breaking bad news, from "Your stock options are now worthless" to "Honey, I wrecked the car today." To choose a template, select it and click OK, or just double-click the one you want. (If the List View icon at the bottom of the window is selected, click the name of a slideshow to see its preview.)

If you find a promising suggestion, double-click its icon. After a moment, you arrive in the three-pane Normal view (Figure 16-1), with the outline and design of your slideshow already in place. You're ready to go about replacing the dummy text of this outline with phrases specific to your pitch, as described on page 605.

Custom-Built Slideshows Based on Your Input

If starting your presentation from a completely formatted, ready-to-go slideshow feels too much like cheating, you may prefer to take advantage of the AutoContent Wizard. This feature draws upon the same set of canned slideshow designs as the Content list described in the previous paragraphs, but gives you the opportunity to tailor the starter slides up front, rather than after PowerPoint has created them.

In the Project Gallery, click Blank Documents in the Category list. Then double-click AutoContent Wizard in the list to its right. The wizard proceeds to take you through the following steps:

1. **Choose a presentation type.**

   The first screen of the AutoContent Wizard asks you what kind of presentation you're planning. Start by using the Category pop-up menu to tell PowerPoint the overall nature of the presentation you're planning (General, Corporate, Projects, or whatever). You'll see a list of design templates appropriate for the category you've chosen; click each to see a preview of that slide design at the bottom of the window. Click Next to continue.

2. **Specify the presentation medium.**

   The wizard screen asks you to choose how you're going to deliver your slide-show—on a computer screen, as black-and-white overheads, as color overheads, or as 35mm slides. Your choice affects both the measurements of the slides and the color scheme: darker colors for computer screens and 35mm slides, lighter colors for color overheads, and, of course, black and white for black-and-white overheads. Click Next.

Tip: You can adjust the dimensions of your slideshow later by choosing File→Page Setup (when reusing the show for a different projection method, for example). However, as the graphics and text boxes on each slide may shift in the process, it's best to pick the appropriate size for your slides at this early phase.

---

3. **Give your show a name.**

   On the final wizard screen, you're asked to enter the presentation's title, descriptive information, and any "footer" text that you want to appear at the bottom of each slide (such as your name or your department name).

When you finally click Finish, you wind up with a slideshow document containing several ready-to-customize slides. A quick examination will show that they're filled with bogus information, such as dummy numbers in the charts and irrelevant data plotted in the graphs—but the point is that the designs and sequence are already in place. Now's your chance to change the actual text and numbers to suit your purpose. After all, you probably don't want to start off a motivational presentation with a slide that says, "Title goes here."

Starting from Scratch

Although the Project Gallery can save you hours of work, there's a downside to using it, too. Since you'll be choosing from the same repertoire as millions of other Power-Point users, there's a chance your slideshow will look just like someone else's, maybe even the speaker who came before you. The only surefire way to guarantee a unique look is to design your presentation yourself. Fortunately, it's not as hard as it sounds. To access a blank presentation from the Project Gallery, click the Blank Documents category and then double-click PowerPoint Presentation. Or, if you're already in PowerPoint, choose File→New Presentation (⌘-N).

Either way, you're now facing the New Slide dialog box, from which you can choose a layout for your first slide (see page 604). Then you can use PowerPoint's various text and drawing tools to build each slide from scratch. Although designing slides this way involves a lot more work than simply choosing a template, you'll be rewarded with a presentation that doesn't *look* like it came out of a can.

Changing Designs in Midstream

Unlike, say, home decorating, changing your presentation's color scheme and other elements requires nothing more than a few quick mouse clicks. In the Formatting Palette, open the Change Slides panel by clicking on its title bar, if it's not already open. Next, click on the Slide Design tab on the left to reveal thumbnails of all the canned templates; click on one to apply it to your presentation. (They're the same ones that you saw in the Project Gallery.) If you don't like the change, choose Edit→ Undo Slide Design (⌘-Z) to revert. (You can also change the design by choosing Format→Slide Design.)

The pop-up menu below the Change Slides panel lets you apply a color scheme to the text, graphics, and other elements on your slides. Most of the canned templates only offer one or two choices that are compatible with the design's background and layout, but you can customize your own colors by selecting Custom Scheme from the menu (see Figure 16-3).

POWER USERS' CLINIC

Adding Your Own Templates

In many corporations, PowerPoint slideshows are an every-day occurrence. You may need to use a PowerPoint template, approved and designed by your company, as the basis for all slideshows you give. (Don't worry if your company is Windows-based—templates for the Windows version of PowerPoint work just fine on Macs.)

It's easy to make one of these templates show up in your Project Gallery, ready for easy access each time you begin to create a slideshow. Just drag the template file into Microsoft Office 2004→Templates→My Templates folder. It'll show up in the Project Gallery under the My Templates group. In fact, you can transform *any* PowerPoint file into a template by dragging it into this folder.

When you open it, you'll get a blank copy of that file (called "Presentation1," for example), even if it wasn't a PowerPoint template to begin with. PowerPoint is smart enough to figure: "If it's in the Templates folder, I'm probably supposed to treat it as a template."

CHAPTER 16: BASIC POWERPOINT **603**

The New Slide Dialog Box

When you create a new presentation, whether by using the Project Gallery or by choosing File→New Presentation, the first thing you see is the New Slide dialog box (Figure 16-4). This box offers 24 slide designs in a scrolling list, each with a place for some text, a picture, a table, a chart, or a media file—or some combination of these

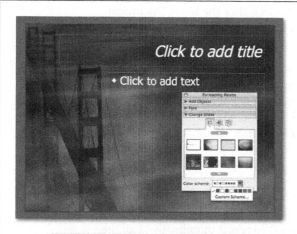

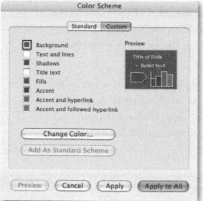

Figure 16-3:
Top: The Change Slides panel of the Formatting Palette lets you select various canned design templates and color schemes. Choosing a color scheme is as easy as picking one from the list. (Selecting a new color scheme changes the colors of all of the elements on a slide.) If you want to create your own color collection, choose Custom Scheme from the "Color scheme" pop-up menu. Bottom: In the resulting Color Scheme dialog box, you can choose new colors for the slide's background, text, shadows, fills, accents, and links.

elements. Each layout has been predesigned with centered text, neatly framed graphics, and so on. When you choose a layout and click OK, PowerPoint creates a new slide with those elements. (If you turn on the box at the bottom of the New Slide dialog, you won't be bothered by it every time you add a slide, and new slides will automatically inherit the layout of the preceding one.)

Which layout you choose for each slide depends on what you want to do with that slide, as shown in Figure 16-4.

Tip: You can always change a slide from one of these canned layouts to another by choosing Format→Slide Layout, or by opening the Slide Layout tab in the Formatting Palette's Change Slides panel.

Step 2: Writing the Outline

A picture may be worth a thousand words, but it's the rare presentation that doesn't include at least some text. Deciding how to transform boring facts into compelling word slides is often the most challenging part of creating a presentation, so words are a good place to begin before you get too hung up on design.

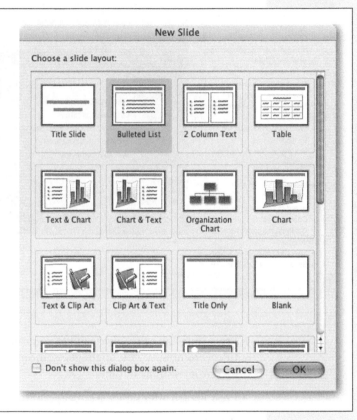

Figure 16-4:
When you add a new slide to your presentation, you'll be presented with the New Slide dialog box, from which you can choose one of 24 different layouts. These layouts make it easy to add various elements to your slides by providing placeholders for bullet lists, charts, artwork, tables, and even movies.

A smart way to go about this is to use PowerPoint's Outline view, which looks much like Normal view, except that the Outline pane is wider. You switch into Outline view by clicking the Outline View button near the bottom left of the main window.

Each numbered slide icon at the left of the Outline pane represents an individual slide. Whatever you type adjacent to the slide icon becomes the corresponding slide's title, whether or not there's a title placeholder in the slide's layout (see Figure 16-5). Indented lines below the title correspond to the slide's subtitle and bullet text. (Bullet points refer to lines of text denoted by special markers called *bullets*—see page 616).

To generate more outline text, you can:

- Press Return after typing a title to start another title. Each title corresponds to a slide.

- Press Tab to *demote* a title into a bullet point under the previous title or bullet point. If you continue pressing Tab, you can continue the demotion, down to five levels below the title. (Demote is outlining jargon for "make less important," or "move down one level in the outline.")

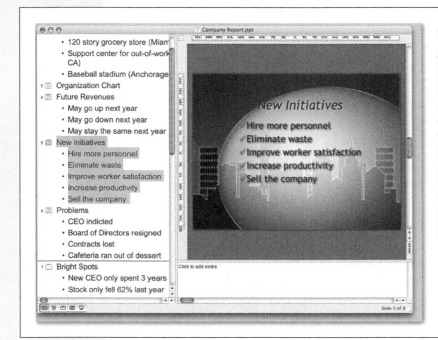

Figure 16-5:
You can drag topics or bullet points into a different order as you build your outline. The cursor changes to crossed arrows when you mouse over a draggable slide or bullet icon. A horizontal line indicates where PowerPoint thinks you want to place the item when you release the mouse. As you work on your outline in the left-hand Outline pane, you get to see the matching slide in the Slide pane.

- Press Shift-Tab to *promote* a bullet point into a more important bullet point or a title. (Promote, as you might guess, means to "make more important," or "move up one level in the outline.")

- Press Return after typing a bullet point to start another bullet point.

- Press Control-M after typing a bullet point to start a title for a new slide.

If you create more than an occasional PowerPoint show, you'll make your life much easier if you master a few of these key combinations:

Keystroke	What it does
Tab	Demotes a heading
Shift-Tab	Promotes a heading
Return	Creates a new heading at the same level
Shift-Option-right arrow	Demotes a heading
Shift-Option-left arrow	Promotes a heading
Shift-Option-+	Expands (shows) the points below the current heading (use the + on the numeric keypad)

Shift-Option-minus sign	Collapses (hides) the points below the current heading (use the - on the numeric keypad)
Shift-Option-down arrow	Moves a heading down by one line in the outline
Shift-Option-up arrow	Moves a heading up by one line in the outline
Option-arrow (any direction)	Moves the cursor one word or line in that direction

If all these keyboard shortcuts are too much to remember, you can promote, demote, and rearrange by simply dragging slide icons or bullet points left, right, up, and down. Also, if pushing buttons is your thing, you can use the Outlining toolbar. (Choose View→Toolbars→Outlining to make it appear.)

As you're creating word slides, remember that your audience will probably be reading everything for the first time, so it's important not to pack too much text into each frame. Generally, it's best to limit your slides to about seven lines, with no more than seven words on each line. As you type your slideshow's outline, you can watch the slide being built in the Slide pane—handy feedback to avoid typing too much text for a bullet.

Using a Word Outline

The PowerPoint outliner isn't the only outliner in Office 2004. If, having cuddled up with Chapter 6 for several evenings, you're already proficient with the outliner in Word 2004, you may prefer to write up your slideshow in Word. Fortunately, you can easily import your outline into PowerPoint.

To do so, launch PowerPoint and choose File→Open to bring up the Open dialog box. Select All Outlines in the Show pop-up menu, and then select the Word document that you want to import.

After you click Open, the Office Assistant asks if you want to open the outline in Word or in PowerPoint; choose PowerPoint. PowerPoint now converts your outline into the basis for a slideshow; each top-level heading becomes the title of a new slide, and subheadings become bullet points on each slide.

POWER USERS' CLINIC

Typing Directly into Your Slides

Not everybody uses the Outline pane to hash out the shape of a presentation. Some people prefer to type their text directly onto the slides themselves.

If you fall into that category, begin the slideshow by choosing only a design template, not a content template as described at the beginning of this chapter. Then, each time you want to add a slide to your show, choose Insert→New Slide (Control-M) or click the New Slide button in the Standard toolbar.

The New Slide window appears (Figure 16-4). Double-click the slide layout you want. After PowerPoint returns you to the main window, you can fill in the details by clicking the various text or graphics placeholders and then typing or importing text to fill those placeholders.

Tip: You can perform this trick from inside Word, too. With the outline open in Word 2004, choose File→
Send To→Microsoft PowerPoint. PowerPoint opens (if it's not already open) and converts the outline into
a presentation automatically, saving you several steps.

Step 3: Building the Show

It's much better to show blank white slides containing an effective message than fancy graphics that don't say anything. That's why it's an excellent idea to begin your presentation planning with the Outline pane.

Once the outline's in good shape, it's time to start thinking about the cosmetics—how your slides look. PowerPoint's tools make it easy to adapt your design (or Microsoft's design) for all the slides simultaneously.

Caution: Choose File→Page Setup and set the Size options *before* you design your slides. A radical change to these options later in the game may result in cutoff graphics or unintended distortions, as though your slides were being projected through a fun-house mirror.

Using Masters

In the same way that design templates let you alter the look of your presentation in a flash, *slide masters* save time by letting you make changes that apply to the entire presentation. *Background master items* appear on every slide, unless you specify otherwise (see page 610). When you add, delete, move, or replace a background master item, you see the change reflected in all of your slides that use it. For example, if you want to add a company logo to all your slides, just place it on the *slide master;* PowerPoint updates all the slides instantly. Other master items serve as placeholders for the title and bullet text. Changes that you make to them on the slide master—the size and color of the font, or the appearance of the bullets, for example—are automatically reflected throughout the presentation.

In fact, PowerPoint offers four different categories of master items: slides, titles, handouts, and notes. Here's how they work.

Slide master

The *slide master*—or, as most people would call it, the master slide—is a special slide whose background, font size and style, bullet style, and footer (whatever appears at the bottom of every slide) determine the look of these elements on every slide it controls.

Editing the slide master

To look at and change the slide master, choose View→Master→Slide Master. Now you're face to face with the slide master itself (see Figure 16-6), which comes with these master items:

- **Title Area.** This usually contains some dummy text, a placeholder for the real text that will appear in your slides. The title area is surrounded by a dashed line.

- **Object Area.** The settings you make in this area determine how the body of your slides—text, charts, pictures, and media clips—will look and where they will sit.

- **Date Area, Footer Area, and Number Area.** These boxes at the bottom of the slide master show where the date and time, slide number, and miscellaneous footer text will appear on each slide. (These same boxes appear in the preview in File→Page Setup→Header/Footer→Slide tab.)

Note: In View→Master→Slide Master mode, the placeholder text (such as "Click to edit Master title style") is irrelevant. Don't bother editing it; doing so has no effect on your actual slides.

Figure 16-6:
The slide master generates certain elements that will be reflected in every slide in the presentation—except for title slides, which have their own title master. The Slide Master view also has a small toolbar of its own with two buttons: Slide Miniature (produces a miniature image of an actual slide in the presentation, which lets you see how your changes to the master slide affect it) and Close (takes you back to the slide you were viewing).

By changing the font size, style, color, and placement of these items, you can change how PowerPoint draws those elements on your slides. For example, if you want all of your slides' titles to be in 24-point Gill Sans Ultra Bold, just click once inside the placeholder text to select the box; then use the Formatting Palette to change the font to 24-point Gill Sans Ultra Bold. Now, any existing slides that have titles (and any *new* slides you make) will display the title in 24-point Gill Sans Ultra Bold.

Adding new elements to a slide master

The title, bulleted text items, and various footers revealed on your slide master can appear on every slide; all you have to do is fill them in. But if you need *additional* text to appear on each slide (such as your department or project name), you can create additional default text blocks on your slide master.

To do so, use the Text Box button on the Drawing toolbar, which usually floats at the left edge of your screen, as shown in Figure 16-9. (If it's not there, choose View→

Toolbars→Drawing.) If you can't find the Text Box button, point to each button in turn without clicking and read the yellow screen tip that appears (the screen tip reveals the button's name). Click the slide master where you want the new text box to appear, type some dummy placeholder text, and then use the Formatting Palette to set its font, color, and style. (To pre-size the text box, click the slide master and drag before you begin to type.)

Title slide master

The *title slide master* is a special kind of slide master. It controls the layout of only one kind of slide: the title slide, usually the first one your audience sees. To view and edit the title master, choose View→Master→Title Master.

Note: The title master inherits the properties of the slide master, so make changes to the slide master first.

Once you understand that this master design applies only to title slides, you can use this slide master exactly like the slide masters described earlier, since elements that you put on the title slide master show up on all title slides. (When you insert a new slide via Insert→Slide, you'll find the Title Slide option at the upper left of the New Slide dialog box. You can also switch any slide to title slide status: While viewing it in the Slide pane, choose Format→Slide Layout, and then double-click Title Slide at the upper left of the Slide Layout dialog box.)

POWER USERS' CLINIC

Expressing a Slide's Individuality

If you're feeling a little oppressed by the idea that slide masters dictate how every slide in a presentation looks, take heart. While it's true that you can't edit text or graphics on an individual slide if they began life on the corresponding master, you can still make the design of an individual slide differ from the master slide in a number of ways.

To change the background fill color of an individual slide, for example, choose Format→Slide Background and make the changes you want in the Background dialog box.

To hide a background graphic that's been supplied by the slide master, choose Format→Slide Background and then turn on "Omit background graphics from master." Click Apply.

PowerPoint also lets you use multiple slide masters, so that, for example, 10 of your slides may be based on one master

design, while 10 of them are based on a different one. (Note, however, that this feature makes life more complicated; now, when you want to make a change to a slide master, you have to remember which one serves as the design basis for a particular slide.)

To apply a different master to a selection of slides, go to the Slide Sorter view by choosing View→Slide Sorter. Select the slide or slides to which you want to apply the second design template. (You can select multiple slides by Shift-clicking them.) Then choose Format→Slide Design.

After a moment, PowerPoint shows you its complete list of design templates, like the ones described at the beginning of this chapter. Make certain that the "Apply to selected slides" radio button is selected and then double-click the design template you want. You'll now find that the selected slides have taken on the look of the second master slide design.

Handout master

You can read more about *handouts* on page 652. For now, it's enough to know that a PowerPoint handout is a special page design that lets you place several slides on a single sheet for printing and distributing to your audience.

Set up the design of your handouts by choosing View→Master→Handout Master, and then adding or editing the elements you want.

Notes master

In PowerPoint terminology, a note is another form of handout—one that features a miniature slide at the top half of the page, and typed commentary at the bottom (see page 652). Once again, you can specify the basic design of your notes printouts by choosing View→Master→Notes Master, and then editing the design you find here (such as altering the font or adding graphics). Predictably, those changes appear on every notes page in the presentation.

View Controls

To get the most out of PowerPoint, you should become familiar with the program's View controls, which are in the lower-left corner of the PowerPoint window (see Figure 16-1). These five buttons let you switch among PowerPoint's five view modes:

- **Normal view** is the standard three-pane view, as illustrated in Figure 16-1.

- **Outline view** expands the Outline pane so that it dominates the main window, shrinking the Slide pane and Notes pane to make room. You may prefer this view when you're working up the contents of your talk and still fiddling with the wording.

- **Slide view** shows only the current slide. You'll probably prefer this view when you're putting the finishing touches (such as the charts and graphics) on your slides, after the outlining process is complete.

Figure 16-7:
You can delete slides in the Slide Sorter view by selecting them and then pressing Delete (or choosing Edit→ Delete Slide). You can also work with transitions (page 627) in Slide Sorter view; a small icon below a slide, shown here on slide 1, represents a transition. Click the transition icon to see a miniature preview.

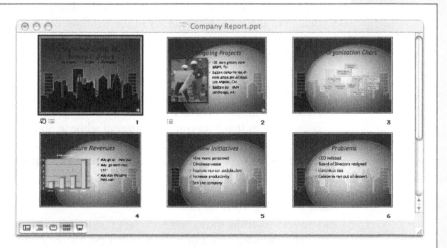

Tip: In any multipane view, you can drag the boundaries between the panes to make individual panes larger or smaller. (A row of four dots in the center of these lines denotes a draggable boundary—but you don't have to put your cursor on the dots themselves.)

- **Slide Sorter view** (Figure 16-7) displays thumbnail images of all the slides that you've created, so that you can rearrange them by dragging. Drag either a single slide or several at once; Shift-click them to select more than one, or ⌘-click the first and last in a range. A vertical "your slide will go here" line appears when you drag selected slides.

  You can use this view as a handy navigational aid. Double-clicking a slide in Slide Sorter view opens the slide in your previous view.

- **Slideshow.** If you click this button, PowerPoint actually begins the slideshow; see page 635 for more detail.

Navigation

No matter which view you're using, moving among the slides in your show is easy. For example:

- **Normal view or Outline view.** The outline is always on the left of the slide; all it takes to move to a slide is a click anywhere within or alongside its outline text. If, for example, you want to go to the fourth slide in the presentation, just click somewhere in the fourth outline element. PowerPoint displays that slide on the right side of the window.

- **Slide Sorter view.** In the Slide Sorter view, you can move from slide to slide by clicking the slide, or by using the arrow keys to move the selection rectangle around. If you double-click a slide, PowerPoint switches to the previous view with that slide selected.

- **Slide view.** The Slide view shows a single slide, filling the window. To move to the next slide in the show, you can click the scroll down arrow, or click the Next Slide button in the lower-right corner of the window, or press the Page Down key. To move to the slide *before* the current slide, click the scroll up arrow, or click the Previous Slide button (also in the lower-right portion of the window), or press the Page Up key.

- **Slideshow.** When you're in Slideshow view, each individual slide takes up the entire screen or window—no menus, no scroll bars, no controls. There are lots of key combinations that help you move around while in Slideshow view (see page 636). For now, you can use the right or down arrow key to move to the *next* slide in a slideshow, or the left or up arrow key to move to the *previous* slide. Press the Esc key to return to the previous view.

Manipulating Your Slides

As you construct the show, new ideas will inevitably pop into your head. Topics you originally expected to fill only three bullet points on a single slide may expand to require several slides—or vice versa. Fortunately, it's no problem to adjust the slide sequence as you go.

Inserting new slides

Inserting a new slide into the lineup once you've created a few is easy. Just click any-place in the outline topic or the slide *before* the spot where you want the new slide to appear, then choose Insert→New Slide (Control-M). The New Slide dialog box appears, as described on page 604.

Inserting slides from other presentations

You can also recycle slides from other presentation files simply by choosing Insert→ Slides from File. The Choose a File dialog box appears; locate and single-click the PowerPoint file whose slides you want to import.

At the bottom of the dialog box, choose "Import all slides" or (if you want to hand-pick the slides worth importing) "Select slides to insert." Then click Open.

If you chose "Select slides to insert," you now see a dialog box offering miniatures of the slides. If you want to import slides with their existing design intact, as opposed to letting them inherit the new presentation's master slide design, turn on "Keep design of original slides." Shift-click the slides you want, click Insert, and then—after PowerPoint inserts the slides behind the dialog box—click Close.

Tip: You can drag slides from one presentation to the other by opening them in the Slide Sorter.

Deleting a slide

In Slide Sorter view, click the slide and then press Delete, or choose Edit→Delete Slide. In Normal view, simply choose Edit→Delete Slide.

Moving slides around

The easiest ways to rearrange your slide sequence are by dragging the tiny slide icons up and down in the Outline pane or by dragging thumbnails around in Slide Sorter view. In either case, the Cut, Copy, and Paste commands work.

Tip: The trick in Slide Sorter view is, before pasting, to select the slide just *before* the spot where you want the pasted slides to appear.

How to Build a Slide

The outliner is an excellent tool for creating the overall flow of your slideshow. But sooner or later, you'll probably want to work on the slides themselves   to add charts or other graphics, to edit your concluding slide when new data becomes available five minutes before a meeting, and so on.

Using Backgrounds

Creating an individual slide is a bit like painting on a canvas: You first paint the background and work your way to the foreground, layer by layer.

For example, PowerPoint lets you set a background color, gradient, pattern, or graphic for your slide. You can also create a backdrop by adding shapes and importing graphics.

Changing backgrounds

Every slide begins life with a backdrop, courtesy of its slide master. If you'd like to override or enhance that backdrop on a particular slide, however, choose Format→ Slide Background, which brings up the Background dialog box (Figure 16-8). In this box, you see a sample slide with the current color scheme. At the bottom, a pop-up menu lets you choose, from a swatch of eight coordinated colors, a new background color.

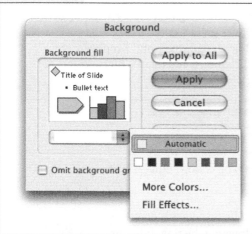

Figure 16-8:
The Background dialog box shows how your background fill color looks when applied to a slide with the current color scheme. (If you feel confident overriding Microsoft's professional color groups, choose More Colors from the pop-up menu. The standard Apple color-picker dialog box appears, offering access to any color under the sun via several different color pickers, as described on page 689.)

WORKAROUND WORKSHOP

Shutting Off Two Annoying PowerPoint Features

If, as you add text to a box, you notice that the words and paragraphs are shrinking, don't be alarmed. PowerPoint is just trying to make your text fit into the placeholder text box. PowerPoint makes the text spill over onto another line only if shrinking the font size and line spacing fails.

If you find this feature annoying, never fear. You can turn it off easily enough: Just choose PowerPoint→Preferences, and, in the dialog box, click the Edit tab. On the Edit panel, turn off the option called "Auto-fit text to text placeholder," and then click OK.

Another feature that sometimes gets in the way: When you select more than one word and end your selection halfway through a word, PowerPoint selects the rest of that word for you. (This feature may sound familiar; the same thing happens in Word.)

This behavior can be frustrating when all you want to do is get rid of an errant suffix. To turn this feature off, choose PowerPoint→Preferences→Edit tab and turn off "When selecting, automatically select entire word." Now you can select as much or as little of a word as you like.

Note: The Background dialog box has two buttons: *Apply* changes only the background of the current slide; *Apply to All* changes every slide in the presentation, even slides with customized backgrounds—use it with caution.

If you want something more elaborate than a solid background color, choose Fill Effects from the pop-up menu, which brings up the Fill Effects dialog box. This box lets you choose one of four effects by clicking one of the tabs along the top: Gradient (a smoothly shifting color blend), Texture (a photograph of some natural material, such as wood grain, marble, or burlap), Pattern (simple, two-color patterns, such as stripes and dots), or Picture (a graphics file from your hard drive). See Chapter 20 for much more on these special tabs.

Tip: Be careful with this feature. Photos, textures, and gradients can make your text very difficult to read. (On the other hand, depending on the news you have to share with your colleagues, that may be exactly what you were hoping.)

Working with Text

There are two straightforward ways to add text to your slides. First, if your slide master includes text placeholders, as shown in Figure 16-6, you can click the individual placeholder text items (which typically read something like "Click to Add Text"), and then type in your own words to replace the dummy text. Because these placeholders are linked to the slide master, they reflect its font characteristics.

The other method is to add new text boxes (with no corresponding placeholders on the master) to a particular slide. Simply click the Text Box button on the Drawing toolbar (Figure 16-9), and then click the slide where you want to add text. PowerPoint adds a text box to the slide in which you can type any text you like.

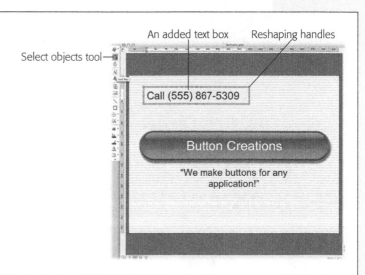

Figure 16-9:
The Select Objects tool (an arrow tool by any other name) lets you select text, pictures, and other items on a slide. The screen tip identifies the Text Box tool, which was used to create the new text box shown here. To move the text box, position the cursor over its border so that the cursor becomes a tiny hand, then drag; to reshape it, drag one of the white handles. (Press Shift while dragging a corner handle to maintain the box's proportions as you resize it.)

An added text box   Reshaping handles

Select objects tool

Call (555) 867-5309

Button Creations

"We make buttons for any
application!"

Editing and formatting text

Adjusting the type characteristics of any kind of text box is easy. First, click the Select Objects tool (see Figure 16-9), and then click the text that you want to adjust. You've just activated the text box. Now you can select part or all of the text to change its font, size, or style, using the Formatting Palette or the Format menu.

Note: *The outline only shows text inside placeholders (titles, subtitles, and bullet points), so it doesn't display text that you add using the Text Box tool. You can change the formatting of text in the outline, but the changes appear only on the slide—after all, an outline with 72-point bold text would look really odd.*

Formatting bullets

Since bullet-point lists play such a big role in business presentations, learning how to format the bullets is a key skill.

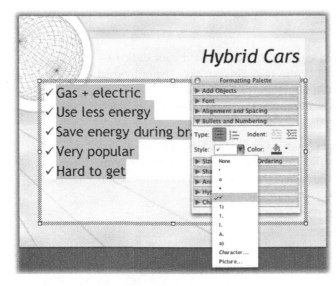

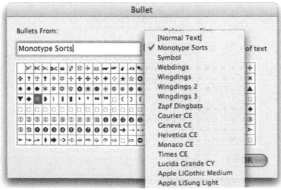

Figure 16-10:
Top: The Bullets and Numbering panel of the Formatting Palette lets you choose the style, color, and size of your bullets.

Bottom: The Bullet dialog box contains a pop-up list of dingbat fonts (fonts whose characters are symbols). Browse these fonts to find just the right bullet for the point you're making. Click the character that you want to use and then click OK. Use the Color pop-up menu to give the bullet a custom color.

To change the bullet style, put the cursor in the text where you want the change to occur. Next, open the Bullets and Numbering panel of the Formatting Palette, and then choose a bullet style from the Style menu you find there.

Other characters as bullets

You don't even have to be content with the mundane dot (•) as your bullet symbol. You can choose any character from a variety of fonts by choosing Character in the menu (see Figure 16-10).

Graphics as bullets

You can even use a little graphic as the bullet, such as a JPEG file that shows a pointing hand, a checkmark, or your boss's head.

To specify a graphics file on your hard drive that you want to use as a bullet, proceed like this:

1. **Click the slide just to the right of the bullet that you want to modify.**

   The insertion point flashes next to the bullet point.

2. **On the Formatting Palette, in the Bullets and Numbering section, open the Style pop-up menu and choose Picture.**

   The Choose a Picture dialog box appears.

3. **Navigate to and double-click the graphic you want to use as a bullet.**

   You return to your slide, where the image automatically replaces the bullet at the same size of the text. To adjust the bullet size, use Format→Bullets and Numbering and enter a new percentage in the "Size: % of text" box.

Adding Graphics, Charts, and Tables

Even if you're delivering good news, a text-only presentation is a surefire way to put your audience to sleep. By inserting graphics, movies, tables, charts, and other objects into your presentations, PowerPoint lets you spice up a dull slideshow, or add information that you can't describe in words. For example, you may want to insert a video clip of your company president explaining why this year's sales numbers aren't *quite* what they should be. Or, if you want to include a picture of your product when giving a marketing presentation, you can import it into your slide. Here's how to go about using these specialized objects.

Graphics

PowerPoint gives you lots of options for bringing graphics into your slides via the Insert menu—from Office's Clip Art collection, from a file on your hard drive, by inserting a Word table, by using an AutoShape, from an Office Organization Chart, from WordArt, or by capturing an image directly from a scanner or digital camera. Use the Insert→Picture command (or the buttons on the Standard toolbar) to insert these special graphics, which Chapter 20 describes in detail. (The Add Objects panel in the Formatting Palette also lets you insert objects into slides.)

Microsoft Word tables

If you've mastered (or even toyed with) the flexible table-making tools in Microsoft Word, here's an instant return on your investment: PowerPoint stands ready to teleport you into Microsoft Word, wait while you design a table for your slide, and then slurp the result into the PowerPoint slide. It works like this:

1. **Choose Insert→Picture→Microsoft Word Table.**

   The Insert Table dialog box appears.

2. **Type the number of rows and columns you want, then click OK.**

   Strangely, enough, you're no longer in PowerPoint; you've been deposited in Microsoft Word, in a window called Document in *Sales Pitch* (or whatever your PowerPoint file is called). Now you can use all of the Word table tools described on page 161.

3. **Design your table. When you're finished, close the Word document.**

   You return to PowerPoint. Your Word document vanishes as though it never even existed, but the table itself materializes on whatever PowerPoint slide you were editing. Want to work on the table some more? No problem—just double-click the table on the PowerPoint slide to return to Word.

PowerPoint tables

If you don't have the patience to flip into Microsoft Word every time you want to slap a table onto a slide, you may prefer to use PowerPoint's own table-making tools. Granted, they're not as flexible as those in Word, but they're more than adequate for most modern slideshows.

When you choose Insert→Table, a small window lets you specify how many columns and rows you want in your table; when you click OK, PowerPoint inserts the table into your slide. Or, for even less fuss, use the pop-up button on the Standard toolbar, shown in Figure 16-11.

Once the table appears, you can adjust its size by dragging the resize handles at each corner, and you can move it or rearrange its interior by dragging the table's borders.

Tip: You can also *draw* a table directly on your slide by calling up the Table toolbar (View→Toolbars→ Tables and Borders) and then using the Draw Table tool. It works just like its Word counterpart, detailed on page 162.

Inserting a table also brings up the Table toolbar. It contains just enough tools to let you make changes like these to your PowerPoint table:

- **Change border lines.** To change a border's style, width, or color, make your selections using the Border Style, Border Width, and Border Color controls in the upper part of the toolbar, and then click the borders you want to change using the Draw Table tool.

- **Change text alignment.** To change how text is aligned in a cell, select the cell (or cells); then click the Text Alignment buttons in the toolbar, which let you align text at the top, center, or bottom of the cell. (You can also use the text-alignment buttons in the Formatting Palette to do this job, as well as to modify the left-right alignment.)

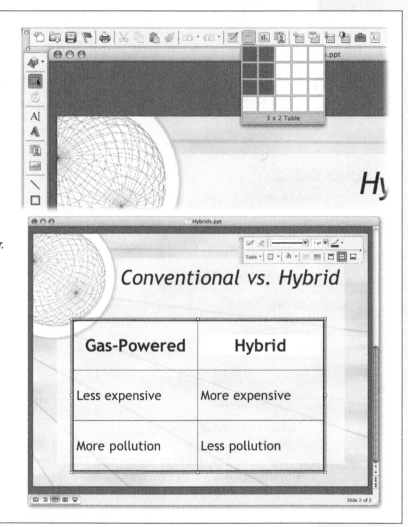

Figure 16-11:
Top: You can create a table very quickly using the Insert Table pop-up button on the Standard toolbar. Drag downward from this icon to specify how many rows and columns you want.

Bottom: Custom tables are plenty easy using the Table toolbar. With the Draw Table tool, you can draw new cells anywhere you like within a table. You can also control almost all aspects of the table from this toolbar as well, including line weight and color.

- **Merge or split cells.** By erasing the line between two cells using the Eraser tool, you can tear down the barrier between them, creating one long cell. (Another method: Select the cells that you want to merge by Shift-clicking them, and then click the Merge Cells button.)

On the other hand, you can also split a cell in two. Click the Draw Table tool and then drag to "draw in" the new border (Figure 16-11). Alternatively, select the cell you want to split and then click the Split Cell button, which vertically divides the cell.

- **Add or remove columns and rows.** The menu commands in the Table pop-up button (see Figure 16-12) let you insert columns and rows as well as delete them. They also let you merge and split cells, set how borders look, and specify how cells are filled.

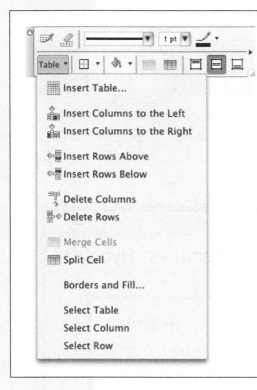

Figure 16-12:
In addition to its toolbar buttons, the Table toolbar has a menu of commands that let you insert and remove columns and rows as well as split and join cells. You can also select a row, a column, or an entire table using this menu.

Movies and sounds

These days, showing your colleagues a bunch of motionless pictures isn't very flashy (if indeed flashiness is what you're after). Via the Insert menu, PowerPoint can import movies and sounds in six different formats—from the Clip Gallery, from files, and from CD audio tracks. You can also record your own sounds directly into PowerPoint.

- **Movie from Gallery.** Microsoft's Clip Gallery has lots of animated GIF files (short cartoons) that illustrate typical business situations, such as a stock ticker and a checklist. To insert a motion clip from the Gallery onto one of your slides, choose Insert→Movies and Sounds→Movie from Gallery. Use these animated GIFs sparingly, as they can quickly turn an otherwise fine presentation into something tacky.

  When, during a slideshow, you arrive at a slide containing a movie from the Gallery, it plays automatically, looping over and over until you move on to the next slide.

Tip: From within the dialog box that appears when you choose Insert→Movies and Sounds→Movie from Gallery, you can visit Microsoft's clip art Web site to search for more animated GIFs. Just click the Online button, which automatically takes you to Microsoft Office Online.

- **Movie from File.** The Insert→Movies and Sounds→Movie from File command lets you select a movie of your own to import into your presentation. It brings up an Open File dialog box, in which you can choose a QuickTime-compatible movie.

  When you insert a movie, PowerPoint asks if you want it to play automatically when the slide comes up during the slideshow. If you click No, the movie won't play until you click it.

  In either case, embedding a movie brings up the Movie toolbar, whose buttons let you insert a movie, play a movie, show its controller scroll bar, make the movie loop over and over, specify the movie's poster frame (a frame of the movie which serves as its icon), and bring up the Format Picture dialog box.

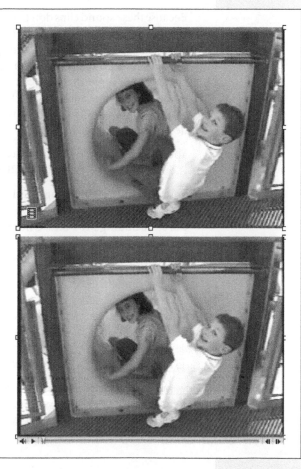

Figure 16-13:
The small filmstrip icon in the lower-left corner of an embedded movie (top) is actually a switch that, when clicked, reveals a simple movie controller (bottom).

Tip: Be careful when you embed movies in your PowerPoint presentation. These movies are *not* saved inside your PowerPoint presentation. Instead, the presentation maintains a *link* to the movie on your hard drive. If you copy your presentation to, say, your laptop, but forget to copy the movie file as well, you'll be in for a rude surprise when the conference-room lights dim. The slide will appear showing the "poster frame" icon of the movie, but nothing will happen when you click it.

Avoid this problem by saving your multimedia PowerPoint presentation as a *package*—a single folder that contains the PowerPoint file and every linked file it needs, ready for backing up, burning to CD, copying to your laptop, and so on. Choose File→Save As, and then, in the Format pop-up menu, choose PowerPoint Package.

- **Sound from Gallery.** The Insert→Movies and Sounds→Sound from Gallery command opens the Clip Gallery and lets you browse for the appropriate sound clip, much as though you're browsing for motion graphics in the Gallery. Turn on the Preview checkbox to display a small Preview window; then you can play a sound in the Clip Gallery by clicking the triangle in the Preview window. These embedded sound files show up as small speaker icons in your presentation; click to play.

  Because these sound clips don't take up much space, PowerPoint generally embeds them directly in the PowerPoint file. This time, you generally *don't* have to worry about bloating your presentation or losing the link to the sound file when you move the presentation to a different disk. (If you choose PowerPoint→Preferences→ General, you'll see that you can specify the sound-file threshold for automatic embedding. For example, PowerPoint makes sounds smaller than 101 K part of your presentation's file, but it leaves larger ones on the hard drive, like the movies described in the previous tip.)

  You *do* have to worry about the cheese factor when embedding sound files, however. It doesn't take many to ruin an otherwise fine presentation.

- **Sound from File.** Choosing Insert→Movies and Sounds→Sound from File brings up an Open File dialog box, which lets you choose your own audio file to import—including MP3 files. Once again, PowerPoint asks if you want the sound to play automatically when its slide appears during your slideshow. If you click No, you'll have to click the sound icon (a small speaker) to make it play.

  You can drag this icon anywhere on the slide.

Note: Planting a large sound file on a slide is like planting a movie there: you're actually installing a *link* to the sound file on your hard drive, not the file itself. This feature keeps the size of your presentation much smaller, but it also means that you have to remember to move the sound file when you move the presentation to another machine. Otherwise, you'll find yourself with a soundless presentation.

Once again, the best way to be sure your sounds travel with you is to save your show as a PowerPoint package (see the Tip on page 622). To do so, choose File→Save As and then name your show. Now pop up the Format menu and choose PowerPoint Package.

- **Play CD Audio Track.** Although the recording industry may not particularly appreciate it, you can also grab a track from a music CD to serve as a soundtrack for your slideshow. When you select Insert→Movies and Sounds→Play CD Audio Track, PowerPoint displays the Play Options dialog box (Figure 16-14), where you can set the start and end points for your sound. When this slide appears during the actual presentation, the song will begin to play automatically (or when you click it, at your option).

Note: The music won't play unless the actual audio CD is already inserted in your Mac at the time of your presentation.

Figure 16-14:
In Play Options, you can choose which CD tracks are included and which portion of the tracks are played; perhaps you only want 15 seconds of the Rolling Stones' "Satisfaction." You can also turn on "Loop until stopped," which causes the sound to repeat until you click or move to a new slide.

- **Record Sound.** The Insert→Movies and Sounds→Record Sound command lets you record your own sounds that are then inserted into the presentation.

Before you record, you have to verify that your microphone or other sound input device is working. Open the Sound System Preferences panel and click the Input tab. Make sure that the correct device is selected, and adjust the input volume if necessary. Quit System Preferences.

Now, in PowerPoint, choose Insert→Movies and Sounds→Record Sound. PowerPoint presents a Record Sound dialog box. Click Record, speak or sing or squawk into your Mac's microphone, and then click Stop. You can play back the sound by clicking Play to make sure it's just what you want. If so, click Save.

You'll find a little speaker icon on your PowerPoint slide; click it during a presentation to hear your recording. (Unlike imported sounds and movies, these sounds are part of the PowerPoint file rather than links to separate files on your hard drive. Be aware that sound files can greatly inflate the size of your PowerPoint document.)

Charts

If your presentation is just crying out for a chart—and what presentation isn't?—just choose Insert→Chart to launch Microsoft Graph. This little application (a part of Office) lets you quickly create a graph, using a stripped-down, Excel-like spreadsheet window. When you choose Graph→Quit & Return to [Your PowerPoint file's name], PowerPoint *embeds* your chart into the current slide. (Embedding puts the output of one program into a document belonging to another. In this case, Graph's output is appearing in a PowerPoint document.)

Once the chart appears in your slide, you can double-click to edit it, launching Microsoft Graph again in the process. (The fact that you can edit it again in its parent program is key to an embedded object.)

Tip: The true graphing genius in Office lies not in Microsoft Graph, but in Excel. If you want a full-fledged chart, or you've already created one in an Excel workbook, just copy and paste it from the workbook or use the Insert→Object command, described next.

Other objects

The Insert→Object command is the first step to embedding several other kinds of visuals onto a PowerPoint slide. The objects can come from such other Office programs as Equation Editor, Excel, Microsoft Graph, Organization Chart, or Word.

As shown in Figure 16-15, the resulting dialog box lets you either choose an existing document to install onto your slide, or create a new one. If you plan to insert an existing file into your slide, *first* choose the object type and then click "Create from file." The instant you turn on "Create from file," the standard Mac OS X Open File dialog box appears so that you can select the document you want.

What happens next depends on what you do in the Import Object box:

- **"Create new" with "Display as icon" turned on.** An appropriate icon now appears on the slide. You can click the icon to open the corresponding program and create a new document. If you're inserting a Word or Excel document into the slide, choose File→Close & Return to [Your PowerPoint file's name] when you're done. (The other Office applications—Graph, Equation Editor, and Organization Chart—have different commands for returning to PowerPoint, but they're all under the application or File menu.)

- **"Create new" with "Display as icon" turned off.** The appropriate program opens so that you can create your new object. Choose File→Close & Return to [Your PowerPoint file's name] when you finish. Your new object appears on the slide.

- **"Create from file" with "Display as icon" turned on.** PowerPoint takes you back to your slide, where an icon for your embedded object appears. Double-click the icon should you ever want to edit or display the object.

- **"Create from file" with "Display as icon" turned off.** The chart, equation, or document appears on the slide. (For Word or Excel files, you see only the first page or worksheet.) Double-click to edit or view the object in its parent program.

You may reasonably scratch your head at the prospect of placing an entire Word or Excel document onto a slide, especially if the document is larger than the slide itself.

After scratching for a few moments, though, you'll probably realize that Microsoft has provided a dandy way to link supporting documents and reference materials to your PowerPoint presentation. When, during your pitch, some muckraking co-worker objects, "But that's not the marketing plan we talked about last month," you can click the Word document's icon that you've placed on the slide in anticipation of just such a ruckus—and smugly open the actual Word file, in Word, for all to see.

Note: Unfortunately, the "Display as icon" and, indeed, this whole object-embedding business, relies on a message technology called Object Linking and Embedding (abbreviated OLE and often pronounced "o-LAY"). As noted in the more complete discussion on page 694, Object Linking and Embedding has a reputation for behaving oddly, although it's not nearly so dangerous as it was in Mac OS 9. It works best when linking to very small documents on computers that have lots of memory.

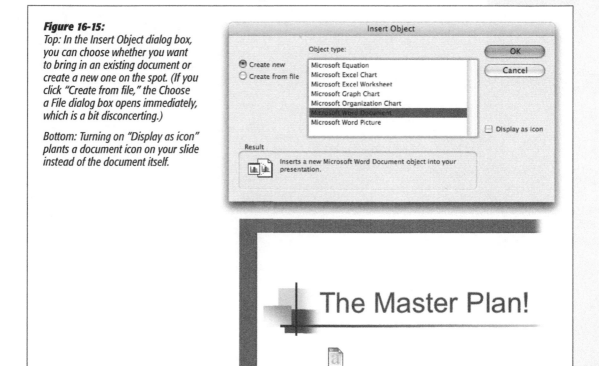

Figure 16-15:
Top: In the Insert Object dialog box, you can choose whether you want to bring in an existing document or create a new one on the spot. (If you click "Create from file," the Choose a File dialog box opens immediately, which is a bit disconcerting.)

Bottom: Turning on "Display as icon" plants a document icon on your slide instead of the document itself.

Hyperlink

The Insert→Hyperlink turns the selected text or graphic into a clickable link, capable of opening another PowerPoint file, any Macintosh file or program, or a specified Web page on the Internet. You'll find a complete description of this feature on page 300.

Advanced PowerPoint

Building individual slides in PowerPoint can be lots of fun, if that's your idea of a good time. But the real muscle of the program lies in its ability to pull those images together into a running slideshow. Although good taste sometimes suffers as a result, you can dress up your slide presentations with flashy cinematics, music, sound effects, and voice narration. You can then rehearse your PowerPoint shows to work out the split-second timing. You can even turn your masterpieces into printouts or a Web site for the benefit of those who missed the presentation, or save your slideshows as QuickTime movies, then edit them again later (back in PowerPoint).

This chapter shows you how to harness these potent PowerPoint features.

Making a Slideshow

Chapter 16 discusses building slides and finding your way around PowerPoint. Now it's time to dig in and look at the big picture—how to bring those images together into a complete slideshow with all the trimmings.

Transitions
PowerPoint gives you broad artistic license in the way you switch from one slide to the next. By varying the *transitions*—the between-slide special effects—you can create a sense of movement or put some zip into otherwise lackluster material such as tables, flowcharts, and scenes from your Cancun honeymoon. PowerPoint transitions range from simple *cuts* (with one slide quickly replacing another) to fancier effects such as *dissolves* (where one slide melts into the next) and checkerboard *wipes* (where slides

transmogrify with a moving checkerboard effect). Even with all this variety, though, it's a good idea to rely on simple transitions and use the pyrotechnics sparingly.

How transitions work

Transitions, as the term implies, appear in the spaces between slides in a show. To add a transition in PowerPoint, you first need to specify the location by selecting the slide that *begins* the switcheroo. If, for example, you want to insert a transition between the fourth and fifth slides in a show, select slide four in one of the following ways:

- In Normal view, click in the outline heading.
- In Slide view, summon the slide.
- In Slide Sorter view, click the slide thumbnail.

After selecting a slide, you can add a transition in any of several ways (see Figure 17-1):

- On the Formatting Palette, open the Change Slides panel and click the Slide Transition tab (the middle icon). Pick the transition you want to use.
- Choose Slide Show→Slide Transition; or in Slide Sorter view, Control-click a slide and choose Slide Transition from the contextual menu.

    The Slide Transition dialog box appears, offering a pop-up menu with a list of transitions. Scroll down the list and make your choice, then click Apply.

- In Slide Sorter view, use the Slide Sorter toolbar that appears automatically; it offers a Transitions pop-up menu. (If you don't see the toolbar, choose Tools→ Customize→Customize Toolbars/Menus and make sure that Slide Sorter is turned on.)

Kinds of transitions

Although you'll probably end up using simple cuts and other tried-and-true favorites over the course of your slideshow career, PowerPoint dangles before you a mouth-wateringly long list of special effects.

PowerPoint gives you a total of 65 transitions, grouped into 23 basic types (described here by their visual effects):

UP TO SPEED

Avoiding the Cheese Factor

PowerPoint makes it easy to load up your presentations with funky transitions, sounds, and other cheesy gimmicks. But with power comes responsibility. While you may be tempted to show off all the program's entertaining features in a single presentation, bear in mind that old design adage:

Less is more. It's usually best to keep your transitions and sounds simple and your designs basic. This way, you won't distract the audience from the important part of the presentation—your message—with a bunch of dazzling effects.

- **Blinds.** The first slide closes like a set of blinds, either horizontally or vertically. As that image moves out, the next one emerges in its place.

- **Box.** The incoming slide wipes over the previous image with an expanding or contracting box, opening from either the center or the edges.

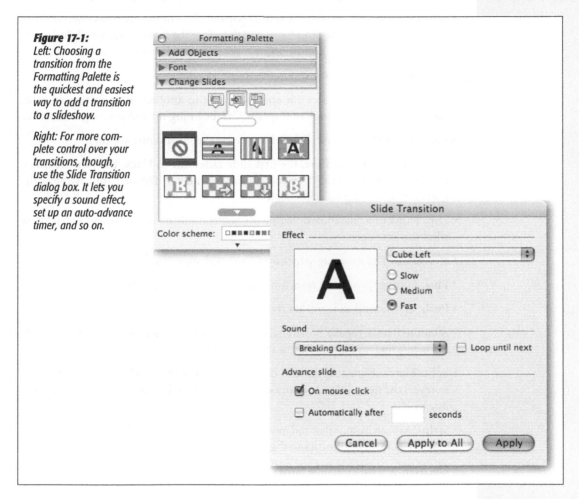

Figure 17-1:
Left: Choosing a transition from the Formatting Palette is the quickest and easiest way to add a transition to a slideshow.

Right: For more complete control over your transitions, though, use the Slide Transition dialog box. It lets you specify a sound effect, set up an auto-advance timer, and so on.

- **Checkerboard.** The first image breaks up into a pattern of adjacent squares, which turns into the next image as it sweeps across or down the screen.

- **Circle.** An expanding circle reveals the next slide.

- **Comb.** The second slide comes into view as interlocking strips that approach from opposite sides of the frame.

- **Cover.** The new slide scoots in from offscreen to cover the previous image with a framed, three-dimensional effect. The eight variations in this group match the directions from which the incoming slide can enter: top, bottom, left, right, and the four corners.

- **Cube.** The slide becomes the face of a 3-D cube, which rotates to reveal the upcoming slide.

- **Cut.** The next slide in the show simply pops in place of the previous one. No frills, no fireworks. This is the most basic, and therefore the most useful, of all the transition types; it's also the "transition" you get if you don't specify *any* transition.

- **Diamond.** Like the Circle, but in the shape of a diamond.

- **Dissolve.** One slide fizzles out and morphs into another in an impressionistic, "pixellated" fashion. Think of Captain Kirk beaming up and you've got the idea.

- **Fade Smoothly.** The first slide fades away as the second one appears.

- **Fade Through Black.** Here, the first slide fades out to black, then the next one materializes in its place. This transition is similar to Dissolve, but without the granulated, melting-in-acid effect.

- **Flip.** Think of a chalkboard that pivots horizontally or vertically and you'll know what this one does.

- **Newsflash.** The spinning-page effect from old-style newsreels.

- **Plus.** Another geometric transition, like Circle, but in the shape of a cross.

- **Push.** The second slide pushes the first one away.

- **Random Bars.** Irregular horizontal or vertical slats appear across the image, quickly disintegrating and giving way to the next slide.

- **Split.** The first image splits into doors that open either horizontally or vertically to reveal the next slide. Or, doors showing the second image close in over the first image.

- **Strips.** As seen in countless old movies, the incoming image wipes across the screen diagonally from one corner to the opposite corner.

- **Uncover.** The existing slide moves offscreen to expose the next image lying behind it. Shrewd readers will recognize this as the reverse of Cover.

- **Wedge.** Invisible clock hands rotate in opposite directions to wipe away the current slide and reveal the one after it.

- **Wheel.** Similar to Wedge, but rotating wheel spokes erase the current frame and show the next slide.

- **Wipe.** In an effect that's similar to Cover but with more of a squeegee effect, the incoming slide moves vertically or horizontally into view as it wipes away the previous slide.

Note: Most of these transitions can come from more than one direction (Wipe Right and Wipe Left, for example.) You choose the one you want from the Effect pop-up menu in the dialog box shown in Figure 17-1.

Customizing your transitions

Once you've chosen a transition effect, you can tinker with its settings to add variety or to make them conform to your presentation's overall style. Customizing transitions is also an effective way to set your slideshow apart from the efforts of less-creative PowerPoint users. (Just allow yourself enough time before the big pitch to refine your transitions.)

Using the Slide Transition dialog box (Slide Show→Slide Transition), you can control just about every aspect of how transitions behave. Here's a look at some of the things you can manipulate in this box (see Figure 17-1):

- **Effect.** Use this section to preview transition effects by choosing a new transition or selecting a new speed. PowerPoint responds by playing your new effect in the preview box. This is an extremely useful feature, because most transition types have several, sometimes subtle, variations, and the names of some transitions give few clues to their exact function. Also, some of the more intricate effects, like Cover and Checkerboard, look more impressive at slower speeds.

- **Sound.** In the gratuitous-bells-and-whistles department, nothing beats the Sound section. Using this pop-up menu, you can add a sound effect to your transition: applause, breaking glass, a car driving by, or anything else you find in your Microsoft Office 2004→Office→Sounds folder. (You can also choose Other Sound to use a sound located elsewhere. PowerPoint recognizes sounds in many common file formats; search for "sound" in the online help to see the full list.)

Tip: You can add new sounds to the pop-up menu by dropping your own WAV (.wav) sound files into the Microsoft Office 2004→Office→Sounds folder.

The occasional explosion or whoosh can bring comic relief, help you underscore a point, or draw special attention to an image. But for the sanity of those viewing your slideshow, go easy on the noise. Don't apply sound to every transition, or the next sound you hear will be the silence of an empty auditorium.

Tip: Don't use these sound effects for background music. For that purpose, insert a sound object in a given slide using the Insert command, as described on page 622, or use a CD as a soundtrack (page 623).

- **Advance slide.** Here's where you tell PowerPoint the method you want to use for advancing to the next image in your slideshow. You have two basic choices: advance when you click the mouse, or advance automatically after a number of seconds that you specify (the preferred choice of trade-show booth personnel worldwide). You can also turn on both options, thereby instructing the program to change slides after a number of seconds *unless* you click the mouse first.

Putting On the Show

Now that you know how to build individual slides and insert transitions, it's time to make the presentation itself.

Setting up

Before you slick your hair and strut out on stage, the first preparatory step is to choose Slide Show→Set Up Show. In the dialog box that appears (see Figure 17-2), you can choose the *type* of presentation you want it to be—a typical full-screen slideshow, a small show for an individual reader to browse, or a self-running kiosk-style show that keeps playing until you (or the police) shut it off.

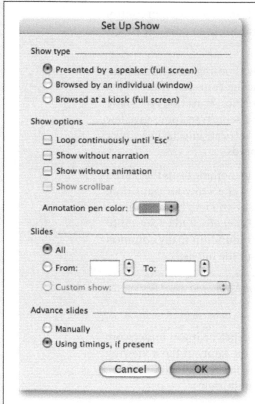

Figure 17-2:
The Set Up Show dialog box also lets you choose which slides to use and how you want them to be advanced: manually, with a mouse click; or automatically, using preset timings. You can also choose an annotation pen color for the onscreen writing tool that allows you to scrawl arrows, circles, cartoons, or quaint Latin expressions on your slides to underscore a point (or keep yourself entertained while the audience is napping).

Rehearsing your presentation

As P-Day (Presentation Day) draws near, you can use PowerPoint's *rehearsal mode* to run through the slideshow and work out the timing. It can be very helpful to know how long it takes to show each slide, especially if you have a tight presentation schedule. This handy feature even allows you to factor in sufficient time for the laughter to subside after your well-rehearsed "off the cuff" jokes.

To begin the rehearsal, choose Slide Show→Rehearse Timings. The screen fills with the first slide, and PowerPoint shifts into presentation mode. A timer appears in the lower-right corner of the slide, ticking off the number of seconds the slide is spending onscreen. Each time you advance to a new slide, the timer resets itself to zero and begins the count anew for *that* slide.

When you've gone through the whole show, PowerPoint asks if you want it to record those timings for use later in an automated show. If you answer yes, PowerPoint logs the timings automatically in the "Advance slide" portion of the Slide Transition dialog box (Figure 17-3). The program then asks if you want it to note those timings in Slide Sorter view, as shown in Figure 17-3. You may as well do this; it's pretty

Figure 17-3:
After you've completed your timing run, PowerPoint marks the slide duration beneath each slide in Slide Sorter view. The duration of transitions is not factored into the timing of each slide, so if you've chosen some of the slower, transitions, take their length into account when calculating the timing of your show.

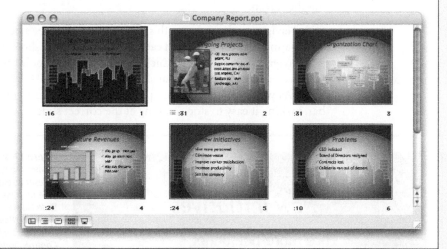

UP TO SPEED

Using a Projector

The screen on Apple's PowerBook G4 may be big, but it's still not big enough for a conference room full of your colleagues. Yes, the day will come when you're faced with displaying your presentation on a big, TV-style monitor or a projector that throws the slides onto a large screen.

If you have access to a projector that can take VGA, DVI, or miniDV cables, you're in business, since every current PowerBook, iBook, Power Mac, and iMac model has a video-out connector on the back or side panel for these kinds of cables. If you have a recent model laptop, you'll probably have to use the adapter that came with the computer. (Some portable Macs also sport S-video jacks, but neither you nor

your audience will be satisfied with the quality.)

Start by connecting your Mac's video out port to the projector's video-in port. If you see the same desktop on both screens, you have video mirroring turned on. (Mirroring duplicates the primary and secondary displays. To turn off mirroring, so you can view your Presenter Tools on the laptop screen, for example, open the System Preferences→Displays→Arrangement tab and uncheck the Mirror Displays checkbox. If you don't see the checkbox, your computer only supports mirroring.)

Once you've got your Mac's video desktop showing up on the projector, you can run your slideshow on the big screen.

handy to see those time allotments, even if you decide to ignore them and advance the slides manually.

Choosing a navigation scheme

If you choose PowerPoint→Preferences→View tab, you'll find some useful preference settings that affect the appearance of the show you're about to give. In the Slide Show area, for example, you'll find a pop-up menu with choices including:

- **Pop-up menu button.** Turning on this option means that when you twitch the mouse during your slideshow, PowerPoint will make a subtle toolbar appear in the lower-left corner. Clicking it gives you the same pop-up menu of useful controls (Next, Previous, End Show, and so on) that you usually get only by Control-clicking the screen.

- **Slide Navigator.** If you choose this option, then you'll see a peculiar, detached scroll bar floating near the bottom of each slide (Figure 17-4 shows the bar). You can use it to navigate your slideshow: Click the left- and right-pointing triangle buttons to advance or retreat through your slides, or use the scroll bar to jump around in the show. As you scroll, PowerPoint pops up slide miniatures on the Slide Navigator bar, making it easy to stop scrolling at the correct slide.

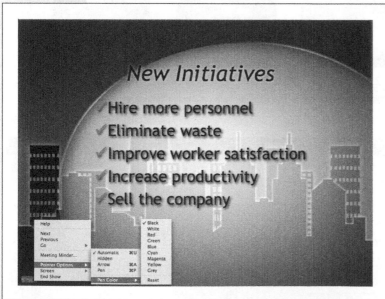

Figure 17-4:
To view the contextual menu in a slideshow, either Control-click a slide or, if you've turned on the Slide Navigator bar (top left) in the PowerPoint→Preferences→ View tab, click the Slide Show Controls button on the bar. The resulting menu (shown here) gives you a lot of power. For example, you can choose Pen from the Pointer Options submenu and then scribble circles, arrows, underlines, and other real-time doodles on your slides during the presentation. (You can later erase your additions by choosing Screen→Erase Pen from the contextual menu.)

The Preferences→View tab also offers an "End with black slide" checkbox, which is well worth turning on. That way, when you reach the end of your slideshow, you won't awkwardly drop back into the disorganized world of icons and menus that will shatter the illusion of tidiness you've so carefully projected.

Tip: While you're at it, go ahead and manually create a black slide at the *beginning* of your presentation. This way, your audience won't see the first slide until you're really ready.

Presenting onscreen

Your formal wear is clean and pressed. Now the moment has come—it's time to run your show. Any one of the following options starts the slideshow:

- Click the Slide Show view button in the lower-left corner of the main window. (It looks like an old-time home movie screen—the rightmost button.)

- Choose Slide Show→View Show.

- Choose View→Slide Show.

What happens next depends on your computer setup. If you have only one monitor, PowerPoint fills the screen with your first slide (or, if you clicked the Slide Show view button, with the slide that was previously selected). Unless you've chosen to use preset timings, the first slide stays on the screen until you manually switch to the next one (by clicking the mouse or pressing the Space bar, for example).

If you have two screens, and your computer supports non-mirrored video, the slide only appears on the secondary monitor. The main display—typically your laptop's screen—turns into a command center called Presenter Tools (see page 638).

PowerPoint gives you several ways to move around inside a full-screen show. A simple mouse click or a press of the Space bar moves you to the next slide, as does pressing the down arrow or right arrow key. (One exception: If you've set up an animation on a slide, these advance keys trigger the animation instead of summoning the next slide. More on animations later.)

After you've reached the end of the show, PowerPoint returns you to its previous view.

Note: If you rehearsed your slideshow and chose to save your timings, the show will play automatically to the end, displaying each slide for the predetermined number of seconds.

While your slideshow is running, you can Control-click anywhere on the screen to bring up a contextual menu that offers such self-explanatory navigation options as Next, Previous, and End Show. It also gives you some less obvious options that are worth pointing out:

- **Meeting Minder** opens a floating window in which you can enter minutes of your meeting or list action items to be taken up after the meeting.

- **Pointer Options,** as you might imagine, let you pick the kind of onscreen cursor you want to use—Automatic, Hidden, Arrow, or Pen. (Automatic gives PowerPoint the authority to choose a pointer for you; Hidden makes the pointer go away; Arrow is the standard Mac arrow-shaped pointer; and Pen turns the pointer into a writing tool; see Figure 17-4.)

- Finally, the **Screen** submenu's commands let you pause a running slideshow that's otherwise on autopilot, put up a black screen during a discussion, or erase any graffiti that you made with the aforementioned pen tool.

Controlling the show

Here's the rundown on helpful keystrokes you can use while the slideshow is running:

What to do	How to do it
Next slide (or start an animation)	Mouse click, Space bar, Return, N, Enter, right arrow, down arrow, Page down
Previous slide or animation	Left arrow, up arrow, Page up, P, Delete
End a slideshow	⌘-period, hyphen, Esc
Jump to a certain slide number	A number key and then Return
Jump to the first slide/last slide	Home, End
To/from a black screen	B, period
To/from a white screen	W, comma
Erase drawing onscreen	E
Show or hide arrow pointer	A, =
Change pointer to pen	⌘-P
Change pointer to arrow	⌘-A

Putting Controls on Slides

If you don't feel like memorizing keystrokes, you can embed a host of useful command buttons (for advancing slides, jumping to the end of the show, and so on) right on the slide when you're preparing the show. You can place buttons on individual slides or many slides at once.

- If you want to add a button to just one slide, switch into Normal view or Slide view, and bring up the slide in question.

- If you want to add a button to the same location in a group of slides—or all of them—place it on the slide master. Start by choosing View→Master→Slide Master. (See page 608 for a refresher on working with the slide master.)

Note: Don't try this shortcut if you'll be saving your presentation as a QuickTime movie. For QuickTime movies, you must put the buttons on each slide individually.

Once the slide where you want to stick your button is showing, make sure the Drawing toolbar is also showing. (Choose View→Toolbars→Drawing if it's not.) On the Drawing toolbar, use the AutoShapes pop-up button to choose from the Action Buttons submenu (see Figure 17-5).

On the Action Buttons palette are 12 buttons. The four in the middle of the palette help you jump around during the show: Previous Slide, Next Slide, First Slide, and Last Slide.

To put an Action Button on your slide, click the button you want. (Alternatively, choose a button name from the Slide Show→Action Buttons submenu.) Then drag diagonally on the slide as though using one of PowerPoint's drawing tools. Power-Point draws the button for you, then opens up the Action Settings dialog box shown in Figure 17-5.

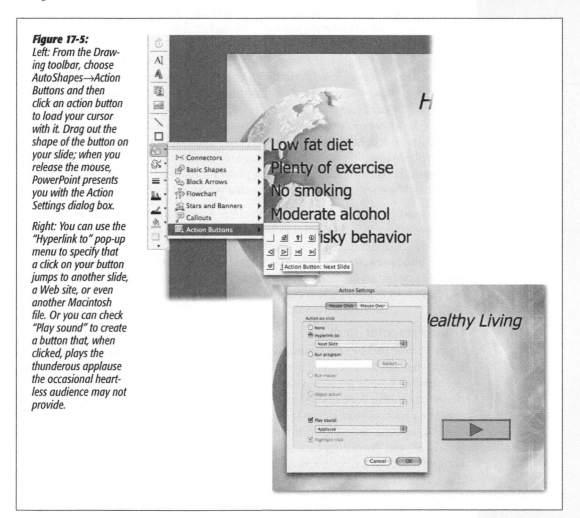

Figure 17-5:
Left: From the Drawing toolbar, choose AutoShapes→Action Buttons and then click an action button to load your cursor with it. Drag out the shape of the button on your slide; when you release the mouse, PowerPoint presents you with the Action Settings dialog box.

Right: You can use the "Hyperlink to" pop-up menu to specify that a click on your button jumps to another slide, a Web site, or even another Macintosh file. Or you can check "Play sound" to create a button that, when clicked, plays the thunderous applause the occasional heartless audience may not provide.

In this box, you can specify exactly what your newly created button will do. The proposed settings are fine for most purposes, so you can generally just click OK. It's worth noting, however, that you can use these controls to make your button do much fancier tricks, as described in Figure 17-5.

(By default, your action will be triggered when you *click* the corresponding button. But if you click the Mouse Over tab in the Action Settings dialog box, you can also specify that something happens when you just point to it instead.)

Later, when the slideshow is running, press the A key to make the arrow cursor appear, then click your newly created button to trigger the associated event.

Caution: Planning to save your show as a QuickTime movie? Watch out for action settings that don't work out well with movies! For example, Microsoft recommends that you avoid all mouse overs; hyperlinks to last slide viewed, end of show, custom show, other PowerPoint presentation, other file, and email address; run program and run macro; object action; play sound; and highlight click.

You can put any of eight other Action Buttons on your slides. Some come with preset icons and some have preset Action Settings that match their individual functions. **Custom** lets you customize your own action button (by running a macro or launching a program); **Home** zips back to the first slide in the show; **Help** lets you create a link to a help slide that you've designed; **Information** creates a link to an information slide that you've added; **Last Slide Viewed** takes you back to the last slide you saw (which, if you've been jumping around, isn't necessarily the slide before this one in sequence); **Document** launches a Macintosh file or program that you specify; **Sound** triggers a sound; and **Movie** starts rolling a movie that you've set up beforehand.

If you want to change the appearance of an Action Button—or any other Auto-Shape—double-click the button to bring up the Format AutoShape dialog box.

Tip: You don't have to use one of the predrawn shapes on the Action Buttons palette as your visible button; PowerPoint can turn *any* graphic object into a button. Just Control-click it and choose Action Settings from the contextual menu, then proceed as described in the preceding paragraphs.

Using Presenter Tools

If you've ever had to rush through a presentation because you lost track of time or forgot what was coming up on the next slide, PowerPoint's Presenter Tools new feature is a blessing. While the video projector or other external monitor shows a full-screen presentation, this feature displays the current slide, notes, and upcoming slides in separate panes on your laptop (Figure 17-6). A clock at the top of the screen counts the elapsed time since the beginning of the slideshow, so it's easy to pace yourself. Best of all, you don't even have to do anything extra to use Presenter Tools. If your computer supports non-mirrored video and you have a second monitor connected, this feature starts up automatically when you begin the slideshow.

All the shortcuts that work in full-screen mode also work in Presenter Tools. For example, you can advance to the next slide by pressing Return or Space bar. Or if you prefer, you can also navigate by clicking the green arrows at the top of the screen.

Tip: To practice using Presenter Tools on a single monitor, Choose Slide Show→View Presenter Tools.

The Presenter Tools notes pane would be handy even if it only let you read your notes during a slideshow—after all, you can't be expected to remember *everything* when you're at the podium. But Presenter Tools goes a step further by letting you *edit* the notes during your presentation, too. It's the ideal way to keep track of which jokes work and which slides make your audience wince in pain.

Note: If you mouse off the Presenter Tools screen onto the slideshow screen, you can Control-click to bring up the shortcut menu that includes Meeting Minder and other options.

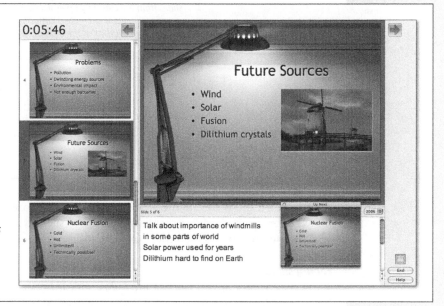

Figure 17-6:
New in PowerPoint 2004, Presenter Tools divides the screen into three panes, much like Normal view. The largest, at the top, shows you exactly what the audience sees, in real time. The pane on the left shows thumbnails of the entire presentation; to go to any slide, click it. The notes pane at the bottom shows your slide notes. The Up Next window shows the next animation on the current slide or the next slide in the presentation.

Recycling Your Presentations

PowerPoint lets you create multiple custom shows in a single document. This feature comes in handy if, for example, you want to have both long and abbreviated versions of the same show, or if you want to tailor some material you've used before to a different audience. It's also great for creating shows that *branch.* Anyone who's using your document in a one-on-one situation can follow different branches by clicking hyperlinked buttons. You could even get fancy and give each branch a different slide master.

But let's take the first case. Suppose you're going to address two different groups on the topic of deer. You have lots of engaging slides on the topic. But there's a good chance the group from the Bambi Fan Club wouldn't sit through the show you've got planned for Hunters Anonymous. You could solve this moral dilemma by creating a *customized* show for each group, each of whose slides are a subset of the complete deer presentation.

To build such a custom show, choose Slide Show→Custom Shows. The resulting dialog box offers four choices: New, Edit, Remove, and Copy.

When you click New, a dialog box pops up that lets you choose the slides you want to include in the custom show (Figure 17-7). You can also reorder the slides in your custom show and give your custom show a name.

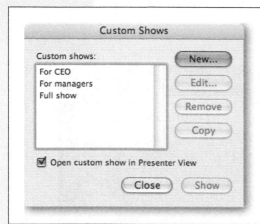

Figure 17-7:
Using the Custom Shows dialog box, you can choose a subset of slides from the currently open slideshow and reorder those slides any way you want to create a customized presentation. If you turn on the checkbox at the bottom, the show opens in Presenter Tools.

Then, when it's time to give the actual presentation, choose Slide Shows→Custom Shows to bring up a window that lists the custom shows you've built. Click the one you want to present and then click Show; your custom show now begins.

Hiding slides

There may be times when you want to hide a slide from view without actually deleting it. The slide needs more work, for example, or it's not appropriate for a certain audience. There are a couple of ways to go about preventing a slide from showing up in slideshows. First, you can select the slide you want to hide and then select Slide Show→Hide Slide. You can also use the Slide Sorter view to hide slides by selecting the slides you want to hide and then clicking the Hide Slide button in the Slide Sorter toolbar. (If that toolbar isn't visible, choose View→Toolbars→Slide Sorter.) Power-Point simply skips over hidden slides when you run the slideshow. (Hidden slides show up in the Slide Sorter with a slash through their number.)

To bring a hidden slide back into view, Control-click it in Slide Sorter view and select Hide Slide to turn off the checkmark.

Tip: Hidden slides appear dimmed in Presenter Tools' slide gallery. To show a hidden slide, click it, or press H when you're on the preceding slide.

Multimedia Effects

PowerPoint puts at your disposal a Spielbergian selection of special effects. In addition to the transitions you insert between slides, the program lets you animate particular elements in an image. It also enables you to add a soundtrack or voice narration to your slideshow—features that are especially useful if you want to save the presenta-tion as a standalone movie.

Adding Animations

One of the simplest ways to jazz up a PowerPoint presentation is to animate an ele-ment in a slide—be it text, an image, or even a movie. You can make objects appear and disappear with precision timing, change their shape or color, or add sound effects for emphasis.

As always, these effects do nothing to make up for the lack of a meaningful message in your presentation, and seem primarily designed for making glitzy demos of Power-Point at trade shows. Therefore, use them sparingly and with good taste.

Caution: You've been warned: Animations may not show up when you export your PowerPoint presenta-tion as a QuickTime movie (as described on page 646), especially if you've also created transitions between slides.

Preset animations

To animate an object using one of PowerPoint's ready-made special effects, first select the object you want to animate—click inside a block of text or click an image, for example.

Note: Not all standard animations work with all kinds of objects. Laser Text and Typewriter, for instance, affect only text, not graphics. If a particular effect isn't applicable to the object you've selected, that option is grayed out on the Animations menu.

Then choose an animation style from the Slide Show→Preset Animations submenu, which offers 12 different animations (plus an Off option to remove an animation). A few examples:

- **Fly In.** The selected object shoots in from the left with a *swish* sound and comes to rest at its rightful spot in the layout.

- **Fly In/Out.** The selected object flies onto the slide from the left and lands in its proper position, then, with another mouse click or keypress, rockets off to the right. An audible *swish* accompanies both motions.

- **Drive-In/Out.** The selected object enters the slide from the right and, with the sound of a car motor and screeching tires, skids into its resting place. Another keypress or click sends the object off the slide to the left with the same infernal racket.

- **Flash Once.** No sound here. The selected object simply flashes once in a silent, subliminal kind of way.

- **Dissolve.** The selected object gradually materializes before your eyes, a few pixels at a time.

- **Laser Text.** Characters fly onto the screen from the upper-right corner, accompanied by a sound like a laser gun from a bad science fiction movie.

- **Appear.** In this, the simplest of all PowerPoint's animations, the selected item just pops into its predetermined spot on the slide.

Tip: To preview an animation, choose Slide Show→Animation Preview. A little window pops up, showing you just how the animation looks when it kicks in. (Click the window to replay the animation.)

Custom animations

If none of the preset animations suits your fancy, you can fiddle with them to create an effect you like better. The Custom Animation dialog box is the shop where you soup up animations and control multiple animations on the same slide. To open this window, choose Slide Show→Custom Animation, or click the Customize button in the Animation section of the Formatting Palette.

In the Custom Animation dialog box (Figure 17-8), you can exercise control over almost every aspect of an animated object, such as how it enters or exits a slide and what sounds it makes. This is also where you let PowerPoint know which animations to trigger if you have *more* than one per slide.

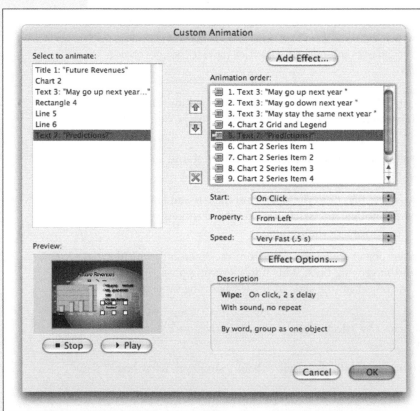

Figure 17-8:
The Custom Animation dialog box is animation headquarters, your personal Dreamworks studio. Its pop-up menus give you access to tons of animation effects and options. The box at the bottom provides a summary of the animation you're working on.

The left side of the Custom Animation dialog box shows a list of all the text boxes, graphics, and other objects on the slide. To animate one of these objects (or adjust the animation style you've already applied), click the one you want to work with. Below that list is a Preview pane with Stop and Play buttons; use these, if you wish, to see how your adjustments affect the slide.

After you choose the text or graphic you want to give life to, click the Add Effect button. The Animation Effects dialog box appears, offering these three tabbed sections:

- **Entrance.** Use this tab to select how the element makes its appearance on the slide. The effects are grouped into four categories—Basic, Subtle, Moderate, and Exciting—that describe how eye-catching the effect is. If an effect is grayed out, it's not an option for that element.

- **Emphasis.** This option, new to PowerPoint 2004, lets you choose an effect that calls attention to an element that already appears on the slide. For example, Lighten makes the object turn brighter.

- **Exit.** This tab lets you choose an effect to apply when an element disappears from the slide. Aside from options that don't apply to disappearing objects, and a few extra ones that do, the list is identical to the one in the Entrance tab.

After you apply an animation to a text box or graphic element, it shows up in the Animation Order box on the right. This list shows not only the animations you've applied, but the order in which they occur. To change the sequence, select an element and click the up or down arrow buttons to the left. You can also delete one or more animations by selecting them and clicking the red X icon.

Tip: You can apply as many animations to an object as you like, so an element can appear in the Animation Order box more than once.

POWER USERS' CLINIC

Using Animations for Special Effects

It's all too easy to dismiss animations as flashy add-ons that don't belong in a serious slideshow. But, if you use your imagination, you can use PowerPoint's effects repertoire to enhance *any* presentation. Here are two examples:

To teach a science class how a mirror works, you can use a simple animation to make a light ray bounce off the bottom of the screen. First, draw two lines that meet at the bottom of the slide to form a "V" shape. Next, group them (select both lines and choose Group from the Draw pop-up in the Drawing toolbar). Finally, animate the grouped object with a Wipe

effect from the left. When you click or hit a key to advance, the light beam looks like it's being reflected upward.

Animations also make it easy to highlight any part of a photograph. Begin by drawing a circle around the area of interest. (Pick a color that contrasts with the picture, and make sure to select No Fill from the Fill Color pop-up menu in the Drawing toolbar.) Animate the circle with a Wedge effect in the Custom Animation dialog box. When you click or hit the advance key, the circle materializes to focus your audience's attention.

To edit an existing animation, double-click it in the Animation Order list to reopen the Animation Effects box. Once you're satisfied with your choice of effects, click OK to return to the Custom Animation dialog box.

You can go a long way just using PowerPoint's animations as they come, but someday you may want to exert more control over what they do. Three pop-up menus below the Animation Order box let you control what starts the animation, how it looks, and how long it takes:

- **Start.** This menu lets you choose whether the animation triggers when you click or press the advance key, at the same time as the previous animation, or after the preceding animation finishes.

- **Property.** Here, you specify how the animation works. For example, if you've chosen Fly-Out, you can pick where you want the element to zip when it exits the slide.

- **Speed.** This pop-up menu lets you indicate how fast (or slow) you want the animation to occur, from half a second to five seconds, start to finish.

The button below the pop-up menus calls up the Effect Options dialog box, which has two tabs:

- **Effect.** Pop-up menus let you pick a sound to accompany the animation, as well as specify whether the animated object should disappear, change color, or remain unchanged after the animation.

- **Timing.** Here, you can fine-tune the animation's timing, as well as set it to repeat as many times as you like. (The "Rewind when done playing" checkbox resets the animation after it's finished.)

Narration

If you're worried about laryngitis on the day of your presentation, if you're creating a self-running kiosk show, or if you have an unnatural fear of public *squeaking*, you might want to record voice narration for your slideshow ahead of time. This way,

---

FREQUENTLY ASKED QUESTION

Bullet-by-Bullet

I've seen these really tall, smart, good-looking people do presentations where their bullet lists don't show up all at once. Instead, each point whooshes onto the screen on command. Can I do that too?

It's easy to animate the arrival of your bullets. Choose Slide Show→Custom Animation, and select the text object (the one that contains your bullets) in the box to the left. Click Add Effect, select Fly In from the Entrance tab, and click OK. Choose From Left and Fast from the Property and Speed pop-up menus, respectively. (For a more subtle effect, try Fade or Dissolve In.)

If you click OK, your bullet points will now fly in one at a time, each time you click the mouse (or press an advance key). If you click Effect Options and click the Timing tab, you can specify instead that they appear a certain number of seconds apart. And, if you click the Text Animation tab, you can choose the bullet level that you want to group together—something that will make sense only if you've actually created bulleted lists within bulleted lists.

OFFICE 2004 FOR MACINTOSH: THE MISSING MANUAL

you can sit back and relax while your confident, disembodied voice plays along with the show.

To add recorded narration to your presentation, you need a Mac with a microphone, of course. (PowerBooks and iMacs have built-in mikes; USB microphones are available for Power Macs, Cubes, and iBooks; and older Power Macs came with a small plastic microphone and corresponding jack.) You might want to visit the Sound panel of System Preferences (click the Input tab) to make sure that you've selected the correct microphone for input. Quit all other sound-recording programs, if any are running. Then:

1. **Choose Slide Show→Record Narration to bring up the Record Narration dialog box.**

   This box shows the current recording settings, including your maximum recording time based on your free hard-drive space. Since sound files can be huge, the "Link narrations" checkbox lets you save your narration files to any location you like, such as an external hard drive with plenty of free space, rather than embedding them in the presentation file. Click Set to choose where PowerPoint saves linked narrations. When you finish recording, that location will contain one AIFF sound file for each slide in your presentation.

Note: If you link your narrations, moving your presentation to another machine will break the links. (As always, the PowerPoint Package format avoids this problem, as discussed on page 622.)

---

2. **Click Record.**

   PowerPoint starts running through your presentation. As you advance through the slides, PowerPoint makes a separate, linked AIFF sound file for each slide. Or, if you didn't link the recording, PowerPoint attaches the audio you recorded as a sound object on each slide.

   There's no easy way to re-record just one flubbed slide; for most purposes, it's simplest to start over with a new "take." To start over, end the slideshow using whatever method you normally use (press Esc, for instance). Then, choose Slide Show→Record Narration and begin again. (And if you're *really* having trouble, you can always record individual sound files for each slide, then attach them as described on page 623.)

Note: These voice clips override any other sound effects in the slideshow, so if you're using a recorded narration, embedded sound effects (including transition sounds) don't play.

---

3. **Record whatever you want to say for each slide, then advance the slides as you normally would (by clicking the mouse, for example).**

   When you reach the end of the slideshow, PowerPoint asks if you want to save the timings (to record the amount of time you spent on each slide) along with your narration. If you click No, PowerPoint saves only the narration. If you click Yes,

PowerPoint saves the timings along with the narration, overwriting any existing timings.

If you choose not to include the timings, each sound will play when you manually advance to a given slide. In this way, you can let the narration play and then have some discussion with each slide, moving on only when you're ready.

Warning: Voice recordings can eat up a lot of disk space, so be sure you have enough room on your hard drive to hold the sound. If not, consider saving your voice files to an external hard drive or some other industrial-strength storage area.

Once you're done recording your narration, you've got a self-contained slideshow, suitable for parties or board meetings.

Saving Presentations as QuickTime Movies

PowerPoint 2004 retains the previous version's ability to save presentations as Quick-Time movies. This is a nifty idea for two reasons. First, anyone with QuickTime installed—Mac users, Windows users, whoever—can play these movies even if they don't have PowerPoint. This is a great way for your associates and underlings to give the same kinds of pitches you give without having to spring for a copy of Office. Second, a presentation movie thus converted can be opened and edited in PowerPoint as if it were a PowerPoint file.

Note: You can still go to Microsoft's Web site to download PowerPoint Viewer 98, a utility that lets you play PowerPoint presentations on Macs that don't have PowerPoint. Alas, the viewer doesn't run under Mac OS X, and it isn't compatible with many features in recent versions of PowerPoint. In general, the Save as Movie option described on these pages is far more flexible and compatible with far more computers.

Before you proceed, remember that not every bell and whistle of a PowerPoint slideshow survives the conversion into a QuickTime movie. As noted here and there throughout this chapter, things like action buttons on master slides, many PowerPoint transitions, and certain actions (mouseovers, certain kinds of links, play sound, and so on) won't work at all.

To turn an open PowerPoint presentation into a QuickTime movie, choose File→ Make Movie. This brings up a Save dialog box, which you can use to name your movie file and choose a folder location for it.

As you save your movie, PowerPoint gives you a chance to fine-tune some of its settings. To begin, click the Movie Options button. PowerPoint responds by opening the Movie Options dialog box shown in Figure 17-9.

The most important settings worth examining here are Movie Dimensions (see Figure 17-9) and the Optimization pop-up menu. The latter lets you specify which you value more: compact file size, smooth playback of animations, or picture quality. Depending on the complexity of your file and the screen size you've specified, these virtues may be mutually exclusive. If you want the highest quality animations, for example, the file won't be very small on your hard drive, and the quality of animated photos may suffer.

Tip: After you've saved your slideshow as a QuickTime movie, you may notice your PowerPoint transitions acting flaky. Because the PowerPoint Movie format doesn't actually support PowerPoint transitions, they get translated to a QuickTime equivalent that may be very different from what you intended. For the best results, use simple transitions like Fade Smoothly, or don't use any transitions at all.

Figure 17-9:
This dialog box lets you specify the size of the QuickTime movie; 640 x 480 won't fill most of today's 15-inch or larger screens. Using the "Background soundtrack" pop-up menu, you can choose an MP3 file or another file to play during the whole slideshow—a handy option in self-running, kiosk situations. Notice the radio buttons in the Save area that let you select whether PowerPoint should use your new settings for just this presentation or use them for future presentations as well.

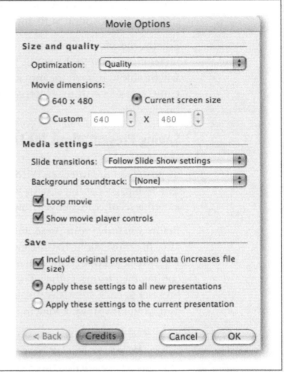

WORKAROUND WORKSHOP

Mac Presentations on Windows PCs

If you're really in demand as a speaker, you'll eventually have to bite the bullet and show a Mac PowerPoint presentation on a Windows computer. Although the QuickTime movie format offers one workaround, it's usually better if you can use the Windows version of PowerPoint to run your slideshow. When you're preparing your presentation, use fonts that you know will be installed on the Windows PC—Arial and Times New Roman, for example. Import graphics in cross-platform

formats like JPEG and GIF, and convert movies to AVI format using Apple's QuickTime Pro application.

Finally, if you can, do a dry run on the actual computer that you'll be using for your presentation, just to make sure that there aren't any last-minute glitches. Copy your slideshow, along with movies and other linked files, to the PC's desktop and double-click the presentation file. (If the movies don't play, you may need to reinsert them manually.)

This dialog box also lets you import a sound file to use as a soundtrack. Chosen tastefully, music or some other nondistracting sound (rainfall or ocean waves, perhaps) can make your movie a more well-rounded presentation. Tread carefully, though, to avoid crossing that fine line between "nondistracting" and "sleep-inducing." These background sound files can be in any number of formats, including AIFF, QuickTime audio, WAV, and MP3.

To add a background soundtrack, choose Select Soundtrack in the Background soundtrack pop-up menu. PowerPoint asks you to locate the sound file that you want to use, which it then attaches to your presentation when you click OK. PowerPoint will mix the soundtrack sound with any embedded sounds, including voice narration.

Finally, the Movie Options window lets you decide whether PowerPoint adds the *presentation data* to the movie file. If you choose this option, you or your colleagues will be able to reopen the movie file *right back into PowerPoint* for further editing—a truly impressive stunt. However, you'll make the resulting movie file much bigger on the disk.

Saving Presentations for the Web

PowerPoint lets you create presentation files that are formatted, coded, and ready to be posted on the Internet. With just a few mouse clicks, you can save your slideshow as a Web page, complete with some nifty JavaScript programming that gives viewers a high level of control over how they watch your show.

Before you move your presentation onto the Web, you'll first want to see how it looks after the conversion. To preview your presentation as a Web page, choose File→Web Page Preview. PowerPoint generates all the necessary graphics, HTML, and JavaScript coding, then transfers the whole enchilada into your browser. You can then use your browser to click your way through the presentation, which actually looks very much as it would if you were viewing it in PowerPoint's Normal (three-pane) view.

To save your presentation as a Web page (or rather, a set of them), choose File→ Save as Web Page. PowerPoint asks where you'd like to save your show. Clicking Web Options opens a dialog box that lets you tell the program such things as what colors

---

TROUBLESHOOTING MOMENT

Funky Fonts

When viewing a presentation that's been converted into a Web page, you may notice that the fonts don't fit quite right—a by-product of the fact that the HTML language of Web pages isn't terrifically brilliant about managing fonts. Although PowerPoint does its best to compensate, sometimes type rendered in HTML is just too large for the allotted space, so chunks of text bump down to the next line.

You can do a couple of things to combat this fat-font problem. Keep your font sizes a shade smaller than you ordinarily would, and try not to squeeze too much copy on a single line. And whenever possible, avoid tables with multiple lines of text; these babies are just waiting to bunch together and run over.

---

to use, where to place navigation buttons, and how to encode images. Once you're satisfied with the options you've chosen, click OK. To actually save the presentation, click Save. PowerPoint automatically renders your presentation as HTML files complete with embedded JavaScript and accompanying Web-ready graphics files. You wind up with a home page and a folder full of HTML files, graphics files, and sound files. You can upload these files to your Web server as you would any other Web page files (see page 311).

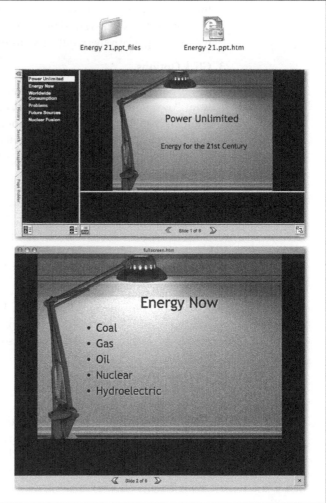

Figure 17-10:
Top: After you've saved your presentation as a Web page, you can find it in the Finder as a single, "home page" file and a folder containing secondary pages and supporting media files. In this example, the presentation was named Energy 21.ppt.htm. PowerPoint also applied that name to the folder.

Middle: In Internet Explorer, buttons at the bottom let you hide (or show) the Outline and Notes panes, switch slides, or see the show at full-screen size.

Bottom: The slideshow runs in Safari, but the full-screen option doesn't work properly. The look of a Web presentation on any individual computer depends on many factors: operating system, fonts installed, screen resolution, browser preferences set by the user, and so on.

Saving Slides as Graphics

Among its many other gifts, PowerPoint allows you to save individual slides—text and all—as graphics files. This can be a handy little feature whenever you want to make sharp-looking, high-resolution images of your presentation to pass along to your friends (or your agent).

To save a PowerPoint slide as a graphics file, first open the slide you want to convert, then follow these few steps:

1. **Choose File→Save As.**

   A dialog box appears, offering several options.

2. **From the Format pop-up menu, select a graphics file format.**

   JPEG is an excellent choice for photos; PICT is good, too, but it's a Macintosh-only format. Use GIF or PNG (see the box on page 296) for smaller files, especially if you intend to use the resulting still images on a Web page and if your audience will be using relatively recent versions of the popular Web browsers.

3. **Click Options.**

   At the bottom of the resulting Preferences window, you can choose whether you want PowerPoint to save *all* the slides in the show as graphics or just this one. In addition, you can set up the file resolution and dimensions. (The file's dimensions is an important setting, since you don't want your monitor to chop off part of the slides.) Finally, you can specify whether to compress the file (smaller files, worse quality).

Tip: You don't need to set up these options time after time; you can set up your preferred settings only once, on the PowerPoint→Preferences→Save tab. There you'll find the identical graphics-saving options, which affect the proposed values for all your subsequent graphics-saving exploits.

---

4. **Change the settings as desired, click OK, then name the still image and click Save.**

   If you opted to save all of the slides, PowerPoint automatically creates a *folder* bearing your file's name. Inside the folder are the individual graphics files, with names like Slide1.jpg, Slide2.jpg, and so on.

Printing Your Presentation

Although PowerPoint is primarily meant to throw images onto a monitor or projector, you can also print out your presentations on good old-fashioned paper—which is especially useful, of course, for printing handouts, overheads, and notes. Whatever the format, all printing is done through the same basic procedure: Open the presentation you want to print, make a few adjustments in the Page Setup dialog box and the Print dialog box, then fire away.

Page Setup

Before printing your presentation, you should pop open the hood and take a peek at the Page Setup dialog box (see Figure 17-11). After all, this important window is the engine that controls the size of your slides, whether they're for onscreen viewing or printing. Be sure to make any size adjustments early in the game; if you fiddle with the knobs in Page Setup *after* the slide has been made, it'll stretch to fit, possibly giving the image a warped or distorted look, or knocking certain graphics off the edges altogether.

You can use the settings in this dialog box to morph your slideshow into something appropriate for another format—taking it from an overhead projector to a Web banner, for instance. Also, if you want to send your presentation out to be printed, you can adjust the presentation's resolution by clicking the Options button in the Save dialog box.

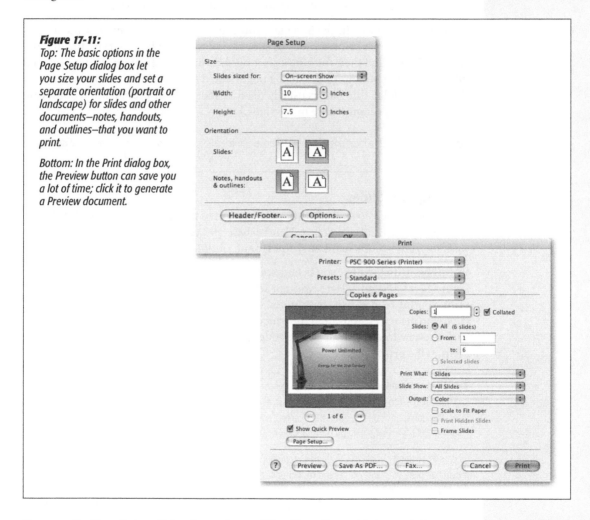

Figure 17-11:
Top: The basic options in the Page Setup dialog box let you size your slides and set a separate orientation (portrait or landscape) for slides and other documents—notes, handouts, and outlines—that you want to print.

Bottom: In the Print dialog box, the Preview button can save you a lot of time; click it to generate a Preview document.

To open the Page Setup dialog box, choose File→Page Setup. Doing so brings you face to face with Microsoft's version of the Page Setup box, which presents you with a pop-up menu offering several preset slide sizes: On-screen show, US Letter, US Ledger, A3, A4, B4, B5, 35mm slides, Overhead, and Web banner (Figure 17-11, top). If you have a custom slide size in mind, you can set its width and height here as well.

Tip: If you need the options available in the familiar Mac OS Page Setup dialog box, you can get there quickly by clicking Options in Microsoft's version of the Page Setup dialog box.

Click Header/Footer to make text (such as a slide number, page number, or date) appear on the top or bottom of every slide, or every note and handout. On each tab in the Header and Footer dialog box, click the checkboxes and watch the Preview at the lower right to see where the different text elements appear. Once you've turned on a checkbox, select the box's related options and enter text as appropriate.

For example, working in the Slide tab, you can insert a slide number at the lower-right corner of each printed slide (or slide thumbnail on a handout) by turning on "Slide number" and then entering a starting slide number. Turn on "Don't show on title slide" at the bottom of the dialog box if you'd like that number hidden on *title* slides. (Although a title slide is usually the first slide in your presentation, but it can theoretically appear anywhere in the show.)

Tip: You can change the locations of the footer boxes on the Slide tab by dragging them on the slide master (see page 608).

Printing Your Slides

When you're ready to commit your presentation to paper, choose File→Print (⌘-P) to bring up the Print dialog box. Here's where you tell PowerPoint exactly what you want to print—slides, handouts, notes, or an outline.

In the Print dialog box, you'll find special, PowerPoint-related print settings (see Figure 17-11, bottom). Here, you can select which chunks of your presentation you want to print (slides, handouts, notes, or the outline). From this spot you can also choose to print a custom show, provided you created one earlier. When you're ready, click Preview to check your choices one last time, or click Print to send your document to the printer.

Tip: The beauty of the Mac OS X Preview function is that it lets you convert your PowerPoint document—or *any* document—into a PDF file (otherwise known as an Acrobat file). Anyone with almost any kind of computer (Mac, Windows, or Unix) can open the resulting document using the free Acrobat Reader program. (You can create a PDF file immediately by clicking Save As PDF in the Print dialog box.)

Of course, sending people a PDF file of your presentation isn't quite as exciting as sending them a QuickTime movie complete with animations and multimedia. But a PDF document is compatible with far more computers. (Plus, it's less detrimental to forests than distributing printouts on paper.)

Notes and Handouts

It didn't take the world long to dispel the myth of the paperless office, and that's evident every time your audience asks you for a hard copy of your presentation. Sure, you can steer some audiences to the Web version of your presentation that you've cleverly posted to the Web in advance (be sure to point this out to your boss as a cost-saving measure you've adopted). But when that approach fails, PowerPoint can print out your notes and handouts or convert them to PDF files for electronic distribution.

Every PowerPoint slide can have *notes* attached to it: written tidbits to help you get through your presentation, or to clarify points for your audience. As you build your presentation, the Notes pane in PowerPoint's Normal view provides a place to type notes for each slide as it's active. (These notes appear on Web pages if you leave "Include slide notes" turned on in the Appearance tab of the Web Options dialog box when saving your presentation as a Web page.)

Handouts are printouts of your slides, usually featuring multiple slides per sheet of paper. They let your audience take your entire show away with them on paper, to spare them from having to take notes during the meeting. Handouts don't include notes; you'll have to print those out separately.

Note: Both notes and handouts have master pages, which work the same as slide masters; see page 608 for details.

To print your notes and handouts, choose File→Print (⌘-P). This brings up the settings specific to PowerPoint. In the Print What pop-up menu, you can choose to print notes or handouts in layouts that contain two, three, four, six, or nine slide miniatures per sheet. Here again, if you click Preview, you'll be shown an onscreen preview of the printout-in-waiting, which you can then save as a PDF file in the Mac OS X program called Preview.

Tip: You can choose the Layout item in the Copies & Pages pop-up menu to print one, two, four, six, nine, or 16 slides per page. With Layout chosen, use the "Pages per Sheet" pop-up menu; your printer will substitute one slide per page. (You won't see your custom layout in Preview, but it will still print.)

Part Five:
Microsoft Office as a
Whole

4

Chapter 18: The Project Gallery and Toolbox

Chapter 19: Customizing Office

Chapter 20: The Graphics Programs of Office

Chapter 21: AppleScripting Office

The Project Gallery and Toolbox

The Project Gallery

Every time you launch an Office program (by clicking its dock icon, for example), you're greeted by a special document-launching screen, elegantly named the Project Gallery.

Since Office 2001, the Project Gallery has been the repository for icons that represent the kinds of Word documents and other types of files Office can create for you. (Use the scroll bar to see all of them.) You'll see canned *templates* for mailing labels, resumés, budgets, brochures, fax cover letters, and dozens of others—not to mention Excel, PowerPoint, and Entourage documents like spreadsheets and blank email messages. The idea is that you don't have to launch (or even know) the Office program you're going to use for the document. From anywhere in Office, you can create or open any kind of document. Choose File→Project Gallery in any Office program, or memorize the keystroke Shift-⌘-P.

Tip: Instead of wasting valuable dock real estate with those bulky Excel, Word, and PowerPoint icons, you can simply drag the Project Gallery Launcher (in your Applications→Microsoft Office 2004→Office Folder) to the dock. Whenever you want to work in Office, just click the Project Gallery launcher, and away you go.

The 2004 edition of Project Gallery also boasts the nifty new ability to access projects you create in Entourage's new Project Center. These projects are powerful organizational tools—just the thing you need to keep track of everything involved in designing games, writing a recipe book, or crafting a lengthy business proposal. Projects track all emails, documents, and files associated with the project and place them in a handy location accessible from Word or any other Office 2004 program. See Chapter 10 for more details on projects.

Tip: If you'd rather not visit the Project Gallery every time you launch Word, turn off "Show Project Gallery at startup." You can also choose Word→Preferences, click the General button (in the list at left) and turn "Show Project Gallery at startup" on or off.

Opening Documents

Opening any kind of document in the Project Gallery works the same way: Click the list items in the Category list on the left (see Figure 18-1) until you see the desired template or document type on the right. Then double-click the document icon to open it.

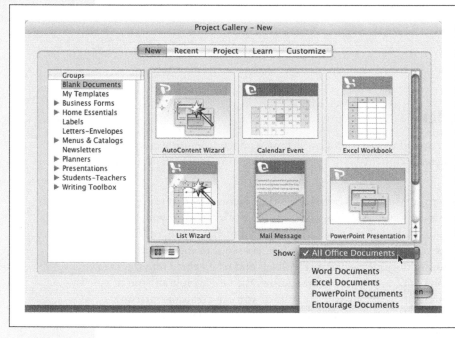

Figure 18-1:
When you launch an Office program, the Project Gallery appears, assuming that you want to open a new, blank document in Word, Excel, PowerPoint, or, in this case, Entourage. If you'd rather see a list of recent documents each morning, you can customize the Project Gallery's startup screen, as described on page 662.

To see how it works, let's first assume you're writing a letter. Click the flippy triangle next to the Business Forms category (or double-click Business Forms). Then click Letterheads; an assortment of colorful stationery templates appears in the window. (Catalog view is the best way to get an overview of what's available.) Double-click a template; a new document opens, all formatted and ready for you to input your own address and other information.

Note: In the icon view, clicking on any category adjacent to a flippy triangle splashes the generic Project Gallery screen. The screen identifies each of the Project Gallery tabs (see page 659 for details). Click on the flippy triangle adjacent to a category, and then a template group under it to remove the screen.

Choosing Made Easy

Whether you're composing a magnum opus to rival Stephen King's *Dark Tower* series, or just a thank you note to your grandmother, the tabs at the top of the Project Gallery window are a perfect place to start.

New

Well, you can guess what the icons on this tab do: open brand new, empty documents, waiting for you to fill with your own words. Ah, but what kind of document? Several categories of new documents await your perusal:

- **Blank Documents.** Contrary to the name, these are not all fresh-linen-flapping-in-the-breeze blank. This category not only includes blank Word documents, PowerPoint presentations, Entourage emails, and Excel Workbooks, but also a List Wizard for creating tailgate party lists, a shortcut to enter Entourage calendar events, a blank Web page, or a spanking-new Word Notebook.

- **Business Forms.** From agendas to invoices, you'll find everything that you need for your business, whether it's running the local Boy Scout troop or managing a multi-million-dollar firm.

- **Home Essentials.** These documents help with the ever-more-complex task of home management. They include specially formatted Excel spreadsheets waiting for you to enter your home budget, financial or medical information, and even lists to leave for your babysitter.

- **Labels, Letters, and Envelopes.** Create custom versions using these templates.

- **Menus and Catalogs.** Use these templates to create restaurant menus, or catalogs of, say, heavy equipment that your small business sells. (Why Microsoft put these two in the same category is anybody's guess.)

- **Newsletters.** Just as you might expect, this category includes multiple newsletter templates. Sixteen in all, if you're counting along.

UP TO SPEED

Keystrokes of the Very Busy

Within the Project Gallery, after you have selected a template type—such as Agendas—you can jump from the category list at left to the templates in the right or middle panel by pressing Tab. Once you've highlighted one of these lists, a blue box surrounds the list, indicating that it's active. Pressing the up and down arrow keys moves you up or down the lists. When the templates are in icon view, you can press all four of the arrow keys to highlight successive icons. Don't try this if you have big fingers or work on a laptop. The arrows are

just too small; there's no telling what your Mac will think you are trying to tell it. (Sorry, Mac OS purists: You can't jump to a particular template by typing the first letters of its name.)

When you've highlighted a category (in the left-side list) marked by a "flippy triangle," press ⌘-right arrow to expand it, or ⌘-left arrow to collapse it again. And when you've finally highlighted the template you want, pressing Return or Enter, of course, opens it.

- **Planners.** An incredibly diverse category that includes buckets of templates. Checklists, diet plans, tournament bracket charts, shopping lists, party/wedding plans (guaranteed to be less expensive than hiring J-Lo), to-do lists (including a child's chore lists), and workout logs are all present and accounted for.

- **Presentations.** Simply tens upon tens of PowerPoint presentations, preformatted for situations like training sessions and the oh-so-subtle "Communicating Bad News."

- **Students-Teachers.** Aids for students and teachers, including several types of graph paper and lesson planners.

- **Writing Toolbox.** Consists of four kinds of infinite-page documents: Bibliographies, Guides, Journals, and Reports. Unlike ordinary one-page templates, these can grow according to your needs. With some of the templates each page is different. For instance, the Term Paper template contains a ready-made table of contents and example footnotes, which you replace with your own information (See Figure 18-2).

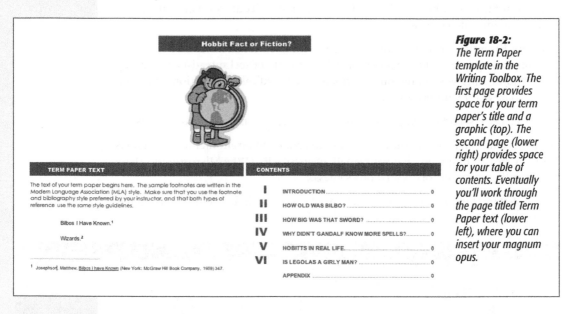

Figure 18-2:
The Term Paper template in the Writing Toolbox. The first page provides space for your term paper's title and a graphic (top). The second page (lower right) provides space for your table of contents. Eventually you'll work through the page titled Term Paper text (lower left), where you can insert your magnum opus.

Recent

Clicking this button displays a list of recent documents you've worked on categorized by relative dates (today, yesterday, last week, and so on). Double-click one of these document icons to open the document. Alternatively, you can select the document and then mouse over to the Open as Copy button.

You might want to open a copy if, for instance, you're writing a letter of complaint to the phone company, and you can base it on the complaint letter you sent to the cable company last week. Since most of your choicest phrasings will probably remain the same, there's no need to start the letter from scratch. (The Open Copy option in the standard Open file dialog box serves the same purpose, but it's nice to have it in the Project Gallery.) Conversely, if you're writing the great American novel (or European, or Asian, depending on where you live), you'll probably want to keep the novel in one document, so you'll use the Save As command and save over the original document.

Project

Clicking here displays the projects that you've created in the Project Center as shown in Figure 18-3. The Project Center is Office 2004's new, gee-whiz tool that allows you to organize complete projects, including email, Excel files, contacts, documents, and so on in one centralized location. For example, you can place your proposal document for a new fast food restaurant, a picture of the location, and all the emails concerning the enterprise in the same project. For more detail, see Chapter 9.

Tip: You can also access your projects from the Projects panel of the Toolbox palette, also new in Office 2004. See page 667.

Figure 18-3:
Right here in the Project Gallery, you can see every project you've created in the new Entourage Project Center (Chapter 10), complete with all the relevant photos, emails, notes, and documents related to the project. If you have a little trouble getting oriented before your second cup of coffee, this screen is a great place to start your day. Use the Project Gallery's Custom-ize feature (page 662) to open to this screen when you first launch Office for the day.

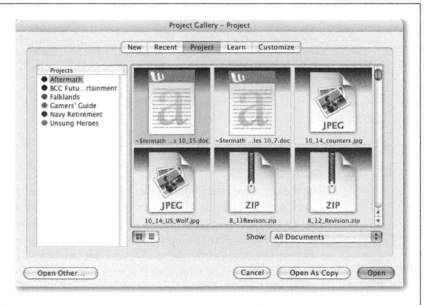

Learn

Not sure where to begin? Clicking the Learn button reveals a slew of sample Office 2004 documents, as described in Figure 18-4, to help you see your Office options in greater detail. Although instructive, these files aren't interactive tutorials, watersheds in your life, or an epiphany, but rather examples of what you might do using Office's main features. Each includes not only the sample proper, but also annotations that explain how the document was put together.

Tip: While you're in the Learn panel, don't miss the Discovering Microsoft Office document. This 152-page PDF file covers the basics of using Office, from creating a spreadsheet, to chatting with your friends using MSN messenger. Discovering Microsoft Office is a convenient place to learn the basics and unearth features and even programs you didn't know were in there. To open it, click Discovering Office in the Topics panel and then double-click Discovering Microsoft Office. The PDF downloads and opens automatically in Acrobat Reader, which comes installed on all new Macs. (You can also open it in Mac OS X's Preview program.)

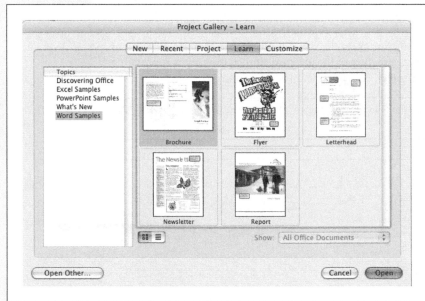

Figure 18-4:
Clicking Learn displays categories of topics on the left, and specific documents on the right. Click a topic that piques your curiosity, double-click the sample document in the Project Gallery, and you're off to the learning races. Click the Excel, PowerPoint, or Word sample categories, and the Project Gallery displays sample documents from the chosen program. features and programs.

Customize

For the first time, the Project Gallery is under your command. From the Customize panel, new in Office 2004, you can choose whether you want to show Project Gallery on startup, which documents/files you wish it to show, how many recent files to remember, and where to keep your local and workgroup templates. For example, you can have Office remember virtually every document you've used for the past year, or make it show only the templates that your department is supposed to use.

Tip: The Project Gallery lists simply reflect whichever files are in the Microsoft Office 2004→Templates folder on your hard drive. If you'd like to add to, trim down, rename, or reorganize the options in the Project Gallery, just return to the Finder, open the Applications→Microsoft Office 2004→Templates folder, and go to town. For example, you might add your corporate logo letterhead, after first saving it as a template (see page 226. You can also use the Show checkboxes described below to specify which document options your Project Gallery displays.

Tweaking the Project Gallery

You can also customize the Project Gallery using the following buttons and menus found at the bottom of the dialog box:

- **View.** These buttons let you choose to view the Project Gallery either in icon view or list view. In icon view, each document is represented like a big square, just like the squares on the button. In list view (click the button with the lines on it), the panel of large document icons is replaced by a list of smaller icons. At the right, a preview panel opens where you can see a more detailed view of what you're about to open.

- **Show.** This pop-up menu is like a filter. If you want to view *only* templates for Word documents, for example, choose All Word Documents from here. You won't see Excel templates, PowerPoint templates, and so on.

  On the other hand, the setting called All Office Documents has its advantages. From this one panel, you can open up any kind of Office document or template without having to visit your dock, for example, to launch the appropriate program.

- **Open Other.** Click this button to display Office's standard Open dialog box. If you access the Project Gallery through the Project Gallery launcher (page 657), this button doesn't appear.

Tip: If you tinker with the Project Gallery settings and have a subsequent change of heart, you can always return to the original settings by clicking on the all-powerful Restore Defaults button.

Ditching the Project Gallery

To dismiss the Project Gallery, click Cancel or press the Esc key (or ⌘-period). Word automatically opens a new blank document. If you'd rather open an existing document, click Open Other or use one of the methods described below. Word, a prince among Mac applications, always closes its default blank document whenever you open one of your own.

Toolbox

Unlike the toolbox in the corner of your garage, Office 2004's Toolbox is easy to find and is never missing a 9/16" socket wrench. Better still, it can do many things your rusty, red toolbox could never do. For example, it can store your snippets of inspiration (pictures, text, and so on), provide definitions and other research aids, check your document's compatibility, or provide a window into Office's Project Center. The Toolbox consists of four sections: Scrapbook, Reference Tools, Compatibility Report, and Project Center.

Scrapbook

Think of the Scrapbook as, well...a scrapbook. It's a location where you can drag copied snippets from documents or pictures, or Excel spreadsheets.

After opening the Scrapbook, as described in Figure 18-5, copy your text (or whatever) into the Scrapbook window by dragging it or using any of the conventional cut, copy, and paste methods (see page 58). To reuse the material, click the Paste button (near the middle of the Scrapbook) to paste the material shown in the Scrapbook window into your cursor's current location. There are three pasting options:

- **Paste.** This most common option pastes the material in the exact same format that you copied it.

Walk Where They Fought: The Battle of Guilford Courthouse

Figure 18-5:
You can open the Scrapbook from any Office 2004 program by selecting Tools→Scrapbook or clicking the Toolbox icon on the Standard toolbar (but not on the Entourage toolbar), and then clicking the Scrapbook icon at the top left of the Toolbox. Paste text, pictures, or Excel spreadsheets into the Scrapbook—and there they'll stay until you need them. Scroll through your scraps (called clippings *in the Office world) using the scroll bar. Copy a clipping from the Scrapbook by dragging it onto your document (or by using any of the usual keyboard shortcuts). If the scrap you're attempting to paste to the Scrapbook is larger than a megabyte, you'll get this warning.*

- **Paste as Plain Text.** By golly, they weren't kidding. This is the button to use if you want to remove all the formatting from the text and paste it as just plain text.

- **Paste as Picture.** This command pastes the stuff as a picture that you can format using any of Word's picture tools like color adjustment and shadowing, as described in Chapter 20. You can use this to turn, say, a drawing object into a picture and thus avail yourself of the picture tools.

On the other hand, the Add button takes the selected text, picture, table, or whatever, and transfers it to the Scrapbook. There are four options:

- **Add Selection.** An alternative to the Copy command, this option instantly adds your current selection to the Scrapbook. This is handy if you've highlighted a piece of text—a clever email joke, for example—that you wish to paste into other Office programs.

- **Add File.** Adds the current file to the Scrapbook. It can be any Office document, but remember, there's a one-megabyte limit here.

- **Add From Clipboard.** Pastes whatever is in your clipboard to the Scrapbook.

- **Always Add Copy.** This is a good one for the time-challenged among us. After you click this, anything you copy or cut is pasted directly into the Scrapbook. Pretty cool.

If you have a scrap you no longer need, you can delete it with the delete key or by pressing the Delete button. Three delete options exist on the Delete pop-up menu:

- **Delete.** This choice is the plain, garden-variety delete. It deletes the currently selected clipping.

- **Delete Visible.** Deletes the clipping in the preview window.

- **Delete All.** Deletes all clippings.

Note: When you delete a clipping, it's gone—a part of history. There's no way to get it back. Kind of like the dot-com boom.

Organizing Clippings

If you have a lot of clippings to keep track of—or you're one of those people who sorts their socks by color—you might want to click the Organize title bar. Doing so lets you place the currently selected clipping into categories and projects (by clicking the appropriate pop-up menu and selecting the desired category or project).

You may also add keywords, which is a great idea when you have tons of clippings. Assigning a Keyword allows you to search for the clipping by that word. For example, you might want to add the words, *Christmas*, *apple*, and *uncle*, as keywords for the recipe to your Uncle John's apple pie that he brought to Christmas dinner. To do so, type the words in the box and click Add. Highlighting words and clicking Revert removes them.

Reference Tools

Like a pocket dictionary, Word's built-in Reference Tools are handy, easy to use, and out of the way until you need them. Because it's electronic, it also has some unexpected features. Click the Toolbox, and then the book icon to open the Reference Tools. Below are the most commonly used dictionary features.

To look up a word in a document, highlight the word, and then choose Tools→Dictionary or type the word into the window at the top of the Reference Tools, (If no word is highlighted, you can still click to open the dictionary.) You can also control-click or (and this is a PC-user trick) right-click the word right in your document and choose Look Up→Definition from the shortcut menu.

Now all of the tens of thousands of words in the dictionary are listed in the upper pane of the dictionary window, as shown in Figure 18-6. When you click a word in the upper pane, the definition appears in the Definition pane. Here are some other ways to use the dictionary:

If you began this process with a highlighted word, the Reference Tool opens to that word, or to the most similar Reference Tool entry. When you open the Reference Tool as you're typing, it opens to the word (or word fragment) you've most recently typed.

To go directly to a word, type it in the small box at the top and press Return or click Go! The word list scrolls to match the word, and the lower pane automatically jumps to the current definition. The thesaurus section provides similar words and synonyms. Replace your original word with the selected synonym by clicking Insert. Choosing Look Up provides a definition of the currently selected word.

Searching the Encarta Encyclopedia or MSN provides additional information about the word. This is useful when you want additional information on a word or when the kids are working on a report. Type the word in the upper box and then click Search Encarta Encyclopedia or Search MSN.

All the panes have arrows for scrolling at top and bottom. If you're unsure how a word is spelled, just scroll through the word list until you find it.

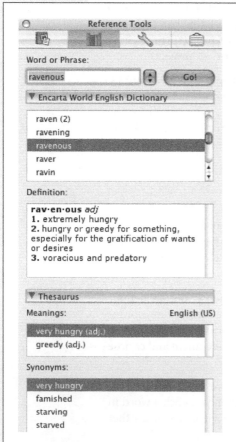

Figure 18-6:
After you type a word into the small box at the top of the Reference Tools, you may click the small flippy triangle next to Thesaurus to browse the synonyms. Type a word, such as Pyramids, *and click Search MSN; Word starts your browser, tools over to MSN, and searches for articles on Pyramids. Same thing for "Search Encarta," but you end up at Encarta.*

You can copy the text of the definition to paste in a Word document, your Scrapbook, email message, and so on. Just drag to select the text in the definition window and then press ⌘-C (or Control-click the definition and choose Copy Article or Copy Selection from the shortcut menu).

Projects Palette

Clicking the Projects Palette button (it looks like a sleek metal briefcase) opens a window into the wonderful world of Projects, a cool new Office 2004 feature extensively covered in Chapter 10. The abbreviated Projects palette available through the Toolbox lets you page through your projects by clicking next to the current project (the small triangle, to be exact), and selecting the project you wish to view from the pop-up menu.

There's also quite a bit more that you can do from this panel, without actually going to the Project Center window. Below the title and picture is a bar that displays when the project is due along with four buttons:

- **Add Current File.** Adds your current file to the list of files in the project.

- **Remove Current File.** Removes current file from the list of files in the project.

- **Open Entourage Project Watch Folder.** Opens the project watch folder in Entourage that is associated with the project.

- **Open Finder Project Watch Folder.** This opens the actual folder where your project watch files are stored.

Below these buttons is the schedule section. This is like a mini-day-by-day calendar. It shows the events relating to your currently selected project. Click the blue star to schedule a new event, and the arrows to click through the days.

The Notes to Self are just that. You can type directly into this box, or drag highlighted text into it. Scroll the text using the scroll bar.

Underneath the schedule are the tasks associated with the project. Double-click any of them to open it. You can click to place a checkmark in the box, in order to celebrate a task's completion. Right-click the task itself, select Priority, and choose one from the shortcut menu. Any changes you make here are reflected in the Project Center itself.

And finally is a list of email messages associated with the project. Double-click to open and read the message in a separate window.

Although you can do a lot from the Toolbox, sometimes you just need the big picture. Click the big "Go to Project Center" button at the bottom of the Projects palette, and Entourage opens to the Project Center—easy as that.

Compatibility Checker

The Compatibility Checker checks to see if the document that you are emailing to your boss will actually open in his ancient copy of Word 97 (for example). The vagaries of document compatibility—even if they were all created in one version of Microsoft Office or another—can be incredibly complex. Sometimes a feature works fine, other times it doesn't. Sometimes a document just looks and works different for no apparent reason. The Compatibility Checker makes it simple to figure out what's going on—and even do something about it.

Note: If you open a document that was created in another program or another version of Office, there probably are compatibility issues. The Toolbox icon on the Standard toolbar throbs when Office detects any incompatibility, even something so minor that you may not notice. Click the icon to open the Toolbox and find out what's going on.

In addition to checking on the current document, you can also utilize this feature to make a document "backwards compatible" to someone with an older version of Office. The Compatibility Report warns you if you're using features that may not work in other versions.

Open the Toolbox, click the wrench icon to open the Compatibility Report panel (or just choose Tools→Compatibility Report), and proceed as follows:

1. **From the "Check compatibility with" pop-up menu, choose the document type with which you want to compare your open document.**

   Office checks your document for compatibility. In a few seconds, it displays a list of potential problems in the top (Results) window. (Click Check Document if the check doesn't begin immediately.)

2. **Click one of the items in the Results window for more information.**

   A fuller explanation appears in the bottom window.

3. **Choose an action.**

   You can click the buttons in the middle of the panel to either Fix or Ignore the error. Sometimes, there is no fix, but Office just wants to explain that some new features may not be available in older documents. If there is something you can do to remedy the problem, such as find the correct document template, the Explanation window often provides a link you can click to go right to work. You can also click on the Help button to get more information.

Just click the Recheck Document button anytime to repeat the process.

Customizing Office

Customizing Your Toolbars

Like Britney Spears, Microsoft desperately wants the approval of its fans—especially its relatively new legion of Mac fans. The Redmond, Washington programmers seem willing to do almost anything to make Office a hit. Its software design seems to subscribe to the theory, "If you don't like something, change it yourself."

Very few elements of the way you work with Office are set in stone. Word, Excel, and PowerPoint each let you redesign the toolbars and even rework the menus. In Word and Excel, you can also choose different keyboard equivalents for commands. (Only Entourage is off-the-rack software. You can't work it over in the same ways.)

Even if you're a novice, customization is worth exploring. There will almost certainly come a day when you wish you could choose an easier function keystroke than the one Microsoft chose. With this chapter as your guide, you can. One way to customize your toolbars is to drag them around the screen and change their shapes to fit your whims (and your monitor shape). To move a toolbar, just drag it, using its skinny title bar (next to the close button) as a handle.

You'll soon discover that toolbars are "magnetic." That is, they like to snap against the sides of the monitor, other toolbars, the Formatting Palette, or to the Office Assistant's window—just about anywhere except an actual document window.

Tip: This snappiness is designed to help you keep your screen tidy, but if you want to stifle your toolbars' social tendencies, press Shift as you drag them.

You can also reshape your toolbar by resizing it as if it were a window: Just drag the diagonally striped area in the lower-right corner, as shown in Figure 19-1.

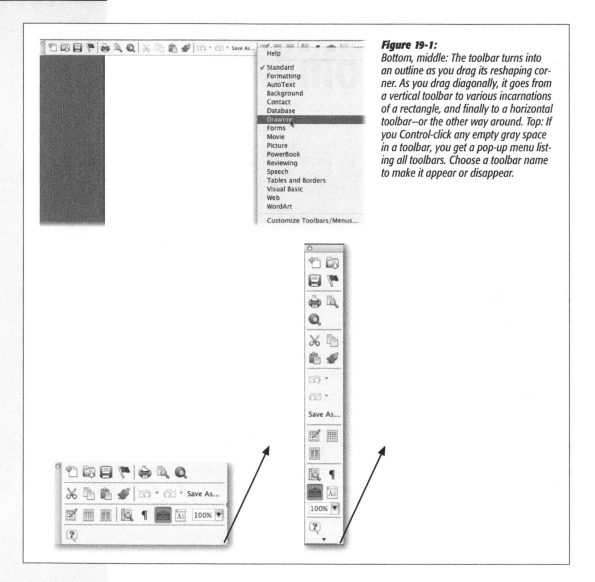

Figure 19-1:
Bottom, middle: The toolbar turns into an outline as you drag its reshaping corner. As you drag diagonally, it goes from a vertical toolbar to various incarnations of a rectangle, and finally to a horizontal toolbar—or the other way around. Top: If you Control-click any empty gray space in a toolbar, you get a pop-up menu listing all toolbars. Choose a toolbar name to make it appear or disappear.

Showing Other Toolbars

Excel, PowerPoint, and Word each come with a toolbar or two that pop up when the program opens, but that's just the beginning. In fact, Word has 31 toolbars, Power-Point has 17, and Excel has 23, each dedicated to a certain purpose (such as graphics work, Web design, or reviewing comments). Some toolbars appear automatically when you use a related command or open a corresponding editing area. Others you can summon or dismiss, as you need them.

You can open and close toolbars in any of three ways:

- Control-click (or right-click) the More Buttons toolbar icon (usually at the far right or bottom edge of an open toolbar or palette), or Control-click (or right-click) an empty area on any open toolbar or palette. As shown in Figure 19-1, you get a pop-up menu of what Microsoft considers to be the most useful toolbars. Choose the name of the one you'd like to open or close.

- Choose from the View→Toolbars submenu. Here again, you see about 23 toolbars.

- Choose Tools→Customize→Customize Toolbars/Menus. Now you see a list of *all* of the toolbars, even the obscure ones. Turn on a checkbox to make the corresponding toolbar appear or disappear instantly. (Because you don't even have to close the dialog box between experiments, this is the fastest way to have a quick look at all the available toolbars.) Click OK to close the dialog box.

Creating Custom Toolbars

The likelihood of Microsoft *perfectly* predicting which buttons you'd like on which toolbars is about the same as finding the wrench you want, the first time you reach into your highly disorganized pile of tools, while laying on your back under the '57 Chevy, with transmission fluid dribbling on your chin. Fortunately, it's very easy to delete or add buttons on Excel, PowerPoint, or Word toolbars—much easier than crawling out from under that Chevy. In fact, you can, and should, create entirely new toolbars that contain nothing but your own favorite buttons. If you use Word's styles, as described on page 137, for example, it's a no-brainer to create a palette of your favorite styles, so that you can apply them with single click.

To move a button or delete it from a toolbar

To move a button, open the Customize dialog box by choosing Tools→Customize→ Customize Toolbars/Menu and then just drag the button to a new spot on the toolbar—or even to another toolbar. (You can ignore the Customize dialog box itself for the moment. Although it seems counterintuitive, the Customize dialog box needs to be open for this dragging to work). The button assumes its new place, and the other buttons rearrange themselves to make room.

To get rid of a button, Control-click the button you wish to remove, and then choose Hide Command from the shortcut menu that appears. If you already have the Customize dialog box open, you can delete a button by dragging it off the toolbar to the desktop or anywhere else in the document window. (Either way, you can get the button back later if you like; read on.)

To add a button or design a new toolbar from scratch

Every now and then, you'll wish you had a one-shot button that triggers some useful command—for inserting the current date into your document, for example.

To add a button to an existing toolbar, choose Tools→Customize→Customize Toolbars/Menu and then click the Commands tab. A list of command categories appears, grouped by menu. Click a category in the left box, and a list of associated commands appears on the right, along with an icon for each command, if one exists. It's a staggeringly long list that includes almost every command in the program.

If you click the All Commands category, you'll notice that the names of Office's commands in the All Commands list are a tad user-hostile. No spaces are allowed, and the name of the command often runs together with the menu that contains it (such as ToolsSpelling). You'll also notice that each of your Office programs offers *hundreds* of commands that don't appear in the regular menus. Furthermore, the names of some commands don't quite correspond to their menu-bar equivalents. For example, the command for Insert→Comment is InsertAnnotation in the All Commands list. So check the menu categories before you resort to the All Commands list.

Tip: Trying to move around quickly in the All Commands category? You can type a letter (or letters) to move to the part of the list beginning with that letter. For instance, type *v* to scroll to commands for viewing or *ins* to jump to commands for inserting.

You can drag *any* of the command icons (and hence the command) in the Customize dialog box onto a toolbar, as shown in Figure 19-2. Some of them even take the form of pop-up menus, such as Font Color, which then become part of your toolbar. In fact, if you drag the command at the bottom of the Categories list called New Menu onto a toolbar, it turns into a pop-up menu that you can fill with any commands you like. You might decide to set up several custom pop-up menus filled with small lists of related styles—one just for headings, for example. The more logical the arrangement, the quicker the access. You can rename your homemade pop-up menu as described in the Tip on the next page.

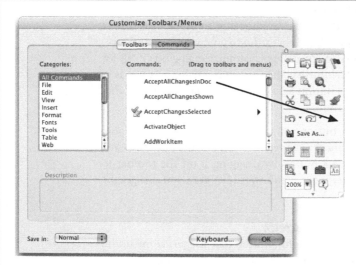

Figure 19-2:
Adding commands to a custom toolbar is as easy as dragging them from the Commands section of the Customize window to the toolbar. Once you let go, feel free to drag it or its toolbar-mates around into a more pleasing arrangement, or drag the lower-right corner of the toolbar to reshape it.

Weirder yet, look at the top of your screen—there's a *duplicate menu bar* there, floating on its own toolbar! Click one of these phony menus to open it. Now you can drag any menu command *right off the menu* onto your new toolbar, where it will be available for quicker access. Once buttons are on the toolbar, you can drag them around, or even drag them off the toolbar to get rid of them, as long as you don't close the Customize dialog box.

Tip: If you double-click a toolbar button or pop-up menu while the Customize dialog box is open, you summon the Command Properties dialog box. Here's where you get to specify how you want the command to look in the toolbar: as a little icon, as a plain English word, or both (see the box below). You can also add a separator line before the button (above it or to its left) by turning on "Begin a group."

You can even perform this kind of button editing when the Customize window *isn't* open—in the middle of your everyday work. The trick is to Control-click the button and choose Properties from the shortcut menu.

Designing a completely new toolbar works much the same way. Choose Tools→ Customize→Customize Toolbars/Menus, select the Toolbars tab, and then click the New button. You'll be asked to name your new toolbar, which then appears as an empty square floating oddly above the Customize dialog box—a toolbar just waiting for you to provide commands. Now click the Commands tab and begin populating your new toolbar with commands and buttons, just as described earlier. Click OK when you're finished.

OBSESSIVE USERS' CLINIC

Drawing Your Own Buttons

Not all commands that you drag onto your toolbars come with associated picture buttons (Save As is a good example). Most of the time, all you get is a text button. If you'd prefer an icon, though, you can add one.

The trick is to Control-click the new button and choose the Properties command. You get the Command Properties dialog box, shown here, where you see a little blank button icon in the upper-left corner. Click the pop-up menu attached to find 42 alterative button icons vying for your affection. If one of Microsoft's ready-made buttons

will do, choose it from this pop-up menu.

If you don't care for any of Microsoft's microscopic masterpieces, you can design your own button in some other program (Photoshop or AppleWorks, let's say). Copy it, switch to the Office program you're editing, and then paste the graphic onto a button by choosing Paste Button Image from the menu. Microsoft recommends a 20 x 20 pixel image for maximum good looks. To restore the button's original icon (or lack of icon), choose Reset Button Image at the bottom of the menu.

Attaching Custom Toolbars to Documents

In Word, a toolbar you've created or edited is stored in the Normal template (see page 232), so that it will be available for use in any new documents you create. But after spending 20 minutes handcrafting the world's most brilliant toolbar, the last thing you want is to confine it forever to your own Mac.

Fortunately, you can pass on your brilliance to other people just by attaching the custom toolbar to an Excel workbook or Word document (PowerPoint lacks this feature).

- **In Excel.** Choose Tools→Customize, then click the Toolbars tab. Click a toolbar's name in the pane on the left side of the Customize window, and then click Attach.

  The Attach Toolbars window appears. It works exactly like the Organizer, described and illustrated on page 230. Use it to select the destination document and copy the toolbar into it.

- **In Word.** Choose Tools→Templates and Add-Ins. Click the Organizer button. Use the Organizer described on page 230 to copy any toolbar into any document *or* template.

Note: When you open a Word document in which someone has embedded a homemade toolbar, a dialog box offers a word of caution. It lets you know that the toolbar could conceivably contain a macro virus (see page 595).

Redesigning Your Menus

Not only can you build your own toolbars in Excel, PowerPoint, and Word, you can also twist and shape the *menus* of these programs to suit your schemes. You can add and remove menu items from the various menus, and you can even move the menus themselves so that they appear in different places on the menu bar.

More than one Excel owner, for example, has found happiness by stripping out over half of the default commands that he found he never used. Conversely, you're missing out in Word if you don't *add* commands to the menus that you usually need to trigger by burrowing through nested dialog boxes.

As noted earlier, choosing Tools→Customize→Customize Toolbars/Menus doesn't just open the Customize dialog box. It also opens a strange-looking *duplicate* menu bar just beneath the real one. If you click a menu name on this Menu Bar "toolbar," the menu opens, revealing all of the commands in that menu.

Adding a command

To add a command to a menu, choose Tools→Customize→Customize Toolbars/Menus, and click the Commands tab. Find the command that you want to add (by clicking the appropriate category on the left side first, for example). Then drag the command out of the Commands list and straight onto the *name* of the desired menu (on the *duplicate* menu bar), as shown in Figure 19-3.

Note: Excel has *two* menu bars—a Worksheet Menu Bar and a Chart Menu Bar. They're listed individually in the Customize dialog box's Toolbars tab. That's because Excel's Data menu changes into a Chart menu when a chart is selected. These menu bars are independent, so if you make changes to the Insert menu item on the Chart Menu Bar toolbar, those changes *won't* be reflected in the Insert menu item on the Worksheet Menu Bar.

As you drag your command over the duplicate menu, the menu opens automatically. As you drag down the menu, a line shows you where the new command will appear when you release the mouse.

Tip: You can even rename your newly installed menu command. Open the duplicate menu bar, then double-click your command to open the Command Properties dialog box. Type the new name and press Return.

Removing a menu command

Suppose that you never use the Dictionary command in Excel's Tools menu; the only word *you* need to know is "Profit."

Getting rid of a menu command—whether you put it on the menu or not—is easy. Choose Tools→Customize→Customize Toolbars/Menus to summon the strange duplicate menu bar shown in Figure 19-3. Now click the menu title (in the duplicate menu bar) that contains the offending command. Finally, drag the command itself off the menu.

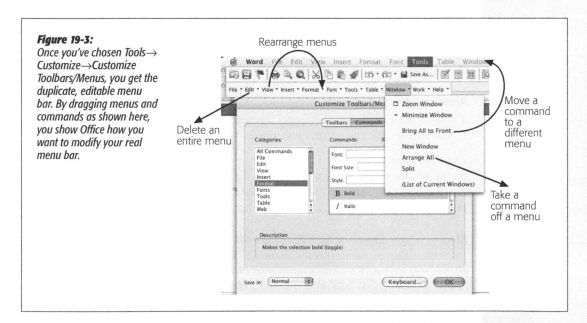

Figure 19-3:
Once you've chosen Tools→ Customize→Customize Toolbars/Menus, you get the duplicate, editable menu bar. By dragging menus and commands as shown here, you show Office how you want to modify your real menu bar.

Rearrange menus

Delete an entire menu

Move a command to a different menu

Take a command off a menu

Tip: In Word only, there's a faster way to remove a menu command, one that doesn't even involve the Customize dialog box. Start by pressing Option-⌘-hyphen (on the main keyboard, not the number pad). The cursor is now "loaded," as reflected by its status as a big, bold – sign. Now just *choose* the menu command you want to nuke, using the regular menus. When you release the mouse, the command is gone, and your cursor returns to normal.

Removing commands from menus doesn't delete them from the program, of course. To restore a command you've removed from a menu, reinstall it as described in the previous section.

Adding a menu

You can do more than just add commands to existing menus. You can also create completely *new* menus, name them whatever you please, and fill them with any commands you like, in any order you like. This feature opens up staggering possibilities of customization: You can create a stripped-down "just the commands you really need" menu for an absolute novice, for example, or build a menu of your macros.

To do so, choose Tools→Customize→Customize Toolbars/Menus, click the Commands tab, scroll to the bottom of the Categories list, and click New Menu. Drag the New Menu command from the Commands list (right side of the window) to the Menu Bar toolbar. Put it anywhere you want—between the File and Edit menus, for example, or to the right of the Help menu.

With the new menu still selected, Control-click your new menu and choose Properties from the shortcut menu (or click the Modify Selection button in the Customize dialog box). Type a name for your new menu into the Name field. Finally, press Return. (Control-clicking also offers the Begin Group command, which inserts a separator line into your menu-under-construction.)

Your new menu is installed. Now you can add to it any commands you want, using the same technique described in "Adding a command," on page 674.

Removing a menu

You don't have to stare at Microsoft's complex menus if you rarely use one of them. If you never use tables in Word, for example, by all means get rid of the Table menu.

Doing so couldn't be easier. Choose Tools→Customize to make the phantom double menu bar appear. Point to the name of the menu you no longer need and drag it directly downward and off the menu bar. Once it's gone, the other menus close up to fill its space. (Never fear: You can always bring it back, as described below.)

Moving whole menus, or specific commands

Even the order of menus on the menu bar isn't sacrosanct in Office 2004. If it occurs to you that perhaps the Fonts menu should come before the Edit menu, choose Tools→Customize→Customize Toolbars/Menus. Now you can start dragging around the menu titles themselves (on the duplicate menu bar) until you've reached an arrangement that you like.

While you're at it, you can also drag individual commands from menu to menu. As shown in Figure 19-3, start by choosing Tools→Customize→Customize Toolbars/Menus. Then bring the menu command to the screen by opening its current menu in the duplicate menu bar. Now drag the command to the *name* of a new menu, which opens automatically; without releasing the mouse, drag downward until the command is positioned where you want it. Finally, release the mouse button.

Resetting everything back to normal

When you delete a command, it's not gone from Office. You've merely removed it from its menu or toolbar, and it's easy enough to put it back—a handy fact to remember when you've made a mess of your menus through overzealous exploration.

Open the Customize window (by choosing Tools→Customize→Customize Toolbars/Menus). Click the Toolbars tab. In the list at left, click Menu Bar, and then click Reset. You've just restored your menus and commands to their original, factory-fresh condition.

Tip: You can use this technique to reset any of the factory toolbars, too. On the Tools→Customize→Toolbars tab, just turn on the checkbox next to the toolbar you want to restore, and then click Reset.

Reassigning Key Combinations

Pressing an equally staggering number of keyboard shortcuts can trigger a staggering number of Office commands. The only problem arises when you discover that Microsoft has chosen something bizarre (like Option-⌘-R for Thesaurus) instead of something more natural (like ⌘-T).

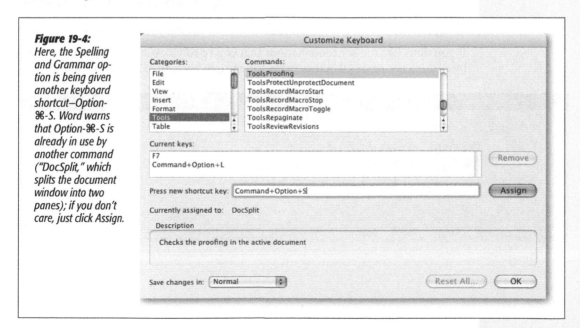

Figure 19-4:
Here, the Spelling and Grammar option is being given another keyboard shortcut–Option-⌘-S. Word warns that Option-⌘-S is already in use by another command ("DocSplit," which splits the document window into two panes); if you don't care, just click Assign.

The good news is that you can reassign key combinations for any menu command—in Word and Excel, anyway. You can't fiddle with the keyboard commands in PowerPoint or Entourage.

To begin, choose Tools→Customize→Customize Keyboard. In the Customize dialog box, click the Keyboard button.

Now the Customize Keyboard window appears (see Figure 19-4). It works much like the toolbar-editing dialog box described earlier in this chapter. At left, click a command category; at right, click the name of the command you want to reassign. (After clicking or tabbing into one of these lists, you can jump to a particular category or command by typing the first couple letters of its name.)

After highlighting the command for which you'd like to change or add a key combination, click in the box beneath the "Press new shortcut key" field. Now press the keys you'd like to use as the new key combo, using any combination of the Shift, c, Option, and Control keys, along with a letter, F-key, or number key.

If that keystroke already "belongs" to another command in the Office 2004 program you're using, the Customize dialog box shows you which command has it (Figure 19-4). To reassign that keystroke to the new command anyway, click the Assign button. To keep the current setting, press Delete, and then try another keystroke.

Obviously, you can't have two commands linked to a single keystroke. However, you *can* create more than one keyboard shortcut for a single command. For instance, in Word 2004, both ⌘-B and Shift-⌘-B are assigned to Bold.

Tip: If you find yourself frequently triggering a command *accidentally,* you may want to *remove* its assigned keystroke. To do so, click the command name in the list, highlight the keystroke in the "Current keys" list, and then click the Remove button. Click OK to save the changes.

If you don't like the key combinations that you've edited, you can always reset them by clicking the Reset All button in the lower-right portion of the dialog box.

GEM IN THE ROUGH

Faster Keyboard Reassignment in Word

Word offers a shortcut for assigning a keyboard shortcut to a menu. Press Option-⌘ and the + sign on your numeric keypad (at the right side of your keyboard). The mouse pointer changes into a large ⌘ symbol.

Now click the toolbar button, or choose the menu command, for which you want to set up a keystroke. A special keyboard-reassignment box appears, looking something like the one in Figure 19-4. Just press the keystroke you want as described above. There–you've just saved yourself several steps.

The Graphics Programs of Office

O ffice comes with Word for text, Excel for numbers, PowerPoint for slides, and Entourage for email and scheduling. From reading the box, you might conclude that Office is therefore missing one of the cornerstone Macintosh programs: graphics software.

In fact, however, Office comes with a minor army of graphics tools, including the Clip Gallery, AutoShapes, WordArt, and more—built right in and shared among Word, Excel, and PowerPoint.

Inserting a Graphic

You can drag, paste, or insert a picture into a Word, Excel, or PowerPoint document. To insert a graphic, choose Insert→Picture or click the Insert Picture button on the Drawing toolbar (in Entourage chose Message→Insert→Picture) and then select one of the following from the submenu:

- **Clip Art** opens the Office Clip Gallery, as described below.

- **From File** opens a dialog box where you can choose any graphics file on your Mac.

- **Horizontal Line** (Word only) is a quick way to put a horizontal line between paragraphs without opening the Borders and Shading dialog box. These lines are actually GIF files. They're more decorative than standard lines and borders, and ideal for use on Web sites (see Chapter 8).

- **AutoShapes** are an expanded, elaborate version of the familiar circles and squares that you create with drawing tools. For instance, AutoShapes include arrows, cubes, banners, and speech balloons.

- **WordArt** allows you to change the look of text in a number of wacky, attention-getting ways. After typing the text, you can stretch, color, and distort it, using Office's drawing tools (page 684).

- **From Scanner or Camera** lets you import directly from one of these devices connected to your Mac—sometimes. Its success depends on your model of digital camera or scanner.

The Clip Gallery

Clip art refers to a canned collection of professionally drawn, cartoonlike illustrations designed for use in a wide variety of documents. Designing a birthday card for a child? You can count on finding a soccer ball or kite in any self-respecting clip-art collection. Need a sketch of people at the office for a newsletter article about business travel? Off you go to the clip-art collection.

Fortunately, Office comes with about 200 pieces of ready-to-use art in a collection called the Clip Gallery. To review them, choose Insert→Picture→Clip Art. The Clip Gallery opens, as shown in Figure 20-1. (Clicking the Insert Clip Art button near the middle of the Drawing toolbar opens it, too.)

Note: In Entourage, you get a Choose a File dialog box instead of the Clip Gallery. You must actually browse over to the Applications→Microsoft Office 2004→Clipart folder in order to select your clip art.

UP TO SPEED

Pictures and Drawings

There are two distinct kinds of graphics in the computer world, which, in Office, are known as pictures and drawings.

Pictures include bitmap files, raster graphics, painting files, JPEG or GIF images, photographs, anything scanned or captured with a digital camera, anything grabbed from a Web page, and Office clip art. What all pictures have in common is that (a) they're composed of individual, tiny colored dots, and (b) you can't create them using the tools built into Office. You *can* make pictures larger or smaller, but if you stretch something larger than its original size, it might look blotchy.

Drawings include AutoShapes, Word Art, and any graphics you create using Office's own drawing tools. Drawings, also known as vector or object-oriented graphics, are stored by the Mac as mathematical equations that describe their size, shape, and other characteristics. That's a fancy way of saying that you can resize, rotate, squish, or squeeze drawings as much as you like without ever worrying that they'll print jagged or blotchy.

Keeping these distinctions in mind might help you understand why your Office programs function like they do when you work with graphics.

Categories

The Categories button in the Clip Gallery window opens a dialog box where you can delete categories from, or add categories to, the Clip Gallery. Neither process deletes or adds any actual pictures; they stay where they always were—in the Microsoft Office 2004→Clipart folder. You're just deleting or adding category names into which the pictures can reside.

Figure 20-1:
Click a category in the list at the left to see thumbnails of the available clips, one of which is Search Results (after you've done a keyword search, as shown here). Click a thumbnail and then click Insert (or just double-click the thumbnail) to place the full-size version in your document. (Turn on the Preview box to see the full-size image in a separate window.) You then have to click Close to ditch the dialog box.

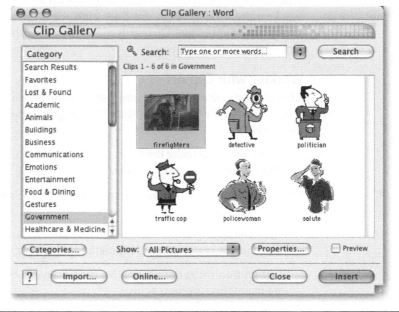

Online

If you click the Online button, Office asks your permission to launch your Web browser and connect to the Microsoft Design Gallery Live Web site, which offers thousands of additional clip-art files in a searchable database. You can download them individually or in groups by turning on their boxes.

Adding Your Own Clips

You're not limited to clip art from Microsoft. Not only can you transfer your own images into any Word document with the Insert→From File command, but you can also make them part of the Clip Gallery. This gives you the opportunity to use the Clip Gallery's search function and organizing features and see thumbnails of your own clip art, too. (iPhoto it ain't, but this feature can be handy.)

To do so, choose Insert→Picture→Clip Art to open the Clip Gallery; click Import. Use the Open window in the Import dialog box to navigate on your Mac to the graphics files that you want to bring into the Clip Gallery. (Make sure the Show menu shows "Clip Gallery Images"; the kinds of images you can import are JPEG, TIFF, PICT, GIF, PNG, or Photoshop files, as well as clip art from Microsoft.)

Deleting Clips

If you want a clip out of your life forever, click it in the Clip Gallery and choose Edit→ Clear. Word asks for confirmation before nuking it.

Search

When you enter a word in the Search box at the top of the Clip Gallery and click Search, Word finds all the clips that match (or are related to) that keyword. For instance, if you type in *automobile*, Word pulls up all the clips that have "automobile" as a keyword. Cooler yet, it also finds clips with "car" or "vehicle" as keywords—it relies on the Office 2004 Thesaurus to figure out which possible keywords mean the same thing as what you typed!

Working with Clip Art

After placing a piece of clip art into your document, you can click it to produce eight tiny square handles at its perimeter. By dragging these handles, you can resize the illustration in a variety of ways:

- **Drag** a handle to resize the figure in that dimension—drag the top one to make it taller, a side one to make it wider, and so on.

- **Shift-dragging** a corner handle keeps an object in its original proportions as you resize it.

- **Option-dragging** any handle resizes the object from the center outward in the direction you're dragging. (This method does not maintain proportion.)

- **Shift-Option-dragging** a corner handle resizes an object from the center outward *and* maintains its proportions.

- **⌘-dragging** any handle overrides the *drawing grid* (see page 686).

You can also move a graphic around the screen by dragging it freely.

AutoShapes and WordArt

There are two kinds of drawings in Word: those you make yourself using Word's drawing tools (see page 684), and those Word makes for you, through features such as AutoShapes and WordArt.

AutoShapes

An AutoShape is a ready-made drawing object. As with the simple circle, square, and triangle of times past, you simply drag to size and place them in your document. However, you now have many more choices courtesy of Office 2004.

To use an AutoShape in your document, click the AutoShapes button on the Drawing toolbar. (If it's not already open, choose View→Toolbars→Drawing. Or, if you can't get enough of that genie effect, click the Drawing button on the Standard toolbar.)

As shown in Figure 20-2, each AutoShape menu provides a palette of choices. Click one, then release the mouse; now drag in your document to place the AutoShape—you can always resize or move it later.

Tip: As you drag to create an AutoShape, press Shift to keep the shape in equal length-to-height proportion. For instance, select the rectangle shape and Shift-drag to create a square, or select the oval and Shift-drag to create a perfect circle. As noted earlier, you can also press Shift when dragging to resize such an object without distorting its original proportions.

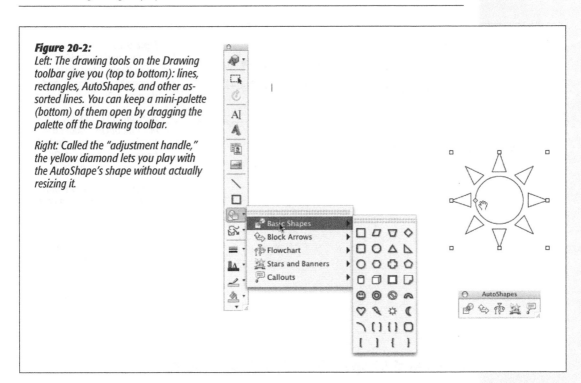

Figure 20-2:
Left: The drawing tools on the Drawing toolbar give you (top to bottom): lines, rectangles, AutoShapes, and other assorted lines. You can keep a mini-palette (bottom) of them open by dragging the palette off the Drawing toolbar.

Right: Called the "adjustment handle," the yellow diamond lets you play with the AutoShape's shape without actually resizing it.

WordArt

Like an AutoShape, a piece of WordArt is a type of ready-made drawing object. In this case, it's used for special text effects—3-D, wavy, slanting, colored, and various other permutations—that would be just right on a movie poster (but should be used sparingly in other situations). Figure 20-3 illustrates some examples.

To create some WordArt, choose Insert→Picture→WordArt. (Alternatively, you can click the Insert WordArt button on the Drawing toolbar, which looks like a three-dimensional A.) Then proceed as shown in Figure 20-3.

When you click a piece of WordArt, the WordArt toolbar appears (Figure 20-3, lower right). Most of its tools take you to dialog boxes for formatting WordArt. Clicking Edit Text takes you back to the Edit WordArt dialog box; double-clicking the WordArt itself does the same thing. There are also buttons for the WordArt Gallery and the Format→WordArt dialog box.

The bottom row contains tools—spacing and alignment, for example—that format the actual text of your WordArt. The most powerful button here is the second one, Vertical Text, which takes the WordArt and strings it downward, so that one letter appears below the other. Clicking the first one, Same Letter Heights, stretches the nonascending and descending letters of the selected WordArt so that all letters line up, top and bottom.

Figure 20-3:
Top left: In the WordArt Gallery, choose a text design that strikes your fancy, and then click OK.

Top right: In the dialog box that opens, choose a typeface, then type your text banner message; click OK when you're finished.

Lower left: Your new WordArt instantly appears in your document.

Lower right: The WordArt toolbar. If you can't find the WordArt toolbar, it's probably not open. Click a WordArt object or choose View→Toolbars→WordArt.

Lines and Shapes: The Drawing Toolbar

Even with the immense variety of AutoShapes and WordArt, some days you just need to unleash your creative spirit. With Office's drawing tools, you can draw free-form lines and shapes and combine them with arrows and AutoShapes to build your own masterpieces.

To get started, summon the Drawing toolbar by choosing View→Toolbars→Drawing, or by right-clicking on the line dividing the toolbars and then selecting Drawing. Click the Line, Rectangle, or Lines toolbar icon, as shown in Figure 20-4. Choose a line type from the Line Style pop-up menu; then drag in your document to place the line, rectangle, or shape you've selected from the Lines pop-up button. (As with AutoShapes and WordArt, lines lie *on top of* text in Word—and are invisible in Normal view—unless you wrap them around the text, as described on page 156.)

If you've opted for the Lines tool, you'll find that each of the options in its pop-up button menu works a bit differently:

- **Line.** Drag for the position and length of the straight line you want; the cursor turns into a tiny cross. To resize the newly drawn line, drag the handles on each side, or reposition it by dragging the line itself (at which time the cursor turns into a hand).

Figure 20-4:
When a toolbar menu has a strip of dotted lines at the top, you can drag it off the toolbar (left) to create a floating palette (right). The Lines palette contains tools for straight lines, arrows, double arrows, curved lines, free-form shapes, and scribbled lines.

- **Arrow** and **double arrow** work just like lines. When you draw a single arrow, the point appears where you stop dragging; a double arrow automatically springs points on both sides.

- **Curve.** Unlike lines, you draw curves by clicking, not dragging. Click to create a starting point; as you move the mouse, the curve follows. When you click a second time, the line gently curves from the first point to the second. Continue in this same manner. (The curve tool works best for wiggles and waves rather than closed shapes.) When you're done, double-click to finish off the curve. To enclose the shape, click as close as you can to your starting point.

- The **Freeform** tool is a two-in-one special. When you drag with it, the cursor turns into a pencil and works like a pencil—you can draw lines with any bend and direction without the limitations of the Curve tool. The instant you let go of the mouse button, the cursor turns into a cross and becomes a line tool. Clicking the mouse again now draws a straight line, just as with the Line tool. Hold down the mouse button again to go back to freehand drawing. (Nobody ever promised that Office would be a simple program!)

- The **Scribble** tool is like Freeform without the straight-line feature. You drag it to draw a freehand line; the line ends when you let go of the mouse button.

Editing Drawn Objects

To change the color and thickness of lines and the shapes you've drawn, use the Line formatting tools on the Formatting Palette or Drawing toolbar. Here are some of the other options on the Drawing toolbar or, if you Control-click the object, the shortcut menu:

- **Edit Points.** Don't worry if your line or drawn object doesn't come out perfect on the first try. Just do the best you can, and then select the shape and choose Edit Points from the Draw pop-up menu at the top of the Drawing toolbar (or from the shortcut menu). You can then drag the little black dots to resize and reshape the line. This trick is especially useful for the Curve, Freeform, and Scribble tools.

- **Open Curve.** This unusual command (available on the shortcut menu only) "disconnects" the point where you closed a Curve, Freeform, or Scribble object. Now you can use the edit points to reshape the object. Should you ever want to close the gap again, Control-click the shape again and choose Close Curve.

- **Nudge.** Although you can always move a picture or drawing object by dragging with the mouse, your hand movements on the mouse may not be precise enough. Fortunately, Office offers finer control.

  To give your object a more controlled nudge, click the pop-up menu triangle at the end of the drawing toolbar and choose Nudge→Up, Down, Left, or Right. If you've got Snap to Grid turned on (see below), you'll nudge the object one gridline at a time. If Snap to Grid is turned off, each nudge moves the object only one pixel at a time. Of course, it's far less effort to simply tap the arrow keys, which also moves a selected object one pixel at a time.

Aligning Drawn Objects

When you have multiple drawing objects on a page, you may want them to be equally spaced or evenly aligned by their top edges. Instead of working out the measurements and aligning them yourself, use Office's built-in alignment features.

To do so, select the objects that you need to line up or arrange (Shift-click each one). Then choose one of the following options from the Align or Distribute menu of the Draw pop-up button (on the Drawing toolbar). Use the tiny icons on this menu as a visual clue to their functions.

- **Align Left, Center, or Right.** These commands bring the selected objects into perfect vertical alignment by their left or right edges, or centerlines.

- **Align Top, Middle, or Bottom.** These commands bring the selected objects into perfect *horizontal* alignment by their top or bottom edges, or centerlines.

- **Distribute Horizontally or Vertically.** Use these commands to spread your drawing objects across the page or from top to bottom—with an equal amount of space between each one.

You can also use the above commands on a single object, to place it at either side or in the center of a page.

The Drawing grid

Even without using the alignment commands, you might have noticed that it's fairly easy to pull objects into alignment with one another just by dragging. That's because each Word page has an invisible alignment grid that objects "snap to," as if pulled into line by a magnetic force.

To see the grid, choose Draw→Grid on the Drawing toolbar. Turn on "Display gridlines on screen" in the Drawing Grid dialog box, specify a gridline separation in the "Horizontal every" box (and the "Vertical every" box too, if you like), and then click OK. Now you can see the grid's faint gray lines superimposed on your document.

Note: In Excel, the gridlines are the cell boundaries themselves. You can either snap to these gridlines or "To Shape" (see "Snap objects to other objects," below).

Now that you know what the grid looks like, here's how to use it:

- To turn the grid off so that you can drag objects around with no spatial restriction whatsoever, turn off the "Snap objects to grid" box.

Tip: When the grid is turned off, ⌘-drag an object when you *do* want it to snap to the grid. Conversely, when the grid is turned on, ⌘-dragging a graphic moves it exactly where you put it, *without* snapping to the grid.

- You can use the "Snap objects to other objects" box with or without snapping to the grid. When this box is turned on, a dragged object snaps into alignment with the edges of the closest nearby object. If the grid is on, the nearest object overrides the grid.

- Change the default grid spacing (an eighth of an inch) by changing the measurements in the "Grid settings" boxes.

Click OK to apply the grid changes to your document.

Rotating drawing objects

You can rotate drawing objects in either of two ways: freely with the mouse, or in precise 90-degree increments.

- To Free Rotate, click the object, and then click the rotation tool (a curved-around arrow) on the Drawing toolbar. The handles on the object become green dots. Drag any dot to rotate the object on its own axis. The object jumps into its new orientation when you let go of the mouse button. (*Option*-drag to rotate the object on its end instead.)

- To rotate in 90-degree increments, click the object, and then choose Draw→Rotate or Flip→Rotate Left or Rotate Right on the Drawing toolbar. Repeat the process to continue rotating the object a quarter turn at a time.

- To flip a selected drawing object, choose Draw→Rotate or Flip→Flip Horizontal or Flip Vertical on the Drawing toolbar. Flip Horizontal reverses the object from side to side; Flip Vertical turns it head-over-heels.

Formatting Pictures and Drawings

Once you've placed a graphic into a document, you can touch it up in a number of ways, from fixing a scanned photo to fattening up an arrow you've drawn.

Microsoft offers these image tools in triplicate, just to make sure you can't miss them.

- **The Formatting Palette.** When you click a picture or drawing, whichever sections you're used to seeing there (Font, Borders and Shading, and so on) are replaced by an arsenal of graphics controls (Fill, Line, Size, and so on).

- **The Drawing or Picture toolbar.** This toolbar appears on your screen whenever you click a graphic of the corresponding type. The formatting controls available to you are different for each kind of graphic (*drawing* or *picture;* see page 680).

Note: In Word the Picture toolbar doesn't appear when the Formatting Palette is open. Just this once, Microsoft is saving you a scrap of redundancy. It does, however, appear in Excel and PowerPoint.

- **The Format dialog box.** When you *double-click* a drawing or picture in Word or Excel, this massive, multitab dialog box appears (see Figure 20-5). Its various panes let you specify every conceivable aspect of the selected graphic.

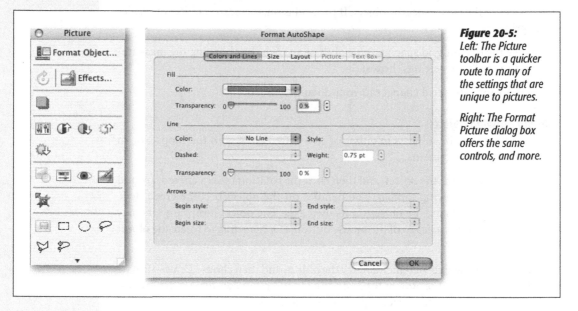

Figure 20-5:
Left: The Picture toolbar is a quicker route to many of the settings that are unique to pictures.

Right: The Format Picture dialog box offers the same controls, and more.

The following discussion focuses on the Format dialog box, since it's the most complete. Most of the choices described in this section also appear, however, in the Formatting Palette and the appropriate toolbar.

Colors and Lines Tab

On this tab of the Format dialog box, you can specify a color, picture, or pattern that will fill in the interior of your picture or drawing.

Note: The Colors and Lines tab is designed to fill in the background of *drawing objects* and *Office clip art.* It generally has no effect on other kinds of pictures.

Fill Color: Standard palette

Office comes with a standard palette of 40 colors, which you can access from all kind of places, like the Drawing toolbar and the Formatting Palette (see Figure 3-3, for example). Click the color you want to apply it.

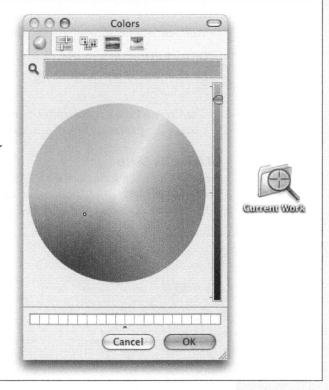

Figure 20-6:
The Colors dialog box offers five color pickers. They're all easy to use, especially the Color Wheel shown here. Click the magnifying glass in the upper-left corner, then move it anywhere on the spectrum wheel and click to choose the color you see in the middle of the "glass." You can even move it anywhere on your Mac's screen—even over, say, a Web-browser window or a desktop icon—and click any color that strikes your fancy. The picker "captures" whichever color you click on, even the clear, delicate blue of a Mac OS X desktop folder.

Fill Color: More Colors

If none of the 40 meets with your artistic standards, choose More Colors from the Fill Color pop-up menu. This opens the Mac OS X color picker, which offers five different ways to select almost any color in existence. First of all, you can choose any color that you currently see on the monitor, like a sample from your desktop picture, by clicking the "magnifying glass" icon, and then clicking anywhere onscreen, as discussed in Figure 20-6.

The five square buttons at the top of the color picker reveal different panels, each of which provides a unique way to see and even blend colors. Choose the one that best matches how you're used to looking at color. Here are the various color pickers you can try:

- On the **Color Wheel** panel, you can click anywhere in the circle to choose a color from the spectrum. Use the slide on the right to make the hues brighter or darker.

- The **Color Sliders** panel gives you access to traditional color systems, like CYMK, which lets you blend the ink color used in the printing business—Cyan, Yellow, Magenta, and Black. Choose your favorite color system from the pop-up menu near the top of the panel.

- The **Color Palettes** panel lets you choose, from the pop-up menu, lists of color swatches such as Apple's standard palette or the set of colors that you can use on Web pages. Scroll through the list and click your desired color.

- **Image Palettes** lets you select colors from the spectrum in the big square on the panel. You can also choose to import a graphics file into the square and then pick from it, too.

- The **Crayon Picker** is the simplest one to use—as easy as picking a crayon out of a box. (The names are lots of fun, too.)

Fill Color: Fill Effects

If you choose Fill Effects from the Fill Color pop-up menu, you get the secret dialog box shown in Figure 20-7. It offers four tabs of its own, each offering a dramatic way to fill in the background of the selected drawing object.

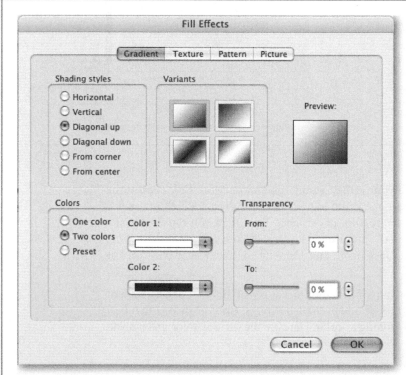

Figure 20-7:
Clicking the Colors radio buttons on the Gradient tab lets you use any of Word's color-picking tools to choose the colors to apply to the gradient effects. The Preset choice gives you a list of preinstalled custom color combinations with poetic names such as Late Sunset and Fog. The Transparency sliders add transparency to either end of the gradient effect.

- For example, the **Gradient** tab lets you apply smoothly shifting colors within the interior of the drawing object—for rainbowlike, shimmery effects. Use the top controls to specify the colors you want to shift from and to; use the bottom controls to indicate the direction of shifting. And because you're in the world of Office 2004, you can apply transparency to the gradient colors by using the sliders at the lower right.

- The **Texture** tab is your personal Home Depot for marble, granite, burlap, and other building materials. When you need to dress up, say, a title or heading by "mounting it" on a stately, plaque-like rectangle, these squares are just the ticket. (Click Other Texture to choose a graphics file on your Mac that you'd like to use instead as a tiled, repeating background pattern.)

- The **Pattern** tab offers a variety of two-color patterns. Using the pop-up menus at the bottom of the dialog box, you can specify which is the dark color and which is the light one.

- Finally, when you click the **Picture** tab, you'll find no pictures to choose from—at first. Click Select Picture to choose any picture file on your Mac, including but not limited to Office clip art. Click Insert to bring the picture into the Picture tab, where you can see what it will look like. Click OK to use the picture as a fill for your drawing object.

Transparency

This slider, found on the Colors and Lines tab and the Formatting Palette, changes whatever color you've chosen into a transparent version. The text or objects layered above or below it remain visible through the color, courtesy of Mac OS X's Quartz graphics technology.

Line pop-up menus (drawing objects only)

In the Line section of the Colors and Lines tab, you can choose colors, dash and dot patterns, styles (single, double, and so on), weight or thickness, and transparency. All of it applies to the lines that constitute the selected drawing. (*Weight* is measured to the nearest .25 point.)

As you'll soon discover, this option is dimmed for picture objects like clip art and digital photos.

Pick Line Color/Pick Fill Color

Choosing this eyedropper tool on the line or fill color *palettes* (not the Format dialog box) lets you click to pick a color anywhere on your Mac's screen. It can be in any open window, such as a Web page in your browser. When you click a color with the eyedropper, the line or fill takes on that color to match. That color is then added to the bottom of all Office color palettes for your future use.

Arrows (drawing objects only)

If you've drawn a simple line (as opposed to an enclosed shape), you can add an arrowhead to one or both ends, using the Arrow controls here.

Size Tab

While you can always resize a picture right in your document by dragging its handles, the Size tab offers other invaluable features. For example:

- **Height, Width.** These boxes let you specify precise measurements for the height and width of your drawing object, in hundredths of an inch.

- **Rotation.** This option lets you rotate a drawing object (not a picture) to any angle.

- **Scale.** These controls let you enlarge or shrink a selected graphic by a specified percentage. (If you turn on **Lock aspect ratio** before adjusting size, the drawing's original height-to-width proportions remain the same. The **Relative to original picture size** box applies only to pictures, not drawings; it lets you use the boxes in the Scale section to change the picture's size by a percentage of the original size. Thus, by changing the percentage to 200, you can double a picture's size without calculating the exact measurements.)

Tip: Making bitmapped images (like digital photos) *larger* than they originally appear is a recipe for blotchiness. Simply stated, you can't have more dots per inch than the image's original resolution. And if you intend to print such graphics, be aware that their standard screen resolution, 72 dots per inch, isn't fine enough to produce high-quality prints. For that purpose, use digital images of 150 dots per inch or higher.

- **Reset.** Word remembers the original size and aspect ratio (proportion of height to width). Click this button to restore the picture to its original size and shape, no matter how much you've played with it. (This option isn't applicable to drawings.)

Picture Tab (Picture Objects Only)

The tools on the **Picture** tab, as shown in Figure 20-5, provide a great deal of control over how your image looks. For example:

- Use the **Crop from** boxes to specify, in hundredths of an inch, how much you'd like to trim off each side of a picture. (There's a crop tool on the Picture toolbar, of course, but it doesn't permit this kind of numerical accuracy.)

- The **Color** menu lets you turn your color graphic into grayscale, black and white, or watermark. (The watermark setting produces an extremely faint image, light enough that you can still read text that flows over it.

  These choices affect only the image itself, not the fill. You adjust the fill on the Colors and Lines tab as described above.

- **Brightness and Contrast** are mainly useful for touching up photographs, but they do affect clip art and other images. Increase brightness and contrast for a crisper look; decrease them for a softer effect.

If you change your mind about anything you've done to a picture, remember you can undo your changes one by one by choosing the Edit→Undo command. Or, to start all over again, click the **Reset** button here; this will restore your picture to its original, pristine condition.

The Picture Toolbar

The Format Picture dialog box described in the previous pages may be overrun with features, but when it comes to touching up pictures (scans, JPEG images, Office clip art, and so on), it's only the beginning. The Picture toolbar, which appears automatically when you click a picture, offers many more ways to dress up your images. (You can also summon it by choosing View→Toolbar→Picture. And by the way, this command is not available if the Formatting Palette is open, because the same tools automatically appear there if you select a picture.)

Move the cursor over the buttons on the toolbar to see their pop-up labels, as identified here:

- **Picture Effects** applies Photoshop-like filters to a photograph, allowing you to radically change its look with a single click. You can make it look as if it were drawn in charcoal, for example, or made of stained glass. Click the Picture Effects button to see the full gallery of choices.

- The **Shadow** button puts a shadow behind any type of picture, making it look as though it's floating just above the surface of your document. Click Shadow Settings to open a toolbar where you can choose a different color for the shadow, and nudge it closer to or further away from the picture.

- When you click the **Set Transparent Color** button, the cursor turns into an arrow pointer. When you click that pointer on a solid color in your picture, everything of that color turns transparent. When your picture is a photograph, this is the way to eliminate its background and wrap text tight against the foreground image. It works best if the photograph's background is a solid color. (This tool is not available on clip-art pictures.)

- The **Color Adjustment** tool works for both photographs and clip art. Clicking it opens a dialog box where you can increase or decrease the *saturation* (making the image colors appear more intense or washed out), or adjust the amount of red, blue, or green in the image. You can do this just for effect, or to correct a photograph that has a distorted tint from improper lighting.

  It's OK if you've never done this before; just click one of the radio buttons and watch what happens in the preview windows. Now you can see exactly how the image has changed. Click Reset Settings to return to the original, or Apply to make the change permanent. If you click Color Adjustment again, your altered image becomes the new "normal," so that you can adjust the color further. (To return to the true original color, use Edit→Undo as many times as necessary.)

- **Fix Red Eye** and **Remove Scratch** are, of course, special tools for correcting photographs once you've inserted them in a Word document.

- The **Marquee** tools along the bottom of the Picture toolbar are for selecting parts of photographs and other bitmap images. Click on one of the tools and drag it over the image to select the desired area. (To cancel a marquee selection, double-click anywhere in the document.) Now you can click the Cutout button to remove that area, or use the Cut, Copy, and Paste commands to place that part of the picture somewhere else.

- The **Magic Lasso** tool (at the lower right) is the most exciting. It lets you click repeatedly around an irregularly shaped item in your picture (a person, for example); the shimmering selection marquee hugs the outline of the item. To close the marquee and complete the selection, double-click back at the starting point.

  Once you've highlighted a portion of the picture in this way, you can cut out the selection, removing your ex from the picture forever, for example. You can also apply certain effects to that portion of the picture inside or outside the lasso, applying a dry brush effect to the background while leaving the people inside the lasso clear.

Object Linking and Embedding (OLE)

Linked and *embedded* objects are both chunks of data, like drawings or spreadsheets, nestled within a document in one Office program but actually created by another.

You edit them in whatever program created them, but behind the scenes, there's a big difference in where their data is stored. A *linked* object's data is stored in a separate file (what Microsoft calls the *source* file). An *embedded* object, on the other hand, is an integral part of the file in which it appears. All its data is stored right there in the document. That's why an embedded object bloats the file size of the document that contains it. However, embedding an object means that you'll never have to endure that sickening jolt when you realize you're missing an important speech that you copied to your laptop (as you might if you had only used linking).

The whole process is called Object Linking and Embedding, or OLE for short. You can't get very far on a Microsoft newsgroup or discussion board without seeing that acronym. At user group meetings, the preferred pronunciation is olé.

Creating Linked Objects

To add a linked object to your Office document, you first must create that object in a program that offers OLE features. On the Mac, that includes Word, Excel, and Power-Point 2004. For example, you can use linking to incorporate a drawing, spreadsheet, or chart into a Word document; weirdly enough, even another Word document can be incorporated into a Word document.

When you've created the source document, save the file, open the destination Word document, and choose Insert→Object. Click From File to open the Insert as Object dialog box (Figure 20-8), where you can navigate to the source document.

When you've located the source document, select it, turn on Link to File, and click Insert. The entire contents of the source file appear in the destination document inside a resizable border. You can format this object using Word's picture-formatting tools—but to edit the *content* of the linked object, you must open the actual source file.

Figure 20-8:
Checking the "Display as Icon" box in the Insert as Object dialog box creates an icon (left) that links to the source document. Both linked and embedded objects can be displayed as icons.

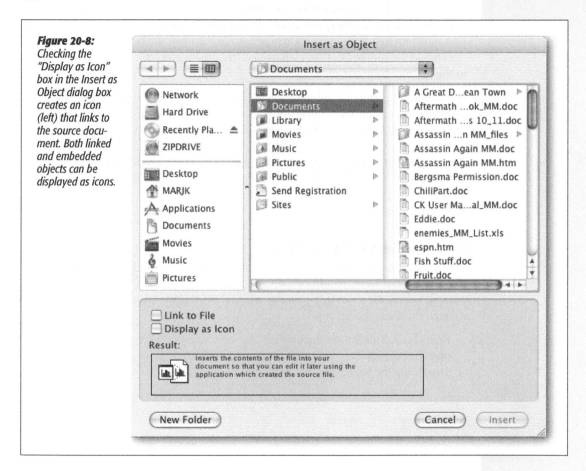

Editing Linked Objects

To edit a linked object, simply double-click it. (If you have many linked objects in one document, choose Edit→Links, and then click the link you want to edit in the list box. Links can be identified by the name of the source file.)

If it isn't already running, the source program launches, and the source document opens. Now you can edit the story, rotate the drawing, or revise the numbers in the spreadsheet. When you close the source document, the linked object is automatically updated.

It's easy to see the limitation of linked objects: Without the source file and the destination file on the same Mac, you can't edit the linked object. If you copy a document containing a linked object to a Zip disk, email it, or transfer it to your iBook, you'll be able to see, but not edit, the linked object. The bottom line: If you must edit it on the road, be sure to copy the source file onto the same disk or laptop.

Repairing a broken link

If Office can't find the source file for a linked object, perhaps because you've moved or renamed it, there's a way to remind Office of its location. Choose Edit→Links and select the link in question; click Change Source. An open file box appears where you can choose the source file; this is what tells Office to reconnect it to that link. Navigate to the file and double-click it.

You can use the same technique to change a linked object to a new source file altogether—such as a different illustration or a new fiscal year's ledger. Bear in mind that the new source file must be in the same program as the original one.

Tip: This is also the technique to use if you want to create a link to only a certain part of a source file—for example, a range of cells in an Excel spreadsheet or an excerpt of a Word document that you've marked with a bookmark. (See page 242 for details on bookmarks.) Type the name of the range or bookmark in the Range/Bookmark box.

Overriding Automatic Updating

Office automatically updates linked objects every time you edit the source document. If, however, you want the linked object to remain unchanged (permanently or temporarily), there are a number of ways to go about it. Begin by choosing Edit→Links to open the Links dialog box.

- **Break Link.** This button uncouples the connection between source document and object. (Because this choice is irrevocable, Office asks if you're sure.) From now on, editing the source document does nothing at all to the destination document.

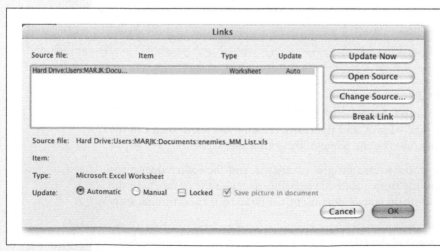

Figure 20-9:
When you click a link in the "Source file" box, the full file name and location appear just under the box.

You can't even repair the link, since the object no longer *is* a link. It becomes a picture, however, and still can be formatted as such (see page 687).

Tip: If you act quickly, you can reinstate a broken link by choosing Edit→Undo Links or pressing ⌘-Z.

- **Locked.** This box prevents changes to the source document from affecting the destination object. You can still double-click the link to open the source document, but any editing you perform there won't have any effect until you turn off the Locked box again *and* click the Update Now button in the Links dialog box.

- **Manual Updating.** Automatic is Office's default way of updating linked documents. When you choose the Manual radio button at the bottom of the Links dialog box, Word updates the linked object only when you click Update Now.

Creating Embedded Objects

Creating an embedded object from an existing file is the same as creating a linked object, except you do *not* turn on Link to File.

To bring in an external file using this technique, choose Insert→Object. In the dialog box, proceed like this:

- **If the file you want to embed already exists:** Click From File. Navigate to and open the source document to embed a copy of it in your Office document.

- **To create a new file (for embedding) on the spot:** In the list box, double-click the kind of object you want to create: Chart, Worksheet, Picture, or whatever. A new window opens, complete with menus and toolbars, where you can begin creating the object. When you're done, close the window; the object appears in your document.

Tip: When creating an embedded picture, you can use any of Word's drawing tools, as described earlier in this chapter. However, when you close the window, the result is a *picture,* not a drawing. To edit it with picture tools, you must double-click to open its window, as described below. This is a great way to use both drawing tools and picture tools (picture effects, brightness, and so on) on the same object.

If, on the other hand, you simply want to insert a drawing object in a Word, Excel, or PowerPoint document, just open the Drawing toolbar (see page 684) and draw away!

Editing Embedded Objects

Like a linked object, an embedded object has a surrounding frame. You can format it using Office's picture tools (see page 687).

To edit it, though, you must double-click it. (Or click it and choose Edit→Object→ Edit. The Edit menu changes to specify the type of object you've selected—Document Object, Worksheet Object, and so on.) The object opens in a separate document window, where you can edit it using the appropriate menus and toolbars.

You can edit an embedded object in any compatible program on your Mac. Just click the object and then choose Edit→Object→Convert. Choose a program in the list that appears, and then click OK. (Most of the time, the Microsoft Office programs will be the only ones available.)

CHAPTER
21

AppleScripting Office

If you're like most people, you probably didn't upgrade to Office 2004 because of its vastly improved ability to work with AppleScript. But if you're not using AppleScript to streamline your complex or repetitive tasks, you're not tapping Office's true potential for efficiency and speed. For the first time, you can control all four Office programs with AppleScript—the Mac's very own programming language. (In other words, Microsoft just gave PC owners yet another reason to switch to the Mac.)

To the delight of experienced scripters, the potential for unleashing the power of AppleScript on Office 2004 is now boundless. Fortunately, you don't have to become a scripter to reap all the benefits, since there are hundreds of ready-made scripts you can download and use. This chapter will give you a taste of what you've been missing and get you started with a few ready-to-use scripts.

Microsoft has significantly enhanced the AppleScript prowess of Word, Excel, and PowerPoint and enormously expanded each program's AppleScript *dictionary* (the lexicon of a program's own specific commands and objects). Word's dictionary is about 100 times its previous size, arguably the largest AppleScript dictionary in existence, and Excel's almost as big, with a fairly hefty PowerPoint dictionary bringing up the rear. (Compare that to Apple's own Keynote, which doesn't even recognize AppleScript.)

Entourage has had an outstanding relationship with AppleScript—among the very best on the Mac—ever since its inception in Office 2001, and it's gotten better and better in Office X and 2004. Earlier versions of Excel had pretty good scriptability too, but

Word had a very primitive AppleScript dictionary, and was very, very buggy, which made it mostly unusable. And PowerPoint didn't work with AppleScript at all.

Note: The only way you could use AppleScript with previous versions of Word (and in PowerPoint X) was to learn another programming language–Visual Basic for Applications (see Microsoft's Other Programming Language on page 701)–and then convert it to use within AppleScript via the magic command *do Visual Basic*. Older scripts written exclusively as *do Visual Basic* still work in Office 2004, but now you have full–and virtually identical–control available via native AppleScript.

What is AppleScript?

AppleScript is the Mac's built-in *scripting*—that is, programming—language. (It's been around since 1993, with System 7.1, but you had to pay for it as an add-on until Apple made it part of the operating system with System 7.5.) Even without learning to write your own scripts, you can use scripts to control any application (Apple's or otherwise) whose developers have made it *scriptable,* meaning that they've built the necessary code into their program and provided an AppleScript dictionary. That's right. Although the AppleScript language is built right into Mac OS X, you can only use it to control scriptable applications like Entourage, Word, iCal, iTunes, Adobe InDesign, and Photoshop.

Apple intended AppleScript to be more English-like and easier to learn than other programming languages—although some would say that the resulting "English" is a very unusual dialect indeed. Well, it certainly is easier to read than to write.

If you know nothing about AppleScript and would like to learn, skim this chapter to see what you're missing, and then go to a primer such as O'Reilly's *AppleScript: The Missing Manual* to learn the basics of the AppleScript language before venturing into writing Office scripts.

Why Use AppleScript?

The vast majority of Office fans never dip a toe into AppleScript. But if you use Office to run a business or manage a department, you're failing to live up to your true computing potential.

The great advantage of AppleScript is that you only need to learn one programming language to communicate to *every* scriptable application on your Mac. You can create a workflow that takes data from the Entourage Address Book and puts it into both Excel and FileMaker Pro, then prepares a Mail Merge in Word using the same information to type personalized form letters and envelopes, and then sends out an email back in Entourage. And Entourage is AppleScript only—you couldn't use VBA even if you wanted to. You can also use AppleScript to run macros, which are VBA, in Word (page 279) and Excel (page 592) documents via the *run VB macro* command (which somehow was omitted from PowerPoint).

AppleScript lets you:

- **Automate.** Perform repetitive tasks automatically in a few seconds, instead of spending minutes or even hours plowing through them yourself. For example, you can run a script in Entourage to set the default address to the Home address, rather than Entourage's built-in default of Work address. If you have 1000 contacts, this script will take about a minute to run, as opposed to multiple hours opening and changing each contact manually. Now you can print address labels for your Flag Day cards without skipping the folks whose work addresses you don't know.

- **Customize.** Devise your own routines, sometimes even doing things that are impossible to do yourself onscreen in the first place. The world is your oyster: You can write scripts to duplicate calendar events (Entourage can't do that on its own), add a BCC to your boss on all email messages you send out (see page 706), add a contact to a particular group without messing about finding or opening the group, remove all single carriage returns pasted into a Word document in one fell swoop without affecting double-returns at ends of paragraphs (see page 710), and much, much more.

- **Interact.** Control several different applications in one workflow. You can take a letterhead document you've created in Word and have it open as a new letter addressed to a selected Entourage contact, complete with date, address, salutation, and signature already in place. Or you can export full contact information (street, city, state, phone numbers, email addresses, and so on) for every member of a group or category to an Excel worksheet or FileMaker Pro database—or both.

UP TO SPEED

Microsoft's Other Programming Language

This chapter makes several references to VBA—*Visual Basic for Applications*. VBA is the language Microsoft provides for programming Word, Excel, and PowerPoint both on Mac and Windows. (It's also used in many other Windows-only Microsoft applications.) If you happen to know VBA already, or you want to create automations that work cross-platform, you'll probably prefer VBA macros over AppleScript scripts. Since Office 2004's AppleScript essentially mirrors its VBA model, it really makes no functional difference which language you use—as long as you stick with Office applications. As soon as you want to combine more than a very minimal reference to another Mac application, including the Finder, you need to use AppleScript instead. (VBA actually has a special method—*Macscript*—that lets you include some AppleScript within macros written for the Mac—a sort of *do Visual Basic* in reverse. But it's very cumbersome to use for more than a single line or so.)

You can refer to guides such as O'Reilly's *Writing Word*

Macros to get going on VBA. The VBA Help in the Virtual Basic Editor in Word, Excel, or PowerPoint (go to Tools→Macro→ Visual Basic Editor then to Help→Visual Basic Help) is excellent, too. You also might someday want to create AutoExec macros that run automatically when you open Word, Excel, or PowerPoint, something AppleScript can't do. (For more on VBA and the Visual Basic Editor, see page 283.)

If your office has both PCs and Macs, it makes sense to create your cross-platform VBA macros on a Mac rather than on a PC. That's because Office's VBA for the Mac is at an earlier version, so a few items available in Windows—but very few—aren't available in Office for the Mac. (For instance, VBA in Office Mac does not include any ActiveX controls—which is actually good news since ActiveX has been the conduit for most Office Windows viruses.) In other words, if you create your macros on a Mac, they'll run in Windows, but not necessarily vice versa. See the *Strategies for Developing Cross-Platform Solutions* topic in VB Editor Help for details.

Installing and Running Office Scripts

Whether you choose to write your own scripts or not, you can always run scripts that others have written. Since Word, Excel, and PowerPoint 2004 scripting is so new, there are only a few scripts available for them—for now. There are bound to be a great many scripts written and distributed as time goes on. Entourage already has hundreds of scripts, almost all of them free, some of which can do amazing things and make your life easier in the process. If you can drag and drop, you can install and run an AppleScript.

Downloading Scripts

1. **Download the script package from the Web site. Unstuff or unzip it if necessary.**

   You'll usually end up with a folder containing a script file, a ReadMe document, and perhaps one or more supporting files.

   The script file will look like one of the icons in Figure 21-1.

Sample Applet

Add Bcc.scpt

Merge Columns

Figure 21-1:
Left: Script applications (applets) bear a hidden .app extension. You run them by double-clicking them, or you can put them in the Dock and click them there, like any application. Some applets have a downward arrow included in the icon indicating that they're droplets. These scripts run when you drag and drop files onto them. Applets and droplets take a few seconds to start up; you'll see them bounce in the Dock.

Right: Script files, or documents, which may bear the .scpt extension, have no such overhead. They start immediately, but to run them you have to install a special Script menu (page 703).

2. **Read the ReadMe—or at least any installation and setup sections it may have—for any special instructions.**

Scripts come in two basic forms—applications, known as *applets*, or as *scripts* (*script documents*), as shown in Figure 21-1. Developers create their scripts in either of these two forms when they save them.

Installing Applets (Script Applications) and Droplets

If the icon is an applet (or droplet) as shown in Figure 21-1, you can store it, and its folder, anywhere at all on your computer. You can move it to your Applications folder or to a subfolder for scripts within it, or to your Microsoft User Data folder (even though it's not data) or to a subfolder for Office script applets you can make there.

You can also drag the applet icon to your Dock, as with any application, so you can launch it from there. If it's a script you'll be using often, dock it.

Run the applet by double-clicking it, like any application, or by clicking it in the Dock if it's there. Or if it's a droplet (with the down arrow), drag one or more files of the appropriate type—usually a Word, Excel, or PowerPoint document—onto it. You can even store droplets in the Dock and drop files onto it there.

If the icon is a script document (see Figure 21-1; it may or may not bear an .scpt extension), then you have to put it in a specific place depending on whether it's a script for Entourage or for one of the other Office applications. Read on.

Installing Entourage Script Menu Scripts

When you're in Entourage, you'll notice a dark, scroll-shaped icon just to the right of the Help menu in the menu bar. That's Entourage's exclusive Script menu, and it comes preloaded with a few scripts that automate multi-step Entourage processes, like turning the selected email message into an Entourage note. Word, Excel, and PowerPoint don't come with their own Script menus, so you have to install Mac OS X's Script menu, as described in the next section.

Here's how to add to this menu any AppleScripts you've downloaded from the Web or written yourself.

1. **If the script is a script document for Entourage, drag the icon into your Home→ Documents→Microsoft User Data→Entourage Script Menu Items folder (see Figure 21-2).**

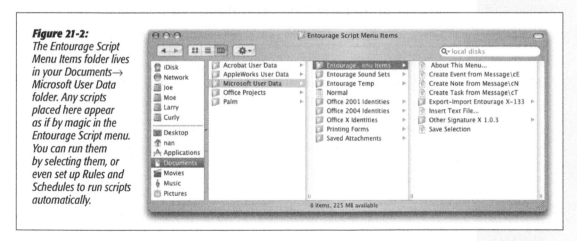

Figure 21-2:
The Entourage Script Menu Items folder lives in your Documents→ Microsoft User Data folder. Any scripts placed here appear as if by magic in the Entourage Script menu. You can run them by selecting them, or even set up Rules and Schedules to run scripts automatically.

In the Entourage Script menu, You now see a menu item with the name of the script (see Figure 21-3).

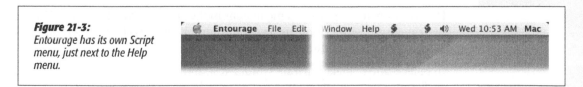

Figure 21-3:
Entourage has its own Script menu, just next to the Help menu.

2. **Select the menu item to run the script.**

   You can also set up an Entourage rule to run the script when messages are downloaded or sent (see page 353), or an Entourage schedule to run the script automatically at startup, when you quit, or on a repeating regular schedule (see page 328).

3. **If you wish, you can create a keyboard shortcut for the script if it doesn't already have one. See page 677.**

Installing Word, Excel, and PowerPoint Scripts

To use your Mac OS X Script menu, you first need to make it visible if you haven't already done so. Go to your Applications→AppleScript folder and double-click the Install Script Menu file. (In Mac OS X 10.2, the file is called Script Menu.menu.) Skip this step if your menu bar already shows a Script menu.

Once you've installed the menu, you'll see a Script menu icon over on the right side of your menu bar (see Figure 21-3). It looks just like the Entourage Script menu but is visible always, in all applications. Now that you've activated the menu, you can install (and organize) the scripts that will appear on it. Here's how:

1. **Open the appropriate Scripts folder, Library→Scripts folder at the main level of your hard drive, or your Home folder→Library→Scripts folder.**

   You can choose whether to put your script where anyone who uses your Mac can access it (the one at the main level of your hard drive) or where you alone see it when logged into your own account (the one in your Home folder). You can also arrive at your account's Scripts folder by selecting the top menu item in the Script menu: Open Scripts Folder.

Note: Scripts placed in your hard drive's Library→Scripts folder appear in the upper part of the Script menu, and scripts placed in your Home→Library→Scripts folder appear in the lower part of the folder.

   You now have a choice as to whether you want the script to be available from all applications, or only when you're in the Office application where the script will run. Unless you use dozens of scripts in your daily work, you may not need to worry about organizing your Script menu in such great detail. But if you do, skip to step 3.

2. **If you want the script to be always available, drag the script icon to the Scripts folder you opened in step 1.**

   The script's name appears as a menu item in the Script menu at all times. When you choose the script, it opens its application (Word, Excel, or PowerPoint) if necessary and brings it to the front.

3. **To reduce clutter, make separate Word, Excel, and PowerPoint subfolders within the Scripts folder and drag the script icon to the appropriate subfolder.**

The subfolders now appear in the Script menu, just like Apple's preinstalled subfolders. Each script is a submenu item of its folder. To reduce clutter further, so that you'll only see the scripts you can use in the current Office application, go on to the next step.

4. **To make scripts only appear in the Script menu when you're using the correct application, make a subfolder in the Scripts folder and name it Applications.**

   Use whichever Scripts folder you chose in step 1.

5. **Inside this new Applications subfolder, make three sub-subfolders and name them exactly as shown here:** *Microsoft Word, Microsoft Excel,* **and** *Microsoft PowerPoint.*

6. **Drag the script icon to the appropriate sub-subfolder.**

   You see the script as a menu item, in the lower part of the Script menu, only when you're in Word, Excel, or PowerPoint.

POWER USERS' CLINIC

Reuse, Recycle, Recompile

If you have old Excel or Word scripts that won't run in 2004, and display Excel and Word keywords as incomprehensible «raw codes» when you open them in Script Editor, follow these steps to get them working again. For Excel:

1. Quit Excel 2004. Quit Script Editor. Log out (from the Apple menu) and log in again.

2. Open Excel X (if necessary, reinstall it from the Office X CD). Open Script Editor.

3. Open your Excel X scripts in Script Editor.

4. With each script, go to File→Save As. Choose Text from the File Format pop-up menu. You'll notice the extension changes to .applescript. Save it anywhere on your Mac.

5. Quit Excel X and Script Editor. Log out and then in again (again).

6. Open Excel 2004, then launch Script Editor.

7. Open the .applescript Text versions of your scripts in Script Editor. You now see—in uncompiled text—the original text of the scripts (not the strange «raw codes» of the compiled script versions).

8. Open the Excel 2004 dictionary in Script Editor (choose File→Open Dictionary→Microsoft Excel). If you are in any doubt as to which Excel dictionary is the one for 2004, instead click the Browse button at the bottom of the window and navigate to Applications→Microsoft Office 2004→Microsoft Excel.

9. Most of the Excel X commands and classes—which look like SquishedTogetherWords from the Excel X version—have very close equivalents in the Excel 2004 dictionary, except they're separate lowercase words, like 'squished together words.' Change your old text to the new dictionary commands as needed. Make sure to check through all the suites in the dictionary to find the terms you need: the Microsoft Excel Suite and the Table Suite are the ones you need most often.

10. Click the Compile button, and debug (fix the line in which a highlighted word appears if you get an error—it may be the preceding word that has the problem), as necessary.

11. When properly compiled so the styled formatting appears when you click the Compile button, Save As a Script or Application.

To run a script you've installed using these steps, select it in the Script menu.

Running the Scripts

Once you've installed a script, it's ready to run. Here's a quick review of the many ways you can run an AppleScript script.

- To run an applet, just double-click its icon in the Finder or click it once in the Dock

- To run a droplet, drag and drop files on it.

- To run a Script menu script, just select it in the menu.

- To run an Entourage script automatically, set up a Rule (page 353) or Schedule (page 328) to Run AppleScript.

Starter Scripts

Here are a few short scripts to get you going, with some explanations to follow each. You can copy them straight from the "Missing CD" page at *www.missingmanuals. com* and paste them into Script Editor, or you can type them yourself, being careful to get all the spelling correct. Click the Compile button in Script Editor to ensure you've made no errors in typing. If styled formatting suddenly appears, you've done it right. If you get an error, fix the line in which the highlighted word appears (often it's the word preceding the highlighted one that's the problem). You can test the scripts from Script Editor if you wish, as long as you have Entourage or Word set up to go (for example, a new message window in Entourage, a document with extra carriage returns in Word).

Save the Entourage and Word scripts as a script. (When you choose File→Save in Script Editor, that's what usually appears for the file format.) Save the Entourage scripts to the Entourage Script Menu Items folder as described earlier—you'll find them in Entourage's Script menu. Save the Word script either to your Home→Library→Scripts folder or to your hard drive's Library→Scripts folder, also described earlier, so it will appear in the Mac's Script menu. Run your scripts from the appropriate Script menu by selecting the name there. As for the Excel script, save it as an application; choose Application from the File Format pop-up menu when saving.

Note: In all the scripts on the following pages, the comments–which appear *in italics*–have no effect on the script. They're just there for human beings to read. In AppleScript, you can make single-line comments by typing two hyphens (--). Anything following the double-hyphen on that line is a comment. You can make multi-line (or single-line) comments by enclosing the text within *(* asterisk parentheses*)*. You'll see both in the scripts below.

Add BCC (Entourage)

This Entourage email-message script adds a BCC name and address of your choice to a new message you're about to send. Perhaps you're required to BCC your boss or supervisor on messages to certain people. Instead of having to click in the BCC address pane and type your boss's email address every time, you can just run this script. Even better, add a keyboard shortcut to the script's name (see page 677), and then simply press the keys.

If you need to BCC *every* message you send out, you could even run a variation of the script from a schedule (see page 328) that runs every minute. (But you'd first want to remove the *beep* and *display dialog* lines so you don't get them in your face every, well, minute.) There's no way to make this script run when you click the Send button. By that time it's too late, since Entourage's Outgoing Rules run *after* the message has already gone out. But a schedule running every minute will catch virtually any message you're writing before you send it off.

```
-- insert the BCC's real name and email address below
property theBCC : "\"My H. Boss\" <pointyhair@mywork.com>"

tell application "Microsoft Entourage"

    activate -- brings Entourage to the front if you're running
this from Script Editor
    if class of window 1 is draft window then
        set newMsg to window 1
    else -- no new message window
        --!!remove beep and display dialog lines if running auto-
matically from a schedule!
        beep
        display dialog "Add BCC script only works when there is a
new message window in the front." buttons "OK" default button
"OK" with icon 0
        return -- quits
    end if


    set bccRecips to BCC recipients of newMsg


    -- don't wipe out BCC recipients already added manually
    if bccRecips ≠ "" then -- ≠ means "is not equal to"
        if bccRecips does not contain theBCC then -- don't add it a
second time
            set bccRecips to bccRecips & ", " & theBCC
        end if
    else -- no BCCs
        set bccRecips to theBCC
    end if


    set BCC recipients of newMsg to bccRecips


    (* Entourage leaves the BCC address pane invisible. If you'd
like to see it, you need to prod the window to display: the next
```

```
try/on error block does that. If not, remove the block, or put
asterisk parentheses around it.*)
    try
        select progress window -- brings it forward momentarily if
it's open
        select newMsg --brings new message forward again, showing
BCCs
    on error -- progress window isn't open
        open progress window
        close progress window
    end try
end tell
```

The first part of the script checks whether the front window is a new draft message window, simply known as **draft window** in the AppleScript dictionary. If it's not, the script alerts you via a beep and a dialog box, then quits prematurely via the **return** command. (Remove the **beep** and **display dialog** lines if you're running the script from a repeating schedule.)

The next part of the script checks whether you've already entered any BCC recipients and makes sure not to erase them. Instead, the script appends a comma, space and your boss's email address ("**,** " **& theBCC**). Otherwise, if there's no BCC yet, it simply sets the variable **bccRecips** to the saved property (boss's email address). Any which way, **bccRecips** now represents the desired BCC line, which now contains the **BCC recipients** of the **newMsg** message window.

Finally, there's a peculiar tail to this script. If you stop after you set the BCC recipients, the script works perfectly and includes the BCC you set in your new message. But you would have no visual confirmation: Since you haven't clicked the BCC field manually (the whole point of the exercise), it's still hidden. To make it appear, this script uses a trick: flashing the miniature progress window to the front and away again. It's so fast you won't even notice it, but when it's gone, the BCC field, complete with "My H. Boss," suddenly appears. If you don't need this visual cue or find it disruptive, just remove this part of the script.

Attach vCard (Entourage)

Surprisingly, Entourage has no simple setting to add a vCard to messages you send out. This script makes or updates a vCard file for you in your Microsoft User Data folder, then attaches it to the message. Again, you could also run this script automatically from a schedule every minute to catch virtually all messages you send out. The script gets your own contact information from the Entourage Address Book, creates the vCard file, tells the Finder to give the file the correct creator code and file code—so the Entourage vCard icon now appears for the file—and then goes back to Entourage to add the file as an attachment to the message. It's a nifty learning script that covers a lot of ground in just a few lines.

```
tell application "Microsoft Entourage"
    activate
```

```
    set MUDpath to (path to MUD) -- finds the Microsoft User Data
folder on your hard disk
    set meContact to me contact -- that's your contact
    set vcInfo to vcard data of meContact
    set myName to name of meContact
end tell


set pathName to (MUDpath & myName & ".vcf") as Unicode text --
adds a .vcf extension


try -- just in case something goes wrong, like a locked file
    -- will create a new file or open an existing one
    set f to open for access file pathName with write permission
    set eof f to 0 -- updates the file if it exists already
    write vcInfo to f -- does the deed
    close access f -- never forget to close access


    tell application "Finder" -- setting creator and file type
sets the Entourage icon for the vCard
        set creator type of file pathName to "OPIM" -- Entourage's
creator code
        set file type of file pathName to "vCrd"
    end tell


    set theVcard to alias pathName


on error errmsg number errNum
    try
        close access f
    end try
    beep 2
    display dialog "There was a problem with accessing the vCard
in the Microsoft User Data folder for Attach vCard script."
& return & return & "Remove any vCard you see there and try
again." & return & return & errmsg & return & return & errNum
buttons {"OK"} default button 1 with icon 0
    return


end try


tell application "Microsoft Entourage"


    if class of window 1 ≠ draft window then return -- quit si-
lently
    set newMsg to window 1
```

```
    set theAttachments to every attachment of newMsg
    repeat with theAttachment in theAttachments
        if name of theAttachment = (myname & ".vcf") then return --
the vCard is there already
    end repeat

    make new attachment at newMsg with properties {file:theVcard}
-- adds the attachment


end tell
```

You'll notice several interesting Entourage items in this script. **path to MUD** finds your Microsoft User Data folder in your Home→Documents folder and identifies your own contact (the one with the little "i" icon in the Address Book). It would be nice if Entourage had a command to export the contact as a vCard, but, failing that, this script shows how to do it by writing this vCard data to a file. Finally, at the end, the script accesses the **attachment** element of the **draft window** class in the Entourage Mail and News Suite, first to check for existing attachments (you don't want to duplicate the vCard if the script is running automatically from a schedule) and then to make a new attachment by specifying the **file** property of **attachment** class. The script also shows you an example of a try/error block in the very remote chance there's a problem (perhaps a locked file, or permissions issues).

Remove Extra Carriage Returns (Word)

Let's say you've gone to the trouble of formatting your Normal and Body Text styles to include a proper 6-point space after each paragraph (see page 119). Isn't it annoying to then find that pasting in text from other people's less elegant documents or from email messages results in all those extra, unwanted blank lines? You may know how to remove these in Edit→Replace using the special ^p (paragraph break) characters, but it can get rather tedious since you also have to replace single carriage returns in the email text with spaces so adjacent words don't squish together. That in turn requires substituting some special placeholder for the double returns before replacing the single returns and then, finally, replacing the placeholder with single returns. Quite a lot of work just to get a properly formatted document.

This little script will do it all for you in the flash of an eye. It makes use of Word's rather complex **find** object—which is a class, not a command—in the enormous Microsoft Word Suite, and introduces you to the **text object** property. The **text object** property returns a *text range*—which you can find in all its glory in the Text Suite of the Word Dictionary. It's a good idea to become acquainted with text ranges as soon as possible, since you'll be spending most of your time in Word dealing with them.

Note to more experienced scripters: To get or set the actual plain text of a word, or paragraph, or entire document–which isn't necessary in this script–you would specify the content property of its text object. The text object, a text range, contains dozens of properties in addition to the simple text content. It knows details of the range's font, size, color, paragraph formatting (like space after), borders, Word style, language, whether you've done a grammar check, and so on and so on–everything that makes Word a sophisticated word processor and not the simple text editor that you may be more accustomed to scripting. So to get just the plain text, remember to get the content property.

```
tell application "Microsoft Word"
   activate
   set textObject to the text object of active document
   -- get the find object, and use 'tell' to avoid having to re-
peat 'of find object of docText' with every command targeting it
      tell (find object of textObject)
         --clear all unusual options from the Find panel
         set {forward, wrap, format, match all word forms, match
case, match sounds like, match whole word, match wildcards} to
{true, find continue, false, false, false, false, false, false}
         clear formatting
         clear all fuzzy options
         clear formatting (its replacement) -- note 'its' to avoid
confusion with replacement class
         -- first replace all double carriage returns with a place-
holder ("!_REPLACE_RETURN_TEXT_!")
         execute find find text "^p^p" replace with "!_REPLACE_RE-
TURN_TEXT_!" replace replace all
         --now replace all single returns with a space
         execute find find text "^p" replace with " " replace re-
place all
         -- finally replace placeholder text with single returns
         execute find find text "!_REPLACE_RETURN_TEXT_!" replace
with "^p" replace replace all
      end tell
end tell
```

Note that AppleScript can set or get a whole slew of an object's properties all at once by using a list (the items in the {list braces} above) for both properties and their values. That's an advantage AppleScript has over VBA, by the way. Also, note that this script uses the same special ^p character that you'd use in the Find/Replace panel onscreen. If it used the standard AppleScript term for carriage returns—**return**—when replacing, in the final line of the script, you'd end up with "manual" line breaks (like the ones you can type in Word by pressing Shift-Return). These break a line but are not true paragraph marks. You'd also lose your "space after" paragraph setting, as well as anything else identifying your paragraph formatting, and you'd end up with just one single, long paragraph for the whole document. Word's AppleScript can find and replace true paragraph marks happily enough when you instruct it to *search* for the return character—it just can't *insert* them this way. This script is a great example of one of Word's nifty AppleScript tricks (technically known as a *coercion*) that gets the job done by letting you use ^p (instead of **return**) in an AppleScript **find**.

Tip: Learn about ^p and all the other special characters you can use this way by choosing Help→Word Help→Advanced search methods→"Find and replace items by typing codes."

If you want to do a Find and Replace just on the selection (highlighted text) in a document, rather than the whole document, just replace the third line of the script with:

```
set textObject to the text object of the selection
```

Merge Columns (Excel)

Excel has a cool way to merge two columns into one using a formula (see page 484); this script combines that formula with the power of AppleScript automation. Perhaps you're receiving hundreds of Tab-Text or .CSV (Comma Separated Value) files from a CGI form, where people have entered one item at a time and each answer is assigned to a field, and then hundreds or thousands of such records are assembled in one text file, each on its own line. But now you'd like to combine two of these fields—for example the two lines of a street address—before storing the data as an Excel workbook or importing it into FileMaker Pro. This script does just that. It's incredibly fast, largely due to its ability to use an Excel formula, and the fact that it doesn't on a repeat loop for each pair of adjacent cells.

If you save this script as an application, it becomes a droplet with the telltale down arrow in its icon (the **on open** handler is what ensures it's a droplet). You can drag and drop any number of Excel files onto it, and it takes care of them all and then closes them again. The script puts a space (" ") between the combined adjacent cell values—but you can change that to any punctuation you like. As a precaution, it converts any dates or numbers it finds into text first to avoid errors. This script uses a *handler,* or subroutine, called **MergeColumns()** to do its work. (Read up on handlers in any of the books listed on page 715.)

```
--Enter the pair of columns to be merged, from left to right
property columnPair : {"B", "C"}

-- on open makes this a droplet : theItems (a list of aliases)
are the files dropped on it
on open theItems
   repeat with theItem in theItems -- for each file
      repeat 1 times -- a trick to allow skipping items, Apple-
Script has no "Next" command
         tell application "Microsoft Excel"
            try -- works with .xls (Excel), .csv, and tab-delim-
ited .txt files
               open workbook workbook file name (theItem as Uni-
code text)
```

```
            on error -- if it's a file that can't open in Excel,
just skip it silently
                exit repeat -- exits the 1 time repeat; go on to
next file
            end try
        end tell
        my MergeColumns() -- calls the MergeColumns() handler
(subroutine)
    end repeat
  end repeat
end open


on MergeColumns()
  tell application "Microsoft Excel"
    set screen updating to false -- speeds up execution
    tell active workbook
      --you'll need these when saving:
      set fileFormat to file format
      set folderPath to path
      set filePath to full name
    end tell
    set {a, b} to columnPair -- a is first item ("B" here), b
is second item ("C" here)
    --get the column index as a number (3) from the range using
column letter (range "C:C")
    set y to first column index of range (b & ":" & b) of ac-
tive sheet

    --insert an empty column to the left of column D : i.e. a
new empty column D
    insert into range column (y + 1) of active sheet

    (* set the formula of cell D1 to be B1&" "&C1 or B1&C1
(i.e. it concatenates B1 and C1, inserting a space between them
if neither is empty ) using the variables a and b for the column
letters and an Excel formula; \'' is AppleScript for literal
quotes (the quote must be escaped by a backslash) *)
    set formula of cell 1 of column (y + 1) of active sheet to
("=IF(AND(" & a & "1<>\"\"," & b & "1<>\"\")," & a & "1&\" \"&"
& b & "1," & a & "1&" & b & "1)")
        -- in other words: =IF(AND(B1<>"",C1<>""),B1&" "&C1,B1&C1)
    --[if neither B1 nor C1 is empty, insert a space between them]
when concatenating them

        -- new column in used range, expressed as a range for fill
down command; 'get address' returns "D1:D100" or however many
```

```
rows there are in the used range
    set newRange to range (get address of column (y + 1) of
used range of active sheet)
    --fill the new column D of the used range with the same
formula for each cell
    fill down newRange
    (* convert the formula references in new column D to hard
text to avoid error when the old columns are deleted:
    'get value' gets just the text values as a list; then set
the range's values to that list of strings to remove formula
references *)
    set value of newRange to (get value of newRange)

    delete range range (a & ":" & b) of active sheet -- deletes
the old columns B and C

    (* if the file is a normal Excel Workbook (.xls) file, you
can just save it.
    If it's another sort of file, like Tab-Text, you need to
delete the original and make a
    new file of the same type, to avoid annoying Save dialog
boxes on screen. *)
    if fileFormat = workbook normal file format then
      save workbook
    else
      tell application "Finder"
        delete alias filePath
        -- sometimes the Finder gets confused if you don't up-
date
        update alias folderPath
      end tell
      -- now you can save the workbook using the same file
path
      save workbook as (active workbook) filename filePath
file format fileFormat
    end if
    close active workbook saving no -- !!! otherwise you get
another Save dialog box
    set screen updating to true -- restore
  end tell


end MergeColumns
```

You'll notice the peculiarities with saving and closing workbooks. If you've opened a normal Excel Workbook .xls file, you can just save it. For most other sorts of files (like tab-delimited files), however, trying to do so brings up a dreaded Save As dialog box. You either have to make a new file with an altered name, or do what the script does and delete the original file replacing it with a new one of the same name (using the **save workbook as** command).

Learning More

Let's face it: These few pages can't teach you AppleScript. If you've already done some scripting, they may have given you a few glimmers into some of the particulars of Office 2004. If you've never written a single line of code, you may have gleaned a sense of the exciting power and possibilities of AppleScript. If this chapter has whetted your appetite to learn to write scripts of your own, there are lots of books that can teach you, some of which are listed below. And consider joining the AppleScript-Users mailing list (URL below) to ask questions when you're stuck.

Part of the versatility of AppleScript—and also one of its oddities—is that every application has its own unique "dialect." Each has its own vocabulary defined in its own dictionary, and its own syntax peculiarities too, sometimes defined nowhere. General AppleScript books don't help much with that aspect: Where they touch on application scripting, it's mostly just a few basic Apple applications such as Address Book and iTunes. With the exception of Entourage, Office scripts are extremely unorthodox since they mirror the VBA model, not a usual AppleScript model. Their scripting can be daunting even for those of you fully up to speed on AppleScript.

Happy to say, there's help at hand. Microsoft is creating free AppleScript References and sample scripts for each Office application. These References go into all the detail and explanation you could possibly want. The first, Word AppleScript Reference, is 526 pages long, and available at this writing in PDF format at *www.microsoft.com/mac/resources/resources.aspx?pid=asforoffice*. Future Office AppleScript References will be available at the same location, and may be there already as you read this book. You can also get a lot of help at the AppleScript-Users mailing list and at the newsgroups for each Office Mac application, also listed below. See you there!

Basics of AppleScript

These books provide an introduction to how AppleScript works, and then get you started scripting:

- **AppleScript: The Missing Manual** by Adam Goldstein (O'Reilly).

- **AppleScript for Absolute Starters.** Free PDF tutorial on the very basics; *www.applescriptsourcebook.com/tips/AS4AS.html*.

AppleScript in Depth

These volumes cover AppleScript from start to finish:

- **AppleScript: A Comprehensive Guide to Scripting and Automation on Mac OS X** by Hanaan Rosenthal (Friends of ED). A thorough tutorial from beginner to advanced.

- **AppleScript: The Definitive Guide** by Matt Neuburg (O'Reilly). The best book, especially if you already know some AppleScript or another programming language. It offers a stimulating presentation of how the language actually works.

- **AppleScript Language Guide** (Apple). Free PDF download (1999: somewhat out of date); *http://developer.apple.com/documentation/AppleScript/Conceptual/Apple-ScriptLangGuide/AppleScriptLanguageGuide.pdf*

Office 2004 AppleScript

Here are some helpful resources tailored to Entourage, Word, Excel, and Power-Point:

- **Microsoft AppleScript Reference Guides.** Free PDF downloads; *www.microsoft.com/mac/resources/resources.aspx?pid=asforoffice*

- **Do Visual Basic.** Web article by Paul Berkowitz; *http://word.mvps.org/MacWord-New/WordAppleScript.htm*

- **Entourage Help.** In Entourage, choose Help→Entourage Help and search for "About the script menu."

Scripts for Entourage, Word, Excel, PowerPoint

These Web sites offer free Office scripts:

- **Macscripter.net.** Hundreds of scripts for Entourage; some for Word and Excel are on the way. Use the Categories pop-up menu and the Search field to find your way around, then download and run the scripts as described in this chapter; *http://macscripter.net/scriptbuilders/*

- **Scriptable Applications: Microsoft PowerPoint.** Scripts for PowerPoint 2004—from Apple! Copy and paste the scripts you find here into Script Editor, and save to your Mac; *www.apple.com/applescript/powerpoint/*

All orders are governed by the Terms & Conditions of Sale of John Wiley & Sons Ltd at: http://eu.wiley.com/WileyCDA/Section/id-302258.html Click on Change location and then select UK, which terms shall prevail over all other terms and conditions. A hard copy can be provided upon request. Title to goods passes upon payment in full and not upon delivery.

Total weight 1.214 kgs

1

For internal use

Enclosures code(s)

Delivery arranged by WDS Ltd.

Totals	13.95
VAT	.00
Total Payable Great Britain Pounds	13.95

Copies: In 1
No. of Parcels 1

Initiator: Amazon
CSENDOFDAY PRTINVR QPGMR 01/10/13 JWINV1 3:56:43

WILEY

Publishing Offices and Accounts

John Wiley & Sons Limited
The Atrium, Southern Gate
Chichester, West Sussex
PO19 8SQ, UK

Telephone +44 (0) 1243 779777
Facsimile +44 (0) 1243 775878
SAN   GB 001 2279

VAT No   GB 376 7669 87

Service, Distribution and Returns

John Wiley & Sons Limited
European Distribution Centre
New Era Estate, Oldlands Way
Bognor Regis, West Sussex
PO22 9NQ, UK

Telephone +44 (0) 1243 843291
Facsimile +44 (0) 1243 843302
E-Mail   cs-books@wiley.com
www.wiley.com

Bill to

Amazon EU Sarl
5 Rue Plaetis Luxembourg
C/O PO Box 4558
Slough
SL1 0TX

Carrier

Chi Haulage - Amazon Ridgemont

Customer Notes   V8652191
V8652191

Special Instructions

Ship to VAT No.   / 727255821

Ship to

AMAZON EU SARL
5450534000109
MARSTON GATE
FULFILMENT CENTRE
RIDGEMONT
MK43 0ZA

INVOICE No.

7760383

Tax Point Date	1/10/13
Account No.	GB 727255821
Customer VAT No.	GB 727255821
Terms	90 days
EORI Number	GB376766987000
Page No.	1

		Run No.	210
		Order Type	05

Bankers Details

National WestminsterBank Plc
5 East Street, Chichester
West Sussex PO19 1HH, UK
IBAN GB05NWBK60052496190175

Account No.	96190175
Sort Code	60-05-24
Swift Code	NWBKGB2L600524
BIC No.	NWBKGB2L

Author/ Title	Binding	ISBN/ EAN
Walker	PAPER	059600820
Office 2004 for Macintosh		9780596008208

Index

(Excel), 475

A

absolute references in Excel, 495

Address Book (*see* Entourage Address Book)

Add Current File button (Projects Palette), 667

Advance slide option (Slide Transition dialog box), 631

aligning drawn objects, 686

All Caps, 111

All Commands list, 672

animations (PowerPoint), 641–644

  custom, 642–644

  editing exiting, 644

  preset

    Appear, 642

    Dissolve, 641

    Drive-In/Out, 641

    Flash Once, 641

    Fly In, 641

    Fly In/Out, 641

    Laser Text, 642

  using for special effects, 643

Animation Effects dialog box, 643

Appear animation (PowerPoint), 642

AppleDouble encoding scheme, 367

AppleScript, 699–716

  advantages of, 700

  capabilities, 700

    in Entourage, 460

  dictionary, 699

  online resources, 461

  overview, 700–701

  resources, 715

applets

  installing, 702

  running, 706

arrows, drawing, 685

attachments, 349–353

  adding, 364–367

    encoding and compression options, 367

  Entourage

    actions, 349

    when attachments don't open, 351–353

  file name extensions, 351

Audio Notes (Word), 197–198

Audio Notes Toolbar functions (Word), 198

AutoCaptioning (Word), 247

AutoComplete

  Excel, 472

AutoContent Wizard (PowerPoint), 602

AutoCorrect (Word), 91–93

  turning off, 90

AutoFill

  Excel, 472–475

Across Worksheets option, 473

Down option, 472

fill handle, 474

Justify option, 474

Right, Left option, 472

Series option, 473

AutoFilter menu (Excel), 496, 504

AutoFormat (Excel), 511

AutoFormat (Word), 99–104

  applying in one pass, 103

  options

    Bold and _italic_ with real formatting, 102

    Automatic bulleted lists, 101

    Automatic numbered lists, 101

    Borders, 101

    Define styles based on your formatting, 103

    Format the beginning of a list item like the one before it, 102

    Headings, 100

    Internet paths with hyperlinks, 102

    Ordinals (1st) with superscript, 102

    Symbol characters (--) with symbols (—), 102

    Tables, 101

  using as you type, 100

    "Straight quotes" with "smart quotes", 102

AutoMark (Word), 262

AutoRecovery (Word), 35

AutoShapes, 680, 682

AutoSummarize (Word), 235–237

AutoSum (Excel), 492

AutoSum button (Excel), 487

AutoText (Word), 93–97

  field, 96

  graphics, 96

  setting up entry, 94

  toolbar, 95

  triggering entry, 95

AutoType (Word), 91

AVERAGE (Excel), 487

B

Background dialog box (PowerPoint), 615

Background Sound dialog box (Word), 299

.bat file name extension, 352

BinHex encoding method, 367

bitmap files, 680

Blinds transition (PowerPoint), 629

.bmp file name extension, 352

Borders and Shading dialog box (Word), 142

  extra features, 126

  Horizontal Line button, 129

Box transition (PowerPoint), 629
bulleted lists, 112
   customizing, 115
   pictures as bullets, 115
Bullets and Numbering dialog box (Word),
   114–116, 142
buttons
   adding to toolbars, 671
   drawing your own, 673
   moving or deleting from toolbars, 671

C

Calculator (Excel)
   using to assemble formulas, 489
Calendar (*see* Entourage Calendar)
Categories button (Clip Gallery), 681
cells (Excel), 467
   data entry, 468–470
   difference between Cut command and Copy
      command, 478
   erasing, 481
   inserting and removing, 479
   merging, 525
   number formats (*see* Excel, number formats)
   protecting, 518
   referencing, 467
   selecting all, 477
   selecting block, 476
   selecting noncontiguous group of, 476
   selecting single, 476
   typing data into, 467
Change Slides panel (Formatting Palette), 628
charts, 528–543
   3-D
      move series in, 538
      rotating, 537
   advanced charting, 541–543
   Axes tab, 534
   axis, 536
   axis labels, 536
   creating in one step, 542
   Data Table tab, 535
   deleting elements, 536
   effective chart making
      adding more series, 533
      choosing chart style, 530–532
      customizing chart, 533–536
      placing chart, 536
      selecting data, 529–530
      setting up rows or columns, 532–533
      tweaking charts, 536–540
   error bars, 541
   legend, 536
   moving, 536
   PowerPoint, 624

   repositioning elements, 537
   resizing, 536
   styles of, 530–532
      3-D column charts, 530
      area charts, 531
      bar charts, 530
      bubble charts, 532
      column charts, 530
      cone, cylinder, and pyramid charts, 532
      doughnut charts, 532
      line charts, 531
      pie charts, 531
      radar charts, 532
      stock charts, 532
      surface charts, 532
      XY (Scatter) charts, 531
   Titles tab, 534
   transparent bars, 540
   trend line types, 542
      Exponential, 543
      Linear, 542
      Logarithmic, 542
      Moving Average, 543
      naming your own, 543
      Polynomial, 543
      Power, 543
charts (Word), 160
Chart toolbar, 539
Chart Type dialog box, 542
Chart Wizard, 528–543
Checkerboard transition (PowerPoint), 629
Circle transition (PowerPoint), 629
Clear key, 67
Clipart folder, 681
clippings, organizing, 665
clip art
   adding your own, 681
   Entourage, 680
   working with, 682
Clip Art command, 679
Clip Art Gallery (Word)
   Web page design, 295
Clip Gallery, 680–682
   Categories button, 681
   deleting clips, 682
   Online button, 681
   searching, 682
Color Adjustment tool (Picture toolbar), 693
Color Palettes panel, 690
Color Sliders panel, 690
Color Wheel panel, 689
columns, hiding and showing, 515–549
columns (Word), 146–149
   adding using Columns dialog box, 147
   adding using Standard toolbar, 146

look and flow, 148
resizing, 148
Columns dialog box (Word), 147
Comb transition (PowerPoint), 629
Communicating Bad News template (Power-Point), 601
.com file name extension, 352
Conditional Formatting (Excel), 500, 513
conduits, 444–450
HotSyncing, 447–451
how data differs, 448–450
installing, 444
private records, 447
settings, 445–450
Do Nothing, 446
Entourage overwrites handheld, 445
Handheld overwrites Entourage, 445
Synchronize, 445
special settings, 447
COUNT (Excel), 488
Cover transition (PowerPoint), 629
Create Data Source dialog box (Word), 265
Cube transition (PowerPoint), 630
curves, drawing, 685
Customize Keyboard dialog box (Word), 143
customizing Office, 669–678
Custom Animation dialog box, 642–644
Custom List filter (Excel), 504
Custom Outline dialog box (Word), 206
Cut transition (PowerPoint), 630

D

data
types in Excel, 470–472
databases and Excel, 567–572
FileMaker Pro, 568–570
importing database, 568
selecting data, 569
importing from text file, 572
pulling from Web sites, 571
Data menu (Excel), 583–586
Consolidate command, 586
Filter command, 584
Sort command, 584
Subtotals command, 584
Text to Columns command, 586
data merges, 263–279
creating main document, 268–270
creating new data source, 264–267
Data Merge Manager, 264–279
delimiting numerous fields, 270
header rows and header sources, 267
labels and envelopes, 273–279
editing labels, 276
merging onto envelopes, 277

merging onto labels, 274
propagating labels, 276
merge printing, 271
customizing, 271
query options, 271
merging to email, 272
merging to new document, 272
preparing data source, 264
previewing, formatting, preparing to merge, 270
using existing data source, 267–268
Data Merge Manager, 264–279
Delete key, 67
Diamond transition (PowerPoint), 630
dictionaries, 699
Dissolve animation (PowerPoint), 641
Dissolve transition (PowerPoint), 630
Document Map (Word), 207–209
customizing, 209
viewing and navigating, 208
.doc file name extension, 352
Double strikethrough text effect, 110
drag-and-drop (Word), 63–66
between programs, 64
to desktop, 65
drawings (see images)
Drawing command, 682
drawing grid, 686
Drawing or Picture toolbar, 688
Drawing tool
editing drawn objects, 685
Drawing toolbar, 679, 684–687
aligning drawn objects, 686
Edit Points command, 685
Nudge command, 686
Open Curve command, 686
rotating drawn objects, 687
Draw Table tool (Word), 162
Drive-In/Out animation (PowerPoint), 641
droplets
installing, 702
running, 706
drop caps, 111

E

Edit Points command (Drawing toolbar), 685
Effect option (Slide Transition dialog box), 631
email etiquette, 368
email messages, 357–368
addressing message, 357–359
alignment, 362
attachments, 364–367
encoding and compression options, 367
Bcc field, 358
bullets and indents, 362

Cc field, 357
color, 362
composing body, 360
fonts, 361
HTML versus plain text, 360–364
inserting pictures, sound, or movies, 363
rules, 362
sending, 367
signatures, 363
    adding, 364
spam, 366
SpamCop, 366
styles, 361
subject line, 359–360
embedded objects
creating, 697
editing, 697
embedding and linking objects, 694–698
Emboss text effect, 111
Encarta Encyclopedia, 666
End key, 66
Engrave text effect, 111
Entourage, 315–381
Address Book (*see* Entourage Address Book)
advanced features, 443–461
Advanced Find dialog box, 454
AppleScript capabilities, 460
Calendar (*see* Entourage Calendar)
Categories, 458–459
    assigning, 459
    setting up, 458
clip art and, 680
conduits (*see* conduits)
creating new identity, 451
custom views, 455
directory services, 356
Exchange Server and, 380
finding messages, 452–456
Find Related command, 456
Find window, 453–454
functions, 316–318
    Address Book (*see* Entourage Address Book)
    Calendar (*see* Entourage Calendar)
    Mail (*see* Entourage Mail)
    Notes (*see* Entourage Notes)
    Project Center (*see* Project Center (*see* Entourage Project Center)
    Tasks (*see* Entourage Tasks)
installing Script menu scripts, 703
interface, 317
Junk Mail Filter, 354
Link command, 456–458
Mail (*see* Entourage Mail)
multiple indentities, 450–452

News
    Compose panel, 378
    preferences, 377–381
    Reply & Forward panel, 379
    View panel, 380
    (*see also* newsgroups)
Notes (*see* Entourage Notes)
overview, 315–316
Palm synchronization, 443–444
Preview Pane, 334
scripting resources, 716
scripts
    attach vCard, 708–710
    email-message, 706
Script menu, 460–461
    adding keyboard shortcuts for items, 460
sending and receiving mail, 325–370
setting up, 318–323
setting up account manually, 324
setting up second email account, 324
spell checker, 459
synchronizing with handhelds (*see* conduits)
Tasks (*see* Entourage Tasks)
toolbar, 318
using links, 457
using your .Mac account with your ISP, 323
viruses, email, 351
Entourage Address Book, 425–440
adding picture for contact, 430
calendar icon, 439
capitalization of names, 428
Create Contact window, 427
creating contacts, 426–433
creating groups, 432
dialing contact's telephone number, 438
exporting contacts and archives, 435
flagging contacts, 437
importing contacts, 433–435
    cross-platform, 435
    Import Assistant, 434
information icon, 438
long form, 428–431
    Categories, 429
    Certificate, 430
    Find Related, 429
    Home tab, 429
    Instant Message, 429
    Name & E-mail tab, 429
    New Message To, 429
    Other tab, 430
    Personal tab, 430
    Projects, 429
    Summary tab, 429
    Work tab, 430
message icon, 438

opening, editing, and deleting contacts, 432
overview, 426
printing, 439–440
sending email, 436
small magnifying glass icon, 438
synchronizing, 447
using contacts, 436–438
using contacts in Word, 437
vCards, 431
Web page icon, 438
Entourage Calendar
appointments, 392–399
    deleting events, 395
    editing events, 392
    example of creating, 388–392
    lengthening/shortening events, 393
    printing events, 394
    receiving invitations, 395
    receiving RSVPs for invitations, 396
    rescheduling events, 392
    sending invitations, 395–397
detail calendar, 385
holidays, adding, 397–401
Holidays file, 398
overview, 383–386
overview calendar, 384
recording events, 386–392
saving as Web page, 399–401
synchronizing, 447
viewing days, weeks , and months, 384
Entourage Mail
adding/removing recipients of message, 340
advanced features, 328–334
attached images, sounds, or movies, 335
attachments (*see* attachments, Entourage)
automatic checking on a schedule, 328–331
Compose panel, 378
creating new folders, 344
Custom Arrangements, 348
Deleted Items folder, 338
deleting messages, 337–339
editing messages, 341
email answering machine, 357
filing messages, 344
fixing message database, 339
flagging messages, 346
forwarding messages, 342
headers, 334
History link, 344
linking messages, 347
mailing lists, 341
marking messages as unread, 336
message icons, 336
message rules, 353–357
offline access, 334

options
    Delete Mail, 330
    Excel Auto Web Publish, 330
    Launch Alias, 330
    Receive Mail, 330
    Receive News, 330
    Run AppleScript, 330
    Send All, 330
prefab schedules, 330
preferences, 377–381
printing messages, 344
prioritizing messages, 349
reading messages, 334–337
Read panel, 377
redirecting messages, 343
reformatting messages, 341
replying to messages, 339–341
Reply & Forward panel, 379
restricting download size, 333
selecting messages, 338
Send and Receive All, 325–328
spam filter, 357
threads, 337
types of replies, 340
View panel, 380
writing an email message (*see* email mes-
    sages)
Entourage Notes, 440–442
creating notes, 441
printing notes, 442
Entourage Project Center, 409–421
accessing projects from other Office programs,
    422
Clippings view, 419
Contacts tab, 419
Custom Views, 412
Files tab, 417
getting around, 413–420
Mail tab, 417
New Project Wizard, 410, 416
Note view, 419
Overview tab
    Add icon, 415
    Backup icon, 414
    Calendar, 413
    Properties icon, 415
    Recent Items and Files, 414
    Remove icon, 415
    Share icon, 414
    Tasks, 414
Project Center views, 412
Project Center window, 411
Project Gallery and, 657
Schedule tab, 416
    Calendar, 416

Tasks, 416
sharing projects, 420–421
starting a project, 410–411
Entourage Tasks, 401–406
All Tasks view, 402
changing views, 402
checking off tasks, 405
creating tasks, 403–404
deleting tasks, 405
Due This Week view, 402
Due Today view, 402
editing tasks, 405
filtering tasks, 402
Category and Project, 402
Changed in Last Seven Days, 402
Due Immediately, 402
High Priority, 402
Overdue, 402
Incomplete Tasks view, 402
linking tasks, 405
printing tasks, 405
synchronizing, 447
equations (Word), 160
Esc key, 66
Excel
#####, 475
aligning text, 523–525
Horizontal, 524
Indent, 524
Merge cells, 525
Orientation, 525
Shrink, 525
Vertical, 524
Wrap text, 525
analyzing data, 576–588
(*see also* PivotTables)
attaching custom toolbars, 674
AutoComplete, 472
AutoFill (*see* AutoFill, Excel)
AutoFormat (*see* AutoFormat, Excel), 511
AutoSum, 492
basics, 465–507
calculation order, 491
changing default fonts, 510
charts (*see* charts, Excel)
columns
inserting, 480
selecting, 477
comments, 591
Conditional Formatting, 513
copying, 477
creating styles, 524
Custom List filter, 504
custom views, 588

cutting, 477
data
(*see also* cells; formulas)
entering, 481–484
databases, working with (*see* databases and
Excel)
data forms, 586
Data menu (*see* Data menu)
data tables, 576–577
dates, 471
Dictionary, 591
difference between Cut command and Copy
command, 478
drag-and-drop, 478
erasing borders, 519
exporting files, 560–562
spreadsheet properties, 562
tab-delimited text, 560
templates, 560
Web pages (*see* Excel, Format Web Page
options)
Find and Replace features, 480
flag for follow-up feature, 591
formatting cells manually, 512–519
changing borders and colors, 514
changing cell size, 512–514
hiding and showing rows and columns,
515
formatting numbers as dates, 471
Format Painter, 511
Format Web Page options
Automate, 561
Web Options, 561
Workbook, Sheet, Selection, 561
formulas (*see* formulas)
Goal Seek, 577–579
images and movies, 526–527
inserting by Add Objects palette, 527
inserting by Picture submenu, 526
importing data from text file, 572
installing scripts, 704
lists (*see* lists, Excel)
List Manager (*see* List Manager)
List Wizard (*see* List Wizard)
macros, 592–596
Personal Macro Workbook, 593
playing, 594
problems with, 595
recording, 593–594
sharing, 596
using in menus and toolbars, 595
named ranges, 494
navigation keystrokes, 468–470
number data, 470

number formats, 520–522
  Accounting, 520
  Currency, 520
  Custom, 522
  Date, 521
  Fraction, 521
  General, 520
  Number, 520
  Percentage, 521
  Scientific, 521
  Special, 522
  Text, 521
  Time, 521
one-variable tables, 576–577
outlines, 589
Page Layout view, 467
Paste Special command, 477
pasting, 477
Personal Macro Workbook, 593
Picture toolbar, 526
PivotTables, 572–576
printing (*see* printing, Excel)
proofing tools, 591
pulling data from Web sites, 571
references, 565
  (*see also* formulas, circular references)
references, absolute and relative, 495
reports, 589
rows
  inserting, 480
  selecting, 477
scenarios, 579–581
scripting resources, 716
scripts
  merge columns, 712–715
Solver, 582–583
Spelling dialog box, 591
text, 470
text formatting, 519–526
times, 471
tutorials
  entering data, 481–484
  yearly totals, 491–496
two-variable tables, 576–577
types of data, 470–472
validating data, 587
viewing data, 588–591
workbooks (*see* workbooks)
worksheets (*see* worksheets)
yearly totals tutorial, 491–496
Exchange Server, 380
.exe file name extension, 352
extensions, file name, 351
eyedropper tool, 691

F

Fade transition (PowerPoint), 630
Field dialog box (Word), 238
FileMaker Pro and Excel, 568–570
  importing database, 568
  selecting data, 569
file name extensions, 351
Find and Replace dialog box (Word), 72–78
  finding invisible characters, 77
  Special menu, 77
Fix Red Eye tool (Picture toolbar), 693
Flash Once animation (PowerPoint), 641
Flip transition (PowerPoint), 630
Fly In/Out animation (PowerPoint), 641
Fly In animation (PowerPoint), 641
fonts, 106–112
  All Caps, 111
  changing default in Excel, 510
  choosing, 106
  color type, 110
  drop caps, 111
  sizes, 108
  Small Caps, 111
  styles of type, 108
  text effects, 110
Font dialog box (Word), 142
font issues
  converting slideshows for web display, 648
Footnote and Endnote dialog box (Word), 222
Formatting Palette, 688
  Change Slides panel, 628
  Note Flags panel, 196
Formatting Palette (Excel), 516–519
  Borders and Shading
    Color control, 518
    Draw border control, 518
    Fill color control, 518
    Pattern control, 518
    Style control, 518
    Type control, 517
  changing fonts, 522
  decimal places, 522
  specialized formatting controls, 539
Formatting Palette (Word), 105–135
  All Caps, 111
  character formatting, 106–112
  choosing fonts, 106–108
  color type, 110
  document formatting (*see* document formatting)
  drop caps, 111
  font sizes, 108
  hidden text, 112
  lists (*see* lists)

page numbering across sections, 134
paragraph formatting (*see* paragraph formatting)
section formatting, 132–135
    formatting within sections, 133
    section breaks, 132
Small Caps, 111
text effects, 110
type styles, 108–109
Format Cells dialog box (Excel), 500
formatting numbers, 520–522
protecting cells, 518
Format dialog box, 688
Colors and Lines tab, 688–691
    arrows (drawing objects only), 691
    fill color, fill effects, 690
    fill color, more colors, 689
    fill color, standard palette, 689
    Line pop-up menus (drawing objects only), 691
    pick line color/pick fill color, 691
    transparency, 691
Picture tab, 692
Scale tab, 692
Format Painter (Excel), 511
Format Painter (Word), 28, 121
formulas, 467
advanced, 562–567
auditing, 566
basic calculations, 484–486
    error checking, 485
circular references, 564–565
    iterations, 564
connecting to other workbooks, 566
correcting errors, 566
difference between Cut command and Copy command, 478
error checking, 485
functions, 486–490
    anatomy of, 488
    AutoSum button, 487
    Looking up, 488
    screen tips, 487
linking, 566
nested, 562
overview, 484–496
using Calculator to assemble, 489
Formula Palette, 563–564
Forward Delete key, 67
.fp5 and .fp7 file name extensions, 353
Freeform tool, 685
From Scanner or Camera command, 680
function keys, 67

G

GIF files, 650
.gif file name extension, 352
GIF images, 680
Goal Seek (Excel), 577–579
Gradient tab, 691
Grammar Settings dialog box (Word), 85
graphics (*see* images)
graphics programs, 679–698
grids
drawing, 686

H

handhelds and synchronization (*see* conduits)
Handheld Sync Installer, 444
Help key, 68
Holidays file, 398
Home key, 66
horizontal lines
inserting, 679
HotSyncing, 447–450
how data differs, 448–450
HTML documents (*see* Web pages)
.html or .htm file name extension, 353
hyperlinks, 300–307
email hyperlinks, 305–306
linking to another Web site, 303–305
    by dragging URL, 303
    by typing URL, 303
    by using Favorite or History, 304
linking to application or Mac file, 303
linking to other place or Word document, 300–302
removing, 307
screen tips, 306
selecting and editing, 306
hyphenation (Word), 149–151
hard hyphens, 150
manual, 150
settings, 150

I

images
distinction between pictures and drawings, 680
downloading from Web, 295
Excel (*see* Excel, images and movies)
formats on Web, 296
formatting, 687–693
inserting, 679
photographs, 680
    removing red eye and scratches, 693
pictures as bullets in bulleted lists, 115
PowerPoint, 617

saving PowerPoint slides as graphics, 649
text wrapping
Web page design, 296
transparency, 691
Word, 158–159
converting inline into page graphics, 159
inline versus page graphics, 158
Image Palettes, 690
IMAP email, 319
configuring IMAP options, 326
Insert Picture button, 679
Ins key, 66

J

JPEG files, 650
JPEG images, 680
.jpg file name extension, 352

K

keyboard shortcuts
Excel, 468–470
Keynote, 699

L

Laser Text animation (PowerPoint), 642
lines, drawing, 684–687
Lines tool, 684
linked objects
creating, 694
editing, 695
overriding automatic updates, 696
repairing broken links, 696
linking and embedding objects, 694–698
lists
Excel, 496–507
adding rows or columns, 503
deleting rows or columns, 503
moving or deleting whole list, 505
rearranging rows or columns, 503
sorting and filtering, 504
total row, 505
Word, 112–116
bulleted, 112
Bullets and Numbering dialog box,
114–116
numbered, 114
List Manager (Excel), 497, 505, 507, 551, 570
List menu (Excel)
Chart command, 506
Filter command, 506
Form command, 506
PivotTable Report command, 506
Refresh Data command, 506
Remove List Manager command, 506
Sort command, 506

List toolbar (Excel), 503
List Wizard (Excel), 497, 498, 501, 502, 505, 659
Looking up functions (Excel), 488

M

Mac
using as Web server, 400
macros
Excel, 592–596
Personal Macro Workbook, 593
playing, 594
problems with, 595
recording, 593–594
sharing, 596
using in menus and toolbars, 595
Word, 279–283
creating, 279–282
Macros dialog box, 281, 283
Organizer, 283
running, 282
Visual Basic, 283
.Mac account with your ISP, using, 323
Mac OS X's handwriting recognition program,
191
Mac OS X Script menu
making visible, 704
Magic Lasso tool (Picture toolbar), 694
mailing lists
etiquette, 369
mail (*see* Entourage)
Make Movie command (PowerPoint), 646
Marquee tools (Picture toolbar), 694
Master Documents (Word), 209–215
assigning passwords, 214
creating subdocuments, 210
deleting subdocuments, 214
formatting, 214
locking and unlocking subdocuments, 214
opening and expanding subdocuments, 212
removing subdocuments, 213
security, 214–215
sharing on network, 215
splitting and combining subdocuments, 213
turning existing Word document into subdocument, 211
viewing, 211–212
viewing and renaming subdocuments, 212
MAX (Excel), 488
Meeting Minder, 635
menus
adding, 676
adding commands, 674
assigning keyboard shortcut in Word, 678
moving specific commands, 676
moving whole, 676

redesigning, 674–677
removing, 676
removing commands, 675
resetting, 677
Microsoft User Data folder, 702
MIME/Base64 encoding method, 367
MIN (Excel), 488
movies
embedded in Word for Web, 297
Excel (*see* Excel, images and movies)
QuickTime (*see* QuickTime movies)
.mp3 file name extension, 352
.mpg file name extension, 352
MSN, 666
MSN MoneyCentral
Currencies (Excel query), 571
Major Indices (Excel query), 572
Stock Quotes (Excel query), 572

N

named ranges, 494
narration, 644–646
Newsflash transition (PowerPoint), 630
newsgroups, 370–381
composing, forwarding, and replying to messages, 375
downloading list of, 373
etiquette, 375
finding, 374
reading messages, 374–375
Read panel, 377
setting up account, 371–372
New Project Wizard (Entourage), 410, 416
New Slide dialog box, 600, 603, 604, 605, 610,
613
Normal (PowerPoint View control), 611
Notebook Layout view (Word), 34, 189–200
Audio Notes, 197–198
Audio Notes Toolbar functions, 198
changing appearance of lines, 200
flagging actions items, 196
labelling sections, 199
lined or unlined, 199
Mac OS X's handwriting recognition program,
191
opening, 190–192
non-Notebook Word document, 191
organizing notes, 193–196
setting text levels with Formatting Palette,
194
setting text levels with keyboard and
mouse, 194
sorting headings, 195
placing notes besides notes, 196
toolbar, 192–193

Audio Note Toolbar, 193
Eraser, 193
Quick Search, 193
Scribble, 192
Select Objects, 193
tracking in Entourage, 196
Notes (*see* Entourage Notes)
Note Flags panel of Formatting Palette, 196
Nudge command (Drawing toolbar), 686
numbered lists, 114
customizing, 115
number formats (*see* Excel, number formats)

O

ODBC (Open Database Connectivity), 567
Office Clip Gallery (*see* Clip Gallery)
Office Notifications, 406–409
acting on notifications, 407–409
alerts, 407
Complete checkbox, 408
configuring, 409
Dismiss button, 408
Notifications window, 406–407
Open Item button, 407
Snooze button, 408
turning on/off, 409
turning sound on/off, 409
OLE (Object Linking and Embedding),
694–698
Online button (Clip Gallery), 681
Open Curve command (Drawing toolbar), 686
Open Database Connectivity (ODBC), 567
Open dialog box (Word)
Enable, 16
finding files, 16
Folder Selection Menu, 17
New Folder, 18
Open, 17
View Buttons, 17
Open Entourage Project Watch Folder button
(Projects Palette), 667
Organizer (Word), 231
Organizing Clippings (Toolbox), 665
Outliner (Word), 200–207
building outlines, 201–203
Breaking up headings, 203
Inserting body text, 202
Promoting and demoting, 202
Rearranging headings, 202
Choose from the Previous level number menu,
206
choosing new level in Level box, 207
customizing outlines, 205–207
Custom Outline dialog box, 206
expanding/collapsing outlines, 203

Follow number with menu, 206
Legal style numbering box, 207
Link level to style menu, 206
ListNum field list name box, 207
numbering outlines, 204
Number Format panel, 206
Number position panel, 206
outlining existing document, 204
renumbering numbered outlines, 205
Start at box, 206
Text position box, 206
Outline (PowerPoint View control), 611
Outline text effect, 111
Outline view (PowerPoint), 605–608

P

page borders, 127–128
Page Layout view (Excel), 467
Page Setup dialog box (Excel), 545–549
Header/Footer tab, 547
Margins tab, 546
Page tab, 546
Sheet tab, 548
Page Setup dialog box (PowerPoint), 650
Page Up and Page Down keys, 68
painting files, 680
Palm synchronization with Entourage,
443–444
Paragraph dialog box (Word), 142
paragraph formatting, 116–129
Borders and Shading, 125–130
extra features, 126
page borders, 127–128
shading, 128
text and paragraph borders, 125
horizontal alignment, 117
indentation, 120–122
first line indent, 121
hanging indent, 121
left and right indent, 121–122
line spacing, 117
orientation, 119
spacing, 119–120
widows and orphans, 118
Paste as Hyperlink command (Word), 62
Paste Function dialog box (Excel), 489
Paste Special command (Word), 60–61
Formatted Text (RTF), 60
HTML Format, 61
links, 60
Microsoft Word Document Object, 60
Picture, 61
Styled Text, 61
Unformatted Text, 61
Word Hyperlink, 60

Pattern tab, 691
.pdf file name extension, 352
Personal Macro Workbook, 593
photos (see images)
pictures (see images)
Picture Effects (Picture toolbar), 693
Picture tab, 691
Picture toolbar, 693–694
Picture toolbar (Excel), 526
PICT files, 650
.pif file name extension, 352
PivotTables
creating, 572–576
Plus transition (PowerPoint), 630
PNG files, 650
Pointer Options (slideshows), 635
POP email, 319
PowerPoint
adding images, 617
advanced features, 627–654
animations (see animations)
AutoContent Wizard, 602
backgrounds, 614
Background dialog box, 615
basic, 599–625
building slides, 613–625
bullets, 616
changing designs, 603
charts, 624
deleting slides, 613
dictionary, 699
editing and formatting text, 616
inserting new slide, 613
inserting slides from other presentations, 613
installing scripts, 704
movies, 620–623
Movie from File, 621
Movie from Gallery, 620
multimedia effects, 640–650
Play CD Audio Track, 623
printing, 650–653
notes and handouts, 652
page setup, 650
slides, 652
Project Gallery, 600
rearranging slides, 613
Record Sound, 623
saving slides as graphics, 649
scripting resources, 716
Select Objects tool, 615
sound, 620–623
Sound from File, 622
Sound from Gallery, 622
starting from scratch, 603
tables, 618–620

templates, 600
    adding your own, 603
    Communicating Bad News, 601
Text Box tool, 615
turning off features, 614
using Word outline, 607
View controls, 611–612
Word tables, 618
working with text, 615
writing outline, 605–608
(*see also* slideshows)
.ppt file name extension, 352
presentations (*see* slideshows)
Presenter Tools, 638–639
printing
    Entourage
        messages, 344
    Entourage Address Book, 439–440
    Entourage Calendar, 394
    Entourage Notes, 442
    Entourage Tasks, 405
    Excel, 543–549
        page setup, 545
        Print Preview (Apple), 545
        Print Preview (Microsoft), 543–545
    PowerPoint, 650–653
        notes and handouts, 652
        page setup, 650
        slides, 652
    Word, 38–53
        envelopes, 48
        labels, 50
        Page Setup, 43–44
        Print button, 38
        Print dialog box (*see* Print dialog box)
        Print Preferences, 46–48
        Print Preview, 44–46
Print dialog box (Word)
    advanced settings, 40
    Cancel, 43
    Copies and Pages, 39
    FAX, 43
    Layout, 39
    Microsoft Word panel, 40
    Output options, 40
    Preview, 42
    Print settings, 40
    Save as PDF, 43
    Saving custom settings, 42
    Summary, 42
projectors, using, 633
projects, 667
    (*see also* Entourage Project Center)
Projects Palette button, 667
Project Center (*see* Entourage Project Center)

Project Gallery, 657–663
    accessing projects from, 422
    closing, 663
    composing documents, 659–663
    Customize panel, 662
    customizing, 662
    document templates, 659
    Entourage's new Project Center and, 657
    Learn button, 661
    New tab, 659
    opening documents, 658
    Open Other button, 663
    PowerPoint, 600
    Project button, 661
    Recent button, 660
    Show pop-up menu, 663
    templates, 97–99
    View buttons, 663
Project Gallery (Word), 14–15
.psd file name extension, 352
Push transition (PowerPoint), 630

Q

Quick Time movies
    embedded in Word for Web, 297
    saving slideshows as, 638, 646–648
    specifying dimensions, 647
quotes, curly and straight, 74

R

.ra, .rm, or .ram file name extension, 352
Random transition (PowerPoint), 630
raster graphics, 680
Reference Tools, 665–667
relative references in Excel, 495
Remove Current File button (Projects Palette), 667
Remove Scratch tool (Picture toolbar), 693
Reviewing toolbar (Word), 176
rows
    hiding and showing, 515
.rtf file name extension, 353

S

Save Version dialog box (Word), 186
scenarios (Excel), 579–581
Scrapbook, 663–665
    accessing projects from, 423
scripting (*see* AppleScript; scripts)
scripts
    downloading, 702
    installing and running, 702–706
    installing Entourage Script menu scripts, 703
    installing Word, Excel, and PowerPoint, 704
    running, 706

starter, 706–715
    Entourage attach vCard script, 708–710
    Entourage email-message script, 706
    merge columns in Excel, 712–715
    remove extra carriage returns in Word, 710–712

Script menu, 460–461
    adding keyboard shortcuts for items, 460
    scripts
        Create Event from Message, 460
        Insert Text File, 461
        Save Selection, 461

Script menu scripts
    installing Entourage scripts, 703
    Mac OS X, 704
    running, 706

.scr file name extension, 352

section formatting (*see* Formatting Palette, section formatting)

Select Objects tool (PowerPoint), 615

servers
    using Mac as Web server, 400

Set Transparent Color button (Picture toolbar), 693

Shadow button (Picture toolbar), 693

Shadow text effect, 111

shapes, drawing, 684–687

shortcut keys (Word), printing out list of, 68

signatures (email), 363
    adding, 364

slideshows
    adding button to just one slide, 636
    adding button to same location in group of slides, 636
    building, 608–613
    changing appearance of Action Button, 638
    control-clicking while running, 635
    converting for web display, 648–649
        font issues, 648
    handouts, 611
    helpful keystrokes, 606, 636
    hiding slides, 640
    making, 627–640
    making presentations, 632–636
        choosing navigation scheme, 634
        presenting onscreen, 635
        rehearsing, 632
        setting up, 632
    masters
        adding new elements, 609
        editing, 608
        handout, 611
        notes, 611
        title slide master, 610
        using, 608–611
    Meeting Minder and, 635
    moving around inside full-screen show, 635
    narration, 644–646
    navigation, 612
    notes, 611
    placing Action Button on slide, 637
    placing controls on slides, 636–638
    Pointer Options, 635
    Presenter Tools, 638–639
    presenting Mac version on PC, 647
    printing, 652
    projectors, using, 633
    recycling, 639–641
    saving as QuickTime movies, 638, 646–648
    Screen submenu, 636
    transitions (*see* transitions)
    (*see also* PowerPoint)

Slideshow (PowerPoint View control), 612

Slide (PowerPoint View control), 611

Slide Sorter (PowerPoint View control), 612

Slide Sorter toolbar, 628, 640

Slide Transition dialog box, 628, 629, 631, 633
    Advance slide option, 631
    Effect option, 631
    Sound option, 631

Small Caps, 111

Smart Cut and Paste (Word), 65

Solver (Excel), 582–583

Solver Parameters dialog box, 582
    By Changing Cells, 583
    Equal To, 583
    Set Target Cell, 583
    Subject to the Constraints, 583

sound, embedded in Word for Web, 299–300

Sound option (Slide Transition dialog box), 631

SpamCop, 366

special effects
    using animations for, 643

special keys
    Clear key, 67
    Delete key, 67
    End key, 66
    Esc key, 66
    Forward Delete key, 67
    function keys, 67
    Help key, 68
    Home key, 66
    Ins key, 66
    Page Up and Page Down keys, 68

Split transition (PowerPoint), 630

spreadsheets (*see* workbooks; worksheets)

Strikethrough text effect, 110

Strips transition (PowerPoint), 630

StuffIt, 367

styles (Word), 137–144
 Add to templates, 142
 applying, 139–140
 Automatically update, 142
 changing, deleting, or copying, 143–144
 creating by example, 140
 creating in dialog box, 141–143
  Name, 141
  Style based on, 141
  Style for following paragraph, 142
 deleting multiple styles, 144
 Formatting panel, 142
 Format pop-up menu, 142
 Paragraph in the Style type menu, 142
 storage location, 139
 transferring, 144
Subscript text effect, 110
Superscript text effect, 110
symbols in Word, 224
synchronizing handhelds (*see* conduits)

T

tables (Word), 160–173
 adding column of figures, 172
 adding rows and columns, 165
 alignment, 169
 AutoFit, 169
 Autoformatting, 167
 automatic sizing, 164
 background shading, 167
 balanced columns, 164
 Borders and Shading, 166
 cell margins and spacing, 167
 converting table to text, 171
 converting text to table, 171
 creating, 160–166
 deleting cells, 166
 deleting rows and columns, 166
 deleting whole table, 166
 Draw Table tool, 162
 formatting, 166–173
 formulas, 171
  cell references, 172
  functions, 173
  operators, 173
 headings, 167
 merging and splitting cells, 170
 navigation shortcuts, 163
 nested tables, 169
 resizing whole table, 165
 selecting cells, 163
 setting rows and columns to exact sizes, 164
 size, 169
 sizing rows and columns, 164
 sorting, 173

 text formatting within cells, 168
 text wrapping, 169
 thin gray lines, 166
 typing into, 163
tabs (*see* Word, tabs)
Tabs dialog box (Word), 142
templates
 PowerPoint, 600
  adding your own, 603
  Communicating Bad News, 601
 Project Gallery, 97–99, 659
 Word (*see* Word, templates)
text
 copying, 58
 drag-and-drop, 63–66
  between programs, 64
  to desktop, 65
 effects, 110
 finding and replacing, 71–78
 Paste Special (*see* Paste Special command)
 pasting, 59
 selecting, 55–58
 selecting multiple items, 58
Texture tab, 691
text boxes (Word), 151–158
 changing background color, 154
 changing border styles, 154
 changing text direction, 153
 creating, 152
 formatting within, 153–155
 linked, 155
  copying, 155
  deleting, 155
  grouping, 155
 linking and unlinking, 152
 navigating, 153
 sizing, 154
Text Box toolbar (Word), 152–153
Text Box tool (PowerPoint), 615
text wrapping
 Web page design, 296
.tif or .tiff file name extension, 352
toolbars
 adding buttons, 671
 changing shapes of, 669
 creating custom, 671–673
 custom
  attaching to Excel workbook, 674
  attaching to Word document, 674
 customizing, 669–674
 designing from scratch, 671–674
 moving, 669
 moving or deleting buttons, 671
 Notebook Layout view (Word), 192–193
 showing other, 670

Toolbox, 663–668
  accessing projects from, 422
  Organize title bar, 665
  Scrapbook, 663–665
Tools menu
  accessing projects from, 422
transitions (PowerPoint), 627–631
  Blinds, 629
  Box, 629
  Checkerboard, 629
  Circle, 629
  Comb, 629
  Cover, 629
  Cube, 630
  customizing, 631–632
  Cut, 630
  Diamond, 630
  Dissolve, 630
  Fade, 630
  Flip, 630
  how they work, 628
  Newsflash, 630
  Plus, 630
  Push, 630
  Random, 630
  Split, 630
  Strips, 630
  types of, 628–631
  Uncover, 630
  Wedge, 630
  Wheel, 630
  Wipe, 630
transparency, 691
typing less, 90–104
  AutoCorrect (Word), 91–93
  AutoFormat (see AutoFormat)
  AutoText, 93–97
  click and type, 90
  Project Gallery templates, 97–99

U

Uncover transition (PowerPoint), 630
Usenet (see newsgroups)
UUEncode, 367

V

vCards, 431
.vcfm file name extension, 353
Versions dialog box, 186–188
viruses, email, 351
Visual Basic, 283

W

Web, downloading images from, 295
Web-based email, 319

Web forms, 307–308
Web pages
  design in Word (see Word, Web page design)
  posting online, 311
  pulling data into Excel, 571
  saving as Word document, 310
  saving Entourage Calendar as, 399–401
  saving from Word, 308–311
    options, 309
  translation problems saving from Word, 310
Web servers
  using Mac as, 400
Wedge transition (PowerPoint), 630
Wheel transition (PowerPoint), 630
Wipe transition (PowerPoint), 630
.wmf file name extension, 352
Word
  Advanced Find, 74
  All Caps, 111
  assigning keyboard shortcut to menus, 678
  as Web browser, 286–287
  attaching custom toolbars, 674
  AutoCaptioning, 247
  AutoCorrect (see AutoCorrect)
  AutoFormat (see AutoFormat)
  AutoMark, 262
  AutoRecovery, 35
  AutoSummarize, 235–237
  AutoText (see AutoText)
  AutoType (see AutoType)
  backing up files, 37
  bookmarks, 242–244
    adding, 242
    deleting, 242
    hidden, 244
    navigating by, 243
    viewing, 244
  Borders and Shading dialog box, 142
  Bullets and Numbering dialog box, 142
  captions, 244–248
    adding text to, 246
    AutoCaptioning, 247
    deleting and editing, 246
    inserting, 244–246
    labels, 244
    numbering, 245
    positioning, 244
    updating, 247
  change tracking, 178–184
    accepting or rejecting all changes, 183
    identifying yourself, 179
    making changes, 180–182
    merging tracked changes, 184
    options, 181
    preparing, 179–180

reviewing changes one by one, 182–183
turning on, 179
character formatting, 106–112
charts, 160
choosing fonts, 106–108
Clip Art Gallery
Web page design, 295
color type, 110
columns, 146–149
adding using Columns dialog box, 147
adding using Standard toolbar, 146
look and flow, 148
resizing, 148
comments, 175–178
adding, 175–177
deleting, 178
navigating, 178
reviewing, 177
comparing documents, 185
copying text, 58
Create Data Source dialog box, 265
creating and opening documents, 13–19
cross-references, 248–251
inserting, 249–250
modifying and deleting, 250–251
Customize Keyboard dialog box, 143
custom dictionaries, 86–89
adding and removing, 88
choosing before spell checking, 88
creating new, 87
editing, 86
exclude dictionaries, 88
foreign language, 88
Custom Outline dialog box, 206
Data Merge Manager, 264–279
dictionary, 699
document formatting, 130–131
headers and footers (see Word, headers
and footers), 130
margins, 130
mirror margins, 131
document protection, 20
downloading images from Web, 295
drag-and-drop, 63–66
between programs, 64
to desktop, 65
Draw Table tool, 162
drop caps, 111
equations, 160
fast saves, 37
fields, 237–242
building in Field dialog box, 238
displaying, 241
inserting, 237
locking, unlocking, and unlinking, 241

modifying with switches, 239
printing options, 242
updating, 241
what fields do, 240
finding and replacing, 71–78
finding files with Open dialog box, 16
finding invisible characters, 77
find by format, 75–77
Find command, 72
Font dialog box, 142
font sizes, 108
footnotes and endnotes, 221–225
controlling flow, 223
deleting, 223
nonstandard numbering, 222
Formatting Palette (see Formatting Palette)
Formatting panel, 142
Format pop-up menu, 142
Frame around a paragraph, 142
Go To command, 68–69
Grammar Settings dialog box, 85
gutters, 131
headers and footers, 130, 217–221
bound-book pages, 220
different for different sections, 221
page numbers, 219
positioning, 220
title page, 220
hidden text, 112
hyphenation, 149–151
hard hyphens, 150
manual, 150
settings, 150
indexes, 256–263
AutoMarking long documents, 262
cleaning up, 263
creating index entries, 257–259
cross-references, 258
deleting, 263
editing index field codes, 260
generating the index, 261–262
page-range entries, 259
inserting breaks, 144–146
column, 145
line, 145
page, 145
paragraph, 144
section, 145
installing scripts, 704
Internet and, 285–311
language choices, 142
line numbering, 225–226
linking to Web, 63
lists (see lists)
margins, 130

Master Documents (*see* Master Documents)
mirror margins, 131
navigation buttons, 22
Navigator buttons, 69
    Browse by Comment, 70
    Browse by Edit, 71
    Browse by Field, 70
    Browse by Footnote, 70
    Browse by Graphic, 70
    Browse by Heading, 71
    Browse by Page, 70
    Browse by Section, 70
    Browse by Table, 70
Notebooks (*see* Notebook Layout view)
opening Web pages from hard drive, 286
opening Web pages from Web, 286
Open command, 15–18
Organizer, 231
Outliner (*see* Outliner)
page layout, 144–149
page numbering across sections, 134
page numbers, 219
Paragraph dialog box, 142
Paste as Hyperlink, 62
Paste Special (*see* Paste Special command)
pasting text, 59
posting Web pages online, 311
preparing to send a reviewed document, 186
printing (*see* printing, Word)
Project Gallery (*see* Project Gallery)
Recent Files list, 18
Replace command, 73
Reviewing toolbar, 176
ruler, 22
Save As options, 36
Save Version dialog box, 186
saving files, 35–38
saving Web pages, 308–311
    as Word document, 310
    options, 309
    translation problems, 310
scripting resources, 716
scripts
    remove extra carriage returns, 710–712
scroll bar, 22
selecting multiple items, 58
selecting text, 55–58
Send To command, 52
shortcut keys, printing out list of, 68
Small Caps, 111
Smart Cut and Paste, 65
spelling and grammar, 79–89
    checking all at once, 80–83
    checking spelling as you type, 79
    options, 83–85

Split box, 22
spreadsheets, 160
Standard toolbar, 27–32
    Close, 32
    Columns, 30
    Cut, Copy, Paste, 28
    Envelopes, 32
    Flag for Follow Up, 27
    Formatting Palette, 31
    Format Painter, 28
    Hyperlink, 32
    Insert Excel Spreadsheet, 32
    Insert Table, 29
    Links, 32
    magnifying glass icon, 32
    Navigation Pane, 30
    New Blank Document, Open, Save, 27
    Office Assistant, 31
    Print, 28
    Print Preview, 28
    Redo, 29
    Scrapbook, 32
    Show/Hide, 30
    Spelling and Grammar, 31
    Tables and Borders, 29
    Toolbox, 30
    Undo, 28
    Web Page Preview, 28
    Web Toolbar, 32
    Zoom, 31
status bar, 24–26
styles (*see* styles)
symbols, 224
tables in PowerPoint, 618
Table of Authorities, 255
Table of Contents (TOC), 251–256
    built-in headings, 251–253
    custom formatting, 254
    updating or deleting, 254–256
    using other styles, 253–254
Table of Figures, 255
tabs, 122–125
    applying to paragraphs and styles, 124
    bar, 123
    centered, 123
    decimal, 123
    default, 123
    left, 123
    right, 123
    setting, 123
    types, 123
Tabs dialog box, 142
templates, 226–234
    document templates, 227
    document templates, attaching, 229–230

global templates, 228
global templates, loading as, 233
modifying, 228
Normal template, 232–233
Organizer, 230
text boxes (*see* text boxes)
Text Box toolbar, 152–153
text effects, 110
text wrapping and layering, 156–158
    layering text with graphics, 157
title bar, 21
type styles, 108–109
typing less, 90–104
    AutoCorrect, 91–93
    AutoFormat (*see* AutoFormat)
    AutoText, 93–97
    click and type, 90
    Project Gallery templates, 97–99
using Address Book contacts in, 437
using Word outline in PowerPoint, 607
versioning, 186–188
    automatically saving a version, 187
    deleting a version, 188
    opening a version, 187
    saving a version, 186
    spinning off a version, 187
viewing HTML code, 287
views, 32–35
    Master Document, 34
    Normal, 33
    Notebook Layout (*see* Notebook Layout
        view)
    Online Layout, 33
    Outline, 34
    Page Layout, 33
Web page design, 287–295
    animated text, 292
    backgrounds, 291
    basic layout, 288–295
    bullets, 296
    designing site map, 288
    dividers, 296
    font color, 291
    horizontal lines, 297
    hyperlinks (*see* hyperlinks)
    movies, 297–299
    scrolling text, 292
    sound, 299–300
    Style Gallery, 290
    tables, 294
    text effects, 292
    text wrapping, 296
    Themes, 288
    Web forms, 307–308
    Web page preview, 300

Window menu, 23
word processing basics, 19–21
Work menu, 19
writing styles, 85–86
WordArt, 680, 683
word processing basics, 19–21
workbooks (Excel), 465
    connecting to other, 566
    merging, 558–559
    Protect Sheet command (*see* worksheets,
        Protect Sheet command)
    referring to other, 565
    requiring passwords, 556
    shared
        limitations, 555
        protecting, 557
    Share Workbook command, 554–557
        Conflicting changes between users, 555
        Include in personal view, 555
        Track changes, 554
        Update changes, 554
    worksheets and, 551–562
worksheets (Excel)
    adding, 552
    data (*see* cells; formulas)
    deleting, 552
    formatting, 509–527
    hiding and showing, 552
    moving and copying, 553
    opening, 465–467
    printing (*see* printing, Excel)
    Protect Sheet command
        Allow selection of only certain parts of a
            worksheet, 557
        Hide rows, columns, or sheets, 557
        Protecting a shared workbook, 557
        Protect a sheet from changes, 556
        Protect a workbook from changes, 556
        Protect individual cells from changes, 556
        Require a password to open a workbook,
            556
    renaming, 467, 553
    scrolling through sheet tabs, 553
    showing more or fewer tabs, 554
    size limits, 467
    tracking changes, 557–558
    tricks, 469
    workbooks and, 551–562
    working with multiple, 551–554
.wpd file name extension, 353
.wps file name extension, 353

X

.xls file name extension, 352

Colophon

This book was written in Word 2004 on various Macs around the country and edited using the tracking feature described in Chapter 5. The screenshots were captured with Ambrosia Software's Snapz Pro X (*www.ambrosiasw.com*).

Phil Simpson designed and produced the cover of this book, based on a series design by David Freedman. Rose Cassano created the cover illustration with Adobe Illustrator CS. The fonts used for the cover include Adobe's Minion and Gill Sans font families. Simpson designed and laid out the interior of the book in Adobe InDesign 3.0 on a Macintosh PowerMac G5 and PowerBook G4. The fonts used include Formata (as the sans-serif family) and Minion (as the serif body face). To provide the and ⌘ symbols, Simpson created a custom font using Macromedia Fontographer.

Rob Romano and Lesley Borash created the illustrations using Adobe Photoshop CS and Macromedia Freehand MX.

John Cacciatore and Stephanie English proofread the book in PDF files generated by Adobe Acrobat. Julie Hawks created the index and Caroline Savello cross-referenced the book in Adobe InDesign

The book was transmitted to the printing plant in the form of PDF files.

Related Titles Available from O'Reilly

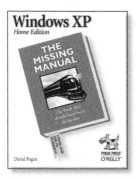

Missing Manuals

AppleWorks 6: The Missing Manual

Dreamweaver MX 2004: The Missing Manual

GarageBand: The Missing Manual

Google: The Missing Manual

iLife '04: The Missing Manual

iMovie 4 and iDVD: The Missing Manual

iPhoto 4: The Missing Manual

iPod & iTunes: The Missing Manual, *2nd Edition*

Mac OS X: The Missing Manual, *Panther Edition*

Windows 2000 Pro: The Missing Manual

Windows XP Pro: The Missing Manual

Windows XP Home Edition: The Missing Manual

POGUE PRESS™
O'REILLY®

Our books are available at most retail and online bookstores.
To order direct: 1-800-998-9938 • *order@oreilly.com* • *www.oreilly.com*
Online editions of most O'Reilly titles are available by subscription at *safari.oreilly.com*

Keep in touch with O'Reilly

1. Download examples from our books

To find example files for a book, go to:

www.oreilly.com/catalog

select the book, and follow the "Examples" link.

2. Register your O'Reilly books

Register your book at *register.oreilly.com*

Why register your books?
Once you've registered your O'Reilly books you can:

- Win O'Reilly books, T-shirts or discount coupons in our monthly drawing.
- Get special offers available only to registered O'Reilly customers.
- Get catalogs announcing new books (US and UK only).
- Get email notification of new editions of the O'Reilly books you own.

3. Join our email lists

Sign up to get topic-specific email announcements of new books and conferences, special offers, and O'Reilly Network technology newsletters at:

elists.oreilly.com

It's easy to customize your free elists subscription so you'll get exactly the O'Reilly news you want.

4. Get the latest news, tips, and tools

www.oreilly.com

- "Top 100 Sites on the Web"—PC Magazine
- CIO Magazine's Web Business 50 Awards

Our web site contains a library of comprehensive product information (including book excerpts and tables of contents), downloadable software, background articles, interviews with technology leaders, links to relevant sites, book cover art, and more.

5. Work for O'Reilly

Check out our web site for current employment opportunities:

jobs.oreilly.com

6. Contact us

O'Reilly & Associates
1005 Gravenstein Hwy North
Sebastopol, CA 95472 USA

TEL: 707-827-7000 or 800-998-9938
(6am to 5pm PST)

FAX: 707-829-0104

order@oreilly.com
For answers to problems regarding your order or our products. To place a book order online, visit:

www.oreilly.com/order_new

catalog@oreilly.com
To request a copy of our latest catalog.

booktech@oreilly.com
For book content technical questions or corrections.

corporate@oreilly.com
For educational, library, government, and corporate sales.

proposals@oreilly.com
To submit new book proposals to our editors and product managers.

international@oreilly.com
For information about our international distributors or translation queries. For a list of our distributors outside of North America check out:

international.oreilly.com/distributors.html

adoption@oreilly.com
For information about academic use of O'Reilly books, visit:

academic.oreilly.com

POGUE PRESS™
O'REILLY®

Our books are available at most retail and online bookstores.
To order direct: 1-800-998-9938 • order@oreilly.com • www.oreilly.com
Online editions of most O'Reilly titles are available by subscription at *safari.oreilly.com*

Buy *Office 2004 for Macintosh: The Missing Manual* and access the digital edition

FREE on Safari for 45 days.

Go to **www.oreilly.com/go/safarienabled**
and type in coupon code **0MI2-TAIH-DP5C-VVHY-SCW1**

Better than e-books

Search
over 2000 top
tech books

Download
whole chapters

Cut and Paste
code examples

Find
answers fast

Read books from cover
to cover. Or, simply click
to the page you need.

**Search Safari! The premier electronic reference
library for programmers and IT professionals**

Addison
Wesley

Sun
microsystems

ALPHA

Java

Microsoft
Press

Peachpit
Press

O'REILLY

que

macromedia
PRESS

PRENTICE
HALL
PTR

AdobePress
SAMS
New
Riders
Cisco Press

Part# 40421

Get even more for your money.

Join the O'Reilly Community, and register the O'Reilly books you own. It's free, and you'll get:

- $4.99 ebook upgrade offer
- 40% upgrade offer on O'Reilly print books
- Membership discounts on books and events
- Free lifetime updates to ebooks and videos
- Multiple ebook formats, DRM FREE
- Participation in the O'Reilly community
- Newsletters
- Account management
- 100% Satisfaction Guarantee

Signing up is easy:

1. Go to: oreilly.com/go/register
2. Create an O'Reilly login.
3. Provide your address.
4. Register your books.

Note: English-language books only

To order books online:
oreilly.com/store

For questions about products or an order:
orders@oreilly.com

To sign up to get topic-specific email announcements and/or news about upcoming books, conferences, special offers, and new technologies:
elists@oreilly.com

For technical questions about book content:
booktech@oreilly.com

To submit new book proposals to our editors:
proposals@oreilly.com

O'Reilly books are available in multiple DRM-free ebook formats. For more information:
oreilly.com/ebooks

Spreading the knowledge of innovators   oreilly.com

©2010 O'Reilly Media, Inc. O'Reilly logo is a registered trademark of O'Reilly Media, Inc. 00000

Have it your way.

O'Reilly eBooks

- Lifetime access to the book when you buy through oreilly.com
- Provided in up to four DRM-free file formats, for use on the devices of your choice: PDF, .epub, Kindle-compatible .mobi, and Android .apk
- Fully searchable, with copy-and-paste and print functionality
- Alerts when files are updated with corrections and additions

oreilly.com/ebooks/

Safari Books Online

- Access the contents and quickly search over 7000 books on technology, business, and certification guides
- Learn from expert video tutorials, and explore thousands of hours of video on technology and design topics
- Download whole books or chapters in PDF format, at no extra cost, to print or read on the go
- Get early access to books as they're being written
- Interact directly with authors of upcoming books
- Save up to 35% on O'Reilly print books

See the complete Safari Library at safari.oreilly.com

Spreading the knowledge of innovators.   oreilly.com

©2011 O'Reilly Media, Inc. O'Reilly logo is a registered trademark of O'Reilly Media, Inc. 00000

Lightning Source UK Ltd.
Milton Keynes UK
UKOW06f1103230913

217740UK00002B/102/P

9 780596 008208